# PSALMS

## Volume 1

# PSALMS

Volume 1

## Evangelical Biblical Theology Commentary

General Editors

T. Desmond Alexander, Thomas R. Schreiner,
Andreas J. Köstenberger

Assistant Editors

James M. Hamilton Jr., Kenneth A. Mathews,
Terry L. Wilder

# James M. Hamilton Jr.

 LEXHAM
ACADEMIC

*Psalms: Volume 1*
Evangelical Biblical Theology Commentary

Copyright 2021 James M. Hamilton Jr.

Lexham Academic, an imprint of Lexham Press
1313 Commercial St., Bellingham, WA 98225
LexhamPress.com

Print ISBN (2-volume set) 9781683595649
Print ISBN (Volume 1) 9781683595694
Library of Congress Control Number 2021942469

General Editors: T. Desmond Alexander, Thomas R. Schreiner, Andreas J. Köstenberger
Assistant Editors: James M. Hamilton Jr., Kenneth A. Mathews, Terry L. Wilder
Lexham Editorial: Derek Brown, James Spinti, Abigail Stocker, Mandi Newell, Justin Marr,
    James Weaver
Cover Design: Joshua Hunt, Brittany Schrock
Typesetting: ProjectLuz.com

*For Kenwood Baptist Church at Victory Memorial and my fellow elders there:*
*Denny Burk, Matt Damico, J. O. Oesterling,*
*Chris Burtch, Gabe Molnar, Matt Pierce,*
*Randall Breland, and Colin Smothers*

*Blessed are the people whose God is the L*ORD *- Ps 144:15*

*Those who look to him are radiant, and their faces*
*shall never be ashamed - Ps 34:5*

*Your testimonies are my delight; they are my counselors - Ps 119:24*

*Behold, how good and pleasant it is when brothers dwell in unity! - Ps 133:1*

*I am a companion of all who fear you, of those*
*who keep your precepts - Ps 119:63*

*Let the peoples praise you, O God; let all the peoples praise you! - Ps 67:3, 5*

*Kiss the Son, lest he be angry, and you perish in the way - Ps 2:12*

*May he have dominion from sea to sea, and from the*
*River to the ends of the earth! - Ps 72:8*

*May the whole earth be filled with his glory! Amen and Amen! - Ps 72:19*

# CONTENTS

# GENERAL EDITORS' PREFACE

I n recent years biblical theology has seen a remarkable resurgence. Whereas, in 1970, Brevard Childs wrote *Biblical Theology in Crisis*, the quest for the Bible's own theology has witnessed increasing vitality since Childs prematurely decried the demise of the movement. Nowhere has this been truer than in evangelical circles. It could be argued that evangelicals, with their commitment to biblical inerrancy and inspiration, are perfectly positioned to explore the Bible's unified message. At the same time, as D. A. Carson has aptly noted, perhaps the greatest challenge faced by biblical theologians is how to handle the Bible's manifest diversity and how to navigate the tension between its unity and diversity in a way that does justice to both.

What is biblical theology? And how is biblical theology different from related disciplines such as systematic theology? These two exceedingly important questions must be answered by anyone who would make a significant contribution to the discipline. Regarding the first question, the most basic answer might assert that biblical theology, in essence, is *the theology of the Bible*, that is, the theology expressed by the respective writers of the various biblical books *on their own terms* and *in their own historical contexts*. Biblical theology is the attempt to understand and embrace *the interpretive perspective of the biblical authors*. What is more, biblical theology is the theology of the *entire* Bible, an exercise in *whole-Bible theology*. For this reason biblical theology is not just a modern academic discipline; its roots are found already in the use of earlier Old Testament portions in later Old Testament writings and in the use of the Old Testament in the New.

Biblical theology thus involves a close study of *the use of the Old Testament in the Old Testament* (that is, the use of, say, Deuteronomy by Jeremiah, or of the Pentateuch by Isaiah). Biblical theology also entails the investigation of *the use of the Old Testament in the New*, both in terms of individual passages and in terms of larger Christological or soteriological themes. Biblical theology may proceed *book by book*, trace *central themes* in Scripture, or seek to place the contributions of individual biblical writers within the framework of the Bible's larger overarching *metanarrative*, that is, the Bible's developing story from Genesis through Revelation at whose core is *salvation,* or *redemptive history*, the account of God's dealings with humanity and his people Israel and the church from creation to new creation.

In this quest for the Bible's own theology, we will be helped by the inquiries of those who have gone before us in the *history of the church.* While we can profitably study the efforts of interpreters over the entire sweep of the history of biblical interpretation since patristic times, we can also benefit from the labors of scholars since J. P. Gabler, whose programmatic inaugural address at the University of Altdorf, Germany, in 1787 marks the inception of the discipline in modern times. Gabler's address bore the title "On the Correct Distinction between Dogmatic and Biblical Theology and the Right Definition of Their Goals." While few (if any) within evangelicalism would fully identify with Gabler's program, the proper distinction between dogmatic and biblical theology (that is, between biblical and systematic theology) continues to be an important issue to be adjudicated by practitioners of both disciplines, and especially biblical theology. We have already defined biblical theology as whole-Bible theology, describing the theology of the various biblical books *on their own terms* and *in their own historical contexts*. Systematic theology, by contrast, is more topically oriented and focused on contemporary contextualization. While there are different ways in which the relationship between biblical and systematic theology can be construed, maintaining a proper distinction between the two disciplines arguably continues to be vital if both are to achieve their objectives.

The present set of volumes constitutes an ambitious project, seeking to explore the theology of the Bible in considerable depth, spanning both Testaments. Authors come from a variety of backgrounds and perspectives, though all affirm the inerrancy and inspiration of Scripture. United in their high view of Scripture and in their belief in the underlying unity of Scripture, which is ultimately grounded in the unity of God himself, each author explores the contribution of a given book or group of books to the theology of Scripture as a whole. While conceived as stand-alone volumes, each volume thus also makes a contribution to the larger whole. All volumes provide a discussion of introductory matters, including the historical setting and the literary structure of a given book of Scripture. Also included is an exegetical treatment of all the relevant passages in succinct commentary-style format. The biblical theology approach of the series will also inform and play a role in the commentary proper. The commentator permits a discussion between the commentary proper and the biblical theology it reflects by a series of cross-references.

The major contribution of each volume, however, is a thorough discussion of the most important themes of the biblical book in relation to the canon as a whole. This format allows each contributor to ground biblical theology, as is proper, in an appropriate appraisal of the relevant historical and literary features of a particular book in Scripture while at the same time focusing on its major theological contribution to the entire Christian canon in the context of the larger salvation-historical metanarrative of Scripture. Within this overall format, there will be room for each individual contributor to explore the major themes of his or her particular corpus in the way he or she sees most appropriate for the material under consideration. For some books of the Bible, it may be best to have these theological themes set out in advance of the exegetical commentary. For other books it may be better to explain the theological themes after the commentary. Consequently, each contributor has the freedom to order these sections as best suits the biblical material under consideration so that the discussion of biblical-theological themes may precede or follow the exegetical commentary.

This format, in itself, would already be a valuable contribution to biblical theology. But other series try to accomplish a survey of the Bible's theology as well. What distinguishes the present series is its orientation toward Christian proclamation. This is the Biblical Theology *for Christian Proclamation* commentary series! As a result, the ultimate purpose of this set of volumes is not exclusively, or even primarily, academic. Rather, we seek to relate biblical theology to our own lives and to the life of the church. Our desire is to equip those in Christian ministry who are called by God to preach and teach the precious truths of Scripture to their congregations, both in North America and in a global context.

The base translation for the Biblical Theology for Christian Proclamation commentary series is the Christian Standard Bible (CSB). The CSB places equal value on faithfulness to the original languages and readability for a modern audience. The contributors, however, have the liberty to differ with the CSB as they comment on the biblical text. Note that, in the CSB, Old Testament passages that are quoted in the New Testament are set in boldface type.

We hope and pray that the forty volumes of this series, once completed, will bear witness to the unity in diversity of the canon of Scripture as they probe the individual contributions of each of its sixty-six books. The authors and editors are united in their desire that in so doing the series will magnify the name of Christ and bring glory to the triune God who revealed himself in Scripture so that everyone who calls on the name of the Lord will be saved—to the glory of God the Father and his Son, the Lord Jesus Christ, under the illumination of the Holy Spirit, and for the good of his church. To God alone be the glory: *soli Deo gloria*.

# ACKNOWLEDGMENTS

T he best art points beyond itself to the true, good, and beautiful, and so the Psalms point beyond themselves to the one they praise. His glory is past my power to tell, and so it is with the splendor of the Psalter that sings his praise. Every individual psalm is a masterpiece, and these individual treasures have been carefully arranged to resonate in relationship to one another, to harmonize when heard together, to echo when their architecture is considered, to reprise and retell as they prophesy and prefigure, and the symphony not only makes its own incomparable music, it sings the story of the rest of the Scriptures as well.

My eyes fill with tears of gratitude when I reflect that it has been my privilege not only to read, study, mark, and inwardly digest the Psalms but also to teach, preach, and write on them. I have not done them justice, but I have done my best.

Between March 22, 2015, and June 17, 2018, I preached through the Psalms at Kenwood Baptist Church at Victory Memorial in Louisville, Kentucky. My goal was to have the section of the commentary on the Psalms to be preached written by the time I went to the pulpit on Sunday morning. I am thankful for the weekly deadline, which enforced a disciplined schedule of study and writing. Two churches, Kenwood and Victory Memorial, merged to become one in the fall of 2016. God has been so good to us, and I dedicate this commentary to the members of Kenwood and my fellow elders there. The battle belongs to the Lord (1 Sam 17:47), and I am honored to shepherd this flock of God, which he purchased with his own blood (Acts 20:28), with these men.

The Lord's mercies are too numerous to recount (Ps 40:5), as are the many who deserve thanks. The Lord in his favor gave me a good wife

(Prov 18:22), and I thank them both for the life I enjoy with the wife I love (Eccl 9:9). We are blessed by the olive shoots around our table (Ps 128:3b), and we pray they will always walk in the truth (3 Jn 4).

What a privilege, too, to teach the Psalms at the Southern Baptist Theological Seminary in PhD seminars, in MDiv Hebrew exegesis and English Bible courses, and then to have spoken and taught on Psalms in various other settings. I am thankful for the sabbatical from teaching I received from Southern in the spring of 2018, and I am honored to serve under Dr. Mohler's leadership of the school.

Just as I completed this commentary and prepared to submit it to the original publisher, they decided to shut down the series. My soul was cast down and in turmoil within me (Ps 42:6), but lifting up my eyes to the hills, knowing whence cometh my help (121:1), I kept working on the final edits to the completed manuscript (translation and commentary exceeding 900 pages of word document, well over 400,000 words), trusting the Lord would bring new life to the now-dead series, and that even if never published my labor would not be in vain. The work was well worth doing for its own sake, but great was my rejoicing when Lexham Press resurrected and remade the series. I praise God for—and offer my thanks to—Derek Brown, Jesse Myers, Scott Corbin, and Lindsay Kennedy for their enthusiasm as they brought this work to its new birth in its new home. I am also glad to thank James Spinti for his work editing this project—catching many errors, making excellent suggestions, and bringing everything into conformity with the series protocols.

My friends Stephen Dempster and Dan Phillips carefully, thoughtfully, attentively read every word of the commentary and my translation of the Psalms, often sharing insights from their own analysis of the Hebrew text. I am so thankful for their labor of love.

"Your steadfast love, O Lᴏʀᴅ, extends to the heavens, your faithfulness to the clouds" (Ps 36:5). "If you, O Lᴏʀᴅ, should mark iniquities, O Lord, who could stand?" (130:3). "He does not deal with us according to our sins, nor repay us according to our iniquities. For as high as the heavens are above the earth, so great is his steadfast love toward those who fear him" (103:10–11). "The friendship of the Lord is for those who fear him, and he makes known to them his covenant" (25:14).

May the Lord bless his word.

Jim Hamilton

November 16, 2020

# ABBREVIATIONS

| | |
|---|---|
| ABRL | Anchor (Yale) Bible Reference Library |
| AcBib | Academia Biblica |
| ACCS | Ancient Christian Commentary on Scripture |
| ArBib | Aramaic Bible |
| BASOR | *Bulletin of the American Schools for Oriental Research* |
| BBR | *Bulletin for Biblical Research* |
| BCOTWP | Baker Commentary on the Old Testament Wisdom and Psalms |
| BDB | Brown, Francis, S. R. Driver, and Charles A. Briggs. *The Brown Driver Briggs Hebrew and English Lexicon: With an Appendix Containing the Biblical Aramaic Coded with the Numbering System from "Strong's Exhaustive Concordance of the Bible."* Peabody, MA: Hendrickson, 1997. |
| BHS | *Biblia Hebraica Stuttgartensia*. Edited by Karl Elliger and Wilhelm Rudolph. Stuttgart: Deutsche Bibelgesellschaft, 1983. |
| BibInt | Biblical Interpretation Series |
| BJSUCSD | Biblical and Judaic Studies from the University of California, San Diego |
| BSac | *Bibliotheca Sacra* |
| BTCB | Brazos Theological Commentary on the Bible |
| BZAW | Beihefte zur Zeitschrift für die Alttestamentliche Wissenschaft |
| CBET | Contributions to Biblical Exegesis and Theology |
| CTJ | *Calvin Theological Journal* |
| EBC | Expositor's Bible Commentary, rev. ed. |
| ESVEC | English Standard Version Expository Commentary |

| | |
|---|---|
| FAT | Forschungen zum Alten Testament |
| GDBS | Gorgias Dissertations, Biblical Studies |
| GKC | Gesenius, Wilhelm. *Gesenius' Hebrew Grammar.* Edited by Emil Kautzsch. Translated by Arthur E. Cowley. 2nd edition. Oxford: Oxford University Press, 1910. |
| HALOT | Koehler, Ludwig, Walter Baumgartner, and Johann J. Stamm. *The Hebrew and Aramaic Lexicon of the Old Testament.* Translated and edited under the supervision of Mervyn E. J. Richardson. 2 vols. Leiden: Brill, 2001. |
| HBM | Hebrew Bible Monographs |
| impv. | imperative |
| JANESCU | *Journal of the Ancient Near Eastern Society of Columbia University* |
| JBL | *Journal of Biblical Literature* |
| JETS | *Journal of the Evangelical Theological Society* |
| JSOT | *Journal for the Study of the Old Testament* |
| JSOTSup | Journal for the Study of the Old Testament Supplement Series |
| LHBOTS | Library of Hebrew Bible/Old Testament Studies |
| LNTS | Library of New Testament Studies |
| NETS | *A New English Translation of the Septuagint and the Other Greek Translations Traditionally Included under That Title.* Edited by Albert Pietersma and Benjamin G. Wright. New York: Oxford University Press, 2007. |
| NICOT | New International Commentary on the Old Testament |
| NPNF | *A Select Library of Nicene and Post-Nicene Fathers of the Christian Church.* Edited by Philip Schaff and Henry Wace. 28 vols. in 2 series. 1886–1889. Repr., Grand Rapids: Eerdmans, 1983. |
| NSBT | New Studies in Biblical Theology |
| OECS | Oxford Early Christian Studies |
| OTS | Old Testament Studies |
| PBM | Paternoster Biblical Monographs |
| pers. comm. | personal communication |
| pl. | plural |
| RTR | *Reformed Theological Review* |
| SBET | *Scottish Bulletin of Evangelical Theology* |

| | |
|---|---|
| *SBJT* | *Southern Baptist Journal of Theology* |
| SBLDS | Society of Biblical Literature Dissertation Series |
| SBT | Studies in Biblical Theology |
| SBTS | Sources for Biblical and Theological Study |
| SCS | Septuagint and Cognate Studies |
| SSLL | Studies in Semitic Languages and Linguistics |
| SubBi | Subsidia Biblica |
| SVTG | Septuaginta: Vetus Testamentum Graecum |
| *Them* | *Themelios* |
| *TJ* | *Trinity Journal* |
| TOTC | Tyndale Old Testament Commentaries |
| *TynBul* | *Tyndale Bulletin* |
| *VT* | *Vetus Testamentum* |
| VTSup | Supplements to Vetus Testamentum |
| WBC | Word Biblical Commentary |
| *WTJ* | *Westminster Theological Journal* |
| WUNT | Wissenschaftliche Untersuchungen zum Neuen Testament |
| *ZAW* | *Zeitschrift für die Alttestamentliche Wissenschaft* |

# INTRODUCTION

D oes any literature in the world compare with the book of Psalms? The Greeks have Homer, the Romans Virgil, the Italians Dante, and the British Shakespeare. But nothing sings like the Psalms. As Ronald B. Allen has written, "Only a Philistine could fail to love the Psalms."[1]

No other body of poetry lyricizes the epic deeds of the living God, celebrating the past, signifying the future, interpreting the present, making God known. No other body of poetry both claims to be the word of God and has the Holy Spirit bear witness to that claim, a claim recognized by the people of God across space and through time. No other body of poetry has as its principle author God's chosen king, whose line of descent traces back through Judah to Abraham, and further still to Shem, Noah, and Adam. Nor can any other poetic or literary tradition lay claim to the fact that King David, in writing of his own experience with God in the world, simultaneously wrote as a type of the one to come, Jesus, the world's best and only hope (see further on interpretive culture in §5 of "Biblical and Theological Themes," below). We love the Psalms because in them we encounter God, and as Scott Hafemann affirms, "knowing God is not a means to something else."[2]

In addition to its biblical theological significance, in the words of Othmar Keel, the book of Psalms sings an "unsentimental power and

---

[1] Ronald B. Allen, *And I Will Praise Him: A Guide to Worship in the Psalms* (Grand Rapids: Kregel, 1999), 17. For a dated but still useful survey of scholarship, see Thorne Wittstruck, *The Book of Psalms: An Annotated Bibliography*, 2 vols., Books of the Bible 5 (New York: Garland, 1994).

[2] Scott J. Hafemann, "The Covenant Relationship," in *Central Themes in Biblical Theology: Mapping Unity in Diversity*, ed. Scott J. Hafemann and Paul R. House (Grand Rapids: Baker Academic, 2007), 36.

1

beauty."[3] The splendor and truth of the Psalter leaves us speechless, until our hearts begin to swell with the song it sings, and we join the chorus of hallelujahs prompted by these pages.

The Psalms are true history, fulfilled prophecy, and enduring praise. The book of Psalms is a school of prayer, a fountain of truth, and a revelation of God himself. We will not master this book, but oh that it might master us, becoming the pulse to which our hearts beat, the soil in which our souls take root.

The Psalms speak the words of a loyal son recounting and responding to the promises of a loving Father.[4] This statement makes many assumptions, as does the opening psalm.[5] The opening psalm assumes the wider canonical context, both the story of the world told in Torah (Gen–Deut) and the narratives of how that story continued in the Former Prophets (Joshua–Kings).[6] In this story everything starts with Adam, implicitly a king-priest son of God (Gen 1:26–28; 2:15; 5:1–3; cf. Luke 3:38), whose line of descent goes down to Noah (Gen 5:1–32), then from Noah's son Shem to Abram (Gen 11:10–26), and from Abraham through Isaac to Jacob's son Judah and on down to David (see Gen 49:8–12; Ruth 4:18–22).[7]

God told Abraham that kings would come from him (Gen 17:6), and the biblical authors expected one to arise from the line of Abraham through

---

[3] Othmar Keel, *The Symbolism of the Biblical World: Ancient Near Eastern Iconography and the Book of Psalms* (New York: Seabury, 1978), 14.

[4] The sonship is corporate/national: "Israel is my firstborn son" (Exod 4:22); and also individual, granted to the king, the nation's covenant head: "My son are you" (Ps 2:7; cf. 2 Sam 7:14; Gen 5:1–3; and Luke 3:38).

[5] See Elizabeth Robar's discussion of the way language and grammar work, the Gestalt Effect (humans search for coherent wholes from the parts they experience), the Zeigarnik Effect (we do not rest until we understand the coherent whole), and how these relate to consciousness, memory, and attention in *The Verb and the Paragraph in Biblical Hebrew: A Cognitive-Linguistic Approach*, SSLL 78 (Leiden: Brill, 2015), 1–18.

[6] For my own account, see James M. Hamilton, *God's Glory in Salvation through Judgment: A Biblical Theology* (Wheaton, IL: Crossway, 2010).

[7] For discussion of Adam as a king-priest son of God, see Peter J. Gentry and Stephen J. Wellum, *Kingdom through Covenant: A Biblical-Theological Understanding of the Covenants*, 2nd ed. (Wheaton, IL: Crossway, 2018), 181–217. See also Scott W. Hahn, *Kinship by Covenant: A Canonical Approach to the Fulfillment of God's Saving Promises*, ABRL (New Haven: Yale University Press, 2009), 279. Perhaps the best expositions of the ideas in this paragraph can be found in T. Desmond Alexander, "Genealogies, Seed, and the Compositional Unity of Genesis," *TynBul* 44 (1993): 255–70; Alexander, "Further Observations on the Term 'Seed' in Genesis," *TynBul* 48 (1997): 363–67; and Stephen G. Dempster, *Dominion and Dynasty: A Biblical Theology of the Hebrew Bible*, NSBT 15 (Downers Grove, IL: InterVarsity Press, 2003).

Judah to fulfill Gen 3:15 by crushing the head of the serpent and his seed (Num 23:21, 24; 24:7, 9, 17–19).[8] This king was to be a man of Torah, making his own copy in his own hand that he would diligently study (Deut 17:14–20).[9]

Situated in this wider canonical context, the first two psalms introduce the whole collection and set the framework for it.[10] The first psalm describes the blessing of the beloved son (the sonship made explicit in 2:7), which blessing he has by obeying the Father and abiding in his words. The second psalm develops the character of the wicked (who were introduced in 1:1), explaining that they are rebels plotting insurrection (2:1–3). In response, the Father asserts that he has installed his begotten son as king, and the wicked are warned that they should surrender themselves to his mercy (2:4–12). The wording of the Ps 2:7–9 decree clearly identifies the future king with the one promised to David in 2 Sam 7:12–14.

So begins the saga in song form, and throughout the blessing of God's promises to the king and his people inform their trust, their hope, and their prayer in the face of rebel persecution and ongoing enmity (see Gen 3:15). The prayers are based on the promises, to which the praises likewise respond, because there is none like Yahweh.

### I. An Overview of the Psalter

This commentary seeks to interpret the book of Psalms *as a book*, that is, as a purposefully ordered collection of poems that build on and interpret one another.[11] The first two psalms introduce the whole collection, which

---

[8] James M. Hamilton, "The Seed of the Woman and the Blessing of Abraham," *TynBul* 58 (2007): 253–73.

[9] Jamie A. Grant, *The King as Exemplar: The Function of Deuteronomy's Kingship Law in the Shaping of the Book of Psalms*, AcBib 17 (Atlanta: Society of Biblical Literature, 2004).

[10] Robert L. Cole, *Psalms 1–2: Gateway to the Psalter*, HBM 37 (Sheffield: Sheffield Phoenix, 2013).

[11] David C. Mitchell suggests, "The writers of the Dead Sea Scrolls would probably have regarded the canonical Psalter as a purposefully shaped collection. This is evident not so much from their endorsing the MT-type sequence, although they probably did, but also, conversely, from their practice of producing alternative purposefully shaped collections," *The Message of the Psalter: An Eschatological Programme in the Book of Psalms*, JSOTSup 252 (Sheffield: Sheffield Academic, 1997), 21. Mitchell also discusses "evidence that the rabbis regarded the Psalter's sequence of lyrics as purposefully arranged" (29).

is divided into five books as follows:[12]

**Table 1. The five books of the Psalter.**

| Book 1 | Book 2 | Book 3 | Book 4 | Book 5 |
|--------|--------|--------|--------|--------|
| Pss 1–41 | Pss 42–72 | Pss 73–89 | Pss 90–106 | Pss 107–150 |

The movement of thought within the Psalms has tantalized interpreters across the ages. Commenting on Augustine of Hippo's *Enarrationes in Psalmos*, David Gundersen writes,

> Before his reflections on Psalm 150, Augustine comments briefly on the structure of the Psalter. He admits that "the arrangement of the Psalms … seems to me to contain the secret of a mighty mystery" which "hath not yet been revealed unto me." Because his generation has "not as yet pierced with the eye of our mind the depth of their entire arrangement," he does not want to be "over-bold." He likewise admits that "when I endeavoured to make out the principle of this [five-book] division, I was not able."[13]

In the introduction to his treatise *On the Inscriptions of the Psalms*, the fourth-century Cappodocian church father Gregory of Nyssa [ca. 335–394] writes,

> I have thought it necessary to begin, not by examining the inscriptions, but by setting forth first an approach to the systematic observation of the concepts concerning the Psalter in its totality, through which approach the subject matter [λόγος] of the inscriptions will subsequently be made clear to us.
>
> First, one must understand the aim [σκοπός] to which this writing looks. Next, one must pay attention to the progressive arrangements of the concepts in the book under discussion.

---

[12] Gregory of Nyssa recognized that "the entire treatise of the Psalms has been separated into five sections, and there is a systematic arrangement and division in these sections," *Gregory of Nyssa's Treatise on the Inscriptions of the Psalms*, trans. Ronald E. Heine, OECS (Oxford: Clarendon, 1995), 95, ch. 5, §37. For further discussion of patristic comments on the order of the Psalms, see Mitchell, *Message of the Psalter*, 33–36.

[13] David Alexander Gundersen, "Davidic Hope in Book IV of the Psalter (Psalms 90–106)" (PhD diss., Southern Baptist Theological Seminary, 2015), 11; citing Augustine of Hippo, "Expositions on the Book of Psalms," *NPNF* 1/8:681–82.

These are indicated both by the order [τάξις] of the psalms, which has been well arranged in relation to knowledge of the aim, and by the sections of the whole book, which are defined by certain distinctive conclusions. The entire prophecy in the Psalms has been divided into five parts.[14]

Ronald Heine comments on Gregory's words: "He means that methodologically one must first grasp the goal of the Psalter as a whole, then one must give attention to the arrangement of the materials in the individual books of the Psalter in relation to its overall goal."[15] With the recent interest in the narratival interpretation of the book of Psalms, Gregory's ancient approach of reading every individual psalm in light of the whole Psalter is new again.

Gregory believed that the goal of the Psalter was blessedness. He writes, "The whole teaching which turns us away from evil and attracts us to virtue has been delivered to us through the psalms."[16] Heine cites M. Simonetti on the point that "the theme of Gregory's treatise is 'the progressive ascent of man from the moment when he turns away from sin, until the attainment of the final beatitude,' and remarks that 'we could say that the whole of Gregory's later exegesis tends to develop the theme which we have found in his treatise *On the Titles of the Psalms.'* "[17]

Remarkably, here too Gregory's ancient Christian conclusions on the Psalter match those of modern scholarship. Gordon Wenham has advocated the "canonical" and "narratival" reading of the Psalter as a book that stems largely from Gerald Wilson's 1985 dissertation, and Wenham also claims that "the Psalter is a sacred text that is intended to be memorized," using the work of David Carr to show that the point of memorizing ancient texts was "enculturation."[18] Wenham writes, "Memorization and

---

[14] Gregory of Nyssa, *Inscriptions of the Psalms*, 83 Part 1, intro, §§2–3.

[15] Gregory of Nyssa, *Inscriptions of the Psalms*, 83 n. 3, see also Heine's remarks in the introduction, 12.

[16] Gregory of Nyssa, *Inscriptions of the Psalms*, 87 ch. 2, §16.

[17] Gregory of Nyssa, *Inscriptions of the Psalms*, 1. For examples of other pre-Enlightenment explorations of the order of the Psalms and the Psalter as a book, see Adam D. Hensley, *Covenant Relationships and the Editing of the Hebrew Psalter*, LHBOTS 666 (New York: T&T Clark, 2018), 20–22.

[18] Gerald Henry Wilson, *The Editing of the Hebrew Psalter*, SBLDS 76 (Chico, CA: Scholars Press, 1985). For a recent discussion of the state of Psalms studies dealing with "editorial criticism's crisis of credibility," see Michael K. Snearly, *The Return of the King: Messianic Expectation in Book V of the Psalter*, LHBOTS 624 (New York: T&T Clark, 2016), 9–22. David M.

recital of these texts thus served to transmit the values of this culture more widely among the people at large and to ensure that future generations followed it."[19]

Interpreting the psalms in relationship to one another requires close attention to the superscriptions of the psalms, the link words that connect them, and the thematic relationships between them. Along with superscriptions, link words, and themes, the literary structures and message of both individual psalms and the way groups of psalms are indicated, by common superscription, for instance, are significant for determining the contours of the movements of thought within the Psalter. Establishing the beginning and end and the turning points in flow of thought requires attention to all relevant information. Michael Snearly writes that

> scholars emphasize a variety of textual features in organizing [Book V]. No one feature is consistently ascendant—sometimes superscriptions are dominant, other times it is the form of the psalms, and then there are lexical and thematic parallels. Often, the same author will employ different criteria for different sections. Thus, this approach is labeled "variegated"—that is, variegated in the sense that no one criterion supersedes the others and all the criteria work together to yield the book's division.[20]

This is admittedly very difficult, and the material is open to more than one interpretation.[21] Here I offer a brief overview based largely on the information in the superscriptions (more on the superscriptions in "The Superscriptions of the Psalms," below), and in the commentary on each psalm to follow I consider its literary structure and verbal and thematic links with neighboring psalms. An overview of literary structures across the Psalter's five books can be found below in "The Literary Structure and Meaning of the Psalter."

---

Carr, *Writing on the Tablet of the Heart: Origins of Scripture and Literature* (New York: Oxford University Press, 2005).

[19] Gordon J. Wenham, *Psalms as Torah: Reading Biblical Song Ethically* (Grand Rapids: Baker Academic, 2012), 41–43. See also Wenham, *The Psalter Reclaimed: Praying and Praising with the Psalms* (Wheaton, IL: Crossway, 2013).

[20] Snearly, *Return of the King*, 62–63. Snearly adopts this approach for his own study, 78.

[21] Cf., e.g., the similar approaches but different emphases in O. Palmer Robertson, *The Flow of the Psalms: Discovering Their Structure and Theology* (Phillipsburg, NJ: P&R, 2015); and James Hely Hutchinson, "The Psalter as a Book," in *Stirred by a Noble Theme: The Book of Psalms in the Life of the Church*, ed. Andrew G. Shead (Nottingham: Apollos, 2013), 23–45.

Most of the psalms, 116 of the 150, carry a superscription (see below, "The Superscriptions of the Psalms"), and 13 of the 116 superscriptions contain references to historical situations. Twelve of these 13 are in Books 1 and 2, none are in Books 3 and 4, and the thirteenth is in Book 5 (Ps 142).

Along with the historical information in the superscriptions of Books 1 and 2, most of the psalms in Books 1 and 2 are Davidic, creating the impression that in the psalms of Books 1 and 2 David prays through his life, an impression strengthened by the words found at the end of the last psalm in Book 2, "The prayers of David the son of Jesse are completed" (Ps 72:20).[22]

To reiterate because of the significance of this point, three pieces of evidence thus create the impression that Books 1 and 2 trace David's life from God's promise that he would be king (Ps 2) through his sufferings at the hands of Saul (Ps 52:ss[23] [MT 52:1]) and Absalom (Ps 3:ss [MT 3:1]):

1. The attribution of fifty-five of the seventy-two psalms of Books 1 and 2 to David;
2. The concentration of historical superscriptions that link up with biblical narratives of David's life (again, twelve of the thirteen historical superscriptions are in Books 1 and 2, the thirteenth being in Book 5); and
3. The statement that David's prayers are ended in Psalm 72:20.

Interestingly, in the books of Samuel, Saul persecuted David (1 Sam 16–31), then Absalom tried to usurp his father's throne (2 Sam 15–18). These persecutions are reversed in the Psalms. After the poetic re-presentation of God's promise to David in Ps 2, Absalom's persecution is introduced in the superscription of Ps 3. Later in the Psalter, following the superscription about David's sin with Bathsheba in Psalm 51, Saul's persecution is introduced in Ps 52 (see the expositions of Pss 3 and 52 below). This arrangement suggests that the psalmist means for Saul and Absalom to

---

[22] Unless otherwise noted, translations of biblical texts are my own.

[23] When I refer to superscriptions, which English translations do not number, I will use the abbreviation "ss" as here. Since the Masoretic Text (MT) numbers the superscriptions, the numbering of the verses in English and Hebrew does not always match. Where there are discrepancies, as in the reference above, I add the Hebrew verse reference after the English, prefacing the Hebrew verse reference with the abbreviation MT for Masoretic Text. See further "The Numbering of the Psalms and Their Verses," below.

be interpreted as parallel figures.[24] Saul and Absalom are similar to one another in several significant ways: both are impressive and attractive in worldly terms; both set themselves against Yahweh and his anointed; both continue in unrepentant sin; both are rejected by Yahweh; and both die shameful deaths, testifying to the truth of the warning in Ps 2:10–12.

Psalm 1 presents the blessed man who meditates on God's word, and Ps 2 follows with God's promises regarding his anointed king. Psalm 3's superscription sets the scene for Book 1 of the Psalter, Pss 1–41, and these can be understood as the blessed king's prayers, based on God's promises, in response to rebellious attacks on God and his anointed.

Book 2 opens with a series of psalms of the sons of Korah (Pss 42–49) and a psalm of Asaph (Ps 50), followed by the reference to David's sin with Bathsheba in Ps 51. The sequence creates a noticeable alignment with the history known from the books of Samuel and Chronicles. We read of a "son of Korah" and "Asaph" in 1 Chr 6, in the listing of the "men David put in charge of the music in the Lord's temple after the ark came to rest there" (1 Chr 6:31, CSB). David brought the ark into Jerusalem in 2 Sam 6, received the promise from Yahweh in 2 Sam 7, began to conquer in every direction in 2 Sam 8–10, then sinned with Bathsheba in 2 Sam 11, bringing down God's judgment (2 Sam 12) through the sins of Amnon and Absalom (2 Sam 13–14) that led to Absalom's revolt (2 Sam 15–18).

The impressionistic narrative in Psalms seems to have David suffering in Book 1 until his establishment as king (cf. 1 Sam 16–2 Sam 5; Pss 3–41), then bringing the ark into Jerusalem at the beginning of Book 2 (Pss 42–50; 2 Sam 6), sinning with Bathsheba (Ps 51; 2 Sam 11), suffering the consequences (Pss 52–60; 2 Sam 12–20), and slowly recovering from them toward the end of Book 2 (Pss 61–72; cf. 2 Sam 21–24).

The majority of the psalms in Books 1 and 2 are psalms of David: fifty-five of the seventy-two. The last psalm in Book 2, Ps 72, bears the superscription "Of Solomon" and ends with the notice that "The Prayers of David ... are ended." These features of Ps 72 join with the dearth of psalms of David in Books 3 and 4—only one psalm of David in Book 3 (Ps 86) and only two in Book 4 (Pss 101 and 103)—to suggest that in Book 3 we move from the reign of David to that of Solomon and his descendants (cf. 1 Kgs 1–2, and on from there).

---

[24] See Roger T. Beckwith's discussion of "homiletical identification" in "The Early History of the Psalter," *TynBul* 46 (1995): 18–19.

Book 3 seems to begin from Solomon and work down through the kings descended from David to the exile from the land and the destruction of city and temple in Ps 89 (cf. 2 Kgs 25), noting various attacks on the temple along the way (Pss 74, 79; cf. 1 Kgs 14:25; 2 Chr 12:1–12). With the anointed king cast off and rejected (Ps 89:38), crown in the dust (89:39) and city walls breached (89:40), it looks as though God's wrath has brought an end to the covenant with David (cf. 89:49–51).

At this point a brilliant and powerful theological statement is made by the final editor of the book. Twice in Israel's time in the wilderness Yahweh told Moses that because Israel had broken the covenant, he would judge Israel by destroying the nation and beginning anew with Moses (Exod 32:10; Num 14:12). On both occasions Moses interceded with Yahweh, appealing to God's concern for his own glory, and on both occasions Yahweh showed mercy to Israel, forgiving them (though there were consequences) and continuing in covenant with them. Now after Ps 89, the covenant with David seems to be in the same jeopardy posed to the covenant made at Sinai. Who better to intercede for Israel than Moses?

Book 4 thus begins with "A prayer of Moses, the man of God" (90:ss [MT 90:1]), and in the midst of his intercession Moses prays the very words in 90:13 that he prayed in Exod 32:12, "turn" (שוב), "relent" (נחם). O. Palmer Robertson observes, "Only in these two passages of Scripture [Exod 32 and Ps 90] and no others is Yahweh urged to 'turn' and 'relent.' "[25] The result of the prayer of Moses in Ps 90 matches the result of his prayers in Exod 32 and Num 14. Psalm 91 celebrates the individual who dwells in the shelter of the Most High and experiences his deliverance. Satan quoted Ps 91 to Jesus (Matt 4:6; Luke 4:10–11), rightly discerning that Ps 91 speaks of the king from the line of David (see the exposition of Ps 91 below). Yahweh will enact his reign (Pss 93–100) through David's son and Lord (110:1).

The Former Prophets (Joshua–Kings) narrate the nation's persistence in sin that led to exile from the land. The Latter Prophets (Isaiah, Jeremiah, Ezekiel, and the Twelve [Hosea-Malachi]) proclaimed that God would do a new exodus salvation for his people after the exile that would eclipse the exodus from Egypt (Jer 16:14–15; 23:7–8). The prophets set up a parallel between slavery in Egypt and exile to Babylon on the one hand, with the exodus from Egypt and the new and greater exodus God would do

---

[25] Robertson, *Flow of the Psalms*, 152. Cf. Jonah 3:9.

in the future on the other (see, e.g., Isa 11:16; 52:4; Hos 11:5). The whole Psalter reflects the same hope for a new exodus and return from exile, not least the end of Book 4 (Ps 106:47, "gather us from the nations") and beginning of Book 5 (107:2–3, "those he redeemed ... from the lands he gathered them").

Referencing the threat that Yahweh would scatter his people among the nations when he exiled them (e.g., Deut 4:27), the last psalm of Book 4 closes with the words, "Save us, O Yahweh our God, and gather us from the nations" (106:47). Book 5 then begins with a declaration that sounds like the longed for salvation has happened: "The redeemed of Yahweh must speak, those he redeemed from the hand of distress. Even from the lands he gathered them: from the east and from the west, from the north and from the sea" (107:2–3).

The plea that Yahweh would do the new exodus at the end of Ps 106 finds its answer in the celebration that he has done just that at the beginning of 107. Psalm 108 then reprises Pss 57 and 60, projecting the life of the historical David into the future, David typifying the one to come. Indeed, the wording of Ps 108 sounds like a new conquest. Psalm 109 prays an imprecation against enemies, focusing on one in particular, and then Ps 110 celebrates the enthronement of the future priest-king from David's line at Yahweh's right hand.

The conquest of the future king in Ps 110 issues in the "hallelujahs" of Pss 111–118, followed by the celebration of God's law for the good of God's people in God's place in Ps 119. The Songs of Ascent (120–134, literally, songs of "the goings up") appear to reference the "let him go up" that permitted the historical return to the land (2 Chr 36:23; Ezra 1:3). The exiles come streaming home to Zion, celebrating Yahweh's lovingkindness (Ps 136), calling for the seed of the woman to bring final triumph against the seed of the serpent (Ps 137), hoping in the new king from the line of David (Pss 138–145), and at the end of all things, praising God (Pss 146–150).[26] As Adam Hensley has written,

> The Psalter and its books are crafted around the hope of a coming "David" through whom YHWH would renew his people and

---

[26] Joachim Schaper, *Eschatology in the Greek Psalter*, WUNT 2/76 (Tübingen: Mohr Siebeck, 1995), has argued that the Greek translation of the Psalter was messianic and eschatological. If I am correct, the Hebrew book the translators rendered into Greek was itself already thoroughly oriented toward messianic eschatology.

Zion (e.g., Pss 102–103) and lead them in the thanksgiving and praise of God (Ps 145 et al.). Announced as YHWH's "anointed" and "son" in Ps 2, the king both conquers his enemies (Pss 2, 101, 110, 118; cf. 143:12) and suffers as he identifies with the people as YHWH's servant (Pss 78, 86, 88–89, 102; cf. 18:1). This "David" is instrumental in YHWH's fulfilment of his covenant promises to Abraham and exodus-like salvation of his people, announcing YHWH's grace and favor as YHWH himself had done before Moses (Ps 103).[27]

## II. The Psalms in the Canon

Before we can interpret a text, we must establish the text to be interpreted. This section addresses both the text this commentary seeks to interpret and the implications of the canonical status of that text for the interpretive task. Here we address the canonical form of the text, the enumeration of its verses, the implications the canon has on the interpretive task, and the canonical worldview in which the Psalms make sense.[28]

### A. The Canonical Form of the Text

The inspired text is the canonized text. On this point I follow Peter Gentry, who writes,

> What is authoritative as inspired Scripture is the canonical text. Factors defining a canonical text according to Nahum Sarna, are "a fixed arrangement of content" and "the tendency to produce a standardized text."... The text of the OT in arrangement, content, and stability was fixed by the time of Ben Sira or more probably, at the end of the fifth century BC by Ezra and Nehemiah.[29]

---

[27] Hensley, *Covenant Relationships*, 271.

[28] This section does not deal with the position of the Psalms in the arrangement of the Old Testament canon, but for my view on that question see James M. Hamilton, "Canonical Biblical Theology," in *God's Glory Revealed in Christ: Essays in Honor of Thomas R. Schreiner*, ed. Denny Burk, James M. Hamilton, and Brian Vickers (Nashville: Broadman & Holman, 2019), 59–73.

[29] Peter J. Gentry, "The Text of the Old Testament," *JETS* 52 (2009): 19; see also Gentry, "The Septuagint and the Text of the Old Testament," *BBR* 16 (2006): 193–218. See also Nahum M. Sarna, "The Order of the Books," in *Studies in Jewish Bibliography: History and Literature in Honor of I. Edward Kiev* (ed. Ch. Berlin; New York: KTAV, 1971), 407–13, esp. 411 and 413, n. 15.

Gentry elaborated on his position in private communication with me:

> I affirm that the texts in the canon of the Old Testament were inspired and authoritative from the beginning. Nonetheless, we have no access historically to the demarcation of the canon prior to the work of Ezra and Nehemiah who are responsible for the arrangement later described in *Baba Bathra* 14b. And since Ezra and Nehemiah formulated the rational literary arrangement that was firmly in place by the time of Judas Maccabeus and considered authoritative by Jesus Christ, this is the canonical form of the inspired text.[30]

Having taken these positions, in this commentary I will not speculate on the form or content of individual psalms prior to the final canonical form we now possess, nor will I speculate on how individual psalms might have been grouped prior to the recognition that the Psalter belonged with the growing collection of canonical writings.[31] I will comment on the canonical text and the groupings we find in it. Since the superscriptions comprise part of the canonical text, I receive and interpret them the same way I do the rest of the canonical text (see further "The Superscriptions of the Psalms," below).

The object of interpretation in this commentary, then, is the canonical text of the book of Psalms witnessed to by the Masoretic Text (MT), which I mainly access through the *Biblia Hebraica Stuttgartensia* (*BHS*). As David Mitchell notes, "The New Testament seems to regard the MT-type Psalter as definitive."[32]

---

[30] Peter J. Gentry, email message to author, May 15, 2018.

[31] For discussion of the so-called Elohistic Psalter, the fact that "אלהים [is] used almost exclusively within Pss 42–83," see Terrance R. Wardlaw, *Elohim within the Psalms: Petitioning the Creator to Order Chaos in Oral-Derived Literature*, LHBOTS 602 (New York: Bloomsbury, 2015), quotation from p. 1. Surveying previous proposals, Wardlaw starts from the observation that "the use of the divine names seems to be integral to the canonical presentation and rhetoric of this unit" (6). He is sensitive to "the significance of the present canonical order" and interprets the text as it stands (13). Wardlaw demonstrates how "the Psalter was both composed and collected within the circles where Pentateuchal traditions were well known and in some sense determinative of religious life and institutions" (27), which puts him in position to argue that whereas Yahweh is God's covenant name, when the psalmists refer to him as אלהים (God) they evoke Gen 1:1–2:3, God as Creator, and Exod 20:1 (with 21:6; 22:7–8 [ET 6–7]), God as "ethical re-creator or judge" (31–33).

[32] Mitchell, *Message of the Psalter*, 26.

Some contend that evidence from the Qumran scrolls indicates that the Psalter had not achieved its canonical, fixed arrangement by the time the covenanters went to Qumran. The debate is complex, but the evidence indicates that the variant orders at Qumran themselves presuppose the already established MT order of the 150 psalms as we now have them. The variant order at Qumran can be compared to the way a church today might print selections of Scripture on a weekly handout for use in worship. Such a handout is not intended to replace the Bible but merely to facilitate worship. Along these lines, having surveyed the debate, Hensley writes,

> The relationship of Qumran MSS to the canonical Psalter as Wilson and Flint interpret it remains highly speculative, and others more convincingly explain them as liturgically inspired arrangements that presuppose an existing MT Psalter. Since there is little to commend a wider provenance for 11QPs[a], the difference in its arrangement is best explained by the Qumran community's idiosyncratic liturgical needs.[33]

There is evidence within the Old Testament itself that the book of Psalms achieved recognition as the word of God very early. Will Kynes writes regarding Job's quotation of Ps 107,

> The authoritative status of the psalm, the verbatim citation of Ps 107:40 (Job 12:21, 24), the nearly exact repetition of Ps 107:42 (Job 5:16; 22:19), and the widespread allusions to the psalm all seem to suggest that the author of Job had the text of Psalm 107 before him. ... By examining cognitive theories of memory, Cynthia Edenburg has argued that, because of the "complex cognitive process" of making and identifying allusions, certain forms of involved intertextuality would be inaccessible to an oral audience, instead requiring texts fixed in writing that can be perused.[34]

---

[33] Hensley, *Covenant Relationships*, 39. See Hensley's summary of the discussion (33–39), as well as his discussion of what the Greek translation of the Psalms contributes to the debate (39–41). See also Beckwith, "Early History of the Psalter."

[34] Will Kynes, *My Psalm Has Turned into Weeping: Job's Dialogue with the Psalms*, BZAW 437 (Berlin: de Gruyter, 2012), 95–95. Kynes here cites Cynthia Edenburg, "Intertextuality, Literary Competence and the Question of Readership: Some Preliminary Observations," *JSOT* 35 (2010): 131–48. Kynes extends the kinds of statements he makes here to the other psalms Job quotes (140, see the footnote at the end of the exposition of Ps 39 below where

I regard the final, canonical form of the book of Psalms, the one received into the collection of Scriptures we now call the Old Testament, as breathed out by God (2 Tim 3:16).[35] I would thus attribute inspiration not only to the individual authors of each psalm but also to the editor(s)/anthologist(s) who put the book of Psalms into its canonical form.[36]

## B. The Numbering of the Psalms and Their Verses

The editor of the final form of the Psalter did not enumerate the verses of the psalms, though the enumeration of the individual psalms could indeed have gone back to him or further.[37] The individual psalmists often used internal structuring devices such as *inclusios* and chiastic structures to mark the boundaries of a psalm, and we will see that the five books of the Psalter are punctuated by distinctive beginnings and conclusions.

In the Masoretic Text (MT) the superscriptions are always numbered as verse 1. The superscriptions have not been numbered in English translations. This results in a discrepancy between the Hebrew and English verse numbers. The superscriptions are part of the inspired text of Scripture and in my view should be numbered, not least to create consistency for

---

he is quoted on that point). Kynes also comments in his conclusion, "These allusions suggest these psalms were in written (though not necessarily complete) form when Job was composed and that the book itself was a written composition. Not only had the psalms likely reached a written form by this time, but they also seem to have taken on the status of 'Scripture'" (188). See also the quotation from Zipora Talshir in the first paragraph of "The Canonical Shape of the Psalter," below.

[35] See the magisterial work of Roger T. Beckwith, *The Old Testament Canon of the New Testament Church and Its Background in Early Judaism* (Grand Rapids: Eerdmans, 1985).

[36] I cannot agree with Anthony Gelston, who suggests, "The existence of occasional overlap between some individual psalms, and the virtual duplication of Pss. 14 and 53, indicate one negative conclusion that can be drawn. It is evident that there was no final process of editing the Psalter, by which such duplications might have been removed, and textual inconsistencies between parallel passages ironed out" ("Editorial Arrangement in Book IV of the Psalter," in *Genesis, Isaiah and Psalms: A Festschrift to Honour Professor John Emerton for His Eightieth Birthday*, ed. Katharine J. Dell, Graham Davies, and Yee Von Koh, VTSup 135 [Leiden: Brill, 2010], 165). I find it more plausible that such duplications and overlaps are intentional, along the lines of the way melodies and rhythms are reprised in modern musicals such as *Les Miserables* or *Hamilton*, and thus we should seek to understand what they signify and relish their beauty.

[37] Note Acts 13:33, "as also it has been written in the second psalm" (the textual variant that reads "the first Psalm" does not alter the point made here, which is that the enumeration of the psalms is ancient). For discussion of the variations in the enumeration of individual psalms, see Nancy deClaisse-Walford, Rolf A. Jacobson, and Beth LaNeel Tanner, *The Book of Psalms*, NICOT (Grand Rapids: Eerdmans, 2014), 3–7.

those dealing with the original Hebrew and English translations. In my translation of the Psalms that accompanies this commentary, I have followed the numbering of the verses in Hebrew. In my comments, however, aware that most readers will access the Psalms primarily in English, I first list Scripture references according to their enumeration in English. Where there is a discrepancy, I follow the English enumeration with the Hebrew in parentheses, prefaced by "MT" for "Masoretic Text." For instance, in the Hebrew text the superscription of Ps 3 carries the number 1. This makes the first verse in the body of the psalm verse 2. English translations do not follow the Hebrew numbering scheme, giving the superscription no number. As a result, what is verse 2 in Hebrew is verse 1 in English. In this commentary the verse will be noted as follows: Psalm 3:1 (MT 3:2).

There are also discrepancies between the enumeration of the Psalms in the Masoretic Text and their enumeration in the Greek translation. Karen Jobes and Moisés Silva summarize the problem succinctly:

> The Septuagint, followed by the Vulgate and Roman Catholic Bibles, treats Psalms 9 and 10 as a single psalm, while Psalm 147 is divided into two psalms: 146 and 147. This means that the chapter numbering is off by one from Psalm 10 to 147, with Psalms 1–8 and 148–50 being the same in both traditions.[38]

Jobes and Silva do not note that in the Greek translation Pss 114 and 115 are also combined in LXX Ps 113, and Ps 116 has been split into LXX Pss 114 and 115.[39] When I reference the Greek translation where the Psalm is enumerated differently, I will preface it (as already in this paragraph) with the abbreviation "LXX," for instance, LXX Ps 11.

C. The Canonical Text and the Interpretive Task

Interpreting the Psalter *as a book* found *in the canon* sets us on a different course than the one charted by Hermann Gunkel, who wrote,

> It is not sufficient to deal only with the biblical book of Psalms, … rather, we are convinced from the outset that our presentation must include also those songs which do not belong to the Psalter, whether these are found in the Bible or, indeed, outside

---

[38] Karen Jobes and Moisés Silva, *Invitation to the Septuagint* (Grand Rapids: Baker Academic, 2000), 78–79.

[39] Rightly, Mitchell, *Message of the Psalter*, 16–17.

of Israel, insofar as they show any real inner relationship with the Psalms.[40]

Against Gunkel, my concern here is with the biblical book of Psalms.[41] The primary context in which an individual psalm must be interpreted is the canonical Psalter in which we find it, and then the broader backdrop is that of the Old Testament canon, which was recognized as an authoritative collection very early. I am consciously choosing not to investigate the history of religion, as Gunkel did, but rather to engage in biblical theology.[42]

James Muilenburg writes,

> Gunkel recognized that the earliest psalms were all cultic in character, but he believed that many of them were later liberated from their cultic setting into spiritual songs and prayers. His student, Sigmund Mowinckel, took issue with him there. Mowinckel was convinced that all the psalms were cultic, and in six important monographs ... he sought not only to define their cultic provenience and *Sitz im Leben*, their cultic terminology and imagery, but also the occasions of celebration and festival, of mourning and lamentation, and their relation to other contexts in the life of ancient Israel.[43]

Like Gunkel's, Mowinckel's project involves no small amount of speculation. Since we lack detailed reports that tell us how the individual psalms were used in ancient Israel, interpreting the Psalter as a book in the context of the canonical collection of books is a far safer procedure.

Whereas Gunkel's and Mowinckel's interests were in the history of religion, genre classification, and the life setting in which the psalms were used, my interest is in what the canonical form of the text was intended

---

[40] Hermann Gunkel, *The Psalms: A Form-Critical Introduction*, trans. Thomas M. Horner, Facet Books 19 (Philadelphia: Fortress, 1967), 1.

[41] For an overview of the ways scholars have approached study of the Psalter as a book, see Michael K. Snearly's discussion of "Best Practices in Editorial Criticism," in *Return of the King*, 23–38, esp. the helpful table 3.1 on 37.

[42] For the difference between the history of religion and biblical theology, see Robert Morgan, ed., *The Nature of New Testament Theology: The Contribution of William Wrede and Adolf Schlatter*, SBT 2/25 (Naperville, IL: Allenson, 1973).

[43] James Muilenburg, "Introduction," in Gunkel, *Psalms*, viii.

to communicate.[44] Gunkel and Mowinckel took on a historical task. I take on a textual one. So much of Gunkel's program is based on assumptions he makes, which then become assertions. For instance, he writes,

> Very frequently the Hebrew Hymn will begin: "Give praise," "Sing" (Exod. 15:21), "Give thanks" (Ps. 105:1, etc.). These phrases were originally the precentor's address to the choir. Then the hymn proceeds as the precentor invokes God's name ("Praise Yahweh" or "Sing to Yahweh") and at the same time addresses the singers, who are variously called "you righteous ones " (Ps. 33:1), "Daughter of Zion" (Zeph 3:14).[45]

One of the problems with these assertions is that all we have is what the text tells us, and the text neither explicitly names a "precentor" (see "The Superscriptions of the Psalms" below, esp. the discussion of "to the Choirmaster") nor indicates that a choir is being directed. No stage-directions come with the words of the Psalms, making the reconstruction of the "life setting" in which they were employed necessarily speculative. Terrance Wardlaw puts it well: "The place of privilege should be given to the text before us rather than to its hypothetical antecedent forms."[46] Once again: my purpose is to interpret the canonical text.

## D. The Psalms in the Old Testament Canon

A full discussion of the Old Testament canon, dealing with contents, authorship, dating, and arrangement, is obviously beyond the scope of this commentary.[47] Because my views on these questions will be reflected both here in the introduction and throughout the commentary, and because more than one reader of prepublication versions of this project has flagged the issue, I want to offer some rationale for my position. In

---

[44] See Will Kynes, *An Obituary for "Wisdom Literature": The Birth, Death, and Intertextual Reintegration of a Biblical Corpus* (Oxford: Oxford University Press, 2019).

[45] Gunkel, *Psalms*, 11.

[46] Wardlaw, *Elohim within the Psalms*, 13.

[47] For my attempt to explain and defend the view that the sixty-six books of the Old and New Testaments are inspired by God and therefore inerrant, see James M. Hamilton, "Still Sola Scriptura: An Evangelical View of Scripture," in *The Sacred Text: Excavating the Texts, Exploring the Interpretations, and Engaging the Theologies of the Christian Scriptures*, ed. Michael Bird and Michael W. Pahl, Gorgias Précis Portfolios (Piscataway, NJ: Gorgias, 2010), 215–40. As noted above, my views on the arrangement of the Old Testament canon can be found in "Canonical Biblical Theology."

the same way that choosing to do one thing often entails choosing not to do another, being open to one explanation necessitates being skeptical of another. In much post-enlightenment biblical scholarship one finds an openness and generosity toward scholarly theories, especially those regarded as established, and this sometimes comes with a skepticism toward the primary source data. So, for instance, in much biblical scholarship there is a high degree of skepticism toward the idea that Moses wrote the Pentateuch, and this comes with an open-minded and charitable attitude toward a variety of theories as to how the Torah—the first five books of the Old Testament—came into existence. The primary sources, meanwhile, make assertions like the following (all texts here ESV):

- "Moses wrote down all the words of the Lord" (Exod 24:4).
- "Moses wrote down their starting places ..." (Num 33:2).
- "Moses wrote this law ..." (Deut 31:9).
- "Moses wrote this song ..." (Deut 31:22).
- "When Moses had finished writing the words of this law in a book to the very end, Moses commanded the Levites ... 'Take this Book of the Law and put it by the side of the ark of the covenant ...'" (Deut 31:24–26).
- "as it is written in the Book of the Law of Moses" (Josh 8:31).
- "a copy of the law of Moses, which he had written" (Josh 8:32).
- "the law that Moses the servant of the Lord commanded you" (Josh 22:5).
- "Therefore, be very strong to keep and to do all that is written in the Book of the Law of Moses" (Josh 23:6).
- "... as it is written in the Law of Moses ..." (1 Kings 2:3).
- "him of whom Moses in the Law and also the prophets wrote" (John 1:45).
- "For if you believed Moses, you would believe me; for he wrote of me" (John 5:46).

Many more biblical texts like these could be cited, statements that refer to "the Law of Moses" or refer to the law that "Moses wrote." In my own thinking, when it comes to weighing out the balance of openness and generosity on the one hand, and skepticism on the other, my inclination is to be open and generous to statements in the primary sources and skeptical of scholarly theories that contradict them. And I not only weigh out the balance this way in theory but incorporate it into my practice, which will be reflected in this commentary by the frequent capitalization of the term Torah. The term Torah is an English transliteration of the Hebrew term typically translated law. When I capitalize it, it is because I am inclined to think that the referent is the Pentateuch, the first five books of the Old Testament, the Torah of Moses. I think that Moses wrote the Torah, and that would make the Torah of Moses available to David and the other Psalmists, who, it seems to me, regard the Torah as a most foundational and shaping document for all of life.

The privileging of the primary sources also leads me to the conclusion that within the Old Testament we see a "canonical consciousness" developing. The texts themselves indicate that the believing remnant recognized certain books as coming from God, having divine authority. The Psalter was received into that collection at an early stage.

The fact that the Psalter was included in the collection of books we now recognize as the Old Testament canon tells us several things.[48] First, it tells us that the people of God recognized the book to be inspired by the Holy Spirit. That in turn tells us that they regarded the book as holy, belonging with the other books God had given to them. Further, and perhaps most significantly, this means that the people of God understood the Psalter to comport with their own worldview, to advocate their perspective, to see the world the way they saw it (see further "Biblical and Theological Themes," below). Commenting on the way the psalmists "tapped their [pagan] predecessors for verbal formulas, imagery, elements of mythology, and even entire sequences of lines of poetry," Robert Alter rightly asserts: "The Hebrew poems were manifestly framed for Israelite purposes that were in many regards distinctive and at best no more than loosely parallel to the polytheistic texts that served as poetic precedents."[49]

Biblical theology is the attempt to understand and embrace the interpretive perspective of the biblical authors, and the importance of

---

[48] That the Psalms were accepted into the canon is not disputed. For recent discussion and an accessible presentation, see Edmon L. Gallagher and John D. Meade, *The Biblical Canon Lists from Early Christianity: Texts and Analysis* (Oxford: Oxford University Press, 2018).

[49] Robert Alter, *The Book of Psalms: A Translation with Commentary* (New York: Norton, 2007), xiv, xv. For a catalogue of possible points of contact, see Roger O'Callaghan, "Echoes of Canaanite Literature in the Psalms," *VT* 4 (1954): 164–76.

understanding the worldview of the biblical authors cannot be over-stated.[50] There may have been Israelites who were idolaters, who had embraced foreign worldviews, but the biblical authors understood themselves to be faithful to Yahweh, God of Israel. The self-understanding of the biblical authors receives validation from the believing old covenant remnant that likewise rejected idolatry and preserved and perpetuated the writings that comprise the Old Testament canon.

What goes into a worldview? To summarize briefly, a worldview consists of the story through which people interpret the world (meta-narrative), the truths derived from the story (doctrine), the behaviors promoted and discouraged by the story (ethics), the symbols that summarize and interpret the story (imagery, typology, etc.), and the worship the story intends to promote (liturgy).[51]

As the worship prompted by the story is incomprehensible apart from the story, so the Psalms are unintelligible apart from the rest of the Old Testament. The psalmists understood themselves to be celebrating the God revealed in the Old Testament. For the psalmists, God's character, which he stated plainly on his own behalf in Exod 34:6–7, determines everything. Out of God's character, his goodness, steadfast love, and righteousness, flows the very good world he made. God's character means evil will not prevail in the world. God will defeat sin and death and the serpent and his seed, and he will make the world his own holy dwelling place, a clean place of life, where he will reign over those who fear and love him.

On the basis of these considerations about worldview, unless we have explicit statements to the contrary, we should assume that the truths and doctrines of the Psalter will be the truths of the Law (Torah) and the Prophets. So, for instance, we should assume that what the Psalms tell us about Yahweh will correspond to what Genesis tells us about Yahweh. Similarly, the attitudes and actions promoted in the ethical statements of the Psalter will comport with the ethical statements made in the Ten Commandments, elaborated upon throughout Exodus through Deuteronomy. As with doctrine and ethics, we should assume that the imagery and typology of the Psalter will be rooted in earlier Scripture.

---

[50] James M. Hamilton, *What Is Biblical Theology?* (Wheaton, IL: Crossway, 2014).

[51] N. T. Wright, *The New Testament and the People of God*, Christian Origins and the Question of God, vol. 1 (Minneapolis: Fortress, 1992).

The Hebrew title for the book of Psalms is "Praises" (תהלים). These praises respond to Yahweh, whose character and mighty works of creation and redemption are detailed in the rest of the Old Testament. The praises should be read, then, in relationship to the rest of the Old Testament.

Keel has written, "Faced with words and ideas, the individual hearer conceives their meaning in terms supplied primarily by his own preunderstanding."[52] And Wenham observes,

> The terseness of poetry means that there are many gaps, which thereby force the reader to puzzle over the connection between one line and the next ... the absence of many details within the psalms gives them a general validity that allows their sentiments to be appropriated by readers in a variety of circumstances. ... The absence of precision opens up a psalm to a broad range of situations and invites readers to make its sentiments their own.[53]

So far as possible, my aim has been to bring my preunderstanding into line with what I read in the Bible, to fill in the gaps with information from the Psalms and the rest of the Scriptures. In the same way that the lyrics of Don McLean's 1971 song "American Pie" evoke a backstory that people in our culture recognize, the lyrics of the Psalms evoke a backstory. That backstory is not spelled out in every detail, but it is no less there. The strategy that we instinctively use when we think about McLean's lyrics, or any other poetry, is the same strategy that we must use when interpreting the Psalms.

I want to understand what the authors of these texts intended to communicate.[54] My goal is for the worldview of the biblical authors to be my worldview, and my intent is to interpret the Psalms from that perspective. As Elizabeth Robar has written,

> The discourse unit ... has as its purpose to help another person develop her own corresponding mental representation. ... To

---

[52] Keel, *Symbolism of the Biblical World*, 8.

[53] Wenham, *Psalms as Torah*, 62.

[54] Note Mitchell's comment: "Calvin, aware of the abuses of mystical interpretation, regards authorial intention and historical context as essential to correct interpretation," Mitchell, *Message of the Psalter*, 40.

the extent that the reader construes the text as the author intended, successful communication has taken place ... though the reader is at first provided with inadequate information, she will continually attempt to construct a whole that will explain the available data.[55]

### III. The Canonical Shape of the Psalter

We noted above the division of the Psalter into five books (see table 1. "The five books of the Psalter"), and at the end of each book we find a doxology. Some regard these doxologies as editorial additions, but the doxology at the end of Ps 41 is an integral piece of the psalm, standing as the closing statement in the psalm's chiastic structure (see the "Overview and Structure" of Ps 41 in the commentary below). The same point can be made about the chiastic structures of Pss 72 and 106 (see the "Overview and Structure" section on each below). Note also that the doxology that closes Book 4, Ps 106:48, is quoted with the verse that precedes it (106:47) in 1 Chr 16:35–36—the Chronicler quotes the last two verses from Ps 106, which includes Book 4's doxology. Zipora Talshir writes, "The juxtaposition of these verses suggests that the Chronicler ... knew the Psalms as a collection already organized in five books."[56]

It looks to me, therefore, like the doxologies that close Books 1, 2, and 4 are integral elements of the psalms in which they are found, not extraneous additions tagged on by editors at a later time. The doxology at the end of Ps 89, closing Book 3, could stand by itself, but it seems more likely that Ps 89's doxology is just as original to that psalm as are those that conclude Pss 41, 72, and 106.[57]

These doxologies provide essential components of the architecture of the psalms they conclude, implying that the authors of the individual psalms themselves included the doxologies, perhaps because they

---

[55] Robar, *Verb and the Paragraph in Biblical Hebrew*, 39, 41, 45.

[56] Zipora Talshir, "Several Canon-Related Concepts Originating in Chronicles," *ZAW* 113 (2001): 398. I wish to thank Peter Gentry for drawing my attention to this article.

[57] On a similar issue, Hensley comments, "It therefore seems best to conclude that lexical and thematic links between psalms generally reflect editorial selection of psalms rather than 'redactional' manipulation of their contents." Hensley, *Covenant Relationships*, 71. See Leslie McFall, "The Evidence for a Logical Arrangement of the Psalter," *WTJ* 62 (2000): 223–56, esp. 236.

composed these psalms to play the part they do in the movement of thought that flows through the whole collection.[58]

The doxologies at the end of each book are as follows:

Table 2. The doxologies at the end of each book.

| Book 1 | Book 2 | Book 3 | Book 4 | Book 5 |
|---|---|---|---|---|
| Ps 41:13 (MT 41:14) | Ps 72:18–19 | Ps 89:52 (MT 89:53) | Ps 106:48 | Pss 146–150 |
| Blessed be | Blessed be | Blessed be | Blessed be | |
| Yahweh God of Israel! | Yahweh God, God of Israel, who alone does wonders. | Yahweh | Yahweh, God of Israel, | |
| | And blessed be the name of his glory | | | |
| From the age and unto the age, | to the age, | to the age. | from the age unto the age! | |
| | and may his glory fill the whole of the earth. | | | |
| | | | And all the people said, | |
| amen and amen. | Amen and amen. | Amen and amen. | "Amen!" Hallelujah! | |

These doxologies have four elements in common: (1) *blessed be*, (2) *Yahweh*, (3) *to the age* (forever), and the benediction concludes with (4) *amen*. These benedictions stand as punctuation marks at the end of the books within the Psalter, and then the first psalm of each book is attributed to a different author (the lack of attribution at 1 and 107 differing from attributions at 42, 73, and 90). The various figures to whom the psalms are attributed can be seen on table 3.

---

[58] Psalm 41 is attributed to David, 72 to Solomon (or, in view of 72:20, to David), 89 to Ethan, and 106 has no superscription.

Table 3. Authors to whom the psalms are attributed.

| Book 1 | Book 2 | Book 3 | Book 4 | Book 5 |
|---|---|---|---|---|
| 1–2, none<br>3–9, of David<br>10, none<br>11–32, of David<br>33, none<br>34–41, of David | 42, Korah*<br>43, none<br>44–49, Korah*<br>50, of Asaph<br>51–65, of David<br>66–67, no name<br>68–70, of David<br>71, none<br>72, of Solomon | 73–83, Asaph<br>84–85, Korah*<br>86, David<br>87–88, Korah*<br>88, Heman<br>89, Ethan | 90, Moses<br>91, none<br>92, no name<br>93–97, none<br>98, no name<br>99, none<br>100, no name<br>101, David<br>102, no name<br>103, David<br>104–106, none | 107, none<br>108–110, David<br>111–119, none<br>120–121, no name<br>122, David<br>123, no name<br>124, David<br>125–126, no name<br>127, Solomon<br>128–130, no name<br>131, David<br>132, no name<br>133, David<br>134, no name<br>135–137, none<br>138–145, David<br>146–150, none |
| 37/41 Attributed to David | 18/31 attributed to David | 11/17 attributed to Asaph<br><br>1/17 attributed to David<br><br>1/17 attributed to Ethan<br><br>1/17 attributed to Heman | 2/17 attributed to David 1/17 | 15/44 attributed to David |
|  | 7/31 attributed to Korah | 4/17 attributed to Korah |  |  |
|  |  |  | attributed to Moses |  |
|  | 1/31 of Solomon |  |  | 1/44 attributed to Solomon |
| Grand total attributed to David: 73/150 | | | | |

*Of the sons of Korah

After thirty-seven of the forty-one psalms of Book 1 being "of David," Book 2 opens with a series of psalms "of the Sons of Korah" (Ps 42, 44–49). Psalm 50 is then "of Asaph," and 51–65 and 68–70 are "of David." The last words of Book 2, following its doxology, are "the prayers of David the son of Jesse are completed" (72:20). That reference to the prayers of David casts a Davidic shadow over the whole of Books 1 and 2, and then Book 3 opens with a series of psalms of Asaph (73–83). The opening psalm of Book 4 introduces a new attribution, Ps 90 being "a prayer of Moses." Like the first psalm of Book 1, the first psalm of Book 5 has no superscription. Just as the benedictions mark the ends of the books within the Psalter, the changes in ascription mark the beginnings of Books 2, 3, and 4. With no speaker named in the opening psalms of Books 1 and 5, a change in ascription marks the beginning of each book.

We will give further consideration to the literary structure of the Psalter below, at this point we turn our attention to the superscriptions of the psalms.

## IV. The Superscriptions of the Psalms

The overwhelming majority of individual psalms bear a superscription. Only 34 of the 150 stand without one, while 116 of the 150 psalms are prefaced by a superscription.[59] I will first set forth the data, then discuss what we can conclude from the superscriptions regarding the authorship of the psalms and the authenticity/originality of the superscriptions.

In terms of their distribution across the Psalter, as can be seen on the following table, all but seven of the first eighty-nine psalms (Books 1–3) have superscriptions, while only thirty-three of the sixty-one psalms in Books 4 and 5 have them. In table 4, "Number of superscripted psalms by book," the first number is the number of superscripted psalms in the book, the second the total number of psalms in that book. So under Book 1, we have 37/41, indicating that thirty-seven of the forty-one psalms in Book 1 have superscriptions:

---

[59] The following psalms lack superscriptions: 1, 2, 10, 33, 43, 71, 91, 93–97, 99, 104–106, 111–119, 135–137, 146–150.

**Table 4. Number of superscripted psalms by book.**

| Book 1 | Book 2 | Book 3 | Book 4 | Book 5 |
|--------|--------|--------|--------|--------|
| 37/41  | 28/31  | 17/17  | 7/17   | 26/44  |

As can be observed from table 6: "The psalm superscriptions in the MT," the superscriptions present specific information in a particular order. The information can be described in different ways, but for convenience I will describe it as representing roughly six different kinds of information that can be placed in certain slots. No psalm has a superscription that fills every slot, but the following composite superscription, combining material from the superscriptions of Pss 62, 45, and 63, illustrates the kind of information found in each slot:

**Table 5. Superscription information slots.**

| Slot 1: "For the Preeminent One" | Slot 2: Other information and instructions | Slot 3: Genre/psalm type | Slot 4: Author | Slot 5: Genre/psalm type | Slot 6: Historical information |
|---|---|---|---|---|---|
| For the Preeminent one (Ps 62) | On Jeduthun (Ps 62) | A Psalm (Ps 62) | of David (Ps 62) | A Maskil. A Song of Beloveds (Ps 45) | When he was in the wilderness of Judah (Ps 63) |

Here is the full table:[60]

---

[60] This table presents my literal translation of the superscriptions, in which I depart from many English translations in the following ways: (1) preserving the order in which the information is presented; (2) not adding interpretive words to the terms in the superscriptions (e.g., I maintain "For the Preeminent One" without the interpretive addition of a word like "choir" to "director." Choir is not in the text. It is an interpretive addition); and (3) not adding words to the superscriptions (e.g., the superscription of Ps 145 reads simply, "A praise of David," but English translations tend to add either "song" [ESV: "A song of praise"] or "psalm" [KJV, NAS, NET, NIV: "A psalm of praise"]). I have capitalized words that seem to be technical terms for genres or psalm types in the superscriptions. These include terms such as Psalm, *Shiggaion*, *Miktam*, Song, *Maskil*. Italicized terms are transliterations.

Table 6. The psalm superscriptions in the Masoretic Text.

| Ps | For the Preeminent One (למנצח) | Other information/ instructions | Genre/ psalm type | Author | Genre/ psalm type | Historical information |
|---|---|---|---|---|---|---|
| 1 | | | | | | |
| 2 | | | | | | |
| 3 | | | A Psalm | of David. | | When he fled from before Absalom, his son. |
| 4 | For the Preeminent One. | With stringed instruments. | A Psalm | of David. | | |
| 5 | For the Preeminent One. | To the *Nechilloth*. | A Psalm | of David. | | |
| 6 | For the Preeminent One. | With stringed instruments upon the eighth. | A Psalm | of David. | | |
| 7 | | | A *Shiggaion* | of David. | | Which he sang to Yahweh concerning the words of Cush, a Benjaminite. |
| 8 | For the Preeminent One. | On the *Gittith*. | A Psalm | of David. | | |
| 9 | For the Preeminent One. | On the Death of the Son. | A Psalm | of David. | | |
| 10 | | | | | | |
| 11 | For the Preeminent One. | | | of David. | | |
| 12 | For the Preeminent One. | Upon the eighth. | A Psalm | of David. | | |
| 13 | For the Preeminent One. | | A Psalm | of David. | | |

| Ps | For the Preeminent One (למנצח) | Other information/ instructions | Genre/ psalm type | Author | Genre/ psalm type | Historical information |
|---|---|---|---|---|---|---|
| 14 | For the Preeminent One. | | | Of David. | | |
| 15 | | | A Psalm | of David. | | |
| 16 | | | A *Miktam* | of David. | | |
| 17 | | | A Prayer | of David. | | |
| 18 | For the Preeminent One. | For the Servant of Yahweh. | | Of David. | | When he spoke to Yahweh the words of this song on the day Yahweh delivered him from the hand of all the ones at enmity with him and from the hand of Saul. |
| 19 | For the Preeminent One. | | A Psalm | of David. | | |
| 20 | For the Preeminent One. | | A Psalm | of David. | | |
| 21 | For the Preeminent One. | | A Psalm | of David. | | |
| 22 | For the Preeminent One. | Upon the Doe of the Dawn. | A Psalm | of David. | | |
| 23 | | | A Psalm | of David. | | |
| 24 | | | | Of David. | A Psalm. | |
| 25 | | | | Of David. | | |
| 26 | | | | Of David. | | |
| 27 | | | | Of David. | | |
| 28 | | | | Of David. | | |
| 29 | | | A Psalm | of David. | | |
| 30 | A Psalm. | A Song for the dedication of the house. | | Of David. | | |

| Ps | For the Preeminent One (למנצח) | Other information/ instructions | Genre/ psalm type | Author | Genre/ psalm type | Historical information |
|----|----|----|----|----|----|----|
| 31 | For the Preeminent One. | | A Psalm | of David. | | |
| 32 | | | | Of David. | A *Maskil*. | |
| 33 | | | | | | |
| 34 | | | | Of David. | | When he changed his taste before Abimelech; and he drove him out, and he went. |
| 35 | | | | Of David. | | |
| 36 | For the Preeminent One. | For the Servant of Yahweh. | | Of David. | | |
| 37 | | | | Of David. | | |
| 38 | | | A Psalm | of David. | For causing remembrance. | |
| 39 | For the Preeminent One. | Of Jeduthun. | A Psalm | of David. | | |
| 40 | For the Preeminent One. | | | Of David. | A Psalm. | |
| 41 | For the Preeminent One. | | A Psalm | of David. | | |

**Book 2**

| 42 | For the Preeminent One. | | A *Maskil* | of the sons of Korah. | | |
|----|----|----|----|----|----|----|
| 43 | | | | | | |
| 44 | For the Preeminent One. | | | Of the sons of Korah. | A *Maskil* | |

| Ps | For the Preeminent One (למנצח) | Other information/ instructions | Genre/ psalm type | Author | Genre/ psalm type | Historical information |
|---|---|---|---|---|---|---|
| 45 | For the Preeminent One. | On Lilies. | | Of the sons of Korah. | A *Maskil*. A Song of Beloveds. | |
| 46 | For the Preeminent One. | | | Of the sons of Korah. | On *Alamoth*. A song. | |
| 47 | For the Preeminent One. | | | Of the sons of Korah. | A Psalm. | |
| 48 | | | A Song. A Psalm. | Of the sons of Korah. | | |
| 49 | For the Preeminent One. | | | Of the sons of Korah. | A Psalm. | |
| 50 | | | A Psalm | of Asaph. | | |
| 51 | For the Preeminent One. | | A Psalm | of David. | | When Nathan the prophet went to him, just as he had gone to Bathsheba. |
| 52 | For the Preeminent One. | | A *Maskil* | of David. | | When Doeg the Edomite went and declared to Saul, and said to him, "David went to the house of Ahimelek." |
| 53 | For the Preeminent One. | On *Mahalat*. | A *Maskil* | of David. | | |
| 54 | For the Preeminent One. | With stringed instruments. | A *Maskil* | of David. | | When the Ziphites went and said to Saul, "Is not David hiding with us?" |
| 55 | For the Preeminent One. | With stringed instruments. | A *Maskil* | of David. | | |
| 56 | For the Preeminent One. | On Dove of Silence, Distances. | | Of David. | A *Miktam*. | When the Philistines seized him in Gath. |

| Ps | For the Preeminent One (למנצח) | Other information/ instructions | Genre/ psalm type | Author | Genre/ psalm type | Historical information |
|---|---|---|---|---|---|---|
| 57 | For the Preeminent One. | Do Not Destroy. | | Of David. | A *Miktam*. | When he fled from before Saul, in the cave. |
| 58 | For the Preeminent One. | Do Not Destroy. | | Of David. | A *Miktam*. | |
| 59 | For the Preeminent One. | Do Not Destroy. | | Of David. | A *Miktam*. | When Saul sent, and they watched the house to kill him. |
| 60 | For the Preeminent One. | On *Shushan Edut* [On the Lily of Testimony] | A *Miktam* | of David. | For teaching. | In his struggle with Aram Naharaim [Aram of the two rivers, Mesopotamia] and with Aram Zobah, and Joab returned and struck Edom in the Valley of Salt, twelve thousand. |
| 61 | For the Preeminent One. | On the String. | | Of David. | | |
| 62 | For the Preeminent One. | On Jeduthun. | A Psalm | of David. | | |
| 63 | | | A Psalm | of David. | | When he was in the wilderness of Judah. |
| 64 | For the Preeminent One. | | A Psalm | of David. | | |
| 65 | For the Preeminent One. | | A Psalm | of David. | A Song. | |
| 66 | For the Preeminent One. | | A Song. | | A Psalm. | |
| 67 | For the Preeminent One. | With stringed instruments. | A Psalm. | | A Song. | |

| Ps | For the Preeminent One (למנצח) | Other information/instructions | Genre/psalm type | Author | Genre/psalm type | Historical information |
|----|----|----|----|----|----|----|
| 68 | For the Preeminent One. | | | Of David. | A Psalm. A Song. | |
| 69 | For the Preeminent One. | On Lilies. | | Of David. | | |
| 70 | For the Preeminent One. | | | Of David. | For causing remembrance. | |
| 71 | | | | | | |
| 72 | | | | Of Solomon. | | |

**Book 3**

| Ps | For the Preeminent One | Other information/instructions | Genre/psalm type | Author | Genre/psalm type | Historical information |
|----|----|----|----|----|----|----|
| 73 | | | A Psalm | of Asaph. | | |
| 74 | | | A *Maskil* | of Asaph. | | |
| 75 | For the Preeminent One. | Do Not Destroy. | A Psalm | of Asaph. | A Song. | |
| 76 | For the Preeminent One. | With stringed instruments. | A Psalm | of Asaph. | A Song. | |
| 77 | For the Preeminent One. | On Juduthun. | | Of Asaph. | A Psalm. | |
| 78 | | | A *Maskil* | of Asaph. | | |
| 79 | | | A Psalm | of Asaph. | | |
| 80 | For the Preeminent One. | To Lilies. | A Testimony | of Asaph. | A Psalm. | |
| 81 | For the Preeminent One. | On the *Gittith*. | | Of Asaph. | | |
| 82 | | | A Psalm | of Asaph. | | |
| 83 | | | A Song. A Psalm | of Asaph. | | |

| Ps | For the Preeminent One (למנצח) | Other information/ instructions | Genre/ psalm type | Author | Genre/ psalm type | Historical information |
|---|---|---|---|---|---|---|
| 84 | For the Preeminent One. | On the Gittith. | | Of the sons of Korah. | A Psalm. | |
| 85 | For the Preeminent One. | | | Of the sons of Korah. | A Psalm. | |
| 86 | | | A Prayer | of David. | | |
| 87 | | | | Of the sons of Korah. | A Psalm. A Song. | |
| 88 | | | A Song. A Psalm | of the sons of Korah. | | |
| | For the Preeminent One. | On Mahalath Leannoth. | A Maskil | Of Heman the Ezrahite. | | |
| 89 | | | A Maskil | of Ethan the Ezrahite. | | |

**Book 4**

| | | | | | | |
|---|---|---|---|---|---|---|
| 90 | | | A Prayer | of Moses, the man of God. | | |
| 91 | | | | | | |
| 92 | | | A Psalm. | | A Song for the day of the Sabbath. | |
| 93 | | | | | | |
| 94 | | | | | | |
| 95 | | | | | | |
| 96 | | | | | | |
| 97 | | | | | | |
| 98 | | | A Psalm. | | | |
| 99 | | | | | | |

| Ps | For the Preeminent One (למנצח) | Other information/ instructions | Genre/ psalm type | Author | Genre/ psalm type | Historical information |
|---|---|---|---|---|---|---|
| 100 | | . | A Psalm | | for thanks-giving. | |
| 101 | | | | Of David. | A Psalm. | |
| 102 | | | A Prayer | of one afflicted, when he is faint. | | |
| 103 | | | | Of David. | | |
| 104 | | | | | | |
| 105 | | | | | | |
| 106 | | | | | | |

**Book 5**

| | | | | | | |
|---|---|---|---|---|---|---|
| 107 | | | | | | |
| 108 | | | A Song. A Psalm | of David. | | |
| 109 | For the Preemi-nent One. | | | Of David. | A Psalm. | |
| 110 | | | | Of David. | A Psalm. | |
| 111 | | | | | | |
| 112 | | | | | | |
| 113 | | | | | | |
| 114 | | | | | | |
| 115 | | | | | | |
| 116 | | | | | | |
| 117 | | | | | | |
| 118 | | | | | | |
| 119 | | | | | | |
| 120 | | | A song of the goings up. | | | |

| Ps | For the Preeminent One (למנצח) | Other information/ instructions | Genre/ psalm type | Author | Genre/ psalm type | Historical information |
|---|---|---|---|---|---|---|
| 121 | | | A song of the goings up. | | | |
| 122 | | | A song of the goings up. | Of David. | | |
| 123 | | | A song of the goings up. | | | |
| 124 | | | A song of the goings up. | Of David. | | |
| 125 | | | A song of the goings up. | | | |
| 126 | | | A song of the goings up. | | | |
| 127 | | | A song of the goings up. | Of Solomon. | | |
| 128 | | | A song of the goings up. | | | |
| 129 | | | A song of the goings up. | | | |
| 130 | | | A song of the goings up. | | | |
| 131 | | | A song of the goings up. | Of David. | | |

| Ps | For the Preeminent One (למנצח) | Other information/ instructions | Genre/ psalm type | Author | Genre/ psalm type | Historical information |
|---|---|---|---|---|---|---|
| 132 | | | A song of the goings up. | | | |
| 133 | | | A song of the goings up. | Of David. | | |
| 134 | | | A song of the goings up. | | | |
| 135 | | | | | | |
| 136 | | | | | | |
| 137 | | | | | | |
| 138 | | | | Of David. | | |
| 139 | For the Preeminent One. | | | Of David. | A Psalm. | |
| 140 | For the Preeminent One. | | A Psalm | of David. | | |
| 141 | | | A Psalm | of David. | | |
| 142 | | | A Maskil | of David. | | When he was in the cave. A prayer. |
| 143 | | | A Psalm | of David. | | |
| 144 | | | | Of David. | | |
| 145 | | | A Praise | of David. | | |
| 146 | | | | | | |
| 147 | | | | | | |
| 148 | | | | | | |
| 149 | | | | | | |
| 150 | | | | | | |

Slots 1–6 and the information they present will now be discussed in order.

Slot 1 is always reserved for the term למנצח (the one exception to this is found at Psalm 30), which I have translated "For the Preeminent One." When this appears in a superscription, it always stands first.[61] Occurring fifty-five times across the Psalter, its distribution is as follows: nineteen times in Book 1, twenty-five times in Book 2, eight times in Book 3, none in Book 4, and three times in Book 5.

The only instance of this form (למנצח) outside psalm superscriptions is Hab 3:19 ("For the Preeminent One. With my stringed instruments"), which reads like a psalm superscription, though in this case it is a subscription, standing at the end of Habakkuk's psalm-like prayer (cf. Hab 3:1). The fact that the form is not used elsewhere makes it difficult to establish meaning from usage. Frank-Lothar Hossfeld and Erich Zenger write:

> As regards the first piece of information, למנצח = "For the Music Master," we gladly associate ourselves with Tate's conclusion: "No one really knows what this term meant, and it probably had different meanings at different times. ... I have chosen the traditional 'for the leader' on the basis that (1) the meaning of מבצח [*sic*] is that of the leader or an official responsible for the selection and recitation of a psalm ... and (2) there seems to be no more persuasive option."[62]

Because of the references to music (songs, singing, instruments, etc.) that pervade the Psalter, this term has been interpreted by English translations as referring to one preeminent in music, thus the CSB's "For the choir director" and the ESV's "To the choirmaster." The JPS, however, is more restrained: "For the Leader."

The root נצח has to do with extremity or perpetuity when used as a noun, with leadership when used as a verb. Interestingly, in 1 Sam 15:29, Samuel describes Yahweh as the נצח ישראל, and CSB renders this "the Eternal One of Israel," taking it to refer to Yahweh's perpetuity; the ESV,

---

[61] The one exception being Ps 88. The superscription of Ps 88 is practically a double-superscription, however, and למנצח (*lamenatseach*) does stand in the initial position of the second line:
Line 1: A song. A psalm of the sons of Korah.
Line 2: For the Preeminent One. On Mahalath Leannoth. A Maskil of Ethan the Ezrahite.

[62] Frank-Lothar Hossfeld and Erich Zenger, *Psalms 2: A Commentary on Psalms 51–100*, Hermeneia (Minneapolis: Fortress, 2005), 30; quoting Marvin E. Tate, *Psalms 51–100*, WBC 20 (Nashville: Nelson, 1991), 5.

NAS, and NIV seem to understand this as a reference to Yahweh's extreme glory, rendering the phrase "the Glory of Israel." The form that appears in the Psalm superscriptions (למנצח) is a *piel* participle with a *lamed* prefix, thus something like "for the one who stands out," and the "standing out" seems to reference leading. This can be seen from the related *piel* infinitive construct, לנצח, used on several occasions to describe Levites leading worship with their lyres (1 Chr 15:21), Levites overseeing work on the house of Yahweh (1 Chr 23:4), Levites repairing the temple (2 Chr 34:12), and Levites supervising the rebuilding of the temple (Ezra 3:8–9). David set the Levites over the musical praise of God, and the son of David would be the temple builder, realities that—in view of the promise that the son of David would build a house for God's name (2 Sam 7:13)—forge interesting connotations and associations between the future king and this term. Used as a participle, perhaps to distinguish it from the infinitive construct form often used to describe the Levites, למנצח ("For the Preeminent One") seems to carry connotations of Davidic initiative in temple building and the praise of Yahweh that would take place there.

When the Psalms were translated into Greek, this term was rendered εἰς τὸ τέλος, which Brenton translated "For the end" and Pietersma "Regarding completion" (NETS).[63] As mentioned above, when used as a noun נצח has to do with perpetuity, and the form לנצח (*lamed* prefix on the noun) often means "forever."[64] This common form may have influenced the Greek translation of the superscriptions.

I have chosen to render the form under discussion (למנצח) as "For the Preeminent One," because I take it as one of the many references to the king from the house of David. The king in view could be David himself, a member of the house God promised to build for him, or the seed who would be his Lord (110:1) and sit on his throne forever (2 Sam 7:12–13). Mitchell notes, "The participle מנצח could indicate a chief musician, precentor, or *hazzan*. But it could be understood in other ways. The *leader*

---

[63] Lancelot C. Brenton, *The Septuagint with Apocrypha: Greek and English* (Peabody, MA: Hendrickson, 1986), ad loc.

[64] See Job 4:20; 14:20; 20:7; 23:7; 36:7; Pss 9:6 (MT 9:7), 18 (MT 19); 10:11; 44:23 (MT 44:24); 49:9 (MT 49:10); 52:5 (MT 52:7); 68:16 (MT 68:17); 74:1, 10, 19; 77:8 (MT 77:9); 79:5; 89:46 (MT 89:47); 103:9; Prov 21:28; Isa 13:20; 25:8; 28:28; 33:20; 34:10; 57:16; Jer 3:5; 50:39; Lam 5:20; Amos 8:7; Hab 1:4.

could mean Messiah, especially in the post-exilic period, when נצח is
attested as having the meaning *conquer*."[65]

Slot 2 is filled only in Books 1–3 (Pss 1–89). Nothing is placed in this slot
in Books 4 and 5 (Pss 90–150). Material placed here provides the following
kinds of "Other information and instructions" (in order of appearance):

- the phrase "with stringed instruments" occurs six times (Pss 4,
  6, 54, 55, 67, and 76);
- "upon the eighth," twice (Pss 6 and 12);
- "on the *Gittith*," thrice (Pss 8, 81, 84);
- "On the Death of the Son," once (Ps 9);
- "For the Servant of Yahweh," twice (Pss 18 and 36);
- "Upon the Doe of the Dawn," once (Ps 22)
- "A Song for the dedication of the house," once (Ps 30);
- "Of Jeduthun," once (Ps 39) and "On Jeduthun," twice (Pss 62
  and 77);
- "On Lilies," twice (Pss 45 and 69, see also 60); "To Lilies," once
  (Ps 80);
- "On *Mahalat*," once (Pss 53); "On *Mahalath Leannoth*," once (Ps 88);
- "On Dove of Silence, Distances," once (Ps 56);
- "Do Not Destroy," four times (Pss 57, 58, 59, 75);
- "On *Shushan Eduth*" ["On the Lily of Testimony"], once (Ps 60);
- "On the String," once (Ps 61);

Some of these are difficult to understand (e.g., Pss 22 and 56), and at
points I have simply transliterated (e.g., Pss 39 and 53) because it is not
clear what these terms mean.[66]

Slots 3 and 5 tend to provide the same kinds of information, identifying
the genre or type of psalm. The terms used here include:

- "Psalm," forty-one times in slot 3; fifteen times in slot 5;
- "*Shiggaion*," only in Ps 7;

---

[65] Mitchell, *Message of the Psalter*, 19, citing BDB, 663, and noting the LXX rendering of
Hab 3:19, "where למנצח becomes τοῦ νικῆσαι."

[66] See the discussions in Derek Kidner, *Psalms 1–72: An Introduction and Commentary*, TOTC
(London: InterVarsity Press, 1973), 47–59; and Allen P. Ross, *A Commentary on the Psalms: 1–41*
(Grand Rapids: Kregel, 2012), 47–50.

- *"Miktam,"* twice in slot 3, Pss 17 and 60; four times in slot 5, Pss 56–59;
- "Prayer," four times in slot 3, Pss 17, 86, 90, and 102; once in slot 6, Ps 142;
- *"Maskil,"* ten times in slot 3; three times in slot 5;
- "Song," five times in slot 3; nine times in slot 5;
- "Testimony," only in Ps 80;
- "Praise," only in Ps 145;
- "A Song of the goings up," fifteen times in slot 3, Pss 120–134;
- Psalms 38 and 70 have "For causing remembrance" in slot 5;
- Psalm 60 has "For teaching" in slot 5;
- Psalm 100 has "for thanksgiving" in slot 5;
- Psalm 102 has "when he is faint" in slot 5;
- Some psalms have more than one of these terms in either slot 3 or 5, for example, "A Song. A Psalm" in Ps 48 (see also Pss 45, 46, 83, 87, 88).

Psalms 3–23 place information of this sort in slot 3, so that when Ps 24 places it in slot 5, it feels as though the pattern has been broken. After that, however, the material occurs often enough in slot 5 to constitute a pattern unto itself. When information of this kind is placed in slot 3 and the ascription of authorship follows in slot 4, I render the phrase along the lines of, "A Psalm of David" (e.g., Ps 3). When genre information comes in slot 5, by contrast, after the authorship ascription in slot 4, I render it, "Of David. A Psalm" (e.g., Ps 24). In my view it is unfortunate that standard English translations ignore the distinctions in word order (cf. CSB and ESV on Ps 24, "A Psalm of David"). Translating exactly what is there in the order it appears would give readers of English the opportunity to see that the psalm superscriptions follow a fixed formula regarding what kind of information can be put where.

When authorship is attributed in a psalm superscription (see below, "Authorship"), the name always stands in slot 4. The first psalm of each book has a different author (see table 3 above), adding emphasis, it would seem, to the seams between the books: Book 1, Ps 1, no attribution; Book 2, Ps 42, "of the sons of Korah;" Book 3, Ps 73, "of Asaph;" Book 4, Ps 90, "Moses;" Book 5, Ps 107, no attribution.

Every psalm with a superscription in Book 1 (thirty-seven of forty-one) names David in this information slot. Eighteen of the thirty-one psalms in Book 2 name him, but then only one psalm in Book 3 (86) and two in Book 4 (101, 103) do so. Fifteen of the forty-four psalms in Book 5 attribute authorship to David.

Seven psalms in Book 2 are attributed to the "sons of Korah," with another four in Book 3 and none in either Book 4 or 5. One psalm in Book 2 is attributed to Asaph, with another eleven in Book 3, and none in Books 4 or 5. Two psalms name Solomon (72 and 127); one Heman (88) and Ethan (89), Ezrahites both; one Moses (90); and one "one afflicted" (102).

The sixth slot is reserved for historical information that allows us to find context for the psalm's content in biblical narratives. Only thirteen psalms contain such information: four in Book 1 (Pss 3, 7, 18, and 34); eight in Book 2 (Pss 51, 52, 54, 56, 57, 59, 60, 63); none in Books 3 or 4, and only one in Book 5 (Ps 142).[67]

## A. Authorship

I will begin this discussion with evidence from within the Scriptures, then set forth the conclusion to which this evidence leads me, before considering arguments for positions at odds with my own conclusions.

Within the Old Testament itself we find evidence that the superscriptions were interpreted as indicating authorship. The Chronicler writes, "Then King Hezekiah and the officials told the Levites to sing praise to the Lord in the words of David and of the seer Asaph" (2 Chr 29:30, CSB). This verse seems to indicate that the Levites were instructed to employ psalms of David and Asaph as they sang praise to Yahweh.[68]

Along these lines, 2 Sam 22 attributes what amounts to Ps 18 to David (2 Sam 22:1–51). The author of Chronicles likewise recounts how David appointed the Levites over the service of song at Yahweh's house (1 Chr 6:31 [MT 6:16]; see also 15:16), and that he gave parts of what we know as Pss 105, 96, and 106 to Asaph to sing to Yahweh (1 Chr 16:7–36; see the "Context" section in the commentary below on Pss 96, 105, and 106).[69]

---

[67] Kidner, *Psalms 1–72*, 58, includes Ps 30 from Book 1, but the placement of the information seems to me to indicate that the phrase "for the dedication of the house" modifies the Psalm's genre, "A song." Being then followed by the ascription, "Of David," this notice does not come last as the other historical superscriptions do.

[68] Cf. Mitchell, *Message of the Psalter*, 91–92.

[69] See Talshir, "Canon-Related Concepts," 398: "As far as the Chronicler is concerned, he is citing from an existing and accepted collection of psalms, attributed to David and to his contemporary poets Asaph, Heman and Jeduthun. ... The Chronicler, then, originates

The author of Samuel further presents David referring to himself as "the sweet psalmist of Israel" (2 Sam 23:1), and Amos 6:5 refers to people who "like David devise for themselves instruments of song," indicating that David invented some musical instruments. These Old Testament authors viewed David as a psalm-writer.

Jesus, whom I confess with the one holy and apostolic church as the only begotten Son of God the Father Almighty, understood the attribution of a psalm to David to mean that David himself wrote that psalm (see, e.g., Mark 12:35–37 and parallels). Note that in context the argument Jesus makes turns on Davidic authorship. I do not believe that Jesus could have been wrong about this, nor do I find it plausible that he accommodated his way of speaking to the mistaken ideas of his audience. For him to do that would seem to entail him in a deception, and I do not think it plausible that he would deceive his audience on such a point. We see no indication in the Gospels that he was hesitant to offend people whose erroneous traditions he rejected.

The New Testament writers also indicate that psalms attributed to David were in fact written by David, and in several instances they say that the Holy Spirit spoke through David (see, e.g., Acts 1:16; 2:25; 2:34; Rom 4:6; 11:9). In some cases a biblical author will attribute a psalm to David even when there is no superscription, as Luke does with Ps 2 in Acts 4:25. The author of Hebrews does the same with Ps 95 in Heb 4:7. Because I understand Luke and the author of Hebrews to be inspired by the Holy Spirit and therefore inerrant, I think this means that David wrote Pss 2 and 95.

In my view, biblical theology is the attempt to understand and embrace the interpretive perspective of the biblical authors.[70] I want to believe what the biblical authors believed. From the evidence presented above, it seems to me that Old Testament authors, Jesus, and authors of the New Testament believed that when authorship is attributed in the superscriptions of the psalms, the person to whom the psalm was ascribed did in fact write the psalm. As a follower of Jesus, I seek to believe what he believed about the Bible (see esp. Matt 4:4; 5:18; John 10:35). Jesus believed that David wrote the psalms attributed to him, and so do I.

---

the tradition which accredits David and his chief singers with the writing of the Psalms, or alternatively reflects an already extant tradition of this sort."

[70] See Hamilton, *What Is Biblical Theology?*

It gives me no pleasure to see people contradict Jesus and the Bible, nor do I enjoy pointing out when they have done so. Jesus is Lord, and every knee will bow to him (Phil 2:10–11). When people deny that the authors to whom the psalms are ascribed in the superscriptions did in fact write the psalms, they contradict the evidence of the Old and New Testaments and the testimony of the Lord Jesus himself.

Are these contradictions warranted? We will now survey some of the evidence presented by those who reject the Bible's own testimony on the authorship of the psalms, and we will then briefly consider how this evidence has been interpreted through the ages. *Grammatical, historical,* and *theological* evidence has been cited against the ascriptions of authorship in the superscriptions, and each kind of evidence will be briefly considered in turn

Mitchell makes a *grammatical* case when he writes, "Those headings, for instance, that claim their psalms were composed by David in a particular situation, clearly come from a later hand than their lyrics, for they refer to the psalmist in the third person."[71] The case amounts to this: would David write a superscription like the one we find on Ps 3, "A psalm of David. When he fled from before Absalom, his son." Would David speak of himself in the third person? For Mitchell, the answer is no. I would suggest, however, that the biblical authors regularly speak of themselves in the third person, and that it is not difficult to imagine David doing so. The Bible universally attributes the Torah—the first five books of the Old Testament—to Moses, and Moses often refers to himself in the third person (e.g., Num 12:3). Isaiah speaks of himself in the third person (e.g., Isa 1:1; 13:1; 38:1, 21; 39:5). Hosea describes himself in the third person (e.g., Hos 1:1, 4) and the first (e.g., 3:1). Micah speaks in both the third and first person of himself (Mic 1:1; 3:1). Daniel speaks of himself in both the first (e.g., Dan 9:2) and third (e.g., Dan 10:1) person.[72] Ezra speaks of himself in the third person (e.g., Ezra 7:1–10). Long-standing Jewish and Christian tradition has accepted the Bible's own claims about the authorship of these books, but after the so-called Enlightenment many straightforward biblical assertions have been rejected. We have two options. We can invent a rule that says authors do not speak of themselves in the third

---

[71] Mitchell, *Message of the Psalter*, 16.

[72] See my discussion of the authorship and date of Daniel in James M. Hamilton, *With the Clouds of Heaven: The Book of Daniel in Biblical Theology*, NSBT 32 (Downers Grove, IL: InterVarsity Press, 2014), 30–40.

person: a rule this author admits he finds to be rather arbitrary. Or we can allow the Bible to tell us who wrote its parts, allowing its authors to describe themselves according to their wont.

Another grammatical facet of these discussions involves surveys of all the possible meanings of the *lamed* prefix (on forms such as לדוד, "of David"), possible meanings no one disputes.[73] The issue at hand is whether we are to throw out the indications we find *within the Bible itself*—from other Old and New Testament authors and Jesus—about how the *lamed* prefix in the psalm superscriptions is to be understood. We noted above that "For the preeminent one" (למנצח) occurs in psalm superscriptions and in Hab 3:19. Habakkuk 3:1 also reads like a psalm superscription, "A prayer of Habakkuk" (תפלה לחבקוק).

The formula in Hab 3:1 looks to be modeled on the one found in Pss 17:1; 86:1; 90:1; and 102:1 (see also 142:1). Habakkuk seems to have employed a recognized formula for designating oneself as the author of a psalmic prayer. It seems to me that figures such as Habakkuk, the author of Chronicles, Jesus, Paul, and the author of Hebrews were in a better position to understand what was intended by these *lamed* prefixes than anyone living in modern times.

Moving from grammatical to *historical* reasons for rejecting the authorship claims in the Psalms, the authors of the recent commentary on Psalms in the New International Commentary on the Old Testament (NICOT) series, Nancy deClaissè-Walford, Rolf A. Jacobson, and Beth LaNeel Tanner write,

> We believe that it is likely that the superscription [of David] did not originally indicate authorship—particularly, it did not originally indicate authorship by King David. There are several reasons for this conclusion. The primary reason is the many anachronisms in the psalms that preclude the idea of Davidic authorship. The most obvious of these anachronisms are the frequent references to the temple (Pss. 23:6; 27:4; 36:8), which was built after David's time.[74]

---

[73] See deClaisse-Walford, Jacobson, and Tanner, *Psalms*, 10; and Peter C. Craigie, *Psalms 1–50*, WBC 19 (Waco, TX: Word, 1983), 33–34.

[74] DeClaisse-Walford, Jacobson, and Tanner, *Psalms*, 10.

This claim of anachronism does not stand up to examination. In each of the texts they cite, Pss 23:6, 27:4, and 36:8, we find references to the "house" (בית) of Yahweh. We should first note the possibility that David could be speaking of God's house metaphorically, referring to all creation as the dwelling place of God because the tabernacle and later the temple symbolized the cosmos.[75] Aside from that, however, before David's birth Samuel was sleeping in the "temple" (היכל) of Yahweh when Yahweh called him into service (1 Sam 3:3). There are several possibilities: (1) a later author could be speaking anachronistically, referring to the tabernacle as the temple; (2) an earlier narrative could have been updated in light of later terminology; or (3) the terms later used to refer to the temple Solomon built, terms like temple/palace (היכל) and house (בית) were in use prior to the construction of the temple to describe the tabernacle and other places where God was understood to be specially present, such as the place Jacob named "Bethel," "house (בית) of God," "gate of heaven" in Gen 28:17–19.[76] The charge of anachronism in the Psalms can only stand if we assume that the texts of Genesis and Samuel have been altered or do not accurately reflect the time they describe. If, on the other hand, we take the texts of Genesis and Samuel at face value—and the texts themselves are our primary sources—then these instances attest to references to the temple of Yahweh and the house of Yahweh long before the time of David.

As for claims of *theological*" or "cultic" anachronisms, the NICOT authors allude to these but cite no specific examples.[77] Claims of this nature tend to be very subjective, usually based on what modern scholars deem the ancient authors could have or would have known, and sometimes such claims are made in spite of what the ancient texts themselves say. At any rate, the conclusion that David and the others to whom the psalms are attributed in the superscriptions could not have written what the psalms say for "theological" or "cultic" reasons does not necessarily follow from the evidence itself.

---

[75] G. K. Beale, *The Temple and the Church's Mission: A Biblical Theology of the Dwelling Place of God*, NSBT 17 (Downers Grove, IL: InterVarsity Press, 2004).

[76] For the Old Testament's various ways of describing the presence of God among his people, see James M. Hamilton, "God with Men in the Torah," *WTJ* 65 (2003): 113–33; and Hamilton, "God with Men in the Prophets and the Writings: An Examination of the Nature of God's Presence," *SBET* 23 (2005): 166–93.

[77] DeClaisse-Walford, Jacobson, and Tanner, *Psalms*, 10.

The more time one spends reading modern critical scholarship, the less likely Davidic authorship of the Psalms seems. On the other hand, if the biblical texts themselves eclipse modern critical biblical scholarship in priority, one will likely agree with the authors of the Old and New Testaments—and the vast majority of the "democracy of the dead"—that the people to whom the psalms are attributed did in fact write them. As G. K. Chesterton wrote, "Tradition means giving votes to the most obscure of all classes, our ancestors. It is the democracy of the dead. Tradition refuses to submit to the small and arrogant oligarchy of those who merely happen to be walking about."[78]

Rolf Rendtorff notes, "In later tradition David is seen to be the author of the psalms in general. 2 Macc 2:13 mentions the 'writings of David,' and according to the large Qumran scroll (11QPs^a col. 27) David 'wrote' and 'spoke' no less than 3,600 psalms ... and 450 'songs.' "[79]

Consider the way the NICOT authors summarize the tradition:

> Beginning in antiquity, communities of faith began to associate the Psalter with King David. ... In the Talmud, it is stated that "David wrote the Book of Psalms ..." (*b. Bava Batra 14b–15a*). In this tradition of interpretation of Davidic authorship, the super-scriptions ... are taken as expressing authorship. ... Throughout premodern interpretation of the Psalms, David was assumed to be the author of those psalms that began with the superscription *ledawid*. ... The New Testament also associates David with the psalms. ... The Septuagint, Syriac, and Qumran Psalters indicate that this tradition was expanding very early.[80]

These authors acknowledge the antiquity and ubiquity of the tradition, and yet they set aside the following facts: native speakers of Hebrew living very close to the time when the Psalter was put in its final form (Habakkuk, author of Chronicles, translator of the Greek Psalter, those at Qumran) interpreted the *lamed* prefixes as attributing authorship; the Old and New Testaments claim to be inspired and interpret the *lamed*

---

[78] From ch. 4, "The Ethics of Elfland," in G. K. Chesterton, *Orthodoxy* (Colorado Springs: Waterbrook, 2001), 64–65.

[79] Rolf Rendtorff, "The Psalms of David: David in the Psalms," in *The Book of Psalms: Composition and Reception*, ed. Peter W. Flint and Patrick D. Miller, VTSup 99 (Leiden: Brill, 2005), 53.

[80] DeClaisse-Walford, Jacobson, and Tanner, *Psalms*, 9.

prefixes as attributing authorship; and Jesus understood the *lamed* prefixes this way, as did the long history of interpretation down to the so-called Enlightenment.[81]

In spite of this evidence, the NICOT authors write, "for practical purposes, all of the psalms are anonymous."[82] Peter Craigie similarly concludes,

> the conjunction of the preposition ל with certain personal names (David, Solomon, Moses, et al.) need not, and probably does not, imply authorship ... it may be safest to recognize that the majority of psalms are anonymous and that no certain statements can be made concerning their authorship.[83]

Against Craigie, the safest course is to accept the testimony of the primary sources, as understood by Spirit-inspired interpreters. The New Testament, moreover, presents Jesus understanding the psalm superscriptions to attribute authorship. There is no safety in setting aside the Bible's testimony and contradicting it. Less safe still to disregard the testimony of the Son whose wrath is quickly kindled (Ps 2:12). It was not his opinion that superscripted psalms are anonymous, so to say they were seems to suggest he was in the wrong.

## B. THE AUTHENTICITY OF THE SUPERSCRIPTIONS

The question of whether the psalm superscriptions are authentic and authoritative turns on the question of the canonical and authoritative form of the text of the Old Testament. My analysis of the psalms leads me to the conclusion that the superscriptions were not later additions but integral to the original composition of the individual psalms.[84] Further, I hold the canonical form of the biblical text to be inspired by the Holy Spirit and therefore inerrant and authoritative (see "The Numbering of the Psalms and Their Verses," above).

---

[81] See the critique of the Enlightenment and the biblical scholarship that flows from it in Craig A. Carter, *Interpreting Scripture with the Great Tradition: Recovering the Genius of Premodern Exegesis* (Grand Rapids: Baker Academic, 2018).

[82] DeClaisse-Walford, Jacobson, and Tanner, *Psalms*, 11.

[83] Craigie, *Psalms 1–50*, 35.

[84] Dan Phillips has pointed out to me in private correspondence that the Greek translation of the Psalms seems at times to guess at the meaning of the Hebrew terms in the superscriptions, pointing to the antiquity of the terms. Further, the disparity between some superscriptions and the content of the psalms they head points to the originality of the superscriptions. Would a later editor adding a superscription to Ps 34, e.g., title it as it reads?

Mitchell summarizes the post-Enlightenment rejection of the super-scriptions as being based on two arguments: first, "the text of some psalms was said to date from long after the time of the person named in the heading." And second, "LXX additions to the Hebrew headings were thought to indicate an increasing tendency in scribal circles to create headings at all costs. Hence it was surmised that the whole tradition of the headings was itself of late origin."[85] Taking the second objection first, the multiplication of superscriptions in the Greek translation cannot be disputed. As Pietersma notes, "When one compares the titles in the Greek (LXX) with those of the Masoretic text (MT), it becomes immediately apparent that the process was essentially an additive one."[86] But the conclusion that the superscriptions were added long after the author to whom they were attributed does not follow from the fact that when the Psalms were translated into Greek more superscriptions were added.[87]

The first objection, that the superscriptions were later additions, amounts to a proposal about what the precanonical text may or may not have included, or how it may have been arranged. Such proposals are extrapolations from the text as it has come down to us. In his 2009 article on "The Text of the Old Testament," Gentry catalogues "the surviving witnesses to the text of the OT," listing them as (1) the Dead Sea Scroll texts from the Judean desert, (2) the Cairo Genizah fragments, (3) the Masoretic tradition, (4) medieval manuscripts, and (5) the ancient versions.[88] The superscriptions are attested in every form of the text of the Old Testament in our possession.

Those who reject the authenticity of the superscriptions sometimes distinguish between the canonical form of the text and what they refer to as the "original" form of the text. I am not sure how they know what form this original text took, since the only form of the text in our possession is the canonical. That is to say, the distinction between the canonical form of the text and its original form is not based on an earlier manu-script that witnesses to a Psalter that lacked superscriptions but rather

---

[85] Mitchell, *Message of the Psalter*, 41–42.

[86] Albert Pietersma, "Exegesis and Liturgy in the Superscriptions of the Greek Psalter," in *X Congress of the International Organization for Septuagint and Cognate Studies*, ed. Bernard A. Taylor, SCS 51 (Atlanta: Society of Biblical Literature, 2001), 100.

[87] For discussion of how the older objections from Driver and Mowinckel do not succeed, see Kidner, *Psalms 1–72*, 58–61.

[88] Gentry, "Text of the Old Testament," 20–26.

on a hypothetical reconstruction based on the canonical text we actually have.[89] For instance, referring to the superscriptions as "Psalm Titles," Peter Craigie writes,

> The titles form a part of the canonical text of the Hebrew Bible. ... In many cases, however, the titles do not appear to form an integral part of the psalm to which they are attached; they may represent the work of the editors of the early collections, or of the Book of Psalms as a whole. Thus, they are frequently of more importance for understanding the role of particular psalms in the context of the Psalter and in the historical context of Israel's worship than they are for understanding the original meaning and context of the individual psalms.[90]

Most of what Craigie says here reflects his *interpretation* of the evidence. The only objective fact Craigie states comes in his first sentence, when he affirms that the superscriptions are part of the canonical text. His interpretation that the superscriptions are not integral to their psalms is subjective and open to question, and he acknowledges that he does not know from whose hand they come when he says "they *may* represent the work of the editors" (emphasis added).

Against the conclusions Craigie articulates, consider the evidence of Ps 145, the only psalm with "A Praise" (תהלה) in the superscription, and the same term occurs in the final verse of the psalm, forming an *inclusio* (145:ss, 21 [MT 145:1, 21]). Because this superscription serves with the psalm's final verse to form a literary bracket around the whole psalm, it provides evidence that directly contradicts Craigie's claim that the titles are not integral to the psalms.[91]

---

[89] See Jeffrey H. Tigay's discussion of the way that the existence of "documented forms of each stage of" the Epic of Gilgamesh makes possible a kind of analysis not available for biblical scholars, who have "to hypothetically reconstruct those earlier stages, and, finally, to infer the processes by which the texts reached their present form. Since actual copies of these earlier stages were almost never available for consultation, the results, though impressive, remained hypothetical." Jeffrey H. Tigay, *The Evolution of the Gilgamesh Epic* (Philadelphia: University of Pennsylvania Press, 1982), 1–2.

[90] Craigie, *Psalms 1–50*, 31.

[91] Stephen Dempster points out that Psalm 34 provides another example (private communication): the phrase the CSB renders "pretended to be insane" in the superscription (ESV "changed his behavior"), employs the same term rendered "taste" in 34:8 (MT 34:9). The superscription of Psalm 52 is likewise integral to that Psalm's chiastic structure, as can be seen in the analysis below.

In the final sentence from this quotation, Craigie draws a distinction between "the role of particular psalms in the context of the Psalter," which is to say, the canonical form of the text, and "the original meaning and context of the individual psalms." Craigie does not specify what access he has to "the original meaning and context of the individual psalms." Since the canonical form of the text is the only form of the text in our possession, what Craigie calls "the original meaning and context of the individual psalms" seems to exist in his imagination.

I will be working from the hypothesis that a psalm's superscription comes from the hand of the psalm's author, and that the editor/anthologist who put the Psalter in its final form exercised a light editorial touch that followed trajectories he discerned in the materials. Elaboration of that working hypothesis belongs to the next section on the authorship and design of the Psalter.

## C. The Authorship and Design of the Psalter

At this point I want to introduce a hypothesis about (1) how the whole book of Psalms came to be and (2) how the strategy to communicate a unified message across a series of poems was accomplished.

To be clear, in agreement with many past and present, I am suggesting that the whole book of Psalms has been purposefully arranged so that the individual Psalms join together to tell a wider story in the way a collage of photographs can be arranged to portray a narrative development.[92] The simplest hypothesis is that the narrative message of the Psalter was David's own idea, and that he began the work of arranging the individual psalms. Later psalmists, having understood what David was doing, added to the project in ways that exposited, developed, enriched, and completed what he began.

---

[92] See, e.g., Mitchell, *Message of the Psalter*, 15: "The Hebrew Psalter was designed by its redactors as a purposefully ordered arrangement of lyrics with an eschatological message." For an excellent review of Psalms interpretation, see Mitchell, where he concludes that "the great majority of interpreters, historically speaking, endorse the MT-type arrangement of Psalms" and "the great majority of interpreters, historically speaking, regard the Psalms as foretelling eschatological events, interpreting them of Messiah, eschatological war, the ingathering of Israel, and so on." Mitchell further observes, "The great exception to the general dominance of these two views is the period c. 1820–1970," and he calls that period "a hiatus in Psalms interpretation, during which scholarly opinion diverged sharply from what must be considered, historically speaking, the dominant views" (quotations from 64–65; the whole discussion, 15–65, deserves consideration).

Consider an illustration: I could arrange a set of snapshot photographs that depicted a narrative presentation and interpretation of my own life. My choice of photographs and their meaning would be obvious to anyone from the way that my physical growth would be evident from baby pictures to school photos to graduation and wedding photos then to pictures that would include my children and on from there. Photos of my coffin would have to be added by those who came after me, and as the years passed, other photographs that communicated the significance of different events and the era in general might be added as people who knew what the collage was about and shared my perspective on life and its meaning gained historical perspective. In the kind of presentation I am describing, the narrative development would be impressionistic and interpretive. I might put things out of strict historical sequence in order to make a certain point, and I might also employ labels or other devices to connect my experience to the experience of others like myself.

The collage of the Psalter is not merely about David's own life but God's purposes in the world and how and where David fits in that wider project. For my summary of the overarching story the Psalter tells, see "An Overview of the Psalter," above.

If we allow the Scriptures to tell us their story, we know that David would have had access not only to the Torah but likely also Joshua, Judges, and Ruth. He further had access to prophets such as Samuel, Nathan, and Gad (1 Sam 16:13; 22:5; 2 Sam 7:4–17; 12:1–15, etc.; and cf. 1 Chr 29:29), who would have revealed God's will to him and helped him understand the Scriptures. David himself, moreover, was a prophet (Acts 2:30), inspired by the Holy Spirit of God (2 Sam 23:2).

My proposal, then, is that David not only wrote the individual psalms attributed to him but also began the process of setting them in order. Earlier Scripture would have informed not only his understanding of Israel's past but of his own life and (because passages like Lev 26 and Deut 28–32 prophesy Israel's future) the future of God's people. The trajectory set by David would have been understood by those who followed him not only in time but in perspective. Those who, like David, were enculturated by the Scriptures, those who understood *both* what David had written *and* the significance of David in God's purposes, who like him were not only poets but inspired by the Holy Spirit, saw what David had initiated, understood it, and complemented it with the psalms that God prompted them to write. On this understanding, those who wrote and added psalms to the broader project were complementing and contributing to the work of creative genius inaugurated by the sweet psalmist of Israel. This kind of process would naturally lead to the whole being mainly associated with David, just as the work of some great painter or sculptor is associated with the master himself, even if his apprentices and associates later added touch-ups and highlights.[93]

The symbolic universe in which David and the other Spirit-inspired psalmists operated would have been derived from the Scriptures, which likely would have been memorized (Deut 6:6–7), and which served to enculturate, educate, and elucidate those who knew them. The Bible was written to have world-shaping, mind-building, life-determining impact.[94] For my summary of how the Psalms fit with the wider message of the Old Testament, see "The Psalms in the Old Testament Canon" above and "Biblical and Theological Themes" below.

When we read the Bible sympathetically, we see a natural development from the earlier to the later parts of Scripture. In this commentary I pursue that kind of sympathetic reading of the Psalms, assuming that the inspiration of the Holy Spirit ensured that later biblical authors correctly interpreted earlier biblical authors whose message they developed and clarified.

## V. The Literary Structure and Meaning of the Psalter

How did I arrive at the material to be presented in this section? I began with a fair amount of confidence that Pss 15 and 24, being so similar to one another, were intended to bracket the material between them. I then found the suggestion that this material formed a chiasm persuasive.[95]

---

[93] Stephen Dempster has pointed out to me in private communication that Antoni Gaudi oversaw the beginning of the construction of the Sagrada Familia Basilica in Barcelona in 1882. The project has been under construction since then, and though Gaudi died in 1926, it is considered his work.

[94] Cf. C. Hassell Bullock, "The Shape of the Torah as Reflected in the Psalter, Book 1," in *From Creation to New Creation: Essays in Honor of G. K. Beale*, ed. Daniel M. Gurtner and Benjamin L. Gladd (Peabody, MA: Hendrickson, 2013), 31: "Judging from the many allusions in the Psalms to the Torah (also to the Prophets and Writings ...), I suggest that the psalmists were steeped in the language of those writings, especially the poetic sections, and the images of the Torah stories."

[95] I have been thinking about these matters for years. I was persuaded of Grant's proposal regarding Psalms 15–24 as evidenced by my citation of it in my 2010 book, *God's Glory in Salvation through Judgment*, 280 (citing Grant, *King as Examplar*, 11, 73–74).

The next step was the thought that if someone (David, as likely as not) had structured Pss 15–24 as a chiasm, might he not have done the same with surrounding material? Persuaded that it would be reasonable for a poetic genius to make broad use of a literary convention of such beauty and mnemonic power, I began to watch for repetitions and look for ways those repetitions in language or theme might indicate structure.[96]

Rather than assume that the authors of the psalms and the editor(s) who put them in order simply made haphazard statements or arranged the Psalms for little or no reason, I thus began to work from the assumption that there were, in fact, guiding intentions. These intentions, it seems, can be teased out by careful attention to repeated language, thematic shifts, and other cues authors build into texts. Mary Douglas writes, "As I see it, the tracing of the total scheme from beginning to end and the concern for a coherent pattern would correspond to the biblical authors' own preoccupations, and implicitly to their criteria of literary excellence."[97]

In a chiastic structure, the first and last elements correspond to one another, as do the second and second-to-last, and so forth to the central turning point. That center point will often recall the beginning and anticipate the end. The architecture of such a literary structure enables an author to indicate what is most important, whether by placing that idea in the very center or by reiterating it throughout. When an interpreter rightly understands how an author has structured his material, he knows where things start, where things end, and how things are balanced in between.

The biblical authors seem to have made great use of the chiastic form when organizing their material. Chiasms accomplish a number of powerful effects: by establishing starting and end points, the form ensures that the development of thought comes full circle. The corresponding sections (second and second-to-last, third and third-to-last, etc.) likewise become mutually interpretive, and the interpreter who recognizes the structure can and should read these balancing sections in light of one

---

[96] Having completed my work on the Psalter, I came across this study that confirms and runs in the same direction as the methodology I pursued: Wayne Brouwer, "Understanding Chiasm and Assessing Macro-Chiasm as a Tool of Biblical Interpretation," *CJT* 53 (2018): 99–127.

[97] Mary Douglas, *Thinking in Circles: An Essay on Ring Composition*, The Terry Lectures (New Haven: Yale University Press, 2010), 11. For another study of the biblical authors' use of symmetrical repetition balanced on a center point in chiastic structures, see Victor M. Wilson, *Divine Symmetries: The Art of Biblical Rhetoric* (Lanham, MD: University Press of America, 1997).

another. In this way chiasms become exegetically productive, showing the reader how the meaning of the whole communicates more than the sum of its individual parts. Similarly, authors often center their main idea(s) so that the chiastic structure functions to spotlight the particular contribution of the composition.

Douglas emphasizes the "ring composition's exegetical function," noting how "it controls meaning, it restricts what is said, and in doing so it expands meaning along channels it has dug."[98] Referring to the fact that "chiastic forms are probably the most common rhetorical device in Scripture," Victor Wilson speaks of "their enormous utility and range of application."[99] Just as idioms and grammatical constructions inform our understanding of phrases and sentences, wider literary structures inform our understanding of longer units of text. Douglas puts it well,

> You can compare the functions of ring composition to syntax: it tames wild words and firmly binds their meanings to its frame. Another function is greatly to deepen the range of reference by playing on the double meanings of words. Another of its benefits is that it is a form of play; it gives the pleasure of a game to the composer and the reader.[100]

Again, the chiastic form presents corresponding elements at the beginning and the end, and in each corresponding section down to the central turning point. As Wilson observes, "The center of a chiasm is its *theological* heart. The idea of a theological center gives an identifiable focus to the author's intentions and is a tremendous aid to interpretation."[101] Wilson continues by enumerating other advantages that accrue when interpreters rightly discern an author's chiastic structure:

> A second theological point is that viewing a text without knowledge of its chiastic structure can give the appearance of a text in disarray. ... The *mnemonic* advantage may be the most compelling reason for the longevity of the chiasm and the universality of its use. Here is a mechanism that responds to the listener's need for a generic frame of reference to guide the

---

[98] Douglas, *Thinking in Circles*, 13.
[99] Wilson, *Divine Symmetries*, 45.
[100] Douglas, *Thinking in Circles*, 14.
[101] Wilson, *Divine Symmetries*, 49 (emphasis original).

memory in the process of recollection. The chiasm is self-tu-
toring, prodding the memory to fill in the elements of the form
with balanced pairs. ... Finally, we can note the *aesthetic* attrac-
tion of the chiasmus. The pattern conveys the cyclic orderli-
ness of a perceived reality. ... As the artist seeks a visual balance
in composition, the chiasm obliges an oral world with an aural
balance. So, in a chiasm's return to its point of departure a resolution satisfies the ear's anticipation, like music's return to
the opening key.[102]

In this vein, David Carr writes regarding ancient Greek literature,

The very structure of texts facilitated their own memorization.
In Homer we see the use of chiastic structure for ordering material. ... In addition, as Parry, Lord, and others have observed,
literature like Homer is dense with other elements that would
have aided memorized recall of the text: use of standard sequences of epithets, repetition of the same sequence at the out-
set of several lines, repetition of broader speeches, and so on.[103]

Wilson similarly observes,

Chiasms appear at the micro and macro level of composition
from Homer to *Beowulf* and beyond. Herman Melville, Dylan
Thomas, James Joyce and Carlos Fuentes have all utilized the
construction, as have artists in other media (see Peterson, Por-
ter, and Nanny). Salvador Dali's concentric arrangement of the
apostles in his painting of the Last Supper is a good example.[104]

Both individual psalms and groups of psalms have been carefully structured and chiastically arranged. In this section of the introduction I have
gathered together the chiasms I see in units of material within the Psalter.
For explanation of these units, readers are referred to the "Context" sections in the commentary on relevant psalms.

These chiasms are proposals. They represent my attempt to describe
what the editor of the Psalter seems to have intended. At some points
these things can be described in different ways, and I do not claim to have

---

[102] Wilson, *Divine Symmetries*, 51 (emphasis original).
[103] Carr, *Writing on the Tablet of the Heart*, 98–99.
[104] Wilson, *Divine Symmetries*, 46.

found *the definitive* treatment of these topics. Different possibilities exist, and in some cases the chiastic proposal presented here in the introduction differs from the one presented in the commentary, precisely because both capture aspects of what the psalms present.

A. The Chiastic Structure of Book 1, Psalms 1–41

Psalms 1–2, Introduction to the Blessed Man, Yahweh's Messiah
Psalms 3–9, Absalom's Revolt
    Psalms 10–14, The Wicked
        Psalms 15–24, The King
    Psalms 25–33, God's Word and Glory
Psalms 34–41, Saved through Judgment[105]

## 1. Psalms 3–9

For discussion, see the "Context" section at the beginning of the commentary on Ps 9.

Psalm 3, Absalom's Night of Opportunity
    Psalm 4, David's Morning Prayer
        Psalm 5, They Are Wicked Not I
            Psalm 6, Don't Give Me What They Deserve
        Psalm 7, Plea of Innocence
    Psalm 8, Begotten Son of Adam
Psalm 9, Absalom's Death

## 2. Psalms 10–14

For discussion, see the "Context" section at the beginning of the commentary on Ps 10.

Psalm 10, The Wicked Says in His Heart
    Psalm 11, Yahweh in His Temple
        Psalm 12, Yahweh's Pure Word
    Psalm 13, How Long?
Psalm 14, The Fool Says in His Heart

---

[105] The significant similarities between Pss 25 and 34, along with other features of these psalms, make this proposal more persuasive to me than Grant's, which sees three units arranged ABA: Pss 1–14, 15–24, and 25–41 (*King as Exemplar*, 239).

### 3. Psalms 15–24

For discussion, see the "Context" section at the beginning of the commentary on Pss 15 and 18.

Psalm 15, Who Shall Ascend?
    Psalm 16, Comfort
        Psalm 17, Resurrection
            Psalm 18, Deliverance for David and His Seed
                Psalm 19, The Glory of God
            Psalms 20–21, The King
        Psalm 22, Death and Resurrection
    Psalm 23, Comfort
Psalm 24, Who Shall Ascend?

### 4. Psalms 25–33

For discussion, see the "Overview and Structure of Psalm 25" as well as the "Context" section at the beginning of the commentary on Pss 25, 29, and 30.

Psalm 25, Teaching
    Psalm 26, Vindication
        Psalm 27, Confidence
            Psalm 28, Plea
                Psalm 29, Glory
            Psalm 30, Praise
        Psalm 31, Refuge
    Psalm 32, Forgiveness
Psalm 33, Word

### 5. Psalms 34–41

For discussion, see the "Context" sections on each psalm in this unit, but especially 34, 35, and 41.

Psalm 34, Salvation
    Psalm 35, Defend Me!
        Psalm 36, Sin and Worship
            Psalm 37, Blessed/Cut Off
        Psalm 38, Save me!
    Psalm 39, Wisdom

Psalm 40, Delivered
Psalm 41, Blessed

B. The Chiastic Structure of Books 2–3, Psalms 42–89

Psalms 42–49, Sons of Korah
  Psalm 50, Asaph
    Psalms 51–72, David
  Psalms 73–83, Asaph
Psalms 84–89, Sons of Korah

The constituent parts of this chiasm extending across Books 2–3 of the Psalter may also be chiastic unto themselves. If this is so, the psalms of Korah in 42–49, those of David in 51–72, those of Asaph in 73–83, and those of Korah in 84–89 may have chiastic structures as follows:

### 1. Psalms 42–49, Of the Sons of Korah

See the "Context" sections in the discussion of these psalms in the commentary.

Psalms 42–43, Why So Downcast?
  Psalm 44, Remnant
    Psalm 45, King
    Psalm 46, City
  Psalms 47–48, Praise
Psalm 49, Wisdom

Psalm 50 being a lone psalm of Asaph can stand by itself or be grouped with Ps 49 (see the Context discussion on Ps 49).[106]

### 2. Psalms 51–72, Of David

These psalms of David can be grouped in different ways. I will start with possibilities for smaller units then make a proposal for the whole.

---

[106] Cf. Hensley's observation: "Recent scholarship has become more sensitive to the structural possibilities like chiastic or concentric arrangements of psalms. For example, Zenger sees chiastic arrangements within Pss 3–14, 15–24, 25–34, and 42–49, wherein each group centers around hymns (Pss 9, 19, 29, and 46 respectively). Arguments vary in strength from case to case, but the possibility seems well demonstrated, especially in Pss 15–24." Hensley, *Covenant Relationships*, 31.

In Ps 51 David confesses his sin with Bathsheba and prays for mercy and restoration, but Pss 52–59 detail the persecution David endured at Saul's hands (see the exposition for why the Psalter presents this persecution coming from Saul, rather than Absalom).

Psalm 52, Doeg (Saul's Executioner)
  Psalm 53 (cf. 14), The Fool Says in His Heart
    Psalm 54, Ziphite Treachery
      Psalm 55, The Traitor
        Psalm 56, Cast Down the Peoples, O God
      Psalm 57, When He Fled from Saul
    Psalm 58, Those Who Do Injustice in Their Hearts
Psalm 59, Saul Sent Men

In Ps 60 Yahweh proclaims his sovereignty over the land, and then follow four Psalms in which David cries out for Yahweh (see "Context" on Ps 61):

Psalm 61, Hear, O God
  Psalm 62, For God Alone
  Psalm 63, My Soul Thirsts for You
Psalm 64, Hear, O God

David's prayers are answered when God shoots his enemies in Ps 64, prompting the praises of Pss 65–68 (see "Context" on Ps 65):

Psalm 65, For the Preeminent One. A Psalm of David. A Song.
  Psalm 66, For the Preeminent One. A Song. A Psalm.
  Psalm 67, For the Preeminent One. With stringed instruments. A
    Psalm. A Song.
Psalm 68, For the Preeminent One. Of David. A Psalm. A Song.

As much as David's life typified the one to come, David himself was not the one to come. Book 2 closes with David in difficulty again, praying that the seed God raises up from his line might experience the fulfillment of all God promised. In Ps 72, that seed is Solomon, for whom David prays (see "Context" on Ps 69 and "Exposition" on 72:1).

Psalm 69, The Rejected King
  Psalm 70, Make Haste to Help Me

Psalm 71, Let Them Be Put to Shame (Not Me)
Psalm 72, Give the King Your Justice and Blessing

The whole unit of Davidic Psalms may also comprise a chiasm as follows:

Psalm 51, Bathsheba
  Psalm 52, Doeg
    Psalm 53, Fool (Ps 14)
      Psalm 54, Ziphite Betrayal
        Psalm 55, The Traitor
          Psalm 56, Cast Down Enemy Peoples
            Psalm 57, Be Exalted above the Heavens
              Psalm 58, Against Influencers
                Psalm 59, Assassins
                  Psalm 60, Restore Us!
                    Psalm 61, The King
                    Psalm 62, Wait
                  Psalm 63, Better Than Life
                Psalm 64, Deliverance
              Psalm 65, Blessing
            Psalm 66, Praise
          Psalm 67, Gladness
        Psalm 68, From Sinai to Zion
      Psalm 69, The Rejected King
    Psalm 70, Make Haste to Help Me
  Psalm 71, Let Them Be Put to Shame
Psalm 72, Solomon

Note here that Bathsheba (Ps 51) was Solomon's mother (Ps 72), and that
the attack of Doeg (Ps 52) relates to a cry for enemies to be put to shame
(Ps 71), as the unbelieving fool (Ps 53) prompts a cry for hasty help (Ps
70) and Ziphite betrayal (Ps 54) is connected to the rejected king (Ps 69).
The prayer against the traitor (Ps 55), the casting down of enemies (Ps 56),
the exaltation of Yahweh over the heavens (Ps 57), the prayers *against*
wicked influencers (Ps 58) and assassins (Ps 59) *for* restoration (Ps 60) are
all related to the transfer of Yahweh's throne from Sinai to Zion (Ps 68),
the gladness (67), praise (Ps 66), blessing (Ps 65), and deliverance (Ps 64)
of God's people who know his love is better than life (Ps 63). The whole

sequence turns on the prayer for the ever-reigning king (Ps 61), who will deliver those who wait for and trust in God (Ps 62).

### 3. Psalms 73–83, Of Asaph

The psalms of Asaph may be structured chiastically as follows:[107]

Psalm 73, Response to Perceived Injustice
 Psalm 74, Destruction of Temple
  Psalm 75, Judgment Appointed
   Psalm 76, Judgment Accomplished
    Psalm 77, I Will Remember
     Psalm 78, History of Disobedience
    Psalm 79, Destruction of Temple
   Psalm 80, Plea for Restoration
  Psalm 81, Feasts Anticipate Restoration
 Psalm 82, Gods Judged
Psalm 83, Peoples Judged

### 4. Psalms 84–89, Of the Sons of Korah

The psalms of the sons of Korah in 84–89 may reflect the following chiastic structure:

Psalm 84, Korah: Jerusalem
 Psalm 85, Korah: Hesed and Emet
  Psalm 86, David
 Psalm 87, Korah: Peoples in New Jerusalem
Psalm 88, Korah: Darkness
Psalm 89, Exile

### C. The Chiastic Structure of Book 4

Psalms 90–92, Mosaic Intercession and Reaffirmation of Davidic Covenant
 Psalms 93–100, Yahweh Reigns: Guaranteeing the Davidic Covenant

---

[107] Though Hensley does not present chiastic arrangements, he does speak of Pss 78 and 86 as "central" to their respective units: "Central to the Asaph group, Ps 78 identifies God's election of David and Zion as his divine response to Israel's covenant unfaithfulness. Central to the Korahite group, Ps 86 presents 'David' as the faithful servant of YHWH who appeals to the grace formula," Hensley, *Covenant Relationships*, 269.

Psalms 101–103, Davidic Commitment, Prayer, and Forgiveness
Psalms 104–106, Creation, the Covenant with Abraham, and Israel's Sin[108]

Alternatively, the structure of Book 4 could be depicted as follows:

Psalm 90, Moses
   Psalm 91, The Future King
      Psalm 92, Psalms 1–2
         Psalm 93, Enthroned above the Flood
            Psalm 94, Justice
               Psalm 95, Come Worship
                  Psalm 96, Praise
                     Psalm 97, Yahweh, of Sinai, Reigns
                        Psalm 98, The World's Savior and Judge
                     Psalm 99, Yahweh the Holy One Reigns
                  Psalm 100, Praise
               Psalm 101, Davidic Integrity
            Psalm 102, Prayer of One Afflicted
         Psalm 103, Far as the East Is from the West
      Psalm 104, Creation
   Psalm 105, Redemption
Psalm 106, Save Us! (and gather us from the lands, including reference
   to Moses)

D. The Chiastic Structure of Book 5

In *God's Glory in Salvation through Judgment*, I adapted Zenger's proposed chiasm for Book 5, and here in light of continued reflection I simplify it further:[109]

Psalms 107–112, Davidic King
   Psalms 113–118, Hallelujah
      Psalm 119, Torah

---

[108] Mckelvey presents a similar structure: A 90, B 91–92, C 93–100, C′ 101–104, B′ 105, A′ 106. Michael G. Mckelvey, *Moses, David and the High Kingship of Yahweh: A Canonical Study of Book IV of the Psalter*, GDBS 55 (Piscataway, NJ: Gorgias, 2010), 273; see also 276.

[109] Hamilton, *God's Glory in Salvation through Judgment*, 288; citing Erich Zenger, "The Composition and Theology of the Fifth Book of Psalms, Psalms 107–45," *JSOT* 80 (1998): 98. See esp. Snearly, *Return of the King*, 66–68, 72–74.

Psalms 120–137, Let Him Go Up
Psalms 138–145, Davidic King

Psalms 146–150, Final Hallels

## 1. Psalms 120–134

For discussion, see the "Context" section in the commentary on Ps 134.

Psalm 120, Exilic Distress
  Psalm 121, Help from Yahweh
    Psalm 122, To Yahweh's House and David's Throne
      Psalm 123, Eyes Lifted up to the One Enthroned
        Psalm 124, Saved from Flood-like Enemies
          Psalm 125, The Scepter of Wickedness Will Not Reign
            Psalm 126, Restored Fortunes
              Psalm 127, Yahweh Builds the House
            Psalm 128, Blessed Are All Who Fear Yahweh
          Psalm 129, Put the Wicked to Shame
            Psalm 130, More than Watchmen Wait for the Morning
        Psalm 131, Eyes Not Lifted Too High
      Psalm 132, Yahweh's Oath to David
    Psalm 133, Unity Like Oil on Aaron's Beard
Psalm 134, Bless Yahweh in the Temple

## 2. Psalms 137–145

For discussion, see the "Context" section in the commentary on Ps 137.

Psalm 137, Weeping
  Psalm 138, Answer
    Psalm 139, God
      Psalm 140 Traps
        Psalm 141, Reproof
      Psalm 142, Traps
    Psalm 143, Remember
  Psalm 144, Deliverance
Psalm 145, Praise

### 3. Psalms 146–150

Psalm 146, Blessed Are Those Who Trust the Maker
  Psalm 147, Yahweh Restores Jerusalem and Takes Pleasure in
  Fearers
    Psalm 148, Praise Yahweh from Heaven and Earth
  Psalm 149, Let the Hasid Exult and Do Psalm 2 Justice
Psalm 150, Let Everything That Has Breath Praise the Lord

E. THE CHIASTIC STRUCTURE OF THE BOOK OF PSALMS

This proposal overgeneralizes, but "chunking" the material into thematic groups in this way can make the general direction of the whole book's movement of thought easier to remember and contemplate.[110] Therefore, I propose the following chiastic structure for the Psalter's five books:

Book 1, Pss 1–41, The Suffering of the Historical David
  Book 2, Pss 42–72, The Reign of the Historical David
    Book 3, Pss 73–89, The End of the Historical Davidic House
  Book 4, Pss 90–106, Moses Intercedes for the Davidic Covenant
Book 5, Pss 107–150, The Conquest of the Future Davidic King

### VI. Translating the Psalms

Throughout this commentary I supply my own very literal translation of the Psalms. My intention is to make the link-words between psalms explicit in an effort to allow the author-intended innerbiblical resonance to reverberate in fullness.

Different translations have different goals, and those goals set the priorities and parameters for the work. A translation seeking to produce a powerful literary experience in the target language will do things differently than one seeking to be as faithful as possible with the original. Such a translation will achieve its purpose when readers relish the beauty

---

[110] Robar, *Verb and the Paragraph in Biblical Hebrew*, 12–13, writes: "Chunking is the packaging of multiple bits of information so as to be able to hold them all in memory and manipulate them as a unit. ... A chunk is a packet of information ... a 'gestalt or integrated whole.' ... This is the cognitive version of the Gestalt effect: in chunking, the mind seeks to generate a whole from the parts perceived ... when a chunk has been formed, the mind will then focus on that form, that Gestalt, at the expense of the details of the smaller bits of information ... chunking makes possible the construction of coherence."

of the Psalms in their own language, but such translations are not always helpful for close analysis of how particular terms are used in the Psalter.

As Article 10 of the Chicago Statement on Biblical Inerrancy affirms, "translations of Scripture are the Word of God to the extent that they faithfully represent the original." Because the Bible is God's word, God's people will always be eager to know exactly what the Holy Spirit inspired the biblical authors to say, and God's people will always value the original texts in the original languages. Those who cannot access the original languages will likewise be interested in different ways the text can be translated. There are good ways to make use of free renderings that seek to achieve functional equivalence, and there are good ways to make use of more exact renderings that aim more at formal equivalence. In the translation I have produced I seek to be as direct and formal as possible. Those who want to study exactly what the authors themselves wrote, what the Spirit himself inspired, will always seek more exact renderings (see, e.g., the way initial loose renderings into Greek were later revised to be closer to the original Hebrew), and the impetus to look at the very word of God will continue to drive people to study the Bible in the original languages.

I have chosen to create my own very literal translation of the Psalms for an important interpretive reason. The case that I will be making about the unfolding narrative storyline in the psalter depends heavily upon the way that thematic and linguistic points of contact create a wider web of meaning, linking one psalm to those that surround it, forging connections that make the individual psalms seem like different verses of the same song. In music small flourishes can recall and reprise earlier notes and movements, creating both continuity and development of theme. So it is with poetry: word choice, word order, rhythm, morphology, and even etymology are often pregnant with meaning.

Every word of the Psalms matters, even words whose meanings we do not know, such as selah and other terms in the superscriptions that we can only transliterate. This term selah is part of the sacred text, so we should at least transliterate it. We should not, as the NIV 2011 does, relegate the word selah to footnotes on the translation. In many psalms the placement of the word selah is one of the features the psalmists have used to indicate units of thought within the psalm. So the fact that we do not know what the word means does not mean that it communicates nothing to us.

Continuity between individual psalms is created and sustained in many ways: superscriptions, repeated phrases, the assumption of the wider theology of the Old Testament, ongoing reliance on the promise to David and the truth of God's word, and the reliable character of the God who spoke the word and made the promise. Within the web of meaning created by the devices and shared assumptions, the repetition of even seemingly incidental, everyday words becomes important. In some cases, the reuse of a rare suffix will recall to mind the earlier use of that suffix, forging connections between Psalms, electrifying a dynamic between them (cf. the use of the irregular third-person plural suffix ימו in Pss 2 and 6; for discussion see on Ps 6).

The reader of the Psalms in the Hebrew original has a direct encounter with the raw material that weaves this web of meaning: the sounds and suffixes, rhythms and repetitions, terms and constructions that forge the phrases and fasten the clasps that bind one psalm to another.[111] The resulting panorama displays rich meaning that thickens and deepens, transcending anything that could be derived from one psalm read in isolation from the whole canonical Psalter.

It is all too easy to miss these features and their combined effect if the Psalms are only read in English translation, particularly if the translation presents functional rather than formal equivalents. Sometimes even the more literal translations inexplicably introduce variations that obscure the interconnectedness of the Psalter. For instance, the phrase "all workers of iniquity" (כל פעלי און) occurs in Pss 5:5 (MT 5:6) and 6:8 (MT 6:9), forging a linguistic and thematic link between the two Psalms. The ESV fails to preserve this connection, rendering the phrase "evildoers" in 5:5 and "workers of evil" in 6:8. Translations that are more "free" than the ESV will naturally multiply instances of variation and discontinuity. Stylistic variation is a good principle for original composition in English. The authors of these ancient Hebrew poems, however, intentionally used and reused words and phrases that built strong bridges between psalms. When modern translators introduce stylistic variants, those bridges get burned.

Because of the differences between Hebrew and English, it is impossible to rebuild every one of these bridges in English. This is why, again, biblical scholars and pastors will continue to need to learn Hebrew and also why seminaries and Bible colleges must continue to teach it. As C. S.

---

[111] See esp. the discussions in Cole, *Psalms 1–2.*

Lewis wrote, "Nothing about a literature can be more essential than the language it uses. A language has its own personality, implies an outlook, reveals a mental activity, and has a resonance, not quite the same as those of any other."[112]

Discussing a difficulty in moving from Russian to English, Mirra Ginsburg writes in the preface to her translation of Dostoevsky's *Notes from Underground*, "This, alas, disappears in translation, unless the translator arrogates to herself the entirely inadmissible right to interpolate."[113] Alter apparently agrees with Ginsburg that for a translator to assume the "right to interpolate" is "entirely inadmissible," and he complains at length about the way English translations commit "the heresy of explanation." Alter writes, "The unacknowledged heresy underlying most modern English versions of the Bible is the use of translation as a vehicle for *explaining* the Bible instead of representing it in another language, and in the most egregious instances this amounts to explaining away the Bible."[114] We cannot bring everything in the Hebrew into English, but a formal equivalent translation philosophy coupled with an attempt to render terms and phrases consistently will be more successful than other translation philosophies, avoiding the impulse to "arrogate" the "inadmissible right to interpolate," and seeking to avoid "the heresy of explanation."

The Psalms were not composed in our culture by our contemporaries in our language. Because this is an ancient, foreign book, I am content for my translation to have an initially foreign feel to the English reader, for the English reader to need to give some thought to what he is reading, for him to need to read the poetry closely, compare phrases with surrounding psalms, and for him to feel that he is encountering something that was not composed by someone living in his culture, in his time, speaking his language. This is preferable, in my judgment, to an English reader coming to the Psalms and finding nothing that he does not already know, finding what can too often—in translation—feel like a bland and banal book.[115]

---

[112] Lewis, *Discarded Image*, 6.

[113] Mirra Ginsburg, "On the Translation," in *Notes from Underground*, by Fyodor Dostoyevsky (New York: Bantam, 1974), xxviii.

[114] Robert Alter, "Introduction," in *The Five Books of Moses: A Translation with Commentary*, trans. Robert Alter (New York: Norton, 2004), xix, the whole section runs from xvi to xlv.

[115] Peter Leithart has complained of the way some translation philosophies do not allow the Bible "to say anything we do not already know." *Deep Exegesis: The Mystery of Reading Scripture* (Waco, TX: Baylor, 2009), 6.

The fresh power of the Psalms cannot be captured by the commitments of some translation philosophies.

The intentions of the authors of the Psalms will dictate the terms of my translation of the Psalms. That is to say, rather than allowing the parameters of the translation to be set by my understanding of the abilities of those who might read this translation, the words of the Psalms' authors will be the controlling consideration as I make this translation. I agree with Peter Leithart, who views translation philosophy as an issue of

> authority: which language, which idiom, determines the rendering of the Hebrew into English? For the KJV, the Hebrew text forces itself onto the English. ... Older translations refreshed the target language (English) by bringing in the Hebrew as much as possible. The KJV enlarged not only the language but also the conceptual apparatus of English speakers. ... For *The Message*, by contrast, contemporary English dictates what the Bible may and may not say. ... For most earlier translators, and for commentators, preachers, and Bible scholars, the original Bible set the agenda, while the target language and the target culture were expected to make room for it. They did not believe that the Bible needed to adjust to our prior concepts and institutions.[116]

The Psalms were written by ancient Hebrew poets who did not view the world the way our contemporaries do. The freer the translation, the easier it is for a reader to assume that the psalmists are just like us. The psalmists are not just like us, and those who encounter the Psalms in English translation should be helped by the translation to discern that reality.

We learn the meaning of words from the way they are used in context. My time with the words of the psalms—in the context not only of the Psalter but also of the Old and New Testaments—has led me to the following proposals about what (some of) these terms connote.

First the term מזמר, with the cognate verb זמר: these terms were rendered into Greek with the noun ψαλμός and the verb ψάλλω. For the noun form, מזמר, which only occurs in Psalm superscriptions, English translations have transliterated the Greek term to form the English word *Psalm*. For the verb form זמר, however, English translations alternate between "sing" and "sing praises," and the lexicons will indicate that

---

[116] Leithart, *Deep Exegesis*, 4–6.

perhaps this is a song to be accompanied by a stringed instrument. One of my desires is to allow readers to distinguish between the terms under discussion (זמר/מזמר) and other terms, particularly the noun and verb forms that mean "song" and "sing" (e.g., שיר). Because the verb זמר is used exclusively of the celebration Yahweh's mighty acts, in my translation I have chosen to do with the verb form what English translations have done with the noun form. This results in the transliteration of the Greek root, "psalm," and its use as a verb. For instance, I have rendered Ps 7:18b (ET 7:17b), "And I will psalm the name of Yahweh Most High!" In the same way that the term "epic" derives from a Greek word that simply means "word, story, or poem," but comes to refer to a genre characterized as a long narrative poem celebrating heroic deeds of gods and extraordinary men, the term "psalm" connotes the celebration of Yahweh, the God of Israel's mighty deeds on behalf of his covenant people. It seems to me that when the psalmists declare their intent to זמר Yahweh, they indicate that they will be making a מזמר, and to help English readers see this, I render both noun and verb as "psalm."

Another term rendered somewhat distinctively in my translation is the verb איב, "be hostile to" (BDB). The masculine cognate noun, which is pointed like the participle of the verb, means simply "enemy," and the feminine form of the noun, איבה, refers to "enmity." This feminine noun occurs significantly as the first word of Gen 3:15, "And enmity I will put between you and the woman and between your seed and her seed." I am convinced that all conflict between God's people and their persecutors stems from that first line of Gen 3:15, and thus I think that David's use of the masculine participle (איב) and the noun derived from it to describe his enemies recalls the enmity between the seed of the woman and the seed of the serpent instituted in Gen 3:15.[117] I grant the etymological connection between the English words "enemy" and "enmity," but I do not think that connection will draw those who read English translations that render איב as "enemy" to Gen 3:15. We are dealing, however, with a lexical point of contact that establishes a thematic point of contact. The "seed" theme is prominent in the Psalms, and so is the "enmity" that exists between the seed of the woman and the seed of the serpent. For this reason, rather than rendering this as "enemy," I will employ the word "enmity" ("ones at enmity," etc.) in an effort to capture the allusion to Gen 3:15.

---

[117] See Hamilton, *God's Glory in Salvation through Judgment*, 75–80.

Also related to the significance of Gen 3:15, rather than render זרע as "offspring," I always render it "seed." Along similar lines, rather than "anointed one" for משיח I prefer "messiah."

Whereas translations sometimes render אמת as "faithful" and sometimes as "truth," I have rendered אמת as "truth" ("true," etc.) and אמנה as "faithful" (or "faithfulness," sometimes "trustworthy").

The Greek translation renders עולם ("long duration," "antiquity," "futurity," "age" BDB, 762) as αἰών ("age"), and in Mishnaic Hebrew the term comes to be used in references to "this age" and "the age to come."[118] Such an understanding of the ages can also be seen in the New Testament (see Matt 12:32; Mark 10:30; Luke 18:30; 20:34–36; Eph 1:21). Because of the way these earliest interpreters of the Old Testament seem to have understood the term עולם, I render it "age" in my translation.

The Hebrew phrase typically translated along the lines of "bend the bow" (e.g., Ps 11:2) is a phrase that describes "treading" or "stepping" on the bow, as when one holds the top end of the bow with the bottom on the ground, putting a foot in the middle to bend it that it might be strung. I have rendered this "tread the bow" to maintain the mental image, because the phrase is not so difficult to understand that the vivid phrase must be eliminated.[119]

Because of the way that the Hebrew word for "man" is also the name of the first man, Adam (אדם), I have translated "son of Adam" where translations do "son of man," and at points even where I have rendered אדם "man" I will place "Adam" after "man" in brackets. I do this because of the way that poets often play on the multiple senses their words may convey.

The book of Psalms is one of the world's great treasures. Working through the Psalms for this project has been like living at one of the world's natural wonders, beholding the glory of the one who herein reveals his own character and purposes. The Psalms seek to draw us deeper into him, higher up and further in, and my prayer is that this commentary will aid people in their efforts to understand the Psalms, for the glory of God and the good of his people, in the name of Jesus and by the power of his Spirit.

---

[118] Anthony Tomasino, "עולם," in *New International Dictionary of Old Testament Theology and Exegesis*, ed. Willem VanGemeren, 5 vols. (Grand Rapids: Zondervan, 1997), 3:345–51, esp. 350.

[119] See the ancient depiction of a figure doing just this in Hossfeld and Zenger, *Psalms 2*, 133.

# BIBLICAL AND
# THEOLOGICAL THEMES

T hough uttered in an entirely different context, the adage holds true for the Psalms: "Songs make history, and history makes songs."[1] The Psalms were forged in the history of God's people. God's mighty acts made his people sing, and those songs informed hearts, created expectations, and provided interpretive frameworks.

In his introduction to the literature of the Middle Ages and Renaissance, C. S. Lewis described "the medieval synthesis" as "the whole organization of their theology, science, and history into a single, complex, harmonious mental Model of the Universe." He then states his intention to argue "not only that this Model of the Universe is a supreme medieval work of art but that it is in a sense the central work, that in which most particular works were embedded, to which they constantly referred, from which they drew a great deal of their strength."[2] In the same way, the biblical authors rely on and contribute to the Bible's big story.

Biblical theology seeks to understand the biblical worldview. This has been addressed briefly above. Here we give more attention to the components of a biblical worldview: the master narrative with its characters, setting, and themes; the truths derived from the narrative; the behaviors it encourages and discourages; and the liturgy and culture all this produces. The way of life produced by the writings of the Old Testament is

---

[1] This quotation was a header in the Saturday/Sunday, June 29–30, 2019 print edition of *The Wall Street Journal*, C12, attributed to "Irving Berlin, on the coming of World War II."

[2] C. S. Lewis, *The Discarded Image: An Introduction to Medieval and Renaissance Literature* (New York: Cambridge University Press, 1964), 11, 12.

the cultural stream in which Jesus and his followers understood themselves to swim. If we understand the interpretive perspective of the Old Testament authors, we will see that their perspective has been embraced by the New Testament authors. The Psalms are particularly significant in this regard, for as William P. Brown has noted, "Of all the books regarded as Scripture in the New Testament, the Psalms is the most widely cited. Of the 150 canonical psalms, 129 make their appearance in some form in the New Testament."[3]

### §1. The Master Narrative

What Snearly says of the Psalter applies to the whole of the Old Testament: "The trajectory of the storyline is consistent throughout: Yahweh is king; he has appointed an earthly vice-regent who represents his heavenly rule on earth; the earthly vice-regent and his people travail against the rebellious of the earth."[4]

God created the world very good (Gen 1:31). Man transgressed and incurred judgment (Gen 2–3), but the words of Gen 3:15 bring a promise of triumph over the one who tempted man to sin, and that promise hints that the judgments might be rolled back (cf. Gen 3:17–19 with 5:29) and the world made new. This hope includes the reversal of death itself. As T. Desmond Alexander correctly notes, "death was indeed perceived by the Hebrews as a punishment for man's rebellion against God," but "whereas the wicked were thought to remain in the dark, silent region of *Sheol*, the righteous lived in the hope that God would deliver them from the power of death and take them to himself (*cf.* Ps. 49:15)."[5]

God made promises to Abraham in Gen 12:1–3 that answered the judgments of Gen 3:14–19 point for point, and the promises to Abraham were passed down and expanded upon through the rest of Genesis.[6] Eventually

---

[3] William P. Brown, "The Psalms: An Overview," in *The Oxford Handbook of the Psalms*, ed. William P. Brown (New York: Oxford University Press, 2014), 6.

[4] Snearly, *Return of the King*, 1.

[5] T. Desmond Alexander, "The Old Testament View of Life After Death," *Them* 11.2 (1986): 42, 45.

[6] Hamilton, "Seed of the Woman and the Blessing of Abraham."

God made promises to David that show that the blessing of Abraham will be brought about through the future king from David's line (2 Sam 7).[7]

In addition to the growing collection of promises that develop and build upon one another, we have narratives of Israel's history, most particularly the exodus from Egypt, that have been interpreted and presented in light of the promises. The oppressive Egyptians are the seed of the serpent, and the Gen 3:15 promise that the seed of the woman would bruise the serpent's head receives an anticipatory fulfillment at the exodus. In this vein, Ps 74:13–14 interprets the parting of the Red Sea as a crushing of the serpent's head (see also 89:9–10 [MT 89:10–11]). The exodus from Egypt points forward to a greater defeat of the serpent and his seed through which God will liberate his people. The Sinai covenant likewise builds on previous covenants and anticipates a new covenant that will follow the new exodus.[8] The pilgrimage through the wilderness to the land of promise also anticipates an even greater march on a better country, a new heaven and new earth. Israel's prophets use Israel's past as the paradigm for predicting Israel's future.[9]

§1.1. CHARACTERS

My comments here will be limited to the main characters in the Psalter: Yahweh, the messiah, the people of the messiah, and their enemies, the wicked.

Yahweh is the most important character not only in the Psalms but in the whole of the Bible. Robar rightly refers to him as "the protagonist of the Hebrew Bible."[10] The psalms that rehearse history celebrate his mighty deeds. The psalms that are prayers petition him. And the praises extol his goodness. His *character* is communicated through his word, and his character ensures that his word will be kept. One could argue that God's ultimate goal, the center of biblical theology, is the display of his character, seen most clearly when his justice serves as the backdrop for

---

[7] For an excellent exposition of the theme, see T. D. Alexander, *The Servant King: The Bible's Portrait of the Messiah* (Leicester: Inter-Varsity Press, 1998).

[8] Before leaving Sinai Israel had already broken the covenant and the Aaronic priesthood had failed (Exod 32–34). Moses repeatedly tells Israel that they will break the Sinai covenant but that Yahweh will remember the Abrahamic covenant (the covenant with the fathers, Lev 26:27–45; Deut 4:25–31; 28–32).

[9] Here I have been very brief. See further Hamilton, *What Is Biblical Theology?*; and for much more detail, Hamilton, *God's Glory in Salvation through Judgment*.

[10] Robar, *Verb and the Paragraph in Biblical Hebrew*, 33.

the demonstration of his stunning mercy, which he accomplishes when he shows his glory in salvation through judgment.[11] More on Yahweh's character in §2.1, below.

Yahweh's world has come under attack, and the messiah comes as the hero through whom Yahweh's reign will be reestablished. Explicitly introduced as the one against whom Yahweh's enemies rage in Ps 2, the anointed king from David's line is the subject of key psalms at or near the Psalter's seams: Psalm 2 joins with Ps 1 to introduce the whole collection, and then Ps 72 prays for the fulfillment of God's promises concerning the messiah at the end of Book 2. Psalm 89 rehearses the covenant with David concerning his reigning seed and asks how long the promises will be deferred at the end of Book 3. Near the beginning of Book 5, in Ps 110 David recounts how his Lord was invited to sit at Yahweh's right hand and installed as the Melchizedekian high priest. More on the messiah in §5, below (culture of interpretation).

Those who have experienced Yahweh's character, which can be most prominently identified with the term *hesed* (חסד), lovingkindness (see esp. Ps 136), come to be referred to as the *hasidim* (חסידים), which English translations render as "saints" (ESV, KJV) "godly ones" (JPS, NAS), or "faithful ones" (CSB). In my translation I refer to this group as those "marked by" Yahweh's lovingkindness, his "lovingkind ones." These people embrace Yahweh as God, believe his promises because they trust his character, and live out their commitments by identifying with the king from the line of David. They are not perfect, but when they fail they confess their sin and repent of it. This puts them on the side of the angels.

The enemies do the opposite at every point. They do not take Yahweh as their God, believe what Yahweh has said, follow Yahweh's instructions, trust Yahweh's character, or submit to Yahweh's king. Whether they worship themselves, idols, or something else, they do not love God or his people. This puts them in constant conflict with God, his purposes, and his people.

As Keel has written, "The view which a particular group or culture holds of its enemies is crucial to an understanding of that group or culture."[12] The authors of the Old Testament believe what Yahweh has revealed about his character, his goodness, his righteousness, and they

---

[11] Hamilton, *God's Glory in Salvation through Judgment*.
[12] Keel, *Symbolism of the Biblical World*, 78.

have embraced Yahweh's revealed instructions for life. The wicked, by contrast, worship idols instead of Yahweh, replace his righteousness with their own standards, and depart from his instructions to fulfill their own selfish desires. Their actions dishonor God and harm people, and the people of God—for whom the psalmists speak—denounce their treachery and pray against their agenda.

### §1.2. SETTING

The most significant thing to say about the setting of the Psalms has to do with the Old Testament's presentation of creation as a cosmic temple.[13] This explains the comparison of the temple to the heavens and earth (78:69). The references to the heavens being spread out like a tent likewise reflect tabernacle imagery (104:2), and these concepts inform the way that David can describe the upheaval of creation at the flood (29:3–8) before saying that everything in Yahweh's temple cries, "glory!" (29:9)—Ps 29 depicts everything in Yahweh's cosmic temple shouting that word, glory. This idea also has suggestive implications about David saying that he will dwell in Yahweh's house forever (23:6), implications that would entail a renewal of the cosmic temple (102:25–26) in the form of a new heaven and a new earth and a resurrection from the dead (cf. 17:15).

If the setting is a cosmic temple, the human characters are the visible *image* and *likeness* of the invisible God (Gen 1:26), placed in the cosmic temple to make manifest God's own character, presence, and reign. In a significant sense, Adam was God's son, and the messiah comes as a new Adam. See especially the exposition of Pss 2, 8, and 80.

### §1.3. THEMES

Because a full discussion of the Psalter's themes could be as long as the body of this commentary, here I will briefly discuss three themes: first, God's word and the promises in it; second, the suffering righteous servant; and third, the sudden destruction of the seemingly powerful wicked.

The Psalter makes the same kinds of claims about God's word found in other parts of Scripture. It promises blessing and success to those who meditate on it constantly (Ps 1:2–3; Josh 1:8), affirming its pure truth (Ps 12:6; 18:30 [MT 12:7; 18:31]; Prov 30:5), and asserting that by it God made the world (Ps 33:6; Gen 1). God's word has life-giving, wisdom-imparting,

---

[13] Beale, *Temple and the Church's Mission*.

enlightening, and lasting power (Ps 19:7–9 [MT 19:8–10]). God's word teaches people how to think rightly about God's world.

God's word also makes promises about how and what God will do to redeem, cleanse, and renew his world, and with these promises come instructions on how to please God. The instructions are as sound as the promises are reliable. The Psalms begin the rehearsal of the promises in Ps 2, setting up a pairing of psalms celebrating God's word with psalms celebrating his promise to the king from David's line, a pairing that runs across the Psalter (Pss 1 and 2, 18 and 19 and 20 and 21, and 118 and 119).[14] God's promise to redeem centers on God's promise to the king from David's line, and the Psalter's strategic arrangement puts a spotlight on the reliability of God's creative word guaranteeing the reliability of his promise to redeem.

Much, much more could be said about God's word in the Psalms, but a lot of that can be found in the exposition in the commentary below (see esp. on Ps 119). God's word made the world. God's word instructs his people on how to live in his world. God's word heals and cleanses his people, renewing and reviving them after they have experienced the life-destroying power of sin. God has promised to redeem, and the promise to redeem is as certain as the command for creation to come into being.

Those who believe God's creating and saving word always seem to be in the minority, and the majority always seem to resent them. Cain killed Abel. Ishmael mocked Isaac. Esau wanted to kill Jacob, and Joseph's brothers sold him into slavery. Then the Hebrews rejected Moses, and even after the exodus they wanted to stone him. David steps right into this line and receives the same kind of treatment from Saul and then Absalom.

Psalm 2 speaks of the nations raging against the Lord's anointed, and then Ps 3 begins to illustrate that raging. Remarkably, however, the enemy in Ps 3 is not a foreigner but the king's own son (Ps 3:ss [MT 3:1]). This continues throughout the Psalter, as David again and again speaks of the difficulty he faced from his Israelite kinsmen, which include Cush (7:ss [MT 7:1]), Saul (e.g., 18:ss [MT 18:1]; 57:ss [MT 57:1]), the Ziphites (54:ss [MT 54:1]), and the unnamed traitor (e.g., 41:9 [MT 41:10]; 55:12–14 [MT 55:13–15]).

On these occasions, the righteous sufferer often complains that his enemies hate him without cause (35:19 [MT 35:20]; 69:4 [MT 69:5]),

---

[14] See Grant, *King as Exemplar*.

meaning that he has not wronged them (59:3–4 [MT 59:4–5]). Their enmity arises from their own selfish ambition, as did Saul's and Absalom's.

In the exposition to follow, I will argue that David has interpreted his own experience in light of earlier Scripture. He identifies with the likes of Abel, Isaac, Jacob, Joseph, and Moses, and he identifies his enemies with their enemies. David also seems to have understood the conflict as Gen 3:15 enmity between the seed of the woman and the seed of the serpent, and he seems to have expected that the kings who would arise from his line would also experience that enmity, culminating in *the* king from his line, in whose experience the whole pattern would come to culmination. The future king would be righteous, he would suffer at the hands of enemies unjustly opposing him, and his ultimate triumph would be as dramatic as the death and resurrection reversal poetically described in Ps 22 (esp. 22:14–15 [MT 22:15–16]).

I contend that the authors of earlier Scripture intended their audience to see the enmity between the seed of the woman and the seed of the serpent, and further that they wanted to encourage God's people to stand fast as the seed of the woman against the seed of the serpent. For David to see the outworking of the pattern in his own life, then, was in keeping with the intent of earlier biblical authors, and likewise for later kings—including the man from Nazareth—to identify with David's experience, even to see David's experience fulfilled in his own, would be fully in line with David's intent (see further the discussion of interpretive culture in §5 below).

The enemies, the seed of the serpent, are described as the kings of the earth in Ps 2. They seem more numerous and, in worldly terms, more powerful and impressive, than the seed of the woman. Psalm 73 describes the way they enjoy long lives of indulgence. The Psalms, however, speak to the way that though they have power to dig pits, they will fall into them, all their sin will rebound onto their own heads, and suddenly they will be like chaff before the wind (Ps 1), destroyed in the way by the wrath of the king to come (Ps 2).

## §2. Truths Derived from the Master Narrative

Life will triumph over death. Good will overcome evil. The defiled will be cleansed, the broken mended, the wicked judged, the faithful rewarded, and God's creation purposes will be accomplished. All these realities play into biblical hope. From this perspective the psalmists write.

The psalmists have come to understand that Israel will be exiled from the land, but they also believe that Yahweh will keep his promises to show mercy in the form of a new exodus and return from exile (see Deut 4:25–31, and esp. the quotation of Deut 32:36 in Ps 135:14). They know that though the Davidic king may be dethroned (Ps 89), ultimately God will keep his 2 Sam 7 promises to David (Ps 110). Gary Millar concludes, "To pray in the psalter, then, is to call on the name of Yahweh, as the psalms fill out the conviction that has shaped the other material in the Old Testament."[15]

### §2.1. Divine Simplicity

This is obviously not the place for a full-scale treatment of divine simplicity, but the idea that God is simple has profound explanatory power for understanding the Psalms.[16] The psalmists see no conflict between Yahweh's love and his justice because both are simply the application of his character. He shows steadfast love (חסד) by keeping his promises to forgive the repentant (Pss 32, 51) and judge their unrepentant oppressors (Ps 82). In fact, by judging them he teaches them his name (83:17–18 [MT 83:18–19]), and Asaph prays that they would seek Yahweh as a result (83:16 [MT 83:17]).

The one living and true God is not composed of different concerns and impulses. Rather, the mere human words that describe him, words that stem from Exod 34:6–7—merciful, gracious, patient, loving, true, forgiving, judging, punishing—are but different ways he makes known his character, his *hesed* (חסד). This explains, for instance, a statement like Ps 130:4, which asserts that there is forgiveness with Yahweh in order that he might be feared. We would expect God's justice to prompt fear, but the application of God's character to forgive brings the penitent one who has experienced mercy into contact with the God who is whole, simple. And the experience of God's character—the experience of his forgiveness—prompts fear.

---

[15] J. Gary Millar, *Calling on the Name of the Lord: A Biblical Theology of Prayer*, NSBT 38 (Downers Grove, IL: InterVarsity Press, 2016), 166.

[16] For a good introduction to divine simplicity (though too harsh on fellow evangelicals), see James E. Dolezal, *All That Is in God: Evangelical Theology and the Challenge of Classical Christian Theism* (Grand Rapids: Reformation Heritage Books, 2017).

§2.2. The Fear of God

The most important thing that can happen to anyone who studies the Psalms is precisely what their authors intended for their audience: an encounter with God. The reality that God should be feared cannot be limited to the occurrences of the word. The terrifying majesty of the living God pervades the Psalms and the Old Testament.

Recently my family visited a frozen lake in South Dakota, and we climbed up on a large rock that cropped out in the middle of the solid ice. Our youngest child was five years old at the time, and he was not altogether stable in his snow-boots. He had repeatedly slipped and fallen on the lake as we made our way across it to the rock. We began to scramble up the rock, and I noticed that toward the ledge on the backside of the rock there were patches of ice and snow, and the gentle slope fell away to a sheer face with nothing but the unforgiving granite-like surface of the lake below. As I earnestly held to my five-year old and steered him away from the ledge, my friend who had taken us there noticed me looking at the ledge and holding my son close and said: "Yeah, if he goes over he dies." The fear I felt for my son's safety was healthy and good. The delight I felt to be off that rock, and then off that frozen lake, was even better. This is the logic of the delight in Yahweh's Torah (see the note on "Torah" in "Translating the Psalms," above) the blessed man feels in Ps 1.

The undergirding assumption that informs the fear of God is God himself in all his tremendous majesty. He is not an unpredictable terror like the so-called gods, but he is altogether holy and pure in his justice. He has graciously revealed himself in his word, and those who value their lives recognize their need for that word. Those who disregard God care little for his word. They are fools. The ledge is slippery. The ice below will break them.

The perspective of Ps 1 is that life and death depend upon being in right relationship to Yahweh, and the fear of not being in right relationship with him is precisely what makes God's word so delightful, so nourishing, and so preoccupying. When Ps 1:4 says "Not so the wicked," it could as well say that the wicked do not fear God, and as a result they take no delight in his revelation of himself, of what pleases him, and of where his boundaries are.

And so it is with Ps 2. The raging nations and plotting peoples do not fear God, so they do not want to be constrained by God's warnings that the foot can easily slip on the gentle slope where the ice lurks beneath the snow. God has, so to speak, given fair warning that the human body cannot survive a fall from that height, and God has given good instructions on where and how to tread the high places that the glorious views might be relished and the crashing falls avoided. The rebels do not fear God, so they attack his anointed (2:3). The declaration that Yahweh's messiah, the king from David's line, will execute his judgment on the insurrectionists (2:7–9) comes with a warning that they should learn wisdom (2:10), that is, that they should serve Yahweh with fear (2:11). That fear is precisely to avoid the anger in which the enemies will perish (2:12a), for the righteous king's wrath falls quickly on those who deserve it, while those who take refuge in him will be blessed (2:12b), blessed like the man who treasures God's word (1:1).

### §3. Behaviors

The behaviors encouraged and discouraged by the Psalms do not need to be belabored, being obvious to anyone who reads the psalmists' words. What needs to be noted has to do with the way literature works. Whether narrative or poetry, commands do not need to be issued for an author's understanding of virtue to be clear to his audience. Illustrating this point, Carr quotes Nicoratus in Xenophon's *Symposium*, who explained, "My father, wishing me to become a good man made me learn the whole of Homer, so that even today I can still recite the *Iliad* and the *Odyssey* by heart (III.5)."[17] The heroic values illustrated and enacted in those epic poems were transmitted through the literature, and this quotation makes sense to us because even when authors are not giving commands, their perspective on what they want their audience to do can be discerned. For instance, Ps 1 does not command people to delight in the Torah and meditate on it day and night, but by blessing the man who does those things, the psalmist commends that behavior. Similarly, Pss 14 and 53 do not issue the command: do not say in your heart that there is no God! By calling the one who does so a fool, however, the psalmist discourages such thinking.

The Psalms do not read like lectures, and yet they are didactic. Carr writes,

---

[17] Carr, *Writing on the Tablet of the Heart*, 100–101.

The present written Psalter … thoroughly reflects its function as teaching literature, indeed, literature for teaching torah piety. The introductory Psalm 1 … calls for constant recitation of Torah. The call to learn and teach "Torah" in Psalm 78 (78:1), whatever its original referent, now functions to direct its hearers toward oral-written ingestion of the Pentateuch. The longest Psalm (119) is an acrostic poem calling for similar recitation of and devotion to Torah.[18]

In this way the line between description (of the one who meditates on Torah as blessed, or of the one who says there is no God as a fool) and prescription (commanding the one behavior and forbidding the other) begins to blur. The line between description and prescription of course remains, but authors describe from a certain perspective, taking for granted a master story, assuming truths derived from that story. One need only read the Psalms to see that the behaviors they encourage and discourage align with the commands and prohibitions of the Law and the Prophets.

The Psalter commends a whole life integrity that walks in God's ways, eschews transgressing his boundaries, and cultivates habits of gratitude and praise, meditation and self-talk that reinforce the story, celebrate the salvation, and hope for the ultimate realization of all God has promised.

## §4. Liturgy

In earlier Scripture, the word of God built the psalmists' worldview, and their songs in turn sang truths into souls. My purpose here is not to comment on which psalms were sung at which times but to make a broader comment on how the words used in *worship*, the Psalms, re-tell the *story*, reinforce the *truths*, and re-present the promises of consequence and reward for the *behaviors* encouraged and condemned.

Were it not for the way that so much biblical scholarship obscures this point it might not need to be made, but it must be said: the Psalms are thoroughly *biblical*, and by them the people of God through the ages have had their understanding of the Bible's master narrative deepened, their faith in the truths that flow from it strengthened, their behavioral instincts sharpened, and all this comes not through lecture but poetry.

---

[18] Carr, *Writing on the Tablet of the Heart*, 154.

Poetry used in worship has a way of trickling down into our assumptions, building out the things we take for granted, and penetrating to the depths of who we are. As we sing the songs of the faith, our drives and urges, appetites and dispositions are brought into line with the stories and direct instructions of the Torah. With the Psalms we sing the warnings of the prophets and their promises of glory right through the dark nights and busy days. As Millar writes in his discussion of how people began to call on the name of Yahweh, the phrase "is used to depict prayer, but not simply in a generic sense. Rather, the idea of calling on the name of Yahweh is intrinsically related to God's commitment to rescue his people and deliver on his promises."[19]

The Psalms reinforce *biblical faith*. And as Hafemann rightly puts it, " 'faith' is not 'believing the unbelievable,' but trusting in God's word because of the track record of God's faithfulness."[20]

### §5. Culture

When a group of people agree on the world's master *story*, on the *truths* it teaches, the *behaviors* that accord with it, and when their *worship* grows out of it—and everyone worships—that group has a shared *culture*. Alec Basson's conclusion is correct: "The textual information in the biblical Hebrew psalms ... is more than literary information as such; it is also a cognitive and cultural representation of the psalmist's world."[21] I am arguing that the psalmists understood themselves to be sharing in and extending the culture that stems from the Torah of Moses, continues through the Former and Latter Prophets, and receives further elaboration and attention in the Writings. People who embrace this culture do not lament the fact that God has promised that his king will reign over all the ends of the earth. Rather, they long for God's king to do just that, as Ps 2 promises he will. The people opposed to God's empire are the ones warned to learn wisdom by that same psalm.

Operating within a different culture, on the basis of a different worldview, whose foundations and rationale are not explained but assumed, Ellen Charry writes,

---

[19] Millar, *Calling on the Name of the Lord*, 25.
[20] Hafemann, "Covenant Relationship," 43.
[21] Alec Basson, *Divine Metaphors in Selected Hebrew Psalms of Lamentation*, FAT 2/15 (Tübingen: Mohr Siebeck, 2006), 243.

Despite the beauty of the language there are reasons to be shy of the psalms. Many countenance attitudes and policies of empire, conquest, revenge, and violence [that] are deeply disturbing to modern sensibilities when read as Scripture, even when one recalls that most of the poems are not proposed as from God but to or about God. These are not values that one necessarily wants to inculcate in one's children.[22]

Charry's standard of good, whereby she judges the Psalms to be "deeply disturbing," comes from some other culture than the one inculcated by the Scriptures. She does not wish her children to embrace these values? Does she not want God to reign over his cosmic empire through the vice-regency of the king from David's line? What is it that she prefers to this political arrangement—the kingship of the messiah—and why? Does she not believe that God's king should conquer, that he should apply God's righteous standards by liberating the oppressed and visiting judgment upon the wicked? She has some standard of righteousness, evidently, whereby she condemns that of the psalmists, and this leads her to assert: "These are not values that one necessarily wants to inculcate in one's children."

But all who embrace the interpretive perspective of the biblical authors are prepared to make an "as for me and my house" declaration (Josh 24:15). Yes these *are* the values we want our children to embrace, because we want them to fear and know God. The Bible's Spirit-inspired values are to be preferred, however "disturbing" they may be "to modern sensibilities." Modern sensibility needs to be reshaped by biblical wisdom; moderns need to gain sense (Prov 8:1–21, esp. 8:5), and serve Yahweh with fear (Ps 2:10–12). Graeme Goldsworthy is correct:

In fact, we have to recognize that salvation is an act of God's judgment. This explains something of what lies behind the prayers for judgment on Israel's enemies. Sometimes these seem to be vindictive, and have evoked a sense of moral outrage in some people. Of course it is possible for even God's people to allow the baser feelings of revenge to rise within them,

---

[22] Ellen T. Charry, *Psalms 1–50: Sighs and Songs of Israel*, BTCB (Grand Rapids: Brazos, 2015), xix.

but that does not change the fact that no redemption in the Bible occurs without judgment.[23]

The Bible's values are rooted in the soil of God's revelation of himself from Genesis to Revelation, a revelation of his very character. Charry has cast in her lot with those who deem their own thoughts and values superior to the Bible's, and those who do not turn from such opinions will find themselves described by Ps 1, chaff that the wind drives away, and Ps 2, destroyed in the way.[24]

The words that God inspired the biblical authors to write have created an interpretive culture. We can see that culture in the stunning agreement in perspective among Scripture's forty some authors who lived across one thousand five hundred years on three different continents. No biblical author objects to the fact that the others believe in God, or that they think him faithful. None protest that actually people are not sinful but basically good. None seek to "clarify" that in reality no salvation is needed. And on and on we could go.

Not only are the biblical authors in agreement with one another on the big ideas, they also agree with one another on *how to interpret earlier Scripture*. That is, they share a *hermeneutical perspective*. It is as though those who derive their identity from the Scriptures swim so much in the same biblical waters that they develop similar strokes. Mitchell writes: "It is worth noting, in passing, that the New Testament's Psalms hermeneutic seems little different from that of their contemporaries in first-century Israel."[25] This obviously does not mean that every Second Temple author agreed on the identity of the messiah, but none of them seem to have

---

[23] Graeme Goldsworthy, *Prayer and the Knowledge of God: What the Whole Bible Teaches* (Leicester: Inter-Varsity Press, 2003), 139. I wish to thank Matt Searles for reminding me of this quotation.

[24] Critical approaches to Scripture, of course, make seeing the Old Testament's unified hope more difficult. For an unpersuasive example of this kind of discussion, see Harry Potter, "The New Covenant in Jeremiah XXXI 31–34," *VT* 33 (1983): 347–57.

[25] Mitchell, *Message of the Psalter*, 27. Mitchell's conclusion accords with my own findings from analyzing how the book of Daniel was interpreted in Tobit, at Qumran, in 1 Maccabees, 4 Ezra, and 1 Enoch: "In their use of Daniel, the authors of these books sought to do biblical theology. That is, they attempted to apply to their own situation the interpretive perspective they discerned from the Old Testament. At many points the conclusions these authors draw, and the applications they make, are much nearer to those made by the authors of the New Testament than they are to the conclusions and applications made by biblical scholars in recent centuries." Hamilton, *With the Clouds of Heaven*, 156.

needed to be convinced that there would be one. Similarly, while there were disagreements on typological identifications and fulfillments, there was agreement that the Scriptures were to be read typologically, and so forth.

As a Christian, I am convinced that Jesus accurately discerned what the Old Testament authors intended to communicate. Further, I am convinced that Christ's own Spirit inspired those Old Testament authors to write such that they prophesied and typified precisely who Jesus would be and what he would do (not losing sight of Eph 3:4–5 and 1 Pet 1:10–12). Jesus taught his disciples how to understand the Scriptures, and those disciples, in their New Testament writings, continue to instruct followers of Jesus. Moses prepared the ground for this interpretive field, and the prophets and sages and psalmists learned to interpret the Bible and life from him. Jesus then learned to interpret the Bible from Moses and the prophets, and that interpretive culture is the one I seek to understand. If we make progress in this endeavor, I contend that we will not describe the interpretation of the Psalms found in the New Testament as "exegetical license."[26] Rather, as Thomas Schreiner puts it, "The interpretation offered by the New Testament fits what the Old Testament itself teaches, so that the New Testament writers are not guilty of imposing an alien interpretation upon the Old Testament storyline."[27]

In order to know how to get from what David wrote, for instance, to what the New Testament claims, I am convinced that what Luke presents Peter saying in Acts 2:30–31 should inform how we think about David writing the Psalms. Peter says that David was a prophet (Acts 2:30a), thus he wrote under the inspiration of the Holy Spirit (cf. 2 Pet 1:20–21). Peter also says that David knew the promises God made to him in 2 Sam 7 (Acts 2:30b), and that David foresaw and spoke of the Christ (Acts 2:31). I will flesh out the exegetical case for this in the commentary (see esp. on Pss 2 and 16), but here I will provide a sketch of the biblical promises and patterns that seem to have informed David, along with a statement from Jonathan Edwards that indicates he read things along the lines of what I am proposing here.

Regarding the promises, at many points in the commentary below I will argue that David and other psalmists are making significant connections

---

[26] As Brown does, "Psalms," 7.

[27] Thomas R. Schreiner, "The Commands of God," in Hafemann and House, *Central Themes in Biblical Theology*, 72.

between key texts: from what God says at the creation of the man and woman in Gen 1:28, to what he says about the seed of the woman in Gen 3:15, to what God promised to Abraham in Gen 12:1–3, to the blessing of Judah in Gen 49:8–12, and then to the promises to David in 2 Sam 7.

This gathering set of promises also shapes the way that Moses and other biblical authors prior to David (Joshua and possibly the authors of Judges and early narratives of Samuel) interpreted significant patterns of events. I have in mind the way that Moses draws attention to the fact that the pattern of the exodus from Egypt (Gen 37–Exod 15) was foreshadowed in the life of Abraham (Gen 12–15), a pattern to be repeated at the conquest of the land (Josh 1–5).

Along these lines, too, is the presentation of the pattern of the righteous sufferer (see §1.3 above). This involves the individual who either receives God's favor or is designated as God's representative being opposed, persecuted, and afflicted by opponents: there is enmity between the seed of the woman and the seed of the serpent. Cain kills Abel. Ishmael mocks Isaac. Esau wants to kill Jacob. Joseph's brothers sell him into slavery. And the people of Israel first reject Moses, and then in the wilderness they want to kill him at various points. This pattern is also seen when Saul wants to kill David and when Absalom tries to steal the kingdom, and these themes are often echoed in the Psalms.

When the promises and the patterns are read together with what Luke presents Peter saying in Acts 2:30–31, a hermeneutical presupposition begins to take shape that would appear to explain much of the use the New Testament authors make of the Psalms. This presupposition can be spelled out as follows: *David recognized the way that his own experience constituted a new installment in the pattern of the righteous sufferer, and on the basis of the promises stemming from Gen 3:15 and growing into 2 Sam 7, he expected the pattern of the righteous sufferer to be fulfilled in the life of the king God had promised to raise up from his line.*

If we approach Ps 16, for instance, from this perspective, we can maintain that David speaks there of his own experience, conscious of the fact that his own experience is a promissory type that foreshadows and prefigures the experience of the future king from his line. Thus Peter can preface a quotation of David speaking in the first-person singular of his own experience with the words, "David says concerning him" (Acts 2:25–28). David manifestly speaks of *himself* in the first-person singular (I, me, my), but because he knows the promises God has made, because he was a prophet inspired by the Holy Spirit, and because he understood the patterns that typified him, and the way that his own experience typified the one to come, in speaking of *himself* he also spoke of *him*, that is, the one to come.[28]

Granting what Peter says of David in Acts 2—that he understood earlier Scripture and knew what God had promised him—allows us to maintain *authorial intent* at the *human level*. David *meant* to describe his own experience in such a way that the one to come was *prefigured, foreshadowed, typified*.

What I am proposing can also be understood as a biblical-theological and typological way of getting at "prosopology," the idea that David assumes the perspective of Christ as he speaks in the Psalms.[29] This is not a new idea. David P. Barshinger quotes the words of Jonathan Edwards in *Religious Affections*, where Edwards writes that David "in many of the Psalms, speaks in the name of Christ, as personating him in these breathings forth of holy affection, and in many other Psalms, he speaks in the name of the church."[30]

This way of approaching the Psalms would also seem to line up with Millar's comments:

---

[28] I have no objection to the term "figural," but I do not use it to the exclusion of authorial intent, contra Richard B. Hays, *Reading Backwards: Figural Christology and the Fourfold Gospel Witness* (Waco, TX: Baylor University Press, 2014), 2, where he writes: "Figural reading need not presume that the OT authors—or the characters they narrate—were conscious of predicting or anticipating Christ." In Acts 2:25–31 Luke presents Peter asserting that David understood God's promises and intended to speak of the coming Christ. Luke's presentation of Peter, then, maintains that what Peter claims about Ps 16 in Acts 2 is the fulfillment of what David intended to communicate.

[29] What I am describing here should not be confused with the prosopology found in the writings of Matthew Bates, whose approach nullifies the contextual meaning of Old Testament passages cited in the New. For Bates' views, see Matthew W. Bates, *The Birth of the Trinity: Jesus, God, and Spirit in New Testament and Early Christian Interpretations of the Old Testament* (New York: Oxford University Press, 2015); and Bates, *The Hermeneutics of the Apostolic Proclamation: The Center of Paul's Method of Scriptural Interpretation* (Waco, TX: Baylor University Press, 2019). I interact with Bates in more detail in a forthcoming book on typology.

[30] David P. Barshinger, *Jonathan Edwards and the Psalms: A Redemptive-Historical Vision of Scripture* (New York: Oxford University Press, 2014), 2. I owe this reference to Wyatt Graham's excellent review of Barshinger, Books at a Glance, December 19, 2016, https://www.booksataglance.com/book-reviews/jonathan-edwards-psalms-redemptive-historical-vision-scripture-david-p-barshinger/.

The psalms are (largely) *first* the prayers of David the messiah. Presumably, they were then picked up and prayed (or sung) by Israel as "the people of the Messiah." These "prayers of the suffering Messiah," then, find their fullest meaning when read in a biblical-theological context as "prayers of *the* Messiah" Jesus Christ. So can we pray the prayers as Christians? Yes we can—in the same sense that we are enabled by Jesus to share in his prayers to his Father, his death and resurrection enable those who follow in his steps to pray these "messianic" prayers in a derivative sense.[31]

---

[31] Millar, *Calling on the Name of the Lord*, 142–43.

# EXPOSITION

BOOK 1

## Psalm 1

Psalm 1 is strategically linked with Ps 2, and, as will be demonstrated below, together these first two psalms introduce the whole Psalter. No superscription separates these two psalms, and a textual variant in Acts 13:33 actually refers to Ps 2 as "the first" psalm. The two psalms are linked at more lexical, morphological, phonological, and thematic levels than there is space here to develop.[1]

Psalm 1 divides humanity into the righteous and the wicked, the blessed and the cursed, and it shows the lifestyle, fruit, and final judgment of each. Psalm 1 extols the Torah, the law of the Lord, and Ps 2 fills in Ps 1's poetic gaps.[2] Psalm 2 introduces the messiah, the son of David. The two psalms join together to add to Israel's hope and expectation for a king from the line of David who will obey Deut 17 (cf., e.g., Isa 11).[3] The two psalms are great poetry, communicating much with marked economy.

When Ps 1 is read together with Ps 2, the synergy between these two pieces of poetry suggests that the true blessed man who meditates day and night on the Torah (Ps 1:1–2) will be the king that the Lord has installed on

---

[1] See Cole, *Psalms 1–2*. The pervasive and profound impact of Cole's work on my approach to the book of Psalms makes it impractical to cite him at every point.

[2] See "The Psalms in the Old Testament Canon," in the introduction above.

[3] See esp. Grant, *King as Exemplar*.

Zion, his holy hill (Ps 2:6). This does not necessarily limit the application of the psalm to the future king, for the congregation of the righteous (1:5–6) cannot be so designated unless they too follow the ways of the blessed man. Like him they are blessed (1:1; 2:12), as they take refuge in the king messiah (2:12b). The wind-driven chaff wicked ones (1:4) are the raging nations and kings plotting vanity against the Lord's anointed (2:1–3), and they are summoned to learn wisdom and submit to the son (2:10–13).

Psalm 1 can be seen as a thematic chiasm as follows:[4]

1:1–2, The Righteous and the Wicked
    1:3–4, The Fruitful Tree and the Fruitless Chaff
1:5–6, The Saved and the Perishing

SCRIPTURE

| CSB | Author's translation |
|---|---|
| [1] How happy is the one who does not walk in the advice of the wicked or stand in the pathway with sinners or sit in the company of mockers! [2] Instead, his delight is in the LORD's instruction, and he meditates on it day and night. [3] He is like a tree planted beside flowing streams that bears its fruit in its season, and its leaf does not wither. Whatever he does prospers. | [1] Blessed is the man who does not walk in the counsel of the wicked, and in the way of sinners he does not stand, and in the seat of scoffers he does not sit; [2] but in the Torah of Yahweh is his delight, and on his Torah he meditates day and night. |
| [4] The wicked are not like this; instead, they are like chaff that the wind blows away. [5] Therefore the wicked will not stand up in the judgment, nor sinners in the assembly of the righteous. | [3] He will be like a tree, planted by streams of water, which yields its fruit in its season, and whose leaf does not wither. And in everything that he does, he prospers. [4] Not so the wicked, but they are like chaff, which the wind drives away. |

---

[4] Similarly Robert L. Alden, "Chiastic Psalms: A Study in the Mechanics of Semitic Poetry in Psalms 1–50," *JETS* 17 (1974): 14. I had completed my own analysis of the Psalms before reading Alden's article.

⁶For the Lᴏʀᴅ watches over the way of the righteous,
but the way of the wicked leads to ruin.

⁵Therefore the wicked will not rise in the judgment,
nor sinners in the congregation of the righteous
⁶for Yahweh knows the way of the righteous,
while the way of the wicked will perish.

## Cᴏɴᴛᴇxᴛ: Vᴇʀʙᴀʟ ᴀɴᴅ Tʜᴇᴍᴀᴛɪᴄ Lɪɴᴋs ᴡɪᴛʜ Sᴜʀʀᴏᴜɴᴅɪɴɢ Psᴀʟᴍs

I am convinced that the Psalms are profoundly interconnected with one another and that this cohesion arises from a coherent worldview. David set the poetic expression of this worldview in motion by writing and collecting psalms, and those who followed him operated out of the same worldview. As evidence for these claims I have painstakingly documented the use and reuse of terms for the early psalms in the Psalter.⁵ Sometimes these words are significant terms, at other points even the reuse of insignificant terms or phrases creates cohesion between neighboring psalms. Linguistic and thematic ties between Pss 1 and 2 include the following:⁶

1:1 "Blessed" (אשרי)
2:12 "Blessed" (אשרי)

1:1 "the counsel of the wicked"
2:1 "the peoples plot vanity"

1:1 "the way of sinners" (דרך)
2:12 "lest ... you perish in the way" (דרך)

1:1 "in the seat of scoffers he does not sit" (ישב)
2:4 "The one who sits in the heavens laughs" (יושב)

1:2 "on his Torah he meditates" (יהגה)
2:1 "the peoples meditate vanity" (יהגו)

---

⁵ I have done this for most of the psalms in Book 1. The process involved repeated close reading of each psalm and its neighbors, followed by a BibleWorks search on virtually every word of these psalms to see where else each term appeared. When I considered the point sufficiently established, I discontinued the documentation of all the lexical interconnectedness.

⁶ For a full study, see Cole, *Psalms 1–2*.

1:6 "the way of the wicked will perish" (דרך ... תאבד)

2:12 "you perish in the way" (ותאבדו דרך)

EXPOSITION

## 1:1–2, The Righteous and the Wicked

The first word of Ps 1, blessed, is identical to the first word of the last statement of Ps 2 (Ps 2:12b, "blessed are all"), creating an *inclusio* around the two psalms that binds them together. This *inclusio* also forges a connection between the blessed man of Ps 1 and the blessed people who kiss the son and take refuge in him in Ps 2:12, and the reference to "the son" in 2:12 joins with statements in 2:7–9 to recall the promises to David in 2 Sam 7. The CSB renders the first word of the psalm, אשרי, "happy." Against this, however, are the indications in the psalm (esp. 1:3, 6) that Yahweh causes the whole-life flourishing that gives the general sense of happiness described, making "blessed" a better English choice to communicate what the psalm connotes.

The opening statement in Ps 1 says that "the man" is blessed, and then verse 5 speaks of a "congregation of the righteous," with the reference to "the righteous" in verse 6 plural in Hebrew. This group of righteous people in verses 5–6 apparently joins the blessed man, identifying with him and following his way of life: avoiding wickedness by meditating on the Torah.

Psalm 1:1 pronounces a blessing on the man who does not do three things, and then verse 2 states what he does. This pattern—three things not done, one thing done—is reminiscent of the instructions regarding the king in Deut 17:16–20, where there are three things he must not do (acquire many horses, many wives, or excessive silver) and one thing he must do: write out the Torah and read it all his days. It is not hard to imagine wicked counselors urging the king of Israel to sin by acquiring horses, wives, and silver, then scoffing at any suggestion that such should not be done in Israel.

The blessing in Ps 1 is pronounced on the man who does not walk, stand, and sit in the counsel, way, and seat, of the wicked, sinners, and scoffers.[7] These three things the blessed man does not do clearly parallel each other. The walking, standing, and sitting are all metaphorical

---

[7] For the allusions to Ps 1:1 in Job 10:3 and 21:16; to Ps 1:4 in Job 21:18; to Ps 1:1–2 in Job 5:13–14; to Ps 1:3–4 in Job 13:25; and to Ps 1:1, 6 in Job 23:10–11, see Kynes, *My Psalm Has Turned into Weeping*, 145–60.

descriptions of the blessed man's way of life, and there seems to be a progression from moving in the wrong kind of counsel, to standing in the wrong way of life, to sitting in the wrong kind of seat. It is noteworthy that the wicked, sinners, and scoffers constitute three different classes of "fools" in the book of Proverbs—people who oppose God in their attitudes and their behavior.

Psalms 1 and 2 are linked by the references to *sitting* and scoffing: whereas *scoffers* have a seat where the blessed man does not *sit* in Ps 1:1, the one who *sits* in the heavens *mocks* the scofflaws, holding them in derision, in Ps 2:4.

Verse 2 describes *what* the blessed man does and *why* he does it. The why is stated first, seen in the word "delight." The blessed man delights in the Torah ("law") of the Lord. The specific referent of the term "Torah" (CSB "instruction," ESV "law") is the Pentateuch, the five books of Moses.[8] As other books were added to the growing canonical collection (e.g., Josh 24:26), they too came under the umbrella concept of "Torah." This trajectory leads, for instance, to Jesus referring to Ps 82:6 as something "written in your law" (John 10:34). "Torah" includes much more than the various biblical rules and regulations that the English translation "law" might suggest. The Hebrew term connotes the history of God's acts to deliver his people and all of the instruction that he has given in his word.

Psalm 1:2 has two third-person masculine singular pronouns: "but in the Torah of Yahweh is *his* delight, and on *his* Torah he meditates day and night." The referent of the first is clear enough—"his delight" points to the gladness the blessed man introduced in 1:1 feels about the Torah. The referent of the second, in the phrase "his Torah," could point either to Yahweh, which is perhaps most likely, or to the blessed man. Understanding "his Torah" to refer back to Yahweh's Torah makes sense because of the delight the blessed man feels, as stated in the first half of the line, "in the Torah of Yahweh." If, on the other hand, the referent of the first pronoun determines the referent of the second, and in the original Hebrew the two sit side by side in the middle of the verse (his delight, his Torah), the "his Torah" referred to could be the blessed man's Torah.

---

[8] Psalm 1's references to meditating on Torah day and night and prospering (1:2–3) draw language and concepts from Josh 1:8, which refers to the ספר התרה, "scroll of the Torah." Note that Moses is referenced in Josh 1:7, and in Josh 8:31 we read of the ספר תרת משה, "the scroll of the Torah of Moses" (cf. Josh 8:32). First Kings 2:3 depicts David charging Solomon to keep what "is written in the Torah of Moses" (בתרת משה).

If this is the case, the psalmist perhaps assumes that the blessed man is Israel's king, that he has obeyed Yahweh's Deut 17:18–19 instruction to copy out the Torah in his own hand, and that his delight is in *his* Torah, that is, the copy he made for himself.

The blessed man's delight in the Torah results in him meditating on it day and night. The terminology of this phrase recalls Josh 1:8, as does the final statement of verse 3. "Meditate" renders a Hebrew verb for muttering or musing, generating a mental picture of a man going about reciting the words of Torah to himself as he continually contemplates them. Psalm 1 asserts that the man who has memorized Torah and mutters it as he mentally rehearses it day and night will be happy.

In another point of contact with Ps 2, the same term rendered "meditate" in Ps 1:2 is used to describe the vain plotting of the peoples to overthrow the Lord's messiah (2:2). This suggests that we are to understand the "counsel of the wicked," in which the blessed man refuses to walk in Ps 1:1, as illustrated by the vain plotting against Yahweh and his messiah described in Ps 2:1–3 (cf., e.g., Isa 7:1–9).

The idea of meditating on the Torah day and night is reminiscent of Deut 6:6–7, where fathers are instructed to repeat the Torah constantly to their children and discuss its meaning with them throughout the day's comings and goings. Along these lines, in Josh 1:8, Moses commanded Joshua to meditate on Torah day and night, while in Deut 17, the king is required to write out the Torah and read it all his days. The blessing in Ps 1:1–2 is thus pronounced on a Joshua-like man who obeys Deut 6 and 17.

### 1:3–4, The Fruitful Tree and the Fruitless Chaff

Verses 3–4 move from what the blessed man does to the fruits of his lifestyle, comparing him to a flourishing tree planted beside abundant water. The image of a tree or a vine is used in the Old Testament for both the nation of Israel as a whole (e.g., 2 Sam 7:10; Isa 6:13; Ps 80:8) and for individuals within the nation (e.g., Ps 128:3). An indication that those who hope in the future king experience the blessing described in Ps 1 can be seen from the way Ps 92:12–13 (MT 92:13–14) uses the same terminology to describe the righteous (plural) being like trees (92:12 [MT 92:13]) planted in the house of the Lord (שָׁתוּל; 92:13 [MT 92:14]). As these images from Pss 1 and 92 inform one another, the temple context of Ps 92 reinforces the Edenic impression given by the Ps 1 imagery (see below).

Jeremiah is probably reflecting the influence of Ps 1 when he uses verbatim phrases from Ps 1:3 to compare the man who trusts the Lord to a flourishing tree planted by water (Jer 17:7–8; cf. Ezekiel's use of the imagery for the nation of Israel in 17:1–23; 19:10, 13). The term rendered "planted" here can also refer to transplanting, connoting a gardener digging up a sapling to replant it in good soil where it has ready access to "streams of water."

The term rendered "streams" refers to canals dug to provide irrigation, which were often necessary in the dry climate of Israel (cf. Job 38:25; Prov 21:1). The streams of water that nourish the tree in Ps 1:3 represent the Torah on which the blessed man meditates.

For those whose symbolic universe is built from scriptural imagery, the Ps 1:3 picture of trees planted by streams of water yielding fruit in season subtly evokes the trees Yahweh planted in the garden in Eden in the east, where the four rivers ran with the good fruit growing (Gen 2:8–10).[9] The poetic effect suggests that meditating on Torah mediates the presence of God, so that those who walk with God in the word experience a renewal of what life would have been like in Eden.[10] Similarly, those who learn the Torah in Prov 3 (Prov 3:1–12) find wisdom (3:13) to be a tree of life (3:18), and both Prov 11:30 and 15:4 indicate that the words of the righteous are a "tree of life" to others.

A tree planted by irrigation canals would thrive on well-watered roots, bearing its fruit at the right time, leaves not withering from drought. This image communicates that the man who meditates on the Torah day and night will have a life that bears good fruit at the appropriate time, the truths of the Torah sustaining him when the leaves of others would wilt.

Later biblical authors pick up the imagery of withering leaves. Announcing judgment on Israel for not walking in the Torah, Isaiah says they will be "like an oak whose leaf withers, and like a garden without water" (Isa 1:30; cf. 34:4). Jeremiah also describes withered leaves on

---

[9] The targum rendered this line, "He is like the tree of life which is planted by streams of water," translation by David M. Stec, *Targum of Psalms*, ArBib 16 (Collegeville, MN: Liturgical Press, 2004), 29.

[10] Stephen Dempster, "An 'Extraordinary Fact': Torah and Temple and the Contours of the Hebrew Canon, Part 1," *TynBul* 48 (1997): 48, sees this theme as one of the major emphases of the final form of the OT canon: "Obedience to the Word of God leads to the experience of the Presence of God or blessing. Disobedience of that Word leads to the experience of the Absence of God or curse."

the tree that has borne no fruit for the Lord (Jer 8:13). Pointing to the eschatological restoration of the cosmic temple, Ezekiel describes a river flowing from the temple with trees on either side whose leaves will not wither (Ezek 47:12).

The last phrase of verse 3 provides us with another point of contact with Josh 1:8. The term used in the statement "in everything that he does, he *prospers*" is the same used when Joshua was told to "meditate on [this Book of the Torah] day and night ... then you will cause your way to *prosper*" (Josh 1:8).

The psalmist does not come right out and say something like this: *Israel is looking for a leader who will obey Deut 6 and 17 and thereby lead Israel to conquer the land as they did in Joshua's day. As he meditates on the Torah of Yahweh, the presence of Yahweh will be mediated to him through the word, just as Adam and Eve walked with God in the garden. Those who walk in the Torah enjoy God's presence in a way that approximates the experience of Eden.*

The psalmist does not say it this way because that is not how concepts are communicated in poetry. The psalmist hints at and suggests these things, however, by using imagery that recalls Yahweh planting a garden in Eden, where he caused trees to grow, with a river that flowed out of Eden to water the garden (Gen 2:8–10). The reuse of the imagery, employing the terminology of Ps 1, in Isaiah, Jeremiah, and Ezekiel seems to substantiate the idea that the psalmist meant to use Edenic imagery to describe the righteous man. The clear points of contact with Josh 1:8 validate the idea that the blessed man will be Israel's conquering captain.

The simple statement that opens verse 4, "The wicked are not so," returns our attention to those in whose counsel the blessed man does not walk (1:1) and indicates that the wicked do not delight in the Torah, do not meditate on it day and night, do not enjoy the Eden-like experience of being transplanted into a garden where irrigation canals have been dug, do not yield the fruit they should when the time comes, have leaves that wither, and do not prosper like Joshua. However strong the standing of the sinners might seem, however lofty the seat of scoffers be set (cf. 1:1), their leaves will wither, and they will be "like chaff, which the wind drives away" (1:4). Keel explains: "God ceaselessly watches over the order he has established. Just as he upholds the man who submits to it, so too he destroys the man who violates it."[11] The chaff to which the wicked are

---

[11] Keel, *Symbolism of the Biblical World*, 99.

likened presents a strong contrast to the fruitful unwithered righteous, and unlike that rooted tree by streams of water, the wicked are driven off by the wind. In Ps 35:5 David prays that his enemies would be "like chaff before the wind." Isaiah again appears to be influenced by Ps 1 as he repeatedly compares the enemies of God's people to chaff (Isa 17:13; 29:5; 41:15), and Hosea uses the image to describe God's people—who have not kept his word—going into exile (Hos 13:3). Daniel describes overthrown enemy nations in just these terms (Dan 2:35).

### 1:5-6, The Saved and the Perishing

The opening statement of Ps 1:5 stays with the wicked, who were just in view in verse 4, to say that they "will not rise in the judgment." The word "rise" (קוּם) rendered "survive" by the CSB, is translated "arise" in Isa 26:14, "They are dead, they will not live; they are shades, they will not arise." The reference to "the judgment" supports the notion that the rising in view in Ps 1:5 is eschatological.[12] The wicked may seem wise in the eyes of the world; sinners may stand strong in their ways; and scoffers may sit in what seem to be established seats, but they will not rise in the judgment. The judgment will go against them. Whether the judgment in view is in this life or the one at the end of all things, it is future from the point of view of the psalmist.

The psalmist here articulates his confidence that in a future judgment the verdict will go against the wicked. Just as the first half of Ps 1:5 says the wicked will not rise in the judgment, the second half of the line says, "nor sinners in the congregation of the righteous." If rising for eschatological judgment is in view, the congregation of the righteous are those who will be vindicated at that time. Both Isa 26:14 and Ps 1:5 state that the wicked will not rise in the judgment, whereas Dan 12:2 asserts that both the wicked and the righteous will be raised from the dead. John can be seen to resolve this difficulty in Rev 20:4-6, where he indicates that the righteous will be raised at the second coming, with

---

[12] The Greek translator rendered לֹא יָקֻמוּ as οὐκ ἀναστήσονται, and cf. the targum, "Therefore the wicked do not stand in the great day of judgment," trans. Stec, *Targum of Psalms*, 29. Pace Schaper (*Eschatology in the Greek Psalter*, 46–48), who thinks the Greek translator has introduced eschatological thought here; it seems to me that he has provided a valid interpretation of the Hebrew. For discussion of Ps 1:5 in the targum and rabbinic literature, see Timothy Edwards, *Exegesis in the Targum of Psalms: The Old, the New, and the Rewritten*, GDBS 28 (Piscataway, NJ: Gorgias, 2007), 91–95.

the unrighteous raised after the millennium for the final judgment. Paul seems to share this perspective, saying that those who belong to Christ will rise at his coming (1 Cor 15:23) and "the dead in Christ will rise first" (1 Thess 4:16). After the millennium, all are raised (Rev 20:11–15). Understood this way, we can see why Ps 1 and Isa 26 say the wicked will not be raised (when the righteous are), while Dan 12 says they will be (after the millennium).

In Ps 1:6 the "way" of this "congregation of the righteous" points to their way of life, and since they are called "righteous," there can be no doubt that their "way" is the same as that of the blessed man, who in verse 1 did not stand in the "way" of sinners. The "way" of the blessed man and the righteous who are aligned with him is the one prescribed in the Torah of Yahweh rather than the one in which the sinners stand. Yahweh knows the "way of the righteous" because he is the one who has instructed them in the Torah, the one who has caused them to delight in it, and who has walked with them down it. The righteous delight in the Torah of Yahweh because they understand that he alone is God (Deut 6:4); they love him (6:5), so they keep his words on their hearts (6:6), meditating on the Torah day and night like the blessed man (Ps 1:1–2). The other way, that of the wicked, will perish (1:6b). It is interesting to observe that it is not the wicked who are said to perish at the end of Ps 1:6 but their way. This may be more than compressed poetic language, pointing to an eschatological state of affairs when the way of the wicked will no longer be an option.

Bridge

If we read Pss 1 and 2 together, the blessed man who meditates day and night on Torah in Ps 1 can be identified with Yahweh's messiah in Ps 2, and Jesus came evidencing obedience to Deut 17 as he answered Satan's temptations by quoting Deuteronomy (e.g., Matt 4:1–11). The righteous are those who call him blessed, for whom he refused the counsel of the wicked, the way of sinners, and the seat of scoffers. As Christians, our first response to Ps 1 is to bless the Lord Jesus, to see how he did what we fail to do, and through that to begin to imitate him in his delight in the Scriptures, meditating upon them, and thereby enjoying God's presence.

Psalm 1 also encourages the people of God who face what may seem to be overpowering evil. Both Daniel and John depict human governments ranged against God and his people as beasts (Dan 7; Rev 13), and Ps 1 says the wicked will be like chaff, matching the swift demise of the beast in Daniel and Revelation. Whether the wicked are fining, imprisoning, or even killing Christians, they are like chaff. Suddenly, unexpectedly, the wind will drive them away. The judgment will go against them. The challenge for the people of God in every generation is to walk in the Scriptures and trust God, leaving room for wrath. It is the Lord's to avenge. He will repay (Rom 12:19).

## Psalm 2

Overview and Structure of Psalm 2

Acts 4:25 asserts that God spoke by the mouth of David through the Holy Spirit the words of Ps 2, indicating that God inspired David by the Holy Spirit to write Ps 2.[13] Though we cannot be dogmatic on a point like this, the interconnectedness of Pss 1 and 2 seems to indicate common authorship.

The contents of Ps 2 fall out as follows:

2:1–3, The Vain Meditation of the Nations
2:4–6, Yahweh's Confident Purpose to Establish His King
2:7–9, The King's Rehearsal of Yahweh's Decree
2:10–12, Warning to Conspiring Rebels

Psalm 2's content forms a chiastic structure:[14]

2:1–3, The Nations Conspire
   2:4–6, Yahweh Responds
   2:7–9, The King Proclaims
2:10–12, The Rulers Warned

---

[13] Sam Janse rejects the testimony of Acts 4:25 and concludes "that Ps.2 was composed after *the hymn of Isa.49:1–6*. We do not treat this prophetic text within the reception history of Ps.2, but rather think of an influence in the opposite direction"; Sam Janse, *You Are My Son: The Reception History of Psalm 2 in Early Judaism and the Early Church*, CBET 51 (Leuven: Peeters, 2009), 31 (emphasis original). Given the testimony of Acts 4:25, a conclusion better founded on the available evidence is that David's words in Ps 2 communicate themes Isaiah will later trumpet in passages such as Isa 11 and 49.

[14] See the alternative, yet similar, proposal in Alden, "Chiastic Psalms 1–50," 14.

SCRIPTURE

**CSB**

¹ Why do the nations rage
and the peoples plot in vain?
² The kings of the earth take their
stand,
and the rulers conspire together
against the Lord and his Anointed One:
³ "Let's tear off their chains
and throw their ropes off of us."

⁴ The one enthroned in heaven laughs;
the Lord ridicules them.
⁵ Then he speaks to them in his anger
and terrifies them in his wrath:
⁶ "I have installed my king
on Zion, my holy mountain."

⁷ I will declare the Lord's decree.
He said to me, "You are my Son;
today I have become your Father.
⁸ Ask of me,
and I will make the nations your
inheritance
and the ends of the earth your
possession.
⁹ You will break them with an iron
scepter;
you will shatter them like pottery."

¹⁰ So now, kings, be wise;
receive instruction, you judges of the
earth.
¹¹ Serve the Lord with reverential awe
and rejoice with trembling.
¹² Pay homage to the Son or he will be
angry
and you will perish in your rebellion,
for his anger may ignite at any
moment.
All who take refuge in him are happy.

**Author's translation**

¹ Why do the nations rage,
and the peoples meditate vanity?
² The kings of the earth take their
stand,
and the rulers gather together
against Yahweh, and against his
messiah.
³ Let us tear apart their bonds,
and cast from us their ropes.

⁴ The one who sits in the heavens
laughs;
my Lord[15] mocks them.
⁵ Then he will speak to them in his
wrath,
and in his fury he will terrify them,
⁶ "As for me, I have installed my
king on Zion, the mountain of my
holiness."

⁷ I will recount the decree of Yahweh:
He said to me,
"My son are you,
I, today, have begotten you.
⁸ Ask from me, and I will give the
nations as your inheritance,
and the ends of the earth as your
possession.
⁹ You will break them with a rod of
iron,
shatter them like a potter's vessel."

¹⁰ And now, O kings, cause yourselves
to be wise;
receive correction, O judges of the
earth:
¹¹ Serve Yahweh in fear,
and rejoice with trembling.
¹² Kiss the son lest he be angry,
and you perish in the way:
for his wrath flares quickly.
Blessed are all who take refuge in him.

---

[15] On אדוני see Bruce K. Waltke and Michael P. O'Connor, *An Introduction to Biblical Hebrew Syntax* (Winona Lake, IN: Eisenbrauns, 1990), 123–24, §7.4.3e–f.

CONTEXT: VERBAL AND THEMATIC LINKS WITH SURROUNDING PSALMS

For links between Pss 1 and 2, see the corresponding section on Ps 1.

> 2:1–3 The raging, meditating, standing, and gathering against Yahweh and his anointed explain the counsel, way, and seat of the wicked, sinners, and scoffers of 1:1.

> 2:2, 6 The mention of Yahweh's anointed (2:2), who is his king (2:6), clarifies the identity of the individual blessed man from 1:1.

> 2:6 "mountain of my holiness"
> 3:4 (MT 3:5) "mountain of his holiness"

> 2:10 "cause yourselves to be wise" (הַשְׂכִּילוּ)
> 1:3 "in everything he does, he prospers" (יַצְלִיחַ)

The connections between Pss 1 and 2 indicate that the counsel of the wicked (Ps 1:1) informs the conspiratorial attempt to usurp Yahweh's dominion described in 2:1–3. The plot meditated by the wicked is but chaff before the wind (1:4), for though they sit in earthly seats of authority and scoff at Yahweh (1:1), he sits in heaven and mocks their futile rebellion (2:4), proclaiming his purposes (2:5–6) through the enthronement of the Davidic king, whose worldwide reign Yahweh has promised to establish (2:7–9). On this basis the rulers of the earth are advised to learn wisdom that will cause them to prosper (2:10–12). In essence, they are called to recognize that Yahweh will do what he has promised to do in the Torah and in his promises to David. Those who submit to Yahweh's anointed king will not be destroyed in the way of the wicked (2:12; cf. 1:1, 6) but will be blessed (2:12) because they have taken refuge in the blessed man (1:1).

EXPOSITION

## 2:1–3, The Nations Conspire

The line of thought from Ps 1 continues right into Ps 2. Yahweh means to reestablish his dominion over his defiled cosmic temple through the vice-regency of the new Adam, seed of the woman, seed of Abraham, seed of Judah, seed of David. The nations of the earth are not meditating on Torah like the blessed man (cf. Ps 1:2). Instead they meditate on vanity (2:1). The vanity or emptiness in view is the scheme they are depicted articulating in 2:3, and the people doing the scheming are the kings and rulers in 2:2. They conspire together against Yahweh and Yahweh's anointed, a reference to the king from David's line, as 2:7-9 makes clear, and the term rendered *anointed* is the Hebrew word transliterated into English as *messiah* (משיח).

Given the interconnectedness of Pss 1 and 2, the bonds and ropes that the rulers want to tear off and cast away in 2:2 are to be understood as Yahweh's promises and regulations in the Torah. The path to life is the way of accepting Yahweh's rule and indulging in the hope of what he promises. The path to destruction is the path of rejecting Yahweh's declaration of what is right and wrong in his commands and prohibitions and going to war against the king Yahweh has promised to establish.

Those who would reject Yahweh and his anointed want to reign for themselves in the way that seems right in their own eyes, without reference to morality as Yahweh has defined it. The attempt of a creature to throw off the reign of the creator is laughable, thus Yahweh's response to it.

### 2:4-6, Yahweh Responds

Scoffers sit in their seats (1:1) and concoct impossible strategies to throw off the Creator's yoke (2:1-3), while Yahweh sits enthroned in the heavens, impervious to attack, scoffing right back at those who think so little of him (2:4).[16] The psalmist commends the fear of Yahweh (2:11) precisely because those who do not show him due regard arouse his terrifying wrath (2:5). The only explanation for the fact that some do not fear him is that they have not yet experienced that wrath. The term used to describe Yahweh terrifying his enemies is the same used to describe the dismay Joseph's brothers felt when he revealed himself to them (בהל, 2:5; Gen 45:3). When Joseph's brothers sold him into slavery they did not fear him because they had not seen him in terrifying majesty as lord of Egypt. And so it is with those who conspire against Yahweh and his anointed.

In the face of the conspiracy of his enemies, Yahweh announces in 2:6 that he has established his king on Zion, his holy hill. The psalmist

---

[16] Cole argues that the one who sits in the heavens is the messiah; *Psalms 1-2*, 99-103. Psalm 11:4, however, asserts, "Yahweh, in the heavens is his throne." Moreover, the one seated in the heavens in 2:4, who speaks to his enemies in 2:5, is the one who has installed his king in 2:6, and that person is Yahweh, not the king who has been installed.

presents Yahweh referring to Zion as his holy hill because the temple
was built on that mount. Acts 4:25 attributes Ps 2 to David. No temple
was on Mount Zion until Solomon built it. This reference to Zion as the
holy hill where the king is established, then, works with other features
of the passage to point to the one in whom the promises made to David
in 2 Sam 7 would be fulfilled. During his life David knew that Yahweh had
identified the place where the temple would be built (2 Sam 24), so Davidic
authorship of these statements poses no historical difficulty.

### 2:7–9, The King Proclaims

In Ps 2:7–9, the king rehearses Yahweh's decree. We have just noted how
Luke, under the inspiration of the Holy Spirit, attributes this psalm to
David in Acts 4:25. We have also noted how there was no temple in David's
day, and yet Zion is described as Yahweh's holy hill in 2:6. These realities
work with the wording of the decree to suggest that while David is the
author of Ps 2, he presents the speaker as the king from his line, his seed,
the throne of whose kingdom Yahweh promised to establish forever in
2 Sam 7:13. Yahweh said of the seed he promised to raise up for David in
2 Sam 7:14, "I will be to him a father, and he will be to me a son."

David heard the words of 2 Sam 7:14 from the prophet Nathan (2 Sam
7:4) as Yahweh spoke them about the seed he promised to raise up for
David (7:12–14). David would know, therefore, that these words were
spoken to his descendent rather than to him. This would indicate that
the voice speaking in the first-person singular in Ps 2:7, "*I* will tell ... he
said to *me*" is to be understood as the voice of David's seed, the promised
descendent rather than the voice of David himself.

David thus presents the promised king from his line, whose throne
Yahweh swore he would establish forever, speaking of how Yahweh
became his father and he became Yahweh's son. This sonship language
suggests that the king from David's line has taken up the role of Adam,
the son of God (Gen 5:1–3; Luke 3:38). The father-son relationship also
establishes the king from David's line as Israel's representative, for at
the exodus Yahweh denominated Israel as his firstborn son (Exod 4:22).[17]
When Yahweh names the Davidic king his son, he makes him his adamic

---

[17] Interestingly, the Midrash Tehillim [midrash on Psalms] on this passage cites Exod 4:22;
Isa 52:13; 42:1; Ps 110:1; and Dan 7:13. See Edwards, *Exegesis in the Targum of Psalms*, 151–55.

vice-regent, the representative of the nation of Israel, the individual seed of the woman who stands for the collective, the one who will reign in Yahweh's own image and likeness, establishing Yahweh's dominion over all creation.[18]

The rightful claim to dominion over all creation is what Yahweh invites the king to request in Ps 2:8. The inheritance of the *nations* in Ps 2:8 shows the outcome of the plot the *nations* meditated in Ps 2:1. Simultaneously, these words herald the fulfillment of the blessing of Abraham: Yahweh promised to bless those who bless Abraham and curse those who dishonor him, and he promised to bless all the families of the earth in him (Gen 12:2–3). Psalm 2:8 poetically promises that the blessing of Abraham will be fulfilled through the Davidic king.

The possession of the ends of the earth in Ps 2:8 likewise proclaims that the king from David's line will succeed where Adam and Israel failed. Adam was to expand the borders of the garden, being fruitful and multiplying to fill the earth with those in God's image and likeness, but he sinned, was expelled, and the serpent took dominion (cf. Dan 7:1–14; Eph 2:2). Land was promised to Abraham (Gen 12:7) and received by Israel at the conquest, and like Adam, Israel was to expand the borders of the land, be fruitful and multiply, so that all the earth would be filled with Yahweh's glory (cf. Num 14:21). Like Adam, however, Israel sinned and was expelled from the land. The exile was in the future in David's day, but Moses had already prophesied it in Lev 26, Deut 4:25–31, and Deut 28–32. Adam and Israel failed to cover the dry lands with Yahweh's glory, but Yahweh decrees in Ps 2:8 that the king he promised to raise up from David's line will possess the ends of the earth.

Psalm 2:9 portrays the outcome of the conspiracy against Yahweh and Yahweh's anointed depicted in 2:1–3. Yahweh's king will shatter his enemies with a rod of iron (cf. 110:5), and the term rendered *rod* in Ps 2:9 is the same term used to describe the *scepter* that would not depart from Judah in Gen 49:10 and that would arise from Israel in Num 24:17. In the context of Num 24, the Moabites are attempting to curse Israel. God told Abraham that he would bless those who blessed him and curse those who dishonored him (Gen 12:2), tying those who dishonor Abraham to the serpent God himself cursed in Gen 3:14. The Moabites trying to curse Israel,

---

[18] Cf. the targum, "You are as dear to me as a son to a father, pure as though I had created you this day," translation by Stec, *Targum of Psalms*, 30.

then, are seed of the serpent, and Num 24:17 states that the ruler who will arise in Israel will "crush the forehead of Moab." The eschatological king who will inherit the nations and possess the ends of the earth (Ps 2:8) will crush the head of the seed of the serpent (2:9; 110:5; 137:9) who plot a vain rebellion against Yahweh and the seed of the woman (2:1–3).[19]

Those who do not learn from Torah are like chaff before the wind (Ps 1:4). They stand the same chance against Yahweh that a clay pot stands against an iron rod. A creature will no more overthrow the creator than a potter's vessel will break an iron rod. The iron rod in the hand of the mighty king will shatter the clay pot.

## 2:10–12, The Rulers Warned

Lest anyone think Yahweh cruel to mock his enemies (2:4), let it be noted that the enemies receive fair and forthright warning of Yahweh's purposes (2:5–9) and are called to amend their ways (2:10–12). The man who meditates on the Torah day and night will *prosper* (צלח) in all his ways (1:2–3), and the kings and rulers are summoned in 2:10 to *cause themselves to be wise* (שכל). In some key texts these terms "prosper" and "be wise" appear together to speak of the way that meditating on Torah will result in the enjoyment of the good life. Joshua is commanded in Josh 1:7 not to turn from the Torah to the right or the left so that he might cause himself to be wise (שכל). Then in 1:8 he is instructed that meditating on Torah day and night will result in him causing his way to prosper (צלח), with the result that he will cause himself to be wise (שכל). Similarly, as David instructs Solomon to do everything written in the Torah of Moses in 1 Kgs 2:1–4, he tells him that if he does so he will be wise (שכל) in all he does (1 Kgs 2:3). The use of these two terms together in Josh 1:7–8, and the use of the term found in Ps 2:10 in 1 Kgs 2:1–4, indicates that in Ps 2:10 the rulers and kings are being admonished to make themselves wise through the study of what Yahweh has commanded and promised in the Torah. They are encouraged to join the "congregation of the righteous" (1:5) by delighting in the Torah of Yahweh (1:2), which urges them to submit to Yahweh's king (2:6–9). If the kings will obey this admonition, they will be among the blessed (אשרי) who take refuge in the son (2:12).

---

[19] See discussion of Pss 110:5 and 137:9 in the second volume, and note that the same Hebrew verb, נפץ, appears in Pss 2:9 and 137:9. ESV uses "dash" in both places. Unfortunately the CSB has "shatter" in 2:9 and "dash" in 137:9, obscuring the connection.

Proverbs 16:20 encapsulates the instruction of Ps 2:10-12, "The one who causes wisdom by the word [משכיל על דבר] will find good, and as for the one who trusts in Yahweh, blessed is he [ובוטח ביהוה אשריו]."

The kings and rulers are urged to receive correction through the warning in 2:10. Rather than plot against Yahweh and his messiah (2:1–3), in 2:11 they are admonished that they should serve Yahweh with fear because he spoke to them in his wrath, to rejoice in him with trembling because he terrified them in his fury (2:11, cf. 2:5). The form this service and rejoicing should take is articulated in 2:12, where they are told to kiss the son. The son the rebel kings are urged to kiss in 2:12 is the one Yahweh declared to be his son in 2:7. We have another point of contact with the Joseph story (cf. 2:5), for after Joseph revealed himself to his brothers, he kissed them (Gen 45:15). The dreams marked Joseph out as God's chosen (cf. Gen 37), and in the same way that his brothers were reconciled with a kiss, so the rebels in Ps 2 are urged to be reconciled to God's chosen, his son, with a kiss.

BRIDGE

The son will execute Yahweh's wrath, and the rebel kings are warned that rather than conspire against Yahweh and his anointed (2:1–3), they should serve Yahweh (2:11) and kiss the son (2:12) because the anger of the one who will break his enemies with a rod of iron, shattering them like a potter's vessel (2:9), flares up quickly. The king who will obey Deut 17 will be blessed (Ps 1:1–3; 2:6–9). The congregation of the righteous embraces the Torah that promises his reign and establishes Yahweh's commands and prohibitions (1:5–6). And all who take refuge in the Davidic king will be blessed (2:12). The blessing in 2:12 is the same happiness of 1:1 because it arises from the same place: from embracing the interpretive perspective of the biblical authors. They envision a symbolic universe in which Yahweh reigns as king, determines right and wrong, good and evil, forbids the one and commends the other, and promises to establish his lordship over the world through the king from David's line.

Happy are those who learn from the Torah of Yahweh that the world of the Bible is the real world, and happy are those who take refuge in the one of whom the Torah and the Prophets speak.

## Psalm 3

OVERVIEW AND STRUCTURE OF PSALM 3

In Ps 3:1–2 (MT 3:2–3) David's adversaries "rise" against him and declare that there is no salvation for him in God. In 3:7–8 (MT 3:8–9) David calls on Yahweh to "rise" against his enemies and declares that salvation belongs to Yahweh. David communicates his confidence in Yahweh in 3:3–4 (MT 3:4–5), and that confidence gives him fearless sleep in 3:5–6 (MT 3:6–7). Psalm 3 thus evidences a chiastic structure:

3:1–2 (MT 3:2–3), Enemies Rise and Declare No Salvation in God
    3:3–4 (MT 3:4–5), Confidence in Yahweh
    3:5–6 (MT 3:6–7), Fearless Sleep
3:7–8 (MT 3:8–9), Rise Up Yahweh to Whom Salvation Belongs

SCRIPTURE

| CSB | Author's translation |
|---|---|
| A psalm of David when he fled from his son Absalom. | [1] A Psalm of David. When he fled from before Absalom, his son.[20] |
| [1] LORD, how my foes increase! There are many who attack me. [2] Many say about me, "There is no help for him in God." *Selah* | [2] O Yahweh, how my adversaries multiplied! Many are rising up against me. [3] Many are saying of my soul, "There is no salvation for him in God." *Selah.* |
| [3] But you, LORD, are a shield around me, my glory, and the one who lifts up my head. [4] I cry aloud to the LORD, and he answers me from his holy mountain. *Selah* | [4] But you, O Yahweh, are the shield about me, my glory, and the lifter of my head. [5] With my voice to Yahweh I called, and he answered me from the mountain of his holiness. *Selah.* |

---

[20] In this translation I follow the Masoretic enumeration of the verses, numbering the superscriptions of the Psalms as verse 1. English translations do not enumerate the superscriptions, resulting in a discrepancy between Hebrew and English verse numbers. When I refer to verses in the footnotes on the translation, the abbreviation ET means "English Translation" and provides the verse number employed by them.

⁵ I lie down and sleep;
I wake again because the Lᴏʀᴅ sustains
   me.
⁶ I will not be afraid of thousands of
   people
who have taken their stand against
   me on every side.

⁷ Rise up, Lᴏʀᴅ!
Save me, my God!
You strike all my enemies on the
   cheek;
you break the teeth of the wicked.
⁸ Salvation belongs to the Lᴏʀᴅ;
may your blessing be on your people.
*Selah*

⁶ I lay down, and I slept.
I woke because Yahweh sustained me.
⁷ I will not fear because of the myriads
   of people,
who round about set upon me.

⁸ Rise up, O Yahweh, save me, O my
   God!
For you strike all at enmity with me
   on the jaw,
the teeth of the wicked you shatter.
⁹ To Yahweh belongs salvation;
May your blessing be on your people.
   *Selah.*

Cᴏɴᴛᴇxᴛ: Vᴇʀʙᴀʟ ᴀɴᴅ Tʜᴇᴍᴀᴛɪᴄ Lɪɴᴋs ᴡɪᴛʜ Sᴜʀʀᴏᴜɴᴅɪɴɢ Psᴀʟᴍs

Lexical and thematic ties link Ps 3 to Pss 1 and 2. The first two psalms
introduced the righteous king who keeps Torah (1:1–1), and the congregation of the righteous (1:5–6) that takes refuge in him (2:12). Against
them gather together the wicked kings and rulers who would throw off
Yahweh's yoke (1:4; 2:1–3). Yahweh announces in 2:6 that he has set his
king on Zion, the mountain of his holiness, and the righteous sufferer
declares in 3:4 that Yahweh answered him from the mountain of his holiness. This lexical link confirms the impression that the speaker in Ps 3 is
the Ps 1 blessed man who is the Ps 2 anointed king (1:1–3; 2:2, 7–9). The
opposition he faces in Pss 3–4 illustrates the vain meditations of 2:1–3,
and in 4:3 he asks how long his enemies will love "vain words," using the
same term that described the "vain" plot in 2:1.[21]

Psalm 2 had concluded with an admonishment to the rebel kings that
they should "kiss the son," using the Aramaic for "son" (בר) instead of
the Hebrew (בן). The Aramaic may have been chosen in 2:12 to differen-
tiate the future king from David's line from the rebel Absalom, the "son"
of David described with the Hebrew word (בן) in Ps 3's superscription.[22]

---

[21] Cf. Cole, *Psalms 1–2*, 150: "A primary function of Psalm 3 is to provide further details
on the murderous attack of Ps. 2.1–3."

[22] Following Cole, *Psalms 1–2*, 143 and n. 4.

EXPOSITION

### 3:1–2 (MT 3:2–3), Enemies Rise and Declare No Salvation in God

The superscription to Ps 3 sets these words at the time when Absalom led a rebellion against his own father, seeking to usurp not only his living father's throne but the very kingdom of God. That satanic action forced David to flee Jerusalem, and the events narrated in 2 Sam 15–17 allow us to sketch in a backdrop that informs the statements we find in Ps 3. The events of David's life in 2 Sam 15–17, and the poetic statement of the way that God delivered him in Ps 3, typologically foreshadow the eschatological king celebrated in Pss 1–2. A brief review of the narrative of Absalom's rebellion will deepen our understanding of Ps 3.

Because of David's sin with Bathsheba (2 Sam 11), Nathan said that God would raise up evil against David out of his own house (2 Sam 12:11). Eventually Absalom conspired against David and stole the hearts of Israel (15:1–6). Absalom had himself proclaimed king (15:10), and David fled the city (15:14). When David heard that his own revered counselor, Ahithophel (cf. 16:23), who happened to be Bathsheba's grandfather (cf. 2 Sam 11:3; 23:34), had joined Absalom, he prayed that Yahweh would turn Ahithophel's counsel to foolishness (15:31). Then when Hushai the Archite tried to go with David, David sent him back into Jerusalem to thwart Ahithophel's counsel (15:32–34). David prayed, and then David took action.

Ahithophel gave counsel to Absalom against Yahweh and against his anointed in 2 Sam 17:1–4 (cf. Ps 1:1; 2:1–3). That counsel entailed Ahithophel taking a force of twelve thousand and pursuing David the night of his flight (2 Sam 17:1). He reasoned that David was weary, that he could be struck down alone, and that all Israel would then embrace Absalom (17:2–3). Everyone saw the wisdom of Ahithophel's advice (17:4), but David had prayed and acted, and Absalom allowed Hushai to respond (17:5). Hushai countered Ahithophel's shrewd advice (17:6–13), and the narrator explains that Yahweh had ordained to defeat Ahithophel's good counsel to punish Absalom's rebellion (17:14). Yahweh ordained, David prayed and acted, and Yahweh's plan came to pass. The danger David faced the night he fled Jerusalem, danger augmented by Ahithophel's powerful stratagem, sets the scene for Ps 3, whose superscription reads, "A psalm of David, when he fled from before Absalom, his son."

Whereas David's sin resulted in what he suffered at Absalom's hands (cf. 2 Sam 12:10–11), there is no hint in Pss 1, 2, or 3 that would indicate that the king to whom the words of Ps 2:7–9 were spoken had sinned or provoked the enmity of his adversaries. The historical David typifies the eschatological king from his line who will have none of his failures.

The vain plots against Yahweh and his anointed in 2:1–3 are like Absalom's conspiracy in 2 Sam 15, a conspiracy that "was mighty" as the people "were going and increasing [רב] with Absalom" (2 Sam 15:12). This provides a backdrop for David's expression in Ps 3:1 (MT 3:2) that his adversaries have "multiplied" (רב). Neither Absalom nor those aligned with him were concerned about the fact that David was Yahweh's anointed. By their actions Absalom and his henchmen declared that their attempt to overthrow David would be slowed neither by Yahweh's endorsement of David nor the oaths he made to him. David makes this disregard for Yahweh explicit when he relates the way that many were saying of him that there was no salvation for him in God (3:2).

We are not sure what selah means (see BDB, 699–700; and *HALOT*, 756), but it seems to mark turning points in Ps 3.[23] Verses 1–2 (MT 1–3) introduce the situation, then verses 3–4 (MT 4–5) recount how David was delivered, and David reflects on what has taken place in verses 5–8 (MT 6–9). Each of these units is concluded with the term selah.

Pss 1–2 inform David's response to those rising against him (3:1, MT 2) in at least two ways: First, because the blessed man meditates on the Torah (1:1–3), he will know that Yahweh has promised to establish the blessing of Abraham (Gen 12:1–3) through the king from Judah's line (Gen 49:8–12), so no enemies of that king will finally overthrow God's intention to bless the world through that kingdom. Second, Yahweh has decreed to David that the seed of David will prevail over all nations (Ps 2:6–9). These realities result in David's response to his adversaries in Ps 3:3–4 (MT 4–5).

### 3:3–4 (MT 3:4–5), Confidence in Yahweh

On the basis of God's promises to him in 2 Sam 7, promises that have multiple connections to the blessing of Abraham in Gen 12:1–3, David asserts that Yahweh will be for him what he said he would be for Abraham.[24] The

---

[23] With only a few exceptions, the targum renders "selah" as "forever," for the details and brief discussion, see Stec, *Targum of Psalms*, 31.

[24] God promised David a great name, as he had promised to Abraham (Gen 12:2; 2 Sam 7:9), and God told both Abraham and David of the one who would come from their own body (Gen 15:4; 2 Sam 7:12). In all the Hebrew Bible, the full expression, "who will come from the loins of you" (אשר יצא ממעיך) occurs in only these two places (Gen 15:4; 2 Sam 7:12). God

Lord told Abraham that he himself would be his shield (Gen 15:1), and in response to his multiplying enemies, David asserts that Yahweh is the shield about him, his glory, and the lifter of his head (Ps 3:3, MT 3:4). That Yahweh is David's glory means that Yahweh is what is praiseworthy about David, what wins David honor and esteem from others. Rather than David asserting that his intelligence or his ingenuity or his skill with the sling or his derring-do in battle is what wins him a reputation, David asserts that Yahweh is his glory, Yahweh has given him success in battle, Yahweh has ensured his significance. Similarly, David does not say that he has been sustained because he has a sunny disposition, because he has the power of positive thinking, or because he has cultivated the habits of highly successful people. Rather, David asserts that he has been sustained because Yahweh is the one who lifts his head. This reference to Yahweh lifting David's head in Ps 3:3 (MT 3:4, ומרים ראשי) anticipates the statement in Ps 110:7, "therefore he will lift up the head" (ירים ראש).

Because Yahweh is David's protection (his shield), the best thing about his reputation (his glory), and the one who sustains him (the lifter of his head), it is natural for David to cry out to Yahweh (Ps 3:3–4, MT 4–5). When David relates that Yahweh answered his cry "from the mountain of his holiness" in 3:4 (MT 3:5), the phrase recalls the place where Yahweh asserted he had established his king in 2:6—Yahweh's assertions in 2:6–9 thus provide the basis for David's appeal and Yahweh's answer in 3:4 (MT 3:5).

### 3:5–6 (MT 3:6–7), Fearless Sleep

Having described the uprising against him in 3:1–2 (MT 3:2-3) and responded with his confidence in Yahweh, prayer to Yahweh, and Yahweh's answer in 3:3–4 (MT 3:4–5), David's words fit what happened when Absalom drove him from Jerusalem and Hushai's counsel saved his life. Ahithophel was on the verge of destroying the weak and weary David, but because of the counsel of Hushai, Absalom rejected Ahithophel's advice.

That near-death night seems to be the historical backdrop summarized in the poetic line of Ps 3:5 (MT 3:6), in which David asserts that he lay down and slept, waking again because Yahweh sustained him. Yahweh sustained David by thwarting the good counsel of Ahithophel through

---

told Abraham that kings would come from him (Gen 17:6), and God promises to establish the king from David's line (2 Sam 7:12–16). Cf. also Mic 5:2 (MT 5:1).

the loyal counsel of Hushai in answer to David's prayer (2 Sam 15:31, 34; 17:5, 14).

There were multitudes joining Absalom (2 Sam 15:12). Ahithophel wanted to take twelve thousand out against David immediately (17:1). Absalom, however, agreed with Hushai's advice to delay and gather all Israel against David (17:11). Because Yahweh is the shield about him (Ps 3:3, MT 3:4), David asserts in Ps 3:6 (MT 3:7) that he would not fear though myriads gathered around him, setting themselves upon him.

### 3:7–8 (MT 3:8–9), Rise Up Yahweh to Whom Salvation Belongs

There is a both-and dynamic in Yahweh's decree in Ps 2:8–9, which entails Yahweh's action and that of the Davidic king. On the one hand, Yahweh invites the king to request to inherit the nations (2:8); on the other hand, the Davidic king will break and dash the enemies (2:9). This gives rise to the prayer in 3:7 (MT 3:8), where David calls on Yahweh to "rise up" (קומה) against those who are "rising up" (קמים, 3:1 [MT 3:2]) against him. David calls on Yahweh to save him. Whereas the shattering of the enemies in 2:9 may subtly allude to the head wound to the seed of the serpent in Gen 3:15, that connotation seems even stronger in Ps 3:7 where Yahweh strikes the cheek of David's enemies, breaking their teeth.

Many might say that there is no salvation for David in God (3:2 [MT 3:3]), but David recognizes in Ps 3:8 (MT 3:9) that salvation is not in the counsel of the wicked, though they be wise as Ahithophel (cf. 1:1). Nor will salvation be found in the outwardly impressive show of the world's rulers, though they be handsome as Absalom (cf. 2:1–3). The Law and the Prophets teach, as David would know both from his meditation on the Torah (cf. Ps 1:2) and from the promises of Yahweh mediated to him through Nathan (2 Sam 7), that salvation belongs to Yahweh (3:8, MT 3:9).

BRIDGE

Throughout Book 1 of the Psalter David fights his way through affliction and suffering. This suffering corresponds to the difficulties David faced from the moment that Samuel anointed him (1 Sam 16) through the period when Saul was persecuting him (1 Sam 17–31) on to the opposition of Saul's people after his death (2 Sam 1–4) until David was at last anointed king over Israel and Judah in 2 Samuel 5. This being the case, the question naturally arises as to why the third psalm relates difficulty from Absalom rather than Saul.

If the Psalter tracks with the narrative of Samuel, why do we not find a psalm like Ps 52 in the place of Ps 3? Psalm 52 relates to the time when David fled from Saul, and it follows hard on the heels of Ps 51, whose superscription connects it to David's sin with Bathsheba. The sin with Bathsheba resulted in the Lord raising up trouble for David out of his own house (2 Sam 12:11), manifested in Absalom's rebellion. So if the Psalter tracks with Samuel, we would expect Ps 52 where we find Ps 3, and Ps 3 where we find 52.

I propose that the Psalter does track with the narrative of Samuel, and that Pss 3 and 52 are where we find them because their positioning makes an interpretive point. That point being that Saul and Absalom are the same kinds of characters engaged in the same kinds of projects. Samuel had anointed David king, making Saul's persecution of David opposition to Yahweh and Yahweh's anointed. This is the sort of rebellion in which Absalom engages when he attempts to usurp his father's throne, setting himself against Yahweh and Yahweh's anointed king.

The narrative progress of Book 1 of the Psalms, then, can be seen as a poetic representation of David's rise to power. In that rise the righteous sufferer clings to Yahweh's promise as he refuses to seize the kingdom through sin or intrigue but waits on the Lord to depose his adversaries (cf. Matt 4:1–11). In that rise, David's life typifies the one for whom it was necessary that he first should suffer and then enter into glory (cf. Luke 24:26).

## Psalm 4

OVERVIEW AND STRUCTURE OF PSALM 4

As in Ps 3, the selahs in Ps 4 seem to mark turning points in the psalm. The question "how long?" is posed to the enemies in 4:2 (MT 4:3), which ends with a selah, then the enemies are admonished in 4:3–4 (MT 4:4–5), which is also followed by selah, after which the enemies are told to embrace true piety in 4:5 (MT 4:6), and then in 4:6–8 (MT 4:7–9) David prays for God's blessing and speaks of how he enjoys it.

David cries out to the Lord, rehearsing his past faithfulness, in verse 1 (MT 2), then addresses the vain rebellion of the sons of Adam in 4:2

(MT 4:3). He then addresses a series of commands to his enemies in 4:3–5 (MT 4:4–6), before returning to their vain rebellion in 4:6 (MT 4:7) and concluding with a celebration of God's goodness to him personally in 4:7–8 (MT 4:8–9). Psalm 4 reflects the following chiastic structure:[25]

4:1 (MT 4:2), Present Plea Based on Past Faithfulness
    4:2 (MT 4:3), How Long Vanity and Lies?
        4:3–5 (MT 4:4–6), How to Repent
        4:6 (MT 4:7), David's Response to Opponents
4:7–8 (MT 4:8–9), The Gladness and Shalom God Gives

### SCRIPTURE

**CSB**

For the choir director: with stringed instruments. A psalm of David.

¹ Answer me when I call,
God, who vindicates me.
You freed me from affliction;
be gracious to me and hear my prayer.

² How long, exalted ones, will my
    honor be insulted?
How long will you love what is
    worthless
and pursue a lie?
*Selah*

³ Know that the LORD has set apart
the faithful for himself;
the Lord will hear when I call to him.
⁴ Be angry and do not sin;
reflect in your heart while on your
    bed and be silent.
*Selah*

⁵ Offer sacrifices in righteousness
and trust in the LORD.

**Author's translation**

¹ For the Preeminent One.
With stringed instruments.
A Psalm of David.

² When I call, answer me, O God of my
    righteousness!
In the tight place you made it broad
    for me.
Be gracious to me, and hear my
    prayer.

³ O sons of man, how long will my
    glory be made a reproach,
as you love vanity, as you seek
    falsehood? *Selah.*

⁴ But know that Yahweh separated the
    lovingkind one for himself;
Yahweh will hear when I call to him.
⁵ Be in uproar and do not sin;
speak in your hearts on your beds and
    be quiet. *Selah.*

⁶ Sacrifice sacrifices of righteousness,
and trust in Yahweh.

---

[25] Similarly Alden, "Chiastic Psalms 1–50," 15.

<sup>6</sup> Many are asking, "Who can show us anything good?"
Let the light of your face shine on us, LORD.

<sup>7</sup> You have put more joy in my heart than they have when their grain and new wine abound.
<sup>8</sup> I will both lie down and sleep in peace,
for you alone, LORD, make me live in safety.

<sup>7</sup> Many are saying, "Who will cause us to see good?"
Lift up on us the light of your face, O Yahweh!

<sup>8</sup> You gave gladness in my heart, greater than when their grain and new wine abound.
<sup>9</sup> In shalom I will both lie down and sleep,
for you alone, O Yahweh, in trust[26] make me dwell.

### CONTEXT: LEXICAL AND THEMATIC LINKS WITH SURROUNDING PSALMS

Lexical and thematic resonance ties Ps 4 to Pss 3 and 2, which naturally also means that Ps 4 continues to build out the design initiated in Pss 1 and 2. Links between Pss 3 and 4 include the following: The same root used to designate David's "adversaries" in 3:1 (MT 3:2, צר) designates the "tight place" in 4:1 (MT 2, צר). In both psalms, "many are saying" (רבים אמרים) (3:2 [MT 3:3] and 4:6 [MT 4:7]). In both the terms "cry" and "answer" are juxtaposed (אקרא ויענני in 3:4 [MT 3:5], בקראי ענני in 4:1 [MT 4:2]). David speaks of "lying down and sleeping" in both (שכבתי ואישנה in 3:5 [MT 3:6] and אשכבה ואישן in 4:8 [MT 4:9]).

In addition to these lexical links with Ps 3, Ps 4 is linked to Ps 2 through the reference to the "vain" words spoken by the enemies of the king (ריק in 2:1 and 4:2 [MT 4:3]). The relief from distress spoken of in 4:1 (MT 4:2) is most naturally understood as the answered prayer described in 3:4 (MT 3:5), Yahweh's setting apart of the "lovingkind one" (חסיד) in 4:3 (MT 4:4) matches his decree in 2:6–9, as the warning to learn wisdom and true piety in 4:4–5 (MT 4:5–6) matches the same in 2:10–12. Robert Cole has argued for priestly overtones in Pss 1–2, overtones that resonate through the priestly blessing from Num 6:24–26 sounded in 4:6 (MT 4:7).[27]

---

[26] This masculine noun, בטח, is often rendered along the lines of "security" (*HALOT* offers "confidence"), but the cognate verb (בטח, which occurs in 4:6 [ET 5]) means "to trust" and the feminine form of the noun (בטחה) means "trusting" or "confidence" (cf. BDB, *HALOT*).

[27] E.g., Cole, *Psalms 1–2*, 140.

EXPOSITION

### 4:1 (MT 4:2), Present Plea Based on Past Faithfulness

In the superscription to Ps 4 we encounter the term regularly rendered "choir director" (CSB) and the like.[28] This term is a *piel* participle of a verb that connotes preeminence (cf. its use in 2 Chr 2:2 [MT 2:1] for supervisors) with a *lamed* prefix (למנצח). The musical connotation that results in the nuance of "choirmaster" (ESV) comes from the musical terminology with which this form is associated, such as the reference to "stringed instruments" in the superscription to Ps 4. The Greek translation of Psalms, however, renders this form εἰς τὸ τέλος, "For the end" (Brenton), or "Regarding completion" (NETS). Given David's role in the reformation of Israel's worship—organizing singers, providing psalms, and leading in worship—a translation along the lines of "For the preeminent one" might not be far off. In that case, there may be a nod in the direction of the promised seed of David who will lead Israel in battle and in worship as his ancestral namesake did (for further discussion, see this commentary's introduction).

David is in constant difficulty, under constant threat, throughout Book 1. The danger prompts his call in 4:1 (MT 4:2) for Yahweh, God of his righteousness, to answer when he calls. The rest of the verse relates how Yahweh did just that. What is typically rendered along the lines of the CSB, "You freed me from affliction" (4:1 [MT 4:2], cf. ESV, "You have given me relief when I was in distress"), can be more literally rendered, "In the tight place you made it broad for me." The lexical connection between the "tight place" (4:1 [MT 4:2] צר) and the "adversaries" in 3:1 (MT 3:2, צר), joins with the natural effect of reading the two psalms in sequence to give the impression that the Ps 4:1 (MT 4:2) rehearsal of the way Yahweh broadened out the constricted difficulty David experienced refers to the deliverance from Absalom celebrated in Ps 3.

The Psalms are like life: deliverance from one difficulty does not result in immediate enthronement. David rehearses one deliverance, and that joins with Yahweh's promise in 2:6–9 to provide the foundation for more prayer for deliverance. Yahweh's past faithfulness grounds David's prayers in the present.

---

[28] Stec renders targum's לשבחא as "To the singer," *Targum of Psalms*, 32, passim. Cook renders the same as "For praise," see Edward M. Cook, trans., *The Psalms Targum: An English Translation* (2001), http://www.targum.info/pss/tg_ps_index.htm.

David calls on the Lord in 4:1 (MT 4:2) to be gracious to him and hear his prayer. Numbers 6:25 invokes Yahweh's grace on his people, and David prays for that grace here at the beginning of Ps 4. Later in Ps 4 David will pray for the Num 6:26 lifting up of Yahweh's face upon his people (4:6 [MT 4:7]), which connects back to the Ps 3:8 (MT 3:9) plea for Yahweh's blessing to be on his people. The blessings of Pss 3 and 4 hearken back to the blessing on those who take refuge in the Davidic king at the end of Ps 2:12, a blessing enjoyed because the king himself is blessed (1:1).

## 4:2 (MT 4:3), How Long Vanity and Lies?

Confident in the promises of God in the Law (Ps 1:2) and the Prophets (2:6–9), David addresses his enemies in 4:2 (MT 4:3), asking them how long they will treat his glory, which he identified in 3:3 as Yahweh himself, as a reproach (employing a *lamed* of transformation). For those who have rejected Yahweh and his moral authority, the commands and prohibitions, promises and prescriptions of the Lord are worthy only of scorn. They mock the existence of God, suggest that those who believe what he says are harming others, and do all they can to make everyone regard their wicked immorality as righteous good behavior. In such circumstances, Prov 28:4 holds true: "Those who forsake Torah praise the wicked, while those who keep Torah strive against them." Thus it is that the wicked regard Yahweh's glory, and the radiance of righteous behavior, as a reproach.

David's enemies, moreover, are committed to their vain plots (2:1–3), and David asks them in 4:2 (MT 4:3) how long they will persist in their love for conspiracies and lies.

Yahweh's assertions in Ps 2:6–9 inform the Ps 4:3 (MT 4:4) declaration that Yahweh has set apart the "lovingkind one" for himself, and the description of the man in Ps 1 is what makes him *hasid* (חסיד). I have rendered this term the "lovingkind one" to bring out the connection between *hasid* (חסיד) and *hesed* (חסד) and to stress the singularity of this individual. The assertion here is not that Yahweh has set apart the *congregation* of those who live out steadfast love for himself but that he has set apart *the man* who lives that way for himself. That man is the one crying out to Yahweh in 4:1 (MT 4:2) in the face of the vain plots of 4:2 (MT 4:3, cf. 2:1–3).

Reading Ps 4:3 (MT 4:4) in light of what has been said to this point in the Psalms, Yahweh has set him apart by planting him next to Torah streams of water (1:3), by installing him on Zion (2:6), decreeing his reign (2:7–9), being his shield and glory and the lifter of his head (3:3 [MT 3:4]), hearing his prayer (3:4 [MT 3:5]), sustaining him (3:5 [MT 3:6]), and shattering the teeth of his enemies (3:7 [MT 3:8]). All this shows that this man belongs to Yahweh, that Yahweh has chosen him and set him apart for himself, and it guarantees that Yahweh will continue to hear his prayer (4:3 [MT 4:4]).

### 4:3–5 (MT 4:4–6), How to Repent

Having instructed the "sons of man" in Ps 4:3 (MT 4:4), in 4:4–5 (MT 4:5–6) David tells them how to respond to the knowledge he has given them. David uses a term in 4:4 (MT 4:5) that connotes a trembling agitation or perturbation. He instructs his enemies to feel this response, warning them, however, not to sin. It is as though they are being instructed to work through their rage against Yahweh's king, and against the announcement that they will not overcome him, in a way that vents emotion but does not persist in rebellion or transgress God's laws. They can be angry about God's purposes if they can do so in a way that refrains from ongoing sin and refuses future rebellion.

In the rest of 4:4 (MT 4:5) David offers yet more counsel to his enemies on how they can, in the terms of Ps 2:10, cause themselves to be wise: They should speak in their hearts upon their beds and be quiet (cf. Mic 2:1–2; Prov 4:16). The image of someone *speaking* in his heart while being *quiet* on his bed creates a mental picture of a man who has been in rebellion realizing his error, reflecting on the judgment he faces, and thinking his way through to repentance and submission. David advises his enemies to go through this process to get over their rage against Yahweh and his anointed (cf. 2:1–3).

Once the enemies have realized the truth of David's words in Ps 4:3 (MT 4:4) and worked through their anger to arrive at a place of silent, peaceful, quiet acceptance of Yahweh's king, as depicted in 4:4 (MT 4:5), they will be able to do what David advises in 4:5 (MT 4:6). Their sacrifices will be righteous if they have submitted themselves to (i.e., kissed) the son, taking refuge in him (cf. 2:12), and trusting in Yahweh (4:5 [MT 4:6]).

### 4:6 (MT 4:7), David's Response to Opponents

The first words of Ps 4:6 (MT 4:7) are an exact repetition of the first phrase of 3:2 (MT 3:3), "many are saying" (רבים אמרים). This would indicate that the kind of thing being said in 4:6 (MT 4:7) is the kind of thing that was being said in 3:2 (MT 3:3). Those who would assert that God was not going to save David (3:2 [MT 3:3]) are the kinds of people who would ask who would cause the people to see good (4:6 [MT 4:7]). The assumption here is that David will not cause them to see the kind of good they long for, and this indicates that though David has given them true and good counsel in 4:3–5 (MT 4:4–6), that counsel has not been received.

David responds to the skeptical rejection of his rightful authority by crying out to Yahweh, asking him to cause Israel to experience the blessing of Aaron from Num 6:26. David petitions the Lord to lift up the light of his face upon his people (4:6 [MT 4:7]), and just as Num 6:26 ends with a wish for Yahweh to give peace to his people, David will say in Ps 4:8 (MT 4:9) that Yahweh causes him to lie down and sleep in peace (שלום). David, the king from Judah's line, prays for the people in the words of Aaron, anticipating the Ps 110 king who will be priest.

## 4:7–8 (MT 4:8–9), The Gladness and Shalom God Gives

David then speaks in 4:7 (MT 4:8) of how Yahweh has put more joy in his heart than the wicked have when their fields yield much grain and their vines produce much wine. His point is that whereas the wicked relish material prosperity and physical success, walking with God brings a joy that transcends the highest heights possible for the worldly.

In another point of contact with Ps 3, David speaks in Ps 4:8 (MT 4:9) of how Yahweh makes him lie down and sleep in safety. These links with Ps 3 thus bracket the sentiments of 4:6–8 (MT 4:7–9), establishing that having instructed and admonished his enemies in 4:3–5 (MT 4:4–6), in 4:6–8 (MT 4:7–9) David is still dealing with rebels.

Though the rebels would attack him, David lies down and sleeps in peace because Yahweh alone can guarantee safety (4:8 [MT 4:9]). First Samuel 24:14 states, "Saul sought [David] every day, but God did not give him into his hand." David celebrates in Ps 4:8 (MT 4:9) the way that Yahweh steadfastly protects and preserves his people for the purposes to which he has appointed them.

### BRIDGE

David essentially teaches rebels to repent in Ps 4:3–5 (MT 4:4–6), laying out a step-by-step process whereby they (1) acknowledge Yahweh's king (4:3 [MT 4:4]); (2) work through their frustration and anger until they can quiet their hearts and be at peace with Yahweh's purposes (4:4 [MT 4:5]); and (3) begin to worship Yahweh with righteousness and trust that pleases him (4:5 [MT 4:6]). Paul quotes David's Ps 4:4 (MT 4:5) command to the rebels, "be angry, and do not sin," in Eph 4:26. Paul's flow of thought aligns nicely with David's, as Paul teaches former pagans how to leave off wickedness to conduct themselves in ways that please the Lord.

Like David, Paul advises the Ephesian Christians to work through their emotional anger in a way that does not transgress, then he instructs them not to let the sun go down on their anger, dealing with it before they go to sleep, which seems to be what David counsels in the rest of Ps 4:4 (MT 4:5), when he urges, "ponder in your own hearts on your beds, and be silent" (ESV). Paul's previous words in Eph 4:25 urge putting away false-hood and speaking the truth, and this matches the question posed in Ps 4:2 (MT 4:3) as to how long vain words will be loved and lies sought out.

Paul's instructions in Eph 4:25–26 match the flow of thought in Ps 4. The apostle Paul thus models the application of Davidic poetry in the Psalms in the lives of Christians. He applies David's moral exhortation in a context where he sets forth what it looks like to live as those who have heard the good news of Jesus and been taught in him, those who have put off the old and are being renewed in the new, in the image of Christ himself (Eph 4:21–24). Paul shows concern for the wider context of the Old Testament passage he quotes, using it in accordance with the intended meaning of the human author—David. Hereby Paul teaches Christians how to understand and apply the Old Testament.

## Psalm 5

OVERVIEW AND STRUCTURE OF PSALM 5

Psalm 5 opens with a plea that Yahweh hear the psalmist's words (5:1–2 [MT 5:2–3]), and then the two large sections of the psalm, 5:3–7 and 5:8–11 (MT 5:4–8 and 5:9–12), each begin with statements addressed directly to the Lord, "O Yahweh," the divine name (יהוה) coming in the vocative position at the beginning of the poetic line in 5:3 and 8 (MT 5:4 and 9), followed by reasons the psalmist gives for the Lord to hear. These lists of reasons begin with statements of what is not that begin with "For" (כי): "For you are not" in 5:4 (MT 5:5 כי לא); "For there is not" in 5:9 (MT 5:10, כי אין). Both lists make mention of an "abundance"—the abundance of steadfast love by which the David enters Yahweh's presence in 5:7

(MT 5:8), and the abundance of transgressions for which he prays his enemies will be banished in 5:10 (MT 5:11). Both sections conclude these lists with contrastive statements of confidence in how the righteous will be received: the individual righteous man will worship Yahweh in 5:7 (MT 5:8), and the congregation of the righteous will rejoice in Yahweh in 5:11 (MT 5:12). The psalm concludes with a confident assertion that Yahweh will bless the individual righteous man (5:12 [MT 5:13]).

Psalm 5 evidences the following balanced construction:

5:1–2 (MT 5:2–3), Hear Me
   5:3–7 (MT 5:4–8), O Yahweh ... For ... Abundance ... But I
   5:8–11 (MT 5:9–12), O Yahweh ... For ... Abundance ... But Let All
5:12 (MT 5:13), Blessing and Favor

SCRIPTURE

| CSB | Author's translation |
|---|---|
| For the choir director: with the flutes. A psalm of David. | [1] For the Preeminent One. To the *Nechiloth*. A Psalm of David. |
| [1] Listen to my words, LORD; consider my sighing. [2] Pay attention to the sound of my cry, my King and my God, for I pray to you. | [2] Give ear to my words, O Yahweh! Understand my meditation. [3] Give attention to the voice of my cry, my King and my God! For to you I pray. |
| [3] In the morning, LORD, you hear my voice; in the morning I plead my case to you and watch expectantly. | [4] O Yahweh, in the morning you will hear my voice, in the morning I set it before you, and I will watch. |
| [4] For you are not a God who delights in wickedness; evil cannot dwell with you. [5] The boastful cannot stand in your sight; you hate all evildoers. [6] You destroy those who tell lies; the LORD abhors violent and treacherous people. | [5] For not a God delighting in wickedness are you. No evil will sojourn with you. [6] The boastful will not stand before your eyes. You hate all workers of iniquity. [7] You destroy those who speak falsehood. The man of bloodshed and treachery you abominate, O Yahweh. |

⁷ But I enter your house
by the abundance of your faithful
    love;
I bow down toward your holy temple
in reverential awe of you.
⁸ Lord, lead me in your righteousness
because of my adversaries;
make your way straight before me.

⁹ For there is nothing reliable in what
    they say;
destruction is within them;
their throat is an open grave;
they flatter with their tongues.
¹⁰ Punish them, God;
let them fall by their own schemes.
Drive them out because of their many
    crimes,
for they rebel against you.

¹¹ But let all who take refuge in you
    rejoice;
let them shout for joy forever.
May you shelter them,
and may those who love your name
    boast about you.
¹² For you, Lord, bless the righteous
    one;
you surround him with favor like a
    shield.

⁸ But I, in the abundance of your
    lovingkindness, will enter your
    house.
I will bow down to the temple of your
    holiness in the fear of you.

⁹ O Yahweh, lead me in your
    righteousness because of the ones
    who watch me.
Make straight before me your way.
¹⁰ For there is in their mouth no
    reliability.
Within them is destruction.
Their throat is an open grave.
Their tongues cause slipperiness.
¹¹ Declare them guilty, O God.
Let them fall by their own counsels.
In the abundance of their
    transgressions banish them,
for they rebel against you.

¹² But let all who take refuge in you
    be glad.
To the age let them shout with joy.
And cover them.
And let them exult in you—the ones
    who love your name.

¹³ For you bless the righteous, O
    Yahweh.
As with a bodyshield of favor you
    surround him.

CONTEXT: VERBAL AND THEMATIC LINKS WITH SURROUNDING PSALMS

Here follows a list of verbal and thematic connections between Ps 5 and
those in its immediate vicinity.

5:1 (MT 5:2) "meditation" (CSB, "sighing," הגיגי)
1:2 "he meditates" (יהגה from הגה)

5:3 (MT 5:4) "in the morning" (2x)
4:8 (MT 4:9) "lie down and sleep"
3:5 (MT 3:6) "lay down and slept"

5:5 (MT 5:6) "shall not stand" (יתיצבו)
2:2 "take their stand" (יתיצבו)

5:5 (MT 5:6) "all workers of iniquity" (כל פעלי און)
6:8 (MT 6:9) "all workers of iniquity" (כל פעלי און)

5:6 (MT 5:7) "falsehood" (כזב)
4:2 (MT 4:3) "falsehood" (כזב)

5:7 (MT 5:8) "your lovingkindness" (חסד)
4:3 (MT 4:4) "lovingkind one" (חסיד)

5:7 (MT 5:8) "your house ... the temple of your holiness"
3:4 (MT 3:5) "the mountain of his holiness"
2:6 "the mountain of my holiness"

5:7 (MT 5:8) "in the fear of you" (ביראתך)
2:11 "in fear" (ביראה)

5:8 (MT 5:9) "your way"
1:1 "the way of sinners"
1:6 "way of the righteous ... way of the wicked"
2:12 "destroyed in the way"

5:10 (MT 5:11) "their own counsels" (ממעצותיהם)
1:1 "the counsel of the wicked" (בעצת)

5:10–11 (MT 5:11–12) use of rare third-person plural
   (they/their) suffix (ימו; 2x)
2:3–5 use of rare third-person plural (they/their) suffix
   (ימו; 5x)

5:11 "they rebel against you"
2:2 "against Yahweh"

5:12 "all who take refuge in you" (חסי בך)
2:12 "blessed are all who take refuge in him" (חוסי בו; cf. 4:5,
   MT 4:6)

Like Pss 3 and 4, Ps 5 makes use of key phrases and terms that have
been introduced in Pss 1 and 2, along with drawing on the language and
themes of Pss 3 and 4. The next psalm with new historical information
in its superscription is Ps 7 (cf. 2 Sam 16:5–14), and the information it
provides relates to that given in the superscription to Ps 3 (2 Sam 15–17).

This indicates that Pss 3–7 are to be read in light of the reference to David's flight after Absalom's revolt referenced in the superscription of Ps 3 (MT 3:1).

Psalms 3 and 4 both reflect the danger that David was in from the counsel of Ahithophel. He had advised Absalom to attack David the night of his flight (2 Sam 17:1–4), and this seems to inform David's references to lying down and sleeping in safety because the Lord protected him in 3:5 and 4:8 (MT 3:6 and 4:9). If Pss 3 and 4 reflect that night of crisis, Ps 5 is David's prayer on the morning after those difficulties (cf. "in the morning" 2x in 5:3 [MT 5:4]). The prayer of Ps 5 is based squarely on the truths and promises of Pss 1 and 2. David himself typifies the blessed man of Ps 1, the Lord's anointed king of Ps 2, and with his enemies seemingly on the ascent (MT 3:1) David prays the truths of Pss 1 and 2 in Ps 5. In Ps 5 David's prayer functions as a kind of personal reassurance that God will keep his word and do justice against the wicked.

<small>EXPOSITION</small>

### 5:1–2 (MT 5:2–3), Hear Me

The term *nechiloth* (הנחילות) occurs only in the superscription of Ps 5 (MT 5:1). It may be related to the term for "flute" (חליל), resulting in the translation "with the flutes" (CSB, ESV, NAS). That connection was clear to neither the Greek translator nor Jerome, both of whom apparently understood the term as a feminine participle referring to one who inherits (הנחלת) (so BDB, s.v. "נחילה"). For the other terms in the superscription and their arrangement, see the introduction.

After its superscription, Ps 5 opens with David appealing to Yahweh to hear his prayer and understand his meditation. The term at the end of Ps 5:1, "meditation" (הגיגי, "murmuring" or perhaps "musing," the CSB goes with "sighing"), is related to the verb used in Ps 1:2 to describe the blessed man "meditating" (יהגה, whose lexical form is הגה) on the Torah. The use of this term indicates that David is calling on the Lord to consider his meditation on the Torah. David is confident in God's purposes and promises as communicated in Torah, but Absalom's revolt, and its seemingly overwhelming might, have David crying out to be heard by Yahweh in Ps 5:1 (MT 5:2), reminding Yahweh that he is the blessed man who meditates on the Torah (Ps 1), not the wicked one who plots against Yahweh (cf. Ps 2:1–3). The cry to be heard continues into 5:2 (MT 5:3), with David asking for God's attention and asserting that far from plotting against Yahweh (again, cf. 2:1–3), he claims Yahweh as "my King and my God." This declaration of allegiance and fealty is reminiscent of his identification of Yahweh as his shield, his glory, and the lifter of his head in 3:3 (MT 3:4).

### 5:3–7 (MT 5:4–8), O Yahweh ... For ... Abundance ... But I

Why is David asking Yahweh to hear and making protestations of his loyalty in Ps 5:1–2 (MT 5:2–3)? Because his enemies have conspired against him and grown strong (MT 3:1, cf. 2 Sam 15:12). David made it through that first night because Yahweh sustained him (3:5 [MT 3:6]), and now in Ps 5:3 (MT 5:4) he makes his morning prayer to Yahweh. David has asked Yahweh to hear in 5:1–2 (MT 5:2–3), and now the body of Ps 5 consists of two statements, each of which begins with David addressing Yahweh by name (5:3 [MT 5:4] and 5:8 [MT 5:9]).

David tells Yahweh that he will set his prayers before him and watch in 5:3 (MT 5:4) for the reasons that he enumerates in 5:4–7 (MT 5:5–8). David states these reasons as things in which Yahweh does not delight:

- wickedness does not please Yahweh;
- no evil sojourns with him (5:4 [MT 5:5]);
- those who boast do not stand before him;
- he hates all who work iniquity (5:5 [MT 5:6]);
- he destroys those who speak lies;
- and Yahweh abominates those who shed blood and deceive others (5:6 [MT 5:7]).

Yahweh, of course, knows all of these truths about himself. Yahweh knows that he is pleased with righteousness, that only the clean and holy can dwell in his presence, that those who are humble and rely on him will stand before him, that he loves those who do what is right, speak what is true, and love others and help them to flourish in what is true. The fact that David prays through all this means that as he prays David rehearses Yahweh's own character. These statements that Yahweh hates wickedness praise him because they announce his righteous character. At the same time, these statements reassure David that, however things may seem, Yahweh is good and will keep his word.

The fact that Yahweh hates the kinds of satanic schemes that Absalom has attempted in his effort to usurp the kingdom of God and steal it from his own father lead David to the confident assertion in Ps 5:7 (MT 5:8). The affirmations in Ps 5:7 (MT 5:8) match the negations in 5:4–6 (MT 5:5–7) point for point:

- Yahweh hates wickedness, but David experiences Yahweh's abundant lovinkindness;
- no evil sojourns with Yahweh, but David will enter his house;
- the boastful will not stand before Yahweh's eyes, but David will bow down to his holy temple;
- Yahweh destroys liars and abominates those who shed blood and deceive, but David fears Yahweh—and that fear of Yahweh keeps him from such destructive tactics.

In Ps 5:3–7 (MT 5:4–8) David models a character reinforcing prayer that finds strength in the rehearsal of what does and does not please the Lord. David has been forced to flee his throne and city, the threat of death arising from within his own house as a result of his own sin (cf. 2 Sam 12:10–11), and he responds by reminding himself of what does and does not please God. Under such trying circumstances, the knowledge of Yahweh's character keeps David from the wicked ways of responding that he catalogues here: engaging in evil, boasting in pride, working iniquity, pursuing a campaign of misinformation in a bloodthirsty quest for vengeance (cf. 5:4–6 [MT 5:5–7]). The rehearsal of Yahweh's character also assures David that because Absalom *has* pursued this kind of course, he will not prevail, leading to David's confident celebration of God's love for him in 5:7 (MT 5:8).

### 5:8–11 (MT 5:9–12), O Yahweh … For … Abundance … But Let All

Having reminded himself of Yahweh's displeasure with the wicked through his communion with God in prayer in Ps 5:3–7 (MT 5:4–8), David entreats Yahweh to keep him from the way of the wicked by leading him in Yahweh's own righteousness in 5:8–10 (MT 5:9–11). Then just as the previous section concluded with David's confidence about his own ability to go on worshiping Yahweh in 5:7 (MT 5:8), the section in 5:8–11 (MT 5:9–12) concludes with a prayer that the congregation of the righteous (cf. 1:5; 2:12) will ever exult in Yahweh (5:11 [MT 5:12]).

As in 5:3 (MT 5:4), David's first word addresses Yahweh by name in 5:8 (MT 5:9). Whereas in 5:3–7 (MT 5:4–8) David was praying to be heard, in

5:8-11 (MT 5:9-12) he prays that Yahweh will lead him in righteousness (5:8 [MT 5:9]). This prayer for Yahweh to lead him is motivated by David's awareness that he is being watched, and these watchers are so hostile that the term is typically rendered "adversaries."[29] The final clause of Ps 5:8 (MT 5:9) speaks of Yahweh's "way," which David asks Yahweh to make straight before him, as another way of describing Yahweh's "righteousness," in which David has asked to be led.

The reasons David gives for asking to be led in Yahweh's righteousness, having Yahweh make his way straight before him (5:8 [MT 5:9]), are presented in 5:9 (MT 5:10). The three reasons amount to an elaboration on the reference to "those who speak falsehood" in 5:6 (MT 5:7). David does not want to go the way of those who speak no firmness, within whom is destruction, whose throats are an open grave—an expression that seems to indicate that there are dead hearts at the bottom of those open graves—and whose tongues cause slipperiness (5:9 [MT 5:10]). There is a chiastic structure to these four phrases:

For there is in their mouth no reliability.
    Within them is destruction.
    Their throat is an open grave.
Their tongues cause slipperiness.

The first and fourth phrases indicate that what they speak is not firm and gives no stable traction, while the second and third phrases communicate that death and destruction reside within them. Those with dead hearts and destructive impulses speak unreliable slippery words. This is the counsel of the wicked in which David does not want to walk (1:1, cf. "their counsels" in 5:10 [MT 5:11]), the kind of speech that advises rebellion against Yahweh (cf. 2:1-3).

As a result of the words that overflow from their hearts, David calls on Yahweh to declare them guilty in the first statement of Ps 5:10 (MT 5:11). His next words speak to how he would like Yahweh to enact the sentence—letting them "fall by their own counsels." David wants Yahweh to allow the futility of the wicked counsel in which the blessed man does

---

[29] So CSB. All six instances of this term are in the Psalms, and the NAS renders each instance "foes." BDB glosses the term "[insidious] watcher" because they connect the word etymologically to a term meaning "watch stealthily, lie in wait;" see BDB, 1003-4; cf. *HALOT*, s.v.

not walk (1:1) to rebound upon the wicked themselves. Keel observes, "The psalms often attribute the failure of the wicked not to the direct intervention of Yahweh, but to the operation of the order established by God at creation. The evil which originates with the wicked creates a fateful chain of events which ultimately turns against the offender himself (Pss 7:16; 34:21; 37:15)."[30]

Since the focus of 5:9 (MT 5:10) was verbal sin, the "abundance of transgressions" for which David wants the enemies banished in 5:10 (MT 5:9) is likely also verbal, which would tie their "counsels" by which David wants them to fall to the way that they "rebel" against Yahweh, mentioned in the last phrase of the line. This fits naturally with the vain plots of 2:1–3. David calls on the Lord to visit just consequences against the boastful workers of iniquity who spoke their false thoughts that they could throw off the Creator's yoke. To rebel against David as Absalom did is to rebel against Yahweh, for David was Yahweh's anointed king (cf. 2:2; MT 3:1).

Just as the first part of David's prayer in 5:3–7 (MT 5:4–8) concluded with a contrastive positive statement of how David would worship Yahweh in 5:7 (MT 5:8), so now the second part of the prayer in 5:8–11 (MT 5:9–12) concludes with a contrastive prayer that those who align themselves with Yahweh and Yahweh's anointed might always rejoice. The continuity of theme and situation strengthens the linguistic connection between taking "refuge" in Yahweh in 5:11 (MT 5:12) and taking "refuge" in Yahweh's king in 2:12. The blessing pronounced in 2:12, "blessed are all who take refuge in him," is elaborated upon here, as these who take refuge in Yahweh will rejoice in him, shout with joy, and experience the shelter Yahweh provides; and they will exult in him because they love his name (5:11 [MT 5:12]). As in Ps 1, where the blessed man is accompanied by the congregation of the righteous (Ps 1:1, 5), so in Ps 5 David worships in 5:7 (MT 5:8) and he is joined by those aligned with him in 5:11 (MT 5:12).

### 5:12 (MT 5:13), Blessing and Favor

Those aligned with David will be standing with him against the wicked rebels who have gathered themselves together against Yahweh and Yahweh's anointed (2:2). In a real sense, the cause of the congregation of the righteous stands or falls on the success of Yahweh's anointed. If

---

[30] Keel, *Symbolism of the Biblical World*, 98.

he is defeated, they will be defeated. But if he prevails, they prevail with him. This explains the connection between the exulting of those who love Yahweh's name at the end of 5:11 (MT 5:12) and the statement that grounds that exultation in 5:12 (MT 5:13): Yahweh blesses the individual righteous man, and Yahweh surrounds him with favor that acts like a shield covering the whole body.

Those who take refuge in Yahweh are glad in him (5:11 [MT 5:12]) because he guarantees the success of his king (5:12 [MT 5:13]). There is no favor like Yahweh's, and there are no arrows that can pierce that shield.

Bridge

The Psalms are a school of prayer. In Ps 5's class session, David models how to take comfort in the character of Yahweh. This both reinforces David's commitment to live in a way that pleases Yahweh and builds his confidence that his enemies will not prevail (5:3–7 [MT 5:4–8]). In addition, David knows the temptation of the way of the wicked, particularly when circumstances try patience and the world seems set against him. In such a situation, David asks Yahweh to lead him in his righteousness and make his way straight before him (5:8 [MT 5:9]).

Paul quotes Ps 5:9 (MT 5:10) in Rom 3:13. Reading Ps 5 as continuing the themes introduced in Pss 1–2, as I have done here, sharpens the relevance of Paul's use of the thoughts of Ps 5 because he quotes them having asserted that none seek God (3:10) and all have together turned aside and become worthless (3:11). Paul likely saw all sinners as having gathered themselves together against Yahweh and his anointed (cf. Ps 2:1–3), and the open grave of their throats and the deceit of their tongues (3:13) would naturally be their speaking against Yahweh's king. We would expect the seed of the serpent to have the venom of asps under their lips (Rom 3:13).

Psalm 5 portrays Yahweh's king responding to difficulty with prayer to and trust in Yahweh, and the psalm teaches that Yahweh will certainly protect his king (5:12 [MT 5:13]). The portrayal and the teaching of this psalm inspire those who align themselves with Yahweh's king to pray as David did.

## Psalm 6

### Overview and Structure of Psalm 6

Psalm 6 is laced with the language of Ps 2, resulting in a strong impression that David here pleads with God not to treat him the way that Ps 2 declares God will treat his enemies. In 6:1–3 (MT 6:2–4) David asks Yahweh not to rebuke, correct, and terrify him the way Ps 2 declares he will do to his enemies. Then in 6:4–5 (MT 6:5–6) David asks Yahweh to turn from wrath, rescue him, and sustain his ability to give thanks among the living. In 6:6–7 (MT 6:7–8) David recounts his vexation and many tears, prompted by the success of his enemies. The psalm then concludes in 6:8–10 (MT 6:9–11) with David warning the workers of iniquity that Yahweh has heard his prayer, confidently asserting that they will face a sudden comeuppance that will leave them shamed and shucked, with the chaff drifting away in the wind.

There seems to be a chiastic structure here:

6:1–3 (MT 6:2–4) How Long until My Enemies Get What They Deserve?
    6:4–5 (6:5–6) Turn and Give Me Your Lovingkindness So I Can Thank You.
    6:6–7 (MT 6:7–8) My Enemies Cause Me Much Vexation and Weeping.
6:8–10 (MT 9–11) Depart Evildoers Because Yahweh Hears Me and Will Punish You.

### Scripture

| CSB | Author's translation |
|---|---|
| For the choir director: with stringed instruments, according to *Sheminith*. A psalm of David. | [1] For the Preeminent One. With stringed instruments upon the eighth. A Psalm of David. |
| [1] Lord, do not rebuke me in your anger; do not discipline me in your wrath. | [2] O Yahweh, rebuke me not in your wrath, nor correct me in your rage. |
| [2] Be gracious to me, Lord, for I am weak; heal me, Lord, for my bones are shaking; | [3] Be gracious to me, O Yahweh, because I am frail. Heal me, O Yahweh, because my bones are terrified, |

³my whole being is shaken with terror.
And you, Lord—how long?

⁴Turn, Lord! Rescue me;
save me because of your faithful love.
⁵For there is no remembrance of you in death;
who can thank you in Sheol?

⁶I am weary from my groaning;
with my tears I dampen my bed
and drench my couch every night.
⁷My eyes are swollen from grief;
they grow old because of all my enemies.

⁸Depart from me, all evildoers,
for the Lord has heard the sound of my weeping.
⁹The Lord has heard my plea for help;
the Lord accepts my prayer.
¹⁰All my enemies will be ashamed and shake with terror;
they will turn back and suddenly be disgraced.

⁴and my soul is exceedingly terrified.
But you, O Yahweh, how long?

⁵Turn, O Yahweh, rescue my soul.
Save me because of your lovingkindness,
⁶for there is no remembrance of you in death;
in Sheol who will give thanks to you?

⁷I am weary in my groaning.
I cause my bed to swim the whole night;
with my tears I cause my couch to dissolve.
⁸My eye wastes away from vexation;
it grows old on all my adversaries.

⁹Depart from me all workers of iniquity,
for Yahweh has heard the sound of my weeping.
¹⁰Yahweh has heard my supplication
Yahweh receives my prayer.
¹¹They will be ashamed and greatly terrified
—all at enmity with me—
they will turn back and suddenly be ashamed.

CONTEXT: VERBAL AND THEMATIC LINKS WITH SURROUNDING PSALMS

Psalm 6 superscription: "With stringed instruments" (בנגינות)
Psalm 4 superscription: "With stringed instruments" (בנגינות)

6:1 (MT 6:2) "rebuke me not in your wrath" (באפך)
2:5 "he will terrify them in his wrath" (באפו)
2:12 "his wrath flares quickly" (אפו)

6:1 (MT 6:2) "nor correct me" (תיסרני)
2:10 "now O kings ... receive correction" (הוסרו)

6:2 (MT 6:3) "Be gracious to me" (חנני)
4:1 (MT 4:2) "Be gracious to me" (חנני)

6:2 (MT 6:3) "my bones are terrified" (נבהלו)
2:5 "he will terrify them" (יבהלמו)

6:3 (MT 6:4) "my soul is ... terrified" (נבהלה)
2:5 "he will terrify them" (יבהלמו)

6:3 (MT 6:4) "But you, O Yahweh" (ואת יהוה)
3:3 (MT 3:4) "But you, O Yahweh" (ואתה יהוה)
4:8 (MT 4:9) "you..., O Yahweh" (אתה יהוה)

6:3 (MT 6:4) "how long" (עד מתי)
4:2 (MT 4:3) "how long" (עד מה)

6:4 (MT 6:5) "your lovingkindness" (חסד)
5:7 (MT 5:8) "your lovingkindness" (חסד)
4:3 (MT 4:4) "lovingkind one" (חסיד)

6:7 (MT 6:8) "my adversaries" (צוררי)
3:1 (MT 3:2) "my adversaries" (צרי)

6:8 (MT 6:9) "Depart from me"
4:3–6 *instructions for the wicked*
2:10–12 *instructions for the wicked*

6:8 (MT 6:9) "all workers of iniquity" (כל פעלי און)
5:5 (MT 5:6) "all workers of iniquity" (כל פעלי און)

6:8–9 (MT 6:9–10) "Yahweh has heard [2x] ... Yahweh receives
   my prayer"
2:8 "ask of me"

6:10 (MT 6:11) "They will be ashamed" (ויבהלו)
2:5 "he will terrify them" (יבהלמו)

6:10 (MT 6:11) "all who hate me" (כל איבי)
3:7 (MT 3:8) "all who hate me" (כל איבי)

6:10 (MT 6:11) "suddenly be ashamed"
1:4 "they are like chaff"

Psalm 6 moves from the personal reassurances found in Ps 5 (see "Context"
discussion there) to an appeal that Yahweh not treat David the way his
wicked enemies deserve to be treated. By means of the language he uses

in Ps 6, David indicates that he feels the way Ps 2 said his enemies were to feel, but by the end he is confident that the truths of Pss 1 and 2 will obtain. Psalm 7 builds on Ps 6 as a cry for just vindication, and then Ps 8 stands as a confident assertion of Yahweh's purposes for the king from David's line.

Exposition

### 6:1–3 (MT 6:2–4), How Long until My Enemies Get What They Deserve?

The only difference between the superscriptions of Pss 4 and 6 is the additional phrase, "upon the eighth" in that of Ps 6. *HALOT* (s.v.) lists five suggested interpretations of this term, noting that a decision between them is impossible: (1) some take it as an eight stringed instrument; (2) others as a reference to the eighth string of an instrument (cf. 1 Chr 15:21); (3) still others as a reference to a lower octave (cf. 1 Chr 15:20); (4) it could refer to the eighth in a series of festivals or ceremonies; or (5) to a city with a similar sounding name.

As noted above, there is strong lexical resonance between Ps 6 and Ps 2. The terms "wrath" and "correct" (CSB, ESV "discipline") in 6:1 (MT 6:2) are the same terms used in Ps 2:5 and 10. In Ps 2 the wrath and correction were directed at the enemies of Yahweh's anointed. Given the circumstances referenced in the superscription of Ps 3 and the flow of thought in Pss 3–5, it would seem that in Ps 6 David is asking Yahweh not to give him what his enemies deserve. This would place the emphasis on the first-person pronoun in 6:1 (MT 6:2): "O Yahweh, rebuke *me* not in your wrath, nor correct *me* in your rage." The idea seems to be that this rage and correction should be directed not at the anointed but at his enemies.

The first statement of Ps 6:2 (MT 6:3) restates a plea found in 4:2, "Be gracious to me," tying Ps 6 not only to Ps 2 but to the intervening psalms. David's frail state (CSB "weak," ESV "languishing") is understandable in light of the fact that his son has driven him from the palace (MT 3:1). David then calls on the Lord to heal him, and when he describes his bones as "terrified" and his soul as "terrified" in 6:2–3 (MT 6:3–4), he uses the term from Ps 2:5, "in his fury he will *terrify* them." In Ps 2:5 Yahweh replies to the rebellion of his enemies (2:1–3) by terrifying them. In Ps 6:2–3 (MT 6:3–4) David complains that what was supposed to happen to his enemies has happened to him, and he concludes the thought of 6:3 (MT 6:4) by asking the Lord how long this state of affairs will continue.

In Ps 6:1–3 (MT 6:2–4) David cries out to Yahweh, asking how long until his enemies get what they deserve.

## 6:4–5 (MT 6:5–6), Turn and Give Me Your Lovingkindness So I Can Thank You.

The circumstances of his life indicate to David that the way God said things would be is not the way they are, but David neither questions whether God is really there nor joins with those who rebel against God. David sticks to his convictions—that God is good and that his word is true—as he protests, and he calls out to the Lord to turn and set things right in 6:4–5 (MT 6:5–6).

The term David uses to call Yahweh to "turn" in 6:4 (MT 6:5) is the one the prophets use when they call Israel to repent. David is not charging Yahweh with sin, but he has suggested that he suffers what his enemies deserve in 6:1–3 (MT 6:2–4), so he calls Yahweh to turn from allowing things to be contrary to what Yahweh said would be. This entails the "rescue" of David's terrified "soul" (6:4 [MT 6:5]). David identified himself as the "lovingkind one" (חסיד) in 4:3 (MT 4:4), and he said that he would enter Yahweh's house in the abundance of the Lord's "lovingkindness" (חסד) in 5:7 (MT 5:8). Now he appeals to that same "lovingkindness" (חסד) of the Lord as the basis of the salvation he seeks in 6:4 (MT 6:5).

Appealing to Yahweh's lovingkindness in 6:4 (MT 6:5), David adds an application to Yahweh's concern for his own glory in 6:5 (MT 6:6). David understands that Yahweh deserves to be remembered as God and thanked for all he has done. David knows that remembering the Lord and the offering of thanks to him is the best way for people to live: that it is what is right, and that it is what the Lord wants for people. He also knows that the rebels will not remember the Lord or give thanks to him. So David appeals to the Lord's concern for his remembrance among the living when he says, in essence, that if he dies there will be no remembrance of Yahweh, that thanksgiving cannot be offered to Yahweh from Sheol (6:5 [MT 6:6]). In Ps 6:4–5 (MT 6:5–6) David calls on the Lord to turn and show him lovingkindness so that David can continue to remember and thank him.

## 6:6–7 (MT 6:7–8), My Enemies Cause Me Much Vexation and Weeping.

In 6:6 (MT 6:7) David describes his weary groaning and says that he has cried so many tears that his bed has been caused to swim. He depicts rising waters causing the bed to swim in a flood of tears. David changes metaphor slightly in the next line, describing the flowing tears dissolving his couch. The poetry communicates that David's situation has him weeping, and reflection on the events of David's life signaled by the superscription of Ps 3 (MT 3:1) help to explain the excessive weeping David describes in 6:6 (MT 6:7). All the trouble stemmed from David's sin with Bathsheba. He committed adultery, had Uriah murdered, then the child that was conceived died. In the aftermath, and in fulfillment of Yahweh's verdict delivered by Nathan in 2 Sam 12, Amnon abused Tamar, only to be murdered by Absalom, and then Absalom tried to steal the very kingdom of God from his father, David.

Such devastation warrants not only the weeping of 6:6 (MT 6:7) but also the sorrow and vexation David describes in 6:7 (MT 6:8). When David references his "adversaries" in 6:7 (MT 6:8), he uses the same term found in 3:1 (MT 3:2), reinforcing the continuity between Pss 3–6. In Ps 6:6–7 (MT 6:7–8) David's deep emotional turmoil describes the way his enemies cause him to weep.

## 6:8–10 (MT 6:9–11), Depart Evildoers Because Yahweh Hears Me and Will Punish You.

The confidence that returns in Ps 6:8–10 is like a shoot from a stump whose roots are firmly planted in the soil of Pss 1 and 2. Yahweh's decree in Ps 2 and the blessing described in Ps 1 enable David to warn his enemies that Yahweh has heard his prayers and will punish them. When David tells his enemies to depart and refers to them as "workers of iniquity" in 6:8 (MT 6:9), the use of the phrase "workers of iniquity" found in 5:5 (MT 5:6) again makes the point that these psalms are using the same terms to describe the same things. The enemies should flee, David says in 6:8 (MT 6:9), because Yahweh has heard the weeping that David described in 6:6–7 (MT 6:7–8).

Repetition can communicate both relief and certitude, and both come across in Ps 6:9 (MT 6:10) where David says that Yahweh has heard his supplication and received his prayer. The fact that Yahweh has heard David's plea that Yahweh "turn" (6:4 [MT 6:5]) from the situation where David experiences what is due his enemies (6:1–3 [MT 6:2–4]) means that the enemies are about to experience what Yahweh said they would in Pss 1 and 2. Thus David announces in 6:10 (MT 6:11) that they will be shamed and "terrified"—again using the term from 2:5, but this time the right people experience the terror—those who hate the Lord's anointed. When they turn back from their wicked plots (2:1–3) and experience their sudden shaming it will be like wind driving away chaff (1:4), like the way of the wicked perishing (1:6), like those who have received fair warning being destroyed in the way (2:12).

BRIDGE

In this fallen world all of God's children will at times feel that the wicked are blessed while the righteous are cursed. David's response to those feelings is exemplary and typological. It is exemplary in that it models unwavering trust in God, honesty before God, and a boldness to call on God to keep his promises. It is typological in that David's prayer in Ps 6 points to one who, unlike David, will not suffer for his own sins but for the sins of his people (note the allusion to Ps 6:3 [MT 6:4] in John 12:27), one who willingly takes upon himself the punishment due the enemies of God, who weeps over those who have rejected him, and whose vindication will indeed bring about the shamed terror of those who hate him, those who will meet a sudden destruction.

## Psalm 7

OVERVIEW AND STRUCTURE OF PSALM 7

Psalm 7 seems to reflect the following chiastic structure:[31]

7:1–2 (MT 7:2–3), Plea
    7:3–5 (MT 7:4–6), The Innocent
        7:6–8 (MT 7:7–9), Rise up, O Yahweh
            7:9–10 (MT 7:10–11), Desire for Justice
        7:11–13 (MT 7:12–14), God Is a Just Judge
    7:14–16 (MT 7:15–17), The Guilty
7:17 (MT 7:18), Praise

---

[31] Compare the proposal of Alden, "Chiastic Psalms 1–50," 15.

SCRIPTURE

| CSB | Author's translation |
|---|---|
| A *Shiggaion* of David, which he sang to the LORD concerning the words of Cush, a Benjaminite. | ¹ A *Shiggaion* of David, which he sang to Yahweh concerning the words of Cush, a Benjaminite. |
| ¹ LORD my God, I seek refuge in you; save me from all my pursuers and rescue me, | ² O Yahweh God, I take refuge in you! Save me from all who pursue me, and deliver me, |
| ² or they will tear me like a lion, ripping me apart with no one to rescue me. | ³ lest he tear my soul like a lion, rending with none to deliver. |
| ³ LORD my God, if I have done this, if there is injustice on my hands, | ⁴ O Yahweh, if I have done this, if there is iniquity in my hands, |
| ⁴ if I have done harm to one at peace with me or have plundered my adversary without cause, | ⁵ if I have repaid evil to the one at peace with me, and plundered my adversary without cause, |
| ⁵ may an enemy pursue and overtake me; may he trample me to the ground and leave my honor in the dust. *Selah* | ⁶ let the one at enmity with my soul pursue and overtake, and let him trample my life to the earth, and lay my glory in the dust. *Selah.* |
| ⁶ Rise up, LORD, in your anger; lift yourself up against the fury of my adversaries; awake for me; you have ordained a judgment. | ⁷ Rise up, O Yahweh, in your wrath. Be lifted up on the outrage of my adversaries, and awaken for me the judgment you have commanded. |
| ⁷ Let the assembly of peoples gather around you; take your seat on high over it. | ⁸ Let the congregation of the peoples surround you, and over it return on high. |
| ⁸ The LORD judges the peoples; vindicate me, LORD, according to my righteousness and my integrity. | ⁹ Yahweh will judge the peoples. Judge for me, O Yahweh, according to my righteousness, according to my integrity within me. |
| ⁹ Let the evil of the wicked come to an end, but establish the righteous. The one who examines the thoughts and emotions is a righteous God. | ¹⁰ O let the evil of the wicked end, but establish the righteous one, O righteous God, tester of hearts and guts. ¹¹ My shield is with God, Savior of those of upright heart. |

¹⁰ My shield is with God,
who saves the upright in heart.
¹¹ God is a righteous judge
and a God who shows his wrath every
    day.

¹² If anyone does not repent,
he will sharpen his sword;
he has strung his bow and made it
    ready.
¹³ He has prepared his deadly
    weapons;
he tips his arrows with fire.

¹⁴ See, the wicked one is pregnant with
    evil,
conceives trouble, and gives birth to
    deceit.
¹⁵ He dug a pit and hollowed it out
but fell into the hole he had made.
¹⁶ His trouble comes back on his own
    head;
his own violence comes down on top
    of his head.

¹⁷ I will thank the Lord for his
    righteousness;
I will sing about the name of the Lord
    Most High.

¹² God is a righteous judge,
and a God who is indignant the whole
    day.
¹³ If one will not repent, he will
    sharpen his sword.
His bow he treads, and readies it.
¹⁴ And for him he makes ready
    instruments of death.
He makes his arrows as those that
    burn.

¹⁵ Behold: He writhes iniquity and gets
    pregnant.
He goes into labor and gives birth to
    deception.
¹⁶ He dug a cistern and shoveled it,
and he fell in the pit he made.
¹⁷ His labor returns on his own head,
and on his cranium his violence
    comes down.

¹⁸ I will thank Yahweh according to his
    righteousness.
And I will psalm the name of Yahweh
    Most High!

CONTEXT: VERBAL AND THEMATIC LINKS WITH SURROUNDING PSALMS

7:1 (MT 7:2) "I take refuge in you"
5:11 (MT 5:12) "let all who take refuge in you rejoice"
2:12 "blessed are all who take refuge in him"

7:1 (MT 7:2) "save me" (הושיעני)
6:4 (MT 6:5) "save me" (הושיעני)

7:2 (MT 7:3) "my soul"
6:3, 4 (MT 6:4, 5) "my soul"

7:4 (MT 7:5) "my adversary"
7:6 (MT 7:7) "my adversaries"
6:7 (MT 6:8) "my adversaries"

3:1 (MT 3:2) "my adversaries"

7:5 (MT 7:6) "the one who hates my soul" (see "my soul" at 7:2 above)
6:10 (MT 6:11) "all who hate me"
3:7 (MT 3:8) "all who hate me"

7:5 (MT 7:6) "my glory"
3:3; 4:2; 8:5 (MT 3:4; 4:3; 8:6) "glory"

7:6 (MT 7:7) "Rise up, O Yahweh"
3:7 (MT 3:8) "Rise up, O Yahweh"

7:6 (MT 7:7) "in your wrath"
6:1 (MT 6:2) "in your wrath"

7:6 (MT 7:7) "the judgment you have commanded"
Compare 1:5; 2:6–9 "the judgment," Yahweh's decree

7:7 (MT 7:8) "the congregation of the peoples" (עדת לאמים)
1:5 "the congregation of the righteous" (עדת)
2:1 "the peoples meditate vanity" (לאמים)

7:8 (MT 7:9) "peoples" (עמים)
3:6 (MT 3:7) "people" (עם)
3:8 (MT 3:9) "people" (עם)

7:8 (MT 7:9) "Yahweh judges the peoples"
1:5 "the wicked will not rise in the judgment"

7:9 (MT 7:10) "the wicked (pl.) ... the righteous one"
1:5 "the wicked (pl.) ... the congregation of the righteous"
1:1, 4, 5, 6; 3:7 (MT 3:8) "the wicked"

7:10 (MT 7:11) "my shield"
3:3 (MT 3:4) "you, O Yahweh, are the shield about me"

7:11 (MT 7:12) God a righteous judge and indignant
2:4 "The one who sits in the heavens laughs"

7:12–13 (MT 7:13–14) If he does not repent ... Yahweh prepares instruments of death
1:6 "the way of the wicked will perish"

2:10–12 wicked admonished and warned of coming destruction
4:3–5 (MT 4:4–6) wicked instructed
6:8–9 (MT 6:9–10) wicked warned of Yahweh's wrath

7:14 (MT 7:15) the wicked "gives birth to deception"
1:1 "counsel of the wicked"
2:1–3 "the peoples meditate vanity"

7:15–16 (MT 7:16–17) wicked falls into the pit he dug to trap others
5:10 (MT 5:11) "Let them fall by their own counsels"

7:17 (MT 7:18) "I will give thanks ... and I psalm"
6:5 (MT 6:6) "there is no remembrance of you in death; in Sheol who will give thanks to you"

7:17 (MT 7:18) "the name of Yahweh Most High"
5:11 (MT 5:12) "the ones who love your name"
8:1, 9 (MT 8:2, 10) "how majestic is your name"

With these linguistic points of contact, Ps 7 fills in more of the picture being painted in Pss 3–6. Psalms 3–4 dealt with the night of David's flight from Absalom, then Ps 5 presented David's morning-after-crisis-affirmation that Yahweh is just. In Ps 6 David insisted that Yahweh not treat him as Ps 2 said he would treat the enemies of the anointed, and now in Ps 7 David responds to the accusations of his enemies. This cycle of psalms moves toward resolution in the celebration in Ps 8 and the lament over the death of the son in Ps 9.

Exposition

### 7:1–2 (MT 7:2–3), Plea

The term *shiggaion* in the superscription of Ps 7 also appears in Hab 3:1. *HALOT* (s.v.) states that its etymology and meaning are unknown.

The superscription of Ps 7 contains what appears to be historical information in the phrase "concerning the words of Cush, a Benjaminite," but the historical narratives concerning David do not tell us who Cush was or what he said. Given the accusations David addresses in 7:3–5 (MT 7:4–6), the words of Cush would seem to be along the lines of the words of Saul's kinsman Shimei, who cursed David as he fled Jerusalem after Absalom's revolt, charging that Yahweh was avenging the blood of Saul's house on

David (2 Sam 16:5–8).[32] The book of Samuel demonstrates that David was not involved in the death of Saul or anyone related to him, and that would correspond to the innocence David claims in Ps 7:8 (MT 7:9).

As can be seen in the list of lexical points of contact above, there is massive vocabulary continuity between Pss 1–7. Psalm 7 contributes thematically in that it presents David bringing to the Lord the charges his enemies have made against him.

A blessing was pronounced on those who take refuge in the son in 2:12, and David prayed in 5:11 (MT 5:12) that all taking refuge in Yahweh might rejoice. He opens 7:1 (MT 7:2) asserting that he takes refuge in Yahweh, and praying as he did in 6:4 (MT 6:5) that Yahweh would save him from the enemies who pursue his soul (cf. 6:3–4 [MT 6:4–5]). On the metaphor of taking refuge in Yahweh, Basson observes that the psalmist

> uses a model of the concrete world to conceptualise an abstract category. This new conceptualisation of Yahweh is grounded in the experience of going into holy places or hills. … Through this conceptualisation, the metaphor YAHWEH IS A REFUGE is formed.[33]

### 7:3–5 (MT 7:4–6), The Innocent

Having opened with his plea in 7:1–2 (MT 7:2–3), David denies the charges made against him in 7:3–5 (MT 7:4–6). He denies the charges with an oath formula in which he prays that if he has done what they say he did, they might destroy him. The use of this formula asserts both David's innocence and his commitment to justice.

Enemies have charged that David has iniquity in his hands (7:3 [MT 7:4]), that David "repaid evil to the one at peace with" him, and that he plundered his adversary without cause (7:4 [MT 7:5]). These charges could have been leveled against David regarding his conflicts with either Saul or Absalom, and as noted above, in 2 Sam 16:5–8 one of Saul's kinsmen indicted David for David's treatment of Saul when Absalom revolted.

---

[32] Similarly on Shimei, Gert Kwakkel, *According to My Righteousness: Upright Behaviour as Grounds for Deliverance in Psalms 7, 17, 18, 26, and 44*, OTS 46 (Leiden: Brill, 2002), 33–34. Cf. the targum's rendering, "A loud song of thanksgiving of David, which he sang before the LORD, because he uttered the song about the misfortune of Saul the son of Kish, who was from the tribe of Benjamin," so Stec, *Targum of Psalms*, 35.

[33] Basson, *Divine Metaphors in Psalms*, 83.

David's words here constitute a pre-Augustinian assertion of "just war theory." David is saying that he did not fight against those who were at peace with him. Both Saul and Absalom forced David into conflict by initiating hostility against him. Nor did David engage in a war motivated by the acquisition of plunder. He only conquered in an attempt to establish peace and maintain it.

So committed to the righteousness of his cause is David that he brings it before the Lord, being willing to attest to his innocence not only with his freedom but with his very life. David had asked his enemies how long they would treat his glory as a reproach in 4:2 (MT 4:3), and in 8:5 (MT 8:6) he will assert that the Lord crowned man with glory (cf. his assertion that Yahweh is his glory in 3:3 [MT 3:4]). David is ready in 7:5 (MT 7:6) to have himself put on trial, and if he is found guilty he will submit his glory to being caused to lie in the dust. He will have his honor stripped, his majesty removed, and his life ended. David protests his innocence with all he is and all that matters to him.

### 7:6–8 (MT 7:7–9), Rise up, O Yahweh

David had asked Yahweh not to discipline him in the wrath designated for his enemies in 6:1 (MT 6:2), referencing 2:5. Now in 7:6 (MT 7:7) David calls on Yahweh to do what he said he would in 2:5 and rise up in wrath against his enemies (cf. "rise up" in 3:7 [MT 3:8]). The judgment David references in 7:6 (MT 7:7) is the one in which the wicked will not rise in 1:5, the verdict that enacts Yahweh's decree in 2:6–9, which has Yahweh's king ruling with an iron rod. David calls on Yahweh, the righteous judge, to keep his word.

David references Pss 1–2 again when he speaks of the "congregation of the peoples" in 7:7 (MT 7:8). David indicates that this group is the opposite of the Ps 1:5 "congregation of the righteous" by combining the term "congregation" from 1:5 with the term "peoples" from the 2:1 phrase "the peoples meditate vanity." This "congregation of the peoples" in 7:7 (MT 7:8), then, should be understood as those who in 2:2 took their stand and gathered together against Yahweh and his anointed. Over that assembly of rebels bringing charges against him (7:3–5 [MT 7:4–6]), David asks Yahweh to "return on high" at the end of 7:7 (MT 7:8). David asserts in 7:8 (MT 7:9) that Yahweh judges the peoples, again referencing "the judgment" mentioned in 1:5. Psalm 1:6 asserts that Yahweh knows the way of the righteous, and that gives David confidence to invite Yahweh to judge him according to his righteousness and integrity in 7:8 (MT 7:9). David does not claim that he has perfectly obeyed the law but protests that he is innocent of the charges made by the wicked (referenced in 7:3–5 [MT 7:4–6]).

## 7:9–10 (MT 7:10–11), Desire for Justice

David has called on the Lord in 7:1–2 (MT 7:2–3), entered his plea of innocence in 7:3–5 (MT 7:4–6), and beseeched the Lord to rise to up to his defense in 7:6–8 (MT 7:7–9). In 7:9–10 (MT 7:10–11) he asserts the different destinies of the righteous and the wicked and his own trust in God. The contrasting fates of the wicked and the righteous flow right out of the perishing way of the wicked in Ps 1:6 (cf. 2:12) and the flourishing of the righteous, who is like a planted and well-watered tree in 1:3. That imagery likely stands behind the Ps 7:9 (MT 7:10) request that Yahweh would "establish" (CSB) the righteous, while the idea of the wicked coming to an end at the beginning of the verse matches the chaff that the wind drives away (cf. 1:4). Yahweh is in position to judge righteously because he is the "tester of hearts and guts" (7:9 [MT 7:10]). Yahweh knows, literally, the "hearts and kidneys." He knows hearts: commitments and devotions, thought processes and plans. He knows the kidneys: visceral responses and inclinations and dispositions that people might hide from one another.

David restates in 7:10 (MT 7:11) something that he said in 3:3 (MT 3:4), that his shield is with Yahweh, meaning that Yahweh provides his protection. David has just stated that Yahweh tests "hearts" in 7:9 (MT 7:10), and now in 7:10 (MT 7:11) he says that Yahweh saves the upright in heart. In 7:12 (MT 7:13) David will speak of the need to repent, which indicates again that David is not talking about sinless perfection when he speaks of an "upright heart." Rather, to have an upright heart is to repent of sin (7:12 [MT 7:13]) and take refuge in Yahweh (7:1 [MT 7:2]).

## 7:11–13 (MT 7:12–14), God Is a Just Judge

David had asked Yahweh to rise up in anger in 7:6 (MT 7:7), and now in 7:11 (MT 7:12) he asserts that God is righteous and "is indignant the whole day." This indignation is reminiscent of the way Ps 2:4 described the Lord responding to his enemies with mocking laughter. The wicked have repeatedly been warned that they will be destroyed so they should repent (1:6; 2:10–12; 4:3–5 [MT 4:4–6]; 6:8–10 [MT 6:9–11]). David again warns the unrepentant of the fate that awaits them in 7:12–13 (MT 7:13–14). He depicts Yahweh as a mighty soldier, in the words of the NAS translation of Jer 20:11, "a dread champion." He sharpens his sword, strings his bow and makes it firm, preparing the instruments he will use to kill his enemies, with arrows described as flaming, whether from actual fire or as a metaphorical description of the way they burn those who experience them.[34] The point is that the unrepentant will neither conquer nor escape Yahweh. They must either flee their sin in favor of his mercy or face his wrath.

### 7:14–16 (MT 7:15–17), The Guilty

David's protestation of his own innocence near the beginning of this psalm (7:3–5 [MT 7:4–6]) is now balanced by his description of the guilt of the wicked near its end (7:14–16 [MT 7:15–17]). In Ps 7:14 (MT 7:15) David graphically describes the process whereby the wicked dally with evil, are inseminated by it, then gestate the iniquity until it comes to full term, at which point they labor to give birth to it and bear the child of their sinful imaginations in the form of their deception. Then in keeping with his prayer in 5:10 (MT 5:11) that the wicked would fall by their own counsels, David describes in 7:15–16 (MT 7:16–17) how the wicked defeat themselves by their wickedness. The person most hurt by sin is the one who does it. That is to say, as much as the sin may inflict evil and pain on others, the one who does sin is the one most damaged by that sin. The reward sinners gain will be the fruit of their own evil.

### 7:17 (MT 7:18), Praise

This psalm opened with a plea and ends with a matching praise. In Ps 7:17 (MT 7:18) David asserts that the prayer of 6:5 (MT 6:6) has been answered. Praying to be delivered in Ps 6:4 (MT 6:5), David told the Lord that in the event of his own death there would be no one to remember the Lord as God and give thanks to him. Now in 7:17 (MT 7:18) David says that he gives thanks to Yahweh and psalms the name of Yahweh, the Most High. The term rendered "sing about" by the CSB is the verb form of the same word translated "psalm." The verb is *zamar* (זמר), and the noun rendered

---

[34] See comments in "Translating the Psalms" in the introduction on the phrase "tread the bow."

"Psalm" is *mizmor* (מזמור). David is doing what this book, Psalms, is called: he is "psalming" Yahweh.

When David says he is thanking and psalming Yahweh "according to his righteousness" (7:17 [MT 7:18]) he is not throwing around meaningless phrases. Yahweh's justice is at stake when the wicked conspire against Yahweh and against Yahweh's messiah. If Yahweh is to be righteous, he must do justice against the wicked. Yahweh's righteousness is also at stake in the question of whether he will keep the promises he has made to those who take refuge in him by aligning themselves with his king, the one he installed on Zion (cf. Ps 2). When David therefore says that he gives thanks and psalms Yahweh according to Yahweh's righteousness, he asserts that, as dealt with in Pss 3–7, Yahweh upholds the truths of Ps 1 and the promises of Ps 2 in spite of the revolt of those like Absalom.

BRIDGE

The Psalter seems to move through cycles of difficulty that resolve into praise, and that is what we see in this first cycle of Pss 1–8. The difficulties of Absalom's revolt through which David has persevered in Pss 3–7 give way to the celebration of Yahweh's glory in Ps 8. The pattern of first suffering then rejoicing recurs not only in cycles of psalms but individual ones, and the sequence finds fulfillment in Christ, being repeated in the lives of those who follow him.

## Psalm 8

OVERVIEW AND STRUCTURE OF PSALM 8

The chiastic structure of Psalm 8 can be depicted as follows:[35]

8:1 (MT 8:2), The Name of the Lord
   8:2–4 (MT 8:3–5), The Weakness of Man
   8:5–8 (MT 8:6–9), The Authority of Man
8:9 (MT 8:10), The Name of the Lord

---

[35] For a similar analysis, see Alden, "Chiastic Psalms 1–50," 13.

CSB                                          Author's translation

For the choir director: on the *Gittith*. A        [1] For the Preeminent One.
psalm of David.                              On the *Gittith*.
                                             A Psalm of David.

[1] Lord, our Lord,
how magnificent is your name                 [2] O Yahweh, our Lord, how majestic is
    throughout the earth!                        your name in all the earth!
                                             On account of which, put your
You have covered the heavens with                majesty over the heavens.
    your majesty.
[2] From the mouths of infants and           [3] From the mouth of babes and
    nursing babies,                              sucklings you established strength,
you have established a stronghold            because of your adversaries,
on account of your adversaries               to cause the one at enmity and the
in order to silence the enemy and the            avenger to cease.
    avenger.                                  [4] When I look at your heavens,
                                             the works of your fingers,
[3] When I observe your heavens,             the moon and the stars,
the work of your fingers,                    which you made ready,
the moon and the stars,                      [5] what is man [*Enosh*] that you
which you set in place,                          remember him,
[4] what is a human being that you           the son of Adam that you visit him?
    remember him,
a son of man that you look after him?        [6] Yet you caused him to lack a little
[5] You made him little less than God            from the gods,
and crowned him with glory and               and with glory and majesty you
    honor.                                       crowned him.
[6] You made him ruler over the works        [7] You made him rule over the works of
    of your hands;                               your hands,
you put everything under his feet:           all things you put under his feet:
[7] all the sheep and oxen,                  [8] sheep and oxen, all of them,
as well as the animals in the wild,          and also the beasts of the field;
[8] the birds of the sky,                    [9] bird of the heavens and fish of the
and the fish of the sea                          sea,
that pass through the currents of the        passing the paths of the seas.
    seas.
                                             [10] O Yahweh, our Lord, how majestic is
[9] Lord, our Lord,                              your name in all the earth!
how magnificent is your name
    throughout the earth!

## Context: Verbal and Thematic Links with Surrounding Psalms

The familiarity of Ps 8, and the frequency with which it is read in isolation from the psalms that have preceded it, might tempt some readers to question the relevance of the following list of linguistic and thematic points of contact with surrounding psalms. Sensitive to this reality even in my own estimation of the weight of some of these connections, allow me to say that these lists are trying to capture the effect of reading the Psalms in sequence in Hebrew. The student of the Psalms, or better, the worshiper of Yahweh, who proceeds from one psalm to the next in sequence in the original would find the use and reuse of even seemingly incidental terms, phrases, and points of reference such as "all the earth" (8:1 [MT 8:2]) to cause resonance within the broader context, which includes the promise that the Lord's messiah will inherit "the ends of the earth" (2:8).

I submit, therefore, that this list of verbal and thematic links between Ps 8 and surrounding psalms shows that Ps 8 was intended to be read not in isolation but in sequence, not as making abstract statements about humanity in general but as continuing the flow of thought that began with the blessed man in Ps 1, identified him as the Lord's anointed king in Zion in Ps 2, then traced his Davidic difficulties with the wicked haters who rebelled against him in Pss 3–7.[36]

8:1, 9 (MT 8:2, 10) "how majestic is your name"
5:11 (MT 5:12) "the ones who love your name"
7:17 (MT 7:18) "the name of Yahweh Most High"
9:2 (MT 9:3) "your name, O Most High"

8:1 (MT 8:2) "in all the earth"
2:8 "ends of the earth"

---

[36] *Pace* Rolf A. Jacobson's interpretation of Ps 8, where he reads the psalm as pertaining to humanity in general rather than to David himself or the future king from his line. This can be seen from Jacobson's rendering of Ps 8:4 (MT 8:5), "What are human beings that you remember them? Or mortal persons that you attend them?" In keeping with this rendering, Jacobson summarizes the psalm with the words, "The first stanza starts with a focus on the *glory* of God in creation and ends with a question about the value of humanity. The second stanza answers this question by affirming that God has crowned humanity with *glory* and ends with a discussion of the various creatures over whom humans have been given responsibility." DeClaisse-Walford, Jacobson, and Tanner, *Psalms*, 120–28 (emphasis original). To approach Ps 8 as Jacobson does is to fail to read the psalm in context.

8:2 (MT 8:3) "you established strength" (יסדת)
2:2 "rulers gather together" (נוסדו from יסד)

8:2 (MT 8:3) "your adversaries"
3:1 (MT 3:2); 6:7 (MT 6:8); 7:4, 6 (MT 7:5, 7); 10:4 (MT 10:5)
   "adversary(ies)"

8:2 (MT 8:3) "the hater"
3:7 (MT 3:8); 6:10 (MT 6:11); 7:5 (MT 7:6); 9:3, 6 (MT 9:4, 7) those
   who hate

8:3 (MT 8:4) "your heavens"
2:4 "the one who sits in the heavens"

8:3 (MT 8:4) "which you made ready" (כוננתה)
7:9, 12, 13 (MT 7:10, 13, 14); 9:7 (MT 9:8); 10:17 make ready
   (forms of כון)

8:4 (MT 8:5) "man" (אנוש)
9:19, 20 (MT 9:20, 21); 10:18 "man" (אנוש)[37]

8:4 (MT 8:5) "you remember him"
6:5 (MT 6:6); 9:6, 12 (MT 9:7, 13) remembrance/remember

8:4 (MT 8:5) "son of man (Adam)"
80:17 (MT 80:18) "son of man (Adam)"
Compare 144:3; 146:3

8:5 (MT 8:6) "glory"
3:3 (MT 3:4); 4:2 (MT 4:3); 7:5 (MT 7:6) "glory"

8:5 (MT 8:6) "you crowned him" (תעטרהו)
5:12 (MT 5:13) "you surround him" (תעטרנו)

8:6 (MT 8:7) "you put" (שתה)
3:6 (MT 3:7); 9:20 (MT 9:21) "set"
Compare 8:4 (MT 8:5) "son of Adam"—with "Seth's" name, שת

---

[37] Cf. the similar questions in Job 7:17 and 15:14.

EXPOSITION

## 8:1 (MT 8:2), The Name of the Lord

The superscription of Ps 8 refers to "the *Gittith*." The NKJV, reflecting the targum's rendering, takes this to refer to "the instrument of Gath."[38] Gath was Goliath's city, and the circumstances of David's conflict with Goliath correspond to the content of this psalm.

The opening and closing words of Ps 8 make the same assertion: "O Yahweh, our Lord, how majestic is your name in all the earth!" (8:1, 9 [MT 8:2, 10]). David had described the exultation of those who love Yahweh's name in 5:11 (MT 5:12), and he had just concluded Ps 7 by psalming Yahweh's name (7:17 [MT 7:18]). The phrase in Ps 9:2 (MT 9:3) is almost identical to the one at the end of Ps 7. This sequence of statements ties Pss 7–9 together and links them all to Ps 2. Yahweh promised the ends of the earth to the king from David's line in Ps 2:8, and in Ps 8:1 David asserts the majesty of Yahweh's name in all the earth. This is the kind of king Yahweh wants: one who loves Yahweh's name and wants his pervasive glory recognized.

The second line of Ps 8:1 (MT 8:2) is typically rendered, "You have set your glory above the heavens" (ESV). The verb form, however, is an imperative, resulting in the rendering, "put your majesty over the heavens."[39] Reading Ps 8 in sequence with the preceding psalms, such an imperative would make good sense. David asserts that Yahweh's name is majestic in all the earth then makes a command-wish for Yahweh to put his glory over the heavens for all to acknowledge.

## 8:2–4 (MT 8:3–5), The Weakness of Man

In Ps 8:2 (MT 8:3) David uses a poetic expression to communicate that Yahweh uses the weak things of the world to shame the strong (cf. 1 Cor 1:27). In my view, this verse must be interpreted against the thought world of earlier Scripture. To illustrate what I do and do not mean, consider the comments of Jacobson:

> The creation motif of the psalm thoroughly permeates this stanza, as vv. 1b and 3 indicate. But v. 2bc may also reflect the creation motif, as Nahum Sarna has argued. The *enemy and*

---

[38] The targum has "upon the lute that he brought from Gath," so Stec, *Targum of Psalms*, 37.

[39] GKC §66h asserts without argumentation, "in [Psalm] 8² the very strange reading תנה is no doubt simply meant by the Masora to suggest נתנה."

*avenger* in v. 2c are best explained as a reference to the foes that
God overcomes in the process of creation. As is well known, the
mythic concept of creation as a conflict was commonly held
among Israel's neighbors. Within the Old Testament, vestiges
of this mythic idea are found. In Ps. 74:13–14a, 16–17, for example ... [citing those verses],. ... it is particularly enlightening
that both Psalms 8 and 74 refer to God's *might* ([transliterating
Hebrew עז]; cf. Isa. 51:9; Ps 89:11). The term is part of the vocabulary of the creation conflict myth, lending support to the view
that the phrase *you have established might because of your foes, to
put an end to enemy and avenger* is another reference to the act
of creation.[40]

It is true that Israel's neighbors commonly held to "the mythic concept
of creation as a conflict," but this position is foreign to the account in
Genesis. The Hebrew term Jacobson references, "might" (עז), occurs
nowhere in the Genesis creation account but twice in the celebration of
the defeat of Egypt at the Red Sea in Exod 15 (15:2, 13).[41] The claim that
the texts Jacobson references, Pss 74 and 89 and Isa 51, attest to this
creation conflict fails to distinguish between different worldviews.[42] As
Rebecca Watson explains,

> In contradistinction to a polytheistic worldview, it was the Is-
> raelite position to affirm the absolute power of Yahweh over all
> creation. In Ugarit, conflict between relatively equally-matched
> deities could cause frightening and dangerous phenomena on
> earth. By contrast, in the dominant voice in the literature of

---

[40] DeClaisse-Walford, Jacobson, and Tanner, *Psalms*, 123–24, citing Nahum Sarna, *On the
Book of Psalms: Exploring the Prayers of Ancient Israel* (New York: Schocken Books, 1993), 53–61.

[41] A point brought to my attention by Allan M. Harman, "The Exodus and the Sinai
Covenant in Psalms," *RTR* 73 (2014): 12.

[42] Rightly Rebecca S. Watson: "The results of a thorough critical analysis of the relevant
psalm texts, considered individually without recourse to extra-biblical parallels, confirms
that traditional interpretation has grossly overplayed any indications which could be com-
patible with the presence of the *Chaoskampf* theme, and indeed that there is no unequivocal
internal evidence pointing to its existence in any of the texts considered ... there is no clear
causal link between this motif and that of creation ... in none of the passages here examined
can it properly be stated that any form of combat is depicted as taking place." Rebecca S.
Watson, *Chaos Uncreated: A Reassessment of the Theme of "Chaos" in the Hebrew Bible*, BZAW 341
(Berlin: de Gruyter, 2005), 259.

Israel, it was declared ... that Yahweh was the only God ... , and that everything was governed by his power and righteous will.[43]

There is no conflict in Gen 1 and 2, but conflict is introduced in Gen 3:15. In my comments on Pss 74 and 89 in the second volume I will argue that these passages (like Isa 51) interpret the crossing of the Red Sea as a crushing of the serpent's head, an anticipatory fulfillment of Gen 3:15. With Gen 3:15 dealing with the seed of the woman, the Lord establishing strength by means of babies and infants would seem to fit in that context as well. In fact, the term rendered "enemy" (אויב) in Ps 8:2 (MT 8:3) is related to the term rendered "enmity" in Gen 3:15 (איבה). To capture the connection between the enemies who are at enmity, I have rendered Ps 8:2 (MT 8:3),

> From the mouth of babes and sucklings you established
>     strength,
> because of your adversaries,
> to cause the one at enmity and the avenger to cease.

It is not only the lexical connection between "enmity" and "the one at enmity" that ties Ps 8:2 (MT 8:3) to Gen 3:15. There is also the fact that God's adversary is spoken of in the singular. The Psalms regularly acknowledge that God has many enemies, as can be seen in 2:1–3. The singular enemy referenced in Ps 8:2 (MT 8:3) could be the primal enemy, the one who instigated the others, whose downfall will mean their end.

Understanding the singular enemy as the serpent of Gen 3 would explain how God has established strength to silence him through babies. The prohibition on eating of the tree in Gen 2:17 warned that death would result. The man and woman transgressed and ate, and then in a vain attempt to avoid the death penalty, tried to hide from God (Gen 3:8). When God began speaking words of judgment over the serpent, he stated that the seed of the woman would bruise his head (Gen 3:14–15).

The statement that they would have seed that would oppose the serpent revealed that the man and woman would not die immediately, giving them hope for ongoing life and the bearing of children, and the statement that the seed would bruise the head of the serpent revealed that their seed would punish God's enemy.

---

[43] Watson, *Chaos Uncreated*, 167–68.

The Bible locates the conflict in which Yahweh engages not in creation but in redemption. Jacobson's reading, then, has displaced the biblical conflict background for the one assumed in the alternative worldview held by Israel's idolatrous neighbors.[44]

In Ps 8 David no doubt reflects on creation, but his reflections are not limited to Gen 1 but continue into Gen 3. David might even allude to both Gen 1 and Gen 15 in Ps 8:3 (MT 8:4) when he speaks of *looking at* Yahweh's *heavens*, the work of his fingers, the moon and the *stars*. The Gen 1 overtones are obvious. Might there be an allusion as well to Abraham saying that Yahweh had given him no seed in Gen 15:3, in response to which Yahweh takes him outside and tells him to *look at the heavens* and number the *stars* in 15:5?

The poetic statement in Ps 8:2 (MT 8:3), then, may not merely be a figurative way of saying that Yahweh triumphs over the strong by the weak. This verse speaks of God establishing strength from babies and infants *because* of God's adversaries (using the same term found in 3:1 [MT 3:2]; 6:7 [MT 6:8]; 7:4, 7 [MT 7:5, 8]; and 10:5). Moreover, the verse goes on to say that through babes and sucklings God will "cause the one at enmity and the avenger to cease." The reference to the "one at enmity" employs the same term found in 3:7 (MT 3:8); 6:10 (MT 6:11); 7:5 (MT 7:6); 9:3, 6 (MT 9:4, 7), further rooting Ps 8 in surrounding soil.[45] These singulars, "the one at enmity and the avenger," could be collective singulars, or they could be referring to God's one original enemy. In that case, Ps 8:2 (MT 8:3) stands as a poetic way of saying that God's answer to Satan's rebellion is the assertion that the woman would have a child, that there would be enmity between the seed of the woman and the seed of the serpent, and that the woman's seed would bruise the serpent's head (Gen 3:15).[46]

---

[44] As Watson puts it, "The application of the *Chaoskampf* as an overarching theme encompassing such a variety of biblical motifs has, in part, at least, been a product of the comparative method, which has tended to overemphasise putative similarities between religious systems and cultures but, as a result, has obscured the distinctiveness of the imagery and beliefs contained within the Hebrew Bible." Watson, *Chaos Uncreated*, 259.

[45] In response to what I have written here, Stephen Dempster comments (private communication): "I think this is made particularly poignant in the story of Moses' birth when Moses as a baby cries and the Egyptian princess has mercy on him. In this baby's cry can be heard the eventual complete collapse of the Egyptian empire."

[46] There is a strong pattern of unexpected, miraculous births in Genesis and then on through the OT. Adam and Eve were supposed to die, and they were promised seed. Abraham was old and Sarah barren, and they were promised seed. Rebekah too was barren, and God

Contextual factors strengthen the connection between Gen 3 and Ps 8. David inspects creation, the moon, and the stars in 8:3 (MT 8:4), reflects on man's place (with a reference to the son of *Adam*) in creation in 8:5 (MT 8:6), and then exposits Gen 1:28 in 8:6–8 (MT 8:7–9).[47] These considerations indicate that Ps 8 reflects David's profound understanding of Old Testament theology. David understands that God's purpose is to saturate creation with his glory (Ps 8:1, 9 [MT 8:2, 10]). He understands his own place in the line of descent that starts from Adam (cf. 8:4–8 [MT 8:5–9]), and that in the promise of Gen 3:15 God answered Satan's triumphant roar with a baby's cry. Through the king from David's line, who will be a new Adam, David knows that God will reestablish his dominion over creation (8:6 [MT 8:7]).[48]

In Ps 2:4 God was referenced as "the one who sits in the heavens," and in Ps 8:3 (MT 8:4) David relates his reflections on gazing into God's heavens, which he further refers to as "the works of your fingers." The mention of the moon and the stars, whose creation was narrated in Gen 1:14–19, strengthens ties to the creation account and calls up a mental image of the poet gazing into the night sky.

The glory of God's world prompts David to ask in 8:4 (MT 8:5) what man (אנוש) is, the son of man (בן אדם) that Yahweh should attend to him. Here again I want to interact with Jacobson to contend that Ps 8 is best interpreted *in context*—in the flow of thought stemming from Pss 1–2 and *against the backdrop of earlier Scripture.*

Jacobson renders Psalm 8:4 (MT 8:5),

> What are human beings that you remember them?
> Or mortal persons that you attend them?

He footnotes this with the words, "The Hebrew reads, lit.: 'What is man that you remember him? The son of man that you attend him?' The above translation reflects a desire to use inclusive language."[49]

---

opened her womb. Eventually Isaiah prophesies that a virgin will conceive and bear a son whose birth will signify God's presence with his people.

[47] See Gentry and Wellum, *Kingdom through Covenant*, 231–32.

[48] Kynes convincingly argues that it is more likely that Job 7:17–18 parodies Ps 8:5 than that the other way around, arguing that Job holds fast to the psalm's teaching in faith. For further discussion, see Kynes, *My Psalm Has Turned into Weeping*, 63–79.

[49] DeClaisse-Walford, Jacobson, and Tanner, *Psalms*, 121 and n. 10.

In the explanation of his rendering, Jacobson has imposed a concern from our culture—for inclusive language—onto an ancient text whose author does not seem to have shared that concern. The masculine Hebrew terms for "man" were considered to be inclusive, just as "man" in English has long been understood to encompass "man and woman." Only with the rejection of that usage by more recent writers and speakers of English have concerns for inclusive language created these problems for translations.[50] Jacobson's imposition of a concern for inclusive language also shifts the langue from singulars to plurals. Those plurals refer to humanity in general, but consider the import of the *singulars* used by the author of Ps 8. In my literal rendering of the Psalter, I translate Ps 8:4 (MT 8:5) as follows:

> What is man [*Enosh*] that you remember him,
> the son of Adam that you visit him?

The first instance of "man" in the opening question, "What is man?," renders the Hebrew term אנוש, which term is also the name of Seth's son in Gen 5:6. It appears that just as אדם, the name of the first man, came to be used to refer to man in general, so the name אנוש, son of the son of Adam, came to be used to refer to man in general, also supplying the plural form (men) אנשים.

Psalm 8 is poetry. Poetry is often intentionally allusive. In the questions he poses in this verse, David has alluded to the first three generations in the line of descent of the seed of the woman, Adam, Seth, and Enosh, and he has done so in reverse order: first third-generation Enosh, then the second-generation son of Adam, and in that reference we hear of first-generation Adam himself. The reference to the line of descent of the seed of the woman so carefully traced in Genesis would fit nicely with the understanding of the "babies and infants" in Ps 8:2 (MT 8:3) proposed above.

Jacobson's transformation of David's singulars into plurals destroys connections not only to earlier Scripture—the overtones of Genesis just discussed—but also to later Scripture. For instance, in Dan 7, the kingdoms are presented as beasts. At the end of Ps 8, the son of man exercises Adamic dominion (Gen 1:28) over the beasts (8:7–8 [MT 8:8–9]). In Dan

---

[50] See Vernard Eller, *The Language of Canaan and the Grammar of Feminism* (Grand Rapids: Eerdmans, 1982).

7, the dominion of the beasts is taken away and given to one like a *son of man* (Dan 7:11–14). Jacobson's translation, however, obscures any possible connection to the son of man in Dan 7, to say nothing of the connection to the son of man in the Gospels and in Heb 2.

The larger point I am making here is that earlier Scripture is the most important backdrop for understand the Psalms. The Torah of Moses was intended to have a shaping influence on Israel's worldview, and those who wrote Scripture understood themselves to be operating in that worldview. The fact that the believing community recognized what they wrote as Scripture indicates that their self-understanding was validated by others who embraced, promoted, and protected that Mosaic worldview.

My interaction with Jacobson's commentary on Ps 8 also indicates that if earlier Scripture is not treated as the primary background against which the Psalms are to be interpreted, some other background will inevitably prove determinative. Jacobson's comments on Ps 8:2 (MT 8:3) treat ancient Near Eastern myths about the gods engaging in conflict at creation as the primary background for understanding that verse, and his translation of Ps 8:4 (MT 8:5) allows our own cultural context and its concern for inclusive language to eclipse concerns arising from what David intended to say, concerns arising from David's cultural context, concerns for connections David sought to make with earlier Scripture, and concerns for connections later biblical authors sought to make with what David wrote.

If Ps 8 is read out of context, without regard for its relationships with those that precede and follow it in the Psalter, and if the ancient Near Eastern worldview is allowed to eclipse the biblical worldview, then Ps 8 can be taken to refer to humanity in general, with nothing much to say about the coming messiah.

But if we read Ps 8 in context, understanding it in continuity with Pss 1–2 and 3–7 and 9–41 and so forth, then in Ps 8 we can see David contemplating his own new-Adam role as one who is to exercise the dominion that God has given to him. Moreover, David understands the purpose of his dominion to be the extension of Yahweh's glory, and he understands that dominion to be in conflict with the way "the enemy and the avenger" seeks to establish his own dominion through the kings of the nations who set themselves against Yahweh and his anointed (2:1–3). David understands that God chooses the weak things of the world, things like babies and infants, to shame the strong, and David understands that

God made a promise about the seed of the woman, whose descent can be traced down from Adam through Seth and Enosh to Abraham and Judah and Boaz to Jesse. Standing in that line of descent, David knows that God keeps his promises, those made in words of judgment over the serpent and those made to the likes of Abraham, Judah, and himself. The man who wrote Ps 8, after all, also wrote Ps 110.

David has mentioned the first three men in the line of descent through which the seed of promise came: Adam begat Seth, who begat Enosh, and the line continues to Abraham, Judah, and David, eventually culminating in the birth of the carpenter's son, the man from Nazareth. With the allusions to Adam and Enosh, the use of the verb "put" (שׁתה) in the phrase "you put all things under his feet" in 8:6 (MT 8:7) employs the verb from which Seth's name (שׁת) was made, and those verses, Ps 8:6-8 (MT 8:7-9), obviously describe what God did for Seth's father Adam in Gen 1:28.

### 8:5-8 (MT 8:6-9), The Authority of Man

David speaks in Ps 8:5 (MT 8:6) of how God caused man to "lack a little from the gods," meaning that God "made him a little lower than the heavenly beings" (ESV). The CSB renders this, "You made him a little less than God," but the Greek translation took *elohim* to refer to "angels," a rendering quoted by the author of Hebrews (Heb 2:7). This leads me to think that *elohim* here more likely refers to heavenly beings than to God himself.

In the rest of Ps 8:5 (MT 8:6) David describes how God crowned man with glory and majesty. The rest of the psalm exposits this statement, so the glory and majesty should be understood to refer to the vice-regency God gave to Adam at creation. David seems to present himself as Israel's king, standing as a new Adam reigning over God's people, and in keeping with that, he asked in 4:2 (MT 4:3) how long his "glory" will be regarded as a reproach, and in 7:5 (MT 7:6) he risked his "glory" being laid in the dust.

David mused on "the works of your fingers" in 8:3 (MT 8:4), and now in 8:6 (MT 8:7) he asserts, "You made him lord over the works of your hands, all things you put under his feet." The verb I have rendered "you made him lord" (following *HALOT*, s.v.) could be interpreted to mean, "you caused him to rule" (תמשׁילהו *hiphil* of משׁל). Though a different verb is used in Gen 1:28 to grant "dominion" to the man (רדה, though משׁל is used in Gen 1:18 to speak of the great lights "ruling"), from what David says in Ps 8:6-8 it is clear that he has Gen 1:28 in mind. In Gen 1:28 God blessed the man and woman, told them to be fruitful and multiply, fill the earth and subdue it, and then he granted them dominion over (1) the fish of the sea and over (2) the birds of the heavens and over (3) every living thing that moves on the earth. David works backward through the beasts in Ps 8:6–8 (MT 8:7–9), referencing the way that God put (3) all sheep and oxen ... and also the beasts of the field, (2) birds of the heavens, and (1) fish of the sea under the feet of the man who stood over creation as God's representative.[51]

### 8:9 (MT 8:10), The Name of the Lord

David then concludes Ps 8 in verse 9 (MT 10) with a restatement of verse 1 (MT 2), asserting the majesty of God's name over all the earth.

BRIDGE

When Satan tempted Adam and Eve to sin, he sought to usurp dominion over God's creation, dominion God had granted to the man and the woman (Gen 1:28). Satan thereby became "the ruler of this world" (John 12:31). God told the snake, however, that the seed of the woman would bruise his head (Gen 3:15). Adam then begat Seth, who begat Enosh, and from that line came Abraham, to whom God made covenant promises (Gen 12:1–3). Those promises were passed to Isaac, then to Jacob, and then the chief came from Judah (1 Chr 5:2). In the covenant with David articulated in 2 Sam 7, God made clear that the blessing of Abraham would be fulfilled through the king from Judah's line, David's son, the seed of the woman.

God purposed to make his name great in all the earth through the fulfillment of these promises, and in Ps 8 David shows his understanding of these big themes in Old Testament theology. David understands that God's ultimate purpose is his glory (Ps 8:1, 9 [MT 8:2, 10]). David understands that through the seed of the woman, the baby born to those under a sentence of death, God promised to cause the hater and avenger to cease (8:2 [MT 8:3]), and David knows his place in that line of descent, from which his greater son would also come. David understands that as God's king he is a kind of anticipatory new Adam (8:4–8 [MT 8:5–9]). This

---

[51] See Keel, *Symbolism of the Biblical World*, 58: "This dominion consists not only in holding subject, but also in defense of the weaker animal against the attacking lion," and here Keel refers to depictions on p. 59 (figs. 60 and 61) of a man with a domesticated animal under foot as he fights off a predator.

self-understanding will become clear in Ps 110:1, where we see that David knows that his greater son will be the new Adam through whom God's purposes will be realized.

Both Paul and the author of Hebrews see Pss 8 and 110 fulfilled in Christ. Paul alludes to Ps 110:1 when he writes in Eph 1:20 of how God "raised [Christ] from the dead and seated him at his right hand in the heavenly places," and then he alludes to Ps 8:6 [MT 8:7] in 1:22 with the assertion, "And he put all things under his feet." Similarly, the author of Hebrews quotes Ps 110:1 in Heb 1:13 and then Ps 8:4–6 [MT 8:5–7] in Heb 2:5–8. These New Testament interpretations of Ps 8 seem to confirm the idea that in this psalm David both reflects on his role as God's new-Adam vice-regent over creation and looks forward to the promised king from his line, the son of man (Adam) who will be the 2 Sam 7:14 son of God.

Satan's attempt to usurp God's kingdom in Gen 3 is not unlike Absalom's attempt to do the same in 2 Sam 15. The struggles with Absalom reflected in Pss 3–7, then, set up the realization of God's purposes. God's glory will be put above the heavens once the enemy has been defeated by the son of man, the baby born to slay the dragon, like a youth going out to fight a giant knowing the battle belongs to Yahweh. We see God's power perfected in the weakness of those who live and die relying on the one who raises the dead. His glory cannot fail. His kingdom cannot be shaken. His worth cannot be overestimated. His word will ever ring true, his enemies ever fall flat, and his name be ever praised.

# Psalm 9

OVERVIEW AND STRUCTURE OF PSALM 9

9:1–2 (MT 9:2–3), Praise
   9:3–4 (MT 9:4–5), Judgment for the Wicked
      9:5–6 (MT 9:6–7), Destruction of the Wicked
         9:7–8 (MT 9:8–9), Yahweh Sits Enthroned
            9:9–10 (MT 9:10–11), Yahweh a Stronghold
          9:11–12 (9:12–13), Psalm Yahweh
         9:13–14 (9:14–15), Plea for Salvation
      9:15–16 (9:16–17), Destruction of the Wicked
   9:17–18 (9:18–19), Judgment for the Wicked
9:19–20 (9:20–21), Plea

For discussion of this structure, see the exposition of the psalm below.

Scripture .

| CSB | Author's translation |
|---|---|

For the choir director: according to *Muth-labben*. A psalm of David.

<sup>1</sup>I will thank the Lord with all my heart;
I will declare all your wondrous works.
<sup>2</sup>I will rejoice and boast about you;
I will sing about your name, Most High.

<sup>3</sup>When my enemies retreat,
they stumble and perish before you.
<sup>4</sup>For you have upheld my just cause;
you are seated on your throne as a righteous judge.
<sup>5</sup>You have rebuked the nations:
You have destroyed the wicked;
you have erased their name forever and ever.
<sup>6</sup>The enemy has come to eternal ruin;
you have uprooted the cities,
and the very memory of them has perished.

<sup>7</sup>But the Lord sits enthroned forever;
he has established his throne for judgment.
<sup>8</sup>And he judges the world with righteousness;
he executes judgment on the nations with fairness.
<sup>9</sup>The Lord is a refuge for the persecuted,
a refuge in times of trouble.
<sup>10</sup>Those who know your name trust in you
because you have not abandoned those who seek you, Lord.

<sup>11</sup>Sing to the Lord, who dwells in Zion;

---

<sup>1</sup>For the Preeminent One.
On the death of the son.
A Psalm of David.

<sup>2</sup>I will thank Yahweh with all my heart.
I will recount all your wonders.
<sup>3</sup>I will be glad, and I will exult in you.
I will psalm your name, O Most High.

<sup>4</sup>When those at enmity with me turn back,
they will stumble and perish from before your presence,
<sup>5</sup>for you have rendered my judgment and my case:
you sat on the throne judging in righteousness.

<sup>6</sup>You rebuked the nations.
You made the wicked perish.
Their name you blotted out to the age and on.
<sup>7</sup>The one at enmity came to an end in ruins everlasting.
You uprooted cities.
The memory of them perished.

<sup>8</sup>But Yahweh will sit to the age.
He established his throne for judgment,
<sup>9</sup>and he will judge the world in righteousness.
He will render verdict on the peoples in uprightness.

<sup>10</sup>And Yahweh will be a stronghold for the crushed,
a stronghold for times of destitution,
<sup>11</sup>and they trust in you—the ones who know your name—

proclaim his deeds among the nations.
¹² For the one who seeks an
    accounting
for bloodshed remembers them;
he does not forget the cry of the
    oppressed.

¹³ Be gracious to me, Lord;
consider my affliction at the hands of
    those who hate me.
Lift me up from the gates of death,
¹⁴ so that I may declare all your praises.
I will rejoice in your salvation
within the gates of Daughter Zion.

¹⁵ The nations have fallen into the pit
    they made;
their foot is caught in the net they
    have concealed.
¹⁶ The Lord has made himself known;
he has executed justice,
snaring the wicked
by the work of their hands.
*Higgaion. Selah*

¹⁷ The wicked will return to Sheol—
all the nations that forget God.
¹⁸ For the needy will not always be
    forgotten;
the hope of the oppressed will not
    perish forever.

¹⁹ Rise up, Lord! Do not let mere
    humans prevail;
let the nations be judged in your
    presence.
²⁰ Put terror in them, Lord;
let the nations know they are only
    humans.
    *Selah*

for you have not forsaken those who
    seek you, O Yahweh.

¹² Psalm [pl. impv.] to Yahweh, who
    sits in Zion.
Declare his deeds among the peoples,
¹³ for the one who seeks blood
    remembers them:
he will not forget the cry of the
    afflicted.

¹⁴ Be gracious to me, O Yahweh.
Behold my affliction from those who
    hate me,
O you who lift me up from the gates
    of death,
¹⁵ that I may recount all your praises
    in the gates of daughter Zion.
I will rejoice in your salvation.

¹⁶ The nations sank in the pit they
    made.
In the net that they hid their foot was
    caught.
¹⁷ Yahweh has been made known.
He rendered judgment.
In the work of his hands he ensnares
    the wicked. *Higgaion* [meditation]
    *Selah.*

¹⁸ The wicked will return to Sheol
    —all the nations who forget God—
¹⁹ for not forever will the needy be
    forgotten,
the hope of the afflicted perish
    evermore.

²⁰ Rise up, O Yahweh, let not man
    prevail.
Let the nations be judged in your
    presence.
²¹ Appoint, O Yahweh, a terror for
    them.
Let the nations know that they are
    but men. *Selah.*

### Context: Verbal and Thematic Links with Surrounding Psalms

9:1 (MT 9:2) "I will thank Yahweh" (אודה יהוה)
7:17 (MT 7:18) "I will thank Yahweh" (אודה יהוה)

9:1, 14 (MT 9:2, 15) "I will recount" (אספרה)
2:7 "I will recount" (אספרה)

9:2 (MT 9:3) "I will rejoice, and I will exult in you"
5:11 (MT 5:12) "rejoice ... exult"

9:2 (MT 9:3) "I will psalm your name, O Most High"
7:17 (MT 7:18) "I psalm the name of Yahweh Most High"
Compare 9:11 (MT 9:12) "Psalm Yahweh"

9:2 (MT 9:3) "name"
8:1, 9 (MT 8:2, 10) "name"

9:3, 5, 6 (MT 9:4, 6, 7) "perish"
1:6; 2:12; 5:6 (MT 5:7) "perish/destroy"

9:4 (MT 9:5) "you have rendered my judgment and my cause"
7:8 (MT 7:9) "Judge for me, O Yahweh, according to my
  righteousness"

9:4 (MT 9:5) "you sat on the throne judging in righteousness"
9:7 (MT 9:8) "Yahweh will sit forever"
9:11 (MT 9:12) "Yahweh, who sits in Zion"
2:4 "the one who sits in the heavens"
Compare 2:6 "Zion"

9:5 (MT 9:6) "you rebuked the nations"
2:4 "My Lord mocks at them"

9:6 (MT 9:7) "The one at enmity came to an end in everlasting
  ruins ... uprooted"
1:4 "like chaff, which the wind drives away"

9:8 (MT 9:9) "peoples" (לאמים)
2:1 "peoples" (לאמים)

9:9 (MT 9:10) "the crushed"
10:18 "the crushed"

9:9 (MT 9:10) "times of destitution" (לעתות בצרה)
10:1 "times of destitution" (לעתות בצרה)

9:10 (MT 9:11) "they trust in you"
4:5 (MT 4:6) "trust in Yahweh"

9:10 (MT 9:11) "the ones who know your name"
5:11 (MT 5:12) "the ones who love your name"

9:10 (MT 9:11) "those who seek you"
Compare 9:12 (MT 9:13); 10:4, 13, 15; 14:2 "seek"

9:13 (MT 9:14) "Be gracious to me"
4:1; 6:2 (MT 4:2; 6:3) "Be gracious to me"

9:14 (MT 9:15) "rejoice"
2:11 "rejoice"

9:14 (MT 9:15) "your salvation"
3:2, 8; 13:5 (MT 3:3, 9; 13:6) "salvation"

9:15–16 (MT 9:16–17) the wicked caught in their own traps
Compare the same in 5:10 (MT 5:11); 7:15–16 (MT 7:16–17)

9:19 (MT 9:20) "Rise up, O Yahweh"
3:7 (MT 3:8); 7:6 (MT 7:7) "Rise up, O Yahweh"

9:19–20 (MT 9:20–21) terrify the enemies with your judgment
Compare 2:5 "he will speak to them in his wrath, and in his fury
    he will terrify them"

Picking up the discussion from the introduction to this commentary, we turn our attention to the arrangement of groups of psalms. Psalms 15–24 have been recognized as comprising a unit, with 15 and 24 forming an *inclusio*, and there are clear points of contact between Pss 10 and 14, with both psalms referring to the way the wicked disregards God (10:4; 14:1) and to what the wicked says in his heart (10:6, 11; 14:1). This suggests that, while there are points of contact that bind Pss 9 and 10 together, Pss 10–14 nevertheless comprise a unit, as do Pss 3–9. The lack of a superscription between Pss 9 and 10 and the use of similar language in the two psalms serves as mortar between the wider bricks of Pss 3–9 and 10–14.

The unit of Pss 3–9 seems to deal with Absalom's revolt. After the introductory Pss 1–2, the superscription to Ps 3 locates the prayer when David "fled from before Absalom, his son." Corresponding to Ps 3, the superscription of Ps 9 speaks of "the death of the son" and celebrates God's justice.

Like Ps 3, Ps 4 speaks of safety during sleep, hearkening back to Ahithophel's plan to attack David, a plan thwarted by Hushai's counsel, David's prayer, and the Lord's decree. Psalm 4 also speaks of the way "Yahweh separated the lovingkind one for himself" (4:3 [MT 4:4]). This emphasis on Yahweh's king is matched by the emphasis on the son of Adam in Ps 8 (8:4 [MT 8:5]).

In Ps 5 David insists that Yahweh is righteous and does not delight in wickedness as he pleads with God to keep him from the way of the wicked. These emphases match the way that David insists on his innocence in Ps 7.

At the center of this cycle Ps 6 calls on the Lord not to do to David what Ps 2 said he would do to the wicked. The Ps 8 celebration of the majesty of Yahweh's name in all the earth and the dominion of the son of man resolves into the celebration of Yahweh's justice in Ps 9. These psalms seem to be arranged chiastically as follows:

Psalm 3, Absalom's Night of Opportunity
    Psalm 4, David's Prayer
        Psalm 5, They Are Wicked, Not I
            Psalm 6, Don't Give Me What They Deserve
        Psalm 7, Plea of Innocence
    Psalm 8, The Begotten Son of Man
Psalm 9, The Death of Absalom

EXPOSITION

The superscription to Ps 9 contains a unique phrase found in no other psalm that the CSB and ESV render "According to Muth-Labben." This phrase is translated by the NKJV, "To *the tune of* 'Death of the Son.' "[52]

---

[52] Cook renders the targum, "concerning the death of the man who went out between the armies," Cook, *Psalms Targum*. Stec has "concerning the death of the man who went out, a general from among the armies," Stec, *Targum of Psalms*, 38. In verse 6 the targum names Goliath.

Translating (rather than transliterating) the phrase brings out the way that the superscriptions of Pss 3 and 9 refer to the "son." Taking the reference to the "death of the son" in the superscription of Ps 9 as a reference to the death of Absalom ties Ps 9 to the context. David prayed on the night of danger in Pss 3 and 4, the next morning in Ps 5, then cried out for justice in Pss 6 and 7. In Ps 8 he confidently asserts the place of the Davidic king in the wider purposes of God, and then Ps 9 celebrates God's justice.[53]

Just as a number of individual psalms begin by rehearsing affliction and end with celebrations of God's salvation, so Pss 3–9 seem to move through the same pattern of suffering followed by glory (cf. Luke 24:26).

Psalm 9 falls into ten two-verse units that seem to correspond to one another in the chiastic structure presented above. In the exposition that follows I will treat the corresponding elements together, considering the praise of 9:1–2 (MT 9:2–3) with the plea of 9:19–20 (MT 9:20–21), the judgment and destruction of the wicked in 9:3–6 (MT 9:4–7) with the same in 9:15–18 (MT 9:16–19), and the Lord as his people's stronghold in 9:7–14 (MT 9:8–15).

### 9:1–2, 19–20 (MT 9:2–3, 20–21), Praise and Plea

The reference to the death of the son in the superscription of Ps 9 joins with 9:3–6 (MT 9:4–7) to identify the context for what David declares in 9:1–2 (MT 9:2–3). Yahweh has judged David's enemy and brought the rebellion to nothing (9:3–6 [MT 9:4–7]), prompting David to thank Yahweh with his whole heart, recount Yahweh's wondrous deeds, rejoice and exult in him, and psalm the name of the Most High (9:1–2 [MT 9:2–3]). David's references to giving thanks and psalming Yahweh's name in 9:1–2 (MT 9:2–3) match the same in 7:17 (MT 7:18).

The CSB renders the verb zamar (זמר) "sing about" in 7:17 and 9:2. This is the verb from which the word mizmor (מזמר), psalm, is derived. In my translation, I have used the term "psalm" as a verb: "I will psalm your name, O Most High." This verb seems to refer to the act of celebrating the

---

[53] In 2 Sam 18–19 David mourns Absalom's death and Joab rebukes him for saddening the people who risked their lives on his behalf. Psalm 9 perhaps results from David reacting not as a father to the tragic death of a wayward son but as Yahweh's king to the demise of one who revolted against the Lord and his anointed.

epic tales of Yahweh's salvation in poetic form.[54] The Greeks sang their heroes in *The Illiad* and *The Odyssey*, and the Hebrews sang of Yahweh and his king in the Psalms.

David thanks and praises God for deliverance in Ps 9:1–2 (MT 9:2–3), likely the deliverance from Absalom. At the end of the psalm, however, David will call on the Lord to rise up and judge the nations, to terrify them as he promised he would in 2:4–12. The closing plea of Ps 9:19–20 (MT 9:20–21), then, indicates that the body of Ps 9 celebrates not merely the kind of thing God has done in the past for David but the kind of thing he will do in the future for the promised king from David's line. The historical pattern of deliverance celebrated in Ps 9 thus points forward to the end-time deliverance God will accomplish for his people, as the final statement of Ps 9 specifically call upon him to do! (9:19–20 [MT 9:20–21]).

If God does not work that deliverance, wicked people will prevail over God, thwarting his purposes and nullifying his promises. But in Ps 9:19 (MT 9:20) David urges Yahweh to "rise up" (cf. 3:7 [MT 3:8]; 7:6 [MT 7:7]) and "let not man prevail." The psalmist declared that Yahweh would terrify the rebels in his fury in Ps 2:4, and he spoke of how his enemies had been terrified before Yahweh's presence in 9:3 (MT 9:4). Similarly, he wants all rebel nations to be judged in Yahweh's presence in 9:19 (MT 9:20). The terror that David asks God to visit on the nations in 9:20 (MT 9:21) will put the fear of God into them, forcing them to realize that God is God, and they are but men.

David praises God for his deliverance in 9:1–2 (MT 9:2–3), and he pleads with him to make it global, apparently at the end of all things, in 9:19–20 (MT 9:20–21).

### 9:3–6, 15–18 (MT 9:4–7, 16–19), Judgment and Destruction

The fact that David says his enemies "perish" in 9:3 (MT 9:4) recalls the warnings that the wicked would perish in their rebellion in 1:6 and 2:12. The enemies are described here with a term that can be rendered "those at enmity" (אויבי), and it is related to the term used in Genesis 3:15 for

---

[54] Speaking of terms cognate with Hebrew מזמר, זמר, and שיר, Tigay writes, "Several Akkadian myths and epics are termed *zamaru*, 'song,' just as a Hittite myth was known as *The Song* (SIR) *of Ullikumi*. While the terms *zamaru* and SIR were also used for hymns, it remains to be determined whether these terms mean anything more than 'song' or 'poem' when applied to myths and epics." Tigay, *Evolution of the Gilgamesh Epic*, 51–52.

the "enmity" (איבה) God said he would put between the woman and the serpent and her seed and his.

Psalm 9:3 (MT 9:4) speaks as though Yahweh has come in person to David's defense. Seeing him, the enemies turn to flee, stumble, and perish from before Yahweh's presence. David had called on Yahweh to render judgment on his behalf in 7:8 (MT 7:9), and he asserts that Yahweh has done just that in 9:4 (MT 9:5).

What Yahweh did when he showed up to defend David (9:3–4 [MT 9:4–5]) is described in 9:5–6 (MT 9:6–7). Here again there is significant correspondence with what was promised in Ps 2. Psalm 2:4 declared that Yahweh would mock his enemies, speaking derisively to them, and the term rendered "rebuke" (גער) in Ps 9:5 (MT 9:6) carries connotations of insulting speech (cf. its use in, e.g., Isa 17:13; Ps 106:9; and see *HALOT*, s.v.). In keeping with the warnings in Pss 1:6 and 2:12, Yahweh made the enemies perish, and he blotted out their name forever (9:5 [MT 9:6]). The fact that those at enmity with David "came to an end in ruins everlasting" (9:6 [MT 9:7]) is reminiscent of chaff that the wind drives away. That Yahweh uprooted their cities (9:6 [MT 9:7]) shows them to be the opposite of a tree planted by streams of water (cf. Ps 1:3).

Often humans refuse to submit to Yahweh because they are seeking a name for themselves (cf. Gen 11:4). Absalom's reputation was central to his rebellion against David (cf. 2 Sam 15:1–6). The Bible tells the truth that the quickest way to be forgotten, to have one's name blotted out forever, one's memory perish (Ps 9:5–6 [MT 9:6–7]), is to rebel against the Lord and his anointed.

Corresponding to the wicked's experience of judgment in 9:3–4 (MT 9:4–5) and destruction in 9:5–6 (MT 9:6–7) is their experience of destruction in 9:15–16 (MT 9:16–17) and judgment in 9:17–18 (MT 9:18–19). In 9:3 (MT 9:4) the enemies "turn back" (שוב), and in 9:17 (MT 9:18) they "return to Sheol" (שוב). David's assertion in 9:4 (MT 9:5) that Yahweh vindicated him in judgment is the basis for his assertion in 9:18 (MT 9:19) that "not forever will the needy be forgotten."

David's enemies experience Yahweh's personal displeasure in 9:3–6 (MT 9:4–7), and they experience the futility of evil in 9:15–18 (MT 9:16–19). This world was not made as a place where the universe cooperates with evil deeds, nor was life created so that wicked people would find their way to some wicked-man's paradise. Those who set traps for others will have themselves to thank when the traps snap shut on their own feet.

They will fall into their own pits (9:15 [MT 9:16]; cf. 5:10 and 7:14–16 [MT 5:11; 7:15–17]). Psalm 9:16 (MT 9:17) asserts that Yahweh makes himself known when the weapons of the wicked backfire and the shooters are themselves shot. Yahweh's justice is visited when people suffer the consequences of their own evil, when he snares the wicked in what they themselves have wrought.

Psalm 9:16 (MT 9:17) concludes with "*Higgaion Selah.*" The term "*Higgaion*" (הגיון) is translated "meditation" in Ps 19:14 (MT 19:15), and it seems to appear at this point in Ps 9 to invite meditation. *Higgaion* is related to the verb "meditate" (הגה), and the term invites the psalm's audience to reflect and learn wisdom from the outcome of the wicked.

The wicked will not find their way to a place of reward for the clever and intrepid. They will go to Sheol (9:17 [MT 9:18]). They will go to the place of punishment reserved for those who rebel against the Lord and his anointed. Those who forget God—who refuse to fear him, honor him, obey him, and thank him—will be punished. When Ps 9:18a (MT 9:19a) explains that the wicked will go to Sheol because the needy will not be forgotten forever, it implies that the wicked have been oppressing and abusing the needy, for which they will be judged (cf. 9:10, 12 [MT 9:11, 13]). As Prov 14:31 asserts, "The one who oppresses the poor person insults his Maker, but one who is kind to the needy honors him" (CSB). Similarly, when Ps 9:18b (MT 9:19b) says the hope of the afflicted will not perish evermore, the statement implies that the afflicted have been hoping for deliverance from oppression, crying out to the Lord whose ears are attentive to the cries of the needy (cf. 9:12b [MT 9:13b]).

## 9:7–14 (MT 9:8–15), The Lord Our Stronghold

Whereas the name of the enemies and their memory are gone forever (9:5–6 [MT 9:6–7]), Yahweh sits enthroned in heaven forever, having established his throne to uphold justice (9:7 [MT 9:8]). This verse makes plain the connection between Yahweh's throne and his authority to judge. Having established the throne for judgment, on which he will sit until the age of his kingdom comes (9:7 [MT 9:8]), David asserts that Yahweh will judge in righteousness and render his verdict on the people in uprightness (9:8 [MT 9:9]). That he will do so is bad news for the wicked but good news for those who repent of sin and take refuge in him.

Corresponding to Yahweh's throne-justice in 9:7–8 (MT 9:8–9) we see the cry for gracious treatment in 9:13–14 (MT 9:14–15). Here again we have an indication that David recognizes that he has not attained perfect obedience. He recognizes that he needs God to treat him better than he has deserved by his actions, and he calls on God to show kindness and favor to him at the beginning of 9:13 (MT 9:14). As the verse continues, David calls on the Lord to see how the haters have afflicted him. This again appeals to the Lord's decree, recounted in 2:7–9, and David again appeals to God's concern for his glory in 9:14 (MT 9:15). Whereas the enemy has rebelled against Yahweh and his anointed, David calls on God to deliver him from death at the end of 9:13 (MT 9:14) so that he can rehearse the Lord's praise in 9:14 (MT 9:15).

When Yahweh lifts David up from the gates of death (9:14 [MT 9:15]), David asserts that he will praise Yahweh in the gates of daughter Zion and rejoice in his salvation (9:14 [MT 9:15]). The reference to the city as "daughter Zion" personifies the city.[55] With the king being identified as God's son (2:7), the city of David appears to be claimed as God's daughter. Those interested in hearing such praise would not be the congregation of the wicked that has set itself against Yahweh and his anointed but rather the congregation of the righteous that, like the blessed man, loves the Torah (cf. Ps 1–2).

The connection between Yahweh enthroned in justice in 9:7–8 (MT 9:8–9) and the plea for salvation in 9:13–14 (MT 9:14–15) is forged through Yahweh's righteousness being founded on the fact that he establishes his faithfulness to his people by keeping his promises to them. Because Yahweh keeps his word, because he is faithful to his people, the fact that he is enthroned in righteousness means that he will keep his promise to save the humble and repentant who take refuge in him and judge the proud and wicked who refuse to kiss the son (cf. 2:12).

Yahweh's justice seen in wrath on the wicked and salvation for his afflicted people leads naturally to the heart of Ps 9 found at the center of its chiastic structure in 9:9–12 (MT 9:10–13). This is what makes Yahweh a "stronghold for the crushed, a stronghold for times of destitution" (9:9 [MT 9:10]). The "crushed" here are oppressed by the wicked, who in their

---

[55] For the genitive of apposition, see GKC §128k. Alternatively, the "daughter of Zion" may be a reference to an unwalled village near Zion, a suburb of sorts. The difficulty then is that such a "daughter" would have "gates." It may be that a village without walls could nevertheless have a place where business is conducted and elders sit that was referenced as its "gates," as the custom of business conducted in city gates might allow a part of a dwelling place being so called even if there were not literally gates and a wall.

pride disregard what Yahweh has said. David would fit this description ("crushed") when Absalom was wickedly usurping the kingdom, and the statements are general enough to extend to any pious Israelite being exploited or defrauded by those strong in the world's strength. Proverbs 23:10–11 envisions a scenario like this when it warns not to "move an ancient landmark or enter the fields of the fatherless, for their Redeemer is strong; he will plead their cause against you."

Yahweh is not weak. He does not slumber. He is not inattentive. He will plead the cause of those who keep his word. He is their stronghold.

Because he is a mighty fortress, acting on behalf of those who wait for him, those who know Yahweh's reputation, his name, trust him (9:10a [MT 9:11a]). To know Yahweh's name is to know his character: it is to know that he does not forsake those who seek him (9:10b [MT 9:11b]).

Who is like the Lord our God? He does not help those who can help him—as if anyone could. He helps those who can offer him nothing, who cannot defend, enrich, or contribute to him in any way. He helps those who cannot defend their borders, who cannot fund a security force, who cannot devise a clever strategy to entrap intruders, who cannot establish peace through a demonstration of their own strength. Yahweh is their stronghold because they have no other fortress, no other help, no other refuge. He does not help those who help themselves. He helps those who cannot help themselves.

Naturally those so helped recognize what he has done for them, and David responds in 9:11 (MT 9:12) with a command for the epic narratives of what Yahweh has done to be celebrated in poetic song, heralding the might of the Lord, his faithfulness to his word, and his superior wisdom and strategic genius. David calls for Yahweh, who sits in Zion, to be psalmed, for his deeds to be declared among the peoples (9:11 [MT 9:12]). In Gen 9:5 the Lord told Noah that he would "seek" the blood of the slain: whether man or beast did the killing, God would "seek" the blood of the slain, which is to say, establish justice for the slain. Now David declares in Ps 9:12 (MT 9:13) that Yahweh is the one who seeks blood, not forgetting the cry of the afflicted.

BRIDGE

The pattern of events in Pss 3–9, moving from affliction, to confidence in the Lord, to confident vindication, is the pattern of the righteous sufferer, for whom it is necessary first to suffer and then to enter his glory. This is the pattern fulfilled in the Lord Jesus, and this is the example he left, that we should follow in his steps.

John does not quote the Greek translation of Ps 9:3 (MT 9:4) in John 18:6, but when Jesus identifies himself to those who have come to the garden to arrest him, they experience exactly what Ps 9:3 (MT 9:4) says. In fact, John 18:6 may reflect a loose allusion to the Hebrew of Ps 9:3 (MT 9:4).

Ps 9:3 (MT 9:4), "When those at enmity with me turn back, they will stumble and perish from before your presence."

John 18:6, "When Jesus said to them, 'I AM,' they turned back and fell to the ground."

The historical deliverance of David from Absalom was a visitation of God's justice. Jesus spoke of the hour of his crucifixion as "the judgment of this world" (John 12:31), and the patterns of history will be fulfilled:

When the Lord Jesus is revealed from heaven with his mighty angels in flaming fire, inflicting vengeance on those who do not know God and on those who do not obey the gospel of our Lord Jesus. They will suffer the punishment of eternal destruction, away from the presence of the Lord and from the glory of his might, when he comes on that day to be glorified in his saints, and to be marveled at among all who have believed (2 Thess 1:7–10).

## Psalm 10

OVERVIEW AND STRUCTURE OF PSALM 10

Whereas Ps 9 was a confident acclamation of Yahweh's rebuke of the nations (9:1–6, 15–16 [MT 9:2–7, 16–17]) with a prayer for more of the same in the future (9:19–20 [MT 9:20–21]), Ps 10 opens on a discordant note, asking why Yahweh holds back and hides himself. The final phrase of Ps 10:1 is an exact repetition of a phrase in 9:9 (MT 9:10), but the thought of the two verses could not be more different. Psalm 9:9 (MT 9:10) asserts that Yahweh is "a stronghold for times of destitution." Psalm 10:1, by contrast, asks Yahweh, "Will you hide in times of destitution?" The statement in Ps 9 celebrates the comfort of God's presence; in Ps 10 it bewails God's absence.

From there the contrasts between Pss 9 and 10 continue, with Ps 10 often reusing language from Ps 9. Whereas Ps 9 gave thanks and praise to Yahweh because he judged and destroyed the wicked (9:1–6 [MT 9:2–7]), Ps 10 describes the impudent arrogance of the wicked man in all his scheming potency (10:2–11), calling on the Lord to do justice against the evil in their strength (10:12–15). Psalm 10 concludes with a confident assertion that Yahweh is king and will establish righteousness (10:16–18).

The movement of thought in Ps 10 proceeds as follows:

10:1–5, The Pride of the Wicked
  10:6–11, The Plans of the Wicked
  10:12–15, The Prayers of the Righteous
10:16–18, The Humility of the Righteous

SCRIPTURE

CSB                                    Author's translation

[1] LORD, why do you stand so far
   away?
Why do you hide in times of trouble?
[2] In arrogance the wicked relentlessly
   pursue their victims;
let them be caught in the schemes
   they have devised.

[3] For the wicked one boasts about his
   own cravings;
the one who is greedy curses and
   despises the LORD.
[4] In all his scheming,
the wicked person arrogantly thinks,
"There's no accountability,
since there's no God."
[5] His ways are always secure;
your lofty judgments have no effect
   on him;
he scoffs at all his adversaries.
[6] He says to himself, "I will never be
   moved—
from generation to generation I will
   be without calamity."

[1] Why, O Yahweh, do you stand far off?
Will you hide in times of destitution?

[2] In majesty the wicked one burns the
   afflicted.
Let them be seized in the schemes
   they have devised,
[3] for the wicked boasts over the desire
   of his soul.
And the one who cuts in greed he
   blesses.
He spurns Yahweh.

[4] The wicked according to the height
   of his nose does not seek;
there is no God in any of his schemes.
[5] His ways always writhe.
On high are your judgments from
   before him.
As for all his adversaries, he snorts at
   them.

[6] He says in his heart, "I shall
   not totter for generation and
   generation,
because there will be no calamity."

⁷ Cursing, deceit, and violence fill his
    mouth;
trouble and malice are under his
    tongue.
⁸ He waits in ambush near settlements;
he kills the innocent in secret places.
His eyes are on the lookout for the
    helpless;
⁹ he lurks in secret like a lion in a
    thicket.
He lurks in order to seize a victim;
he seizes a victim and drags him in
    his net.
¹⁰ So he is oppressed and beaten down;
helpless people fall because of the
    wicked one's strength.
¹¹ He says to himself, "God has
    forgotten;
he hides his face and will never see."

¹² Rise up, Lord God! Lift up your hand.
Do not forget the oppressed.
¹³ Why has the wicked person despised
    God?
He says to himself, "You will not
    demand an account."
¹⁴ But you yourself have seen trouble
    and grief,
observing it in order to take the
    matter into your hands.
The helpless one entrusts himself to
    you;
you are a helper of the fatherless.
¹⁵ Break the arm of the wicked, evil
    person,
until you look for his wickedness,
but it can't be found.

¹⁶ The Lord is King forever and ever;
the nations will perish from his land.
¹⁷ Lord, you have heard the desire of
    the humble;
you will strengthen their hearts.
You will listen carefully,

⁷ An oath fills his mouth, with
    treacheries and oppression.
Under his tongue are labor and
    iniquity.

⁸ He sits in ambush in the villages.
In the secret places he murders the
    innocent.
His eyes treasure the hapless.
⁹ He will ambush in the secret place
    like a lion in a thicket.
He will ambush to seize the afflicted.
He will seize the afflicted when he
    draws him into his net.
¹⁰ He will crush.
He will bow down.
And the hapless have fallen by his
    mighty ones.

¹¹ He says in his heart, "God has
    forgotten.
He has hidden his face.
He will never see."

¹² Rise up, O Yahweh!
O God, lift your hand!
Do not forget the afflicted.

¹³ Why has the wicked spurned God?
He says in his heart, "You will not
    seek."
¹⁴ You have seen!
For you note labor and vexation to
    give by your hand.
To you the hapless abandons [his
    cause].
As for the fatherless, you are his
    helper.
¹⁵ Shatter the arm of the wicked and
    evil.
Seek his wickedness that will not be
    found.

¹⁶ Yahweh is king of the age and on.
The nations have perished from his
    land.

<sup>18</sup> doing justice for the fatherless and
the oppressed
so that mere humans from the earth
may terrify them no more.

<sup>17</sup> The desire of the afflicted you
heard, O Yahweh.
You will establish their heart.
You will incline your ear
<sup>18</sup> to judge for the fatherless and the
crushed,
that man from the earth might not
again cause trembling.

CONTEXT: VERBAL AND THEMATIC LINKS WITH SURROUNDING PSALMS

As noted above, there are many points of contact between Pss 9 and 10, and no superscription divides the two psalms. The Greek translation of the Psalter even joins the two, numbering both as Ps 9 and Ps 11 as Ps 10. Whereas many commentators today think that Pss 9 and 10 should be read as one psalm, several factors convince me that they are not to be read as one. A better solution, I contend, is that Pss 3–9 form one unit, with Pss 10–14 forming another. The points of contact and the lack of a superscription on Ps 10 create coherence between the two units.[56]

Reasons for seeing Pss 9 and 10 as distinct psalms include the following: First, the tone of Pss 9 and 10 differs in that Ps 9 is an outright celebration of the display of God's justice, whereas Ps 10 reflects on the pride of the wicked (10:1–11) and calls on the Lord to do justice (10:12–18). Second, as argued above, Pss 9 and 10 each appear to be self-contained chiasms.[57] Third, some have attempted to establish an acrostic encompassing Pss 9 and 10, but the alleged acrostic breaks down on the details.[58] Each letter of the Hebrew alphabet is not represented at the head of successive lines of Pss 9 and 10: while some letters are missing, those that do appear are not in alphabetic order. Fourth, Pss 3 and 9 share references to the "son" in the superscription, and then as discussed above, that unit of psalms can be seen to deal with Absalom's revolt. Similarly, Pss 10 and 14 share the strikingly unique features of relating what the wicked "says in his

---

[56] Contra, e.g., deClaisse-Walford, Jacobson, and Tanner, *Psalms*, 129; and John Goldingay, *Psalms 1-41*, BCOTWP (Grand Rapids: Baker Academic, 2006), 162, 166, who reads the two psalms together under the heading, "How to Pray against the Powerful," and claims that the "MT reflects a later division of the Psalm in usage."

[57] Alden, "Chiastic Psalms 1–50," 16, sees a chiasm in Ps 9, but he does not venture one for Ps 10.

[58] The *BHS* text reflects this tradition with letters of the Hebrew alphabet in the margin of Pss 9 and 10. Anyone who knows the order of those letters can thereby see that some are skipped while others listed in the margin are manifestly out of order.

heart" (10:6, 11, 13; 14:1) and the declaration that "there is no God" (10:4; 14:1; cf. 53:2), which suggests that Pss 10–14 also comprise a unit. On this reading, the verbal links between Pss 9 and 10 do not mean that the two psalms are to be read as one, but they do bind together the two units (3–9 and 10–14). Fifth, in Pss 10 and 14, the wicked are disregarding God in what they say in their hearts, and Pss 11–13 fit such a context. Psalms 10–14 can be depicted chiastically as follows:

Psalm 10, The Wicked Says in His Heart: There Is No God
    Psalm 11, Flee as a Bird to Your Mountain
        Psalm 12, I Will Arise, Says Yahweh
    Psalm 13, How Long, O Yahweh
Psalm 14, The Wicked Says in His Heart: There Is No God

Over against what the wicked say in Pss 10 and 14, with the taunts and the prayer of how long in Pss 11 and 13, in the center of this unit stands God's promise to arise to defend his own in Ps 12.

Here is a selection of significant linguistic and conceptual points of contact between Ps 10 and surrounding psalms:

10:1 "in times of destitution" לעתות בצרה
9:9 (MT 9:10) "for times of destitution" לעתות בצרה

10:2, 3, 4, 13, 15 (2x) "the wicked"
Compare 1:1, 4, 6; 3:7 (MT 3:8); 5:4 (MT 5:5); 7:9 (MT 7:10); 9:5, 16, 18 (MT 9:6, 17, 18)

10:2, 9 (2x), 12 "the afflicted"
Compare 9:12, 13, 18 (MT 9:13, 14, 19); 12:5 (MT 12:6); 14:6

10:4, 13, 15 "seek"
Compare 9:11, 13; 14:2

10:4 "there is no God" אין אלהים
14:1; 53:2 "there is no God" אין אלהים

10:5 "judgment"
1:1; 7:6 (MT 7:7); 9:4, 7, 16 (MT 9:5, 8, 17)

10:5 "he snorts" יפיח
12:5 (MT 12:6) "he pants" יפיח

10:6, 11, 13 "he says in his heart"
14:1 "The fool says in his heart"

10:6 "totter"
13:4 (MT 13:5)

10:6 "generation"
12:7 (MT 12:8); 14:4 (MT 14:5)

10:7 "tongue"
Compare 12:3–4 (MT 12:4–5)

10:11 "never" לנצח
9:6, 18 (MT 9:7, 19) "everlasting," "forever" לנצח

10:12 "Rise up, O Yahweh!" קומה יהוה
3:7 (MT 3:8); 7:6 (MT 7:7); 9:19 (MT 9:20); 17:12 (MT 17:13); 132:8
קומה יהוה

10:12 … 15 "Rise up, O Yahweh … Shatter the arm of the wicked"
3:7 (MT 3:8) "Rise up, O Yahweh … the teeth of the wicked you
shatter"

10:16 "The nations have perished from the earth"
9:3, 5, 6 (MT 9:4, 6, 7) "perish"
1:6; 2:12; 5:6 (MT 5:7) "perish/destroy"

EXPOSITION

**10:1–5, The Pride of the Wicked**

The Psalms are honest, and they deal with the vicissitudes of life. Psalm
9 sang the justice the Lord did against the wicked in vindication of those
the wicked were oppressing. Because the Lord had defended him, the
psalmist celebrated the Lord as his stronghold (9:9 [MT 9:10]).

The situation reflected in Ps 10 is different. When your face is lacer-
ated because an oppressor is dragging you by the hair through gravel,
the Lord may not feel like a fortress. In fact, as the wicked flex, smirk,
taunt, and strut, it can seem that the Lord is distant, hiding even. That is
precisely what the psalmist communicates in 10:1, asking why the Lord
stands far off, asking if he will hide himself in times of destitution. The
psalmist does not, however, give up on the Lord. To cry out to the Lord
as he does in 10:1 is to declare confidence in God's goodness, ability, and

love. The opening questions in Ps 10:1 are informed by the description of the wicked's bold impertinence in 10:2–5.

In Ps 10:2 the psalmist complains that "in the majesty of the wicked he will burn the afflicted." When the wicked are strong the weak will be harmed. Thus people hide themselves when the wicked rise (Prov 28:12). Having asserted this in the first half of the line, the psalmist then prays, "Let them be seized in the schemes they have devised." This prayer asks for what has been described in Pss 5:10 (MT 5:11); 7:15–16 (MT 7:16–17); and 9:15–16 (MT 9:16–17), namely, for the wicked to suffer the consequences of their own plots. Here, however, the psalmist asks for the wicked to be taken in the hidden evil of their plans: for them to be caught in the act.

The psalmist explains why he prays in 10:3. Whereas the righteous boast in Yahweh, the verb often used to communicate praise for Yahweh (הלל, cf. e.g., Ps 44:9) appears in 10:3 in the assertion that the wicked "boasts over the desire of his soul." The word used to refer to the "desire" of the wicked in 10:3 (תאוה) will be used in 10:17 to describe the "desire" of the afflicted. This shows us the religious character of the irreligious. That is to say, everyone will boast in something, and everyone will desire something. The righteous will boast in the Lord and desire to see his justice, his victory, his righteousness. The wicked will boast in whatever their souls crave, and in the craving they celebrate what they desire, worshiping it. Sin is a worship problem. Wickedness is a worship problem. We were created to boast over the desire of our souls. The souls of the wicked desire what will never satisfy them, and they boast in what is not worthy of their praise.

I have rendered the second statement in Ps 10:3, "And the one who cuts in greed he has blessed." This rendering understands the participle (בצע) as a substantival direct object, "the one who cuts in greed," of the following finite verb whose subject is the wicked referenced in the first part of the line (ברך), "he has blessed." This rendering fits the context. Just as the wicked man "praises" and "desires" so he "blesses," another term used to describe how the righteous respond to the Lord. Against the CSB, ESV, and NAS, there is no reason to suppose that "he blesses" is a kind of coded expression for "curses," as though this were an emendation of the scribes known as a *tiqqune sopherim*.[59] In the same way that the righteous man speaks well of the Lord and people who act like the

---

[59] So also Goldingay, *Psalms 1–41*, 164. For brief discussion of *tiqqune sopherim* scribal emendations, see Ellis R. Brotzman, *Old Testament Textual Criticism: A Practical Introduction* (Grand Rapids: Baker, 1994), 54–55.

Lord, so the wicked man speaks well, that is, blesses, those who engage in extortionary practices in an effort to achieve dishonest gain. This is precisely the problem: the wicked bless what Yahweh has cursed. Thus the final sentiment in 10:3, "He has spurned Yahweh." To worship anything other than Yahweh is to spurn him. The problem with us sinners is that we desire the wrong things, praise the wrong things, and bless the wrong things, when we should desire, praise, and bless the Lord.

The prayer at the end of Ps 9 that Yahweh would appoint a terror for the wicked is an expression of love for the wicked (9:20 [MT 9:21]), because if Yahweh terrifies them, they might fear him. Far from fearing Yahweh, Ps 10:4 describes how the wicked lift up their noses. Behind the CSB's phrase "the wicked arrogantly thinks" stands a pictographic reference to the height of the wicked's nose. Apparently the arrogant in the ancient world were inclined to the same mannerisms as the arrogant in our own day. According to the height of his nose—which is to say, according to his own high opinion of himself—"he does not seek." In my translation, I have supplied what the wicked man does not seek—Yahweh. He does not seek because of his pride, because of the inclination of his head, with his nose in the air. He does not see the wrath awaiting him, so he feels neither need for Yahweh nor compulsion to seek him. Following the Masoretic accentuation of the text, I have rendered the next line of Ps 10:4, "There is no God in any of his schemes." The wicked man praises what he desires and blesses those who take advantage of others. He spurns Yahweh, lifts up his nose, does not seek Yahweh, and Yahweh plays no role in any of his plots.

BDB (298) takes the verb (חיל) at the beginning of Ps 10:5 to go with a root that means "be firm, strong." HALOT (311) takes this instance with the same root but suggests that the verb "prosper" should be read: "Ps 10₅ rd. יצלח or יצלחו." The only other place this verb is used is in Job 20:21. I have translated the text as it stands, taking the verb as the far more commonly used root that often designates the writhing or twisting of a woman in childbirth.[60] The twisting and turning characterizes the tortuous way of the wicked, as opposed to the straightness of the way of the upright.

Psalm 10:5 goes on to specify that the Lord's judgments are on high, out of the wicked's line of sight and therefore not part of his consideration.

---

[60] See BDB, 296–97; and HALOT, 310–11. Cf. Goldingay, Psalms 1-41, 164, who follows the Greek translation to the conclusion that another root altogether is in use here.

The reference to him snorting at his adversaries, showing no regard for the danger they pose, communicates the arrogance of the wicked.

The first two commandments are to love God and neighbor. The wicked has regard for neither, and hubris so deludes him that he thinks himself unassailable.

### 10:6–11, The Plans of the Wicked

Psalm 10:6–11 opens and closes with the phrase, "He says in his heart" (10:6, 11). The first instance, in 10:6, presents the wicked assuring himself that he will never be shaken, suffer no unexpected calamity. This shows a lack of humility, a failure to observe the way the world works, and an absence of imagination.

Psalm 10:7 is typically rendered as though the wicked man is using foul language, uttering curse words of the four letter variety, which are sometimes referred to as swear words. The CSB, for instance, has "cursing, deceit, and violence fill his mouth." The term rendered "cursing," however, is a noun that means simply "oath" (אלה). The Greek translation rendered this with a noun meaning "curse" (ἀρά), but this would seem to reflect the way that "swearing" an oath entails calling down a curse on oneself if one fails to keep the promise being made. We should understand Ps 10:7 as referring to those kinds of oaths and curses rather than to the use of foul language. The wicked will make an oath, but the oaths he makes come with treacheries and result in oppression. That is to say, he does not keep his promises, and what promises he keeps are made in deals designed to abuse and exploit others. This man's mouth works much evil, thus the second half of 10:7 refers to the "labor and iniquity" to be found "under his tongue."

The plans of the wicked extend from the counsel he takes within himself, what he says to his own heart (10:6–7), to the actions he pursues (10:8–10) and excuses he makes (10:11). The false oaths of 10:7 are complemented by the physical ambushes of 10:8. The psalmist describes a thug, someone who fears neither God nor man, who breaks laws and bodies. This wicked man commits crimes that involve schemes and extortion, and he complements that with violence, as 10:8 refers to ambush and murder. When 10:8 says that "his eyes are on the lookout for the helpless" (CSB), the text literally says that his eyes "treasure" them. He loves to see people in need, people he can exploit. He values the sight of people with no defender, whose only option will be to fall into his treacherous hands.

Psalm 10:9 continues this vein of thought comparing the wicked man to a lion seizing its prey, and the wicked man's prey is the "afflicted." The idea at the end of 10:9 that he seizes the afflicted by drawing him into his net recalls the "schemes" of 10:2. The wicked man plots and plans and connives ways to spot what he treasures—people in affliction—and then set them up to be exploited to the full by luring them into his traps. Psalm 10:10 describes how the wicked man crushes, bows, and overcomes the hapless by his gang of enforcers.

In Ps 10:11 the psalmist describes the wicked man responding to stabs of conscience, pangs warning him that "in every place are the eyes of Yahweh, keeping watch on the evil and the good" (Prov 15:3). The wicked man "says in his heart, 'God has forgotten. He has hidden his face. He will never see' " (Ps 10:11). If he believed otherwise, he would not break the commandments.

To this point in Ps 10, the psalmist has focused on describing what the wicked say and do. The rest of the psalm is the psalmist's response to the wicked. That response consists of prayer to the Lord and celebration of his reign.

## 10:12–15, The Prayers of the Righteous

The righteous responds to the wicked by going straight to Yahweh. Psalm 10:12 repeats the petition from Pss 3:7 (MT 3:8), 7:6 (MT 7:7), and 9:19 (MT 9:20): "Rise up, O Yahweh!" The Lord says he will do just that in 12:6, and he will be called on to do so again in 17:13 and 132:8. It is as though the psalmist comes before Yahweh, who is seated on his throne in heaven, and calls on him to rise and come forth to confront the wicked. This would explain the next petitions in 10:12 for him to lift up his hand and forget not the afflicted.

In 10:13 the psalmist resumes three thoughts from 10:1–11 in the question and answer, "Why has the wicked spurned God? He says in his heart, 'You will not seek.' " The question and answer picks up (1) the idea that the wicked spurn God from 10:2, (2) the idea that the wicked has spoken a rationalization to his own heart from 10:11, and (3) the idea that the wicked tells God that God himself will not call him to account for his wickedness in 10:13 ("You will not seek").

Because he was praying in 10:12 and continues to pray in 10:14–15, it appears that he is praying in 10:13 as well. Having recounted the wicked's false thoughts in 10:13, the psalmist objects in 10:14, asserting to the Lord that he has seen—rejecting the lie in 10:11 that the Lord will not see. In 10:14 he goes on to assert that the Lord takes note of human wickedness so that he can repay it by his own hand. He reminds the Lord that the hapless has abandoned himself to Yahweh, that Yahweh is the helper of the fatherless. These latter two appeals at the end of 10:14 communicate that orphans have no father to defend them, that the hapless have no one other than the Lord to whom they can appeal.

In Old Testament terms, the arm or hand is often used as a figure of speech for speaking of the power whereby something is accomplished. Thus Ps 136:12 says that Yahweh brought Israel out of Egypt "by a strong hand and an outstretched arm." This informs the prayer in Ps 10:15, "Shatter the arm of the wicked and evil." The psalmist prays that the means whereby the wicked kill, oppress, and extort would be broken. He continues, again in answer to the wicked thinking God will not call to account in 10:13, praying in 10:15b that the Lord would seek out all the evil of the wicked until no more exists to be found.[61]

Psalm 10:6–11 recounts what the wicked says in his heart, and Ps 10:12–15 details what the righteous says in his. The contrast could not be more clear. Whereas the wicked plot the evil they will do to get what they want at the expense of others, the righteous prays to God for the Lord to defend the afflicted, the fatherless, and the crushed by doing justice against the wicked. As the psalm opened with a description of the pride of the wicked in 10:1–5, it will close with the humility of the righteous in 10:16–18.

### 10:16–18, The Humility of the Righteous

Humility entails a correct, and therefore modest, estimation of one's own status. The psalmist evidences humility by stating in 10:16 that "Yahweh is king forever and ever," because this necessarily subjects the psalmist to Yahweh as king. The wicked nowhere acknowledge subjection to Yahweh in Ps 10. The reference to the nations having perished from the earth in the rest of 10:16 speaks as though the conquest of the land—the conquest Israel never achieved—has finally been completed.

Whereas the wicked praise their desire in Ps 10:3, in 10:17 the psalmist confesses that Yahweh heard the desire of the afflicted. That desire has been expressed in 10:12–15. The psalmist further confesses that Yahweh

---

[61] The final phrase of Ps 10:15, which I have rendered, "Seek his wickedness that will not be found," could alternatively be a prayer for the Lord to seek and find hidden evil.

will establish the heart of the afflicted and that he will incline his ear. Hearing their desire, establishing their heart, and inclining his ear should be interpreted together. The desire springs from the heart, so by hearing their desire and inclining his ear, it appears that Yahweh is here said to grant what the afflicted requests and thereby confirm the rightness of what comes from their hearts. This fits with 10:18 as well, where the defenseless and abused are vindicated by the Lord, as mere humans are put in their places.

Psalm 10:16–18 evidences humility as the psalmist acknowledges that Yahweh is king, recognizes his need for Yahweh to act on his behalf, and celebrates the way that Yahweh will put proud earthlings in their proper place.

Bridge

A good example of the kind of person the wicked in Ps 10 target would be the biblical character Ruth. In the book that bears her name, we read that she was a widow supporting her widowed mother-in-law. These two ladies had neither husbands nor fathers to protect and provide for them, and the wicked of Ps 10 would treasure the sight of them coming, seeing in the vulnerable women an opportunity to exploit, ensnare, and abuse. The diagnosis of the wickedness and the prayer against it in Ps 10 exemplify a godly response for those who would be like Boaz, a defender of the vulnerable, a provider for the needy, in all generations. As the one who descended from him would do, Boaz married a gentile bride and brought the stranger into the covenant, providing for the needy, protecting the weak, and reconciling the stranger, granting unassailable standing in God's people.

Ruth's own response to her predicament likewise instructs. She committed herself to godliness and accepted godly leadership from Boaz. As in the book of Ruth and in Ps 10, the best recourse for those whom the wicked target is the refuge found in Yahweh.

## Psalm 11

Overview and Structure of Psalm 11

The seven short verses of Ps 11 are straightforward. The psalmist rehearses how the wicked threaten him in 11:1–3 and assures himself of Yahweh's presence and character in 11:4–7.[62]

---

[62] For a proposed chiasm in Ps 11, see Alden, "Chiastic Psalms 1–50," 16–17.

11:1–3, The Threats of the Wicked
11:4–7, The Presence and Character of the Lord

SCRIPTURE

| CSB | Author's translation |
|---|---|
| For the choir director. Of David. | [1] For the Preeminent One. Of David. |
| [1] I have taken refuge in the LORD. How can you say to me, "Escape to the mountains like a bird! | In Yahweh I take refuge. How can you all say to my soul, "Flutter to your mountain, O bird. |
| [2] For look, the wicked string bows; they put their arrows on bowstrings to shoot from the shadows at the upright in heart. | [2] For behold, the wicked tread the bow. They ready their arrow on the string to shoot in the dark at the upright of heart. |
| [3] When the foundations are destroyed, what can the righteous do?" | [3] When the foundations are thrown down, what can the righteous one do?" |
| [4] The LORD is in his holy temple; the Lord—his throne is in heaven. His eyes watch; his gaze examines everyone. | [4] Yahweh, in the temple of his holiness. Yahweh, in the heavens is his throne. His eyes see; his eyelids test the sons of Adam. |
| [5] The Lord examines the righteous, but he hates the wicked and those who love violence. | [5] Yahweh will test the righteous and the wicked, and the one who loves violence his soul hates. |
| [6] Let him rain burning coals and sulfur on the wicked; let a scorching wind be the portion in their cup. | [6] He will cause snares to rain on the wicked, fire and brimstone and scorching wind the portion of their cup. |
| [7] For the Lord is righteous; he loves righteous deeds. The upright will see his face. | [7] For Yahweh is righteous. Righteous deeds he loves. The upright will see his face. |

CONTEXT: VERBAL AND THEMATIC LINKS WITH SURROUNDING PSALMS

11:1 "I have taken refuge"
2:12; 5:11 (MT 5:12); 7:1 (MT 7:2)

11:2 "tread the bow ... ready"
7:12 (MT 7:13) "his bow he treads, and readies it"

11:2 "the upright in heart"
7:10 (MT 7:11) "the upright in heart"
Compare 11:7 "the upright"

11:3, 5 "the righteous"
5:12 (MT 5:13); 7:9 (MT 7:10); 14:5

11:4 "Yahweh is in the temple of his holiness"
Compare 2:6; 3:4 (MT 3:5); 5:7 (MT 5:8)[63]

11:4 "Yahweh, in the heavens is his throne"
Compare 2:4; 9:4, 7 (MT 9:5, 8)

11:4 "his eyes see"
5:5 (MT 5:6) "the boastful will not stand before your eyes"

11:4–5 "his eyelids test the sons of Adam. Yahweh will test the
    righteous and the wicked"
7:9 (MT 7:10) "let the evil of the wicked end, but establish the
    righteous one, O righteous God, tester of hearts and guts."

11:4 "the sons of Adam"
12:1 (MT 12:2) "the sons of Adam"
14:2 "the sons of Adam"

11:5 "the one who loves violence his soul hates"
5:5 (MT 5:6) "You hate all workers of iniquity"

11:6 "fire and brimstone"
Compare Gen 19:24 "brimstone and fire"
Compare Deut 29:23 (MT 29:22) "brimstone and burning salt …
    like … Sodom and Gomorrah"

11:7 "For Yahweh is righteous"
Compare 7:9, 11 (MT 7:10, 12); see also Dan 9:14

11:7 "The upright will see his face"
17:15 "in righteousness I will see your face"

Psalms 1–2 introduce the Psalter and set its tone. Psalms 3–9 deal with
Absalom's revolt, and Pss 10–14 present David's reflections on the kind

---

[63] See also Hab 2:20.

of people who engage in the 2:1–3 rebellion against the Lord and his Messiah. Psalm 10 presents the arrogance and plots of the wicked; Ps 11 recounts the threats they make against the king; Ps 12 contemplates what things are like when the wicked are ascendant; Ps 13 asks how long until the Lord keeps his promise; and Ps 14 observes the folly of those who disregard God.

Each of these psalms also includes David's righteous response to the rebels. In Ps 10 he prays with humble vehemence; in Ps 11 he reflects on God's character and presence; in Ps 12 he celebrates the certain purity of God's word; in Ps 13 he trusts, rejoices, and sings; and in Ps 14 he longs for the restoration of the fortunes of God's people.

EXPOSITION

### 11:1–3, The Threats of the Wicked

Even as David recounts the threats of the wicked in Ps 11:1–3, his perspective is one of total confidence. Believing Pss 1–2, David responds to the threats of mere mortals (9:20 [MT 9:21]; 10:18) with incredulity, amazed at the stupidity of those who would attack Yahweh and his messiah. David asserts that he has done what Ps 2:12 called the rebel kings to do by taking refuge in Yahweh.[64] That being the case, he asks how they can utter their threats against him (11:1a), then recounts those threats (11:1b–3).

These threats consist of an opening taunt that urges the king to flutter away like a bird flying to safety (11:1b). After the taunt, the reasons the king should flee are given, and those reasons point to the might, methods, and menace of the wicked. The might of the wicked is illustrated in the reference to the warrior treading the bow, nocking the arrow on the string in 11:2a–b. This mental image of a man of war bending his mighty bow is far more intimidating than the characterization of the king as a little birdie who needs to flutter away to avoid the inevitable conquest of the wicked.

The reference to the wicked shooting in the dark at the upright in 11:2c hints at the methods of the wicked. This seems to point to the way that the wicked feel no qualms about less-than-honorable stealth warfare. He shoots in the dark. He cannot be seen or suspected. Taking his

---

[64] In Ps 2:12 it seems that the rebels are being urged to take refuge in the son, as he is the antecedent of the pronouns. To take refuge in Yahweh's king, however, is to take refuge in Yahweh. David appears to have consciously placed his hope in the promised king from his line.

prey unaware, he has no concern for engaging in a just war according to righteous rules of engagement. If he must murder or assassinate he will do so. The taunt, the might, and the method are all designed to intimidate, yea terrorize, the upright in heart.

The menace of the wicked comes in the question posed in 11:3. This question appears to envision the destruction of the "foundations." Whether those foundations are the cornerstones of the wall or the cornerstones of character, the idea is this: What shields the righteous from the ravages of the wicked has been removed. If the walls are torn down, the righteous cannot defend themselves against the terrorists who seek to conquer by any means necessary. If the character of the people has been compromised, the righteous cannot trust anyone because the public virtue that enables everyone to feel safe has been banished: The city has become a jungle of wild animals. In such a situation, the wicked pose the question, what can the righteous one do?

### 11:4–7, The Presence and Character of the Lord

How does David respond to the taunts, threats, and intimidation of the wicked? He does not begin negotiations with Egypt or Assyria, as faithless kings that followed him would. He does not go out and inspect the city's water supply (cf. Isa 7:1–3). David's mind is not on horses and chariots being made ready for the day of battle but on the Lord, to whom victory belongs (cf. Ps 20:7; Prov 21:31).

David's astonished response to the rebels ("How can you say?!") does not arise from his high estimation of his own prowess and puissance but from his confidence in God. This is why in 11:4a–b he describes Yahweh being enthroned in the temple of his holiness, seated in the heavens, recalling the description of the one seated in the heavens laughing at the rebels in Ps 2:4. In 11:4c David observes that Yahweh, who is righteous, sees everything the wicked do. The darkness from which they shoot (11:2c) will not hide them from Yahweh, who will bring them to justice.

In 11:5a David asserts that Yahweh will test the righteous and the wicked. Sometimes it can seem as though honest people are being held to the righteous standard they embrace, while people see that the dishonest have rejected any standard of righteousness and as a result they are not held accountable for or otherwise disqualified by their infidelities and transgressions. But if Yahweh sees all, and if he tests the righteous and the wicked, meaning that he measures everyone against his own standards of right and wrong, no one will escape justice. This means, as David goes on to assert in 11:5b, that Yahweh is not favorably disposed toward those who love the kind of violence the wicked pursue (cf. 11:2). In fact, just as was asserted in 5:5 (MT 5:6), Yahweh hates those who scorn him, disregard his law, and trample on his people. Yahweh's righteous love is not passive but active, and he is emotionally committed to himself, to his righteousness, and to all that is good for those he loves.

David does not think that this earth sits under a closed heaven, and in 11:6 he describes Yahweh visiting justice. David's imagination is stocked with biblical imagery, and in this verse he speaks as though Yahweh will judge his enemies the way he judged Sodom and Gomorrah, raining down fire and brimstone on them. The scorching wind that will be the portion of their cup is reminiscent of the wind driving away the chaff in 1:4. Whereas David says that Yahweh is his portion and cup in 16:5, he declares that Yahweh's judgment is the portion and cup of the wicked in 11:6.

David's confidence that Yahweh will vindicate his people is grounded in his knowledge of Yahweh's righteous character, which he asserts in 11:7a. Yahweh hates those who love violence (11:5), but he loves righteous deeds (11:7b). Whereas the wicked can expect Yahweh's judgment (11:6), the upright, those at whom the wicked shoot in the dark (11:2), will see Yahweh's face (11:7c).

### Bridge

The message of Ps 11 is timeless and easy to apply. When people who belong to the Lord contemplate the threats of the wicked, they should do so in light of what God has said, in light of God's righteous character, and in light of God's coming judgment. We now know that Jesus is the descendent of David, in whom the promises of Ps 2 are fulfilled. Jesus will judge the wicked, and those who trust in Jesus will behold the glory of God in the face of Christ.

## Psalm 12

### Overview and Structure of Psalm 12

After the description of those who assert that there is no God in Ps 10 and the response to their threats in Ps 11, Ps 12 presents a contrast between the words of the wicked and the words of Yahweh. The psalm appears to fall into a chiastic structure. The opening and closing statements describe a situation where the wicked have the upper hand and the righteous are losing ground (12:1, 8 [MT 12:1–2, 9]). Within that outer frame, 12:2–4 (MT 12:3–5) respond to the lying lips of the wicked and 12:6–7 (MT 12:7–8) marvel at the true words of the Lord. At the center of the psalm's chiastic structure we find the Lord's true words, his declaration that he will arise on behalf of his persecuted and oppressed people in 12:5 (MT 12:6).[65]

12:1 (MT 12:2), The Vanishing Faithful
    12:2–4 (MT 12:3–5), The Empty Words of the Wicked
        12:5 (MT 12:6), Yahweh Promises to Vindicate the Poor and Needy
    12:6–7 (MT 12:7–8), The Pure Words of the Lord
12:8 (MT 12:9), The Strutting Wicked

SCRIPTURE

CSB

For the choir director: according to *Sheminith*. A psalm of David.

[1] Help, LORD, for no faithful one remains;
the loyal have disappeared from the human race.
[2] They lie to one another;
they speak with flattering lips and deceptive hearts.
[3] May the LORD cut off all flattering lips and the tongue that speaks boastfully.
[4] They say, "Through our tongues we have power;
our lips are our own—who can be our master?"

[5] "Because of the devastation of the needy
and the groaning of the poor,
I will now rise up," says the LORD.

Author's translation

[1] For the Preeminent One.
Upon the eighth.
A Psalm of David.

[2] Save, O Yahweh, for the lovingkind one comes to an end,
for the faithful vanish from the sons of Adam.

[3] They speak emptiness, a man to his neighbor,
lips of smooth things in heart and heart they speak.
[4] May Yahweh cut off all the lips of smooth things,
tongue speaking great things,
[5] because they say, "With our tongue we will prevail!
Our lips are with us, who is lord over us?"

[6] "From the destruction of the afflicted,

---

[65] Cf. Alden, "Chiastic Psalms 1–50," 17.

"I will provide safety for the one who
   longs for it."

⁶ The words of the LORD are pure words,
like silver refined in an earthen
   furnace,
purified seven times.
⁷ You, LORD, will guard us;
you will protect us from this
   generation forever.
⁸ The wicked prowl all around,
and what is worthless is exalted by
   the human race.

from the groaning of the needy,
now I will arise,"
says Yahweh.
I will put him in the salvation for
   which he pants.

⁷ The words of Yahweh are pure
   words:
silver refined in a furnace on the
   ground,
purified seven times.
⁸ You, O Yahweh, will keep them.
You will deliver him from this
   generation to the age.

⁹ Round about the wicked walk,
according to the lifting up of
   worthlessness among the sons of
   Adam.

CONTEXT: VERBAL AND THEMATIC LINKS WITH SURROUNDING PSALMS

MT 12:1 "Upon the eighth"
MT 6:1 "upon the eighth" (only at 6:1 and 12:1)

12:1 (MT 12:2) "Save"
Compare 3:7 (MT 3:8); 6:4 (MT 6:5); 7:1 (MT 7:2)
Compare 12:5 (MT 12:6) "salvation"

12:1 (MT 12:2) "the lovingkind one"
4:3 (MT 4:4) "the lovingkind one"

12:1, 8 (MT 12:2, 9) "the sons of Adam"
11:4 "the sons of Adam"
14:2 "the sons of Adam"

12:2, 3 (MT 12:3, 4) "lips of smooth things," cf. "tongue" in 12:3,
   4 (MT 12:4, 5)
5:9 (MT 5:10) "their tongues cause slipperiness"

12:3, 4 (MT 12:4, 5) "tongue"
Compare 5:9 (MT 5:10); 10:7

12:5 (MT 12:6) "afflicted"
Compare 9:12, 13, 18 (MT 9:13, 14, 19); 10:2, 9 (2x), 12; 14:6

12:5 (MT 12:6) "needy"
9:18 (MT 9:19)

12:5 (MT 12:6) "I will arise"
Compare 3:7 (MT 3:8); 7:6 (MT 7:7); 9:19 (MT 9:20) "Rise up, O
Yahweh"

12:5 (MT 12:6) "he pants" יפיח
10:5 "he snorts" יפיח

12:6–7 (MT 12:7–8) The LORD keeps his pure words.
Compare 2:4–9

12:7 (MT 12:8) "this generation" (the wicked one)
Compare 14:5 "the generation of the righteous"

EXPOSITION

## 12:1 (MT 12:2), The Vanishing Faithful

When the wicked are on the rise, the foundations of society are often
under attack (cf. 11:3). In such a situation, a godly leader becomes the
target in a "strike the shepherd, and the sheep will be scattered" sense
(cf. Zech 13:7). This kind of backdrop informs the prayer in Ps 12:1a (MT
12:2a), as David cries out to the Lord for salvation, because "the lovingkind
one comes to an end." This reference to the "lovingkind one" recalls the
same in 4:3 (MT 4:4). The man of God's lovingkindness is the Davidic king.
The fact that he is under attack in 12:1a (MT 12:2a) is complemented by
the diminishing influence of faithful people in 12:1b (MT 12:2b). Psalm
12:1 (MT 12:2) describes a situation where the blessed man from Ps 1, the
Lord's anointed of Ps 2, appears to face certain defeat. It is easy to imagine such a scenario in the midst of Absalom's revolt, and the details will
be filled out in the reference to the wicked prowling the land exalting
worthlessness in 12:8 (MT 12:9).

## 12:2–4 (MT 12:3–5), The Empty Words of the Wicked

All the plots of those who would take God's kingdom from God's king
are, in the words of 12:2a (MT 12:3a), emptiness spoken by one man to
another (cf. 2:1–3). How could such counsel prevail? How could people
be convinced to attack the Almighty and his anointed? Psalm 12:2b (MT
12:3b) recognizes the persuasive power of those whose lips speak smooth
things, and when David refers to them speaking "in heart and heart," he

seems to have their double-mindedness in view. They speak as though they have one heart, but in reality their hearts are elsewhere. David replies with a prayer for Yahweh to cut off all lips speaking smooth things in 12:3a (MT 12:4a), and he elaborates on the way that these tongues are boastful in 12:3b (MT 12:4b), bringing out the weak folly of their cause in 12:4 (MT 12:5), explaining that the only weapon the rebels have is their ability to persuade with words. They have no power to overcome Yahweh, but they can convince people. They think that their army of words will enable them to conquer God and God's king. They assert their certainty that their mouths will give them victory, asking with all the unwarranted overconfidence of fools who will overcome them.

### 12:5 (MT 12:6), Yahweh Promises to Vindicate the Poor and Needy

The answer to the question the wicked ask in 12:4 (MT 12:5), "Who is lord over us?" comes in the words of Yahweh in 12:5 (MT 12:6). Yahweh gives two reasons that prompt him to go into action in 12:5a (MT 12:6a): first, the afflicted are destroyed, and second, the needy groan. The wicked disregard God's concern for the poor and needy, for the stranger and sojourner, so God rises to defend those for whom he cares, stating two ways he will respond in 12:5b (MT 12:6b): first, he will rise from his throne, and second, he will put "him"—probably the "lovingkind one" of 12:1a (MT 12:2a)—in the salvation for which he pants. Yahweh will be Lord over the proud-talking fools whose mouths lie, flatter, deny reality, and seek to unmake the world God made by his word by their own persuasive—but ultimately ineffectual—speech.

### 12:6–7 (MT 12:7–8), The Pure Words of the Lord

Naturally the afflicted and needy are delighted to hear Yahweh speak the words of Ps 12:5 (MT 12:6), and that delight is communicated in the celebration of Yahweh's utterance in 12:6–7 (MT 12:7–8). Rather than simply grunt or shout with gladness at what the Lord has said, David makes a profound comparison in 12:6 (MT 12:7). He takes the image of silver that has been purified in a furnace, and such furnaces appear to have been placed in or on the ground, and asserts that Yahweh's words are as pure as such silver, all dross having been smelted away in a sevenfold purification process.[66]

---

[66] For the placement of the refining furnace, see deClaisse-Walford, Jacobson, and Tanner, *Psalms*, 152 n. 10, following Keel, *Symbolism of the Biblical World*, 184–85.

Having asserted the purity and value of Yahweh's words in 12:6 (MT 12:7), David says that Yahweh himself will guard his words in 12:7a (MT 12:8a). The Lord had asserted in 12:5 (MT 12:6) that he would put "him" in salvation, apparently referring to the "godly one" mentioned in 12:1a (MT 12:2a). This individual is again in view in 12:7b (MT 12:8b), when the Lord declares that he will "deliver him from this generation forever." The reference to "this generation" has the rebels in view, the kind of people who seek to throw off the "bonds" and "ropes" they feel the Lord has put upon them (cf. 2:3).[67]

## 12:8 (MT 12:9), The Strutting Wicked

Psalm 12:8 (MT 12:9) complements the depiction of the scene in 12:1 (MT 12:2). In 12:1 (MT 12:2) the king and his faithful people are on the wane while the wicked wax, and this waxing strong of the wicked is articulated in 12:8 (MT 12:9). David says in 12:8a (MT 12:9a) that the wicked walk around on every side, as though their numbers are increasing, enabling them to surround the righteous. The circumstances that enable the wicked to flex and strut are put succinctly in 12:8b (MT 12:9b), as the prowling of the wicked takes place in accordance with the exaltation of worthlessness (זלות is a *hapax legomenon*) among the sons of man.

### BRIDGE

We still live in the world described in Ps 12. The psalm's statements apply as easily to Jerusalem with Absalom on the rise and David fleeing the city as they do today when people say that this world evolved out of nothing rather than having been created by God, when people say that two men or two women can marry and those who say otherwise are bigots, and when all manner of rebels against God and Christ think that their ability to persuade people will enable them to overcome the Lord himself. As then so now: the Lord's declaration that he will arise to deliver his persecuted and prosecuted faithful is more valuable to believers than the

---

[67] The first-person pronominal suffix in 12:7b (MT 12:8b) is plural, "you will keep them," and the second is singular, "you will deliver him." I have taken these to refer to Yahweh's words and Yahweh's king. The ESV reads the second suffix as a first-person plural, "you will guard us," which is a valid reading of the text. The CSB renders the first as a first-person plural, which is not a valid reading of the text as it stands, and takes the second suffix the same way, "You ... will guard us; You will protect us" (so also NIV 1984). The NIV 2011 takes the first suffix as a reference to the needy and the second as a first-person plural: "You ... will keep the needy ... and will protect us."

purest silver. God's words are true and pure, and he himself will enforce them. That is the message of Ps 12, and that is our hope today.

## Psalm 13

OVERVIEW AND STRUCTURE OF PSALM 13

Psalm 13 opens with a series of four interrogative statements, each beginning with "how long?" (13:1–2 [MT 13:2–3]). David then presents three requests to the Lord in 13:3 (MT 13:4): (1) take note, (2) answer me, and (3) enlighten my eyes. Those three requests are matched by three reasons the Lord should grant them in 13:3–4 (MT 13:4–5): (1) lest David die, (2) lest his enemies boast that they have prevailed over him, and (3) lest they rejoice when he totters. David closes with three assertions of what he does in 13:5–6 (MT 13:6): (1) he trusts in the Lord's lovingkindness, (2) he rejoices in the Lord's salvation, and (3) he sings to the Lord in response to his bountiful treatment.

> 13:1–2 (MT 13:2–3), How Long? Four Times
> 13:3–4 (MT 13:4–5), Three Requests and Three Reasons
> 13:5–6 (MT 13:6), Three Things David Does

SCRIPTURE

| CSB | Author's translation |
|---|---|
| For the choir director. A psalm of David. | [1] For the Preeminent One. A Psalm of David. |
| [1] How long, LORD? Will you forget me forever?<br>How long will you hide your face from me? | [2] How long, O Yahweh, will you forget me forever?<br>How long will you hide your face from me? |
| [2] How long will I store up anxious concerns within me,<br>agony in my mind every day?<br>How long will my enemy dominate me? | [3] How long will I put counsels in my soul,<br>agony in my heart daily.<br>How long will the one at enmity with me be lifted up over me? |
| [3] Consider me and answer, LORD my God.<br>Restore brightness to my eyes;<br>otherwise, I will sleep in death. | [4] Take note; answer me, O Yahweh my God!<br>Enlighten my eyes lest I sleep the death, |

⁴ My enemy will say, "I have triumphed over him,"
and my foes will rejoice because I am shaken.

⁵ But I have trusted in your faithful love;
my heart will rejoice in your deliverance.
⁶ I will sing to the Lord
because he has treated me generously.

⁵ lest the one at enmity with me say, "I have prevailed over him!"
My adversaries will rejoice if I totter.

⁶ But as for me, in your lovingkindess I trust.
Let my heart rejoice in your salvation.
I will sing to Yahweh because he dealt bountifully with me.

CONTEXT: VERBAL AND THEMATIC LINKS WITH SURROUNDING PSALMS

13:1 (2x), 2 (2x) (MT 13:2, 3) "How long?" עד אנה
6:3 (MT 6:4) "How long?" עד מתי

13:1 (MT 13:2) "How long ... will you forget me forever?"
9:12 (MT 9:13) "he will not forget the cry of the afflicted"
9:18 (MT 9:19) "not forever will the needy be forgotten"
10:11 "[the wicked] says in his heart, 'God has forgotten' "
10:12 "Do not forget the afflicted"

13:1 (MT 13:2) "How long will you hide your face from me?"
10:11 "[the wicked] says in his heart, 'God ... has hidden his face' "

13:1 (MT 13:2) "your face"
Compare 4:6 (MT 4:7); 9:3, 19 (MT 9:4, 20); 10:11; 11:7

13:2 (MT 13:3) "counsels"
1:1 "counsel"

13:3 (MT 13:4) "Take note"
10:14 "you note"

13:3 (MT 13:4) "answer me"
3:4 (MT 3:5) "he answered me"
4:1 (MT 4:2) "answer me"

13:3 (MT 13:4) "Enlighten my eyes"
4:6 (MT 4:7) "Lift up the light of your face"

13:3 (MT 13:4) "lest I sleep the death"
6:5 (MT 6:6) "For there is no remembrance of you in death"
9:13 (MT 9:14) "you who lift me up from the gates of death"

13:4 (MT 13:5) "My adversaries will rejoice"
13:5 (MT 13:6) "Let my heart rejoice in your salvation"
2:11 "rejoice with trembling"
9:14 (MT 9:15) "I will rejoice in your salvation"

13:5 (MT 13:6) "I trust"
Compare 4:5, 8 (MT 4:6, 9); 9:10 (MT 9:11)

13:5 (MT 13:6) "in your lovingkindness"
Compare 5:7 (MT 5:8); 6:4 (MT 6:5);

13:5 (MT 13:6) "your salvation"
Compare 3:2, 8 (MT 3:3, 9); 9:14 (MT 9:15); 14:7

13:6 "I will sing to Yahweh"
7:ss (MT 7:1) "he sang to Yahweh"

EXPOSITION

### 13:1–2 (MT 13:2–3), How Long? Four Times

Given the Lord's promise to rise up and save the afflicted and needy in 12:5 (MT 12:6), the questions of "how long?" that open Ps 13 are a natural response. Asking "how long?" assumes that the Lord will do what he said. The only question is how long the psalmist will have to wait. The psalmist knows that Yahweh loves his people and that Yahweh's own reputation is at stake in the lives of his people, so the psalmist knows that Yahweh cares about the very concerns he raises in 13:1–2 (MT 13:2–3). David asks how long he has to wait until the Lord addresses concerns David knows the Lord also has. David's questions, then, seem designed to motivate the Lord to do what he knows the Lord wants to do.

David has already confessed that the Lord will not forget the afflicted forever (9:12, 18 [MT 9:13, 19]), so complementing the question "how long?" with the question of whether the Lord will forget him forever (13:1a [MT 13:2a]) urges the Lord to act. Similarly, in Ps 10:11 the wicked said in his heart that God "has hidden his face" and will not see, which David knows the Lord has not done because 10:14 asserts the Lord does see. So for David to ask how long the Lord will hide his face (13:1b [MT 13:2b]) is also designed to prompt the Lord to intervene as he said he would in 12:5 (MT 12:6). David then asks how long he must agonize and counsel himself over the Lord's delay (13:2a [MT 13:3a]), and how long the one at enmity will be exalted over him (13:2b [MT 13:3b]).

### 13:3–4 (MT 13:4–5), Three Requests and Three Reasons

Having posed his four motivations for the Lord to act in the form of "how long?" questions in 13:1–2 (MT 13:2–3]), David states the three things he wants Yahweh to do in 13:3a. First, David wants the Lord to "take note"—to see the things David is enduring that he has articulated in 13:1–2 (MT 13:2–3). Second, David wants the Lord to "answer me!" And third, David wants the Lord to enlighten his eyes, which is akin to the plea in 4:6 (MT 4:7) for the Lord to lift up the light of his face upon his people (cf. Num 6:24–26).

David accompanies his three requests by articulating three things he knows the Lord does not want to happen in Ps 13:3b–4 (MT 13:4b–5). He knows the Lord does not want the enemy to kill him, so he pleads with the Lord to act lest he sleep the sleep of death (13:3b [MT 13:4b]). He knows that the Lord's own reputation is bound up with how he himself fares, so he pleads with the Lord to act lest the one at enmity boast that he has prevailed over David (13:4a [MT 13:5a]). And finally, David knows that the Lord does not want the enemy to rejoice because David has been shaken, so he pleads with the Lord to prevent that as well (13:4b [MT 13:5b]).

### 13:5–6 (MT 13:6), Three Things David Does

The three things David does in 13:5–6 (MT 13:6) proclaim that his question is neither whether the Lord will act nor whether he can prevail when he does but only *when* the Lord will go into action (cf. 13:1–2 [MT 13:2–3]). David asserts that until the Lord goes into action, he will trust the Lord's lovingkindness, rejoice in the salvation the Lord will accomplish, and sing to Yahweh because of the way Yahweh has treated him (13:5–6 [MT 13:6]).

David does not accuse the Lord, complain about his circumstances, or doubt God's goodness, ability, or concern. Rather, David trusts, rejoices in hope, and sings Yahweh's praise. And this that David does at the end of the psalm is not in conflict with the "how long?" questions he raised at the beginning. Those questions present the Lord's own concerns to the

Lord in full confidence that the Lord will act on them. Like the rest of Ps 13, those opening questions appeal to the Lord's own concerns, reflect the Lord's own priorities, and seek the Lord's own kingdom.

BRIDGE

The sentiments communicated in this psalm asking "how long?" are the same that we see when Paul blesses all who love the appearing of the Lord (2 Tim 4:8), felt by those waiting for the revealing of the Lord Jesus (1 Cor 1:7; 1 Thess 1:10), who will save those eagerly anticipating his return (Heb 9:28). Christians, therefore, rightly identify with David and pray his words, calling on the Lord to act on our behalf, yearning, trusting, rejoicing, singing, and seeking to hasten the day (2 Pet 3:12).

## Psalm 14

OVERVIEW AND STRUCTURE OF PSALM 14

Psalm 14 falls into three parts. The first, 14:1–3, contemplates the folly and wickedness of those who rebel against Yahweh and against his anointed (cf. 2:1–3). The second, 14:4–6, reflects on the culpability and coming judgment of the wicked. The third, 14:7, asks who will give the salvation that will cause gladness and rejoicing for God's people.

> 14:1–3, Folly and Wickedness
> 14:4–6, Culpability and Judgment
> 14:7, Salvation and Gladness

SCRIPTURE

CSB

For the choir director. Of David.

¹The fool says in his heart, "There's no God."
They are corrupt; they do vile deeds.
There is no one who does good.
²The LORD looks down from heaven on the human race
to see if there is one who is wise,
one who seeks God.

Author's translation

For the Preeminent One.
Of David.

The fool says in his heart, "There is no God."
They despoil.
They do abominable work.
There is no one who does good.

²Yahweh from the heavens looks down on the sons of Adam,

³ All have turned away;
all alike have become corrupt.
There is no one who does good,
not even one.

⁴ Will evildoers never understand?
They consume my people as they
   consume bread;
they do not call on the LORD.

⁵ Then they will be filled with dread,
for God is with those who are
   righteous.
⁶ You sinners frustrate the plans of the
   oppressed,
but the LORD is his refuge.

⁷ Oh, that Israel's deliverance would
   come from Zion!
When the LORD restores the fortunes of
   his people,
let Jacob rejoice, let Israel be glad.

to see if there is anyone causing
   wisdom, seeking God.

³ The whole have turned aside.
Together they are corrupted.
There is no one who does good, not
   even one.

⁴ Do they not know, all workers of
   iniquity,
the ones who eat my people like they
   eat bread?
On Yahweh they do not call.

⁵ There they dread with dread,
for God is with the generation of the
   righteous.

⁶ The counsel of the afflicted you all
   put to shame,
but Yahweh is his refuge.

⁷ Who will give from Zion salvation
   for Israel?
When Yahweh restores the captivity
   of his people,
Jacob will rejoice.
Israel will be glad.

CONTEXT: VERBAL AND THEMATIC LINKS WITH SURROUNDING PSALMS

14:1 "The fool says in his heart"
10:6, 11, 13 "he says in his heart"

14:1 (cf. 53:2) "there is no God" אין אלהים
10:4 "there is no God" אין אלהים

14:1 "They do abominable work" התעיבו עלילה
5:6 (MT 5:7) "The man of bloodshed and deceit you abominate,
   O Yahweh" יתעב

14:2 "Yahweh from the heavens looks down"
11:4 "Yahweh, in the heavens is his throne"
Compare 2:4; 9:4, 7 (MT 9:5, 8)

14:2 "the sons of Adam"
12:1 (MT 12:2) "the sons of Adam"
11:4 "the sons of Adam"

14:2 "to see if there is anyone causing wisdom"
2:10 "cause yourselves to be wise"

14:2 "seeking God"
10:4 "does not seek [Yahweh]"
9:10 (MT 9:11) "you have not forsaken those who seek you"
Compare 9:11, 13; 10:13, 15

14:4 "all workers of iniquity"
5:5 (MT 5:6) "all workers of iniquity"
6:8 (MT 6:9) "all workers of iniquity"

14:4 "On Yahweh they do not call"
3:4 (MT 3:5) "I called, and he answered me"
4:1 (MT 4:2) "When I call, answer me"
4:3 (MT 4:4) "Yahweh will hear when I call to him"

14:5 "God is with the generation of the righteous"
Compare 12:7 (MT 12:8) "this generation" (the wicked one)

14:6 "The counsel of the afflicted"
13:2 (MT 13:3) "How long will I put counsels in my soul?"

14:7 "Who will give from Zion salvation for Israel?"
12:5 (MT 12:6) "I will put him in the salvation for which he
     pants"

14:7 "Jacob will rejoice"
Compare 2:11; 9:14 (MT 9:15); 13:5 (MT 13:6)

14:7 "Israel will be glad"
5:11 (MT 5:12); 9:2 (MT 9:3)

EXPOSITION

Psalm 14 rounds out the unit of psalms that opened with Ps 10, with the
links herein to Ps 9 tying the unit consisting of Pss 3–9 to that of 10–14.
After the prayer in Ps 13 that called on the Lord to rise up and save as he
said he would in Ps 12 because of the threats of the rebels in Ps 11, Ps 14

reflects on the foolishness and corruption of the wicked that makes them culpable and will bring about their certain judgment, through which the king from David's line, with all those aligned with him, will be saved.

## 14:1–3, Folly and Wickedness

The arrangement of the sentiments in Ps 14:1–3 creates the impression that David's perspective is the Lord's perspective. David achieves this effect by opening the psalm with his assessment of the wicked in 14:1, then noting how Yahweh also assesses the wicked in 14:2, with Yahweh arriving at the same conclusions in 14:3 that David had articulated in 14:1.

The assessment of the wicked in Ps 14:1–3 is undiplomatic and unsympathetic. David makes no attempt here to justify the wicked, no attempt to suggest that the people of God share some responsibility for the way the wicked have rejected God, and no attempt to soften words of condemnation directed at those who set themselves against Yahweh and his anointed (cf. 2:1–3).

Psalm 14:1 describes what the fool says in his heart (cf. 10:6, 11, 13). As a man thinks in his heart, so he is (Prov 23:7). The psalm starts with what the fool thinks to himself, and what he asserts to himself is that there is no God. This leads naturally to what the fool does, and there is nothing good in it. The fool despoils and does abominable deeds, prompting the assertion that no one who thinks this way does good.

For David, there are no neutral places, no intermediate alternatives between devotion to Yahweh and rebellion against him. There is no in between. There is only wisdom and folly, obedience and rebellion, boasting in the Lord or boasting in one's own sinful desires (cf. Ps 10:3).

Anyone who rejects Yahweh is a fool. Those who reject Yahweh cause the world to be ruined; they commit abominations; and they do nothing good.

Having offered his own assessment of the wicked in 14:1, David writes in 14:2 that Yahweh looks down from heaven on the sons of Adam to see if anyone obeys Ps 2:12 and cultivates the kind of wisdom that produces human flourishing and prosperity, which is to say, to see if anyone seeks God.[68] The reference to the "generation of the righteous" in 14:5 clarifies

---

[68] On Yahweh looking down from heaven Wenham, *Psalms as Torah*, 121, hears echoes of the Lord looking down on Sodom in Gen 18:16 and of him coming down to see the tower the children of man had built in Gen 11:5.

that the people under consideration in 14:1–3 are those who are in rebellion against the Lord and his king, not those who are aligned with David
in submission to Yahweh.

As Yahweh considers the rebels in 14:2, the conclusion he reaches in
14:3 matches David's in 14:1. Rather than follow the Lord and stay on the
path he set before them, they have "turned aside" (14:3a). Rather than
seek to be purified by means of obedience, faith, and perseverance, "they
are corrupted" (14:3b). And then 14:3c repeats 14:1d, "There is no one
who does good," adding, "not even one" (14:3).

David and Yahweh, then, join together on the conclusion that the rebels are foolish, wayward, and corrupting, with none of them doing good.

### 14:4–6, Culpability and Judgment

The rebels were warned in 2:10–12 and admonished in 4:2–5 (MT 4:3–6).
When David commanded them to leave his presence in 6:8 (MT 6:9), he
addressed them as "all workers of iniquity." He references them with
the same phrase in 14:4a when he asks if they do not know. Within the
context of the Psalms, this crowd, the workers of iniquity, has received
fair warning. They should know, but what knowledge they have has not
prompted them to respond as they were urged to in 2:10–12. That they
devour the Lord's people like they eat bread (14:4b) means that they
take advantage of others to benefit themselves. That they do not call on
Yahweh (14:4c) means that they perceive no need for him, feel no fear of
him, and therefore do not seek him.

Psalm 14:5 envisions the time when they will fear Yahweh with a
profound sense of dread, perceiving that Yahweh is with the generation
of the righteous. The reference to the generation of the righteous in 14:5
stands in contrast with the generation from which Yahweh will deliver
the "lovingkind one" (12:7 [MT 12:8]). These two generations, the righteous generation and the wicked generation, are two kinds of people.[69]

Psalm 14:5 is framed as though the wicked have perceived God with
the generation of the righteous, as a result of which they feel the fear of
God. In Ps 14:6 the indictment of the wicked is addressed to them: they
shamed the afflicted by thwarting their plans, but Yahweh is the afflicted
man's refuge. The singular pronominal suffix in the phrase "his refuge"
likely points again to David himself, with whom the generation of the

---

[69] Thus informing what Jesus says about "this generation" in Matt 24:34 and parallels.

righteous are aligned. The relationship between David and his people, and the experiences of David and his people, typify the relationships and experiences of the Lord Jesus and those aligned with him.

### 14:7, Salvation and Gladness

David knows the answer to the question he asks in 14:7. The translations render the expression as a wish, "O that salvation would come," but the text can be rendered literally, "Who will give from Zion salvation for Israel?" That question invites reflection on the decree proclaimed in 2:7–9. When the descendant of David rises to rule, the question "how long?" (13:1–2 [MT 13:2–3]) will be answered, as will the question in 14:7. At that time Jacob indeed will be glad, rejoiced indeed will be Israel.

Bridge

They were fools then, and they are fools now. The awful judgment that awaits the persecutors and afflicters of God's people should prompt us to obey Jesus and pray for them, bless them, preach the gospel to them, and hope they will repent. The teaching of Jesus does not, however, call us to sympathize with evildoers, explain away their wickedness, or join them in the indictment of brothers and sisters in Christ. There is a strange impulse at work in some quarters that results in certain Christians being inclined to side with the wicked against other Christians. Psalm 14 does not teach us to do that. Psalm 14 teaches us that those who reject God and do wicked things are culpable for their folly and wickedness. The psalm also teaches us to say so. We do the wicked no favors if we do not warn them of the wrath to come.

## Psalm 15

Overview and Structure of Psalm 15

Psalm 15:1 raises the question of who will enjoy the presence of Yahweh. In answer the psalm describes what the blameless man does and does not do (15:2–3), how he regards and relates to others (15:4), and how he resists the misuse of money (15:5). Psalm 15:1–3 addresses the blameless king's character, and 15:4–5 speaks to his relationships.[70]

---

[70] On the basis of grammatical forms and correspondences in meaning within Ps 15, Lloyd Barré proposes an interesting chiastic structure for Ps 15, "Recovering the Literary Structure of Psalm XV," *VT* 34 (1984): 207–11.

15:1–3, Character
15:4–5, Relationships

SCRIPTURE

CSB                                    Author's translation

A psalm of David.                      ¹ A Psalm of David.
                                       O Yahweh, who may sojourn in your
¹ LORD, who can dwell in your tent?        tent?
Who can live on your holy mountain?    Who may dwell on the mountain of
                                           your holiness?
² The one who lives blamelessly,
    practices righteousness,           ² He who walks in integrity,
and acknowledges the truth in his      a worker of righteousness,
    heart—                             who speaks truth in his heart.
³ who does not slander with his
    tongue,                            ³ He does not walk on his tongue.
who does not harm his friend           He does not do evil to his friend.
or discredit his neighbor,             And a reproach he does not take up
⁴ who despises the one rejected by the     against his neighbor.
    LORD
but honors those who fear the LORD,    ⁴ A despised person in his eyes is a
who keeps his word whatever the cost,      rejected person,
⁵ who does not lend his silver at      but those who fear Yahweh he will
    interest                               honor.
or take a bribe against the innocent—
the one who does these things will     He makes an oath to do harm and
    never be shaken.                       does not change.
                                       ⁵ His silver he does not give on
                                           interest,
                                       and a bribe against the innocent he
                                           does not take.

                                       Doing these things, he will not totter
                                           to the age.

CONTEXT: VERBAL AND THEMATIC LINKS WITH SURROUNDING PSALMS

Psalm 15 opens with a question that sets up a comparison and contrast
with the previous psalms—the reflections on the wicked and their ways
in Pss 10–14. The fools who say in their hearts that there is no God (10:4, 6,
11, 13; 14:1), who taunt the righteous (11:1–3), plunder the poor (12:5), and
make the righteous cry "how long?" (13:1–2) *will not* abide in Yahweh's
presence. Psalm 15:1, therefore, asks who *will* dwell with Yahweh.

If we ask what motivates the Ps 15 blameless man to relate rightly to God, neighbor, and money, we find answers in Pss 16 and 17.

15:1 "who may sojourn in your tent?"
5:4 (MT 5:5) "no evil will sojourn with you"

15:1 "the mountain of your holiness"
2:6 "I have installed my king on Zion, the mountain of my holiness"
3:4 (MT 3:5) "he answered me from the mountain of his holiness"
11:1 "Flutter to your mountain, O bird."

15:2 "He who walks in integrity"
1:1 "who does not walk in the counsel of the wicked"
Compare 15:3 "He does not walk on his tongue" לא רגל על לשנו

15:2 "does righteousness" פעל צדק
5:5 (MT 5:6); 6:8 (MT 6:9); 14:4 "workers of iniquity" פעלי און

15:2 "speaks truth in his heart"
Compare 10:6, 11, 13; 14:1 [the fool/the wicked] "says in his heart"

15:3 "He does not walk on his tongue"
5:9 (MT 5:10) "Their tongues cause slipperiness"
10:7 "Under his tongue are labor and iniquity"
12:3–4 (MT 12:4–5) "tongue speaking great things. ... With our tongue we will prevail"

15:4 "A despised person in his eyes is a rejected person"
Compare 10:3 "the one who cuts in greed he has blessed"

15:4 "those who fear Yahweh he will honor"
Compare 16:3 "the holy ones ... and the majestic ... all my delight is in them"

15:4 "He makes an oath to do harm and does not change"
Compare 10:7 "An oath fills his mouth with treacheries and oppression."

15:5 "a bribe against the innocent he does not take"
Compare 10:8 "he murders the innocent"

15:5 "he will never totter"
Compare 10:6; 13:4 (MT 13:5); 16:8; 17:5

We have seen that Pss 1–2 introduce the Psalter, followed by Pss 3–9 responding to Absalom's revolt, then 10–14 contemplating the ways of the wicked. Psalms 15–24 turn to consider the ways of the righteous king. The character that enables him to enter Yahweh's presence is described in Pss 15 and 24, the way that Yahweh satisfies him in 16 and 23, the confidence in and need for resurrection life in 17 and 22, the way the Lord delivers in 18 and 20–21, and the glory of Yahweh's general and special revelation is celebrated in Ps 19. This section of Psalms, then, can be seen to have the following chiastic structure:

Psalm 15, The Holy King
    Psalm 16, Yahweh Satisfies
        Psalm 17, Resurrection Confidence
            Psalm 18, Yahweh Delivers
                Psalm 19, Glorious General and Special Revelation
            Psalms 20–21, Yahweh Delivers
        Psalm 22, Need for Resurrection
    Psalm 23, Yahweh Satisfies
Psalm 24, The Holy King

EXPOSITION

**15:1–3, Character**
Yahweh asserted in 2:6, "I have installed my king on Zion, the mountain of my holiness." David likewise averred in 5:4 (MT 5:5), "No evil will sojourn with you." Elements of these two statements are combined when David asks in 15:1,

> "O Yahweh, who may *sojourn* in your tent?
> Who may dwell on the *mountain of your holiness*?"

The question pertains in general to what kind of people can enter Yahweh's presence and remain with him, but given the resonance with the statement in 2:6, the question is particularly interested in the character of the king who will lead God's people into God's presence, there to abide in his glory.

The rest of the psalm describes the king's character (15:2–3) and how he relates to others (15:4–5), with a final assertion that the one who lives this way will never be shaken (15:5c). The three things the king does in 15:2,

1. He who walks in integrity
2. and does righteousness
3. and speaks truth in his heart,

are matched by three things the king does not do in 15:3,

1. He does not walk on his tongue.
2. He does not do evil to his friend.
3. And a reproach he does not take up against his neighbor.

The parallelism between these statements is more apparent if 15:3a is rendered literally, with the term רגל rendered as "walk" (a verb derived from the noun for "foot") rather than the figure of speech being translated "slander" or the like. In our culture we speak of "running people down" with our comments. Apparently in David's day the same could be accomplished by "walking on one's tongue," and this recalls the boasts of 12:4 (MT 12:5), "With our tongue we will prevail! Our lips are with us, who is lord over us?" Those who ask such questions intend to walk on their tongues.

To walk in integrity (15:2a) by contrast is to walk in wholeness, blamelessness, with all the pieces of life corresponding to one another and in harmony. No jarring discord results from one's actual *deeds* being in a different key from one's *words*. It is not hard to imagine a king of Israel insisting on his devotion to Torah before a religious crowd, only to exploit every loophole he can find to benefit his cronies. That would be the opposite of walking in integrity. We might say such a king walks on his tongue, but Ps 15 says such a king cannot sojourn in Yahweh's tent or dwell on his holy mountain

Along these lines, the righteous king does righteousness (15:2b) not evil (15:3b) to his friends.[71] The righteous king who can enter Yahweh's presence is one who treats others how he wants to be treated rather than disregarding how others want to be treated to get what he wants.

We have seen several references to what wicked fools say in their hearts (cf. 10:6, 11, 13; 14:1). All these statements show us how bad people justify their actions to themselves, how they fight off the pangs of conscience and steel themselves against the fear of God. In contrast with this, the righteous king "speaks truth in his heart" (15:2c). He meditates on the Torah day and night (1:2), and he operates in reality as the Bible defines it. He tells himself the truth, not lies. When he is tempted to sin, he does not tell his own heart the lie that this will lead to a stolen pleasure for which he will go unpunished. Rather, he tells his heart the truth, that sin is like diving off a pier into shark-infested water, asking the beasts to bite.

This last item in 15:2 corresponds to the last item in 15:3 because often if we are to take up a reproach against our neighbors we must tell ourselves a series of lies. We must tell ourselves that we are better than we really are and that our neighbors are worse than they really are in order to justify the righteous indignation necessary to take up a reproach against them. If we see our neighbors do something worthy of reproach and recognize in ourselves the inclination to do the same thing, we are less likely to reproach and more likely to admonish with gentle love. If we see our neighbors do something worthy of reproach but also see a young man who never had a father, never heard the gospel, and never had his sinful instincts lovingly disciplined, we will be more inclined to intervene with compassion than with reproach. The righteous king in Ps 15 speaks truth in his heart, and he does not take up unjust reproaches against his neighbor.

These statements in Ps 15:2–3 speak to the king's righteous way of life, and that way of life flows out of the king's character. If we work back from character we find habits, and habits are built out of individual choices. Individual choices result from what we desire. We will see what the righteous king of Ps 15 desires in Ps 16, and what he desires

---

[71] The psalmist has repeatedly referenced his own or God's righteousness (4:1 [MT 4:2], 5 [MT 4:6]; 7:8 [MT 7:9], 17 [MT 7:18]; 9:4 [MT 9:5], 8 [MT 9:9]; cf. 17:1, 15).

determines what he chooses, and those choices become habits, the habits forming character. Character, in turn, operates in all our relationships with others. Having summarized the king's character in 15:1–3, David shows his character in action in relationship with others in 15:4–5.

## 15:4–5, Relationships

There is a direct connection between character and the evaluation of other people. In Israel, a "despised person" should be despised because of the way he profanes God's holiness and harms other people. This assumes, of course, that the Bible defines holiness—sexual chastity, for instance—and that the Bible defines harm. Thus it is not harmful to uphold the sexual morality that God has built into creation and outlined in the Bible. What is harmful is to engage in any kind of sexual activity outside of one man and one woman in covenant marriage, using other people for your own sexual gratification, flaunting God's commands, defiling yourself, inciting God's wrath. Such behavior is despicable. Because of the character of the righteous king, Ps 15:4 declares that he rejects those who should be despised.

This is not a cruel rejection but a righteous response to unrepentant wickedness. It is the opposite of the way the wicked man blesses those who take advantage of others in Ps 10:3 and spurns Yahweh.

In our culture, beautiful young women are being exploited in movies, on billboards, in magazines, and all over the internet. Our response to the images of these women tells us whether in our eyes "a despised person is a rejected person" (15:4a). If your heart soars in response to the images, you are blessing the despised people who exploit attractive, naïve, vulnerable, foolish girls. To reject the despised person is to refuse to indulge in the sins they promote.

The righteous king rejects despised people (15:4a), and he honors those who fear Yahweh (15:4b). Sometimes wicked people are styled as bold, courageous, and interesting, while holy people are seen as restrictive, dour, and boring. Think of the reputation the Puritans have. Our priorities are reflected in our evaluation of people. If the Lord is our priority, and we will see in Ps 16 that the Lord is the righteous king's priority, then holy people who fear God will be interesting, courageous, and exciting to us. If sinful gratification is our priority, then we will be enamored with those who dive into shark-infested waters, encouraging us to try it too. How we respond to people reveals our priorities, and our priorities reveal our character.

Whereas the wicked man in Ps 10:7 had a mouth full of oaths that came with treacheries and oppression—meaning that he betrayed the vows he made and oppressed anyone he could—we read in Ps 15:4c of the way that the righteous king uses an oath formula and keeps his word. The statement, "He makes an oath to do harm," typically rendered, "He swears to his own hurt" (KJV, NAS), probably refers to oath formulas. When making such statements, the one swearing would do something like cut an animal in half, then declare, "may this be done to me if I fail to keep this covenant." The swearing to one's own hurt, or "to do harm," probably refers to the threat made in the making of the covenant. The righteous king "does not change" in that he keeps the covenant and accepts the consequences that come with it. He does not make a promise to get what he wants, only to break the promise when it becomes inconvenient to keep it.

The law of Moses repeatedly prohibits lending money at interest to fellow Israelites (Exod 22:25 [MT 22:24]; Lev 25:36–37; Deut 23:19–20 [MT 23:20–21]; cf. Prov 28:8). Psalm 15:5a declares that the righteous king keeps the Torah. He does not take financial advantage of those who are in need but fears God and obeys God's instructions. Similarly, Torah repeatedly forbids taking bribes to pervert justice (Exod 23:8; Deut 10:17; 16:19; 27:25; cf. 1 Sam 8:3). Psalm 15:5b declares that the righteous king refuses to sell justice for filthy lucre. He cares more about Yahweh and the innocent than the coins he could gain by trading away the Lord and the weak.

Psalm 15:5c asserts that those who possess this character and relate to others this way will not walk on feeble legs over thin ice but will be on firm ground with healthy knees.

### Bridge

As I have indicated above, the rationale for the behaviors described in Ps 15 will be given in Ps 16, where we see that the psalmist lives for the satisfaction found in God's presence. The lifestyle of Ps 15, then, is a lifestyle that refuses the kinds of instant pleasure that lead to long-term pain in favor of temporary sacrifices that lead to lasting satisfaction. In other words, Ps 15 declares that the righteous king embraces the delayed gratification associated with righteous living. He is willing to wait for the reward of righteousness rather than experience the thrill of the shark pool only to be eaten alive because of his wicked foolishness.

Psalm 15 is a convicting series of statements. We Christian readers of the psalm have shown ourselves no more able to live up to its standards of blamelessness than its own author, David. David himself sinned grievously, failing to walk in integrity, doing evil to Uriah, telling his own heart lies. The psalm, then, exposes the reality that were it not for Jesus, the answer to the opening question, "Who may?" would be: no one.

This psalm gives us another occasion to rejoice in the Righteous One, the only man of whom these words ring true, the Lord Jesus, who knew no sin. Once we have seen the glory of the obedience of Jesus, we begin to desire to be like him. How does that work?

If only those who live as Ps 15 describes can sojourn in Yahweh's tent and dwell on his holy mountain (15:1), think what kind of place that must be. Words that describe that fair and happy land include the following: safe, true, loving, kind, uninhibited—this would seem to be the kind of place where one could live naked and unashamed, with no fear of being exploited or mocked or attacked, no fear of being a stumbling block or a distraction. The kind of place where people live this way is the kind of place where the inhabitants have pure hearts and clean hands, where every motive is right, every thought righteous, and every impulse loving.

## Psalm 16

Overview and Structure of Psalm 16

After the plea to God to protect him because he has taken refuge in him, David reflects on the love of God and neighbor in Ps 16:1–4. He expostulates on the way that knowing God results in satisfaction and joy in 16:5–9, before concluding with assertions that God raises the dead and gives fullness of gladness in 16:10–11.

> 16:1–4, The Two Great Commandments
> 16:5–9, Knowing God Results in Satisfaction and Joy
> 16:10–11, God Raises the Dead and Gives Gladness

CSB

Author's translation

A *Miktam* of David.

¹ A *Miktam* of David.
Keep me, O God, because I have taken
    refuge in you.

¹ Protect me, God, for I take refuge in
    you.
² I said to the LORD, "You are my Lord;
I have nothing good besides you."
³ As for the holy people who are in the
    land,
they are the noble ones.
All my delight is in them.
⁴ The sorrows of those who take
    another god
for themselves will multiply;
I will not pour out their drink
    offerings of blood,
and I will not speak their names with
    my lips.

² I say to Yahweh,
"You are my Lord.
My good things are not over you."
³ As for the holy ones who are in the
    land,
they and the majestic ones,
all my delight is in them.
⁴ They multiply their pains who run
    after another.
I will not pour out their drink
    offerings of blood,
and I will not take their names on my
    lips.

⁵ LORD, you are my portion
and my cup of blessing;
you hold my future.
⁶ The boundary lines have fallen for
    me
in pleasant places;
indeed, I have a beautiful inheritance.

⁵ Yahweh is the portion of my
    territory and my cup!
You are the one who upholds my lot.
⁶ The lines fell to me in the pleasant
    places,
surely my inheritance is beautiful to
    me.
⁷ I bless Yahweh, who counsels me,
surely in the nights my guts correct
    me.

⁷ I will bless the LORD who counsels
    me—
even at night when my thoughts
    trouble me.
⁸ I always let the LORD guide me.
Because he is at my right hand,
I will not be shaken.

⁸ I have set Yahweh before me always,
because he is at my right hand I will
    not totter.
⁹ Therefore my heart is glad and my
    glory rejoices,
surely my flesh will dwell in safety.

⁹ Therefore my heart is glad
and my whole being rejoices;
my body also rests securely.
¹⁰ For you will not abandon me to
    Sheol;
you will not allow your faithful one to
    see decay.

¹⁰ For you will not forsake my soul to
    Sheol.
You will not give your lovingkind one
    to see the pit.
¹¹ You cause me to know the path of
    the living,

<sup>11</sup> You reveal the path of life to me;
in your presence is abundant joy;
at your right hand are eternal
pleasures.

satisfaction of gladnesses is your
  presence,
pleasures at your right hand forever.

CONTEXT: VERBAL AND THEMATIC LINKS WITH SURROUNDING PSALMS

16:1 "Keep me"
17:8 "Keep me"

16:1 "I have taken refuge in you"
Compare 2:12; 5:11 (MT 5:12); 7:1 (MT 7:2); 11:1; 17:7

16:2 "You are my Lord"
Compare 12:5 "Who is lord over us?"
See also 2:4; 8:1, 9 (MT 8:2, 10)

16:3 "all my delight is in them"
Compare 1:2; 5:4 (MT 5:5)

16:4 "I will not take their names on my lips"
17:1 "Hear my prayer, which is not from lips of deceit"
17:4 "by the word of your lips"

16:5 "Yahweh is the portion of my territory and my cup!"
11:6 "fire and brimstone and scorching wind the portion of
    their cup"

16:6 "my inheritance is beautiful to me"
2:8 "I will give the nations as your inheritance"

16:7 "I bless Yahweh"
10:3 "the one who cuts in greed he has blessed"

16:7 "who counsels me" יעצני
1:1 "who does not walk in the counsel of the wicked"
    בעצת רשעים

16:7 "in the nights my guts correct me"
1:2 "on his Torah he meditates day and night"
17:3 "you visit in the night"
2:10 "cause yourselves to prosper; receive correction"

16:8 "I have set Yahweh before me always"
10:5 "On high are your judgments from before him"

16:8 "I will not totter"
Compare 10:6; 13:4 (MT 13:5); 15:5; 17:5

16:9 "Therefore my heart is glad"
Compare 5:11 (MT 5:12); 9:2 (MT 9:3); 14:7
4:7 (MT 4:8) "you gave gladness in my heart"

16:9 "my glory rejoices"
Compare "rejoices" 2:11; 9:14 (MT 9:15); 13:4–5 (MT 13:5–6); 14:7
Compare "my glory" 3:3 (MT 3:4, Yahweh); 4:2 (MT 4:3); 7:5 (MT
    7:6, David's exalted position)

16:9 "my flesh will dwell in safety"
15:1 "Who may dwell on the mountain of your holiness?"
Compare 4:8 (MT 4:9) "in safety"

16:10 "you will not abandon my soul to Sheol"
9:10 (MT 9:11) "you have not forsaken those who seek you"
10:14 "To you the hapless abandons [his cause]"
Compare 6:5 (MT 6:6) "in Sheol who will give thanks to you?"
9:17 (MT 9:18) "The wicked will return to Sheol"

16:10 "your lovingkind one"
4:3 (MT 4:4) "Yahweh separated the lovingkind one for himself"
12:1 (MT 12:2) "the lovingkind one comes to an end"

16:11 "satisfaction of gladness"
17:14 "They are satisfied with sons"
17:15 "I will be satisfied"

16:11 "your presence"
4:6 (MT 4:7) "the light of your face"
9:19 (MT 9:20) "in your presence"
13:2 "How long will you hide your face from me?"

16:11 "at your right hand forever"
17:7 "at your right hand"

## 16:1–4, The Two Great Commandments

God put Adam in the garden to work and *keep* it in Gen 2:15, and in Ps 16:1 David prays that God would *keep* him, using the same term (שׁמר). Adam was to protect, defend, preserve, and guard the garden, and David calls on God to defend him from attacks that come from within or without. He declares that he has done what was urged on the kings in 2:12 and has "taken refuge" in Yahweh. Psalm 16:1 is a prayer, and in this prayer David declares to God that he looks to him as his refuge and keeper.

David then opens 16:2 with the words, "I say to Yahweh," and it appears that the rest of the psalm (16:2–11) constitutes what he says to the Lord.

Whereas the wicked asked in 12:5, "who is lord over us?" In 16:2 David says to Yahweh, "You are my Lord." The CSB renders the last phrase of 16:2, "I have nothing good besides you" (similarly ESV, NAS, NIV). The phrase could also be taken as I have rendered it, "My good things are not over you," meaning that David refuses to exalt anything over Yahweh. Either way, David asserts that he values Yahweh supremely.

Having confessed his submission and devotion to the Lord in 16:2, David speaks of his delight in godly people in 16:3. Psalm 16:3 elaborates on 15:4b, which spoke of honoring those who fear God. The people of God delight in one another because of our shared ultimate commitment to love God with all that we are. Love for God, which David articulated in 16:2, results in love for those who love God in 16:3. Because we love God those who scorn and despise him are offensive to us (cf. 15:4a). Because we love God, we appreciate those who honor God. It is natural to be delighted by those who share our ultimate commitment, and that ultimate commitment determines what we value, what we prioritize, what we seek to promote, and what we seek to discourage.

Just as Ps 15:4 spoke of those who were despised and those who were honored, the love for God's people in 16:3 is followed by comments on idolaters in 16:4. David explains that those who commit idolatry only make their own lives more painful. They commit idolatry hoping to help themselves, but by failing to be true to the Lord they only hurt themselves. David then asserts that he will not pour out their offerings of blood nor take their names on his lips. His refusal to speak their names indicates that rather than referring to the names of idolatrous people and the offerings they make, David seems to be referring to the false gods and the drink offerings of blood they require. In all this, David commits himself to obey the first commandment, placing no one and nothing before Yahweh, worshiping him alone.

In Ps 16:1–4, then, David prays for God to keep him obedient to the two greatest commandments: to love God and neighbor.

### 16:5–9, Knowing God Results in Satisfaction and Joy

Why would the righteous king in Ps 15 live the way he does? Why would David articulate the sympathies he does in Ps 16:1–4? Answers to those questions come in Ps 16:5–11. If Ps 15 prompts the question why anyone would live that way—why anyone would forgo pleasure to maintain integrity—Ps 16 answers that there is nothing better than Yahweh. If someone responds to Ps 15 with the assertion that nice guys finish last, the Bible's riposte is that bad guys go to hell, and Ps 16 asserts that good guys know and enjoy God.[72]

Using language familiar from the narratives of Joshua's conquest and allotment of territory to the tribes of Israel, David declares in 16:5–6 that Yahweh is the portion of his territory, who upholds his lot, saying that the boundary lines have marked out pleasant pastures as his, asserting that his inheritance of land is beautiful. The references to boundaries, inherited lands, and allotted portions, however, are metaphorical in 16:5–6, because David here states that Yahweh is his portion. It is as though David would claim Aaron's inheritance as his own.[73] In Num 18:20, "The Lord told Aaron, 'You will not have an inheritance in their land; there will be no portion among them for you. I am your portion and your inheritance among the Israelites' " (CSB).

By saying these things, David colors himself with a priestly, Aaronic hue, and this goes with the way he wore a linen ephod when the ark was brought into Jerusalem (2 Sam 6) and with Ps 110 to shade kingship in Israel with priestly overtones. Adam was a royal priest, Israel was to be a royal priesthood, and now King David speaks of his inheritance in priestly terms, anticipating the King who will come as the great high priest.

Whereas the wicked have "fire and brimstone and scorching wind" as "the portion of their cup" (11:6), David claims Yahweh as his portion

---

[72] This exchange reflects a comment made by Tom Nelson of Denton Bible Church at Southern Seminary chapel in the spring of 2015.

[73] Similarly Bullock, "Book 1," 34.

and cup (16:5a). Because Yahweh himself is his portion, Yahweh himself
is the one who upholds David's allotted territory, defending, guarding,
and maintaining it (16:5b). The lines have fallen to David in the pleasant
places because they mark out Yahweh as what David will inherit (16:6).

Our appreciation of what David says here can be deepened if we consider what land signified to an Israelite. The tribal allotment of ground
constituted his standing in society. The cultivation of that land would
produce his prosperity and become the foundation of his reputation. The
produce and pasturage of the land constituted his livelihood, providing
his food, giving a place for his family and an inheritance for his children.
David says that Yahweh is all this and more for him.

Yahweh made the world. To gain him is to gain the one who made
and controls everything, inventor of every pleasure, insurer of all safety,
definer of right and wrong, and rewarder of those who seek him. To lose
him, even if you gained the world in exchange, would be to lose everything because his wrath and displeasure await. Anyone seeking pleasure,
joy, satisfaction, and happiness should seek Yahweh.

Recognizing that God's word provides heart-mending truth, David
says in 16:7, "I bless Yahweh, who counsels me." David declares that God's
counsel is praiseworthy. I am inclined to think that the counsel of which
David speaks is God's word in the Bible because David speaks of his guts
correcting him in the night in 16:7b, Ps 1:2 speaks of meditating on the
Torah day and night, and in 17:3 he says to Yahweh, "You visit in the
night."[74] These statements indicate that as David reflects on the Torah
day and night, the Lord visits him, and God's biblical counsel corrects
any wayward inclinations he might feel.

In addition to the counsel of God's word in 16:7, David speaks in 16:8a
of making himself mindful of God's presence. He says that he has put
Yahweh before himself. This seems to point to the cultivation of an awareness of God. David reminds himself of God, makes himself conscious of
God, and lives his life before God. The strong connection between awareness of God and the blameless way is forged when David declares in 16:8b
that he will not totter because God is at his right hand. This recalls the
similar statement in 15:5c about the one who walks in integrity never

---

[74] Dan Phillips points out to me in private communication that in Ps 107:11 the phrase
"the words of God" (אמרי אל) is paralleled by "the counsel of the Most High" (עצת עליון),
and in 119:24 Yahweh's testimonies are referred to as "the men of my counsel" (אנשי עצתי).

tottering. The two belong together: those who are conscious of God live in the way that Ps 15 describes precisely because they fear God and are mindful of him, and thereby also they experience God's ongoing presence and protection.

The presence of God is a reward in itself. The presence of God demands virtue, which is also its own reward. Both God's presence and virtue also result in other rewards, such as freedom from guilt, remorse, fear of being found out, and fear of condemnation. To walk with God and know his goodness results in David saying in 16:9a that his heart is glad and his glory rejoices. In Ps 3:3 (MT 3:4) David identified Yahweh as his glory, but in 4:2 and 7:5 (MT 4:3 and 7:6) when David refers to his glory he appears to have his exalted position as Yahweh's king in mind. It seems, then, that for his heart to be glad and his glory to rejoice is for David to feel joy and gladness in his inner being and in his official position as Yahweh's anointed.[75] David then speaks in 16:9b of his flesh dwelling in safety, using the same term for "dwell" found in 15:1b, "Who may dwell on the mountain of your holiness?" Because the Lord is at his right hand, counseling him in the night (16:7–8), David can dwell on God's holy mountain in safety.

Why would anyone live as Ps 15 describes? Because they have experienced God as Ps 16 describes. The sensory temptations that would lead us away from God are exposed as the lying snares that they are. Imagine a situation where you were told that a beautiful but blinding light was about to be passed before your eyes. If you closed your eyes and refused to look, you would be able to see for the rest of your life, and your eyes would grow strong enough to enable you to look on that light eventually. If you open your eyes, however, and look, you will go blind. This is something like the temptation that confronted Adam, and he ate in his weakness, lack of imagination, stupidity, folly, and unbelief.

If the perspective of Ps 16 is ours, however, we will prefer the Lord to anything that would lead us away from him. We will resist temptation and close our eyes rather than sacrifice our sight for the fleeting look. The joy of knowing God in this life described in 16:5–9 is further complemented by the joy of knowing God in the resurrection in 16:10–11.

---

[75] The NET emends the text to arrive at a Hebrew homonym that means "liver," which would indicate that his heart and liver are glad and rejoice. This would fit with the flesh dwelling in safety in 16:9b. In the discussion above I have interpreted the MT as it stands.

## 16:10–11, God Raises the Dead and Gives Gladness

David had prayed to be delivered from death in 6:5 (MT 6:6), reminding the Lord that no one will give him thanks in Sheol. Now he asserts his confidence in 16:10 that his soul will not be abandoned in Sheol, nor will the Lord allow the man of his lovingkindness to see the pit. The reference to the soul not being abandoned to Sheol seems to point to David's spirit not being left there, while the statement that the man of God's loving-kindness will not be given to the pit seems to indicate bodily resurrection. David says that his soul will not be left to Sheol, and his body will not be left in the grave. He goes on to speak of the "paths of the living" in 16:11, and of the "satisfaction of gladness" that is God's presence, the "pleasures" at God's right hand forever. These everlasting pleasures at God's right hand, the fullness of joy in God's presence, and the path of life referenced in 16:11 would seem to be resurrection rewards.

Take just one experience of satisfaction we know in this life. Imagine being in the full sun of a scorching day with no wind, sweltering in the painful heat, only to be welcomed into the breezy shade at the edge of a forest, a cool wind moving, with a tall glass of ice water to greet you. The relief and satisfaction of the pleasure of ice water in the shade is a hint of the fullness of joy that awaits those who will be raised and welcomed into God's presence, there to know the pleasures to be had at his right hand.

### Bridge

Luke presents Peter quoting Ps 16:8–11 in Acts 2:25–28 with reference to the resurrection of Jesus. Peter introduces the quotation with the words, "David says concerning him" (Acts 2:25), but Peter quotes David speaking in the first person, "I saw the Lord always before me" (2:25, cf. 26–28). Having quoted the passage and noted that David's body remains in the tomb (2:29), Peter explains that David was a prophet and was mindful of the promises God had made to him in 2 Sam 7 (2:30), that David saw the future and spoke of Christ's resurrection (2:31), and that the passage is fulfilled in the resurrection of Jesus (2:32). Do these claims match what David actually says in Ps 16:8–11?

The crucial point is the phrase with which Luke presents Peter introducing the quotation of Ps 16:8–11, "David says concerning him" (Acts 2:25). David seems to be speaking *of himself* in the first person. In what sense can Peter assert that David is speaking *of the seed* God promised to raise up from his line?

If David understood himself as a pattern, or type, of the one to come, then *in speaking of himself,* David could have consciously been *speaking of the one to come.* In other words, David could have seen correspondences between figures such as Joseph and Moses and others, then noticed similar patterns in his own life. This could have produced in David the expectation that the promised king to come from his own body would live out the fulfillment of the patterns.

On this understanding, David could have been consciously describing his own experience as well as the pattern of experience he expected to be fulfilled in the life of the one to come. This is one way to account for David speaking in the first-person singular, apparently describing his own experience, and Peter claiming that David spoke concerning Jesus.

With the text of Ps 16:10–11 pointing to resurrection, Peter claims that Jesus has indeed been raised, while the body of David awaits future resurrection. The argument Luke presents Peter making is a sound one that respects the original context and meaning of the Old Testament passage he quotes.

## Psalm 17

Overview and Structure of Psalm 17

In Ps 17:1–7 David cries out to the Lord, pleading with the Lord to hear his just complaint (17:1–2), insisting that he has been blameless (17:3–5), and expressing confidence that God will hear and save (17:6–7). In 17:8–12 David calls on the Lord to protect him from his enemy, describing his vulnerability against the violent (17:8–9), the merciless prowling of the wicked (17:10–11), and likening the wicked to a lion (17:12). In 17:13–15 David beseeches the Lord to rise up and deliver him, making the request (17:13), and then contrasting the way the wicked live for this world with the way that he hopes to be vindicated at the resurrection (17:14–15).

> 17:1–7, Hear and Answer
> 17:8–12, Keep and Protect Me
> 17:13–15, Rise Up and Deliver Me

CSB

Author's translation

A prayer of David.

¹ A Prayer of David.

Hear, O Yahweh, righteousness.

¹ Lord, hear a just cause;
pay attention to my cry;
listen to my prayer—
from lips free of deceit.
² Let my vindication come from you,
for you see what is right.
³ You have tested my heart;
you have examined me at night.
You have tried me and found nothing
evil;
I have determined that my mouth will
not sin.
⁴ Concerning what people do:
by the words from your lips
I have avoided the ways of the violent.
⁵ My steps are on your paths;
my feet have not slipped.

⁶ I call on you, God,
because you will answer me;
listen closely to me; hear what I say.
⁷ Display the wonders of your faithful
love,
Savior of all who seek refuge
from those who rebel against your
right hand.
⁸ Protect me as the pupil of your eye;
hide me in the shadow of your wings
⁹ from the wicked who treat me
violently,
my deadly enemies who surround me.

¹⁰ They are uncaring;
their mouths speak arrogantly.
¹¹ They advance against me; now they
surround me.
They are determined
to throw me to the ground.
¹² They are like a lion eager to tear,
like a young lion lurking in ambush.

Give attention to my cry!
Give ear to my prayer, which is not
from lips of treachery.
² From before you let my judgment
go forth.
Let your eyes see uprightness.
³ You test my heart.
You visit in the night.
You refined me.
You found nothing.
I purposed that my mouth would not
transgress.
⁴ As for the works of man,
by the word of your lips
I kept [myself from] the paths of the
violent.
⁵ Holding my steps in your wagon
tracks
my footsteps do not totter.
⁶ I call to you because you answer me,
O God!
Incline your ear to me.
Hear my word.
⁷ Wondrously show your
lovingkindnesses,
savior of those who take refuge at
your right hand from those who
rise up.

⁸ Keep me as the pupil of the daughter
of the eye.
In the shadow of your wings you will
cause me to be hidden
⁹ from the presence of the wicked
who destroy me,
the ones at enmity with my soul.
They hem me in.
¹⁰ Their fat they close.
Their mouth speaks in majesty.
¹¹ Our steps, now they surround me.

¹³ Rise up, Lᴏʀᴅ!
Confront him; bring him down.
With your sword, save me from the
    wicked.
¹⁴ With your hand, Lᴏʀᴅ, save me from
    men,
from men of the world
whose portion is in this life:
You fill their bellies with what you
    have in store;
their sons are satisfied,
and they leave their surplus to their
    children.

¹⁵ But I will see your face in
    righteousness;
when I awake, I will be satisfied with
    your presence.

Their eyes they set to stretch on the
    ground.
¹² His likeness is as a lion; he will long
    to tear,
and like a young lion he sits in secret
    places.

¹³ Rise up, O Yahweh!
Confront his face.
Cause him to bow.
Deliver my soul from the wicked by
    your sword,
¹⁴ from men by your hand, O Yahweh,
    from men from the world:
their portion among the living,
and with your treasure you fill their
    belly.
They are satisfied with sons,
and they cause their excess to rest
    with their children.
¹⁵ As for me, in righteousness I will see
    your face;
I will be satisfied on waking with your
    likeness.

Cᴏɴᴛᴇxᴛ: Vᴇʀʙᴀʟ ᴀɴᴅ Tʜᴇᴍᴀᴛɪᴄ Lɪɴᴋs ᴡɪᴛʜ Sᴜʀʀᴏᴜɴᴅɪɴɢ Psᴀʟᴍs

17:1 "lips of deceit"
Compare 5:6 (MT 5:7); 10:7

17:3 "you visit in the night"
16:7 "in the nights my guts correct me"

17:3 "you found nothing" בל תמצא
10:15 "wickedness that will not be found" בל תמצא

17:4 "by the word of your lips I am kept from the paths of the
    violent"
Compare 1:1–2

17:5 "In your wagon tracks my footsteps"
23:3 "you lead me in the wagon tracks of righteousness"

17:7 "savior"
7:10 (MT 7:11) "savior"

17:7 "those who take refuge"
Compare 2:12; 5:11 (MT 5:12); 7:1 (MT 7:2); 11:1; 16:1

17:7 "at your right hand"
16:11 "at your right hand forever"

17:8 "Keep me"
16:1 "Keep me"

17:12 "His likeness is as a lion, he will long to tear"
7:2 (MT 7:3) "lest he tear my soul like a lion"
10:9 "like a lion in a thicket"
22:22 "save me from the mouth of the lion"

17:12 "in secret places"
10:8, 9 "in the secret places ... in the secret place"

17:13 "Rise up, O Yahweh!"
3:7; 7:6; 9:19; 10:12; 132:8 (MT 3:8; 7:7; 9:20)

17:13 "by your sword"
7:12 (MT 7:13) "If a man will not repent, he will sharpen his
    sword"

17:14 "their portion among the living"
11:6 "fire and brimstone and scorching wind the portion of
    their cup"
16:5 "Yahweh is the portion of my territory and my cup"

17:14 "They are satisfied with sons"
17:15 "I will be satisfied"
16:11 "satisfaction of gladness"

17:15 "in righteousness I will see your face"
11:7 "the upright will see his face"

EXPOSITION

## 17:1–7, Hear and Answer

The use of Ps 16 in Acts 2, discussed in the "Bridge" section at the end of
Ps 16 above, sheds light on the nature of David's prayer in Ps 17. David
seems to have composed these prayers not merely as a statement of his
own experience but also with an eye to his seed whom God promised

to raise up to reign forever. If we allow Luke's presentation of the use Peter made of Ps 16:8–11 in Acts 2 to inform our understanding of these psalms, we can suggest that David understood that his own prayers would pattern his greater son.

Psalm 17 is one of only two psalms bearing the superscription, "A prayer of David," the other being Psalm 86 (cf. 90:1, "A prayer of Moses"). In light of the superscription of Ps 18, which mentions David being delivered from Saul and all his enemies, Ps 17 should be read against the backdrop of David's perseverance through Saul's persecution narrated in 1 Samuel.

There are three movements in thought in Ps 17:1–7. In the first, David calls on the Lord in 17:1–2 to hear the justice of his cause and vindicate him. From there, David provides evidence for his case in 17:3–5, before stating his confidence that he will be heard and that the Lord is able to save in 17:6–7.

David utters a supplicatory imperative in Ps 17:1 as he commands Yahweh to hear. He has confessed Yahweh's righteousness (e.g., 7:17 [MT 7:18]), so he knows that he is talking about something in which Yahweh himself is invested. Assuming that the verbs and objects in 17:1 are parallel with one another, David calls on Yahweh to "hear," to "give attention," and to "cause to be heard," and what he wants to bring to Yahweh's ears are "righteousness," his "cry," and his "prayer." Paralleling "righteousness" with the references to David's "prayer" creates the impression both that David considers his cause just and that wickedness threatens that just cause.

David buttresses his appeal with the declaration that it does not come from deceitful lips. He is not redefining righteousness, looking for legal loopholes, misrepresenting his opponents, or oppressing those in the right. He speaks the truth in honesty.

David's righteousness, however, is relative. That is to say, from all we know of human experience and the book of Samuel, we can be confident that David claims neither entire perfection nor perfect obedience. He can, however, maintain that he did nothing subversive to Saul's kingship; he did nothing violent to bring about Saul's demise; and he did nothing malicious to the survivors of Saul's house. On those fronts, David was righteous, making all of Saul's persecution of David wicked and any accusations leveled against David after Saul's death false.

David does not want the kind of "vindication" that the wicked sometimes claim for themselves. David does not want laws to be broken, justice to be disregarded, or words to be redefined in his vindication. He calls on the Lord to let his vindication go out from the Lord's own presence in Ps 17:2a, meaning that David's vindication will correspond to truth, establish righteousness, and free the oppressed. When the Lord vindicates David in that way, the Lord's own eyes will behold uprightness, and David calls on the Lord to bring that about in 17:2b.

David supports the 17:1 claim that his cause is righteous by appeals to God's own evaluation of him and his character in 17:3, testimony to his devotion to God's word in 17:4, and a claim that he walked the blameless way in 17:5. David says in 17:3a that the Lord has tested his heart. David here reminds the Lord of the Lord's own evaluation of David's intellect, desires, emotions, and instincts. When David tells the Lord in 17:3b that he himself visited David at night, he seems to have in view the Lord's awareness that David has not used his nights to hatch secret plots, indulge hidden vices, or cultivate corruption under cover of darkness. David asserts that the Lord himself refined him (17:3c), that no dross was found (17:3d), and in keeping with this David says that he purposed in his heart not to transgress with his lips (17:3e). In act, speech, and motive, David avers he has done nothing for which the Lord should condemn him.

David explains the foundation of his integrity in 17:4, asserting that God's word kept him from the ways violent men would resolve the kinds of problems David faced. In accordance with the description of the blessed man in Ps 1, David here asserts that, among countless other possible sins, God's command not to murder kept him from solving the Saul problem that way; God's command not to bear false witness kept him from seditious speech; and God's command to honor father and mother kept him from anything that would disrespect the authority God had put over him. God's word kept David from violent attempts to improve his situation.

David's professed obedience to God's word in the Bible leads naturally to the assertion in 17:5 that rather than tread the "paths of the violent" his steps stayed on the "wagon tracks" of the Lord and thus his footing was firm. The imagery teaches that those who disobey are on slippery ground, that they will totter on unstable steps. By contrast, David asserts that his integrity in his dealings with Saul makes him confident and bold, not merely to walk, but to cry out to the Lord as he does in 17:6.

David states his certainty that the Lord will answer his call in 17:6a and calls on the Lord to hear in 17:6b. He can do these things because he has embraced what the Lord designated to be righteousness (17:1), because the Lord himself evaluated him (17:3), and because the Lord's word has kept him from transgression (17:4–5). There is no conflict between God's love and God's justice. In fact, for God to uphold his word and do justice is for him to show love. Thus David has been appealing to the Lord to show justice in 17:1–6, and in 17:7 he states that for the Lord to do so will be for him to show his lovingkindness in a way that will provoke wonder and admiration from those who experience God's love. The recipients of that love will be "those who take refuge at your right hand" (17:7b). What drove them to take refuge was the fact that their enemies were rising up against them. The Lord's right hand—the place of refuge in 17:7—was the place of everlasting pleasure in 16:11.

The Lord is so good, so powerful, so wise, and so comforting that moments of difficulty and crisis become moments in which God's people celebrate his reliability, his steadfast love, his comforting justice, and his faithfulness to his own word. For those who know him, it is a joy to call on him, and calling on him is enough. If the answer is delayed for the duration of one's earthly life, as David will attest in 17:15, hope will never fail.

### 17:8–12, Keep and Protect Me

David pled for justice in 17:1–7, and now in 17:8–12 he begs for protection from the wicked. David asks the Lord to protect him the way that we protect the most sensitive parts of our bodies, saying, "Keep me as the pupil of the daughter of the eye" (17:8a).[76] We instinctively shield our eyes, and the reference to the "daughter" of the eye brings in connotations of a vulnerable, delicate, female child, one whom a loving father would protect with his very life. David next calls on the Lord to hide him in the shadow of his wings (17:8b).[77] Ruth asked Boaz to spread his wings over her (Ruth 3:9; cf. 2:12). David comes to the Lord humbly, recognizing that he cannot protect himself. Like a widow in need of a kinsman redeemer, David appeals to the protector to be his defense.

---

[76] Cf. Basson, *Divine Metaphors in Psalms*, 92.

[77] Bullock argues that this "draws upon the language of the Song of Moses (Dt 32:10–11)," where Israel is the apple of Yahweh's eye protected under the shadow of his wings, "Book 1," 36–37.

David details what he needs to be protected from in Ps 17:9–12. He called on the Lord to shelter him under his wings (17:8b) from the wicked who would destroy him, those at enmity with his soul who surround him (17:9). In the conflict between the seed of the woman and the seed of the serpent, the seed of the woman calls on the Lord for deliverance.

There is no point in negotiating with the wicked or trying to reason with them because, as David says in 17:10a, "Their fat they close." The term for "fat" here is one associated with kidneys and intestines, the gut, which like the Hebrew term "womb" connotes feelings of sympathy, compassion, and mercy. David describes his enemies as ruthless, merciless. In keeping with their hard-heartedness, in 17:10b David says that "their mouths speak in majesty," referring to the haughty, supercilious, arrogant expressions of their views.

David spoke of the way the wicked surround him in 17:9b, and now in 17:11a he speaks of the way that his steps are compassed round about by his enemies. It is as though David's foes are staking out the parameters of David's movements, scoping out his territory. Their intent is articulated in 17:11b, as David says that his enemies have set their eyes to lay him low. They want him thrown down, subjugated to their power.

David has likened his enemies to prowling lions, seeking whom they may devour, in Ps 7:2 (MT 7:3) and 10:9, and he does so again in 17:12. Their lust for blood and lurking methods do not image forth the character and likeness of God. These men are beastly, not manly. They are killer cats on the hunt, not noble men seeking truth, goodness, and beauty.

### 17:13–15, Rise Up and Deliver Me

Having presented the justice of his cause in 17:1–7 and the evil of his adversaries in 17:8–12, David calls on the Lord to rise up and do justice in 17:13–15. David has called on the Lord to rise up in Pss 3:7 (MT 3:8); 7:6 (MT 7:7); 9:19 (MT 9:20); 10:12, and he will do so again in 132:8.

In Deut 7:10 Moses declared that Yahweh would not be slack toward the one who hates him but would repay him "to his face" (אל פניו). David urges the Lord to deal with his enemy—who is also God's enemy—and he wants Yahweh to "confront his face" (פניו). David knows that God is personally offended by sin and that a personal reckoning will be made.

Whereas David's enemies want to stretch him out on the ground (Ps 17:11b), David calls on the Lord to cause his enemy to bow in 17:13. Interestingly, while "the wicked" are referred to in the plural in 17:9–11, the one likened to a lion is in the singular in 17:12, and the one David wants Yahweh to confront to his face is singular in 17:13, with a return to plural references in 17:14. There is no confusion here. This probably reflects a situation where Saul is the singular wicked man, and all those aligned with Saul are those referenced in the plural. David did not raise his hand against Saul, the Lord's anointed. He did just what we see him do at the end of 17:13, where he prays for Yahweh to use his sword to deliver him from the wicked (cf. esp. 1 Sam 26:9–10).

The thought of Ps 17:13, Yahweh delivering David by his sword, continues in 17:14, as the reference to the singular wicked man is extended to the men of the world in general. David asks the Lord in 17:14 to deliver him by his hand, his power, from men of the world whose portion is in this life. The reference to their portion being in this life is in pointed contrast to David saying Yahweh was his portion in 16:5 (cf. 11:6). This contrast continues through the remainder of Ps 17, and the contrast ties Pss 16 and 17 together.

When David goes on in 17:14 to say that the Lord fills the bellies of the worldly with his treasure, he implies that every good thing people value flows from God's goodness. God gives them good gifts, but they neither thank him nor honor him as God. Whereas David said that "satisfaction of gladnesses" was the Lord's own presence in 16:11, and confesses himself satisfied to behold the Lord himself in 17:15, the worldlings are "satisfied with sons" in 17:14. These are people whose god is their belly, whose minds are set on earthly things (Phil 3:19). They enjoy all God's goodness, are content to surround themselves with their children as emblems of their own prosperity, whom they mean to enrich by their own prowess. Their gaze does not go to the horizon of life to ponder what awaits on the other side of the sleep of death. The wickedness of their cruel malice, which David forcefully described in 17:8–12, is founded on their philosophy that this life is all there is to live (17:14).

David, by contrast, knows that there is more to live for than filling his belly, multiplying one's sons, and enriching them through what he bequeaths. He states this plainly through his reference to waking at the end of 17:15. Death and resurrection are frequently referred to in terms of sleeping and waking (see esp. Isa 26:19; Dan 12:2).[78] Thus the

---

[78] Alexander, "Old Testament View of Life After Death," 45, observes "that death is sometimes described as falling asleep (e.g. Ps 13:3; Dan 12:2) and the resurrection as reawaking

"righteousness" in which David says that he will behold God's face is the righteousness to be enjoyed by those whom God has raised from the dead for everlasting life (cf. Dan 12:2–3). Similarly, David is not speaking of seeing God's face in some metaphorical way during this life. Rather, when he speaks of seeing God's face in righteousness, he is talking about the enjoyment of direct access to the presence of God when the dead are raised, the world is healed, the curse gone, the serpent crushed, the gates to Eden opened, and God's children are embraced in his arms as he wipes away every tear (cf. Isa 25:8).

David lives for more than the satisfaction to be found in the enjoyment of God's good gifts without reference to knowing God himself, more than a bevy of sons who will inherit much. David lives to be satisfied when he wakes with a vision of glory. This hope for the resurrection articulated in Ps 17:15 buttresses David's commitment to faithfulness articulated in 17:3, joining God's commands and prohibitions that David said kept him from the paths of the violent in 17:4, promising a reward richer than any perverse pleasure that would lure him to transgress, to forget God, or to live for the now.

All of God's glory and beauty is reflected and refracted in the world he made. Everything beautiful we have ever seen—a graceful human form, a radiant sunset, a cherished newborn child, the happy sight of home, the smile of a friend, the appeal of everything snazzy-fresh and stylish—all of these beautiful things are but hints and whispers of the beauty of the Creator. Nothing can satisfy us like God can satisfy us. We were made for his presence. Our souls ache for the fulfillment of our longings for the Lord. In Ps 17:15 David articulates his confidence that his every yearning will be satisfied when he sees God's face.

That confidence in the resurrection from the dead and the gratification of gladness, the satisfaction in God's presence, the everlasting pleasures at his right hand (16:8–11; 17:15), makes it enough to call on the name of the Lord. This profound theology undergirds David's commitment to righteousness whatever it costs him reflected in 17:1–7.

David's righteousness provokes the wicked, the seed of the serpent, to be at enmity with him. David's commitment to righteousness prevents him from violent, lawless methods of dealing with his difficulties. But

---

(e.g. 2 Ki. 4:31; Jb. 14:12; Is. 26:19; Dn. 12:2) suggests possibly that the intermediate state of the righteous is one of comparative tranquility and peace."

David's commitment to righteousness also keeps him from being beastly, merciless, cruel, leonine, and evil like the wicked in 17:8–12. David's righteousness makes him bold to call on the Lord to rise up to deliver him in 17:13–15, and David's confidence in the resurrection makes it enough to call on the Lord.

BRIDGE

If we are going to follow in David's sure footsteps and walk the Lord's wagon tracks (17:5), we must follow his example. We need the word of the Lord's own lips to keep us from the paths of the violent (17:4), and we need to have our imaginations fired by the hope of what will be (17:15). As noted above, David's righteousness was relative. He did not attain to sinless perfection.

Given the fact that the world as God made it was sinless, however, and given the promise that God would crush the head of the one who tempted man into sin in Gen 3:15, David would have reason to hope that when God defeated evil through the seed of the woman, the curses would be rolled back (cf. Gen 5:29) and sin would be banished from God's cleansed creation (cf. Dan 9:24).

I have suggested that in Ps 16 David described his own experience, knowing that his own experience would be a type of the one promised to come from his line. Such an understanding would fit with Ps 17 as well. David surely knew that the claims he made to be righteous were claims to relative righteousness (see the many psalms confessing sin, not least Ps 51), and there is reason to think that he could have hoped that his own relative blamelessness anticipated one whose righteousness would be comprehensive, whose integrity would be complete, whose holiness would be like that of Adam prior to sin, but who unlike Adam would never be deceived by the serpent.

Psalm 17 is "a prayer of David" (superscription), but if we put the words on the lips of the Lord Jesus (as the New Testament authors frequently do with the Psalms), they flow even more smoothly than they do from the tongue of David, that sweet psalmist of Israel. If we hear the Lord Jesus speak the words of Ps 17, we need qualify none of the claims, soften none of the assertions, nor walk back any aspect of what it will be for the speaker to behold God's face in righteousness (cf. John 1:18). The Lord Jesus is most qualified to pray this prayer, and we who follow him should strive to have its truths pulse in our own hearts.

## Psalm 18

OVERVIEW AND STRUCTURE OF PSALM 18

Psalm 18 evidences a chiastic structure wherein the opening and closing statements answer one another, inner rings match, interpret, and develop each other, with the center point of the chiasm serving as an explanation of David's success and Yahweh's character. David opens declaring his love for Yahweh and the way Yahweh protects him (18:1–3 [MT 18:2–4]) and closes by stating that Yahweh gives him victory over his enemies because of Yahweh's love for him, David, and his offspring forever (18:47–50 [MT 18:48–51]). In Ps 18:5–6 (MT 18:6-7) David describes how he was threatened by Death, Belial, and Sheol, but the threats were overcome because, as he declares in 18:46 (MT 18:47), Yahweh lives. David's cry for help in Ps 18:6 (MT 18:7) stands across from the subjection of foreign nations to his reign in 18:43–45 (MT 18:44–46). David describes Yahweh hearing his 18:6 (MT 18:7) prayer and going into action in 18:7–15 (MT 18:8–16), and the language and imagery he uses to describe Yahweh intervening is reminiscent of accounts in Exod 15 and 19, evoking the Red Sea and Sinai. The corresponding section of the chiasm, Ps 18:37–42 (MT 18:38–43), develops the imagery by advancing the narrative undercurrent, as David speaks of overcoming his enemies using language and imagery that recalls the conquest of the land under Joshua. Within the exodus and conquest rings, in 18:16–19 (MT 18:17–20) David celebrates the way that Yahweh rescued him and put him in a broad place. This stands across from 18:30–36 (MT 18:31–37), where David speaks of how God shielded and equipped him and set his feet in a broad place. The character of David and Yahweh are described in the center of the chiasm, with David's righteousness and clean hands the focus in 18:20–24 (MT 18:21–25), and Yahweh's mercy to the humble and pure but his judgment on the crooked and proud stated in 18:25–29 (MT 18:26–30).

This chiastic structure can be summarized as follows:[79]

18:1–3 (MT 18:2–4), David's Love for Yahweh
   18:4–5 (MT 18:5–6), Death, Belial, and Sheol

---

[79] Having arrived at this understanding of the Psalm's structure by my own independent analysis, I was pleased to find a similar chiasm in Alison Ruth Gray, *Psalm 18 in Words and Pictures: A Reading through Metaphor*, BibInt 127 (Leiden: Brill, 2014), 201.

18:6 (MT 18:7), David's Cry to Yahweh
18:7–15 (MT 18:8–16), Yahweh Intervenes as at the Red Sea
and Sinai
18:16–19 (MT 18:17–20), Yahweh Rescues David (Broad
Place)
18:20–24 (MT 18:21–25), David's Righteousness and
Clean Hands
18:25–29 (MT 18:26–30), Yahweh Lifts up the Humble
18:30–36 (MT 18:31–37), Yahweh Empowers David (Broad
Place)
18:37–42 (MT 18:38–43), David Conquers as Joshua Did at the
Conquest
18:43–45 (MT 18:44–46), Foreigners Subjected to David
18:46 (MT 18:47), Yahweh Lives
18:47–50 (MT 18:48–51), Yahweh's Love for David

The psalm might also be summarized as follows:

18:1–6, David in Danger
18:7–19, Yahweh in Action
18:20–29, The Character of David and Yahweh
18:30–45, David in Conquest
18:46–50, Yahweh in Praise

SCRIPTURE

CSB

For the choir director. Of the servant
of the LORD, David, who spoke the
words of this song to the LORD on the
day the LORD rescued him from the
grasp of all his enemies and from the
power of Saul. He said:

[1] I love you, LORD, my strength.
[2] The LORD is my rock,
my fortress, and my deliverer,
my God, my rock where I seek refuge,

Author's translation

[1] For the Preeminent One.
For the servant of Yahweh.
Of David.
When he spoke to Yahweh the words
of this song
on the day Yahweh delivered him
from the hand of all the ones at
enmity with him
and from the hand of Saul.
[2] And he said, I love you, O Yahweh,
my strength.

my shield and the horn of my
  salvation,
my stronghold.
³ I called to the Lord, who is worthy of
  praise,
and I was saved from my enemies.

⁴ The ropes of death were wrapped
  around me;
the torrents of destruction terrified
  me.
⁵ The ropes of Sheol entangled me;
the snares of death confronted me.
⁶ I called to the Lord in my distress,
and I cried to my God for help.
From his temple he heard my voice,
and my cry to him reached his ears.

⁷ Then the earth shook and quaked;
the foundations of the mountains
  trembled;
they shook because he burned with
  anger.
⁸ Smoke rose from his nostrils,
and consuming fire came from his
  mouth;
coals were set ablaze by it.
⁹ He bent the heavens and came down,
total darkness beneath his feet.
¹⁰ He rode on a cherub and flew,
soaring on the wings of the wind.
¹¹ He made darkness his hiding place,
dark storm clouds his canopy around
  him.
¹² From the radiance of his presence,
his clouds swept onward with hail and
  blazing coals.
¹³ The Lord thundered from heaven;
the Most High made his voice heard.
¹⁴ He shot his arrows and scattered
  them;
he hurled lightning bolts and routed
  them.
¹⁵ The depths of the sea became visible,

³ O Yahweh, my high ridge and my
  stronghold and the one who
  delivers me,
My God, my rock—I take refuge in
  him—
my shield and the horn of my
  salvation, my secure height.
⁴ The one to be praised, I call on
  Yahweh,
and from the ones at enmity with me
  I am saved.

⁵ Encompassed me the cords of Death;
the torrents of Belial startled me.
⁶ The cords of Sheol surrounded me;
confronted me the snares of Death.

⁷ In my distress I call Yahweh,
and to my God I cry for help.
He hears my voice from his temple,
And my cry for help comes before
  him, in his ears.

⁸ Then reeled and rocked the earth,
and the foundations of the mountains
  quaked and reeled,
for it kindled in him.
⁹ Smoke rose in his nose;
and fire from his mouth devours;
coals burned from him.
¹⁰ Then he bent the heavens and came
  down,
with thick darkness under his feet.
¹¹ And he mounted a cherub and flew,
and he flew swiftly on the wings of
  the wind.
¹² He makes darkness his covering
  round about him,
his shelter darkness of waters,
dark clouds of mist.
¹³ From the brightness before him,
his dark clouds passed over,
hail and coals of fire.
¹⁴ And he caused thunder in the
  heavens,

the foundations of the world were
    exposed,
at your rebuke, Lord,
at the blast of the breath of your
    nostrils.

¹⁶ He reached down from on high
and took hold of me;
he pulled me out of deep water.
¹⁷ He rescued me from my powerful
    enemy
and from those who hated me,
for they were too strong for me.
¹⁸ They confronted me in the day of
    my calamity,
but the Lord was my support.
¹⁹ He brought me out to a spacious
    place;
he rescued me because he delighted
    in me.

²⁰ The Lord rewarded me
according to my righteousness;
he repaid me
according to the cleanness of my
    hands.
²¹ For I have kept the ways of the Lord
and have not turned from my God to
    wickedness.
²² Indeed, I let all his ordinances guide
    me
and have not disregarded his statutes.
²³ I was blameless toward him
and kept myself from my iniquity.
²⁴ So the Lord repaid me
according to my righteousness,
according to the cleanness of my
    hands in his sight.

²⁵ With the faithful
you prove yourself faithful,
with the blameless
you prove yourself blameless,
²⁶ with the pure
you prove yourself pure,

Yahweh, even the Most High, he gives
    his voice,
hail and coals of fire.
¹⁵ And he sent his arrows and
    scattered them,
and flashes multiplied and confused
    them.
¹⁶ Then were revealed the channels of
    the water,
And were uncovered the foundations
    of the world,
from your rebuke, O Yahweh,
from the blast of the breath of your
    nose.

¹⁷ He sends from on high,
he takes me,
he draws me out from many waters.
¹⁸ He delivers me from the strong one
    at enmity with me,
and from the ones who hate me,
for they were stronger than I.
¹⁹ They confront me in the day of my
    distress,
and Yahweh was a support to me.
²⁰ And he brought me out to a broad
    place,
he delivered me because he delighted
    in me.

²¹ Yahweh dealt with me according to
    my righteousness,
according to the purity of my hands
    he restored me;
²² for I kept the ways of Yahweh,
and have not wickedly strayed from
    my God;
²³ for all his judgments were before
    me,
and his statutes I did not cause to be
    turned from me.
²⁴ And I had integrity with him,
and I kept myself from my iniquity.
²⁵ Yahweh restored me according to
    my righteousness,

but with the crooked
you prove yourself shrewd.
[27] For you rescue an oppressed people,
but you humble those with haughty
eyes.
[28] Lord, you light my lamp;
my God illuminates my darkness.
[29] With you I can attack a barricade,
and with my God I can leap over a
wall.

[30] God—his way is perfect;
the word of the Lord is pure.
He is a shield to all who take refuge
in him.
[31] For who is God besides the Lord?
And who is a rock? Only our God.
[32] God—he clothes me with strength
and makes my way perfect.
[33] He makes my feet like the feet of a
deer
and sets me securely on the heights.
[34] He trains my hands for war;
my arms can bend a bow of bronze.
[35] You have given me the shield of
your salvation;
your right hand upholds me,
and your humility exalts me.
[36] You make a spacious place beneath
me for my steps,
and my ankles do not give way.

[37] I pursue my enemies and overtake
them;
I do not turn back until they are
wiped out.
[38] I crush them, and they cannot get
up;
they fall beneath my feet.
[39] You have clothed me with strength
for battle;
you subdue my adversaries beneath
me.
[40] You have made my enemies retreat
before me;

according to the purity of my hands
before his eyes.

[26] With the lovingkind one you show
yourself lovingkind;
with the man of integrity you show
yourself to have integrity;
[27] with the pure you show yourself
pure;
but with the twisted you show
yourself tortuous.
[28] For you cause salvation for an
afflicted people,
but eyes that are lifted up you cause
to be abased.
[29] For you cause light in my lamp, O
Yahweh,
my God, you cause my darkness to
shine.
[30] For in you I run against a troop,
and in my God I leap over a wall.

[31] The God, integrity is his way.
The word of Yahweh has been
refined.
A shield is he to all who take refuge
in him.
[32] For who is God but Yahweh?
And who is a rock except our God?
[33] The God, the one who girds me with
strength,
and he gave integrity to my way.
[34] The one who makes my feet like
those of a deer,
and upon my high places he causes
me to stand.
[35] The one who teaches my hands for
battle,
so that my arms can bend a bow of
bronze.
[36] And you gave to me the shield of
your salvation.
And your right hand supports me.
And your humility causes greatness
for me.

I annihilate those who hate me.
⁴¹ They cry for help, but there is no
    one to save them—
they cry to the Lord, but he does not
    answer them.
⁴² I pulverize them like dust before the
    wind;
I trample them like mud in the streets.

⁴³ You have freed me from the feuds
    among the people;
you have appointed me the head of
    nations;
a people I had not known serve me.
⁴⁴ Foreigners submit to me cringing;
as soon as they hear they obey me.
⁴⁵ Foreigners lose heart
and come trembling from their
    fortifications.

⁴⁶ The Lord lives—blessed be my rock!
The God of my salvation is exalted.
⁴⁷ God—he grants me vengeance
and subdues peoples under me.
⁴⁸ He frees me from my enemies.
You exalt me above my adversaries;
you rescue me from violent men.
⁴⁹ Therefore I will give thanks to you
    among the nations, Lord;
I will sing praises about your name.
⁵⁰ He gives great victories to his king;
he shows loyalty to his anointed,
to David and his descendants forever.

³⁷ You caused a wide place for my
    steps under me,
and my ankles did not buckle.

³⁸ I will pursue the ones at enmity
    with me and overtake them,
and I will not turn back until finishing
    them.
³⁹ I will crush them and they will not
    be able to rise,
they will fall under my feet.
⁴⁰ And you gird me with strength for
    battle,
you cause those who rise up to bow
    beneath me.
⁴¹ And as for those at enmity with
    me, you give to me the back of the
    neck;
and as for those who hate me, I will
    annihilate them.
⁴² They cry for help and there is no
    one to save,
on Yahweh and he does not answer
    them.
⁴³ I grind them like dust before the
    face of the wind,
like the mire of the streets I cause
    them to be emptied.

⁴⁴ You deliver me from the disputes of
    the people.
You put me as head of the nations.
A people I have not known will serve
    me.
⁴⁵ At the hearing of the ear they
    obeyed me.
Sons of the foreigner submitted to
    me.
⁴⁶ Sons of foreigners wither and quake
    from their shut up places.

⁴⁷ Yahweh lives!
And may my rock be blessed!
And may the God of my salvation be
    lifted up!

⁴⁸ The God, the one who gives
   vengeances to me.
And he causes peoples to be spoken
   under me.
⁴⁹ The one who delivers me from
   those at enmity with me,
even from those who rise up against
   me, you lift me up.
From the man of violence you cause
   me to be delivered.
⁵⁰ Therefore I give thanks to you
   among the nations, O Yahweh.
And to your name, I will psalm.
⁵¹ He causes greatness of salvations
   for his king,
and does lovingkindness to his
   messiah,
to David and to his seed unto the age.

CONTEXT: VERBAL AND THEMATIC LINKS WITH SURROUNDING PSALMS

18:2 (MT 18:3) "my deliverer"
17:13 "Deliver my soul"

18:2 (MT 18:3) "I take refuge in him"
2:12 "blessed are all who take refuge in him"
Compare 18:30 (MT 18:31)

18:2 (MT 18:3) "my shield"
3:3; 18:30, 35 (MT 3:4; 18:31, 36)

18:2 (MT 18:3) "my stronghold"
9:9 (MT 9:10) "Yahweh will be a stronghold ... a stronghold"

18:5 (MT 18:6) "confronted me the snares of death"
17:13, "Confront his face"
18:19 (MT 18:20) "They confront me"

18:6 (MT 18:7) "He hears my voice from his temple"
3:4 (MT 3:5) "he answered me from the mountain of his
   holiness"
Compare 2:6; 5:7 (MT 5:8); 11:4

18:9 (MT 18:10) "thick darkness"
Compare Exod 20:21; Deut 4:11; 5:22; 1 Kgs 8:12

18:13 (MT 18:14) "And he caused thunder in the heavens"
Compare 2 Sam 2:10; 7:10

18:14 (MT 18:15) "he ... confused them"
Compare Exod 14:24; 23:27; Josh 10:10; 1 Sam 7:10

18:15 (MT 18:16) "the breath of your nose"
Compare Exod 15:8 "breath of your nose"

18:16 (MT 18:17) "he draws me out from many waters"
Compare Exod 2:10 "I drew him out of the water"

18:20 (MT 18:21) "according to my righteousness"
Compare 4:1 (MT 4:2); 7:8 (MT 7:9); 15:2; 17:1, 15; 18:24 (MT
   18:25)

18:21 (MT 18:22) "ways of Yahweh"
Compare 1:1, 6; 2:12; 5:8 (MT 5:9); 10:5; 18:30, 32 (MT 18:31, 33)

18:22 (MT 18:23) "all his judgments were before me"
10:5 "On high are your judgments from before him."

18:26 (MT 18:27) "you show yourself tortuous"
Compare Job 5:13 "the deceptive" (CSB); so also Prov 8:8

18:30 (MT 18:31) "The word of Yahweh has been refined."
12:7 "The words of Yahweh are pure words: silver refined in a
   furnace on the ground, purified seven times."

18:30b–c (MT 18:31b–c), "The word of Yahweh has been refined.
   A shield is he to all who take refuge in him."
Prov 30:5, "Every word of God has been refined. A shield is he to
   those who take refuge in him."

18:33 (MT 18:34) "makes my feet like those of a deer"
Compare 18:36 (MT 18:37)

18:35 (MT 18:36) "your right hand"
Compare 16:8, 11; 17:7; 20:6; 21:8 (MT 20:7; 21:9)

18:37 (MT 18:38) "I will pursue the ones at enmity with me and overtake them"
7:5 (MT 7:6) "let the one at enmity with my soul pursue and overtake"

18:38 (MT 18:39) "I will crush them ... they will fall under my feet"
Compare Gen 3:15; Num 24:8, 17; Judg 5:26; Ps 68:21 [MT 68:22]; 110:5–6; Hab 3:13

18:38 (MT 18:39) "they will not be able to rise"
1:5 "the wicked will not rise in the judgment"

18:39 (MT 18:40) "you cause those who rise up to bow beneath me"
17:13 "Cause him to bow."

18:40 (MT 18:41) "you give to me the back of the neck"
Compare Gen 49:8 "Your hand will be on the necks of your enemies" (CSB)

18:43 (MT 18:44) "You put me as head of the nations ... serve me"
Compare 2:8, 11

18:43 (MT 18:44) "A people I have not known will serve me"
Compare Isa 55:5

18:45 (MT 18:46) "Sons of foreigners wither"
Compare 1:3 "whose leaf does not wither"

18:49 (MT 18:50) "I will psalm"
Compare 7:17 (MT 7:18); 9:2, 11 (MT 9:3, 12); 21:13 (MT 21:14)

18:50 (MT 18:51) "his anointed"
2:2 "his anointed"

We have seen that Pss 1 and 2 introduce the Psalter by showing us the king of Israel as a blessed man who loves Torah and against whom the nations rebel. Psalms 3–9 then give an example of that rebellion as they deal with Absalom's revolt. In Pss 10–14 David explores and responds to what the wicked says in his heart, and in Pss 15–24 David meditates on the future righteous king he anticipates because of God's promise.

Psalms 15 and 24 celebrate the king's character. Psalms 16 and 23 show how the king is satisfied by knowing the Lord. Psalms 17 and 22 depict the king's resurrection confidence in the face of enemy threats. Psalms 18 and 20–21 herald God's deliverance of the king, and Ps 19 celebrates the revelation of God's glory.

In Ps 18 David draws together themes he has introduced in earlier psalms and also interprets his own life in terms drawn from earlier Scripture. By doing this in combination with the reference to the seed promised to him in 18:50 (MT 18:51), David generates the expectation that the exodus and conquest narratives from earlier Scripture, which he uses to describe his own experience in Ps 18, in turn point forward to what can be expected in the life of the one who is to come. Statements like those in 18:43 (MT 18:44), for instance, might be initially fulfilled in David's life but their ultimate realization awaits the one who will inherit the nations (cf. 2:8).

Exposition

### 18:1–6 (MT 18:2–7), David in Danger

Psalm 18 has one of the longest superscriptions in the Psalms at twenty words. The only one longer is Ps 60 at twenty-one words. Psalm 51 has twelve words, 52 has fifteen words.

Psalm 18 is substantially re-presented in 2 Sam 22:1–51. Taking the historical record indicated within the Old Testament as it stands, assuming that the superscription indicates that David wrote Ps 18, and following on the hypothesis that David is responsible for the architectural design of the collection of the Psalms, a design understood and brought to completion by those who added later psalms (see discussion in the introduction), this psalm would have been composed and placed where we find it prior to the writing of 1 and 2 Samuel.[80] I would suggest, then, that whoever wrote Samuel knew Ps 18 and made use of it as a fitting interpretive summary of his narrative.

The superscription refers to "the servant of Yahweh." The only other instance of this phrase in a psalm superscription is in Ps 36. This phrase is only used with reference to Moses, Joshua, and David (cf. also Isa 42:19)

---

[80] Davidic authorship is what the New Testament indicates when its authors attribute psalms to David, as opposed to other possible interpretations of the Hebrew לדוד, such as the suggestion that it is a psalm "about" or "for" David. See the discussion of authorship in the introduction.

in the Old Testament.[81] Moses is described this way once in Deuteronomy as his death is being narrated (Deut 34:5), and then twelve times in Joshua Moses is described this way (Josh 1:1, 13, 15; 8:31, 33; 11:12; 12:6; 13:8; 14:7; 18:7; 22:2, 4, 5). Moses is called "the servant of Yahweh" once in Kings and twice in Chronicles (2 Kgs 18:12; 2 Chr 1:3; 24:6). The book of Joshua only once refers to Joshua as "the servant of Yahweh," and it finally comes at the end of the book as Joshua's death is narrated (Josh 24:29). This creates the impression that both Moses and Joshua had to complete their course and invest their whole lives before they could be referred to this way. Joshua is granted the title only one other time, in the book of Judges, and again his death is being narrated (Judg 2:8). The overwhelming use of this phrase with reference to Moses, whose stature in the Old Testament is almost unmatched, means that Joshua is being complimented when he is referred to this way. The fact that Moses and Joshua are only described this way once they have completed their lives joins with other features in Ps 18's superscription (especially David being delivered from all his enemies) to indicate that this psalm is a poetic summary of the whole course of David's life.

David's reference to himself as "the servant of Yahweh," a phrase only otherwise used with reference to Moses and Joshua, shows David's understanding of his role in God's plan.[82] It also anticipates the way that David will depict the events of his life in Ps 18 with terms drawn from the exodus from Egypt under the leadership of Moses and the conquest of the land under the leadership of Joshua.[83]

With David describing his own experience as an installation in patterns seen in the *type* of thing God did to save Israel under Moses and Joshua, these patterns naturally shape Israel's expectation of the *type* of thing God would do to save Israel under the promised descendant of David (cf. 18:50 [MT 18:51]).

---

[81] The issue here is the whole phrase, "servant of Yahweh." The Lord refers to Abraham, e.g., as "my servant" in Gen 26:24, and he also calls Moses (Num 12:7–8) and Caleb (14:24) "my servant."

[82] For the significance of the theme in the whole Bible, see Stephen G. Dempster, "The Servant of the Lord," in Hafemann and House, *Central Themes in Biblical Theology*, 128–78.

[83] Another point of contact between Moses and the superscription of Ps 18 is the phrase "the words of this song" (את דברי השירה הזאת), which quotes Deut 31:30 verbatim. I owe this reference to Gray, *Psalm 18 in Words and Pictures*, 57 n. 10.

The superscription to Ps 18 tells us that David here responds to the Lord delivering him from Saul and all his enemies. We know some things about David's escapes from Saul and his enemies from the narratives of Samuel, but David will not be talking about those things in literal, historical terms in Ps 18. Rather than describe cities that would have handed him over (see 1 Sam 23:1–12) or the like, he speaks in spiritual and metaphorical terms of "cords of Death." These metaphors allow David to communicate the theological realities at work as the Lord delivers him.

In Ps 18:1–2 (MT 18:2–3) David describes Yahweh with a series of images: strength, rock, fortress, deliverer, place of refuge, shield, horn of salvation, and stronghold. Yahweh, of course, is not *literally* the muscle in David's arms, a boulder, a shield David holds in his hand, or a fortress into which David flees. None of that is David's point. David is saying that he relies on the Lord in the way that other humans in distress rely on advantages they seek to have, whether those advantages are their own strength, powerful allies, a thick wall, the high ground in battle, or superior weaponry. Saul and David's other enemies may have all those assets, but what David has is the Lord himself. David's perspective is that he would rather have the Lord than be a massive physical specimen like Goliath, be allied with the Egyptians or Assyrians, or have all the best weapons and all the best redoubts.

Note that in Ps 18:1 (MT 18:2) David says he loves Yahweh. Worldly, narcissistic people like Saul might love themselves and all the ways they consider themselves superior to others. Politically connected people love politics, and those with the best equipment and strongholds love what they think will secure their triumph. In place of all such advantages, David looks to the Lord and loves him. Naturally, then, in 18:3 (MT 18:4) David asserts that Yahweh is the one who is worthy of praise. What we talk about, celebrate, and trust in reveals what we think is worthy of praise. David calls on the Lord in 18:3 (MT 18:4), and he is saved from all those at enmity with him.

Psalm 18 opens with David's love for and reliance on Yahweh (18:1–3 [MT 18:1–4]) and closes with Yahweh's deliverance of and love for David (18:47–50 [MT 18:48–51]).

When David describes what threatened him in 18:4–5 (MT 18:5–6), he personifies what appear to be the spiritual forces of evil in heavenly places at work behind the human enemies referenced in the super-scription. Death has cords with which he tries to bind David, and Belial unleashes a flood of water to threaten him (18:4 [MT 18:5]). Sheol also has cords that he tries to wrap around David, and Death has set his snares seeking to entrap David (18:6).

The Hebrew text of Ps 18:4–5 (MT 18:5–6) presents a grammatical chiasm:

Verb-Object-Subject-Genitive
  Subject-Genitive-Verb-Object
  Subject-Genitive-Verb-Object
Verb-Object-Subject-Genitive

This chiastic structure is reflected in my translation of the two verses, and the personification of the forces in the chiastic arrangement argues that rather than being rendered as "destruction," Belial should be understood as a demonic power in the heavenlies:[84]

Death
  Belial
  Sheol
Death

In the wider chiastic structure of the whole of Ps 18, the forces of Death, Belial, and Sheol that threaten David's life in 18:4–5 (MT 18:5–6) are no match for what is asserted in 18:46 (MT 18:47)—Yahweh (whom neither Belial nor Sheol can overcome) lives (unvanquished by Death).

## 18:7–19 (MT 18:8–20), Yahweh in Action

In keeping with what he said in 18:1–3 (MT 18:2–4), when David is threatened by the powers of death and hell in 18:4–5 (MT 18:5–6), he does not rely on his strength, his weapons, or his hideouts. He calls on the Lord, who hears him (18:6 [MT 18:7]). In the chiastic structure of Ps 18, David's calling in the Lord in 18:6 (MT 18:7) corresponds to him being made the head of the nations, to whom foreigners submit, before whom they quiver in 18:43–45 (MT 18:44–46). David describes an anticipatory realization of

---

[84] See the discussion of Beliyaal in 1 Sam 1:16 and 2:12 in David Toshio Tsumura, *The First Book of Samuel*, NICOT (Grand Rapids: Eerdmans, 2007), 122–24, 154–55; cf. also Gray, *Psalm 18 in Words and Pictures*, 71–73.

Ps 2:8 and 11—he has asked of the Lord, and the Lord has given him the nations as his inheritance. They serve him with trembling.

The nations will be subject to the Davidic king because the Lord will act for him as he did at the exodus from Egypt. David describes the Lord going into action on his behalf against Saul and all his enemies in Ps 18:7–15 (MT 18:8–16). Rather than speak of what literally happened, however, such as Saul dying in battle against the Philistines (cf. 1 Sam 31), David speaks of Yahweh acting on his behalf with imagery that recalls the Sinai theophany. In Exod 19 Moses describes the mountain wrapped in smoke because Yahweh had come down on it in fire, with smoke everywhere and the mountain trembling with an earthquake (Exod 19:18) in thick darkness (Exod 20:21). David similarly depicts the shaking of the earth, the smoke and fire, and the Lord coming down in thick darkness (Ps 18:7–9 [MT 18:8–10]).

David portrays Yahweh riding a cherub on the wings of the wind, with a tabernacle consisting of the darkness of watery clouds (18:10–11 [MT 18:11–12]). The references to Yahweh's "tabernacle" (Hebrew סכתו; Greek σκηνή) and the "cherub" evoke images of the tabernacle Israel built at Mount Sinai.

Yahweh's radiance contrasts with the dark clouds surrounding him in Ps 18:12 (MT 18:13), and his thundering in the heavens in 18:13 (MT 18:14) recalls Hannah's song (1 Sam 2:10) and Yahweh's triumph over the Philistines (1 Sam 7:10). Yahweh's lightnings stand in poetic parallelism with his arrows in 18:14 (MT 18:15), and he threw David's enemies into confusion (18:14 [MT 18:15]) just as he did to the Egyptians (Exod 14:24), the Amorites (Josh 10:10), and the Philistines (1 Sam 7:10).

The blast of Yahweh's nostrils parts the waters in Ps 18:15 (MT 18:16 רוח אפך), just as the blast of his nostrils did at the Red Sea (Exod 15:8 רוח אפך). The alignment of David with Moses through the phrase "servant of Yahweh" in the superscription joins with the imagery from Sinai and Red Sea to suggest that David has interpreted his deliverance from his enemies as his own personal exodus from Egypt, crossing of the Red Sea, and covenant-making at Sinai.

All this exodus imagery in 18:7–15 (MT 18:8–16) will be matched by conquest imagery in 18:37–42 (MT 18:38–43).

The connections between David and Moses are only strengthened by the language of 18:16 (MT 18:17), where the drawing of David from many waters recalls the daughter of Pharaoh doing just that and naming the child Moses (Exod 2:10).[85] David seems to present himself as a kind of new Moses, who has experienced his own personal new exodus, and this would suggest that the covenant Yahweh made with David is akin to the covenant Yahweh made with Israel through Moses at Sinai.

Just as Egypt was stronger than Israel, Yahweh delivered David from those stronger than he was (Ps 18:17 [MT 18:18]). In his distress, Yahweh was his support (18:18 [MT 18:19]), and just as Yahweh brought Israel into the land of promise, he brought David into a broad place (18:19 [MT 18:20]).[86] Yahweh chose Israel because he loved them (Deut 7:7–8), and he saved David because he delighted in him (Ps 18:19 [MT 18:20]).

Psalm 18:16–19 (MT 18:17–20) describes Yahweh rescuing David and bringing him into a "broad place." Matching this section is the description of Yahweh empowering David in 18:30–36 (MT 18:31–37) and putting a "wide place" under his feet.

## 18:20–29 (MT 18:21–30), The Character of David and Yahweh

At the center of the chiastic structure of Ps 18 stands a dual unit on the character of David (18:20–24 [MT 18:21–25]) and Yahweh (18:25–29 [MT 18:26–30]).

As seen in Ps 17, David claims here a relative righteousness that pertains to the way that he has not broken God's commandments in the way he responded to Saul or his other enemies. David's relative righteousness hints, however, at the comprehensive righteousness the seed of promise from his line (cf. 18:50 [MT 18:51]) is expected to have.

The structure of the section on David's righteousness highlights the fact that God's word produced David's righteousness. That is to say, David is not righteous in and of himself. Rather, his character has been shaped

---

[85] Gray points out, "The verb משה [draw out] occurs only here [including 2 Sam 22:17] and in Exod 2.10." Gray, *Psalm 18 in Words and Pictures*, 106.

[86] The program of sin, exile, and restoration in Deut 32 is significant in the Psalms, and the restoration will take the form of a new exodus. On this theme, see Roy E. Ciampa, "The History of Redemption," in Hafemann and House, *Central Themes in Biblical Theology*, 254–308. David presents an installment of the exodus sequence of events in his own life in Ps 18; and cf. David's "the day of my distress" (יום אידי) with Deut 32:35's "day of their distress" (יום אידם). Gray (*Psalm 18 in Words and Pictures*, 109) drew my attention to the linguistic point of contact, but the interpretation thereof is my own. Cf. the quotation of Deut 32:36 in Ps 135:14 and the discussion of that passage below.

by God's commands and prohibitions. This can be seen from the chiastic structure of 18:20–24 (MT 18:21–25) which has a reference to God's word at its center point:

18:20 (MT 18:21), David's righteousness and clean hands[87]
    18:21 (MT 18:22), David kept Yahweh's ways
        18:22 (MT 18:23), Yahweh's judgments and statutes were before David
    18:23 (MT 18:24), David kept himself from iniquity
18:24 (MT 18:25), David's righteousness and clean hands

God promises blessing to those who obey and cursing to those who disobey. This section on Yahweh dealing with David according to his righteousness amounts to a declaration that God keeps his word.

The section on Yahweh's character (18:25–29 [MT 18:26–30]) opens with four statements on how Yahweh relates to different kinds of people (18:25–26 [MT 18:26–27]), followed by three assertions that explain Yahweh's ways, each beginning with כִּי in Hebrew (18:27–29 [MT 18:28–30]).

It is not difficult to understand how Yahweh shows steadfast love, integrity, and purity to those who show steadfast love, have integrity, and are pure (18:25–26a [MT 18:26–27a]). It can be difficult, however, to understand what is being stated in Ps 18:26b (MT 18:27b), which the CSB renders, "with the crooked you prove yourself shrewd." The same two terms rendered here "crooked" and "shrewd" are found in Deut 32:5 and Prov 8:8, which the CSB renders, "All the words of my mouth are righteous; none of them are deceptive or perverse." The term the CSB renders "deceptive" in Prov 8:8 (פָּתַל) is the one rendered "shrewd" in Ps 18:26b (MT 18:27b; cf. Job 5:13).

Proverbs 8:8 says "deceptiveness" will not be found in the words of wisdom, but Ps 18:26b (MT 18:27b) ascribes this to Yahweh in his dealings with the twisted. David and Solomon, however, both believe that Yahweh is altogether true and truthful. One way to understand the statement in Ps 18, then, is to interpret the *hithpael* stem as indicating, perhaps, the way Yahweh makes the wicked perceive him. This would appear to explain the ESV's rendering, "with the crooked you make yourself seem

---

[87] Though not the same Hebrew expression as seen in 18:24, the concept of "clean hands" links the two passages.

tortuous." This would suggest that Yahweh is not actually deceptive, he only makes the wicked perceive that he is so, but their perception is distorted by their own perverse hearts.

There are, though, moments in Israel's historical narratives when Yahweh deceives his enemies. How can he be holy and true and never lie and do this? At each point, Yahweh does this with someone who has rejected and rebelled against his authority and declared war on his purposes. If an army can send spies into a land, if a general can make his enemy think he is going one way when he is really going the other, setting up an ambush for his enemy, then it would appear that in war the normal rules of social engagement are suspended. Yahweh repeatedly deceives his enemies who have gone to war against him: Pharaoh has enslaved the Israelites, and Yahweh means to free them permanently. He tells Moses, however, to request a three day journey into the wilderness (Exod 3:8; 5:3). Yahweh instructs Moses to send spies into the land of Canaan (Num 13), and spies are again sent after the forty years in the wilderness (Josh 2). Saul has rejected Yahweh and his prophet Samuel, in response to which Yahweh instructs Samuel to anoint one of the sons of Jesse king. Samuel objects that if Saul hears of it he will kill him. Yahweh instructs Samuel to say that he has gone to sacrifice to the Lord (1 Sam 16:1–5).

Those who go to war against Yahweh will find him an implacable foe. As Alison Ruth Gray puts it, "YHWH's response to the king and actions on his behalf are framed and justified in terms of the concept of *lex talionis* [the law of retaliation]."[88] They should not expect him to telegraph his plans and purposes. Their only hope is to repent of their rebellion, wave the white flag of surrender, and bow the knee to Yahweh's king.

These four statements of how Yahweh deals with people in 18:25–26 (MT 18:26–27) are followed by three explanatory statements. First, Yahweh saves the afflicted and humble but he abases the proud (18:27 [MT 18:28]). What could show greater pride than rebelling against Yahweh and going to war against him? Part of Yahweh's strategy to oppose the proud is the way that he shows himself tortuous against them. By contrast, the humble and afflicted are those who will show lovingkindness, integrity, and purity.

David identifies with the humble, the afflicted, the persecuted, and thus he counts himself among those whom Yahweh saves. The second and third explanatory statements, then, apply Yahweh's ways to the ways that he

---

88 Gray, *Psalm 18 in Words and Pictures*, 128.

helps David: giving him light in darkness (18:28 [MT 18:29]), which probably refers to the way that Yahweh's word brings light into David's moral darkness, and enabling him to overcome his enemies (18:29 [MT 18:30]).

The Lord honors those who honor him (1 Sam 2:30), and Ps 18:20–29 (MT 18:21–30) indicates that Yahweh saves David because by faith in Yahweh's word David's character has been shaped by and conformed to Yahweh's own.

### 18:30–45 (MT 18:31–46), David in Conquest

Yahweh opposes the proud but gives grace to the humble (Ps 18:27 [MT 18:28]; cf. Jas 4:6), so it is natural for David to move into a section that declares how Yahweh has given him grace. Yahweh not only drew David out of many waters, delivering him and raising him up as a new Moses (18:16–19 [MT 18:17–20]), he fits him for battle, empowering him as a new Joshua (18:30–36 [MT 18:31–37]), sending him out to accomplish the new conquest (18:37–42 [MT 18:38–43]), exalting the conquering king over all nations (18:43–45 [MT 18:44–46]).

Psalm 18:30–36 (MT 18:31–37) is unified by the references to Yahweh as a "shield" (18:30 [MT 18:31]) and the giver of the "shield" of David's salvation (18:35 [MT 18:36]). Whereas David begins to speak of himself in the first person in 18:37 (MT 18:38), he speaks of Yahweh in the third person as the subject doing all the action of 18:30–36 (MT 18:31–37). The reference to the "broad place" in 18:36 (MT 18:37 רחב) matches the same at the end of the corresponding section in the chiasm at 18:19 (MT 18:20 מרחב).

Psalm 18:30–32 (MT 18:31–33) is tied together by Yahweh's integrity, which makes his word come through refining fires perfect and pure, fulfilling (18:30 [MT 18:31]) his promise to shield those who take refuge in him (cf. 2:12). Having asserted the incomparability of the Lord (18:31 [MT 18:32]), David acknowledges that God girded him with strength and gave integrity to his way—David's integrity comes from Yahweh's (18:32 [MT 18:33]).[89]

Psalm 18:33–36 (MT 18:34–37) is bracketed by what Yahweh does for David's feet—he makes them like those of a deer that is agile on the craggy heights in 18:33 (MT 18:34), and he puts a wide place under them so that

---

[89] Cf. Ps 18:30 (MT 18:31), "The God, integrity [or *perfect*] is his way," and Deut 32:4, "The Rock, integrity [or *perfect*] is his work." The Hebrew constructions are parallel:
Deut 32:4, הצור תמים פעלו.
Ps 18:31, האל תמים דרכו.
My attention was drawn to this connection by Gray, *Psalm 18 in Words and Pictures*, 138.

his ankles don't buckle in 18:36 (MT 18:37). Yahweh not only empowers David's feet, he trains his hands for war, giving him strength to bend a bow of bronze (18:34 [MT 18:35]). Yahweh gives David his salvation as a shield and supports him by his right hand (18:35 [MT 18:36]; cf. 16:11; 17:7; 20:6; 21:8 [MT 20:7; 21:9]).

Thus empowered, David announces that he will chase his enemies down and pulverize them in 18:37–38 (MT 18:38–39]). The verb for "crush" in 18:38 (MT 18:39 מחץ) is repeatedly used in contexts that allude to Gen 3:15 (Num 24:8, 17; Judg 5:26; Ps 68:21 [MT 68:22]; 110:5–6; Hab 3:13). An allusion to Gen 3:15 would seem to be present in Ps 18:38 (MT 18:39), as the crushed enemies cannot rise but are under the feet of the Davidic king.[90]

Again David attributes his power to Yahweh (18:39 [MT 18:40]), then in 18:40 (MT 18:41) David accesses the blessing of Judah to describe how Yahweh will subjugate his enemies to him. In Gen 49:8 Jacob said, "Judah, your brothers will praise you. Your hand will be on the necks of your enemies; your father's sons will bow down to you" (CSB). David uses the term rendered "necks" in Gen 49:8 to assert in Ps 18:40 (MT 18:41), "as for those at enmity with me, you give to me the back of the neck."

These rebels are joined together against Yahweh and his anointed (cf. Ps 2:1–3). Yahweh will not help them against David (18:41 [MT 18:42]). David will trample them. They will be like chaff before the wind (18:42 [MT 18:43]; cf. 1:4).

David brought the ark into Jerusalem in 2 Sam 6, and then God made the promises to him about his seed in 2 Sam 7. In 2 Sam 8–10 David began to conquer territory in every direction, before his tragic sin with Bathsheba in 2 Sam 11. The celebratory statements of triumph over the nations in Ps 18:43–45 (MT 18:44–46) correspond to David's conquests and anticipate the one who will never fail, who will reign forever. David's words about the people he had not known serving him in 18:43 (MT 18:44) seem to have influenced Isaiah's words about the nations not known who will serve Yahweh in Isa 55:5.

### 18:46–50 (MT 18:47–51), Yahweh in Praise

We have noted above how the living Yahweh, the power in heaven in 18:46 (MT 18:47), stands against the forces of Death, Sheol, and Belial from

---

[90] See the discussion and sketches of enemies under the feet of the conquering king in Keel, *Symbolism of the Biblical World*, 292–99.

18:4–5 (MT 18:5–6). David rightly blesses and exalts the Lord (18:46 [MT 18:47]), and he goes on to give the Lord credit for giving him vengeance against those who opposed him (18:47 [MT 18:48]), for delivering him and raising him up against those who rose up against him (18:48 [MT 18:49]), and for all these reasons David sings the epic song of Yahweh's victories, speaking of what Yahweh has done for him in the terms and categories and images and metaphors that have been used to speak of what Yahweh has done in the past. That is to say, David psalms Yahweh's name (18:49 [MT 18:50] אזמרה).

David summarizes the magnificence of the way the Lord has delivered him and ties God's lovingkindness to himself as God's anointed to the promises made about his seed, the promised king from his line, in 18:50 (MT 18:51).[91] The significance of the reference to the seed at the end of Ps 18 cannot be overstated. This reference suggests that the history of what God did for David in Ps 18 also looks forward to what God will do for the seed promised to David.

BRIDGE

The way that David speaks of God's deliverance of him in terms of the patterns of Israel's history points forward to the one who will bring those patterns and types to fulfillment. As with Pss 15, 16, and 17, if we put the words of Ps 18 on the lips of Jesus, the meaning only grows in depth and power. Whereas David was threatened by the powers of Death, Belial, and Sheol (18:4–5 [MT 18:5–6]), those powers actually got their cords and snares on Jesus, who died and was buried. Whereas the earthquake that accompanied Yahweh's intervention on David's behalf was metaphorical (18:7 [MT 18:8]), earthquakes accompanied the death and resurrection of Jesus (Matt 27:54; 28:2). Whereas David spoke metaphorically of his deliverance in exodus and conquest terms (18:7–19; 30–45 [MT 18:8–20; 31–46]), those events found their fulfillment in the death and resurrection of Jesus, the Lamb of God, who took away the sin of the world. Whereas David began to complete the conquest of the land only to be hampered by his

---

[91] The CSB, NAS, NET, and NIV wrongly render the collective singular "seed," which can refer to one or to many, as "descendants." In view of the hope for the promised king from David's line and the way this is fulfilled in Jesus in the New Testament, the ambiguity should be preserved in translation, whether with the actual term "seed," or with a term such as "offspring" (so ESV). To render this as a plural, "descendants," hides the possibility of this referring to the one king who will arise from David's line.

own sin (2 Sam 8–11; Ps 18:37–45 [18:38–46]), every knee will bow, and every tongue confess that Jesus Christ is Lord.

This psalm also instructs those of us who would live as David did in the hope of the lovingkindess God shows to the seed of David (18:50 [MT 18:51]). We too should love the Lord and look to him as our strength, place of refuge, and hope (18:1–3 [MT 18:2–4]). Like David we must call on the Lord (18:6 [MT 18:7]) and keep his word always before us (18:22 [MT 18:23]), righteously relating to our persecutors with clean hands (18:20, 24 [MT 18:21, 25]), keeping the ways of Yahweh as we keep ourselves from evil (18:21, 23 [MT 18:22, 24]).

Like the Song of Moses sung after Yahweh's victory at the Red Sea, we sing the song of David in Ps 18 in celebration of Yahweh's victory at the cross in anticipation of his victory at the return.

## Psalm 19

OVERVIEW AND STRUCTURE OF PSALM 19

As we approach Ps 19, consider the way that some humans have achieved an immortal name by what they achieved:

- Plato turned the spoken dialogues of Socrates into masterpieces of literary philosophy that made himself and his teacher famous;
- Augustine confessed his sin and prayed through his quest to know God in so searching and profound a way that, after the biblical authors, perhaps no writer has had a deeper influence on Christian thought and spirituality;
- Shakespeare employed nothing more than words to hold the mirror up to nature and help us see the world and ourselves more clearly;
- Mozart surprised and delighted people with the sounds he was able to string together;
- and many others are famous for things they sculpted, painted, engineered, built, or invented.

If the glory of those who make things depends on the splendor of what they have made, how much glory is due to the creator of the world, the giver of life? Can we even begin the process of celebrating what the Creator has achieved in a way that befits what he has done? David sets himself that task in Ps 19, in which his admiration of God as Creator (19:1–6 [MT 19:2–7]) is informed and guided by God's word (19:7–9 [MT 19:8–10]), which woos him to all that is good, true, and beautiful, refines his character, and makes him pleasing to the Lord (19:10–14 [MT 19:11–15]).

After the superscription (MT 19:1), Ps 19 comprises three parts. In 19:1–6 (MT 19:2–7) David celebrates the way the heavens communicate God's glory. Then in 19:7–9 (MT 19:8–10) he pens an encomium on what the Torah is and does, after which in 19:10–14 (MT 19:11–15) he responds to the word of God by describing the affects it has on him.[92]

> 19:1–6 (MT 19:2–7), The Heavens Tell God's Glory
> 19:7–9 (MT 19:8–10), What God's Word Is and Does
> 19:10–14 (MT 19:11–15), Sweeter than Honey, Resulting in Godliness

SCRIPTURE

| CSB | Author's translation |
|---|---|
| For the choir director. A psalm of David. | [1] For the Preeminent One. A Psalm of David. |
| [1] The heavens declare the glory of God, and the expanse proclaims the work of his hands. | [2] The heavens are recounting the glory of God, and, "the works of his hands!" declares the firmament. |
| [2] Day after day they pour out speech; night after night they communicate knowledge. | [3] Day to day pours out speech, and night to night declares knowledge. |
| [3] There is no speech; there are no words; their voice is not heard. | [4] There is no speech, and there are no words; not heard is their voice. |
| [4] Their message has gone out to the whole earth, and their words to the ends of the world. | [5] On all the earth their line goes out, and at the end of the world their utterance; for the sun he put a tent in them. |
| In the heavens he has pitched a tent for the sun. | [6] And he, as a bridegroom, goes out from his chamber, he exults, as a strong man, to run his path. |
| [5] It is like a bridegroom coming from his home; | |

---

[92] For a proposed chiasm in Ps 19, see Alden, "Chiastic Psalms 1–50," 18.

it rejoices like an athlete running a
course.
⁶ It rises from one end of the heavens
and circles to their other end;
nothing is hidden from its heat.

⁷ The instruction of the Lᴏʀᴅ is perfect,
renewing one's life;
the testimony of the Lord is
trustworthy,
making the inexperienced wise.
⁸ The precepts of the Lᴏʀᴅ are right,
making the heart glad;
the command of the Lord is radiant,
making the eyes light up.
⁹ The fear of the Lᴏʀᴅ is pure,
enduring forever;
the ordinances of the Lord are reliable
and altogether righteous.
¹⁰ They are more desirable than gold—
than an abundance of pure gold;
and sweeter than honey
dripping from a honeycomb.
¹¹ In addition, your servant is warned
by them,
and in keeping them there is an
abundant reward.

¹² Who perceives his unintentional
sins?
Cleanse me from my hidden faults.
¹³ Moreover, keep your servant from
willful sins;
do not let them rule me.
Then I will be blameless
and cleansed from blatant rebellion.
¹⁴ May the words of my mouth
and the meditation of my heart
be acceptable to you,
Lᴏʀᴅ, my rock and my Redeemer.

⁷ From the end of the heavens his
going out,
and his circuit upon the ends of them,
and there is nothing hidden from his
heat.

⁸ The Torah of Yahweh has integrity,
restoring the soul.
The testimony of Yahweh is
trustworthy,
making wise the simple.
⁹ The precepts of Yahweh are upright,
rejoicing the heart.
The commandment of Yahweh is
pure,
enlightening the eyes.
¹⁰ The fear of Yahweh is clean,
standing forever.
The judgments of Yahweh are true,
they are righteous altogether.

¹¹ They are more to be desired than
gold,
even much pure gold,
and sweeter than honey,
even flowing from the comb.
¹² Surely your servant is warned by
them,
in the keeping of them is great
reward.
¹³ Errors who can understand?
From hidden things clear me.
¹⁴ Even from presumptuous things
hold back your servant,
let them not rule over me.
Then I will have integrity,
and be cleared from great
transgression.
¹⁵ May the speech of my mouth, and
the meditation of my heart,
be pleasing before you, O Yahweh, my
rock and my redeemer.

19:1 (MT 19:2) "The heavens are recounting the glory of God"
19:6 (MT 19:7) "From the end of the heavens his going out"
2:4 "The one who sits in the heavens"
8:1 (MT 8:2) "put your majesty over the heavens"
8:3 (MT 8:4) "when I look at your heavens"
8:8 (MT 8:9) "birds of the heavens"
11:4 "Yahweh, in the heavens is his throne"
14:2 "Yahweh from the heavens looks down"
18:9 (MT 18:10) "he bowed the heavens and came down"
18:13 (MT 18:14) "he caused thunder in the heavens"
20:6 (MT 20:7) Yahweh answers his messiah from his holy
    heavens

19:1 (MT 19:2) "the works of his hands"
8:3 (MT 8:4) "works of your fingers"
8:6 (MT 8:7) "works of your hands"

19:2 (MT 19:3) "day to day ... night to night"
Compare Gen 1 creation account

19:4 (MT 19:5) "On all the earth" בכל הארץ
8:1, 9 (MT 8:2, 10) "in all the earth" בכל הארץ

19:4 (MT 19:5) "the end of the world"
9:8 (MT 9:9) "he will judge the world"
18:15 (MT 18:16) "the foundations of the world"
24:1 "the world"

19:5 (MT 19:6) "his chamber"
Compare Isa 4:5 "over all the glory a canopy"
Compare Joel 2:16 "the bridegroom comes from his room, and
    the bride from her chamber"

19:7 (MT 19:8) "The Torah of Yahweh"
1:2 "in the Torah of Yahweh is his delight, and on his Torah he
    meditates day and night"

19:7 (MT 19:8) "has integrity"
Compare 15:2; 18:23, 25, 30, 32 (MT 18:24, 26, 31, 33)

19:7 (MT 19:8) "restoring the soul"
23:3 "my soul he restores"

19:7 (MT 19:8) "making wise the simple"
Compare Prov 1:4–6

19:8 (MT 19:9) "enlightening the eyes"
13:3 (MT 13:4) "Enlighten my eyes"
18:28 (MT 18:29) "you cause light in my lamp"

19:9 (MT 19:10) "The fear of Yahweh"
Compare 34:12; 111:10; see also 2:11; 5:7 (MT 5:8)

19:9 (MT 19:10) "is clean"
Compare 12:7

19:9 (MT 19:10) "The judgments of Yahweh"
Compare 7:6 (MT 7:7); 9:4, 7, 16 (MT 9:5, 8, 17); 10:5; 17:2; 18:22
    (MT 18:23)

19:10 (MT 19:11) "pure gold"
Compare 21:3 (MT 21:4)

19:11, 13 (MT 19:12, 14) "your servant"
Compare 18 superscription (MT 18:1)

19:14 (MT 19:15) "speech of my mouth"
Compare Deut 32:1; Ps 54:2 (MT 54:4); 78:1; 138:4

19:14 (MT 19:15) "meditation of my heart"
Compare 1:2; 9:16 (MT 9:17)

19:14 (MT 19:15) "my rock"
Compare 18:2, 46 (MT 18:3, 47)

Psalm 19 stands at the center of the chiasm that begins in Ps 15 and runs through 24 (see "Context" discussion accompanying Ps 15 above). Preceded and followed by psalms that deal with deliverance (Pss 18 and 20–21), resurrection (17 and 22), satisfaction (16 and 23), and the holy king (15 and 24), Ps 19 celebrates the way God has revealed himself in creation and Scripture.

## 19:1–6 (MT 19:2–7), The Heavens Tell God's Glory

The superscription of Ps 19 is the same found on Pss 20 and 21.

The first six verses of Ps 19 (MT 19:2–7) begin and end with references to the heavens (19:1, 6 [MT 19:2, 7]). Within that outer frame the inaudible communication of the day and night is the subject of 19:2–4 (MT 19:3–5), and at the end of 19:4 (MT 19:5) David personifies the sun to celebrate the way it shows God's glory in the sky (19:4c–6 [MT 19:5c–7]).

The creation has inspired awe and wonder in David, and he responds to God's glory in creation by shaping language that celebrates what God has accomplished in making the world. God's prowess inspires David's unmatched poetry. David has carefully arranged a string of words meant to sparkle with the glory of the God he attempts to extol. That is to say, as beautiful as this psalm is, the point is not the beauty of the psalm but the wonder of the one it celebrates.

The greatest works of art point beyond themselves to something higher and deeper and more worthy than themselves. This means that those works of art that celebrate infinite greatness have most potential to inspire. A celebration of some limited greatness or flawed hero will limit our delight: we look at a statue of Zeus, and as magnificent as it may be, it not only reminds us of his power but of his troubled marriage, adulterous philandering, and failures to accomplish his purposes. A celebration of the God of the Bible affords an opportunity for uninhibited, unmitigated delight in absolute perfection, moral probity, and never-failing success.

We want to pay attention to the poetry of the Psalms because the beauty of the poetry is meant to communicate the intricacy and simplicity and pulsating rhythmic magnificence of the one the poet extols. A literal rendering of Ps 19:1 (MT 19:2) brings out the way that the verse is a self-contained chiasm:

The heavens
    are recounting
        the glory of God,
        and, "the works of his hands!"
    declares
the firmament.

The matching elements are obviously parallel. The heavens and the firmament, created by God in Gen 1:1 and 1:6, are personified as speakers who "recount" God's glory and "declare" the work of his hands, as though they are enumerating God's wonder-provoking displays and retelling the skillful craftsmanship of his fingers (cf. Ps 8:3, where "the heavens" are "the work of your fingers," see also 8:6 [MT 8:4, 7]).[93] The upshot of this carefully crafted poetic statement is that God's skill and power and worth are communicated by what he has made.

David began in Ps 19:1 (MT 19:2) with what God made in Gen 1:1 and 6, the heavens and the firmament, and he continues in 19:2 (MT 19:3) with what God made in Gen 1:3-5, where God created light, separated light and darkness, and named light day and darkness night. Just as the heavens and the firmament were personified, so it is with day and night in 19:2 (MT 19:3). They are described in human terms, depicted as great talkers whose words instruct, pouring out speech and declaring knowledge. Here again we have a carefully crafted line of poetry, with subject phrases (day to day, night to night), verbs (pours out, declares), and objects (speech, knowledge) all parallel. Once again the point of the poetic personification is that God reveals and communicates through what he has made.

The day and the night introduced in 19:2 (MT 19:3) remain under consideration through the first two lines of 19:4 (MT 19:5). Having described them as personified speakers in 19:2 (MT 19:3), David clarifies that there are no audible words through the three parallel phrases of 19:3 (MT 19:4). The heavens and the firmament, the day and the night, all speak, but not in words that can be heard with the ears. Other means of sensory perception must be employed to hear what they say, and in view of 19:7-9 (MT 19:8-10), the hearing must be guided by God's word in the Torah.

David had described the way the Lord's name is majestic "in all the earth" in Ps 8:1 and 9 (MT 8:2, 10), and he uses the same phrase in 19:4 (MT 19:5) to describe the way the "line" belonging to heaven and firmament, day and night, goes over "all the earth," by which what they communicate extends to the end of the world. This term "line" is used elsewhere to describe a measuring line (e.g., Ezek 47:3; Zech 1:16), so that may be the intended visual image. Alternatively, it could be that the "line" between light and dark, day and night that passes through the heavens over all

---

[93] For the way the language and themes of Gen 1–3 pervade Ps 19, see Bullock, "Book 1," 44–45.

the earth is depicted here. Either way, the meaning is that there is no place on the earth that is not exposed to what heaven and firmament, day and night communicate.[94] These speakers are heard the world over.

In the final line of Ps 19:4 (MT 19:5) David moves to what God made in Gen 1:14–16 as he begins his personification of the sun. God suspended the sun in the heavens at creation, and David describes the sun as a man for whom God pitched a tent, a tent located in the heavens and the firmament, the day and the night. That tent in 19:4c (MT 19:5c) appears to be the "chamber" from which the sun emerges like a bridegroom in 19:5 (MT 19:6). The term rendered "chamber" here occurs elsewhere only at Joel 2:16 and Isa 4:5, both passages that have overtones of a wedding. The depiction of the sun as a bridegroom in Ps 19:5 (MT 19:6) indicates that the sun comes forth from his chamber with the enthusiasm and anticipation of a man about to be married. The sun is like a man who exults over his new bride, and the second comparison in 19:5 (MT 19:6) complements this picture: The sun is depicted as a strong man running his race with joy. The sun does not slouch onto the scene like a lazy, unkempt freeloader but bursts forth with ready eagerness and focused strength. The sun stands at the starting line like an Olympian sprinter, shaking out his powerful arms and legs ready to display his graceful stride and unflagging stamina. The image of the strong man running his race is maintained in 19:6 (MT 19:7), as the sun is described circling the heavens, with nothing hidden from the light of his presence. Again, God's power in creation is evoked by these images, and again the assertion is made that God has revealed himself in creation everywhere the sun shines, everywhere night falls, and every place that sits under the heavens. There is no place on earth where the voice of these communicators cannot be heard. There is no architectural achievement that compares with the vault of the heavens, no engineering feat that outshines the sun on its circuit.

David uses the poetry of Ps 19 to urge his audience to do the following:

---

[94] KJV and NAS render the text as it stands, "line," while other translations interpret instead of translating: ESV, NET, and NIV have "voice," CSB has "message." The problem with interpreting instead of translating is that it strips away the poetic image of either a measuring line or the line between day and night that passes over all the earth. So instead of a vivid poetic image that the reader has the opportunity to ponder, the interpretation posing as a translation flattens the text with a bland interpretation that restates what has already been communicated instead of translating the fresh pictographic language of the poet.

1. Look at the world.
2. Think about what you see.
3. Give praise to the designer, the architect, the engineer, the enlivener of this all-surpassing project.

As clear a voice as the creation has, apart from the Torah it will fall on deaf ears. Having given this unmatched description of God's glory in creation in 19:1–6 (MT 19:2–7), David turns to the nature and power of the Torah in 19:7–9 (MT 19:8–10).

### 19:7–9 (MT 19:8–10), What God's Word Is and Does

David is able to see God's glory in creation because he has experienced God's glory in Scripture, and the interconnectedness of these perceptive activities is demonstrated in the structure of Ps 19. Only someone whose understanding of the universe has been determined by the Torah's creation account would write Ps 19.[95] Having extolled God by celebrating creation in 19:1–6 (MT 19:2–7), David now extolls God by celebrating Scripture in 19:7–9 (MT 19:8–10). Here again the form of the poetry is part of the point. David's carefully structured statements are designed to reflect the craftsmanship on display in God's revelation of himself in his word.

Psalm 19:7–9 (MT 19:8–10) consists of:

- three verses,
- five references to God's word (Torah, testimony, precepts, commandment, and judgments),
- one response to God (fear),
- five characteristics of God's word (integrity, trustworthiness, uprightness, purity, and truth),
- one characteristic of the fear of God (cleanness),
- four things the word of God changes (the soul, the simple, the heart, and the eyes),
- and six things the word of God does (restores, makes wise, gives joy, enlightens, stands forever, and enacts unified righteousness).

---

[95] Schreiner writes of Pss 19 and 119, "These psalms represent the experience of the remnant. The remnant did not find the law to be a burden or onerous, but a joy. The righteous, who were circumcised in heart, did not sigh when considering the Torah, but found it to be the delight of their hearts." Schreiner, "Commands of God," 78 n. 14.

Every statement in 19:7–9 (MT 19:8–10) follows the same formula in Hebrew: the first three words state what God's word is, and the following two words state what it does. Psalm 19:9a (MT 19:10a) breaks the pattern of thought by referring to the fear of Yahweh instead of the word of Yahweh, but the formula of a three word statement followed by a two word statement is maintained. Then in 19:9b (MT 19:10b) the pattern of thought is resumed with the final instance of the formula.

Psalm 19:7 (MT 19:8) asserts that Yahweh's Torah is perfect, and the term commonly rendered "perfect" connotes integrity and wholeness. It means that there are no internal contradictions, no conflicting perspectives, and no incoherent logical leaps. Unlike ancient myths with their insoluble dilemmas, and unlike modern scientific myths with their claims that stagger imagination and belief, the Torah of Yahweh is complete, whole, flawless, and blameless.

That first assertion states what the law of the Lord is, and the next states what it does:[96] restore the soul. The term rendered "restoring" is a word that means "return" and is often used to describe or call for repentance. This connotation appears to inform the KJV rendering of the phrase, "converting the soul." Other translations opt for "reviving/refreshing" (NIV) or renewing (CSB). The word rendered "soul" is sometimes rendered "life," and seems to denote that inner aspect of who we are that can be distinguished from what the Bible describes as our "heart," where we do our thinking. The inner man is repaired, restored, returned to its right state by the Torah of Yahweh.

Psalm 19:7 (MT 19:8) goes on to state that "the testimony of Yahweh is trustworthy." The two tablets with the Ten Commandments are described as "testimony" (Exod 31:18), the ark of the covenant is called "the ark of the testimony" (Josh 4:16), and the Torah is described as containing statutes, commandments, judgments, and testimonies (1 Kgs 2:3). This term "testimony" is another way to describe God's word, what he says for himself in the Ten Commandments, for instance, and what the "testifiers" (cognate term) have said about him. The claim here is that the testimony from and about God in Torah is trustworthy. God is not telling lies about himself, and the biblical authors are not bearing false witness about him.

---

[96] I first heard these statements in Ps 19 described in these terms (what the law is; what the law does) in a sermon by Josh Philpot preached at Kenwood Baptist Church.

The Bible contains reliable testimony, and reliable testimony swears to how things really are, what really happened, and what really should be done. People do foolish things because they hold false beliefs about how things are, what really happened, or what should be done. The Bible's trustworthy testimony makes simpleminded people wise because it bears witness against false claims about who we are, how we got here, and what results from different behaviors. Flowers of happiness do not spring up from the soil of sin the way simple, foolish people expect. The Bible's testimony imparts the wisdom that the oranges and apples and pears and plums of a happy life only grow in the soils of holy living.

The third and fourth descriptions of God's word come in Ps 19:8 (MT 19:9), where David speaks of Yahweh's "precepts" and "commandments." Dictionary.com defines the English word precept as "a moral injunction" or "a procedural directive." This Hebrew term occurs only in the Psalms, and twenty-one of the twenty-four instances of it are in Ps 119. This word for "regulations for the righteous" (*HALOT*, s.v.) appears to be a synonym of "commandment." The assertion here is that Yahweh's precepts are upright. Whatever a culture in rebellion against God might say to the contrary, God's precepts and commandments determine what is morally upright. God's upright moral injunctions, his precepts, produce joy in the heart.

In the summer after my freshman year of college, I had a nightmare one night in which I had committed a crime, been caught, found guilty, and sentenced to prison. I remember the shame I felt, the guilt, the sorrow. My parents would be devastated. My sisters and brother would be embarrassed. And the Lord, of course, would be displeased with me. And then I woke up innocent, law abiding, and free. Psalm 19:8a (MT 19:9a) is true: the Lord's precepts are upright, and they rejoice the heart.

Not only are the precepts upright, the next line of Ps 19:8 (MT 19:9) asserts that Yahweh's commandments are pure. What Yahweh demands of his people is never immoral, never inappropriate, and never even questionable. Yahweh's commandments enjoy a shining moral rectitude, the rising glory of freedom from any debasing corruption or pollution. The immaculate, unstained, unsullied beauty of holiness is on display in what God commands, and the commandment has the power to enlighten the eyes. David here asserts that apart from God's commands people would be in the wayward darkness of confusions, but when the commandment is given the eyes are enlightened. God's word enables us to see not only where we should go but how we should get there.

In Ps 19:9a (MT 19:10a) the pattern of the material—descriptions of God's word—is broken, but it is broken in a way that does not alter the train of thought but complements it, even as the pattern of expression—three-word statements followed by two-word statements—is maintained. David says that the fear of Yahweh is clean, and the word "clean" connotes ritual purity. This departure from speaking of God's word nevertheless fits perfectly because it is the revelation of God in Scripture that prompts the appropriate response of fear, and the appropriate response of fear likewise prompts further attention to Scripture. No one will be defiled or made ritually unclean by fearing God. And God is so fearsome that it will be appropriate to reverence him, to fear him, forever.

David returns to the pattern in the final statement of this section of Ps 19, saying in 19:9b (MT 19:10b) that Yahweh's judgments are true and righteous altogether. Yahweh will never render an unjust decision, never fail to enact righteousness, and never be tempted by anything unrighteous, corrupt, or clandestine. The judgments that Yahweh has decided that are recorded in Scripture are true. They correspond to reality, they stand against evil, they enact justice.

The truth of the Scriptures (19:7–9 [MT 19:8–10]) enables David to see God's glory in creation (19:1–6 [MT 19:2–7]), and the truth of the Scriptures also enables David to see his need for God's mercy and forgiveness (19:10–14 [MT 19:11–15]).

### 19:10–14 (MT 19:11–15), Sweeter than Honey, Resulting in Godliness

J. K. Rowling's novel, written under the pseudonym Robert Galbraith, *The Cuckoo's Calling*, is a demonstration of the misery brought about by a man who seeks money as the salve of his deepest wounds.[97] The villain in the novel commits murder in a vain attempt to inherit a fortune the victim did not want to give to him, and the villain has no peace, no rest, no security, and no joy.

Having described what God's word is and what it does in Ps 19:7–9 (MT 19:8–10), David responds to God's word in 19:10–14 (MT 19:11–15). He recognizes in 19:10a (MT 19:11a) that the Bible is more desirable than gold. Gold cannot renew the soul, give wisdom, or enlighten the eyes the way the Bible can. Gold is merely a valuable asset, and David recognizes

---

[97] Robert Galbraith, *The Cuckoo's Calling* (New York: Little, Brown, 2013).

that knowing God comes from the Scriptures not from gold. David recognizes that knowing God is the highest good, that the Scriptures reveal God, and that to use gold well one must know God and be taught of him in the Scriptures. God's word, therefore, is more valuable that gold, even a lot of the highest quality.

Similarly, God's word is better than sensory experience—encapsulated here by the reference to the sweetness of honey. David recognizes that he needs God's word more than he needs the satisfaction of his bodily needs and the stimulation of his taste buds that honey brings. Anyone who has encountered God through the Scriptures will resonate with David's assertion in Ps 19:10b (MT 19:11b) that the word of God is sweeter than honey. There is an experiential delight that comes from the experience of the presence of God, whose company we were created to enjoy, that transcends the sweet taste and rush of energy honey provides.

From what David says here we see that exposure to God's word has transformed his desires—because he has encountered God in the Scriptures, he has a greater desire for the Bible than for money and sensory pleasure. The Bible has wooed David away from other sources of pleasure.

As he continues in 19:11 (MT 19:12), David speaks of himself as God's servant (see discussion of the superscription to Ps 18), stating that the Scriptures warn him and promise great reward. The Bible holds out before us the highest joy of knowing God, warns us of the destructive results of sin, and promises rewards for those who obey.

In Ps 19:12 (MT 19:13) David recognizes his need for the moral clarity of the Scriptures, asking literally, "Errors who can understand?" We do not always know the right thing to do, nor are we always able to probe the reasons for which we do the wrong thing. We do not understand our own sinfulness, but into our moral darkness God mercifully shines the light of the Scriptures. When David asks to be declared innocent of hidden things in 19:12b (MT 19:13b), he alludes to Exod 34:6–7, where the Lord asserts that he forgives iniquity, transgression, and sin but does not declare the guilty innocent. David seems to acknowledge that there are hidden things in his life as he asks God to show him mercy.

Again describing himself as God's servant in 19:13 (MT 19:14), David calls on Yahweh to hold him back from presumptuous things. Coming hard on the heels of the reference to "hidden things" in the previous verse, this reference to "presumptuous things" probably refers to the kinds of open, public sins committed by people whose consciences have grown hard by their hidden, private sins, to the point that they sin in plain sight without regard for what others think. To get to this point is to experience the awful reign of sin, the dominion of the dark powers that enslave people to iniquity. David wants the light of Scripture to shine on his hidden sins, and he wants to turn from those things, to be thereby restrained from the hardness of heart that leads to flagrant public transgression, to be delivered from sin's dominion.

When the Lord declares David innocent from his private sins and restrains him from the worst impulses of his nature, he says in 19:13b (MT 19:14b), he will be blameless—having integrity—and he will be freed from the pull of heinous sin. These statements make clear that when David speaks of being blameless he refers not to sinless perfection resulting from perfect obedience. Rather, David sees blamelessness arising from a confession of private sin that leads to God mercifully acquitting him of guilt and restraining him from outrageous behavior.

Hidden sins arise from wicked desires fed by wicked thoughts that lead to wicked choices. Those hidden sins are often hidden by deceitful statements designed to keep the sin secret. These realities seem to prompt David to pray to the Lord to so work on him that what he says and thinks about might be pleasing in God's sight (cf. Ps 1:2). The Bible (19:7–9 [MT 19:8–10]) enables David to see God's glory in creation (19:1–6 [MT 19:2–7]), and the Bible has also enabled David to perceive the sinful inclinations in his own heart, to confess that God's way is most desirable (19:10 [MT 19:11]), that God's word warns of recompense and woos with reward (19:11 [MT 19:12]), that it exposes sin and promises forgiveness (19:12 [MT 19:13]), that it restrains, delivers, and produces godliness, for which David prays in Ps 19:14 (MT 19:15).

Bridge

The word of God still does today what it did for David, opening our eyes to see God's glory in creation, shining the light on the hidden thoughts of our hearts, giving new desires, warning and wooing, convicting and restraining, provoking us to speak and think in ways pleasing to the Lord.

The ultimate means whereby God can declare the guilty to be innocent (Ps 19:12 [MT 19:13]) because they have repented and believed in Jesus

(Rom 3:24–26) awaits the coming of the one whose every word and every meditation would be pleasing to God, the one who always did the will of his Father, who obeyed even unto death. Because of Christ's death on the cross, those who turn from sin and trust in Christ can be declared innocent of their hidden sin, justified by grace through faith.

## Psalm 20

OVERVIEW AND STRUCTURE OF PSALM 20

Psalm 20:1–5 (MT 20:2–6) is a list of prayers David offers on behalf of a singular "you," as in "May Yahweh answer you" (20:1a [MT 20:2a]). In view of the context (esp. 20:9 [MT 20:10]) it seems that the individual for whom David prays is the promised seed, the future king from his line (cf. 2 Sam 7:12–15). These statements are things David wants God to do for his descendant. They take the form of blessings that both ask God to do these things and communicate the prayers to the one on whose behalf they are made. This way of approaching Ps 20 is in keeping with the concluding words of Ps 18, where David spoke of Yahweh's great salvation of his king, the way he showed lovingkindness to his anointed, "to David and his seed forever" (18:50 [MT 18:51]).

After the prayers, in 20:6–8 (MT 20:7–9) David articulates his confidence in God's salvation. With a nod to the futility of trusting anything other than Yahweh, David shows confidence that his prayers will be answered.

Psalm 20 concludes in verse 9 (MT 20:10) with a prayer for God to save the king. The two lines of Ps 20:9 (MT 20:10) summarize the whole psalm. The first line prays for God to save the king, summarizing the blessings on the king in 20:1–5 (MT 20:1–6). The second line boldly asserts that Yahweh will answer, summarizing the confidence based on God's promises in 20:6–8 (MT 20:7–9).

> 20:1–5 (MT 20:2–6) Blessings on the Coming King
> 20:6–8 (MT 20:7–9) The Lord Will Save His Messiah
> 20:9 (MT 20:10) God Save the King

SCRIPTURE

| CSB | Author's translation |
|---|---|
| For the choir director. A psalm of David. | [1] For the Preeminent One. A Psalm of David |

CSB

For the choir director. A psalm of David.

[1] May the LORD answer you in a day of trouble;
may the name of Jacob's God protect you.
[2] May he send you help from the sanctuary
and sustain you from Zion.
[3] May he remember all your offerings
and accept your burnt offering.
*Selah*

[4] May he give you what your heart desires
and fulfill your whole purpose.
[5] Let us shout for joy at your victory
and lift the banner in the name of our God.
May the LORD fulfill all your requests.
[6] Now I know that the Lord gives victory to his anointed;
he will answer him from his holy heaven
with mighty victories from his right hand.
[7] Some take pride in chariots, and others in horses,
but we take pride in the name of the LORD our God.
[8] They collapse and fall,
but we rise and stand firm.
[9] LORD, give victory to the king!
May he answer us on the day that we call.

Author's translation

[1] For the Preeminent One.
A Psalm of David

[2] May Yahweh answer you[98] on the day of distress;
may the name of the God of Jacob set you securely on high.
[3] May he send your help from the holy place,
and from Zion may he support you.
[4] May he remember all your grain offerings,
and make your burnt offerings fat.
*Selah.*
[5] May he give to you according to your heart,
and all your counsel may he fulfill.
[6] May we give a ringing cry at your salvation,
and in the name of our God we will set up our banner.
May Yahweh fulfill all your petitions.
[7] Now I know that Yahweh causes salvation for his messiah;
he will answer him from the heavens of his holiness,
by the powers of salvation at his right hand.

[8] These in the chariots, and these in the horses,
but as for us, on the name of Yahweh our God we will cause remembrance.
[9] They are bowed down and fall,

---

[98] All of the second-person singular pronouns ("you/your") in 20:2–6 (MT 20:3-7) are singular. In view of verses 7 and 10, it seems that David psalms these prayer-wish blessings on behalf of the future king from his line.

but as for us, we rise and bear
witness.

[10] O Yahweh, cause salvation for the
king;
he will answer us on the day we call.[99]

CONTEXT: VERBAL AND THEMATIC LINKS WITH SURROUNDING PSALMS

More significant than particular lexical links between Ps 20 and surrounding material is the flow of thought. We have observed the chiastic
structure of Pss 15–24, with the glory of God's revelation of himself in
creation and Scripture at the center in Ps 19. It is precisely that glory of
God celebrated in Ps 19 that makes David pray as he does in Pss 20 and 21.
God's power, displayed in creation and described in Scripture, guarantees
the answers to David's prayers, which are based on God's promises.

Psalms 20 and 21 also balance David's account of the way the Lord
delivered him in Ps 18. This relationship also indicates that the prayers
of Pss 20 and 21 will be answered. As God delivered David in the past, so
he will deliver the scion of David in the future. David's confidence rests
on Scripture and his own enscripturated experience.

20:1 (MT 20:2) "on the day of distress"
Compare 18:6 (MT 18:7) "in my distress"

20:2 (MT 2:3) "support"
18:35 (MT 18:36) "support"

20:4 (MT 20:5) "counsel"
1:1 "counsel"

20:5 (MT 2:6) "your salvation"
18:50 (MT 18:51) "salvation"

20:6 (MT 20:7) "at his right hand"
18:35 (MT 18:36) "right hand"

20:8 (MT 20:9) "they are bowed down and fall"
18:38 (MT 18:39) "they will fall"
18:39 (MT 18:40) "to bow"

---

[99] Or, "O Yahweh, cause salvation; as for the king, he will answer us on the day we call."

## 20:1–5 (MT 20:2–6), Blessings on the Coming King

All ten blessings in Ps 20:1–5 (MT 20:1–6) are prayed for a particular individual—each second-person reference ("you") in these verses is singular. Having articulated the tenfold blessing, David states that he knows Yahweh will cause salvation for his messiah in 20:6 (MT 20:7), and then he summarizes and concludes the psalm in 20:9 (MT 20:10) with a prayer for God to save the king and a confident statement that God will answer. David here prays for the messiah, the king (20:6, 9 [MT 20:7, 10]). This indicates that in this prayer David offers a prayer-wish-blessing to the individual seed God promised to raise up, place on David's throne, and cause to endure forever in 2 Sam 7:12–15.

In Ps 20:1a (MT 20:2a) David uses language familiar from many psalms to express his wish-blessing that Yahweh might answer "you" on the day of trouble. David rehearsed in Ps 18 the way he called on Yahweh and was saved from his enemies (18:6 [MT 18:7]). He went on in Ps 18 to describe the way the Lord worked a new exodus and conquest style deliverance for him (18:7–15, 37–42 [MT 18:8–16, 38–43]). David clearly hopes that Yahweh will save his descendant the same way.

The language of the second blessing in 20:1b (MT 20:2b) is different, but the concepts are the same as what David said the Lord did for him in 18:33 and 48 (MT 18:34, 49). David articulates the hope that "the name of the God of Jacob" will do this. The reference to Yahweh as "God of Jacob" recalls Israel's history. David's prayer for his descendant to be "set securely on high" attaches to God's reputation, his name. God's reputation, in turn, flows from what the Scriptures say God did for his people in the past.

David said in 18:6 (MT 18:7) that Yahweh heard his cry from his temple (cf. 2:6; 3:4 [MT 3:5]). In 20:2a (MT 20:3a) he articulates his prayerful hope that Yahweh will send his descendent help "from the holy place" (CSB, ESV, "sanctuary"). Along these lines, in 2:6 Yahweh asserted that he had installed his king on Zion, site of the Temple Mount, and in 20:2b (MT 20:3b) David hopes Yahweh will "support" his descendant from Zion. Different terms are used in 18:18 (MT 18:19, משען, a noun) and 20:2 (MT 20:3, סעד, a verb), but in both places David speaks of Yahweh "supporting" his anointed king. David also said God did this for him by his right hand in 18:35 (MT 18:36, סעד).

David articulated his desire for Yahweh to deliver the future messiah in Ps 20:1–2 (MT 20:2–3). In 20:3 (MT 20:4) he makes a statement that assumes the piety of the one to come, which will ground Yahweh's good pleasure in him. David wants Yahweh to remember all the grain offerings the messiah will make, and he wants Yahweh to regard all his burnt offerings as fat (20:3 [MT 20:4]). No skinny malnourished reject animals will the messiah offer to the Lord. Rather, the messiah will faithfully serve God. David prays that God will remember the pious offerings and sacrifices.

Not only do the words of David's blessing in 20:3 (MT 20:4) indicate that the messiah will offer sacrifices, the words of his blessing in 20:4 (MT 20:5) assume that the messiah will desire what pleases God. Only thus could David offer the wish-prayer that God will grant the desires of his heart and fulfill all his counsel.[100] The term "counsel" is the same used in Ps 1:1 to describe the wicked counsel in which the blessed man does not walk. This indicates that the Torah informs and governs the king's counsel.

In Ps 20:5a (MT 20:6a) David prays in the hope that the king's salvation will cause the people to rejoice. Such a prayer assumes that the king will have won the hearts of the people. People groan when the wicked reign (cf. Prov 29:2). But David prays that when his seed reigns, the people will give a ringing cry (20:5a [MT 20:6a]). In God's name David hopes all the people of the messiah will set up their banner in 20:5b (MT 20:6b). This indicates that the king's triumph will be Yahweh's triumph. The banners will be emblazoned with the strong name of the one who reigns, maker, ruler, provider, king, judge, and lawgiver. The one who is worthy.

The last of the ten blessings articulates the sweeping hope that Yahweh will fulfill all the king's petitions (20:5c [MT 20:6c]). The word rendered "requests" (CSB) and "petitions" (my trans., ESV) is built from the same root as Saul's name (שאל, משאלה). Perhaps David chose this word to evoke a contrast between the king from his line, and the prayers he will offer, and rejected Saul, and the unfulfilled requests he made (cf. 2 Sam 7:15). This blessing assumes that the king will be a man of prayer, that he will rely on the Lord and hope in him.

## 20:6–8 (MT 20:7–9), The Lord Will Save His Messiah

Scripture and his own experience produce David's confidence "that Yahweh causes salvation for his messiah," as he puts it in 20:6a (MT 20:7a).

---

[100] Cf. the same construction, כלבבך, in 1 Sam 14:7. It clearly refers to what the messiah desires in the psalm and to what Jonathan desires in Samuel. This means that the king according to God's heart in 1 Sam 13:14, כלבבו, will be the one whom God desires (as opposed to a statement being made about the king's character).

David knows the promise of the seed of the woman (Gen 3:15), the blessing of Abraham (12:1–3), the blessing of Judah (Gen 49:8–12), and he sees their fulfillment in the king God promised would come from his line (2 Sam 7:12–15; Ps 2). David is confident that God will answer the messiah from heaven (20:6b [MT 20:7b]) because God has promised to establish the throne of the seed of David. Just as David said the Lord supported him by his right hand (18:35 [MT 18:36]), David is confident that Yahweh will use "the powers of salvation at his right hand" to deliver his descendant (20:6c [MT 20:7c]).

The king of Israel was not to trust in chariots and horses (Deut 17:16) but in Yahweh.[101] The cause of victory receives the credit for victory. David asserts that those who align with him, those who join him in blessing the king to come from his line, are the people who will cause remembrance of the name of Yahweh rather than the power of chariot wheel or horseflesh.

Those whose trust is in worldly things will delight in worldly counsel rather than Scripture (cf. Ps 1:1), and they will be like chaff that does not rise (1:4–5). That is to say, like David's enemies who are caused to bow (18:39 [MT 18:40]) and fall (18:38 [MT 18:39]), those who cause horse and chariot to be remembered rather than Yahweh will be "bowed down and fall."

I have translated Ps 20:8b (MT 20:9b) "but as for us, we rise and bear witness" rather than the way translations typically render it, "we rise and stand firm" (CSB, cf. ESV).[102] This seems to me to fit the context where God's people will cause Yahweh's name to be remembered in 20:7b (MT 20:8b), and it matches the rising to stand with the congregation of the righteous in 1:5. This understanding would identify the congregation of the righteous (1:5) with "David and his seed" (18:50 [MT 18:51]) as those who will cause remembrance of Yahweh's name (20:7 [MT 20:8]) when they "rise" (20:8 [MT 20:9]): when they are raised from the dead to bear everlasting witness to Yahweh's salvation.

---

[101] So also Bullock, "Book 1," 46.

[102] The decision hinges on different meanings of the root עוד. The context persuades me that "bear witness" is the meaning to be preferred to "help one another up," which is the rendering offered by HALOT, s.v.

## 20:9 (MT 20:10), God Save the King

The blessings of Ps 20:1–5 (MT 20:2–6) are summarized in the prayer of Ps 20:9a (MT 20:10a), "O Yahweh, cause salvation for the king."[103] If Yahweh saves the king, he will indeed "answer" the king in his "distress," setting him "securely on high" (20:1 [MT 20:2]). He will have sent help from the sanctuary and supported him from Zion (20:2 [MT 20:3]). The king's offerings and sacrifices will be remembered (20:3 [MT 20:4]), and his heart's desire and counsel will be realized (20:4 [MT 20:5]), while the people aligned with him celebrate (20:5 [MT 20:6]).

Similarly, 20:9b (MT 20:10b) summarizes the confidence of 20:6–8 (MT 20:7–9). Yahweh will answer the prayers David leads the people in for the king (20:1–5 [MT 20:2–6]), causing salvation for the messiah (20:6 [MT 20:7]), and that will lay low the enemies and raise up God's people so they can testify (20:7–8 [MT 20:8–9]).

BRIDGE

The Lord Jesus cried out to the Father in the words of Ps 22 on the day of his distress. God the Father answered the prayers of David for his promised descendant in Ps 20 by raising Jesus from the dead. The people of God give ringing cries in celebration of God's salvation, just as David hoped we would in Ps 20:5 (MT 20:6).

## Psalm 21

OVERVIEW AND STRUCTURE OF PSALM 21

Psalm 21 evidences a chiastic structure:[104]

21:1–2 (MT 21:2–3), Celebration of Yahweh's Strength
    21:3–7 (MT 21:4–8), Yahweh Blesses the King
    21:8–12 (MT 21:9–13), The King Conquers
21:13 (MT 21:14), Celebration of Yahweh's Strength

---

[103] This rendering privileges the poetic parallelism of the words of the verse over the Masoretic accentuation of the line.

[104] Similarly Alden, "Chiastic Psalms 1–50," 18.

SCRIPTURE

CSB

Author's translation

For the choir director. A psalm of David.

¹ For the Preeminent One. A Psalm of David.

¹ LORD, the king finds joy in your strength. How greatly he rejoices in your victory!
² You have given him his heart's desire and have not denied the request of his lips. *Selah*

² O Yahweh, in your strength the king will be glad,
and in your salvation how he will rejoice exceedingly!
³ The desire of his heart you will give to him,
and the request of his lips you do not withhold. *Selah*.

³ For you meet him with rich blessings;
you place a crown of pure gold on his head.
⁴ He asked you for life, and you gave it to him—
length of days forever and ever.
⁵ His glory is great through your victory;
you confer majesty and splendor on him.
⁶ You give him blessings forever;
you cheer him with joy in your presence.
⁷ For the king relies on the LORD;
through the faithful love of the Most High
he is not shaken.

⁴ For you meet him with blessings of good;
you appoint a crown of pure gold for his head.
⁵ Life he asked from you.
You gave to him length of days to the age and on.
⁶ Great his glory in your salvation;
splendor and majesty you bestow on him.
⁷ For you appoint him blessings forever;
you make him joyful in gladness with your presence.
⁸ For the king trusts in Yahweh,
and in the lovingkindness of the Most High he will not totter.

⁸ Your hand will capture all your enemies;
your right hand will seize those who hate you.
⁹ You will make them burn
like a fiery furnace when you appear;
the LORD will engulf them in his wrath,
and fire will devour them.
¹⁰ You will wipe their progeny from the earth

⁹ Your hand will find all the ones at enmity with you;
your right hand will find the ones who hate you.
¹⁰ You will appoint them a furnace of fire for the time of your face;
Yahweh, in his wrath, he will consume them,
and fire will devour them.
¹¹ Their fruit from the earth you will destroy,
and their seed from the sons of Adam.

and their offspring from the human race.

11 Though they intend to harm you and devise a wicked plan, they will not prevail.

12 Instead, you will put them to flight when you ready your bowstrings to shoot at them.

13 Be exalted, LORD, in your strength; we will sing and praise your might.

12 For they stretched evil over you, they devised a scheme.
They will not prevail.

13 For you appoint them a shoulder, when your bowstring you establish against their faces.

14 Be lifted, O Yahweh, in your strength!
We will sing and psalm your might!

CONTEXT: VERBAL AND THEMATIC LINKS WITH SURROUNDING PSALMS

Psalm 21 is a celebration of the answered prayers of Ps 20. Psalm 20 ended with a statement about the king, and Ps 21 opens with the same (20:9 [MT 20:10]; 21:1 [MT 21:2]). Beyond the lexical connection is a thematic relationship: Psalm 20 is David's confident statement of blessing, a wish-prayer that God will show his power on behalf of his descendant. Psalm 21 is a celebration of God doing that very thing.

> 21:1 (MT 21:2) "the king"
> 20:9 (MT 20:10) "the king"
> Compare 18:50 (MT 18:51); 24:7, 8, 9, 10

> 21:1, 5 (MT 21:2, 6) "your salvation" בישׁועתך
> 20:5 (MT 20:6) "your salvation" בישׁועתך
> Compare 18:50 (MT 18:51); 20:6, 9 (MT 20:7, 10); 22:2

> 21:2 (MT 21:3) "The desire of his heart you will give to him"
> 20:4 (MT 20:5) "May he give to you according to your heart"

> 21:3 (MT 21:4) "meet"
> Compare 18:5, 18 (MT 18:6, 19)

> 21:3, 6, 9, 12 (MT 21:4, 7, 10, 13) "appoint" (שׁית)
> Compare 18:11 (MT 18:12) "makes" (שׁית)

> 21:3 (MT 21:4) "fine gold"
> 19:10 (MT 19:11) "fine gold"

> 21:5 (MT 21:6) "splendor and majesty"
> Compare Ps 8:1, 5 (MT 8:2, 6)

21:6 (MT 21:7) "gladness with your presence"
16:11 "satisfaction of gladnesses is your presence"

21:7 (MT 21:8) "lovingkindness"
18:25, 50 (MT 18:26, 51); 23:6

21:7 (MT 21:8) "Most High"
18:13 (MT 18:14)

21:7 (MT 21:8) "he will not totter"
15:5; 16:8; 17:5

21:8 (MT 21:9) "the ones at enmity"
18:3, 17, 37, 40, 48 (MT 18:4, 18, 38, 41, 49)

21:9 (MT 21:10) "fire"
18:8, 12, 14 (MT 18:9, 13, 14)

21:9 (MT 21:10) "devour"
18:8 (MT 18:9)

21:10 (MT 21:11) "seed"
Compare 18:50 (MT 18:51)

21:10 (MT 21:11) "sons of"
Compare 8:4 (MT 8:5); 18:44–45 (MT 18:45–46)

18:11 (MT 18:12) "they devised a scheme"
Compare 10:2

21:11 (MT 21:12) "they will not prevail"
Compare 18:38 (MT 18:39) "they will not be able"

21:13 (MT 21:14) "Be exalted"
Compare 18:27, 46, 48 (MT 18:28, 47, 49)

21:13 (MT 21:14) "we will ... psalm"
Compare 18:49 (MT 18:50)

EXPOSITION

### 21:1–2 (MT 21:2–3), Celebration of Yahweh's Strength

The two-word phrase that opens Ps 21 is repeated at its end, bracketing Ps 21 with references to Yahweh's strength (יהוה בעזך in 21:1, 13 [MT 21:2, 14]).

Whereas in Ps 20 David prayed that God would cause salvation for the king messiah (20:6, 9 [MT 20:7, 10]), in Ps 21 David describes the king glad in Yahweh's strength and rejoicing in his salvation (21:1 [MT 21:2]). The very thing expressed in the form of a prayer-blessing in 20:5 (MT 20:6), "May we give a ringing cry at your salvation," is envisioned being enacted by the king in 21:1 (MT 21:2), "in your salvation how he will rejoice exceedingly!" The use of the same form (בישׁועתך) in 20:5 and 21:1 (MT 20:6; 21:2) creates the impression that the king's salvation in the former is Yahweh's salvation in the latter.

The unity of theme between Pss 20 and 21 is augmented by 21:2 (MT 21:3), where David asserts that God will grant the desire of the king's heart and not withhold the request of his lips. David addressed the future king with the prayer-blessing in 20:4 (MT 20:5) that Yahweh would give him the desires of his heart, and in 20:5c (MT 20:6c) he said, "May Yahweh fulfill all your petitions." In Ps 21 David says the Lord will do for the king what he, David, asked of him in Ps 20.

### 21:3-7 (MT 21:4-8), Yahweh Blesses the King

In Ps 21:3-7 (MT 21:4-8) David extols the way the Lord will do for the future king the very things God promised to do for the Israel's ultimate king elsewhere in Scripture. David here models confidence in God's word that grows out of familiarity with Scripture and the character of God. David knows the Bible, and David knows God. David's knowledge of God and God's word results in the statements he makes here.

David describes the Lord meeting the king "with blessings of good" (21:3 [MT 21:4]) and appointing him "blessings forever" (21:6 [MT 21:7]) in fulfillment of the promises to Abraham (Gen 12:1-3). David then describes the Lord crowning the future king with "a crown of fine gold" (21:3 [MT 21:4]) in fulfillment of the promise that kings would come from Abraham (Gen 17:6).

The reference to the king asking for life and being granted "length of days forever and ever" in Ps 21:4 (MT 21:5) reflects the Lord's promise to establish the throne of his kingdom forever in 2 Sam 7:13. The phrase "length of days" is used in the promises of reward Solomon makes to his son in Prov 3:2 and 3:16. These promises are based on the Mosaic guarantee that keeping the Torah will result in long life in the land not only for fathers and sons in general (Deut 6:2) but specifically for the king (17:20).

The great glory in God's salvation and the splendor and majesty David describes Yahweh bestowing on the king in Ps 21:5 (MT 21:6) reflect

David's meditation on Adam's role in Gen 1:26–28 being transferred to Israel's king in Ps 8—the terms rendered "splendor and majesty" in 21:5 (MT 21:6) are both used in Ps 8 (8:1, 5 [MT 8:2, 6]).

Psalm 21:6 (MT 21:7) returns to the blessings of Abraham and adds the experiential joyful gladness in God's presence David described himself relishing in Ps 16:11. David expects the king to come from his line to enjoy the highest of pleasures, the presence of God. It is as though this king will reenter Eden to walk with God in the cool of the day.

In Ps 21:7 (MT 21:8) we see that David knows the king will be like Abraham who believed God (Gen 15:6): The conduit of Yahweh's blessing will be the king's trust in Yahweh. David spoke in 18:50 (MT 18:51) of Yahweh's lovingkindness working salvation for the king, his anointed, for David and his seed forever, and he speaks in the same terms in 21:7 (MT 21:8), adding that the lovingkindness of the Most High will ensure that the king will never totter.

David's confidence in God's character and conviction that God will keep his word ground the future hope reflected in these verses. David shows exemplary knowledge of the Bible, and God's character shapes his expectation. The salvation David depicts delighting the king (21:1 [MT 21:2]) is the realization of all biblical promise, expectation, and hope.

### 21:8–12 (MT 21:9–13), The King Conquers

In Ps 20 David prayed in confidence a blessing over the king from his line whose throne God promised to establish. In Ps 21 David celebrates the realization of God's promises. This realization will entail God blessing the king (21:3–7 [MT 21:4–8]), and the king conquering his enemies by Yahweh's might (21:8–12 [MT 21:9–13]). David spoke of the future king in the third person ("he, him," etc.) in 21:3–7 (MT 21:4–8), but in 21:8–12 (MT 21:9–13) he addresses the king directly with second-person singular ("you") statements. An argument could be made that the reference to Yahweh consuming his enemies in 21:9b (MT 21:10b) could make Yahweh the subject of the second-person singular pronouns. The agent, however, of Yahweh's triumph will be Yahweh's king. The king's victory will be Yahweh's victory (cf. again the king's salvation 20:5 [MT 20:6] and Yahweh's salvation in 21:1 [MT 21:2]). Yahweh will achieve his conquest by empowering the faithful king he promised to raise up from David's line.

There are a number of references to the ones at enmity with David in Ps 18 (18:3, 17, 37, 40, 48 [MT 18:4, 18, 38, 41, 49]), and the Lord delivered him from them by enabling him to conquer them. So it is in Ps 21:8 (MT 21:9) as David asserts that the future king "will find out" both those at enmity and those who hate him. David described himself setting Yahweh at his right hand in 16:8 then spoke of the pleasure to be found at Yahweh's right hand in 16:11. David was confident that Yahweh would work salvation by his right hand in 20:6 (MT 20:7; cf. 17:7; 18:35 [MT 18:36]). It is no surprise, then, to read of the king conquering his enemies by his "right hand" in 21:8 (MT 21:9).

Psalm 21:9 (MT 21:10) describes the king appearing in glory by means of the reference to "the time of your face," and when he does his enemies will experience the conflagration of his wrath, which enacts the wrath of Yahweh, as the rebels are consumed in fire. Yahweh's coming was characterized by fire in Ps 18 (cf. 18:8, 12, 13 [MT 18:9, 13, 14]), and in both the Old and New Testaments there are indications that whereas God judged the world by water in the time of Noah he will judge it by fire at the end of all things (cf. Isa 26:11; 66:15–16; 2 Thess 1:7–8; 2 Pet 3:5–7).

When the king visits Yahweh's wrath and consumes his enemies, the conquered will not be like the blessed man whose fruit does not wither (1:3). Instead, all the fruit of the wicked will be destroyed (21:10a [MT 21:11a]; cf. 1:6; 2:12). Whereas the steadfast love of the Lord will last forever to David and his seed (18:50 [MT 18:51]), the seed of the serpent will be put under the ban of God's just judgment: they will be destroyed from the land (21:10b [MT 21:11b]).

Why would God consume people in fire? What could justify putting them under the ban? David answers such questions in 21:11 (MT 21:12). He describes the wicked stretching evil over the king and devising a scheme. They want to color Yahweh's king as evil and themselves as righteous. They want public opinion to condemn Yahweh's king and exonerate them. Their scheme is to have Yahweh's king rejected so that they can maintain power. The concluding words of Ps 21:11 (MT 21:12) comfort all who mourn the depredations of the wicked: "They will not prevail."

Why won't they prevail? The reason is stated in Ps 21:12 (MT 21:13). This reason may seem harsh, so we must set it in context. The enemies of God are the kinds of people who have been exposed in recent days as murdering babies and selling their body parts. They are the kinds of people who finance such brutality with taxes they extract by force from people who would never want to be involved in such outrages. They are the kinds of people who use the power of laws and the verdicts of courts to pervert justice so that they can continue their murderous, deceptive, money-making atrocities.

These are the kinds of people who would use the power of the government to have the King Messiah himself brutally crucified.

How will God respond to such people?

Psalm 21:12 (MT 21:13) can be literally rendered: "For you appoint them a shoulder, when your bowstring you establish against their faces."

The first part of this line, "For you appoint them a shoulder," is typically rendered along the lines of the CSB, "you will put them to flight" (similarly ESV). If the two lines of the verse go together, however, they can be understood as a description of Yahweh's king setting his front shoulder toward his enemies as he nocks the arrow and draws the string. He will "appoint them a shoulder" when he takes aim at them to visit Yahweh's justice.

### 21:13 (MT 21:14), Celebration of Yahweh's Strength

When the true and rightful king punishes the wicked, none of his people will have any qualms about the ferocity of Yahweh's justice brought by Yahweh's king. The indignation will be righteous: the crimes conclusively proved, the criminals convicted beyond doubt, the sentence just.

When Yahweh's king establishes Yahweh's justice, the people of God will cheer him on with words like the ones David penned in Ps 21:13 (MT 21:14). We will respond to the display of God's strength by crying out to him to be exalted in it. And we will sing his praise and psalm the epic story of the consummation of history, the happy ending of history, the most satisfying resolution to the greatest story ever made.

Bridge

The king whose conquest David describes in Ps 21 is the king he blessed with the prayers of Ps 20. Just as Peter described David doing in Acts 2:30–31, David prophetically looks forward to the career of his descendant whom God promised to enthrone. Jesus is the blessed king who has experienced God's goodness in Ps 21:3–7 (MT 21:4–8), and when he returns Jesus will be the agent of Yahweh's wrath whose conquest of his enemies 21:8–12 (MT 21:9–13) psalms. As Ps 21:1–2 (MT 21:2–3) says, King Jesus will be glad in Yahweh's strength, when Yahweh gives him all his desires and requests, and as 21:13 (MT 21:14) describes, God's people will celebrate and sing psalms over the display of God's power in him.

## Psalm 22

OVERVIEW AND STRUCTURE OF PSALM 22

Psalm 22 evidences a chiastic structure that can be depicted as follows:

22:1–2 (MT 22:2–3), Distress
   22:3–5 (MT 22:4–6), Trust and Deliverance
      22:6–8 (MT 22:7–9), Despised
         22:9–11 (MT 22:10–12), Be Not Far
            22:12–13 (MT 22:13–14), Surrounded by Bulls and Lions
               22:14–15 (22:15–16), The Dust of Death
            22:16–18 (MT 22:17–19), Surrounded by Dogs and Lions
         22:19–21 (MT 22:20–22), Be Not Far
      22:22–25 (MT 22:23–26), Not Despised
   22:26–28 (MT 22:27–29), Repentance and Worship
22:29–31 (MT 22:30–32), Celebration

The psalm opens with a God-forsaken cry of anguish (22:1–2 [MT 22:2–3]) that is followed by an immediate confession of God's holiness and trustworthiness (22:3–5 [MT 22:4–6]). David, however, communicates in 22:6–8 (MT 22:7–9) that these truths do not apply to him because he is a despised worm. Forsaken worm though he is, David still cries out to Yahweh for help in 22:9–11 (MT 22:10–12) because of the beastly evildoers who threaten him in 22:12–18 (MT 22:13–19). The section on David's enemies (22:12–13, 16–18 [MT 22:13–14, 17–19]) brackets the central statement of the psalm, where David says that his bones are disjointed, that his heart is wax, and that God has put him in the dust of death (22:14–15 [MT 22:15–16]).

Just as the description of the enemies brackets the central statement of the psalm, cries for Yahweh to "be not far" precede and follow the description of David's enemies as wild beasts, the second of these coming in 22:19–21 (MT 22:20–22). Whereas the first half of the psalm communicated desperation ending in death in 22:15 (MT 22:16), the second half builds to hope and celebration. This is seen not only in the faith communicated by the second cry for Yahweh not to be far but also in the celebration of Yahweh's name in the congregation in 22:22–25 (MT 22:23–26). Particularly relevant here is the way David answers his description of himself as "despised of people" in 22:6 (MT 22:7) with the confession that Yahweh "did not despise" in 22:24 (MT 22:25).

The syntactical similarity in the phrasing of Psalm 22:4 (MT 22:5) and 22:27 (MT 22:28) draws attention to the thematic relationship between 22:3–5 (MT 22:4–6) and 22:26–28 (MT 22:27–29). Consider the way these clauses parallel one another:

| 22:4 (MT 22:5) | 22:27 (MT 22:28) |
| --- | --- |
| In you they trusted, | May they remember and turn to Yahweh, |
| our Fathers; | all the ends of the earth; |
| they trusted, | and may they worship before you, |
| and you delivered them. | all the families of the nations. |

This syntactical resonance points to the thematic relationship between God's faithfulness to the fathers in 22:3–5 (MT 22:4–6) and the blessing of "all the families of the nations" (22:27 [MT 22:28]) in 22:26–28 (MT 22:27–29). On what basis could such a connection be made? On nothing less than God's promise to the patriarch Abraham that all the families of the earth would be blessed in him (Gen 12:1–3).

The beginning and end of Ps 22 could not be further from each other in theological terms. Whereas David cries out that God has forsaken him in 22:1–2 (MT 22:2–3), he celebrates the good life in God's presence as the "seed" serves the Lord in 22:29–31 (MT 22:30–32).

We will pursue the exposition of the psalm in three movements:

> 22:1–11 (MT 22:2–12), The Worm
> 22:12–21 (MT 22:13–22), The Enemies
> 22:22–31 (MT 22:23–32), The Hope

SCRIPTURE

| CSB | Author's translation |
| --- | --- |
| For the choir director: according to "The Deer of the Dawn." A psalm of David. | [1] For the Preeminent One.<br>Upon the Doe of the Dawn.<br>A Psalm of David. |
| [1] My God, my God, why have you abandoned me?<br>Why are you so far from my deliverance<br>and from my words of groaning? | [2] My God, my God, why have you forsaken me?<br>Far from my salvation, from the words of my howling. |

² My God, I cry by day, but you do not answer,
by night, yet I have no rest.
³ But you are holy,
enthroned on the praises of Israel.
⁴ Our ancestors trusted in you;
they trusted, and you rescued them.
⁵ They cried to you and were set free;
they trusted in you and were not disgraced.

⁶ But I am a worm and not a man,
scorned by mankind and despised by people.
⁷ Everyone who sees me mocks me;
they sneer and shake their heads:
⁸ "He relies on the Lord;
let him save him;
let the Lord rescue him,
since he takes pleasure in him."

⁹ It was you who brought me out of the womb,
making me secure at my mother's breast.
¹⁰ I was given over to you at birth;
you have been my God from my mother's womb.

¹¹ Don't be far from me, because distress is near
and there's no one to help.
¹² Many bulls surround me;
strong ones of Bashan encircle me.
¹³ They open their mouths against me—
lions, mauling and roaring.
¹⁴ I am poured out like water,
and all my bones are disjointed;
my heart is like wax,
melting within me.
¹⁵ My strength is dried up like baked clay;
my tongue sticks to the roof of my mouth.
You put me into the dust of death.

³ My God. I cry by day, and you do not answer;
and by night, and there is no silence for me.
⁴ But you are holy,
seated upon the praises of Israel.
⁵ In you they trusted, our fathers;
they trusted, and you delivered them.
⁶ To you they called, and they were rescued.
In you they trusted, and they were not put to shame.

⁷ But I am a worm and not a man,
a reproach of man and despised of people.
⁸ All who see me mock at me;
they separate the lip; they shake the head.
⁹ Roll to Yahweh!
Let him deliver him.
Let him cause his rescue,
if he delights in him.
¹⁰ For you are the one who burst me forth from the womb,
who caused me to trust upon the breasts of my mother.
¹¹ Upon you I was cast from the womb,
from the belly of my mother my God are you.
¹² Be not far from me,
for distress is near,
for there is no helper.

¹³ They surround me, the many bulls,
mighty ones of Bashan, they encircle me.
¹⁴ They open upon me their mouths,
a lion tearing and roaring.

¹⁵ Like water I am poured out,
and all my bones are separated;
my heart is like wax,

16 For dogs have surrounded me;
a gang of evildoers has closed in on
  me;
they pierced my hands and my feet.
17 I can count all my bones;
people look and stare at me.
18 They divided my garments among
  themselves,
and they cast lots for my clothing.

19 But you, Lord, don't be far away.
My strength, come quickly to help me.
20 Rescue my life from the sword,
my only life from the power of these
  dogs.
21 Save me from the lion's mouth,
from the horns of wild oxen.

You answered me!
22 I will proclaim your name to my
  brothers and sisters;
I will praise you in the assembly.
23 You who fear the Lord, praise him!
All you descendants of Jacob, honor
  him!
All you descendants of Israel, revere
  him!
24 For he has not despised or abhorred
the torment of the oppressed.
He did not hide his face from him
but listened when he cried to him for
  help.

25 I will give praise in the great
  assembly
because of you;
I will fulfill my vows
before those who fear you.
26 The humble will eat and be satisfied;
those who seek the Lord will praise
  him.
May your hearts live forever!

27 All the ends of the earth will
  remember

it is melted in the midst of my inner
  parts.
16 My strength dried up like a
  potsherd,
and my tongue was cloven on my
  gums.
You put me as the dust of death.

17 For dogs surrounded me,
a congregation of evildoers caused me
  to be hemmed in.
Like a lion! My hands and my feet.
18 I recount all my bones.
They look; they behold me.
19 They divide my garments among
  them,
and for my clothing they cause the
  lot to fall.

20 But you, O Yahweh, be not far!
My strength, hasten to my help!
21 Rescue my soul from the sword,
my only one from the hand of the
  dog.
22 Save me from the mouth of the lion,
and from the horns of the wild ox you
  have answered me!

23 I recount your name to my
  brothers,
in the midst of the assembly I will
  praise you.
24 Those who fear Yahweh, praise him!
All seed of Jacob glorify him,
and stand in awe of him all seed of
  Israel.
25 For he did not despise, and he did
  not detest the affliction of the
  afflicted,
and he did not cause his face to be
  hidden from him,
and when he cried for help to him, he
  heard.
26 From with you is my praise in the
  great assembly,

and turn to the Lord.
All the families of the nations
will bow down before you,
²⁸ for kingship belongs to the Lord;
he rules the nations.
²⁹ All who prosper on earth will eat
and bow down;
all those who go down to the dust
will kneel before him—
even the one who cannot preserve
his life.
³⁰ Their descendants will serve him;
the next generation will be told about
the Lord.
³¹ They will come and declare his
righteousness;
to a people yet to be born
they will declare what he has done.

my vows I will complete before those
who fear him.
²⁷ May the afflicted eat and be
satisfied.
May they praise Yahweh, those who
seek him.
May your hearts live forever.
²⁸ May they remember and turn to
Yahweh,
all the ends of the earth;
and may they worship before you,
all the families of the nations,
²⁹ for to Yahweh belongs the kingdom,
and he rules among the nations.

³⁰ They ate and they worshiped,
all the fat ones of the earth;
before him they bowed,
all who go down to the dust,
and his soul he does not keep alive.
³¹ May the seed serve him,
may it be recounted of the Lord to the
generation.
³² May they come and declare his
righteousness to a people who will
be born,
that he has done it!

Context: Verbal and Thematic Links with Surrounding Psalms

22:1 (MT 22:2) "Why have you forsaken me?"
9:10 (MT 9:11) "you have not forsaken those who seek you"
16:10 "you will not forsake my soul to Sheol"

22:1 (MT 22:2) "Far from my salvation"
10:1 "Why, O Yahweh, do you stand far off?"
18:50 (MT 18:51) "He causes greatness of salvations for his king"
20:5 (MT 20:6) "May we give a ringing cry at your salvation"
21:1 (MT 21:2) "the king ... in your salvation how he will rejoice"
21:5 (MT 21:6) "Great his glory in your salvation"

22:3 (MT 22:4) "holy, seated"
2:4 "the one who sits in the heavens"

22:4–5 (MT 22:5–6) the fathers trusted
21:7 (MT 21:8) "the king trusts in Yahweh"

22:4, 8 (MT 22:5, 9) "delivered ... deliver"
Compare 18:2, 43, 48 (MT 18:3, 44, 49)

22:6 (MT 22:7) "a reproach ... despised"
Compare 15:3–4; 22:24 (MT 22:25)

22:7 (MT 22:8) "All who see me mock at me"
2:4 "My Lord mocks them"
Compare 1:1 "the seat of scoffers"

22:8 (MT 22:9) "if he delights in him"
18:19 (MT 18:20) "because he delighted in me"
5:4 (MT 5:5) "not a God delighting in wickedness are you"

22:10 (MT 22:11) "my God are you" אלי אתה
Same phrase in 63:1 (MT 63:2); 118:28; 140:6 (MT 140:7)

22:11, 19 (MT 22:12, 20) "Be not far from me"
Same phrase in 35:22; 38:21 (MT 38:22); 71:12

22:12 (MT 22:13) "mighty ones of Bashan"
Compare Og, king of Bashan, in 135:11; 136:20 (cf. Deut 3:11)

22:12, 16 (MT 22:13, 17) "surround ... encircle ... hemmed in"
Compare 17:9, 11; 18:5 (MT 18:6)

22:13, 16, 21 (MT 22:14, 17, 22) "lion"
Compare 7:2 (MT 7:3); 10:9; 17:12

22:23 (MT 22:24) "Those who fear Yahweh"
Same phrase in 15:4

22:23 (MT 22:24) "seed of Jacob"
Compare 14:7; 20:1 (MT 20:2); 24:6

22:24 (MT 22:25) "he did not cause his face to be hidden"
Compare 10:11; 13:1 (MT 13:2)

22:26 (MT 22:27) "be satisfied"
Compare 16:11; 17:14, 15

22:26 (MT 22:27) "all who seek him"
Compare 9:10 (MT 9:11); 10:4; 14:2; 24:6

22:27 (MT 22:28) "all the ends of the earth"
Same phrase in 2:8; 67:7 (MT 67:8); 72:8; 98:3; cf. 1 Sam 2:10

22:27 (MT 22:28) "all the families"
Same phrase in Gen 12:3

22:28 (MT 22:29) "to Yahweh belongs the kingdom"
Same phrase in Obad 21

22:29 "the fat ones"
Compare 20:3 (MT 20:4); 23:5

Psalms 15 and 24 set the direction of this section of the Psalter, inquiring about the identity of the one who can enter into God's presence and dwell with him. The implied answer to David's question is the seed promised to him, whose reign is celebrated in Ps 2, whose blessed character is memorialized in Ps 1. The attention of this section of the Psalter, then, is on the future king from David's line. As David speaks of his own experience of God's comforting presence in Pss 16 and 23, he presents himself as a type of the one to come. Similar dynamics are at work as David writes of his confidence that God will raise the dead in Ps 17, and the desperate need for resurrection in Ps 22. We have seen how Ps 18 typologically interprets the deliverance of David from his enemies in the terms and categories of the exodus and conquest, and Pss 20 and 21 bless the future king and pray for him. At the center of this chiastic section of the psalter is Ps 19, a hymnic ode to the glory of God in general and special revelation.

EXPOSITION
### 22:1–11 (MT 22:2–12), The Worm
Psalm 22:1–2 (MT 22:2–3) presents the Bible's most poignant cry of dereliction. These words encapsulate the post-Eden experience. These two sentences communicate the agony and anguish of life apart from God's favorable presence. David knows the answer to his rhetorical question in 22:1 (MT 22:2). He knows that sin separates him from God's presence, and for that reason he speaks of himself as a worm in 22:6 (MT 22:7). The focus here is not on sin, however, but its awful consequence. However

enticing and tempting sin might seem, it separates us from God, and this God-forsaken cry drips with the dreadful reality of separation from God.

David knows that prior to sin's entrance into the world, God walked with man in the cool of the day (Gen 3:8). He knows that all the affliction and opposition he faces from the seed of the serpent stems from God's word of judgment in Gen 3:14–15. And he knows that somehow the descendent God promised to raise up from his line would enter into this world of enmity, overcome it, and bring blessing to the nations (cf. Gen 3:15; 12:1–3; 2 Sam 7, etc.). It is entirely possible, then, for David to have spoken of his own anguish with a view to the way his descendant would also enter into the very separation from God that caused David so much pain.[105]

David might not have known that Jesus would take the sins of the world upon himself and be separated from God as he died on the cross, but he surely intended his words to communicate the problem his descendent would solve. This makes Jesus' quotation of the line as he suffered on the cross most fitting and appropriate, entirely in keeping with David's intention as he wrote the words.

David asks why God has forsaken him as one who himself does not mean to forsake God. This explains David's groaning in 22:1b (MT 22:2b) and the day and night pleas for deliverance in 22:2 (MT 22:3). The lack of "silence"[106] referenced at the end of 22:2 (MT 22:3) points to the unquiet, unrest of life outside Eden, outside the presence of God (cf. God's "rest" in Gen 2:3, and note that Gen 2:15 could be rendered, "And Yahweh God took the man and caused him to rest in the Garden of Eden").

Having bewailed the fact that he is forsaken in 22:1–2 (MT 22:2–3), David immediately acknowledged God as holy and trustworthy in 22:3–5 (MT 22:4–6). Moreover, he confesses that he himself is a despised worm in 22:6–8 (MT 22:7–9). This amounts to a recognition that because of his sin, he deserves to be forsaken by God. That recognition, however, does not keep David from crying out for God's merciful deliverance. Psalm 22 resolves into a celebration of God's salvation, and thereby teaches that God loves to save repentant sinners who call to him.

---

[105] *Pace* Goldingay, *Psalms 1–41*, 324: "It is harder to imagine its being designed for use by the coming 'David.' "

[106] CSB and ESV render this "rest," but the term is דומיה (which *HALOT*, s.v., glosses "silence, rest") as opposed to שבת (Gen 2:3) or נוח (Gen 2:15).

By confessing that God is holy and rightly enthroned on Israel's praise in 22:3 (MT 22:4), David makes it clear that his own forsakenness does not arise from any flaw in God's character. Similarly, as he recounts the way that the fathers of Israel trusted in God and were delivered in 22:4–5 (MT 22:5–6), David acknowledges that his desperate straits are not the result of God failing to answer prayer. Moreover, this celebration of God's deliverance of those who call on him lays the groundwork for Ps 22's own resolution. This psalm bears witness to the way that God answered David's prayers, along with the prayers of that most forsaken one, the Lord Jesus himself.

If God is holy and answers prayer, as 22:3–5 (MT 22:4–6) says he does, why is David forsaken, as 22:1–2 (MT 22:2–3) says he is? David answers this question by calling himself a "worm" in 22:6 (MT 22:7). This is not excessive self-loathing but accurate recognition of sin. Sin is not the only factor, however: there is also the enmity between the seed of the serpent and the seed of the woman (Gen 3:15).

The seed of the serpent are the ones who reproach and despise David in 22:6b (MT 22:7b), who mock him, make faces at him, and wag the head at him in 22:7 (MT 22:8), and who derisively urge him to trust Yahweh, dismissively calling for Yahweh to deliver him in 22:8 (MT 22:9). Just as David quotes his enemies throwing these words at him in Ps 22:8 (MT 22:9), the seed of the serpent threw these words at Jesus on the cross in Matt 27:43. Ironically, against the expectation of the proud wicked, Yahweh does indeed delight in David and the king from his line, delivering them both.

The taunts of the enemies in 22:7–8 (MT 22:8–9) are followed by David's cry for help in 22:9–11 (MT 22:10–12). The cry for help in 22:11 (MT 22:12) grows out of David's awareness of God's faithfulness to him through his whole life in 22:9–10 (MT 22:10–11).

In Ps 22:9 (MT 22:10) David speaks of his life-long dependence upon the Lord, beginning from the harrowing experience of birth. Perhaps adding to the way the conflict between David and his enemies arises from the enmity introduced in Gen 3:15, David speaks of his own experience of the difficulty in childbirth introduced in Gen 3:16. He uses a vivid image to describe the Lord as "the one who burst me forth from the womb" (see BDB, s.v. "גיח," p. 161). The point seems to be that God preserved David through the life and death struggle of childbirth, and David goes on to depict the Lord as the one who caused him to trust, even as he was placed at his mother's breast. David seems to be saying that the Lord worked through the stability of his experience as an infant with his mother to teach David to trust God. This vein of thought continues in 22:10 (MT 22:11), where David describes himself being cast upon Yahweh from birth. Because he trusts Yahweh, and because his life has always depended upon Yahweh, David pleads in 22:11 (MT 22:12) that Yahweh would not be far from him because distress is near and he has no other helper (cf. 22:19 [MT 22:20]).

Throughout this section of the psalm David evidences implicit trust in Yahweh. He knows that he is an unworthy worm, but that does not keep him from calling out to the only one who can help him.

### 22:12–21 (MT 22:13–22), The Enemies

The enmity from the seed of the serpent that has David feeling God-forsaken is described in Ps 22:12–21 (MT 22:13–22). David here describes the beastly character of his enemies and the mortal danger they pose to him.

David uses metaphors to make his audience feel the powerful, sharp-fanged, razor-clawed nature of those who oppose him. He likens them to bulls (22:12 [MT 22:13]), lions (22:13, 16, 21 [MT 22:14, 17, 22]), dogs (22:16 [MT 22:17]), and wild oxen (22:21 [MT 22:22]). These metaphorical depictions show the strength and influence ("mighty ones of Bashan" 22:12 [MT 22:13]), the ripping and boasting ("tearing and roaring" 22:13 [MT 22:14]), the plundering and stealing ("divide my garments ... for my clothing" 22:18 [MT 22:19]), and the devouring, dominating nature of David's enemies ("the mouth of the lion ... horns of the wild ox" 22:21 [MT 22:22]).

The enemies are dangerous, and from the repeated references to the way they have David surrounded it appears that David is outnumbered and cut off from help: "They surround me ... they encircle me" (22:13 [MT 22:14]); "dogs surrounded me ... caused me to be hemmed in" (22:16 [MT 22:17]).

David describes himself with language that strongly suggests that the enemies left his lifeless corpse stripped naked on the ground: he is poured out like water, all his bones separated, heart melted like wax in 22:14 (MT 22:15). His strength is as dry and lifeless as a broken piece of pottery. His tongue is no longer moist and moving but still and stuck in his mouth, and he has been returned to the dust from which he was made (22:15 [MT 22:16]; cf. Gen 2:7; 3:19); all his bones can be enumerated, and his enemies gawk at him (Ps 22:17 [MT 22:18]); his garments are divided up among those who have killed and stripped him. Lots are cast for his clothing (22:18 [MT 22:19]).

Since David wrote Ps 22 during his lifetime, we should not think that he describes a situation in which he was literally killed. The statements he makes that connote physical death in 22:12–18 (MT 22:13–19) accompany his statement connoting spiritual death in 22:1 (MT 22:2). Perhaps David wrote Ps 22 after an encounter that left him as aching and bruised physically as he felt forsaken and alone spiritually.

Here again we can ask whether and how David might have envisioned his own experience being a typological pattern for that of his descendant. David would have understood that expulsion from Eden and separation from God resulted from sin (see Gen 3). He would further have understood that the seed promised to him in 2 Sam 7:12 would be the seed of the woman to crush the head of the serpent promised in Gen 3:15. It is at least possible that David understood that in order for the seed of the woman to conquer death, he would need to experience its worst and be raised from the dead. Perhaps David suspected that his own near-death experiences of defeat at the hands of the seed of the serpent, through which the Lord brought him and raised him up victorious, would be completed in the way his seed would fulfill the pattern: literally dying at the hands of the seed of the serpent to be raised victorious from the dead. The New Testament would seem to validate this interpretation, as the pattern of suffering David describes is cited as fulfilled in Jesus's God-forsaken cry (Matt 27:46; Mark 15:34), in the taunts and head-wagging of his enemies (Matt 27:39, 43; Mark 15:29), and when the soldiers divide up Jesus' clothing and gamble for his tunic (John 19:23–24; cf. Matt 27:35; Mark 15:24; Luke 23:34).

In this way I would suggest that David spoke of his own experience, knowing full well that the pattern of his experience would be fulfilled in the life of his descendant, whom we know to be Jesus (cf. Acts 2:25, "David says of Him: I saw the Lord"). This suggests that David suspected his descendent would conquer death by dying and rising, but it does not demand that David knew, or had revealed to him, the details of how Jesus would die. I say that because of the translation of Ps 22:16 (MT 22:17). I have translated this verse as follows:

"For dogs surrounded me, a congregation of evildoers caused me to be hemmed in. Like a lion! My hands and my feet."

Tanner observes, "There are no less than ten monographs and count-less attempts in commentaries to untangle the meaning of Ps 22:16."[107] I understand David to be again likening his enemies to lions, and making an exclamation about how his own hands and feet are in danger from them.

Virtually every English translation renders the phrase, "Like a lion! My hands and my feet," along the lines of the CSB, "they pierced my hands and my feet" (cf. ESV, KJV, NAS, NIV, etc.). Such translations would seem to point to the very way Jesus died. The only problem is that as far as I can tell there is no warrant for such renderings in the text.

The *BHS* Hebrew text clearly has the word "lion" (כָּאֲרִי). A few manu-scripts apparently had the verb "dig" (כרו), which may have influenced the Greek translation, which also employs the word "dig" (ὀρύσσω). The NET footnote on the verse observes that the Greek translation of Symmachus employed a verb that means "bind," perhaps coming from a Hebrew root with a similar appearance (כרד). That NET footnote concludes, however, "Neither one of these proposed verbs can yield a meaning 'bore, pierce.' " Goldingay observes of the word that means "dig," "There is no basis for stretching it to mean 'pierce.' "[108] I make the following statement with humility, willing to be corrected by the evidence: I can see no basis for translating this line with the word "pierce." I would also say that no part of my theology is affected by the loss of the word "pierce," and as is evident from what I have said above, I do not need the word "pierce" in the translation to see the text as a typological prophecy of the death and resurrection of Jesus. Whereas several statements from Ps 22 are quoted in the New Testament, the New Testament never cites Ps 22:16 (MT 22:17). This makes me think that the New Testament authors did not interpret either the Hebrew ("lion") or the Greek ("dig") to refer to the piercing of hands and feet.

In Ps 22:12–18 (MT 22:13–19) David describes beastly enemies that strip him naked and leave him in the dust of death (22:15 [MT 22:16]). As he had done in 22:11 (MT 22:12), David cries out in 22:19 (MT 22:20) for Yahweh not to be far away from him but to hurry to his help. We know that the animals threatening David are not dogs and lions and oxen but wicked people from the reference to the "congregation of evildoers" in 22:16 (MT 22:17) and the reference to "the sword" in 22:20 (MT 22:21).

---

[107] DeClaisse-Walford, Jacobson, and Tanner, *Psalms*, 230.
[108] Goldingay, *Psalms 1–41*, 321.

The calls for Yahweh to be near and hasten to help (22:19 [MT 22:20]), to rescue (22:10 [MT 22:21]), and to save and answer (22:21 [MT 22:22]) show David's building confidence as he prays in faith to the God who raises the dead. The celebration in 22:22–31 (MT 22:23–32) reflects David's confidence that his prayers for himself and his seed will be answered.

## 22:22–31 (MT 22:23–32), The Hope

The prayer for deliverance in Ps 22:19–21 (MT 22:20–22) showed confidence that God *can* save, and the celebratory praise that follows in 22:22–25 (MT 22:23–26) assumes that God *will* save. Whereas David was "forsaken" in 22:1 (MT 22:2) and "despised" in 22:6 (MT 22:7), he recounts Yahweh's name to his brothers and praises God in the midst of the assembly in 22:22 (MT 22:23), rejoicing that God did not despise the afflicted (22:24 [MT 22:25]). To recount Yahweh's name is to retell the feats whereby Yahweh established his reputation. In context, the feats in view would be the answers to the prayers David prayed earlier in the psalm as he asked for deliverance from the wild beasts. The assembly that David references in 22:22 (MT 22:23) recalls the "congregation of the righteous" mentioned in 1:5.

The reading of Ps 22 being proposed here appears to be supported by the quotation of Ps 22:22 (MT 22:23) in Heb 2:12. I am suggesting that David describes his own experience as a typological pattern that foreshadows that of his descendent. Thus the near—or perhaps metaphorical—death that David describes for himself in Ps 22:15 (MT 22:16) is answered by God delivering him, as though he has been raised from the dead, in 22:23. This matches the way that the author of Hebrews describes Jesus tasting death and being perfected through suffering in Heb 2:9–10, then presents Jesus speaking the resurrection celebrating words of Ps 22:22 (MT 22:23) in Heb 2:12. Such a reading would also explain the quotation of Isa 8:18 in Heb 2:13—both David and Isaiah spoke of themselves in ways that would be typologically fulfilled in Jesus. These New Testament quotations thus demonstrate a profound and deep understanding of what the Old Testament authors intended to communicate, and the New Testament authors claim that intention fulfilled in Jesus.[109]

---

[109] For a thorough discussion of these issues, see esp. Aubrey Maria Sequeira, "The Hermeneutics of Eschatological Fulfillment in Christ: Biblical-Theological Exegesis in the Epistle to the Hebrews" (PhD diss., Southern Baptist Theological Seminary, 2017).

David addresses the congregated assembly he mentioned in Ps 22:22 (MT 22:23) directly in 22:23 (MT 22:24), calling all who fear Yahweh to praise him, identifying the group he addresses as the "seed of Jacob" and "seed of Israel," urging them to stand in awe of God. On what basis should they praise Yahweh? Because he has answered the distressed prayers David offered earlier in Ps 22. David says as much in 22:24 (MT 22:25), where he declares that Yahweh neither despised nor detested him nor hid his face but heard the cries of the afflicted. David then asserts that the praise he will experience in the great assembly comes from Yahweh, and that he will complete his vows in the presence of those who fear Yahweh (22:25 [MT 22:26]).

In what sense does the respect that other people show to David, their praise for him, come from Yahweh (22:25 [MT 22:26])? Perhaps an example from church history will help: God obviously equipped George Whitefield with unique gifts for preaching, and God obviously blessed Whitefield's efforts with remarkable, perhaps unparalleled, results. Many, many conversions resulted from Whitefield's preaching. Whitefield is remembered, praised, and imitated because of his great success, and Whitefield would be the first to say that all the glory results from God. Whitefield would no doubt say that all the praise he received because of his fruitful labors came from the Lord. David seems to mean the same thing: the Lord delivered David, raised him up, inspired him to write Scripture, and gave him triumphs not a few. David therefore gives God all the glory as the source of the praise he himself receives among the saints.

The statements in Ps 22:26–28 (MT 22:27–29) are typically taken as a mix of indicative statements (e.g., CSB 22:26, "The humble will eat and be satisfied") and prayers (cf. the jussive rendered by the CSB in 22:26, "May your hearts live forever!"). Because the Hebrew forms are not distinct, the imperfect forms could be indicatives or jussives. The interpreter must decide which is intended. The flow of thought in Ps 22:26–28 (MT 22:27–29) inclines me to the view that all of these statements should be understood as jussive forms communicating prayer-wish blessings. For my view of how they should be rendered, see the accompanying translation. For the view that most of these statements are indicatives, see the CSB's rendering of these verses.

Read this way, David prays for a situation when God's promises will be fulfilled and God's presence will be enjoyed by his people. The afflicted will be needy no longer but eat and be satisfied. All who seek Yahweh will praise him, and they will live forever—no more death. The curse will have been rolled back and conquered by the seed of David (22:26 [MT 22:27]). When all this happens, all the families of the earth will be blessed through the seed of Abraham (cf. Gen 12:1–3; 22:18), turning to Yahweh and worshiping him (Ps 22:27 [MT 22:28]). Indeed the kingdom will belong to Yahweh, who will exercise dominion over the nations through the king from David's line (22:28 [MT 22:29]).

Having prayed for the blessing of the nations in Ps 22:26–28 (MT 22:27–29), David describes the way things will be when the king from his line has conquered at last in 22:29–31 (MT 22:30–32). In that day there will be no more discrepancy between the appearance of prosperity and godliness: as 22:29 (MT 22:30) says, the "fat ones of the earth" will worship Yahweh.

The last three lines of 22:29 (MT 22:30) speak of those who go down to the dust and the one who does not keep his soul alive bowing to Yahweh. The bowing is easy enough to understand: these people will do homage to Yahweh. The reference to those who go down to the dust appears to have those who die in mind. The final line is a bit more difficult. Some translations take the singular forms to refer to an individual who does not keep himself alive (CSB, ESV, NAS). Others take this to be a representative statement about how all die (KJV, NET, NIV). The clipped nature of the poetry makes specific interpretation precarious, but in general terms we can say that these lines assert that all mortals will bow to Yahweh.

In Ps 22:30 (MT 22:31) David asserts, "May the seed serve him, and may it be recounted of the Lord to the generation." The mention of the "seed" could refer to the singular seed of the woman, the seed of David, or it could refer to the collective seed of the woman, all who identify with the king from David's line. Rendering this "posterity" (ESV, NAS, NIV), "a whole generation" (NET), or "descendants" (CSB) closes down the possibility that David has the future king from his line in view. If the individual seed serves Yahweh, the collective seed will as well. But the collective seed will only serve Yahweh if the individual seed does.

The "generation" that hears the report of Yahweh's work in 22:30 (MT 22:31) can be identified with the righteous generation mentioned elsewhere (14:5; 24:6). This generation is the one that David describes in 22:31 (MT 22:32). They come and declare the Lord's righteousness to the people yet to be born. They will say that God has done it. What has he done? Accomplished salvation, kept his promises, rolled back the curses, defeated death, and established the king from David's line on the throne forever.

BRIDGE

We see from Ps 22 that David's forsaken state (22:1 [MT 22:2]) did not put him beyond the reach of the help that comes to those who call on the name of the Lord.

Throughout this discussion of Ps 22 I have commented on how David speaks of his own experience. Taking my cues from Acts 2:25, where Luke presents Peter saying, "David says concerning him," then quotes David speaking in the first person, I have suggested that David's intention was to speak of himself as a type of the one to come. The pattern of David's experience foreshadows the pattern of experience that will be fulfilled in Jesus, and the New Testament's quotations of Ps 22 supports this understanding.

David speaks of his sin resulting in him being forsaken by God as his enemies triumph over him, strip him of his clothing, which they take for themselves, and leave him naked in the dust. That is not, however, the end of the story, as David continues to call on the Lord and experiences deliverance. As a result he praises God in the congregation of his brothers, anticipating the blessing of all nations in fulfillment of the promise to Abraham. This pattern Jesus fulfills: he took the sins of his people, and as he died on the cross he was forsaken by the Father. The seed of the serpent enacted the words of Ps 22, sometimes even taunting Jesus with them as he died. Jesus was stripped naked. His clothing was plundered. He was laid in the dust of death. But he rose. He recounts God's name in the great congregation. He turns the nations from the ends of the earth to the worship of Yahweh. And his righteousness has been declared to successive generations. God has worked salvation in Christ.

## Psalm 23

OVERVIEW AND STRUCTURE OF PSALM 23

Psalm 23 begins with Yahweh shepherding in the field (23:1) and ends with David returning to Yahweh's house (23:6). Between the first and last verses, which alone mention Yahweh by name, David speaks of Yahweh in the third person (he) in verses 2 and 3, then he addresses Yahweh, speaking in the second person (you), in verses 4 and 5. Verses 2 and 5 both treat the way that Yahweh provides for David, and verses 3 and 4 both describe Yahweh's protective presence. The chiastic structure of the psalm can thus be depicted as follows:

23:1, Yahweh Is My Shepherd
   23:2, He Ensures Grass and Water
      23:3, He Restores and Conducts for His Name
      23:4, You Are with Me in Danger
   23:5, You Set a Table and Anoint
23:6, I Will Return to Yahweh's House

The subheads under which we will consider these lines reflect the shift in scene, from field to house, and in pronouns, from third (he) to second (you) person:

   23:1–3, He Shepherds in the Field
   23:4–6, You Bring Me to the House

SCRIPTURE

CSB

A psalm of David.

[1] The LORD is my shepherd;
I have what I need.
[2] He lets me lie down in green
   pastures;
he leads me beside quiet waters.
[3] He renews my life;
he leads me along the right paths
for his name's sake.
[4] Even when I go through the darkest
   valley,
I fear no danger,
for you are with me;
your rod and your staff—they comfort
   me.

[5] You prepare a table before me
in the presence of my enemies;
you anoint my head with oil;
my cup overflows.
[6] Only goodness and faithful love will
   pursue me
all the days of my life,

Author's translation

[1] A Psalm of David.
Yahweh is my shepherd.
I shall not want.

[2] In grazing places of grass he causes
   me to lie down.
By waters of resting places he leads
   me.

[3] My soul he restores.
He conducts me on the wagon tracks
   of righteousness
for the sake of his name.

[4] Even if I walk in the valley of the
   shadow of death,
I will not fear evil,
for you are with me.
Your rod and your staff, they comfort
   me.

[5] You lay out before me a table,
in the presence of my adversaries.
You make my head fat with the oil,
My cup is full.

and I will dwell in the house of the
   Lord
as long as I live.

⁶ Surely goodness and lovingkindness
   will pursue me
all the days of my life,
and I will return to the house of
   Yahweh
for long days.

### CONTEXT: VERBAL AND THEMATIC LINKS WITH SURROUNDING PSALMS

23:1 "I shall not want"
Compare Deut 2:7; 28:48, 57; Ps 34:10 (MT 34:11)

23:2 "waters of resting places"
Compare Num 10:33; Deut 12:9; Pss 95:11; 132:8, 14; Isa 11:10;
   66:1

23:2 "he leads me"
Compare Exod 15:13; Isa 40:11; 49:10

23:3 "My soul he restores"
Compare 19:8

23:3 "the wagon tracks of righteousness"
Compare 17:5; 65:12

23:3 "for the sake of his name"
Compare 25:11; 31:3 (MT 31:4); 79:9; 106:8; 109:21; 143:11

23:4 "shadow of death"
Compare 44:19 (MT 44:20)

23:4 "I will not fear"
Compare 3:6 (MT 3:7); 56:4, 11 (MT 56:5, 12); 118:6

23:4 "comfort me"
Compare 71:21; 86:17; 90:13

We have noted how Ps 23 corresponds to Ps 16, both being psalms that
celebrate Yahweh's comforting presence. For further structural comments see the "Context" section to Ps 24.

## 23:1–3, He Shepherds in the Field

Like Abel and Abraham, Jacob, Joseph, and Moses, David was a shepherd. When he declares that Yahweh relates to him the way that he related to his flocks, however, he does not speak merely from personal experience. When Yahweh led his people through the wilderness, providing manna from heaven and water from the rock, he was doing for them what a shepherd does for his flock. Recognizing this, Israel's psalmists and prophets spoke of Yahweh as their shepherd. In this psalm David speaks of the Lord in terms that have historical resonance and that are also deeply personal.[110]

When David declares that he will lack nothing in the second line of Ps 23:1, he employs the same term used in Deut 2:7, where Moses declared, "These forty years Yahweh your God was with you. You did not lack a thing." Later in Deuteronomy, in the curses of the covenant, Moses warns that if the people will not obey Yahweh, they will *lack* everything (Deut 28:48). The Lord threatens that this state of *lacking* everything will result in women eating their own children (Deut 28:57). David gladly embraces Yahweh as his shepherd, submitting to Yahweh's direction and purpose, confident that Yahweh will meet his every need (cf. Ps 34:10 [MT 34:11], "those who seek Yahweh will lack no good thing").

Psalm 23:2–3 exposits the metaphor of Yahweh. David describes the way Yahweh meets physical (23:2) and spiritual (23:3) needs. The meeting of physical needs in 23:2, however, is colored by the meeting of emotional and spiritual needs. Even as David describes the way Yahweh ensures that his sheep have grass and water, it is also clear that Yahweh makes the sheep feel safe to lie down and rest. As the rest of the psalm makes clear, Yahweh's protective presence brings about the psychological stability and soul-quiet: this frees the sheep from worry about lions or climate.

There are promised land overtones that are obscured somewhat by the rendering "quiet waters" in Ps 23:2. More literally, David speaks of "waters of resting places." The term "resting place" (מנוחה) is what the Lord sought for his people when the ark set out from Mount Sinai in Num 10:33. Even further back, the cognate verb is used in Gen 2:15 and could

---

[110] Similarly Bullock, "Book 1," 37: "The archetypal story of the exodus is echoed in its verbal expressions. It is not a recounting of the exodus story as we find it in some psalms (e.g., 106:7–8) but an echo of the story."

be rendered, "And Yahweh God took the man and caused him to rest in the garden of Eden." The term "resting place" is also used in Deut 12:9 to describe the "resting place" and "the inheritance" that the Lord gave his people—the land of promise. This term appears in the Lord's declaration that the wilderness generation will not enter the land, his rest, in Ps 95:11 (cf. 132:8, 14; Isa 11:10; 66:1). When David refers to "waters of resting places" with this term, then, he evokes the way that Yahweh shepherded his people to the good land he promised them. That good land God promised his people was an attempt to renew what was lost when Adam was driven from Eden. The goodness of God's presence, David says, is enjoyed by those who are shepherded by Yahweh to "waters of resting places."

The connections between Israel's history and David's experience are strengthened by the term used in the rest of the statement: "By waters of resting places *he leads* me" (Ps 23:2, emphasis added). This verb appears in Exod 15:13, "You led in your strength to the pasture of your holiness." Perhaps under the influence of Exod 15 and Ps 23, when Isaiah describes the new exodus and return from exile, he says in Isa 49:10, "And by springs of water he will lead them" (cf. Isa 40:11).

Those whom Yahweh shepherds will be led to the place where all God's promises are realized, all needs met, and all fears gone.

David describes the spiritual healing the Lord brings in Ps 23:3, speaking of the way his shepherd restores his soul and conducts him along the "wagon tracks of righteousness for the sake of his name." David wrote in Ps 19:8, "The Torah of Yahweh has integrity, restoring the soul." Thus when he speaks of Yahweh restoring his soul in 23:3, it seems that he refers to the way that meditation on the Scriptures (cf. 1:2) renews his inner man. These Scriptures also show the path worn into the land by the Lord's own wagon, "the wagon tracks of righteousness." God leads his "sheep" on this path "for the sake of his name" (cf. 25:11; 31:3 [MT 31:4]; 79:9; 106:8; 109:21; 143:11) because when David lives out God's own righteous character, God's reputation is magnified. God pursues what is right and good for all people, and David acknowledges that God's glory is at stake in the way he himself lives.

As human beings we have physical needs, and in Ps 23:2 David speaks poetically of how the Lord provides for us everything we need for life and safety. We also have spiritual needs: We need the Lord's presence and direction, and we need an overarching purpose for which to live. Psalm 23:3 depicts the good shepherd meeting those needs for us as well.

### 23:4–6, You Bring Me to the House

Whereas Yahweh was the subject of the verbs—he did the actions described in 23:2–3, in Ps 23:4 David does the action. This shift gently moves us away from the shepherd/sheep metaphor, though David will speak in shepherding terms of the Lord's rod and staff at the end of 23:4. It is as though the metaphor still hovers as David begins to speak of himself in less figurative and more human terms.

The Lord provides physically (23:2) and spiritually (23:3), and in Ps 23:4 David speaks of how the Lord's presence gives him peace in the midst of the most dangerous possible situations. He says that even if he walks "in the valley of the shadow of death" he will not fear evil because Yahweh is with him. Valleys are dangerous places because enemies can ambush from the high ground above them. The reference to the "valley of the shadow of death" calls up an image of a path through a low place, over-shadowed by a high place from which the wicked could waylay travelers. Even in extreme danger the presence of Yahweh drives away fear. The shepherd's rod and staff were his implements for disciplining, rescuing, and protecting his sheep. They could be used to dissuade a sheep from going to a dangerous place or to break the skull of the serpent. The Lord is with David, the Lord has his tools, and thus David feels comfort.

In Ps 23:5 David speaks of Yahweh setting a table before him in the presence of his enemies. Perhaps the image is one of a feast in the field after a battle in which the enemies are defeated. What is certain is that the description has Yahweh endorsing David and providing for him, while the enemies are repudiated and put to shame. This is a picture of vindication.

With the next phrase of Ps 23:5 David says, "You make my head fat with the oil." The image of something being made fat apparently connotes lavish and rich provision, suggesting that as David sits at the table Yahweh has prepared for him, Yahweh anoints his head with oil. With the last phrase of 23:5, "My cup is full," David suggests that his portion is fully satisfying. The "cup" has been used to speak metaphorically of one's lot or portion in life in 11:6 and 16:5. The cup and the table of Ps 23:5 match the grass and water in 23:2 in the psalm's chiastic structure.

Similarly, 23:6 stands across from 23:1, suggesting that Yahweh the shepherd's goodness and lovingkindness are chasing David to ensure his protection and provision (the verb "pursue" is often used of an enemy in pursuit). David is confident that every day of his life his shepherd—he of the good character and loyal heart—will be following him, using the rod to keep him from going over the cliff, the staff to beat off enemies. The good protection of the shepherd ensures that David will enjoy a long life of long days returning to Yahweh's house to worship him there.

BRIDGE

Yahweh the good shepherd who led his people out of Egypt and through the wilderness to the land of promise also protected David. Yahweh the good shepherd then became incarnate, and Jesus the good shepherd has led his people out of slavery to sin by accomplishing the new and greater exodus. Jesus shepherds us through the wilderness to the new and greater land of promise, the new heavens and new earth.

During his earthly life, Jesus lived out the truth of this psalm, entrusting himself to him who judges justly (1 Pet 2:23). Jesus was confident that his Father was his shepherd, that his Father would protect and provide for him. God the Father shepherded Jesus the good shepherd, and as we by faith are united to Christ, God the Father and God the Son will shepherd us all the way home.

Peter refers to the Lord Jesus as the "Chief Shepherd" in 1 Peter 5:4. The pastors that the Lord Jesus has given to shepherd the church (Eph 4:11) are the human means whereby the Lord mediates his shepherding love to his people. Those who would have the Lord as their shepherd today should join themselves to a body of believers united to Christ by faith, and thereby united to one another, guided and cared for by the Chief Shepherd's undershepherds on their sojourn to the land of promise.

## Psalm 24

OVERVIEW AND STRUCTURE OF PSALM 24

After the superscription (on which, see the introduction), Ps 24 opens with two verses that declare that Yahweh owns the world and its inhabitants because he is their creator (24:1–2). Having asserted these realities, David turns to the righteousness God requires in 24:3–6. David begins by asking who may ascend Yahweh's mountain to stand in his holy place (24:3), a question as reminiscent of 15:1 as the answer that follows (24:4–5) is of 15:2–5. David then declares in 24:6 that the generation that seeks Yahweh will live out the righteousness described in 24:4–5. The psalm concludes with a rhythmic celebration of Yahweh the coming king (24:7–10).

We will examine Ps 24 under the following subheads:

24:1–2, The Lord Owns the World (Because He Made It)
24:3–6, The Lord Requires Holiness
24:7–10, The Lord Is the Coming King

SCRIPTURE

CSB

A psalm of David.

¹ The earth and everything in it,
the world and its inhabitants,
belong to the Lord;
² for he laid its foundation on the seas
and established it on the rivers.

³ Who may ascend the mountain of
the LORD?
Who may stand in his holy place?
⁴ The one who has clean hands and a
pure heart,
who has not appealed to what is false,
and who has not sworn deceitfully.
⁵ He will receive blessing from the
Lord,
and righteousness from the God of his
salvation.
⁶ Such is the generation of those who
inquire of him,
who seek the face of the God of Jacob.
*Selah*

⁷ Lift up your heads, you gates!
Rise up, ancient doors!
Then the King of glory will come in.
⁸ Who is this King of glory?
The Lord, strong and mighty,
the Lord, mighty in battle.
⁹ Lift up your heads, you gates!
Rise up, ancient doors!
Then the King of glory will come in.
¹⁰ Who is he, this King of glory?
The Lord of Armies,
he is the King of glory.
*Selah*

Author's translation

¹ Of David. A Psalm.
To Yahweh belongs the earth and its
fullness,
the world and those who dwell in it;
² for on the seas he founded it,
and on the streams he established it.

³ Who may ascend the mountain of
Yahweh,
and who may stand in the place of his
holiness?
⁴ Innocent of hands and pure of heart:
the one who does not lift his soul to
the emptiness,
and he does not make an oath for
treachery.
⁵ He will lift up a blessing from
Yahweh,
even righteousness from the God of
his salvation.
⁶ This the generation of those who
seek him,
who seek your face, O Jacob. *Selah.*

⁷ Lift up your heads, O gates,
and be lifted up, O doors of old!
That he may come, the King of glory.
⁸ Who is this King of glory?
Yahweh, powerful and valorous,
Yahweh, valorous in battle.
⁹ Lift up your heads, O gates,
and lift up, O doors of old!
That he may come, the King of glory.
¹⁰ Who is he, this King of glory?
Yahweh of Hosts.
He is the King of glory. *Selah.*

24:1 "the world"
19:4 (MT 19:5)

24:3–5, "Who may"
Compare 15:1–5

24:4, "innocent of hands and pure of heart"
15:5 "a bribe against the innocent he does not take" (cf. 10:8)
18:20, 24 (MT 18:21, 25) "purity of my hands"
19:9 "The commandment of Yahweh is pure"
73:1 "those who are pure in heart"

24:4 "he does not make an oath for treachery"
Compare 5:6 (MT 5:7); 10:7; 17:1

24:6 "the generation"
12:7 (MT 12:8); 14:5; cf. 10:6; 22:30 (MT 22:31)

24:6 "seek him ... seek your face"
Compare 9:10 (MT 9:11); 10:4; 14:2; 22:26 (MT 22:27)

24:7–10 Yahweh as King
Compare 5:2 (MT 5:3); 10:16; 29:10, etc.

Psalms 1–2 introduce the Psalter with a description of the blessed man in Ps 1, followed by Ps 2's meditation on rebellion against Yahweh and his king, which will come to nothing because of God's promise. Psalms 3–9 present David's response to Absalom's revolt as an example of the kind of rebellion spoken of in Ps 2. In these psalms, David is like the blessed man of Ps 1, meditating on God's promise in Ps 2, calling on the Lord for deliverance. Psalms 10–14 then turn to the way the wicked say in their hearts that there is no God. This set of psalms deals with the threats of the wicked and the longing of the righteous for deliverance. At the chiastic center of Pss 10–14 is God's response to the wicked: his declaration in 12:5 (MT 12:6) that he will arise to save the needy.

Psalms 15–24 turn from Absalom's revolt (Pss 3–9) and what the wicked say in their hearts (Pss 10–14) to the hope of the coming king. Psalms 15 and 24 raise questions about what kind of man this king will be, and the answer is that he will be a king of comprehensive righteousness. As David speaks in the first-person singular in Pss 16 and 23, he seems to be speaking of his own experience. Luke presents Peter saying in Acts 2:25, however, that in speaking of himself David also spoke of the one to come from his line, the seed of promise. These psalms indicate that the king to come would experience the Lord's comfort the way David did. Psalms 17 and 22 present a resurrection hope, and Pss 18 and 20–21 contemplate the redemption God will accomplish for the promised seed. In the middle of this chiastic section of psalms stands the celebration of God's glory in creation and Scripture in Ps 19. Perhaps the most surprising aspect of these psalms is the way that Ps 24 hints that the righteous king to come will be, in some sense, Yahweh himself.

EXPOSITION

### 24:1–2, The Lord Owns the World (Because He Made It)

David opens Ps 24 by asserting that the earth and all its fullness belongs to Yahweh. The first half of Ps 24:1 is paralleled by the second, where David announces that to Yahweh belongs the world and its inhabitants. The statements are as easy to understand as their scope is comprehensive: all the territory in existence and all life forms that inhabit it belong to Yahweh. This means that there is no realm he does not claim as his own, no plot where his sovereignty does not hold sway, and no corner or crevice where he will fail to enforce his will. Moreover, all living beings belong to the God of the Bible. No creature is autonomous. Neither fleas nor flying things are free from his authority. All humans in all places belong to him, along with all rock badgers and rats, bats, and bullfrogs everywhere. David declares in Ps 24:1 that Yahweh owns all territory everywhere, as well as everything that lives. The Lord owns it all.

In Ps 24:2 David explains how he knows this, giving the basis for the claim he made in 24:1. David can assert that Yahweh owns everything in 24:1 because, as he declares in 24:2, Yahweh made the world. The creation of the world is described poetically, with Yahweh depicted as having laid the world's foundations on the watery deep, establishing terra firma on the streams and waterways. If the description of the work of Yahweh's fingers in Ps 8:3 (MT 8:4) showed him to be a master craftsman of intricate detail, the image of him founding the dry land on the waters of the world presents him as a powerful stonemason, manipulator of the mighty rocks that form the world's foundation.

David here asserts the answer to an unsolved riddle in the ancient Near East. Othmar Keel comments on an inadequacy in contemporary artistic attempts to portray the ancient world picture:

> Another fundamental error of these contemporary representations lies in their failure to suggest the extent to which the question of the foundations of the universe—of the ultimate basis and security of existence—remained a problem. The ancient Near East was not conscious of any answer to this question. Again and again, ciphers and symbols were employed ... , expressing nothing other than awe in the face of divine, magical power or divine wisdom and grace.[111]

David learned the theological relationship between Ps 24:1 and 24:2 from the early narratives of Genesis. God created the world and its inhabitants, and his status as their creator gives him the right to make the rules. In Gen 1 God creates, and in Gen 2:17 he tells Adam what he is not permitted to do. When the man sins at the snake's instigation, God calls them to account. There is not some other God who created certain parts of this world, or who gave life to some of its inhabitants. The world has one creator, and the world has one life-giver. Thus in turn the world has one judge and one savior. His name is Yahweh.

### 24:3–6, The Lord Requires Holiness

David learned the truths in Ps 24:1–2 from the early chapters of Genesis, and the same can be said of the contents of Ps 24:3–6. After Adam transgressed God's command, God drove him from his holy presence, banishing him from the garden (Gen 3:24). That primal episode and the accompanying teaching of the Pentateuch is the basis for David's poetic assertion that only the holy can enter God's presence in Ps 24:3–6.

Psalm 24:3–6 parallels Ps 15:1–5 in both form and content. In both cases David asks a question about who can enter God's presence, and in both cases he answers the question with schematic descriptions of righteousness.

The question David asks in Ps 24:1 matches 15:1 by using similar language to ask the same question. He first inquires as to who may ascend Yahweh's mountain. Within the book of Psalms, talk of Yahweh's

---

[111] Keel, *Symbolism of the Biblical World*, 56.

mountain evokes the place where Yahweh declared he had installed his king in 2:6. If we widen our field of reference, Mount Horeb, also known as Mount Sinai, was referred to as the Mountain of God in the book of Exodus. Any consideration of someone ascending Yahweh's mountain recalls the way Moses went up Mount Sinai. Ezekiel described the garden of Eden as God's holy mountain (Ezek 28:13–14), and in Ps 68 David describes a kind of transfer of the significance of Sinai to Mount Zion, Temple Mount (68:15–18, esp. 68:17). These references suggest a relationship between Eden, Sinai, and Zion, implying in turn a connection with the future Mount Zion referenced in Heb 12:22 and Rev 14:1. From the beginning of the Bible to its end, to ascend Yahweh's mountain is to enter his presence.

Whereas the wicked will not rise, or stand, in the judgment in Ps 1:5 (לֹא יָקֻמוּ), David asks in Ps 24:3 who will stand in the place of Yahweh's holiness (וּמִי יָקוּם). This point of connection with Ps 1 on who will stand is an important one, as will become clear as we continue through Ps 24. The reference to the place of Yahweh's holiness, where David is asking who can ascend Yahweh's mountain to stand, evokes thoughts of Temple Mount, connecting the place of Yahweh's holiness to Yahweh's temple on Mount Zion.

Having posed the question in 24:3, David answers it in 24:4–5. He gives four descriptions of the one who can ascend Yahweh's mountain and stand in his holy place in 24:4, then a statement that such a person will receive blessing from Yahweh in 24:5. The first description is, literally, that he is "innocent of hands." To be innocent carries a slightly different connotation than cleanness (and cf. the use of the term in question, e.g., in Gen 44:10 and in the many references to "innocent blood"). One can be ritually defiled, offer sacrifice, and be clean, but to be innocent is to be free from guilt because one has not committed transgression. To have innocent hands is to be one whose hands have not worked deeds that defile.

How could a human maintain innocent hands? Only by having a pure heart, which is the second descriptor in 24:4 of the one who can enter Yahweh's presence. Whereas the statement about innocent hands speaks to the man's actions, the description of the heart speaks to his thoughts, motives, emotions, and inclinations, all of which are pure. This remarkable man who has the right to ascend Yahweh's mountain and stand in his holy place will be "innocent of hands and pure of heart" (24:4).

Having described his actions and his inner life, David next encapsulates the worthy man's worship in 24:4. This man, David says, "does not
lift his soul to the emptiness." To lift up one's soul to something is to
direct one's desire toward that thing (cf. the phrase in Deut 24:15; Prov
19:18; and Hos 4:8). In Ps 25:1 David declares, "To you, O Yahweh, my soul
I lift." The man worthy of ascending Yahweh's mountain and standing in
his holy place does not desire what should not be desired, and he does
not worship what is not worthy. He does not seek satisfaction where
there is none to be found, and he does not try to find joy from what can
only give pain.

The final line of Ps 24:4 declares that this man "does not make an oath
for treachery." He does not take vows that he means to betray, and he
does not make oaths only to achieve surprise and wicked advantage when
he breaks them. He does not sport a fair face only to conceal foul deeds.

God rewards the man who lives out the fourfold description in Ps
24:4, and 24:5 speaks of this man lifting up blessing from Yahweh, and
righteousness from God his Savior. The taking up of the blessing may in
fact be envisioned as taking place within the Lord's holy place on his holy
mountain. Perhaps this could be likened to the experience Moses had of
God's glory that left his face shining in Exod 34 (cf. Exod 33:18–34:29). This
parallel with Moses encountering God "face to face" on the mountain (cf.
Exod 33:11, 20, 23; Num 12:8; Deut 34:10) would seem to be strengthened
by the reference to those who seek God's face in 24:6. If indeed we are
to think of the blessing being received in the holy place on Yahweh's
mountain, then it would be natural for the blessing to be the experience
of Yahweh's own favorable presence (cf. Num 6:24–26).

If this man's hands are innocent and his heart is pure (24:4), in what
sense does he receive righteousness from the God of his salvation (24:5b)?
There are places where a declaration of righteousness amounts to vindication, and that is probably the sense in view here. We are familiar with
the motif of the righteous sufferer in the Old Testament: the man, like
David, who has been marked out by God as his chosen one only to be
persecuted unjustly by the wicked. For God to declare that man in the
right would be for God to vindicate him. For God to vindicate him in that
way would be for God to bring about his salvation.

Psalm 24:6 switches from the individual who meets the description
in 24:4–5 to a group of people. Earlier we saw the idea of standing in
Yahweh's holy place in 24:3 worded in the same terms as the 1:5 reference

to standing at the judgment in the congregation of the righteous. I would propose that the same dynamic between the one and the many at work in Ps 1 is at work in Ps 24. Just as Ps 1 begins by describing the individual blessed man, then moves to the congregation of the righteous, so Ps 24 begins with a description of a man worthy to enter God's presence, then moves to the generation of the righteous. There are places in the Psalms where the word "generation" refers to a group of people alive at a certain time (e.g., 10:6; 33:11; 48:13 [MT 48:14]), but there are also places where "generation" refers to a certain kind of people (12:7 [MT 12:8]; 14:5; 22:30 [MT 22:31]). The wicked generation in 12:7 (MT 12:8) is the seed of the serpent, and the righteous generation in 14:5 is the seed of the woman. The generation spoken of in 24:6 is a certain kind of people, namely, the kind of people who seek God.

The generation of those who seek God in Ps 24:6 is thus a way of referring to the seed of the woman. Psalm 24 seems to indicate that the surpassing righteousness of the man who is worthy will bring about a righteous generation who is like him. David knows that his own righteousness is only relative (see his confession of sin in, e.g., 19:12–13), so when he speaks of this man who has innocent hands and a pure heart he seems to describe someone who has risen above the sinful status of humanity. This connection between the righteous one and the collective seed of the woman who are made righteous by him can also be seen in Isa 53. Yahweh crushes the servant, who made his soul a guilt offering, and who sees his "seed" (53:10). Thereby the righteous one, the servant, makes many to be accounted righteous (53:11), because he bore the sin of many (53:12).

While the details are not worked out in full, Ps 24:3–6 indicates that the generation that seeks Yahweh's face will be made righteous by the one who has the right to ascend Yahweh's mountain and stand in Yahweh's holy place.

The two possible interpretations of 24:6b can be seen in the CSB and the NAS. The CSB understands the reference to "Jacob" to be a shorthand for "the God of Jacob." The NAS, by contrast, renders the second line of 24:6, "Who seek your face—even Jacob," apparently taking "Jacob" as a reference to those who seek Yahweh's face. The Hebrew text does not contain the word "God," though the Greek translator supplied it, as do the CSB, ESV, and NIV. I have tried to present a rendering that reflects the Hebrew and leaves the decision to the reader: "who seek your face,

O Jacob." Either way, it is clear that God's face is being sought and that those who seek God's face are God's people.

Psalm 24:1–2 declare that Yahweh, the creator, owns the earth and all that lives on it. Psalm 24:3–6 teaches that holiness is required of those who would enter Yahweh's presence, and it appears that the holiness of the one man brings about the holiness of the many. Psalm 24:7–10 heralds the coming of the king.

### 24:7–10, The Lord Is the Coming King

With Ps 24:3 seeming to describe Yahweh's mountain, atop which sits his holy place, it would seem natural to think of the gates being addressed in 24:7 as either the gates of Jerusalem in general or perhaps specifically the gates of the temple. Following on the question of who has the right to ascend the mountain and stand in the holy place in 24:3, the call to welcome Yahweh, the king of glory in 24:7–10 seems to present Yahweh himself as the one who meets the requirements and will scale the height and stand in the sacred spot. And yet it would appear from 24:3–5 that the worthy one could be distinguished from Yahweh. Perhaps the resolution of the riddle would await the birth of the babe in Bethlehem.

The man of innocent hands and pure heart ascends the mount as Moses did, a mount not unlike the Edenic holy mountain (Ezek 28:13–14).[112] Finding the gates closed, shut perhaps since a cherubim with flaming sword was stationed there (Gen 3:24), with authority and audacity he calls for the gates to be opened. The gates are to be opened that the king of glory, with whom the holy man seems to be identified, might enter.

Yahweh has been heralded as king prior to this point in the Psalms at 5:2 (MT 5:3) and 10:16 (see also, e.g., 29:10; 44:5; 47:2, 6 [MT 47:3, 7], etc.). Yet Ps 24 seems different in that we seem to expect a righteous *man* to enter Yahweh's presence in 24:3–5, only to find a call to celebrate the entrance of Yahweh himself as king in 24:7–10.

The poetic repetition of 24:7–8 in 24:9–10 is as obvious as it is powerful. The restatement, with variations, of these simple urgent imperatives adds a kind of crescendo effect. It is as though the herald, thrilled with the good news of the high king come at last, cannot stop shouting for the doors to be opened.

In 24:7 and 9 the "gates" and "doors of old" are personified, as though their heads droop in slumber from the long wait for the king to come. At

---

[112] See Edwards, *Exegesis in the Targum of Psalms*, 59.

last the moment of his arrival dawns, and the long-locked points of entry are summoned to lift up their heads, that he may enter, the King of glory himself (24:7, 9). Just as 24:7 and 9 shout the same awakening cry, so 24:8 and 10 present the same rhetorical question and answer. If anyone does not know the identity of the King of glory for whom the gates and doors of old must open, the crier announces in 24:8 that it is Yahweh the man of war, returned triumphant from the battle. In 24:10 the variation is that this is Yahweh of hosts—the head of the armies.

Given the broader story of the Bible, significant parts of which have been engaged by this psalm—creation, God's holy presence, to which only the holy have access—we might suspect something significant about these gates and ancient doors. Perhaps David means to evoke thoughts of doors that have been closed to all who do not live up to the four descriptions in 24:4. Perhaps we are to think of a cherubim and a flaming sword at an eastern entrance. Perhaps this psalm acknowledges that for anyone to enter Yahweh's presence, they need Yahweh's own righteousness. Then if we ask for whom those gates will open, the answer in 24:7–10 is that they will open for Yahweh himself. Yahweh who has won the battle (24:8), Yahweh who enters at the head of his army, and thus is titled "Yahweh of hosts" (24:10). Those hosts are likely comprised of "the generation of those who seek him" (24:6).

### Bridge

Can Ps 24 speak of David's own experience? We saw in our consideration of Ps 8 that David understood himself as a kind of new Adam, Yahweh's vice-regent, made in his image to rule in his stead. We can understand Ps 24 to reflect a situation where David understands that he is Yahweh's king who stands at the head of Yahweh's people as Yahweh's representative. David has a relative righteousness—though he himself acknowledges that he is a sinner—and the people who align with David would join him in devotion to Yahweh. We might think of a situation like the one in 2 Sam 6, where David brought the ark into Jerusalem. The first attempt ended in death because of a failure to abide by all God's instructions. The next attempt was successful, and God's people enjoyed his presence in their midst as he accompanied the ark.

Psalm 24 envisions a situation where the righteous king—a king with not relative but comprehensive righteousness—can boldly enter God's presence because of his unblemished life (24:3–6). This righteous king, moreover, has inspired the seed of the woman, the generation of those who seek God, to follow his example, and somehow he has made them righteous like himself (24:6; cf. Isa 53:10–12).

The surprising development in Ps 24:7–10 is that the righteous king who stands at the head of the host (24:10) to enter the sacred places long gated, shut with ancient doors, is none other than Yahweh himself. I do not know the degree to which David understood the relationship that would exist between Yahweh God and the king who would arise from his line. I suspect that he thought that future king would be a new Adam, vice-regent, image of God, representative of Yahweh par excellence. I tend to doubt that David expected that king to be the very incarnation of God himself. But what David wrote in Ps 24 fits perfectly with the identity of the Lord Jesus.

During his earthly ministry, in anticipation of the way he would ascend the hill of Calvary, Jesus went up on the mountain and sat down. The new and better Moses then taught God's people from the mount, instructing them in the life that pleases God. The teaching in the sermon would be activated by the transforming work accomplished on the cross.

What words can we use to rejoice and exult over the fact that the hands of Jesus are innocent, that his heart is indeed pure (24:4)? How do we begin to render the praise due to the one who had the right to enter the very presence of the Father, ascending Mount Zion, entering the holy place, there not just to stand but even to sit!

And oh the mercy and the goodness and the power, the achievement, the accomplishment, to bear our sins, be crushed for our iniquities, to see his seed, to make many to be accounted righteous, to make it so that the "generation" that seeks God, the seed of the woman, are not only justified but transformed from one degree of glory to another into the same image (24:6; Isa 53; 2 Cor 3:18).

One day the King of glory, Yahweh of hosts, the divine warrior, will come at last. The gates will hear the command to lift up their heads. The ancient doors will open. And the good shepherd will see all his sheep safely to pasture.

## Psalm 25

OVERVIEW AND STRUCTURE OF PSALM 25

Psalm 25 is a nearly complete acrostic psalm, the first word of each new verse beginning with the next letter of the Hebrew alphabet. It skips, however, from the first letter of the alphabet to the third (passing over *bet*), then again skips the sixth letter (*vav*) as well as the nineteenth (*qoph*). Rather than end with the final letter, *tav*, at verse 21, verse 22 opens with a *peh*. Even with the three letters skipped and the additional one at the end, the conclusion that Ps 25 is definitely an acrostic is strengthened by its similarity with Ps 34. Like Ps 25, Ps 34 skips the sixth letter *vav*, though this is the only letter Ps 34's acrostic lacks. But again like Ps 25, Ps 34 does not conclude with the line that begins with the last letter, *tav*, at verse 22, but concludes with a line that begins with *peh* at verse 23.

The formal similarity between Pss 25 and 34 suggests a structural relationship between them. The similarities between Pss 25 and 34 join other features to be discussed in the next section that mark out units within these psalms in Book 1.

In addition to being structured according to the Hebrew alphabet, repetitions of key words and concepts create units of thought in Ps 25 that appear to correspond to one another. Psalm 25:1 both recalls 24:4 and stands across from the plea in 25:22. Within these outer frames, 25:2–3 deals with those who wait for Yahweh not being put to shame, and the same is true of 25:20–21.

David calls on the Lord to cause him to know his *ways*, to teach him his *paths*, and to *cause him to walk* in his truth in 25:4–5. David needs this because he recognizes his own sin and waywardness and because enemies threaten him. Similarly, in 25:16–19 David calls on the Lord to turn to him and take away his sins and see how his enemies hate him.

In 25:6–7 David calls on the Lord to *remember* his mercy and loving-kindness, while asking him *not to remember* his sins and transgression. David then repeats the plea that the Lord *remember* him according to his (the Lord's) lovingkindness and goodness. The repetitions form the basis for a chiastic structure within Ps 25:6–7 that can be depicted as follows:

Remember Mercy
    And Lovingkindness
        Remember Not My Sins and Transgressions
    According to Lovingkindness Remember Me
For the Sake of Your Goodness

This focus on God's character—mercy, lovingkindness, and goodness—in 25:6–7 is matched in 25:14–15 with the reference to Yahweh causing those who fear him to know his covenant and experience intimacy with him.

David speaks of how Yahweh *teaches* in both 25:8–9 and 25:12–13, and at the center of the psalm stands the declaration in 25:10 that all Yahweh's ways are lovingkindness and truth for those who keep his covenant, accompanied by the plea in 25:11 that Yahweh forgive iniquity for the sake of his name.

The chiastic structure of Ps 25 can be reflected as follows:[113]

25:1, I Lift Up My Soul to You
 25:2–3, Let Me Not Be Put to Shame; I Wait for You
  25:4–5, Cause Me to Know and Walk because of Enemies and My Sin
   25:6–7, Yahweh's Character; Remember Not My Sin
    25:8–9, God's Teaching
     25:10–11, God's Character and Forgiveness
    25:12–13, God's Teaching
   25:14–15, Yahweh's Covenant
  25:16–19, Look on My Affliction from My Sin and Enemies
 25:20–21, Let Me Not Be Put to Shame; I Wait for You
25:22, Redeem Israel

We will exposit Ps 25 by approaching its contents in the following three sections:

 25:1–5, Let Me Not Be Put to Shame
 25:6–15, The Lord's Character and Covenant
 25:16–22, Let Me Not Be Put to Shame

---

[113] I find this proposal cleaner and simpler than the one in Alden, "Chiastic Psalms 1–50," 18–20. For a structural proposal similar to my own, see Norbert Lohfink and Erich Zenger, *The God of Israel and the Nations: Studies in Isaiah and the Psalms*, trans. Everett R. Kalin (Collegeville, MN: Liturgical Press, 2000), 72–73.

| CSB | Author's translation |
|---|---|

**CSB**

Of David.

¹ LORD, I appeal to you.
² My God, I trust in you.
Do not let me be disgraced;
do not let my enemies gloat over me.
³ No one who waits for you
will be disgraced;
those who act treacherously without
    cause
will be disgraced.

⁴ Make your ways known to me, LORD;
teach me your paths.
⁵ Guide me in your truth and teach
    me,
for you are the God of my salvation;
I wait for you all day long.
⁶ Remember, LORD, your compassion
and your faithful love,
for they have existed from antiquity.
⁷ Do not remember the sins of my
    youth
or my acts of rebellion;
in keeping with your faithful love,
    remember me
because of your goodness, LORD.

⁸ The LORD is good and upright;
therefore he shows sinners the way.
⁹ He leads the humble in what is right
and teaches them his way.
¹⁰ All the LORD's ways show faithful love
    and truth
to those who keep his covenant and
    decrees.
¹¹ LORD, for the sake of your name,
forgive my iniquity, for it is immense.

¹² Who is this person who fears the
    LORD?

**Author's translation**

¹ Of David
To you, O Yahweh, my soul I lift.

² O my God, in you I trust.
Let me not be put to shame.
Let not those at enmity with me exult
    over me.
³ Surely none who wait for you shall
    be put to shame.
They shall be put to shame who are
    treacherous without cause.

⁴ Your ways, O Yahweh, cause me to
    know;
your paths teach me!
⁵ Cause me to walk in your truth,
and teach me,
for you are the God of my salvation;
for you I wait all the day.

⁶ Remember your mercies, O Yahweh,
and your lovingkindnesses,
for from of old are they.
⁷ The sins of my youth, and my
    transgressions, remember not!
According to your lovingkindness
    remember me,
for the sake of your goodness, O
    Yahweh.

⁸ Good and upright is Yahweh,
therefore he teaches sinners in the
    way.
⁹ He causes the humble to walk in the
    judgment
and he will teach the humble his way.

¹⁰ All the ways of Yahweh are
    lovingkindness and truth
to those who keep his covenant and
    his testimonies.

He will show him the way he should
   choose.
¹³ He will live a good life,
and his descendants will inherit the
   land.
¹⁴ The secret counsel of the Lord
is for those who fear him,
and he reveals his covenant to
   them.
¹⁵ My eyes are always on the Lord,
for he will pull my feet out of the
   net.

¹⁶ Turn to me and be gracious to me,
for I am alone and afflicted.
¹⁷ The distresses of my heart increase;
bring me out of my sufferings.
¹⁸ Consider my affliction and trouble,
and forgive all my sins.
¹⁹ Consider my enemies; they are
   numerous,
and they hate me violently.
²⁰ Guard me and rescue me;
do not let me be disgraced,
for I take refuge in you.
²¹ May integrity and what is right
watch over me,
for I wait for you.

²² God, redeem Israel, from all its
   distresses.

¹¹ For the sake of your name, O
   Yahweh,
forgive my iniquity,
for it is great.

¹² Who is this, the man who fears
   Yahweh?
He will teach him the way he chooses.
¹³ His soul in good will lodge,
and his seed will inherit the land.

¹⁴ Intimacy with Yahweh is for those
   who fear him,
and his covenant he causes them to
   know.
¹⁵ My eyes are continually to Yahweh,
for he causes my feet to go out from
   the net.

¹⁶ Turn to me,
and be gracious to me,
for alone and afflicted am I.
¹⁷ The tight places of my heart are
   made broad,
from straits cause me to be brought
   out.
¹⁸ Behold my affliction and my labor,
and take away all my sins.
¹⁹ Behold those at enmity with me, for
   they are many,
and with violent hatred they hate me.

²⁰ Guard my soul, and cause me to be
   delivered.
Let me not be put to shame,
because I have taken refuge in you.
²¹ Let integrity and uprightness
   deliver me,
for I wait for you.

²² Ransom Israel, O God, from all his
   tight places.

CONTEXT: VERBAL AND THEMATIC LINKS WITH SURROUNDING PSALMS

Psalms 25, 26, 27, and 28 all begin with the simple superscription, "Of David."

25:1 "To you, O Yahweh, my soul I lift" (cf. 86:4)
24:4 "who does not lift his soul to the emptiness"

25:2 "in you I trust"
same in 143:8

25:5 "God of my salvation"
24:5 "God of his salvation"

25:6 "mercies ... lovingkindness"
Exod 34:6 "merciful ... lovingkindness"

25:10 "lovingkindness and truth"
Compare Exod 34:6 "lovingkindness and truth"

25:11 "your name"
Exod 34:6–7

25:18 "take away all my sins"
Exod 34:7 "forgiving iniquity, transgression, and sin"

As noted above, Pss 25 and 34 are similarly constructed acrostic psalms. As such, these two psalms bracket those between them, creating a unit that stretches from Ps 25 through 33, and another that runs from 34 through 41. This corresponds to the way that the similarity between Pss 10 and 14 and 15 and 24 mark out earlier units. We can further observe that Pss 25–28 are personal prayers, whereas Ps 29 is not a prayer but a command directed at heavenly beings who should worship Yahweh. Psalm 29 seems to mark a turning point, with Pss 30–33 mirroring the thoughts of 25–28:

Psalm 25, Teaching
    Psalm 26, Vindication
        Psalm 27, Confidence
            Psalm 28, Plea
                Psalm 29, Glory
            Psalm 30, Praise

Psalm 31, Refuge
Psalm 32, Forgiveness
Psalm 33, Word


EXPOSITION

### 25:1–5, Let Me Not Be Put to Shame

In Ps 25 David cries out to the Lord for help. He needs help because of his sin and his enemies, and his appeal is based on Yahweh's character and covenant. In response to the threats from his enemies, David appeals that the Lord not let him be put to shame but instead put them to shame. In response to his own sin, David seeks forgiveness on the basis of God's steadfast love, and he asks the Lord to teach him to walk in truth.

David had described the righteous one in Ps 24:4 as one who refused to "lift his soul to the emptiness." Those who would avoid idolatry will only succeed by doing what David tells the Lord he does in Ps 25:1, lifting his soul to Yahweh (same in 86:4). All his energy, devotion, creativity, longing, and life—his soul—David directs and submits to Yahweh.

In Ps 25:2 David declares his trust in Yahweh and asks that the Lord not let him be put to shame, keeping his enemies from exulting over him. David's pleas for the Lord to teach him in 25:4–5, and his calls for the Lord to forgive his sin (25:7, 11, 18), provide the context for his request that the Lord spare him from shame in 25:2. David understands that his own sin puts him in danger of Yahweh's discipline, and he knows that discipline could take the form of defeat at the hands of his enemies. If David sins and deserves to be put to shame, his enemies will exult over him when they defeat him. So David's prayer not to be put to shame is concomitant with the following prayers that Yahweh teach him his way (25:4–5) and remember not his sins (25:6–7).

David expresses his confidence in Ps 25:3 that none who wait for Yahweh will be put to shame while those treacherous without cause will be. He will speak of waiting for Yahweh again in 25:5 and 21. Waiting for Yahweh is a strategy for fighting sin and a posture of confidence against enemies. To be "wantonly treacherous" (ESV) would not be like what David did when he deceived Saul about going home to Bethlehem to escape being murdered by Saul (1 Sam 20:6, 28, 33). Wanton treachery would be unjustified unfaithfulness, betraying what is right for no good reason. Traitors will be put to shame.

David knows that the best way to avoid shame is to walk in obedience to Yahweh, so he calls on the Lord to cause him to know his ways, asking Yahweh to teach him his paths in 25:4.[114] This is accompanied by the plea that Yahweh cause him to walk in his truth in 25:5. David wants not only to know the truth but to live it. His requests are grounded in the fact that he looks to God for salvation, waiting for him all the day (25:5).

Knowing the weakness of his flesh and the malice of his enemies, in Ps 25:1–5 David prays that Yahweh will keep him from shame, show him the path of life, and cause him to walk in it.

### 25:6–15, The Lord's Character and Covenant

The lovely and profound chiastic statement in Ps 25:6–7 is the whole message of the Bible. It begins with Yahweh's mercies (A) and loving-kindess (B), then comes sin (C), but rather than sin having the last word, Yahweh's lovingkindness (B′) and goodness (A′) surround and overcome man's transgression:

Mercies
    Lovingkindness
        Sins and Transgressions
    Lovingkindness
Goodness

In 25:6 David asks Yahweh to remember his womblike mercies (רחם) and his loyal covenant love (חסד), for they are "from the age" (מעולם). Yahweh's character is constant, and David appeals to God to remember his everlasting mercy and love.

Repeating the terminology of Ps 25:6 in 25:7, David asks the Lord *not* to remember his youthful sins and his transgressions. David claims nothing about himself that would merit reward rather than punishment, nor does he suggest that his good works have outnumbered the bad. His appeal for his sins not to be remembered stands solely on the character of Yahweh. David asks for Yahweh to forget his sin and instead remember him according to Yahweh's own *hesed* and goodness. David recognizes that

---

[114] Hensley points out the "frequent references to YHWH's 'ways' (cf. דרך in vv. 4, 5, 8, 9, and 12)." Hensley, *Covenant Relationships*, 81.

he does not deserve God's kindness, but that God extends his kindness and forgiveness to those who seek it from him.

The mercy of God is the most astonishing and beautiful truth in the Bible.

God mercifully does not remember sin, and God mercifully teaches godliness to the ungodly. This David celebrates in 25:8–9, as he says that God instructs sinners in the way because he is good and upright (25:8). The proud will confess neither their sin nor their need for instruction, but the humble will do both. Thus in 25:9 David says that God causes the humble to walk in accordance with his judgments and teaches them his way. God opposes proud sinners. God forgives humble penitents. God teaches humble students.

David has described the Lord's merciful forgiveness (25:6–7) and kind teaching (25:8–9), and this leads to the apex of his celebration of God's character in 25:10–11. David's statements about the Lord in Ps 25 reflect awareness of Exod 34:6–7, where Yahweh declared his own covenantal name to Moses. Yahweh had described himself as "merciful" (רחום) in Exod 34:6, and David appealed to God's "mercies" in 25:6. Yahweh also said that he was "abounding in lovingkindness and truth" (ורב חסד ואמת) in Exod 34:6. David takes up that phrase and employs it in his summary of Yahweh's ways in Ps 25:10, noting that Yahweh conducts himself this way for "those who keep his covenant and his testimonies" (cf. Ps 18:25–26 [MT 18:26–27]). To keep God's covenant is to remain in relationship with him, as opposed to rejecting the covenant and forsaking God. To keep God's testimonies is to meditate on the Scriptures that contain the true witness of what God has said for himself and what others have said about him.

Those who understand God as he reveals himself in the Scriptures know that his truth demands justice while his lovingkindness makes forgiveness possible. Having just referenced these Exod 34:6 "lovingkindness and truth" aspects of God's declaration of his own name, in Ps 25:11 David asks the Lord to forgive his iniquity for the sake of his name. This request is thoroughly in keeping with Exod 34:6–7, because God said of himself that he is a God "forgiving iniquity and transgression and sin" (Exod 34:7). In Ps 25:10–11 David has taken up God's declaration of his own name in Exod 34:6–7 and prayed it back to God in personal application of God's words to his own spiritual life.

David knows his sin is great, as he says at the end of 25:11, but he also knows God's name, his reputation, which he himself declared in

Exod 34:6–7. David, therefore, appeals to God's own name, his own reputation, as he prays to be forgiven.

David asked for teaching in Ps 25:4–5, then spoke of how Yahweh
teaches in 25:8–9, just prior to the central celebration of Yahweh's name
in 25:10–11, and now he returns to Yahweh's teaching in 25:12–13. The
celebration of God's lovingkindness, truth, and forgiveness in 25:10–11
is immediately preceded and followed by statements about God teaching
humble people. David commends knowing God, and David commends the
humble reception of God's instruction.

In Ps 25:12 Yahweh teaches the way that he chooses to the one who
fears him. Humility (25:9) springs from an experience of Yahweh's holiness that results in righteous fear. To fear God is to respect him, to know
that he cannot be taken for granted or presumed upon. To fear him is to
avoid infringing upon his holiness because one dreads the consequences.
Living in the fear of Yahweh does not result in a shattered state of psychological duress but in the enjoyment of God's goodness. Thus in 25:12
Yahweh teaches the one who fears him, and in 25:13 that man who fears
Yahweh dwells in goodness and his seed inherit the land. Those who fear
Yahweh need fear neither the consequences nor the ramifications of sin.
They enjoy the blessings of holiness.

The promise that the seed will inherit the land (25:12) recalls God's
promises to Abraham (Gen 15:18), and this comes in a context thick with
references to Exod 34:6–7 (Ps 25:10–11, 18) and two mentions of God's
"covenant" (בריתו in 25:10 and 14). Hensley comments on the "strong
entailments of both Abrahamic promises and Mosaic covenantal life and
obligations," seeing evidence here of "David praying for himself according
to a model of Mosaic intercession, whose importance for the preservation
and renewal of the covenant was well-established."[115]

Moreover, Ps 25:14 declares that Yahweh shares his intimate secret
counsel with those who fear him, causing them to know his covenant. The
kind of fear in view, then, is a pious respect that results in appropriate
behavior. The man who fears Yahweh does not incur Yahweh's wrath
but enjoys his favor and savors an ongoing, deepening relationship with
Yahweh. In Ps 25:15 David says that his eyes are always looking to Yahweh,
which is akin to the lifting of his soul to Yahweh in 25:1. In 25:15 David
explains that he does this because Yahweh delivers his feet from snares.

---

[115] Hensley, *Covenant Relationships*, 82.

The "net" David mentions evokes both the traps of sin and the attempts of his enemies to shame him. David looks to the Lord to deliver him from sin and enemies.

### 25:16–22, Let Me Not Be Put to Shame

David knows that if he has the joy of experiencing God's presence, he will be delivered from both sin and his enemies. Thus he prays to Yahweh in 25:16, asking Yahweh to turn his face toward him and show gracious favor to him. David explains his need: he is lonely and afflicted (25:16). Both loneliness and difficulty result in spiritual and physical vulnerability, opening us up to temptation. David responds to this by asking for God to turn to him. He elaborates upon his difficulty in 25:17, saying that the things in his own heart that incline him away from the Lord are spreading. David responds rightly to the growth of evil inclinations—crying out to the Lord for deliverance.

For the third time in Ps 25, David asks the Lord to take away his sin in 25:18, and here again the expression is reminiscent of Exod 34:6–7 (נשא in Exod 34:7 and Ps 25:18). The focus of 25:18 is David's sin, and the focus of 25:19 is the violent hatred of his enemies. David looks to the Lord for deliverance from both.

David asks for protection and deliverance in 25:20, returning also to the request he made in 25:2 that he not be put to shame. The basis for this request in 25:2 was that David had trusted in Yahweh, and the basis he gives in 25:20 is synonymous: he has taken refuge in Yahweh.

David has sins that he has confessed and for which he has sought forgiveness in 25:7, 11, and 18, but he has not been "treacherous without cause" (25:3). David's words in 25:21 show that he has attempted, however imperfectly, to walk in integrity and uprightness in accordance with Yahweh's teaching, waiting on Yahweh (cf. waiting on Yahweh in 25:3, 5; and Yahweh's teaching in 25:4–5, 8–9, and 12–13). David requests in 25:21 that the evidence of his genuine trust in Yahweh seen in his integrity and uprightness might protect him from the shame of having his enemies exult over him (cf. 25:2–3).

David has spoken of his own experiences and concerns in the first-person singular throughout Ps 25, only to make the request in 25:22 that God might redeem Israel from all his troubles. The dynamic between the very personal prayer and the concern for the nation of Israel reinforces the impression that David sees himself, as Israel's king, as the barometer of

Israel's fortunes. If the king is righteous, the nation will be righteous, because the king is the exemplar for the people, the father of the nation, and the best indication of what kind of culture will prevail in the land. If God answers David's prayers for himself in 25:1–21, he will thereby answer the prayer for the nation in 25:22.

BRIDGE

This relationship between David and Israel is transposed and deepened when the music modulates into an elevated key that finds fulfillment in the one of whom the Psalms do sing. Jesus resisted all sin through his vital relationship with his Father, and Jesus was delivered from all enemies, vindicated by means of his resurrection from the dead. Even as Jesus fulfills the pattern of David's prayer in Ps 25, in his death and resurrection Jesus also makes it possible for God to be just and the justifier of the ungodly, a God committed to truth and justice who can mercifully forgive penitent sinners (cf. Rom 3:24–26). Jesus lived out David's prayer for deliverance from sin and enemies, and Jesus also lived out the theological necessity that enables the logic of the prayer as he was crucified for sin and raised for justification (Rom 4:25).

## Psalm 26

OVERVIEW AND STRUCTURE OF PSALM 26

Psalm 26 falls into four parts. In 26:1–2 David prays for vindication and sanctification. In 26:1 he calls on the Lord to decide the case in his favor because of his integrity and trust in Yahweh and because of his commitment to faithfulness. Then in 26:2 he asks the Lord to test and try him so that his heart and inclinations can be refined and purified.

Having stated the direct requests for vindication and sanctification in 26:1–2, David makes no more requests until the final section of the psalm, when in 26:9–12 he asks the Lord not to sweep him away with the wicked (26:9) but to ransom him and be gracious to him (26:11).

Between the requests made at the beginning and end of Ps 26 are two related sections. In 26:3–5 David describes how the Lord's lovingkindness and truth keep him from sitting with the wicked or sympathizing with their assembly. Then in 26:6–8 David describes the way he frequents the Lord's dwelling place to be cleansed from sin, to offer his thanks, and to celebrate God's great deeds.

The contents of Ps 26 may reflect a chiastic structure as follows (note the references to walking in integrity in 26:1 and 26:11):

26:1–2, Prayer for Vindication and Sanctification
    26:3–5, Yahweh's Lovingkindness and Truth
    26:6–8, David's Thanks and Praise
26:9–12, Prayer for Acquittal and Gracious Redemption[116]

We will pursue the exposition of Ps 26 under the following three headings:

    26:1–2, Vindication and Sanctification
    26:3–8, Worship Not Wickedness
    26:9–12, Acquittal and Redemption

SCRIPTURE

| CSB | Author's translation |
|---|---|
| Of David. | [1] Of David. |
| | Judge me, O Yahweh, |
| [1] Vindicate me, LORD, | for I in my integrity have walked, |
| because I have lived with integrity | and in Yahweh I trusted; |
| and have trusted in the LORD without | I will not buckle. |
| wavering. | [2] Test me, O Yahweh, and try me; |
| [2] Test me, LORD, and try me; | refine my guts and my heart. |
| examine my heart and mind. | |
| [3] For your faithful love guides me, | [3] For your lovingkindness is before |
| and I live by your truth. | my eyes, |
| | and I walk in your truth. |
| [4] I do not sit with the worthless | [4] I do not sit with the men of |
| or associate with hypocrites. | emptiness, |
| [5] I hate a crowd of evildoers, | and with those who hide themselves I |
| and I do not sit with the wicked. | do not go. |

---

[116] In my notes I find that several years ago I worked through Ps 26 and arrived at an alternative, complementary chiastic structure that can be depicted as follows:
    26:1–3, Prayer for Vindication (walked in integrity)
    26:4–5, Refusal to Accompany the Wicked
    26:6, Cleansing at the Altar
    26:7, Thanks and Praise
    26:8, God's Temple and Glory
    26:9–10, Do Not Punish Me with the Wicked
    26:11–12, Commitment to Walk in Integrity.

⁶ I wash my hands in innocence
and go around your altar, Lord,
⁷ raising my voice in thanksgiving
and telling about your wondrous
works.

⁸ Lord, I love the house where you
dwell,
the place where your glory resides.
⁹ Do not destroy me along with
sinners,
or my life along with men of
bloodshed
¹⁰ in whose hands are evil schemes
and whose right hands are filled with
bribes.

¹¹ But I live with integrity;
redeem me and be gracious to me.
¹² My foot stands on level ground;
I will bless the Lord in the assemblies.

⁵ I hate the assembly of those who
cause evil,
and with the wicked I will not sit.

⁶ I wash my hands in innocence,
and I go about your altar, O Yahweh,
⁷ to cause to hear with the voice of
thanksgiving,
and to recount all your wonders.
⁸ O Yahweh, I love the habitation of
your house,
even the place of the tabernacle of
your glory.

⁹ Do not gather with sinners my soul,
nor with men of bloodshed my life,
¹⁰ in whose hands is mischief,
and their right hand is full of a bribe.
¹¹ As for me, in my integrity I walk:
ransom me and be gracious to me.
¹² My foot stands on a level place;
in the great assembly I will bless
Yahweh.

CONTEXT: VERBAL AND THEMATIC LINKS WITH SURROUNDING PSALMS

Psalms 25, 26, 27, and 28 all begin with the simple superscription, "Of David."

> 26:3 "your lovingkindness ... your truth"
> 25:10

> 26:4 "men of emptiness"
> 24:4 "does not lift his soul to the emptiness"

> 26:6 "my hands in innocence"
> 73:13

For the flow of thought in Pss 25–33, see the "Context" section on Ps 25.

EXPOSITION

## 26:1–2, Vindication and Sanctification

David opens Ps 26 with a prayer for God to judge him, and in context it is clear that he wants God to render a judgment that vindicates him. Why would David need to pray for vindication?

In Ps 26, like the surrounding psalms, David prays in response to the accusations and attacks of his enemies. Like Moses before him, David seems to have had plenty of people around him ready to grumble about his leadership. He prays that his enemies will not put him to shame and exult over him in Ps 25 (25:2–3, 20). He prays for vindication in 26:1, and there are evildoers, adversaries, and foes in 27:2 (cf. 27:12). David then prays for justice against his enemies in 28:4–5.

David represents God's kingdom. David seeks to advance God's truth. David prays that his detractors would be shown to be in the wrong, and that he would be declared to be in the right, vindicated.

Whatever the charges might have been that were leveled against him, David asks the Lord to vindicate him in 26:1 for two reasons. First, he says that he has walked in his integrity, and second, that he has trusted in Yahweh.

David's final statement in 26:1 (CSB and ESV "without wavering") is an assertion of his commitment, his devotion. I have rendered this phrase, "I will not buckle."

In 2014 Admiral William H. McRaven gave a commencement address at the University of Texas in which he drew ten lessons from his Navy SEAL training. The tenth is an apt illustration of David's commitment not to buckle:

> Finally, in SEAL training there is a bell. A brass bell that hangs in the center of the compound for all the students to see. All you have to do to quit is ring the bell.
>
> Ring the bell and you no longer have to wake up at 5 o'clock. Ring the bell and you no longer have to do the freezing cold swims. Ring the bell and you no longer have to do the runs, the obstacle course, the PT—and you no longer have to endure the hardships of training. Just ring the bell.
>
> If you want to change the world don't ever, ever ring the bell.[117]

In our struggle against sin, we should follow David's example and commit ourselves, vowing to the Lord that we will not buckle. We should commit ourselves: never ring the bell. Never give up. Never give in.

---

[117] William H. McRaven, "Adm. McRaven Urges Graduates to Find Courage to Change the World," *UT News*, May 16, 2014, http://news.utexas.edu/2014/05/16/admiral-mcraven-commencement-speech.

David accompanies his prayer for vindication in 26:1 with a prayer for sanctification in 26:2. The prayer for vindication is not an excuse to wallow in his weaknesses. David asks the Lord to test and try him, praying for his "kidneys" and his "heart" to be refined. The terms used to refer to the testing and the trying are used elsewhere to refer to the refining of silver and gold (cf. Ps 12:6 [MT 12:7]; Job 23:10; Zech 13:9). David's prayer is for the Lord to purify him, to smelt away the impurities through the difficulties of his life.

### 26:3–8, Worship Not Wickedness

How can David commit himself to an unbuckling devotion? What motivates him to pray that the Lord would turn up the heat, bringing the flames near him to smelt away the dross in his life? David answers those questions in Ps 26:3, and what the Lord said of himself in Exod 34:6–7 (cf. Ps 25:10) informs his statement. David sets the Lord before him, specifically, the Lord's steadfast love. God's loyal lovingkindness keeps David from fixating on his enemies, his difficulties, and his temptations. Because David has the Lord's lovingkindness before his eyes, he walks in the Lord's truth.

David says that he walks in Yahweh's truth in 26:3, and then he says in 26:4 and 5 that he does not sit with the wicked, go with hypocrites, or delight in the assembly of evildoers. All this is reminiscent of Ps 1, where the blessed man does not walk, stand, or sit with the wicked but meditates on the Torah of Yahweh day and night. When David says in 26:3, therefore, that the Lord's lovingkindness is before his eyes, he likely has in view meditation on scriptural texts that speak of Yahweh's *hesed* (not least Exod 34:6–7). When he goes on to say in Ps 26:3 that he walks in Yahweh's truth, he likely has in view the Lord's instructions, prohibitions, commandments, and teaching in the Bible.

The Bible, after all, determines what it means for someone to be a "man of falsehood," or as I have rendered the phrase, a man "of emptiness." The blessed king described in Ps 24:4 is one who "does not lift up his soul to the emptiness." David says in 26:4 that he does not sit with such men, nor does he go "with those who hide themselves." The clear implication is that such people keep their wicked purposes and wicked actions from becoming known lest they be punished or rejected.

In Ps 26:5 David says that he hates "the assembly of those who cause evil." The word of God has defined good and evil for him, and God's word determines David's vision of the good life, of pleasure, and of joy. David refuses, therefore, to take pleasure in evil or in the gathering together of those who cause it.

David said he does not sit with the wicked at the beginning of 26:4, and at the end of 26:5 he says he will not sit with them. He seems to be saying that he will continue on the holy path he is on.

Beholding the Lord's lovingkindness in Ps 26:3 keeps David from cavorting with the wicked in 26:4–5, and it also draws David into the worship of the Lord in 26:6–8. David speaks of the "altar" in 26:6 and of the Lord's "house" and the "place" where God's glory dwells in 26:8. He seems to have the place of God's presence in view. In David's day this would have been a tent-like structure along the lines of a tabernacle, with David wanting to build the temple (cf. 2 Sam 7). Though David was not permitted to build the temple, he nevertheless speaks of the place of God's presence, where the altar and eventually the ark of the covenant would be.

David seems to envision going to the place where God was understood to dwell. Just as the righteous king in Ps 24:4 was "innocent of hands," David says in 26:6 that he will wash his hands in innocence. I would maintain both that the kind of innocence in view is not the kind that comes from having made atonement but the kind that exists because one is untainted by guilt (cf. the phrase in Gen 20:5).[118] Innocence indicates inexperience of evil. Still, this does not require David to be claiming sinless perfection. Given the context, it seems that David is not guilty of the charges leveled against him—thus the prayer for vindication in 26:1—and that he has kept himself from the depredations of the wicked described in 26:4–5. Here again David's words do not demand that he himself is without sin, even as they perfectly describe that descendant of his who would be.

In Ps 26:6 David describes the way that he attains a ritually clean state by washing his hands and by sacrificing at Yahweh's altar. The Lord's kindness and mercy prompt his gratitude, so in 26:7a he speaks of how he causes his voice of thanksgiving to be heard. The Lord's faithfulness to Israel narrated in the Scriptures further prompts David to recount Yahweh's wondrous deeds in 26:7b. All of 26:6–8 pertains to worship in a state of ritual purity. David states his affection for Yahweh in 26:8 when he declares that he loves Yahweh's dwelling place, Yahweh's house, where Yahweh's glory dwells.

---

[118] So also Bullock, "The psalmist washes his hands to symbolize his innocence (v. 6), a practice also observed by Israel's elders with the same objective (Dt 21:6–7)," "Book 1," 47.

David loves God, so David naturally enjoys God's presence. David loves to honor God, to be in a state of ritual purity to make sacrifice to God, to celebrate God with thanksgiving, and to rehearse all God's mighty deeds. David loves to worship the Lord.

My friend Heath Lambert spoke recently of the way that some steps to recovery urge people to change their patterns, their people, and their places. David speaks of these things in Ps 26. He devotes himself to a *pattern of life* that pleases the Lord when he speaks of walking in his integrity in 26:1 and 26:11. He speaks of avoiding *people* who will have a negative influence on him when he describes the way he does not sit with the wicked in 26:4–5. And He speaks of the sanctifying *place* when he celebrates worship at God's house in 26:6–8.

### 26:9–12, Acquittal and Redemption

David prayed for vindication and sanctification in 26:1–2, described his enjoyment of worship not wickedness in 26:3–8, and now in 26:9–12 he prays for acquittal and gracious redemption.

David's prayer in Ps 26:9 that the Lord not "gather" (ESV, "sweep away"; CSB, "destroy") him with the wicked presupposes their condemnation and expects the visitation of justice upon them. David asks the Lord not to judge him with the wicked. He has prayed for a verdict of vindication not condemnation (26:1). First Chronicles 28:3 describes David as a man of war who had shed blood, but that is not the kind of man of bloodshed David describes in Ps 26:9. David pursued the Lord's causes in battle, whereas the "bloodthirsty" (ESV) with whom he does not want to be condemned in Ps 26:9 are not soldiers engaged in just and holy wars but cold killers. David continues to portray the wicked in 26:10, speaking of the way they advance their mischief by their power and wickedly use bribes to corrupt justice.

In contrast with the murderous manipulators whom Yahweh will gather up for judgment, David asserts that as he has walked in his integrity (26:1) so he will continue to do (26:11a). Still, recognizing that he himself is not altogether sinless, David cries out for God to be gracious to him and redeem him (26:11b).

David details his way of life in Ps 26. He is committed to the Scriptures, where he experiences Yahweh's lovingkindness. He enjoys worship and avoids the wicked. All this results in what he says in Ps 26:12a. His foot stands on a level place precisely because it will not slide in due time (cf. Deut 32:35). David hates the assembly of the wicked (26:5), but he loves to bless Yahweh in the great assembly of his people (26:12b).

BRIDGE

No one more deserved Yahweh's just vindication than Jesus (26:1a). No one walked better in integrity than Jesus (26:1b). No one trusted Yahweh more, and no one else could say that he *never* buckled under pressure (26:1c, d). Similarly, Jesus was perfected through what he suffered; he was tested, tried, and refined to completion (26:2; cf. Heb 2:11). Jesus kept the Lord's lovingkindness before himself, walked in the Lord's truth, refused to sit with the wicked, and was innocent like no one else (26:3–6). Jesus gave thanks and caused the voice of thanksgiving to be heard. He celebrated and accomplished the Lord's wonders (26:7), and Jesus himself became the dwelling place of Yahweh's glory, tabernacling among us and causing God's glory to be seen (26:8; cf. John 1:14). Jesus makes it so that the guilty can be acquitted, so that repentant sinners will not be swept away with the unrepentant (Ps 26:9–10). Jesus walked in integrity to accomplish God's gracious redemption (26:11), with the result that we stand on solid ground in the great assembly to bless the Lord (26:12).

## Psalm 27

OVERVIEW AND STRUCTURE OF PSALM 27

Psalm 27 consists of four thematic units.[119] In 27:1–3 David asserts that Yahweh is his light and salvation and speaks of how Yahweh makes him confident even in extreme situations. In 27:4–6 David describes his desire to be near Yahweh and extols the joy and shelter of being in God's house, temple, booth, and tent (twice). In 27:7–10 David sets himself to seek God's face, speaking of the way the Lord called people to do this, his obedience to such instruction, and asking the Lord not to hide his face from him. In 27:11–14 David asks the Lord to teach and lead him, to deliver him from his enemies, and concludes with a call for others to be strong and wait for Yahweh.

---

[119] The Greek translation of Ps 27 (LXX Ps 26) adds πρὸ τοῦ χρισθῆναι, "before he was anointed," to the psalm's superscription. For discussion, see Pietersma, "Superscriptions of the Greek Psalter," 103–5.

The contents of Ps 27 reflect a chiastic structure that can be depicted as follows:[120]

27:1, Trust
   27:2–3, The Wicked
      27:4–5, Seeking Yahweh
         27:6, Praise for Deliverance
      27:7–10, Seeking Yahweh's Face
   27:11–12, The Wicked
27:13–14, Trust

We will pursue the exposition of Ps 27 under the following headings:

   27:1–3, Confidence in God
   27:4–6, Desire for God
   27:7–10, Seeking God's Face
   27:11–14, Waiting for God

SCRIPTURE

| CSB | Author's translation |
|---|---|
| Of David. | [1] Of David |
| | O Yahweh, you are my light and my salvation. Whom shall I fear? |
| [1] The Lord is my light and my salvation— whom should I fear? The Lord is the stronghold of my life— whom should I dread? | Yahweh is the stronghold of my life. Whom shall I dread? |
| [2] When evildoers came against me to devour my flesh, my foes and my enemies stumbled and fell. | [2] When those who cause evil are near upon me to eat up my flesh, my adversaries and those at enmity with me, they stumbled and fell. |
| [3] Though an army deploys against me, my heart will not be afraid; though a war breaks out against me, I will still be confident. | [3] If an army encamps against me, my heart will not fear. If war arises against me, in this will I trust. |
| [4] I have asked one thing from the Lord; it is what I desire: to dwell in the house of the Lord | [4] One thing I asked from Yahweh, it will I seek: |

---

[120] Cf. Alden, "Chiastic Psalms 1–50," 20–21.

all the days of my life,
gazing on the beauty of the Lord
and seeking him in his temple.
⁵ For he will conceal me in his shelter
in the day of adversity;
he will hide me under the cover of his
tent;
he will set me high on a rock.
⁶ Then my head will be high
above my enemies around me;
I will offer sacrifices in his tent with
shouts of joy.
I will sing and make music to the Lord.

⁷ Lord, hear my voice when I call;
be gracious to me and answer me.
⁸ My heart says this about you:
"Seek his face."
Lord, I will seek your face.
⁹ Do not hide your face from me;
do not turn your servant away in
anger.
You have been my helper;
do not leave me or abandon me,
God of my salvation.
¹⁰ Even if my father and mother
abandon me,
the Lord cares for me.

¹¹ Because of my adversaries,
show me your way, Lord,
and lead me on a level path.
¹² Do not give me over to the will of
my foes,
for false witnesses rise up against me,
breathing violence.

¹³ I am certain that I will see the Lord's
goodness
in the land of the living.
¹⁴ Wait for the Lord;
be strong, and let your heart be
courageous.
Wait for the Lord.

that I may dwell in the house of
Yahweh
all the days of my life,
to gaze on the beauty of Yahweh,
and to inquire at his temple.
⁵ For he will treasure me in his booth
on the day of evil.
He will cause me to be hidden in the
hiding place of his tent.
On a rock he will lift me high.

⁶ And now he will lift my head over
those at enmity with me around
me,
and I will sacrifice in his tent
sacrifices with shouts of joy.
I will sing, and I will psalm to Yahweh.

⁷ Hear, O Yahweh, my voice.
I call, so be gracious to me and answer
me.
⁸ For you my heart speaks:
you all must seek my face!
Your face, O Yahweh, I will seek.
⁹ Do not hide your face from me.
Do not turn your servant away in
anger [lit. "in nose"].
My help you have been.
Do not forsake me, and do not
abandon me, O God of my salvation!
¹⁰ If my father and my mother
abandoned me,
then Yahweh will gather me.

¹¹ Teach me, O Yahweh, your way,
and lead me in the path of the level
place
because of the ones who watch me.
¹² Do not give me to the soul of my
adversaries,
for they rise against me, witnesses of
deception, and they breathe out
violence.

¹³ Except for me trusting in seeing the
goodness of Yahweh in the land of
the living ...

<sup>14</sup>Wait for Yahweh.
Be strong, and cause your heart to be
   stout;
and wait for Yahweh.

CONTEXT: VERBAL AND THEMATIC LINKS WITH SURROUNDING PSALMS

27:2 "those who cause evil"
Compare 26:5

27:4 "the house of Yahweh"
Compare 26:8

27:10 "Yahweh will gather me"
Compare 26:9

27:11 "the level place"
Compare 26:12

27:11 "the ones who watch me"
Compare 5:9

David prayed for the Lord not to let him be put to shame in Ps 25 (25:2–3, 20), and he prayed for vindication, purification, acquittal, and redemption in Ps 26 (26:1, 2, 9, 11). The prayer in Ps 27 pulses with absolute confidence in God and utter commitment to seek him.

EXPOSITION

## 27:1–3, Confidence in God

Darkness disturbs us because it makes us aware of our vulnerability and weakness. Without light we cannot see, and we have no ability to flip a switch and cause light to shine out from our own eyes. We do not generate light from our bodies. If we are to have light, it must come from a source external to us, whether the sun or a flame or some other contrivance. Because we cannot see in the darkness, we are often frightened by what it might contain: the unperceived danger lurking in the murky unknown.

David celebrates Yahweh as his light-source and his salvation in Ps 27:1. The Lord who created light shines in the darkness, and none can stop his salvation. This prompts David to ask the question: "Whom shall I fear?"

David does not mean that Yahweh literally functions as a light source. He speaks figuratively of the way his knowledge of God comforts him in any darkness. Similarly, the darkness represents vulnerability that may arise from physical circumstances or the attitudes of people.

Because God is his light and salvation, David fears no one. He then changes the metaphor from light in darkness to a reinforced safe place that will stand against all enemies: Yahweh is the stronghold of his life, whom shall he fear? Same answer: no one. No attackers can overcome Yahweh. No darkness can quench his light. No distress can prevent his salvation. No sin can stop him, and death cannot hold those he means to raise.

To communicate just how confident he is, David gives extreme illustrations in 27:2–3. When Achilles faced Hector in Homer's *Illiad*, he was so furious with Hector for killing Patroclus that he said, "Would to God my rage, my fury would drive me now to hack your flesh away and eat you raw."[121] While David may be speaking hyperbolically and figuratively of those who want to consume him, it is not beyond imagination that the brutal enemies David faced might have intended literally to devour him. Another possibility is the threat that Goliath made—to give David's corpse to birds and beasts to eat (1 Sam 17:44). In the face of savage enmity, David believes that the Lord will turn the evil of the wicked back on their own heads. Because David knows that God is with him, he asserts that his vicious enemies will be the ones to stumble and fall.

Yahweh is the stronghold of David's life in 27:1, making him confident even if an army should encamp against him and war arise in 27:3. David probably considered these circumstances the worst of all possibilities—to face an army of cannibalistic savages intent on war. David's knowledge of God is such that when he contemplates the worst things that could happen to him, he concludes that because he trusts in Yahweh he has nothing to fear.

### 27:4–6, Desire for God

Because of the rock-solid reliability of Yahweh, which David has celebrated in 27:1–3, David indicates in 27:4–6 that he wants to be where Yahweh is. Yahweh is light in darkness, salvation in distress, and stronghold in battle (27:1–3), so naturally David desires Yahweh (27:4–6).

The son of Jesse declares in 27:4 that there is one thing he seeks from Yahweh: to dwell in Yahweh's house, so that he can behold Yahweh's beauty and benefit from Yahweh's revelation. David here asserts that he

---

[121] Homer, *The Iliad*, trans. Robert Fagles (New York: Viking, 1990), 553.

finds no place more satisfying, no sights more gratifying, and no information more edifying than what he experiences in Yahweh's presence.

David referred to Yahweh's "house" and "temple" in Ps 27:4, and he speaks of Yahweh's "booth" and "tent" in 27:5, mentioning Yahweh's "tent" again in 27:6. The point of these terms is not to designate different places but to celebrate one place: where Yahweh is. In 27:5 David says that on the day of evil Yahweh will treasure him in his tabernacle, or booth (CSB, ESV "shelter"), that Yahweh will hide him in the hiding place of his tent.

At the end of 27:5 David makes a statement that indicates that if he finds himself in a dark place, such as the valley of the shadow of death (23:4), and if he finds the terrain under his feet unsteady, he remains confident that Yahweh will lift him high on a rock. Yahweh will move him from a place of uncertainty and vulnerability to a place of advantage and strength.

When Yahweh does this for him, David says in Ps 27:6, it will mean that his head is raised up higher than those who are at enmity with him. God will deliver David and shame his enemies. In response to this, David goes on to say in 27:6 that he will go to Yahweh's tent to offer joyful sacrifices, to sing, and to psalm the mighty deeds of Yahweh.

Note well the logic at work in the first two sections of this psalm: Yahweh is a sure help (27:1–3), so being in his presence is the one thing David desires (27:4–6).

### 27:7–10, Seeking God's Face

Having articulated the one thing that he seeks from Yahweh in 27:4–6, David does not add a new thing but develops the same thing in 27:7–10. David wanted to dwell in Yahweh's house to gaze on Yahweh's beauty in 27:4, and he articulates the same idea with different language as he speaks of seeking Yahweh's face in 27:7–10.

He cries out in Ps 27:7 for Yahweh to hear his voice and to be gracious and answer when he calls. The Hebrew text of 27:8 is somewhat difficult, but the verse appears to be a restatement of Deut 4:29, which indicates that Israel should seek Yahweh. David seems to say that he will speak for God and call everyone to seek Yahweh's face. Thus I take the Hebrew text to read, "For you my heart speaks: you all must seek my face!" Having spoken on Yahweh's behalf and called everyone to seek his face, David then he responds by asserting that he will do just that.

Against all expectation and custom, David does not seek to curry favor with the powerful, to win the hearts of the masses, or to gratify his own vanity. David seeks the face of God.

The positive request for God to be gracious to David and bless his attempt to seek Yahweh's face in 27:7–8 is complemented by the alternative in 27:9. David asks the Lord not to hide his face, not to turn him away. David makes this request because Yahweh has been his help, and he beseeches the Lord not to forsake and abandon him. God had promised not to forsake and abandon his people (Deut 31:6), and David asks the Lord to keep his promise.

The first phrase of Ps 27:10 could be taken as a statement of what has happened, as the ESV renders it, "For my father and my mother have forsaken me," or it could be taken as a possibility in keeping with the way the CSB renders it, "Even if my father and mother abandon me." Because we never read of David's father and mother abandoning him, I am inclined to think that the CSB has a better rendering (so also NET, and see my translation). This would align 27:10 with the statements of 27:2–3, communicating David's confidence in God even in the most dire and distressing circumstances. Even if David's own parents were to forsake him, he is confident that Yahweh will gather him to himself.

### 27:11–14, Waiting for God

The requests and admonitions that close Ps 27 continue the tightly logical flow of thought in this psalm. David knows Yahweh as his light, salvation, and stronghold in 27:1–3, so he speaks of his desire to be in God's presence at the temple in 27:4–6 and of seeking Yahweh's face in 27:7–10. David knows from the Scriptures that Adam and Eve were expelled from God's presence in Eden when they transgressed, and in the blessings and curses of the covenant (Lev 26; Deut 28–29), Israel was warned that they would be expelled from God's presence in the land if like Adam they transgressed.

It follows naturally, then, that if David wants to be in God's presence he must walk in God's ways. Thus he calls on Yahweh to teach and lead him in the level path in 27:11, especially since David has enemies who would like to destroy him. David further requests in 27:12 that the Lord not give him over to his enemies to be destroyed, and he cites the deception and unwarranted violence of his enemies as reasons their desires should not be granted.

David indicates in Ps 27:13 that his trust that he would see the goodness of the Lord in the land of the living preserved him through the difficulties and afflictions his enemies visited upon him. In response to God's faithfulness just articulated in 27:13, David calls on others to wait for Yahweh in 27:14, urging them to be strong and cause their hearts to be stout, repeating the call to wait for Yahweh. Like Joshua who was called to courage (Josh 1:6, 9, 18), David urges his people to strengthen their hearts on the Scriptures that they might stand fast. In that fastness they are to wait for Yahweh to do what he promises to do in the Scriptures.

I have rendered the second line in Ps 27:14, "Be strong, and cause your heart to be stout." The Greek translator rendered the two Hebrew verbs here (חזק and אמץ) "act like a man" (ἀνδρίζομαι) and "be strong" (κραταιόομαι). The same two verbs appear together again in Ps 31:24 (MT 31:25; LXX 30:25), and there the Greek translator rendered them the same way. These two instances of this pair of verbs in the Psalter almost certainly funded Paul's statement in 1 Cor 16:13, "act like men; be strong" (ἀνδρίζεσθε, κραταιοῦσθε).[122]

God is David's savior, his illumination, and his place of refuge (27:1–3). David therefore wants to be in God's presence (27:4–6) and to know Yahweh face to face (27:7–10). To experience God's presence, and to be able to remain there, David knows that he must walk in obedient faith, so he calls on God to teach him and he urges strong-hearted patience (27:11–14).

BRIDGE

The false witnesses against David typify the false witnesses against Jesus, as indicated by the allusion to Ps 27:12 when the enemies of Jesus seek false witnesses against him (Matt 26:59–60; Mark 14:55). Here again David speaks of himself in a way that will be fulfilled when his descendent lives out the pattern of David's own experience. Similarly, the way the enemies of David are breathing out violence in Ps 27:12 seems to influence the description of Saul breathing out threats and murder against the disciples in Acts 9:1. These New Testament allusions to Ps 27 forge connections between David and Jesus (and his body, the church) on the one hand, and the enemies of David and Jesus on the other.

---

[122] I wish to thank Dan Phillips for calling this to my attention.

Jesus was even more confident in the Lord than David, and Jesus declared himself to be the light of the world (John 8:12). Jesus fulfills the pattern of experience David describes in Ps 27, and Jesus is the light, the salvation, and the stronghold for his people. In the face of Jesus we see the image of the invisible God (John 14:9; Col 1:15). And in the teaching of Jesus Yahweh instructs his people and leads them in the level path. These things should make our hearts strong to wait for the coming of our Lord.

## Psalm 28

OVERVIEW AND STRUCTURE OF PSALM 28

In Ps 28 David calls on Yahweh to hear his urgent request (28:1–2), then asks not to be swept away with the wicked as he petitions Yahweh to give them what they deserve (28:3–5). David concludes Ps 28 by blessing Yahweh for hearing his prayer and celebrating him as the saving shepherd of his people (28:6–9).

Psalm 28 reflects a chiastic structure that can be depicted as follows:

28:1–2, Hear the Voice of My Supplications
    28:3, The Wicked Deserve Judgment (Not I)
        28:4, Give the Wicked What They Deserve
    28:5, The Wicked Disregard Yahweh so He Will Judge Them
28:6–9, Blessed be Yahweh for Hearing the Voice of My Supplications

The central statement in 28:4 is a chiasm unto itself (see the exposition below).

We will exposit the contents of Ps 28 under the following subheadings:

    28:1–2, Hear Me
    28:3–5, Judge Them
    28:6–9, Bless You

SCRIPTURE

| CSB | Author's translation |
|---|---|
| Of David. | [1] Of David.<br>To you, O Yahweh, I call. |
| [1] LORD, I call to you;<br>my rock, do not be deaf to me. | My rock, be not deaf to me,<br>lest if you are silent to me, |

If you remain silent to me,
I will be like those going down to the
    Pit.
2 Listen to the sound of my pleading
when I cry to you for help,
when I lift up my hands
toward your holy sanctuary.

3 Do not drag me away with the
    wicked,
with the evildoers,
who speak in friendly ways with their
    neighbors
while malice is in their hearts.
4 Repay them according to what they
    have done—
according to the evil of their deeds.
Repay them according to the work of
    their hands;
give them back what they deserve.
5 Because they do not consider
what the Lord has done
or the work of his hands,
he will tear them down and not
    rebuild them.

6 Blessed be the Lord,
for he has heard the sound of my
    pleading.
7 The Lord is my strength and my
    shield;
my heart trusts in him, and I am
    helped.
Therefore my heart celebrates,
and I give thanks to him with my song.

8 The Lord is the strength of his people;
he is a stronghold of salvation for his
    anointed.
9 Save your people, bless your
    possession,
shepherd them, and carry them
    forever.

I be like those who go down to the pit
    [Or: I be ruled with those who go
    down to the pit]
2 Hear the sound of my supplications
when I cry to you for help,
when I lift my hands
to the innermost chamber of your
    holiness.

3 Do not drag me away with the
    wicked,
nor with the workers of iniquity,
those who speak peace with their
    neighbors,
while evil is in their heart.

4 Give to them
according to their deeds,
and according to the evil of their
    practices,
according to the works of their hands
give to them.
Return their way of dealing to them.

5 For they do not understand the
    deeds of Yahweh,
nor the works of his hands.
He will throw them down,
and he will not build them.

6 Blessed be Yahweh,
for he heard the sound of my
    supplications.
7 Yahweh is my strength and my
    shield;
in him my heart trusts;
and I am helped; and my heart exults;
and from my song I will praise him.
8 Yahweh is strength to them,
and he is a stronghold of salvation for
    his messiah.
9 Save your people;
and bless your inheritance;
and shepherd them and lift them up
    until the age!

CONTEXT: VERBAL AND THEMATIC LINKS WITH SURROUNDING PSALMS

> 28:1 "I be like those who go down to the pit" [Or: "I be ruled
> with those who go down to the pit"]
> Compare 143:7
>
> 28:3 "Do not drag me away"
> Compare 10:9
>
> 28:3 "workers of iniquity"
> Compare 5:5 (MT 5:6); 6:8 (MT 6:9); 14:4
>
> 28:5 "works of his hands" (Yahweh's)
> Compare 8:3, 6
>
> 28:5 "throw them down ... not build them"
> Compare Jer 1:10; 12:15–17; 18:7–10; 24:6; 31:28; 42:10; 45:4

There appears to be a chiastic unit in Pss 25–33 (see discussion in the "Context" section of Ps 25), and in this arrangement the cry for vindication in Ps 26 is matched by celebration of forgiveness in Ps 32, the confidence in Ps 27 by the taking of refuge in Yahweh in Ps 31, and the plea of Ps 28 by the praise of Ps 30, with God's glory in judgment central in Ps 29.

There also seems to be a progression from fear of being put to shame in Ps 25, to prayer for vindication in Ps 26, centering on confidence in Ps 27, flowing out in a desire for justice on the wicked in Ps 28, culminating in confidence in God's just power in Ps 29.

EXPOSITION

**28:1–2, Hear Me**
David begs the Lord to hear him in Ps 28:1–2, and his entreaties here set up the request he makes in 28:3–5.

In 28:1 David implicitly declares that he relies on no one but Yahweh, as he plainly states that he calls on Yahweh. David identifies the Lord as his stable, sheltering protector when he calls him his rock, asking him not to be deaf to his cries. Attempting to motivate Yahweh to grant his request, David then describes what will become of him if Yahweh does not hear and answer him. David says that if Yahweh is silent to him, he could become like others whose prayers Yahweh does not answer, those who go down to the pit. The reference to the "pit" seems to be a symbolic reference to the lowest pit where the dead reside (cf., e.g., 30:3; Prov 28:17; Isa 14:19).

Having both asked the Lord not to be deaf and warned of what will happen if the Lord is silent in Ps 28:1, David directly calls on the Lord to hear in 28:2. He describes the nature of his prayer and his own physical posture. David calls on the Lord to hear the voice of his supplications. Other translations render the word "supplications" as "pleas for mercy" (ESV, cf. NET, NIV). The word is related to terms having to do with grace (Hebrew noun חֵן, verb חָנַן, and the term here is תַּחֲנוּן). David thus describes his prayer as a supplicatory request for God to be gracious, and he further speaks of his prayer as a cry to Yahweh for help.

Having described the nature of his prayer, David speaks of his posture as he prays. He depicts himself lifting up his hands toward the holy of holies. This is the desperate posture of a man whose only help and hope are Yahweh, and it assumes the wider Old Testament understanding that Yahweh dwells in the midst of Israel, inhabiting the innermost sanctuary of the tabernacle. David not only sends his prayers to the Lord, he sends out his arms and hands extended in that direction, like a needy child reaching to be picked up by his father.

In Ps 28:1–2 David presents his urgent plea that Yahweh hear the prayer he will make in 28:3–5.

## 28:3–5, Judge Them

David presents a twofold prayer in this section: on the one hand he asks that the Lord not judge him with the wicked in 28:3; then he petitions Yahweh to give the wicked what they deserve in 28:4, confidently asserting that Yahweh will do so in 28:5.

The request not to be dragged off with the wicked in Ps 28:3 presupposes that those who will be like chaff before the wind (1:4) will indeed by carried away in Yahweh's wrath. David refers to the wicked as the "workers of evil" who hide the evil in their hearts by speaking peace to their neighbors. The wording implies that they present a fair outward appearance to mask the foul purposes of their hearts.

Having asked not to be dragged away with the wicked in 28:3, David calls on Yahweh to give them what they deserve in 28:4. He asks that Yahweh punish them in a way that corresponds to their work, in accordance with the evil of their deeds. He then varies the terms slightly, along with the word order, to restate himself: again David calls on Yahweh that according to the evil of their hands he give to the wicked. He concludes the request by asking that Yahweh return to the wicked their own way of dealing with others. Verse 4 reflects a chiastic structure as follows:

Give to them
   according to their deeds
      and according to the evil of their practices
   according to the works of their hands
give to them

The final phrase of 28:4, "return their way of dealing to them," summarizes the message of the verse and anticipates what David will say in 28:5.

The "deeds" of the wicked reflect their failure to understand the "deeds" of Yahweh, and David uses the same term in Ps 28:5 to describe the deeds of Yahweh that he employed to describe the deeds of the wicked in 28:4. Similarly, David had spoken of the work of the hands of the wicked in 28:4, and in 28:5 he says that they do not understand the work of Yahweh's hands (cf. Ps 8). The reuse of the language of 28:4 in 28:5 creates the impression that David thinks the wicked should be judged because they do not acknowledge the mighty deeds of Yahweh. Yahweh's mighty deeds include creation and redemption, and for these Yahweh expects not only thanks and praise but also obedience. David asserts in 28:5 that because the wicked do not render to Yahweh what he deserves, they will be torn down and not built up. The language David employs for tearing down and building up will later be used and reused by Jeremiah (cf. Jer 1:10; 12:15–17; 18:7–10; 24:6; 31:28; 42:10; 45:4).

David makes the main request of Ps 28 in these verses. He has earnestly beseeched the Lord to hear him in 28:1–2, and he presents his request that Yahweh judge the wicked in 28:3–5. In the rest of Ps 28 David will bless Yahweh for hearing his prayer.

### 28:6–9, Bless You

Immediately prior to the main request in 28:3–5, David called on Yahweh to hear the voice of his supplications in 28:3. Immediately following the main request in 28:3–5, David blesses Yahweh for hearing the voice of his supplications in 28:6. David's confidence in 28:6 looks like anticipation of Yahweh doing what David has requested rather than a response to his prayer being answered. David can be confident that Yahweh will answer his prayer because David has prayed in accordance with Yahweh's own word and character. Yahweh's character and power will also be illustrated and reinforced by the celebration of Yahweh's justice at the flood in Ps 29.

Because Yahweh is faithful and good, David celebrates Yahweh in Ps 28:7 as his strength, shield, and heart's trust, citing the way he has been helped, the way his heart exults, and vowing to thank Yahweh in song. David follows the assertion that Yahweh is his own strength in 28:7 with the assertion that Yahweh is "strength to them" in 28:8, and the people in view are those associated with the messiah. The connection with the messiah is made clear by the next statement in 28:8, where David asserts that Yahweh is the messiah's "stronghold of salvation."

David's confidence in Yahweh culminates in the four staccato prayers in 28:9, where he asks Yahweh to *save* his people, *bless* his inheritance, *shepherd* them, and *lift* them forever. These requests assume the imagery of Yahweh shepherding Israel through the wilderness to the land of promise, delivering them from danger, giving them all good things, caring for them like a shepherd, and even carrying wayward or injured sheep on his own shoulders.

### Bridge

The prayer for justice in Ps 28 sets up the warnings of coming judgment seen in the teaching of Jesus (e.g., Matt 23:13–24:1). The Lord's ability to establish perfect justice at the second coming of Christ will be a major manifestation of the glory Jesus asks the Father to allow the disciples to see in John 17:24.

We long for the appearing of Christ, and the treatment of the flood in Ps 29 indicates that past judgment serves as surety for future judgment.

## Psalm 29

### Overview and Structure of Psalm 29

David opens Ps 29:1–2 with a call for the "sons of God" to honor Yahweh as they should, to bow before him in his splendid holiness. The reference to the flood in 29:10, and the water imagery in 29:3–9 suggest that the "sons of God" in view are the transgressors from Gen 6:2. This call for rebels to honor Yahweh is supported by a sevenfold celebration of Yahweh's effective voice in Ps 29:3–9. The power of Yahweh's voice depicted in 29:3–9 seems to be summarized in the reference to the flood in 29:10, and in 29:10–11 David makes plain the implications of the flood: Yahweh is able to strengthen, bless, and give peace to his people.

The contents of Ps 29 will be discussed with the movements of thought breaking down as follows:[123]

> 29:1–2, Glorify Him
> 29:3–9, The Voice of the Lord
> 29:10–11, Flood King

SCRIPTURE

| CSB | Author's translation |
|---|---|
| A psalm of David. | [1] A Psalm of David. |
|  | Ascribe to Yahweh, O sons of gods, |
| [1] Ascribe to the LORD, you heavenly beings, | ascribe to Yahweh glory and strength. |
| ascribe to the LORD glory and strength. | [2] Ascribe to Yahweh the glory of his name, |
| [2] Ascribe to the LORD the glory due his name; | worship Yahweh in the splendor of holiness. |
| worship the LORD | |
| in the splendor of his holiness. | [3] The voice of Yahweh is over the waters; |
|  | the God of glory causes thunder, |
| [3] The voice of the LORD is above the waters. | Yahweh, over many waters. |
| The God of glory thunders— | [4] The voice of Yahweh in the power; |
| the LORD, above the vast water, | the voice of Yahweh in the splendor. |
| [4] the voice of the LORD in power, | [5] The voice of Yahweh breaks the cedars, |
| the voice of the LORD in splendor. | and Yahweh shattered the cedars of Lebanon; |
| [5] The voice of the LORD breaks the cedars; | [6] and he causes Lebanon to skip like a calf, |
| the Lord shatters the cedars of Lebanon. | and Sirion like the son of a wild ox. |
| [6] He makes Lebanon skip like a calf, | [7] The voice of Yahweh hewing flames of fire. |
| and Sirion, like a young wild ox. | [8] The voice of Yahweh makes the wilderness writhe; |
| [7] The voice of the LORD flashes flames of fire. | Yahweh makes the wilderness of Kadesh writhe. |
| [8] The voice of the LORD shakes the wilderness; | [9] The voice of Yahweh makes the deer writhe, |
| the LORD shakes the wilderness of Kadesh. | |

---

[123] For an irregular proposal for understanding the Psalm's structure, see Alden, "Chiastic Psalms 1–50," 21–22.

⁹ The voice of the Lᴏʀᴅ makes the deer give birth
and strips the woodlands bare.

In his temple all cry, "Glory!"

¹⁰ The Lᴏʀᴅ sits enthroned over the flood;
the Lᴏʀᴅ sits enthroned, King forever.
¹¹ The Lᴏʀᴅ gives his people strength;
the Lᴏʀᴅ blesses his people with peace.

and makes the forest bare;
and in his temple the whole of it says:
Glory!

¹⁰ Yahweh sits over the flood,
and Yahweh sits as king to the age.
¹¹ Yahweh gives strength to his people.
Yahweh blesses his people with the shalom.

Cᴏɴᴛᴇxᴛ: Vᴇʀʙᴀʟ ᴀɴᴅ Tʜᴇᴍᴀᴛɪᴄ Lɪɴᴋs ᴡɪᴛʜ Sᴜʀʀᴏᴜɴᴅɪɴɢ Psᴀʟᴍs

29:1 "sons of God"
Compare 89:6 (MT 89:7)

Amid the deeply personal psalms that surround it, Psalm 29 stands out as something distinct. It is not a prayer. Rather than presenting requests to Yahweh and addressing him directly as Pss 25–28 do, Ps 29 addresses the sons of God with a command (29:1–2), which it then supports with a celebration of the power of Yahweh's voice (29:3–9), followed by assertions that Yahweh is the Flood King who saves his people (29:10–11). This makes Ps 29 similar to Ps 24, which likewise makes no requests of Yahweh but asserts his rights as creator, his holiness, and commands the ancient gates to open at his coming. These realities reinforce the impression that Pss 25–33 comprise a unit centered on Ps 29 (see the discussion of "Context" in the commentary on Ps 25).

This unit is both chiastic and progressive. It progresses from David's fear of his enemies putting him to shame in Ps 25, to his cry for Yahweh to vindicate him in 26, then on to his confidence in Yahweh in 27, which in turn makes him ready to call for Yahweh to judge his enemies in 28, and the whole culminates in the call for rebels in the heavenly realms to ascribe to Yahweh the glory due his name in Ps 29. In this way David's fear of shameful defeat has resolved into confident expectation of Yahweh's victory based on the triumph over rebels at the flood.

Exᴘᴏsɪᴛɪᴏɴ

**29:1–2, Glorify Him**

The term "flood" (מבול) occurs thirteen times in the Old Testament. Twelve of the occurrences are in Gen 6–11, all referring to Noah's flood, and the thirteenth is in Ps 29:10. The use of this term in 29:10, in combination with the reference to the "waters" in 29:3 and the imagery of destructive floodwaters in 29:5–9, indicates that in the whole of Ps 29 David meditates on and responds to the Genesis flood.[124]

Though a slightly different phrase is used in Gen 6:2 to describe the way "the sons of God (בני האלהים) saw that the daughters of man were beautiful, and they took any they chose as wives for themselves," the meaning is the same. In Ps 29:1, David addresses the "sons of God" (בני אלים). Perhaps David alters the phrase to make clear that these figures are not to be associated with Yahweh, the God, as his followers.[125] The flood imagery in the psalm, and the reference to the flood in 29:10, condition David's audience to identify the "heavenly beings" (CSB, ESV) he addresses in 29:1 with the "sons of God" whose transgression immediately preceded the flood in Gen 6:2 (cf. 1 Pet 3:19–20; Jude 6).

David calls the heavenly rebels whose transgressions were not able to withstand the might of God's justice to ascribe to Yahweh the glory due his name in Ps 29:1. What those heavenly beings achieved through their sin did not survive the flood, and they lost their liberty (cf. 1 Pet 3:19–20). David calls on them to honor Yahweh, and any humans tempted to rebel against Yahweh and his anointed (cf. Ps 2:1–3) are provided with an example of mightier powers than themselves whose project came to nothing.

David instructs rebels to turn from their rejection of Yahweh and offer him the glory and honor he is due. In Ps 29:1 he calls them to acknowledge Yahweh's "glory and strength," then in 29:2 they are to recognize "the glory of his name"—his reputation—and they are to bow to Yahweh who resides in the splendor of holiness.

### 29:3–9, The Voice of the Lord

In Ps 29:1–2 David calls the powers who transgressed in Gen 6:2 to repent and worship Yahweh, implicitly calling all who rebel against Yahweh to repent and worship as well. In 29:3–9 David backs up the call to repent

---

[124] Watson writes of Ps 29, "It appears also that any received Canaanite traditions utilised here have been reformulated anew as a vehicle for claiming Yahweh's absolute supremacy. Unlike Baal, his kingship is unchallenged ... it is important that this God of power is the God of Israel: his strength is ultimately theirs." Watson, *Chaos Uncreated*, 64.

[125] Goldingay writes, "These are presumably the same beings as are termed *bene elohim* in Job 1:6; 2:1" (Goldingay, *Psalms 1–41*, 415).

with the reason Yahweh should be honored and obeyed: because of the power of his voice.

David refers to Yahweh's voice seven times in 29:3–9. He emphasizes the power of Yahweh's voice, perhaps because those who rebel against Yahweh's commands and Yahweh's king set themselves against what has been accomplished and established by that very voice.

David asserts that Yahweh's voice is over the waters in Ps 29:3, that he is the God who causes thunder (cf. 1 Sam 2:10; 7:10), that he is over many waters. Yahweh's voice brought all into being as he spoke the world into existence (cf. Gen 1:1–2, 6–8), and Yahweh's voice summoned the flood (cf. Gen 7:4). Yahweh's voice should be obeyed.

David asserts the power and majesty of Yahweh's voice in Ps 29:4, before describing a scene that appears to depict the destructive effects of the Genesis flood in 29:5–9. The whole scene seems to respond to Yahweh summoning the flood (cf. 29:3, 10). The awful wall of water would visit his power and majesty with tremendous force (29:4). As that wall of water met the cedars of Lebanon (29:5), the trees would be snapped like twigs. As the mighty torrent met the line of the forest, the trees that would be tossed up on the waves might give the appearance of mighty logs bouncing around like a calf or skipping like a young wild ox (29:6). No enemy power, not Lebanon, not Sirion, not anywhere, would be able to withstand the might of that flood. Yahweh's voice, his command, caused it all.

With the mighty rains of the flood would naturally come the thunder mentioned in 29:3 and the lightning likely pictured by the "flames of fire" in 29:7. The effects of the water on the wilderness, the animals, and the forests are likely in view in 29:8–9. The same verb (חיל) is used in the descriptions of Yahweh causing the wilderness, the wilderness of Kadesh, and the deer to "writhe." The forests and the animals panic and writhe in anguish in the face of the crushing weight of the overwhelming water. The forests are stripped bare by the purging judgment.

The last line of 29:9 declares that "in his temple the whole of it says, Glory!" G. K. Beale has shown that Israel's temple was a microcosm of creation, symbolizing the heavens and the earth.[126] Several statements in the Psalms clearly reflect such a perspective (esp. 78:69; 104:2). If this is correct, given the fact that Ps 29:3–9 discusses the impact of Yahweh's voice on all creation, the temple in view in 29:9 would seem to be the

---

[126] Beale, *Temple and the Church's Mission*.

creation. On this understanding, everything in Yahweh's cosmic temple, everything in all creation, obeys the commands of 29:1–2 and ascribes glory to Yahweh.

### 29:10–11, Flood King

In Ps 29:10 David asserts that Yahweh sat as king over the flood. He held sovereign sway over the strong waters, and his voice ruled them all. That's not all: he sits as king forever. One with such might to enforce his word will never be dethroned. Yahweh was king at the flood, and Yahweh will be king forever.

The implications for the rebels warned in Ps 29:1–2 are clear, as are those for God's people, whose strength is Yahweh. David prays in 29:11 that Yahweh would indeed give strength to his people and bless them with peace. Because of Yahweh's awesome power displayed at the flood, none of Israel's enemies will be able to destroy them. Yahweh is king. He will conquer, and his people will have shalom.

### Bridge

God brought judgment on the world with water at the flood, and at the second coming he will bring judgment in fire (2 Pet 3:6–7). The one guarantees the other. God's glory is established in creation and redemption, and also in judgment. The glory of God's awesome justice at the flood demands that rebels turn and repent. Jesus was baptized in the floodwaters of God's wrath at the cross (cf. Mark 10:38), so that all who are baptized in him will never face that wrath for themselves. He took it all. When he returns, he will come in flaming fire for vengeance (2 Thess 1:5–10).

## Psalm 30

### Overview and Structure of Psalm 30

The flow of thought in Ps 30 can be analyzed in multiple ways.[127] On the one hand, there are five discernible movements of thought:

1. The opening prayer in 30:1–3 (MT 30:2–4) focuses on how Yahweh raised the psalmist up from Sheol;

---

[127] For a proposal not discussed here, see Alden, "Chiastic Psalms 1–50," 22–23.

2. Followed by a call in 30:4–5 (MT 30:5–6) for the "lovingkind ones" (CSB "faithful ones"; ESV "saints") to praise Yahweh in psalm because he turns momentary weeping into lifelong joy;

3. David then recounts in 30:6–7 (MT 30:7–8) a summary of what appears to be the personal experience that prompted what he said in 30:1–5 (MT 30:1–6);

4. Following on the summary of his experience, in 30:8–10 (MT 30:9–11) David recounts the prayer he prayed in response; and

5. In 30:11–12 (MT 30:12–13), as he had done in 30:1–3 (MT 30:1–4) David celebrates again the deliverance Yahweh accomplished on his behalf, which was like resurrection from the dead.

This fivefold movement of thought reflects the following chiastic structure:

30:1–3 (MT 30:2–4), You Raised Me Up
    30:4–5 (MT 30:5–6), Praise the Lord Who Turns Weeping to Joy
        30:6–7 (MT 30:7–8), The Lord's Favor and Displeasure
    30:8–10 (MT 30:9–11), Raise Me from the Dead!
30:11–12 (MT 30:12–13), You Turn Sorry to Joy

An alternative way to approach the psalm is to observe that in 30:1–5 (MT 30:2–6) David presents his response to the personal deliverance he describes in 30:6–10 (MT 30:7–11). He then closes the psalm in 30:11–12 (MT 30:12–13) by returning to the praise for deliverance with which he had opened in 30:1–3 (MT 30:2–4). Throughout, the psalm celebrates the way Yahweh reverses what looks like certain death and delivers from Sheol, the pit, and the dust of death (30:3, 9 [MT 30:4, 10]).

We will pursue the exposition of Ps 30 under the following subheads:

    30:1–5 (MT 30:2–6), Praise God Who Raises the Dead
    30:6–10 (MT 30:7–11), Prayer in Crisis
    30:11–12 (MT 30:12–13), Raised for Thanks and Praise

CSB

A psalm; a dedication song for the house. Of David.

[1] I will exalt you, LORD,
because you have lifted me up
and have not allowed my enemies
to triumph over me.
[2] LORD my God,
I cried to you for help, and you healed
me.
[3] LORD, you brought me up from Sheol;
you spared me from among those
going down to the Pit.

[4] Sing to the LORD, you his faithful ones,
and praise his holy name.
[5] For his anger lasts only a moment,
but his favor, a lifetime.
Weeping may stay overnight,
but there is joy in the morning.

[6] When I was secure, I said,
"I will never be shaken."
[7] LORD, when you showed your favor,
you made me stand like a strong
mountain;
when you hid your face, I was
terrified.
[8] LORD, I called to you;
I sought favor from my Lord:
[9] "What gain is there in my death,
if I go down to the Pit?
Will the dust praise you?
Will it proclaim your truth?
[10] LORD, listen and be gracious to me;
LORD, be my helper."

[11] You turned my lament into dancing;
you removed my sackcloth
and clothed me with gladness,
[12] so that I can sing to you and not be
silent.
LORD my God, I will praise you forever.

Author's translation

[1] A Psalm.
A Song for the dedication of the
house.
Of David.
[2] I will lift you up, O Yahweh,
because you have drawn me up,
and you will not make those at
enmity with me glad over me.
[3] O Yahweh my God, I cried to you for
help,
and you healed me.
[4] O Yahweh, you raised up my soul
from Sheol,
you caused me to live from those who
go down to the pit.

[5] All psalm to Yahweh, you his
lovingkind ones,
and give praise at the remembrance
of his holiness,
[6] because momentary in his wrath,
lifelong in his favor.
In the evening one passes the night
weeping,
but in the morning the ringing cry!

[7] And as for me, I said in my ease,
I will never totter to the age.
[8] O Yahweh, in your favor you set up
my mountain in strength.
You hid your face;
I was terrified.

[9] To you, O Yahweh, I call,
and to my Lord I make supplication.
[10] What profit in my blood, when I go
down to the pit? [note: diff. word
in v. 4]
Will the dust praise you?
Will it declare your truth?
[11] Hear, Yahweh, and be gracious to
me.

O Yahweh be a helper to me!

[12] You turned my wailing into dancing
for me.
You loosed my sackcloth.
And you girded me with gladness,
[13] so that glory will psalm you and not
be silent.
O Yahweh my God, to the age I will
praise you.

CONTEXT: VERBAL AND THEMATIC LINKS WITH SURROUNDING PSALMS

30:1 (MT 30:2) "you will not make my enemies glad over me"
Compare 25:2

30:3 (MT 30:4) "those who go down to the pit"
Compare 28:1

We have seen that the matching acrostic Pss 25 and 34 each open a subunit within Book 1 (Pss 25–33 and 34–41), and we have further seen a build up from Ps 25 to Ps 29 (see "Context" discussion of Pss 25 and 29). Opening the unit of Pss 30–33, Ps 30 links up with the preceding section at both the terminological and thematic levels. Terminologically, as in 25:2 "those at enmity" will not rejoice over David in 30:1 (MT 30:2). Thematically, this means that David will not be put to shame (25:2; 30:1 [MT 30:2]).

There also appear to be thematic connections between Ps 30 and Ps 29. Psalm 29 spoke of the "many waters" and the "flood" (29:3, 10). Immediately following this, David says Yahweh has "drawn" him "up" in 30:1 (MT 30:2), as though he has been pulled out of the floodwaters, and in keeping with this he has been delivered from death (30:3, 9 [MT 30:4, 10]). Whereas the wicked face the floodwaters of God's judgment in Pss 28 and 29, in Ps 30 David celebrates the way the Lord has rescued him from death.

EXPOSITION

**30:1–5 (MT 30:2–6), Praise God Who Raises the Dead**
The superscription of Ps 30 designates this psalm as one "for the dedication of the house." The term rendered "dedication" (חנכת) is used four times in Num 7 to refer to the dedication of the altar, and this is the term used at the rededication of the temple in the Maccabean era giving rise to the feast of *Hanukkah* ("dedication"). These connotations incline the ESV

to render the term "house" (בַּיִת) as "temple," in spite of the fact that the English term "house" usually renders בַּיִת and "temple" typically renders הֵיכָל. The term "house" (בַּיִת), however, is the one used in 2 Sam 7 to refer not only to the temple David wished to build for Yahweh but for the dynastic "house" Yahweh promised to build for David. This superscription colors Ps 30, then, with associations from 2 Sam 7, shading the psalm with hues of both the temple David desired to build in Jerusalem and the promise of an enduring line of descent—culminating in the seed—to David.

In Ps 30:1–3 (MT 30:2–4) David praises God for raising him from the dead, then in 30:4–5 (MT 30:5–6) he calls the assembly of those marked by God's lovingkindness to join him in doing so.

Psalm 30:1 (MT 30:2) summarizes what will be narrated in more general terms in 30:2–3 (MT 30:3–4). David says in 30:1 (MT 30:2) that he will "exalt" (CSB) Yahweh because Yahweh drew him up—Yahweh lifted David out of difficulty, so David lifts Yahweh up in praise. The other side of Yahweh drawing David up out of difficulty is that David's enemies were not made glad with reference to him.

David spoke of being "drawn up" in Ps 30:1 (MT 30:2), and in 30:2–3 (MT 30:3–4) he will speak of how when he cried out to Yahweh for help, he was "healed" and "raised up ... from Sheol" and "caused ... to live from those who go down to the pit." As with other statements in the Psalms and, for example, Jonah 2, great difficulty is presented as though one is in the grip of Sheol, as though the powers of sin and death are prevailing and the end of physical life is inevitable. Deliverance from such affliction is therefore spoken of as though it is tantamount to resurrection from the dead.[128] Those who go down to the pit are the dead. They will reside in Sheol. David's difficulties were such that he accounted himself among them, but because he called on Yahweh, Yahweh healed him, brought him up from Sheol, restored him to life, and separated him from those going down to the pit.

Having lifted Yahweh up for the way Yahweh raised him from the dead in Ps 30:1–3 (MT 30:1–4), in 30:4–5 (MT 30:5–6) David calls on all those identified by Yahweh's lovingkindness to join him in praise. David urges the Hasidim, those characterized by Yahweh's hesed, to psalm Yahweh and "give praise at the remembrance of his holiness" in 30:4 (MT 30:5). This

---

[128] For more on these concepts, see Jon D. Levenson, *Resurrection and the Restoration of Israel: The Ultimate Victory of the God of Life* (New Haven: Yale University Press, 2008).

assumes that Yahweh's intervention on behalf of those whose character is like his own is a function of his holiness. Anticipating what he will say in 30:7 (MT 30:8), David grounds the praise called for in 30:4 (MT 30:5) with the explanation in 30:5 (MT 30:6) that Yahweh's anger is momentary while his favor is lifelong. David notes that while weeping may come and lodge with one for the night, with the dawn comes the shout of joy. This statement in 30:5 (MT 30:6) complements the resurrection language in 30:1–3 (MT 30:2–4).

David's words reflect a situation where his own sin has brought on Yahweh's momentary wrath (30:5 [MT 30:6]), but David's repentance and faith make it so that God's disciplinary displeasure is not what characterizes his life. David may suffer temporary consequences for his sin, but God raises him from the dead with the joy of the morning after the night of weeping in the near death experience of Sheol's pit.

Having experienced God's resurrection power and mercy in his own life (30:1–3 [MT 30:2–4]), David generalizes from his own experience in 30:4–5 (MT 30:5–6) to call all who repent and believe to join him in praising Yahweh's holiness in psalm.

### 30:6–10 (MT 30:7–11), Prayer in Crisis

Psalm 30:1–5 (MT 30:2–6) are written after the fact, looking back on Yahweh's deliverance and responding to it. In 30:6–7 (MT 30:7–8) David recounts what he felt in the midst of the experience, then in 30:8–10 (MT 30:9–11) he recounts the prayer that he prayed, a prayer that is intimately connected to the resurrection themes in 30:1–5 (MT 30:2–6).

If we allow the narrative of Samuel and the superscription to inform our understanding of Ps 30, the prosperity and confidence David describes in 30:6 (MT 30:7) will have been based on Yahweh's promises to him through Samuel. Those promises were then tested by Saul's raging madness as he attempted to murder David. Having been anointed by Samuel in 1 Sam 16, David was preserved against Goliath and Saul, eventually being anointed king over Israel and Judah (2 Sam 5) and bringing the ark into Jerusalem (2 Sam 6). In all this prosperity and safety, safely ensconced in Jerusalem, David thought he would never totter (Ps 30:6 [MT 30:7]).

At that point in David's own life, he wanted to build a temple for Yahweh but was not permitted to do so (2 Sam 7). This could be what David has in view when he says in Ps 30:7 (MT 30:8) that Yahweh set up David's mountain in strength (cf. 2:6) only to hide his face from him.

There could be other scenarios from David's life out of which this psalm arose, but the reference to "the dedication of the house" in the super-scription of Ps 30 seems to connect this psalm to the 2 Sam 7 narrative where David wanted to build the temple but was not permitted to do so. Perhaps David wrote this psalm to be used when the temple had been built and was ready to be dedicated.

What would be the connection between the temple and the life threat-ening circumstances that inform the resurrection themes in Ps 30? Most fundamentally, life is to be found in Yahweh's presence. To be banished from Eden was to be banished from the realm of life because Yahweh was there. The tabernacle was a small-scale symbol of the cosmos with Yahweh dwelling in its midst. The desire to build a temple was a desire to establish Yahweh's dwelling place in the midst of the people.

Perhaps, then, the terror that David feels when Yahweh hides his face in 30:7 (MT 30:8) results from his fear that Yahweh will not, in fact, grant him the joy of his presence. The polar opposite of life in Yahweh's presence would be death in the pit of Sheol.

In response to the fear of banishment from Yahweh's presence, the dismay of Yahweh hiding his face in 30:7 (MT 30:8), David recounts his prayer for mercy in 30:8–10 (MT 30:9–11). The plea for mercy (cf. ESV) is a supplicatory appeal for favor (cf. CSB). David opens and closes his account of his prayer with descriptions of it that employ terms typically rendered "grace" or "favor" (Hebrew חנן) in 30:8 and 10 (MT 30:9 and 11), and in 30:9 (MT 30:10) he presents his argument as to why Yahweh should hear his prayer.

He directs his prayer to the Lord in 30:8 (MT 30:9), and he asks rhetor-ical questions that urge Yahweh to answer his prayer in 30:9 (MT 30:10). David asks what profit there will be in his death, if he descends to the pit. He then asks if the dust, to which the dead return (cf. Gen 3:19), will praise Yahweh, asking if the dust will declare Yahweh's truth (30:9 [MT 30:10]). David's purpose here is to urge Yahweh to keep him alive so that he can continue to praise Yahweh and proclaim his truth. He is denying neither spiritual life after physical death nor a subsequent bodily resur-rection. David wants Yahweh to keep him alive in his presence *on earth now* so that he can please Yahweh. David does not want to be banished from Yahweh's presence in this life, abandoned in the realm of the dead. He wants to live and worship. Thus he seeks Yahweh's gracious favor and mercy in 30:10 (MT 30:11), asking Yahweh to be his helper.

## 30:11–12 (MT 30:12–13), Raised for Thanks and Praise

If we are correct in linking Ps 30 to 2 Sam 7, the hiding of Yahweh's face would be the denial of David's desire to build the temple. The resurrection from the dead imagery would likewise be informed by the reality that though David did not get to build the temple, he did get to continue in God's presence. Moreover, along with continued life in Yahweh's presence, David received the promise that the Lord would raise up his descendant after him who would rule forever.

On this understanding the mourning in 30:11 (MT 30:12) would be prompted by David's fear that he would be banished from God's life-giving presence to the unclean realm of the dead. For God to turn David's mourning into dancing could be understood as God's life-giving promise to David, a promise that takes it for granted that David will continue to enjoy the Lord's satisfying presence. This in turn would inform the description of Yahweh removing from David the burden of sackcloth—as though Yahweh himself had unlaced the bindings and opened the cloth, removing from him the garment of mourning, replacing it with the tunic of gladness.

Psalm 30:12 literally reads, "so that glory will psalm you and not be silent."[129] Thus David can be understood to be describing what will ensue now that Yahweh has made his promises to David about the seed to come from his line, the dynastic house, which promises imply that David and his descendants will enjoy Yahweh's presence. Under these circumstances implied in 30:11 (MT 30:12), David declares in 30:12 (MT 30:13) that "glory will psalm" Yahweh. The result of Yahweh's resurrection power will be glory, and that glory here seems to be personified as one who will himself sing the psalms of Yahweh's praise.

This glory is naturally connected to David, as God's glory is demonstrated by his power in David's life. The praise that God deserves is not silenced, as David warned it would be if he were to die (30:9 [MT 30:10]) but rather gives its voice. David then declares at the end of 30:12 (MT 30:13) that he will praise Yahweh until the age to come, that is, forever, as long as this world lasts. In the sense that David's songs continue to be used in the praise of God, David has kept his word to praise Yahweh forever.

---

[129] The ESV must supply the first-person common singular pronoun to arrive at "my glory," and other translations emend the Hebrew text to arrive at "I" (CSB), "my heart" (NIV), or "my soul" (NAS).

BRIDGE

David had a near-death experience that he describes in Ps 30. Jesus was crucified and buried. David describes Yahweh's deliverance in terms of Yahweh raising him from the dead. On the third day the stone was found to be rolled back and the corpse of the Nazarene was found to have been given transformed life. The disciples wept through the night but the shouts of joy were heard that morning, when the wailing was turned to dancing, the sackcloth exchanged for gladness, and the praises began that will never be silenced. In fulfillment of the patterns of Ps 30 and the promises on which the psalm itself are based, Jesus rose to reign.

## Psalm 31

OVERVIEW AND STRUCTURE OF PSALM 31

Psalm 31 makes heavy use of terms and phrases familiar from earlier psalms. David declares to Yahweh in 31:1–5 (MT 31:2–6) that he takes refuge in him as his strong fortress. In 31:6–8 (MT 31:7–9) David adds that he hates the wicked but rejoices in the Lord, who has known him in his affliction.

Having spoken of the strength and gladness he has in the Lord in 31:1–8 (MT 31:2–9), David describes the reproach he feels from his contemporaries in 31:9–13 (MT 31:10–14), to which he responds with a declaration to Yahweh that he trusts him, calling on him to save and judge in 31:14–18 (MT 31:15–19).

Having spoken of his sorrow and trust in 31:9–18 (MT 31:10–19), David marvels at God's goodness and power to protect in 31:19–20 (MT 31:20–21), before blessing Yahweh in 31:21–24 (MT 31:22–25).

There seems to be a thematic chiasm that falls out as follows:

31:1–5 (MT 31:2–6), Strength
   31:6–8 (MT 31:7–9), Gladness
      31:9–13 (MT 31:10–14), Sorrow
      31:14–18 (MT 31:15–19), Trust
   31:19–20 (MT 31:20–21), Goodness
31:21–24 (MT 31:22–25), Praise

We will discuss the contents of Ps 31 according to the following movements of thought:

31:1–8 (MT 31:1–9), Strength and Gladness
31:9–18 (MT 31:10–19), Sorrow and Trust
31:19–24 (MT 31:20–25), Goodness and Praise

SCRIPTURE

CSB

Author's translation

For the choir director. A psalm of David.

[1] LORD, I seek refuge in you;
let me never be disgraced.
Save me by your righteousness.
[2] Listen closely to me; rescue me
quickly.
Be a rock of refuge for me,
a mountain fortress to save me.
[3] For you are my rock and my fortress;
you lead and guide me
for your name's sake.
[4] You will free me from the net
that is secretly set for me,
for you are my refuge.
[5] Into your hand I entrust my spirit;
you have redeemed me, LORD, God of
truth.
[6] I hate those who are devoted to
worthless idols,
but I trust in the LORD.
[7] I will rejoice and be glad in your
faithful love
because you have seen my affliction.
You know the troubles of my soul
[8] and have not handed me over to the
enemy.
You have set my feet in a spacious
place.

[9] Be gracious to me, LORD,
because I am in distress;
my eyes are worn out from
frustration—
my whole being as well.

[1] For the Preeminent One.
A Psalm of David.
[2] In you, O Yahweh, I take refuge.
Let me not be put to shame to the age.
In your righteousness deliver me.
[3] Incline to me your ear.
Quickly cause me to be rescued.
Be to me a rock of strength,
as a house of strongholds to cause
salvation for me.
[4] For my high ridge and my
stronghold you are,
and for the sake of your name you
will lead and guide me.
[5] You will bring me out of the net that
they laid for me,
for you are my place of strength.
[6] Into your hand I commit my spirit.
You have redeemed me, O Yahweh,
God of truth.
[7] I hate those who guard vapors of
emptiness,
while I trust in Yahweh.
[8] I will rejoice and be glad in your
lovingkindness,
because you saw my affliction;
you know the distresses of my soul.
[9] And you did not shut me up in the
hand of the one at enmity with me.
You caused my feet to stand in a
broad place.

[10] Be gracious to me, O Yahweh,
because there is distress for me.
My eye wastes away in vexation, my
soul and my belly.

¹⁰ Indeed, my life is consumed with
  grief
and my years with groaning;
my strength has failed
because of my iniquity,
and my bones waste away.
¹¹ I am ridiculed by all my adversaries
and even by my neighbors.
I am dreaded by my acquaintances;
those who see me in the street run
  from me.
¹² I am forgotten: gone from memory
like a dead person—like broken
  pottery.
¹³ I have heard the gossip of many;
terror is on every side.
When they conspired against me,
they plotted to take my life.

¹⁴ But I trust in you, Lᴏʀᴅ;
I say, "You are my God."
¹⁵ The course of my life is in your
  power;
rescue me from the power of my
  enemies
and from my persecutors.
¹⁶ Make your face shine on your
  servant;
save me by your faithful love.
¹⁷ Lᴏʀᴅ, do not let me be disgraced
  when I call on you.
Let the wicked be disgraced;
let them be quiet in Sheol.
¹⁸ Let lying lips
that arrogantly speak against the
  righteous
in proud contempt be silenced.
¹⁹ How great is your goodness,
which you have stored up for those
  who fear you.
In the presence of everyone you have
  acted
for those who take refuge in you.
²⁰ You hide them in the protection of
  your presence;

¹¹ For my life is spent in sorrow, and
  my years in sighing.
My strength stumbles in my iniquity,
and my bones waste away.
¹² From all my adversaries I am
  a reproach, especially to my
  neighbors,
and a dread to those known to me.
Those who see me in the street flee
  from me.
¹³ I am forgotten like a dead man,
from the heart;
I am like a broken vessel.
¹⁴ For I hear the whispering of many,
terror on every side,
when they sit together against me,
they plot to take my life.

¹⁵ But as for me, upon you I trust, O
  Yahweh,
I said, My God you are.
¹⁶ In your hand are my times.
Rescue me from the hand of those at
  enmity with me,
and from those who pursue me.
¹⁷ Cause your face to shine upon your
  servant.
Cause me to be saved in your
  lovingkindness.
¹⁸ O Yahweh, let me not be put to
  shame,
for I call on you.
Let the wicked be put to shame.
Let them be silent in Sheol.
¹⁹ Let the lips of deception be dumb,
the ones that speak against the
  righteous,
arrogant with majesty and contempt.

²⁰ How abundant your goodness,
which you treasured up for those who
  fear you,
worked for those who take refuge in
  you,
before the sons of Adam.

you conceal them in a shelter
from human schemes,
from quarrelsome tongues.
²¹ Blessed be the Lord,
for he has wondrously shown his
faithful love to me
in a city under siege.
²² In my alarm I said,
"I am cut off from your sight."
But you heard the sound of my
pleading
when I cried to you for help.

²³ Love the Lord, all his faithful ones.
The Lord protects the loyal,
but fully repays the arrogant.
²⁴ Be strong, and let your heart be
courageous,
all you who put your hope in the Lord.

²¹ You cause them to be hidden in the
hiding place of your presence
from the conspiracies of man.
You treasure them in the booth
from the contention of tongues.

²² Blessed be Yahweh!
For he caused wonders of his
lovingkindness for me in a besieged
city.
²³ But as for me, I said in my alarm,
I am cut off from before your eyes!
Surely you heard the voice of my
supplications
when I cried to you for help.
²⁴ Love Yahweh, all you his lovingkind
ones:
the faithful Yahweh guards,
but he repays on excess those who act
in majesty.
²⁵ Be strong and cause your hearts to
be stout,
all you who wait for Yahweh.

CONTEXT: VERBAL AND THEMATIC LINKS WITH SURROUNDING PSALMS

31:1–3 (MT 31:2–4)
repeated almost verbatim in 71:1–3

31:3 (MT 31:4) "for the sake of your name"
Compare 23:3; 25:11; 79:9; 106:8; 109:21; 143:11

31:3 (MT 31:4) "lead me and guide me"
Compare 23:2–3

EXPOSITION

**31:1–8 (MT 31:2–9), Strength and Gladness**
The accent in Ps 31:1–5 (MT 31:2–6) is on the strength and safety David
finds in the Lord. David's need prompts him to declare Yahweh's power
to protect. He is again calling on the Lord alone as his refuge and defense
against those who would shame him in 31:1 (MT 31:2). He asks the Lord
to hear and rescue quickly, declaring to Yahweh that he is his "rock of
strength" and his "house of strongholds" in 31:2 (MT 31:3). When David
tells the Lord in 31:3 (MT 31:4) that he is both his "high ridge" and his

"stronghold," he seems to be saying that Yahweh is his redoubt whether he is in the field of battle or in the city under siege. Confessing to the Lord that he knows Yahweh will lead him and guide him for the sake of his (Yahweh's) own name in 31:3 (MT 31:4) restates David's confidence that God will keep the promises he has made to him. God's own reputation is at stake in David's life, so David can be confident that the Lord, his place of strength, will deliver him from the snares, traps, and nets of his enemies (31:4 [MT 31:5]). David's confidence in God prompts him to entrust himself to Yahweh, who has redeemed him and will do so again (31:5 [MT 31:6]).

God will redeem David precisely because he is the "God of truth" (31:5 [MT 31:6]) who faithfully keeps his promises. And when God redeems he will do so in "righteousness" (31:1 [MT 31:2]) because he is not a God who acquits the guilty and condemns the innocent (Prov 17:15). God justly acquits the guilty because their guilt has been dealt with: this was accomplished under the old covenant as believers offered the prescribed sacrifices for atonement; under the new, Christ fulfills those sacrifices and establishes God's justice (cf. Rom 3:24–26). Those who repent of their sin, confess it, and claim the sacrifice appointed as their penal substitute are justly declared to be righteous by faith.

In Ps 31:6–7 (MT 31:7–8) David's words show that his emotions line up with God's. He declares that he hates those whom God hates, namely, idolaters who guard and serve "vapors of emptiness." But David trusts Yahweh and rejoices and feels gladness in Yahweh's steadfast love. Love for Yahweh produces a pure love for righteousness, which will bring about a corresponding hatred for wickedness.

Given the way that David will describe the sorrow he feels from the reproach of those who hate him in 31:9–13 (MT 31:10–14), it would seem likely that "those who are devoted to worthless idols" in 31:6 (CSB, MT 31:7) are those plotting to kill David in 31:13 (MT 31:14). In the midst of the difficulties these enemies create for him, David speaks of the way Yahweh knows him in all his afflictions and protects him in 31:7–8 (MT 31:8–9).

From David's words in Ps 31:1–8 (MT 31:2–9), we can see that he is in great distress (cf. 31:7, 9 [MT 31:8, 10]). The focus of these statements, however, is not the depth of his difficulty but the strength and steadfast love of his God, which makes him able to rejoice in the midst of his affliction.

## 31:9–18 (MT 31:10–19), Sorrow and Trust

David's afflictions not only prompt him to declare to the Lord how strong and heartening he thinks God is, as he does in 31:1–8 (MT 31:1–9). These afflictions also spur David to call on the Lord to be gracious to him as he pours out his troubles to the Lord in 31:9–13 (MT 31:10–14). He will again avail himself the opportunity to declare his trust and plead for more grace in 31:14–18 (MT 31:15–19).

David cries out to the Lord to be gracious to him in 31:9 (MT 31:10), explaining that his distress has caused his eyes to waste away in vexation, along with his soul and body. David's physical and spiritual deterioration has two sources: his own sin (31:10 [MT 31:11]) and opposition from his enemies (31:11–13 [MT 31:12–14]).

David describes his sorrow and sighing in 31:10 (MT 31:11), noting that, as the CSB renders it, "my strength has failed because of my sinfulness." I have rendered the line more literally, "my strength stumbles in my iniquity." The point is that sin has weakened David, as it does to us all. Sin produces death, and on the way to the dust it robs us of physical strength, emotional stability, spiritual power, and logical clarity. Sin destroys us. It promises to build us up, to free us, to give us power, only to tear down, enslave, and enfeeble.

Sin weakens us, and it empowers enemies. David details the way that he is rejected and despised, ostracized and avoided in 31:11 (MT 31:12), forgotten as though dead in 31:12 (MT 31:13), and plotted against by mortal enemies in 31:13 (MT 31:14). We are made for human community, so it is painful when we are avoided and forgotten (31:11–12 [MT 31:12–13]). Even worse is the fearful uncertainty that gathers from knowing that people are talking about you but not knowing what they are saying. David has enough information from the rumors and informants to know that enemies plot to murder him (31:13 [MT 31:14]).

David speaks frankly about his difficulties in 31:9–13 (MT 31:10–14), but having explored and explained them he does not give them the last word. In response to the debilitating results of his sin and the active opposition of his enemies, David declares his trust in and need for the Lord in 31:14–18 (MT 31:15–19).

Yahweh is the only God David acknowledges, thus his declaration of trust in 31:14 (MT 31:15). David further declares that Yahweh sovereignly controls his life in 31:15 (MT 31:16), adding to that confession an appeal for deliverance from enemies and persecutors. David feels no conflict between the knowledge of God's sovereign, predestinating power, and the prayers he knows he needs to pray.

David had confessed his hatred of the wicked and love for the Lord in 31:6–8 (MT 31:7–9), and he similarly prays for God to shine the light of his face on him and judge the wicked in 31:16–18 (MT 31:17–19). The appeal for God to make his face shine stems from the experience of Moses (Exod 34:29) and the Aaronic blessing (Num 6:24–26). David appeals for God to save him in his lovingkindness in Ps 31:16 (MT 31:17), having stated his gladness in the same in 31:7 (MT 31:8). He will reference God's steadfast love for a third time in Ps 31 at 31:21 (MT 31:22).

For a second time in Ps 31 (cf. 31:1 [MT 31:2]) David calls on the Lord to prevent him being put to shame, simultaneously calling for the wicked to be shamed and silenced in their pride (31:17–18 [MT 31:18–19]). David wants God's justice upheld and applied.

From what he says in 31:9–18 (MT 31:9–19), we can see that in the midst of his mingled sorrow (over his own sin) and fear (of those who conspire to kill him), David trusts the Lord and seeks his presence.

### 31:19–24 (MT 31:20–25), Goodness and Praise

David has responded to his difficulties by celebrating Yahweh's strength and rejoicing in him (31:1–8 [MT 31:2–9]), and he has discussed his sorrows and responded to them by declaring that he trusts Yahweh and seeks his presence (31:9–18 [MT 31:10–19]). David concludes Ps 31 by marveling at Yahweh's goodness, blessing him and calling those who know him to love the Lord and wait in courage and strength (31:19–24 [MT 31:20–25]).

David's experience of God's faithful character and loving provision, along with his knowledge of Israel's scriptural history, prompt him to exclaim how abundant God's goodness is in Ps 31:17 (MT 31:18). God's goodness can be seen in the lavish world he made, so delightful to our perception and perfectly fitted to our senses. God's goodness can be seen in the good commandments he has given, so protective of purity and respectful of all that is sacred. And God's goodness can be seen in his mercy to the repentant, so unexpected, tender, and forgiving.

David goes on to say in 31:18 (MT 31:19) that God has treasured this goodness up for those who fear him, then wondrously worked it for those who take refuge in him before other people (cf. 31:1 [MT 31:2]; 23:5). Those others, the "sons of man," are those plotting and striving in 31:20 (MT 31:21), and when God works his stored-up goodness for his people the righteous are delivered and the wicked are shamed (31:17 [MT 31:18]). The righteous take refuge in the Lord, and they find the hiding place of his presence to be their stronghold (31:20 [MT 31:21]).

God's goodness has informed them of what is right and wrong. The threat of punishment from God's justice informs their fear of God. Their fear of God keeps them from joining in the shameful deeds of the wicked. Their enjoyment of God's goodness keeps them from enjoying what the wicked enjoy, and they relish God's goodness in God's presence.

David has experienced God as his strength and gladness (Ps 31:1–8 [MT 31:2–9]). The Lord allows him to pour out the sorrows of his heart and declare his trust (31:9–18 [31:10–19]). All this with the Lord's abundant goodness (31:19–20 [MT 31:20–21]) results in David blessing the Lord in 31:21–24 [MT 31:22–25]).

The Lord's steadfast love gave David gladness in affliction (31:7 [MT 31:8]); it was what David appealed to for salvation (31:16 [MT 31:17]); and it is the reason David blesses the Lord (31:21 [MT 31:22]). The reference to the besieged city at the end of Ps 31:21 (MT 31:22) may refer to his experience at Keilah (1 Sam 23:1–14), though there certainly could have been other occasions when he was besieged that are not recorded in Scripture.

Psalm 31:22 (MT 31:23) appears to be a summary of the emotional upheaval David has described in Ps 31 to this point. His urgency in calling on the Lord in 31:1–8 (MT 31:2–9), as well as his discouragement in 31:9–13 (MT 31:10–14), appear here in 31:22 (MT 31:23) to have been prompted by fear that Yahweh would not look favorably upon him. The dread of being cut off from before the eyes of the Lord in 31:22 (MT 31:23) informs both the joy over the fact that the Lord saw his affliction in 31:7 (MT 31:8) and the prayer in 31:16 (MT 31:17) for the Lord to cause his face to shine on his servant.

At the end of 31:22 (MT 31:23) David recounts that the Lord heard his supplications and cry for help, and as a result he calls on all those marked by the Lord's lovingkindness to love him in 31:23 (MT 31:24). God is just. He will not be unjust. So as David says in the rest of 31:23 (MT 31:24), Yahweh guards those who believe but he repays the proud with interest.

David wants the audience of Ps 31 to learn from his experience, so he concludes by urging in 31:24 (MT 31:25): "Be strong and cause your hearts to be stout, all you who wait for Yahweh."[130]

---

[130] See comments at 27:14 on these two Hebrew verbs, their translation into Greek, and the use of that Greek translation by Paul in 1 Cor 16:13.

David delivered the city of Keilah from the Philistines in 1 Sam 23, and then those whom David had delivered were ready to hand him over to Saul. Saul was plotting evil against David (1 Sam 23:9), and the city of Keilah was ready to join Saul in it. At such a time, we can imagine David, in the words of Ps 31:5 (MT 31:6), committing his spirit into the hands of the Lord.

The pattern of David's experience typified the experience of the one who would be handed over to be crucified by the very people he had come to deliver. As the plots of the wicked appeared to be triumphing over him, on the cross Jesus quoted Ps 31:5 (MT 31:6), committing his spirit into the hands of his Father. Jesus lived out the typological pattern of Ps 31 in fuller and deeper ways than we can conceive. He was killed by the conspirators (cf. 31:13 [MT 31:14]), and his vindication involved nothing less than resurrection, ascension, and session at the right hand of his Father on high.

Jesus also set an example for us. We too should entrust ourselves to the Lord when we face difficulty and persecution. We too should rejoice in the Lord's goodness and lovingkindness and truth, seeking his presence at all times and particularly as our place of strength and safety. This is what it will mean for us to be strong and make our hearts stout as we wait for the Lord.

## Psalm 32

OVERVIEW AND STRUCTURE OF PSALM 32

Psalm 32 celebrates the happy relief of knowing that the load of guilt is gone. After the exclamation that the forgiven are blessed in 32:1–2, David recounts the suffering experienced when he was under conviction in 32:3–4. That suffering forced him to confess in 32:5, and in response to the forgiveness he experienced he announces that all those marked by Yahweh's lovingkindness must pray to him in 32:6, hailing the way Yahweh is a hiding place who rescues and delivers him in 32:7. David addresses his audience with instruction in 32:8–9, urging them not to be stubbornly mulish. The psalm concludes in 32:10–11 with David summarizing the way the wicked will suffer but the righteous rejoice.

Psalm 32 reflects a chiastic structure that can be depicted as follows:

The joy of the righteous is their forgiven status (32:1–2, 10–11), and the conviction David felt for his sin enables him to instruct others not to be stubborn as he was (32:3–4, 8–9). Those who confess their sin find that Yahweh is their safe place, their deliverer (32:5, 7), thus all who would know the Lord must pray to him (32:6).

We will exposit the psalm under the following subheads:

Scripture

CSB                                     Author's translation

Of David. A *Maskil.*                   ¹ Of David.
                                        *A Maskil.*
¹ How joyful is the one                 Blessed is the one whose
whose transgression is forgiven,            transgression is lifted, whose sin is
whose sin is covered!                       hidden.
² How joyful is a person whom           ² Blessed is the man to whom Yahweh
the Lord does not charge with iniquity      does not reckon iniquity,
and in whose spirit is no deceit!       and there is in his spirit no deceit.

³ When I kept silent, my bones became   ³ When I was silent, my bones wasted
  brittle                               away
from my groaning all day long.          in my roaring all the day.
⁴ For day and night your hand was       ⁴ For day and night heavy upon me
  heavy on me;                          was your hand,
my strength was drained                 my juice was overturned in the
as in the summer's heat.                  droughts of summer. *Selah.*
*Selah*

                                        ⁵ My sin I caused you to know,
⁵ Then I acknowledged my sin to you     and my iniquity I did not hide.
and did not conceal my iniquity.

I said, "I will confess my
    transgressions to the Lord,"
and you forgave the guilt of my sin.
*Selah*

⁶ Therefore let everyone who is
    faithful pray to you immediately.
When great floodwaters come,
they will not reach him.
⁷ You are my hiding place;
you protect me from trouble.
You surround me with joyful shouts of
    deliverance.
*Selah*

⁸ I will instruct you and show you the
    way to go;
with my eye on you, I will give counsel.
⁹ Do not be like a horse or mule,
without understanding,
that must be controlled with bit and
    bridle
or else it will not come near you.

¹⁰ Many pains come to the wicked,
but the one who trusts in the Lord
will have faithful love surrounding
    him.
¹¹ Be glad in the Lord and rejoice,
you righteous ones;
shout for joy,
all you upright in heart.

I said, "I will confess concerning my
    transgressions to Yahweh."
And you lifted the iniquity of my sin.
    *Selah.*

⁶ Upon this every lovingkind one must
    pray to you at a time of finding.
Surely at an overflow of many waters,
    to him they will not reach.

⁷ You are a hiding place for me.
From distress you rescue me.
With shouts of deliverance you
    surround me. *Selah.*

⁸ I will cause you [sg.] to be wise,
and I will teach you in the way which
    you will walk.
I will counsel you, upon you my eye.
⁹ Be not [pl., you all] as a horse, as a
    mule,
without understanding,
with bridle and halter his ornaments
    to curb,
not approaching to you [sg.].

¹⁰ Many are the pains of the wicked,
but the one who trusts in Yahweh,
lovingkindness surrounds him.
¹¹ Be glad [pl., you all] in Yahweh,
and rejoice, O righteous ones,
and cause ringing cries all you
    upright of heart.

Context: Verbal and Thematic Links with Surrounding Psalms

32:3 "my bones wasted away"
Compare 31:10 (MT 31:11)

In Ps 30 David appears to praise Yahweh even though he was disappointed
that he was not permitted to build the temple. In Ps 31 David cried out to
the Lord from the distress his enemies and his sin were causing him, with
most of his attention focused on his enemies. That changes in Ps 32, as
David elaborates on the distress his sin caused him and rejoices in God's

forgiveness, urging those who would be marked by God's lovingkindness to pray to the Lord as he has done.

Exposition

### 32:1–5, The Blessing of Forgiveness

Just as David had announced a blessing over the man who walks not in wickedness but meditates on the Torah (Ps 1:1–2), so he now blesses (אשרי again, see 1:1) the one whose sin is forgiven. In Ps 32:1 he speaks of transgression being forgiven in the sense that it is lifted (נשא). This verb is used elsewhere to speak of the guilt that Cain bore for murdering Abel (Gen 4:13) and to speak of the guilt that lawbreakers bear (Lev 5:1, 17, etc.). The verb can also be used to describe sin being carried or borne for others. Aaron and his sons were to bear the iniquity of the congregation (Lev 10:17), and the goat sent into the wilderness on the day of atonement bore the iniquities of the people out of the camp (Lev 16:22). Significantly, this term is used twice in Isa 53 to describe the suffering servant: "our sicknesses he bore" (Isa 53:4); and "the sin of many he bore" (Isa 53:12). In Ps 32:1 David exclaims that the one whose sin has been borne is happy.

Not only has the transgression been "lifted" or borne, and thus forgiven, David also describes the sin being "hidden" or "covered" in 32:1. The idea here is that God has put the sin out of his sight (cf. BDB, s.v.). These two terms, "forgiven" and "covered" are used together to describe God forgiving his people and covering their sin again in Ps 85:2 (MT 85:3).

In Ps 32:2 David uses a term familiar from Gen 15:6. That text speaks of how Yahweh "reckoned" or "counted" Abraham's faith as righteousness. David employs the same verb, חשב, "reckon" or "count," in Ps 32:2 to say that the man to whom Yahweh does not "reckon" iniquity is blessed. Whereas in Gen 15:6 God "reckons" Abraham righteous, in Ps 32:2 God does not "reckon" a man as having iniquity. The reckoning goes in both the positive (righteousness) and the negative (no iniquity) directions. It would seem from the use of the verb חשב that in Ps 32:2 David has Gen 15:6 in mind, and in what would seem to be confirmation of that Paul joins Gen 15:6 and Ps 32:2 together in his argument for the justification of the ungodly by faith in Rom 4:1–8.

The second line of Ps 32:2 speaks of this blessed man as having no deceit in his spirit. In the near context David speaks of what he suffered while he was not confessing in 32:3–4 and of how he decided not to hide his sin but confess in 32:5. From this it seems that the deceit in view in 32:2 is an outward display of righteousness that conceals unconfessed sin.

This context of the man who is harboring deceit by refusing to confess his sin (32:2, 5; cf. 1 John 1:10) informs the wasting away in silence in 32:3 and the sapped strength in 32:4. David had spoken of how his strength failed and his bones wasted away because of his iniquity in 31:10, and in 32:3 he again speaks of his bones wasting away (using a different verb). When he describes the Lord's hand being heavy upon him, sapping his strength as with summer heat in 32:4, it becomes clear that David refers to God convicting, afflicting, and opposing unrepentant sinners.

Having announced the blessedness of experiencing forgiveness in 32:1–2, then narrated the pain of unconfessed sin in 32:3–4, David describes his confession in 32:5. He says that he caused Yahweh to know his sin and that he did not hide his iniquity. The term for not "hiding" his sin in 32:5 is the same Hebrew root used to describe the blessing of having God hide his sin in 32:1. We will not prosper if we hide our own sin, but if we confess and repent God hides our sin and we find mercy (cf. the use of the term in Job 31:33 and Prov 28:13). David relates how he decided to confess his sin to Yahweh in Ps 32:5, and again using a term he employed in 32:1, he celebrates the fact that Yahweh "lifted" or "bore," that is, forgave, the guilt of his sin.

### 32:6–9, Don't Be a Mule

Having recounted his own experience, David applies it to the people of God. He says that because of what he has just recounted in 32:1–5, everyone who is marked by God's lovingkindness (חסיד) must pray to Yahweh while the opportunity lasts. In view of the way the following statements speak of "an overflow of many waters" (cf. 29:3, 10), the expression "at a time that you may be found" (CSB) in 32:6 calls to mind the way that there was an opportunity to join Noah until Yahweh closed the door of the ark. Up until the moment of the visitation of judgment, Yahweh can be sought. Prayer can be made. Sin can be confessed. Forgiveness can be experienced. But once the door of the ark is closed, no more opportunity remains.

The reference to the "overflow of many waters" in 32:6 recalls the "many waters" of God's judgment in 29:3, which likewise point back to Noah's flood (cf. 29:10). Those who heed David's call to pray to Yahweh in Ps 32:6 will not be reached by the floodwaters of Yahweh's wrath.

David buttresses his call to prayer in 32:6 with another statement in 32:7 of how Yahweh was his place of safety (hiding place), and savior (rescuing him from distress), and the one who ensured that he would be surrounded by shouts of celebration. The call to prayer in 32:6 is *preceded* by a celebration of forgiveness in 32:5 and *followed* by a celebration of rescue in 32:7.

Psalm 32:8–9 corresponds to David's description of his own suffering while he stubbornly refused to repent in 32:3–4. In 32:8 terms employed in Pss 1 and 2 ("be wise" 2:10; "counsel" 1:1) are used as David states his intention to teach his audience. He then commands them not to be like a recalcitrant horse or an obstreperous mule that will only obey when forced in 32:9.

## 32:10–11, Sorrow for the Wicked; Joy for the Righteous

David's initial celebration of forgiveness in 32:1–2 is balanced by the pains promised to the wicked and the joy that will surround the righteous in 32:10–11.

David had spoken of the way idolaters multiply their pains in Ps 16:4, and now in 32:10 he says that the wicked have many sorrows. In the logic of the psalm, and of the Bible generally, the hand of the Lord will be against and heavy upon the unrepentant, just as David said in 32:4. Their strength will dry up and be broken by the might of the one to whom they refuse to submit, with whom they refuse to agree.

Those who trust Yahweh, by contrast, will be surrounded by his steadfast, covenantal lovingkindness. The literary structure of the psalm indicates that those who trust in 32:10 are to be identified with those who are forgiven in 32:1–2, and these are also those who pray the way David did in 32:5 as he instructed them to do in 32:6.

The same kinds of things can be said about the "righteous" in 32:11. Here again we can see a connection between Ps 32 and Gen 15:6. God reckoned Abraham's faith as righteousness, and in Ps 32:2 David spoke of the Lord not reckoning iniquity. Now he speaks of those who enjoy that blessing as being righteous in 32:11. The righteous (32:11) are those who trust (32:10) and are forgiven (32:1–2) because they confess their sin (32:5) following David's example and instruction (32:6). Just as 32:11 says, they will be glad in Yahweh, rejoice, and shout for joy. Their hearts will indeed be upright as they conform to Yahweh's standards of right and wrong and follow the course of life set out for them in the Scriptures.

BRIDGE

In Rom 3:24–26 Paul explains that God has made the kind of forgiveness that David describes in Ps 32 possible by putting Christ forward as a sacrifice of propitiation. Paul also displays a thorough understanding of Ps 32 and its relationship with Gen 15:6. The righteous (Ps 32:11) trust Yahweh (32:10) and confess their sin (32:5) whereby Yahweh forgives their transgression (32:1–2). Paul proves the idea that justification by faith (Rom 3:28) does not overthrow but upholds the Law and the Prophets (3:21, 31) by showing the consonance between Gen 15:6 (Rom 4:3) and Ps 32 (Rom 4:7–8).

## Psalm 33

OVERVIEW AND STRUCTURE OF PSALM 33

The flow of thought in Ps 33 is straightforward and strong. The opening call to praise in 33:1–3 is grounded in the character of God revealed in his word in 33:4–5 and the power of his word in creation in 33:6–7. Because of God's character and power, 33:8–9 proclaims that everyone should fear him. Picking up the terms "counsel" and "plots" from Pss 1 and 2, 33:10–11 asserts that Yahweh frustrates the plans of the nations and causes his own to stand, resulting in the blessing on the people whose God is Yahweh in 33:12. Psalm 33:10–12 stands at the center of the psalm, with matching concentric rings flowing out from this central point. Thus the fear of Yahweh called for in 33:8–9 is further motivated by the assertion that Yahweh keeps watch on all men in 33:13–14. The assertion that Yahweh made the heavens and the seas in 33:6–7 is balanced by the description of him as the one who shapes hearts and cannot be defeated in 33:15–17. The earth-saturating steadfast love of the Lord in 33:4–5 is the hope of those who fear him in 33:18–19, and the praise and thanks of 33:1–3 comes from those who wait for Yahweh and hope in him in 33:20–22.

Psalm 33 thus chiastically centers on God's prevailing plans and counsels communicated in his word:

33:1–3, Praise Yahweh!
    33:4–5, Yahweh's Lovingkindness Fills the Earth
        33:6–7, By His Word He Made Heavens and Sea
            33:8–9, Fear Yahweh Because of the Power of His Word
                33:10–12, Yahweh's Prevailing Counsel and Plans

33:13–14, Yahweh Is Watching (So Fear Him)
33:15–17, He Made Hearts and Cannot Be Defeated
33:18–19, Yahweh's Lovingkindness for Those Who Fear Him
33:20–22, We Wait and Hope

We will pursue the exposition of Psalm 33 under the following subheads:

33:1–3, Praise the Lord
33:4–12, For His Word
33:13–19, For His Justice and Mercy
33:20–22, For His Lovingkindness

SCRIPTURE

CSB

¹ Rejoice in the LORD, you righteous ones;
praise from the upright is beautiful.
² Praise the LORD with the lyre;
make music to him with a ten-stringed harp.
³ Sing a new song to him;
play skillfully on the strings, with a joyful shout.

⁴ For the word of the LORD is right,
and all his work is trustworthy.
⁵ He loves righteousness and justice;
the earth is full of the LORD's unfailing love.

⁶ The heavens were made by the word of the LORD,
and all the stars, by the breath of his mouth.
⁷ He gathers the water of the sea into a heap;
he puts the depths into storehouses.
⁸ Let the whole earth fear the LORD;
let all the inhabitants of the world stand in awe of him.

Author's translation

¹ Give a ringing cry, you righteous ones, in Yahweh.
To the upright lovely is praise.
² Give praise to Yahweh on the lyre,
with a harp of ten, psalm [pl. impv.] him.
³ Sing to him a new song.
Cause good music to be played with a shout.

⁴ For upright is the word of Yahweh,
and all his works in faithfulness,
⁵ loving righteousness and justice;
the lovingkindness of Yahweh fills the earth.

⁶ By the word of Yahweh were the heavens made,
and by the breath of his mouth all the hosts of them,
⁷ gathering like the heap the waters of the sea,
giving in storehouses the deeps.
⁸ They must be in fear from Yahweh, all the earth.

⁹ For he spoke, and it came into being;
he commanded, and it came into
   existence.

¹⁰ The Lord frustrates the counsel of
   the nations;
he thwarts the plans of the peoples.
¹¹ The counsel of the Lord stands
   forever,
the plans of his heart from generation
   to generation.
¹² Happy is the nation whose God is
   the Lord—
the people he has chosen to be his
   own possession!

¹³ The Lord looks down from heaven;
he observes everyone.
¹⁴ He gazes on all the inhabitants of
   the earth
from his dwelling place.
¹⁵ He forms the hearts of them all;
he considers all their works.
¹⁶ A king is not saved by a large army;
a warrior will not be rescued by great
   strength.
¹⁷ The horse is a false hope for safety;
it provides no escape by its great
   power.

¹⁸ But look, the Lord keeps his eye on
   those who fear him—
those who depend on his faithful love
¹⁹ to rescue them from death
and to keep them alive in famine.

²⁰ We wait for the Lord;
he is our help and shield.
²¹ For our hearts rejoice in him
because we trust in his holy name.
²² May your faithful love rest on us,
   Lord,
for we put our hope in you.

From him they must be in dread, all
   the inhabitants of the world.
⁹ For he spoke, and it was;
he commanded, and it stood.

¹⁰ Yahweh causes the counsel of the
   nations to be broken;
he causes the plots of the peoples to
   be frustrated.
¹¹ The counsel of Yahweh will stand to
   the age,
the plots of his heart to generation
   and generation.
¹² Blessed is the nation for whom
   Yahweh is its God,
the people he chose as an inheritance
   for himself.

¹³ From the heavens Yahweh looks,
he sees all the sons of the Adam.
¹⁴ From the place where he sits he
   causes his gaze to go out
to all inhabitants of the earth.

¹⁵ The one who shapes together their
   heart,
who understands all their works—
¹⁶ there is no king saved by the
   multitude of the force.
A mighty man is not delivered by the
   multitude of strength.
¹⁷ Vain is the horse for salvation,
and in the multitude of his might he
   does not escape.

¹⁸ Behold the eye of Yahweh is toward
   those who fear him,
to those who wait for his
   lovingkindness.
¹⁹ To deliver from death their soul,
and to keep them alive in the famine.

²⁰ Our soul waits for Yahweh.
Our help and our shield is he.
²¹ For in him our heart will be glad,

for in the name of the holiness of him
we have trusted.
²² Your lovingkindness must be upon
us, O Yahweh,
even as we wait for you.

Context: Verbal and Thematic Links with Surrounding Psalms

Psalm 33 begins where Ps 32 ended, with a call for a "ringing cry" from the "righteous" (cf. 32:11; 33:1). This creates the impression that the celebratory praise in Ps 33 is in direct response to the forgiveness of sins in Ps 32.

David penned the death and resurrection Ps 30 for the dedication of the temple, then called on the Lord in response to threats of enemies in Ps 31, celebrated God's forgiveness in Ps 32, and now praises God for his prevailing word in Ps 33.

Exposition

**33:1–3, Praise the Lord**

The repetition of words from the last verse of Ps 32 in the first verse of Ps 33 brings in the forgiveness of sins in Ps 32 as part of the motivation for the "ringing cry," the "praise," the "thanks," and the "new song" in 33:1–3. The removal of the bone-wasting, strength-sapping hand of Yahweh in judgment brings about such intense relief that shouts are warranted, praise is lovely, and gratitude is natural. So powerful are the feelings that good music is desired, music that reflects a level of skill and depth and freshness that corresponds to the freedom and joy the psalmist feels. Shout and song, harp and lyre, and the psalmist's evident enthusiasm all celebrate Yahweh.

**33:4–12, For His Word**

The praises of 33:1–3 are linked to the forgiveness in Ps 32 and further grounded in the statements about the Lord's character and the power of his word in 33:4–12.

The unnamed psalmist asserts that Yahweh's word is upright, then employs terms from Exod 34:6–7 to herald God's "faithfulness" (different but related Hebrew words in Exod 34 and Ps 33) in his work and his world-saturating "lovingkindness" in Ps 33:4–5. We see that there is no conflict between the Lord's love and his justice when we are told in 33:5 that Yahweh does his work in faithfulness, "loving righteousness and justice." God's absolute justice should make us uncomfortable because, as H. L. Mencken wrote, "Injustice is relatively easy to bear; what stings is justice."[131]

Yahweh does not give bad instructions that deceive or lead astray or turn out to be wrong. His word is upright. Yahweh does not change his principles or go back on his promises. His work is done in faithfulness. He delights neither in wickedness nor in wronging others but loves righteousness and justice. His steadfast love is not applied selectively but fills the earth. The point is not that everyone experiences it equally but that the created order that all enjoy, the norms of right and wrong written on all hearts, these saturate the experience of all who enjoy God's good creation.

The creation comes explicitly into focus in Ps 33:6–7. Having declared that Yahweh fills the earth with his lovingkindness, the psalmist states that the heavens were made by the word of Yahweh and that by the breath (רוח) of his mouth all their hosts came to be. Genesis 1:1 asserts that God "created" the heavens and the earth, then Gen 1:2 says that the Spirit (רוח) of Yahweh was hovering over the waters. Genesis 1:3 and following depict Yahweh speaking things into existence. Yahweh's act of speaking the world into being in Gen 1:3 and following is here (Ps 33:6) applied back onto the creation of the heavens, and the mention of the "breath of his mouth" seems to be informed by his "Spirit" in Gen 1:2.

Genesis 1 also depicts Yahweh separating waters (Gen 1:7) and gathering them (1:9), and that likewise informs Ps 33:7, which has Yahweh heaping up the waters and giving the treasures of the deeps.[132] The governing statement in Ps 33:6 seems to indicate that the Lord did all this by means of his powerful word.

The word is both upright (33:4) and the force by which the Lord created (33:6), so all the earth and its inhabitants are called to fear Yahweh and hold him in dread (33:8). The connection between the fear of Yahweh and his word becomes explicit when 33:9 states the reason for the fear called for in 33:8. People should fear God because he spoke and it happened, he commanded and the world stood firm. Human beings find it difficult to speak words that will convince contemporaries or compel

---

[131] Ned Sherrin, ed., *Oxford Dictionary of Humorous Quotations* (New York: Oxford University Press, 2008), 185.

[132] According to a Google search, there are more than 326 million trillion gallons of water on earth, more than two-thirds of which are frozen in ice caps and glaciers, and less than a third of which is fresh water.

children to obey, but God's word is so powerful that he speaks into the void and all creation springs into being by the power of his voice.

Those who know the Lord fear him and experience his lovingkindness (see 33:18), but the wicked should feel what James Joyce described in *Finnegans Wake*: "All moanday, tearsday, wailsday, thumpsday, frightday, shatterday till the fear of the Law."[133]

Psalm 2 described how the nations contemplate vain plots to overthrow the creator God and his king. Psalm 33:10 declares that Yahweh breaks their counsel and frustrates their plots. This broken counsel is that in which the blessed man of Ps 1 refused to walk. In contrast to the shattered plots and thwarted counsel of the nations, Ps 33:11 asserts that Yahweh's counsel will stand forever, and the plots of his heart from generation to generation. Yahweh's plans for his world will infallibly come to pass, and the instructions that he gives about how to live in his world will never fail.

Having acknowledged in 33:10 the futility of the counsel of the nations, which involved recourse to other stories about other deities, the psalmist celebrates the blessedness of the nation whose God is Yahweh in 33:12. That nation, Israel, is blessed precisely because Yahweh has counseled them and revealed to them true stories about the world's origin and destiny. That nation, moreover, is blessed because Yahweh chose them for himself.

### 33:13–19, For His Justice and Mercy

As noted above in the overview of Ps 33, the psalm is a chiasm that centers on 33:10–12. The remainder of the psalm corresponds to and develops its earlier statements.

Psalm 33:8–9 summoned the world and its inhabitants to fear Yahweh, and the matching statements in 33:13–14 describe Yahweh keeping watch on all people in all places. No one shoplifts while the store clerk is watching. Psalm 33:13–14 asserts that Yahweh is watching. There is no way to distract his gaze, divert his attention, or escape his eyes. He sees it all. The reference to humanity as "the sons of the Adam" locates all humans as descending from Adam. We all descend from him and inhabit the world that God made. We will all answer to the one keeping watch. We should indeed fear the Lord.

---

[133] James Joyce, *Finnegans Wake* (Penguin, 1999), 301.

Whereas Ps 33:6-7 celebrated Yahweh's power to create by his word, 33:15 speaks of how Yahweh likewise shapes the hearts of men and understands all we do. Given the context, the assertions that follow in 33:16-17 indicate that no one will be able to overcome Yahweh and avoid his justice. No king will escape Yahweh, not even if he has a mighty army of many men. No mighty man will overpower the divine warrior who comes in judgment, and no horseman will outpace the hound of heaven. There is no escaping Yahweh's justice.

The psalmist means for this to be terrifying. We are guilty because of our many transgressions, and God has seen every one of them. We have offended the holy God whose almighty power has been demonstrated in the way he spoke the world into being. We have transgressed the word of the one whose word made the world.

At just this point the psalmist provides comfort. The comfort comes in a return to the idea of the Lord's lovingkindness introduced in 33:4-5, where it fills the earth. Now in the corresponding statements in 33:18-19 the psalmist says that the eye of the Lord is on those who fear him, who wait for his lovingkindness, to deliver their soul from death. He not only saves them, he provides for them against the outworking of the curse. The land was cursed because of Adam's sin (Gen 3:17-19), resulting in famines across the book of Genesis down to this day. Yahweh keeps alive those who fear him in the famine, however, which is a poetic way of saying that God's judging curse does not fall on those who fear him and hope in his lovingkindness.

What does it mean to fear the Lord? Here it means that we realize that we are guilty before him and dread his punishment. What does it mean to hope in his lovingkindness? Here it entails acknowledging our sin before him and placing our hope in his character—and he has declared himself to be one who forgives iniquity, transgression, and sin (Exod 34:6-7). How can God forgive and uphold justice? The Lord is just. He cannot be characterized the way Moliere mocked the governing powers of France when he said, "Here [in Paris] they hang a man first, and try him afterwards."[134] God has justice on his side, and he will uphold it. But how can he uphold justice and forgive sinners? By putting Christ forward as a sacrifice of propitiation (Rom 3:24-26).

---

[134] Sherrin, *Oxford Dictionary of Humorous Quotations*, 185.

## 33:20–22, For His Lovingkindness

To hope (33:18) means to wait (33:20), and the waiting and hoping articulated in 33:20–22 corresponds to the praise called for in 33:1–3. Speaking in the first-person plural, the psalmist says that we wait for Yahweh because he himself is our help and shield (33:20), he himself makes our hearts glad (33:21a), and in his name we have put our trust (33:21b).

By speaking of trusting Yahweh's holy name, the psalmist firmly locates himself in the religious tradition that is the opposite of the one Thomas Jefferson preferred:

> "Were I to be the founder of a new sect, I would call them Apiarians, and, after the example of the bee, advise them to extract the honey of every sect," he said. "My fundamental principle would be ... that we are to be saved by our good works which are within our power, and not by our faith, which is not within our power."[135]

If we have the power to save ourselves there is no need for God and no need for the son of David, Jesus. But we cannot save ourselves, and we need the Lord's lovingkindness. Psalm 33 closes with a request for that lovingkindness to be upon us in accordance to the way we have waited for him (33:22). God's lovingkindness fills the earth (33:5), it delivers those who fear and wait for him (33:18–19), and it is what the psalmist prays will cover us (33:22).

### Bridge

The psalmist celebrates God's power to create by his word in 33:6. In the progress of revelation John asserts that the word was in the beginning with God, that all things were made through him, and that the word became flesh and tabernacled among us (John 1:1–3, 14). Jesus is the word made flesh, through whom the Father made the world.

W. S. Gilbert (of Gilbert and Sullivan fame) wrote lines for the opera *Iolanthe* that he meant comically but that ultimately apply only to the Lord Jesus:

> The Law is the true embodiment
> Of everything that's excellent.

---

[135] Jon Meacham, *Thomas Jefferson: The Art of Power* (New York: Random House, 2012), 471.

It has no kind of fault or flaw,
And I, my Lords, embody the Law.[136]

## Psalm 34

### Overview and Structure of Psalm 34

The superscription of Ps 34 is one of the few with information that allows us to locate this psalm at a particular point in David's life. Psalm 34 is like Ps 18, whose superscription spoke of the Lord delivering David from Saul and all his enemies, then the body of the psalm used exodus, Mount Sinai, and conquest imagery to describe the Lord's deliverance of David. So it is with Ps 34: the superscription speaks of the deliverance of David from human enemies, likely Achish king of Gath, then the body of the psalm employs language and imagery from the exodus narrative to get at the significance of God's salvation of David.[137]

In Ps 34 David also extrapolates from his own experience to the way the Lord acts on behalf of his people. He begins with a celebratory call to praise (34:1–3 [MT 34:2–4]), then recounts how the Lord heard his prayer and delivered him (34:4–7 [MT 35:5–8]). From there David summons his audience to experience God's goodness and live in accordance with God's instructions (34:8–14 [MT 34:9–15]). Corresponding to the way the Lord delivered David in 34:4–7 (MT 34:5–8), David describes the way the Lord delivers the righteous in general in 34:15–18 (MT 34:16–19). The individual righteous man and the righteous in general who are aligned with him are both described being protected, redeemed, and acquitted, as the wicked are slain and condemned, in 34:19–22 (MT 34:20–23).

Psalm 34 evidences a chiastic structure:

34:1–3 (MT 34:2–4), Praise
    34:4–7 (MT 34:5–8), Called, Heard, Delivered (esp. 34:6 [MT 34:7])
        34:8–14 (MT 34:9–15), Taste and See
    34:15–18 (MT 34:16–19), Called, Heard, Delivered (esp. 34:17 [MT 34:18])

---

[136] Gilbert and Sullivan, *Iolanthe*, 1882.

[137] Dan Phillips observes (pers. comm.) that it would be unlikely for a later editor to read Ps 34 and connect it to the incident when David pretended madness to escape from captivity. This being the case, the superscription is more easily explained as coming from the hand of the psalm's author.

## 34:19–22 (MT 34:20–23), Judgment and Redemption

We will pursue the exposition of Ps 34 in accordance with its natural divisions as follows:

34:1–3 (MT 34:2–4), Praise
34:4–7 (MT 34:5–8), Deliverance
34:8–14 (MT 34:9–15), Taste
34:15–18 (MT 34:16–19), Deliverance
34:19–22 (MT 34:20–23), Redemption

SCRIPTURE

CSB

Concerning David, when he pretended to be insane in the presence of Abimelech, who drove him out, and he departed.

¹ I will bless the LORD at all times; his praise will always be on my lips.
² I will boast in the LORD; the humble will hear and be glad.
³ Proclaim the LORD's greatness with me; let us exalt his name together.

⁴ I sought the LORD, and he answered me and rescued me from all my fears.
⁵ Those who look to him are radiant with joy; their faces will never be ashamed.
⁶ This poor man cried, and the LORD heard him and saved him from all his troubles.
⁷ The angel of the LORD encamps around those who fear him, and rescues them.

⁸ Taste and see that the LORD is good. How happy is the person who takes refuge in him!

Author's translation

¹ Of David. When he changed his taste before Abimelech; and he drove him out, and he went.
² I will bless Yahweh the whole time, regular his praise in my mouth.
³ In Yahweh boasts my soul, let the afflicted hear and be glad!
⁴ Magnify Yahweh with me, and let us raise his name together!

⁵ I sought Yahweh, and he answered me; and from all my fears he delivered me.
⁶ They looked to him, and they shone; and their faces will not be ashamed.
⁷ This poor man called, and Yahweh heard; and from all his distresses he saved him.
⁸ The angel of Yahweh encamps around those who fear him and delivers them.

⁹ Taste and see that good is Yahweh. Blessed is the man who takes refuge in him.
¹⁰ Fear Yahweh, his holy ones, for there is no lack for those who fear him.

⁹ You who are his holy ones, fear the
  LORD,
for those who fear him lack nothing.
¹⁰ Young lions lack food and go hungry,
but those who seek the LORD
will not lack any good thing.

¹¹ Come, children, listen to me;
I will teach you the fear of the LORD.
¹² Who is someone who desires life,
loving a long life to enjoy what is
  good?
¹³ Keep your tongue from evil
and your lips from deceitful speech.
¹⁴ Turn away from evil and do what is
  good;
seek peace and pursue it.

¹⁵ The eyes of the LORD are on the
  righteous,
and his ears are open to their cry for
  help.
¹⁶ The face of the LORD is set
against those who do what is evil,
to remove all memory of them from
  the earth.
¹⁷ The righteous cry out, and the LORD
  hears,
and rescues them from all their
  troubles.
¹⁸ The LORD is near the brokenhearted;
he saves those crushed in spirit.

¹⁹ One who is righteous has many
  adversities,
but the LORD rescues him from them
  all.
²⁰ He protects all his bones;
not one of them is broken.
²¹ Evil brings death to the wicked,
and those who hate the righteous will
  be punished.
²² The LORD redeems the life of his
  servants,
and all who take refuge in him will
  not be punished.

¹¹ The lions are in want and hunger,
but those who seek Yahweh lack no
  good thing.
¹² Come, sons, hear me: the fear of
  Yahweh I will teach you.
¹³ Who is the man who delights in life,
loving to see good days?
¹⁴ Keep your tongue from evil and
  your lips from speaking deceit.
¹⁵ Turn from evil and do good. Seek
  peace and pursue it.

¹⁶ The eyes of Yahweh to the
  righteous, and his ears to their cry
  for help.
¹⁷ The face of Yahweh against those
  who do evil,
to cut from the earth the memory of
  them.
¹⁸ They cried, and Yahweh heard.
  And from all their distresses he
  delivered them.
¹⁹ Near is Yahweh to the shattered of
  heart, and the crushed of spirit he
  saves.

²⁰ Many are the evils of the righteous,
  and from all of them Yahweh will
  save him.
²¹ He keeps all his bones, not one of
  them is broken.
²² Evil will slay the wicked, and those
  who hate the righteous will be
  guilty.
²³ Yahweh redeems the soul of his
  servants, and none who take refuge
  in him will be guilty.

CONTEXT: VERBAL AND THEMATIC LINKS WITH SURROUNDING PSALMS

In addition to the points of contact with Ps 18, Ps 34 is like Ps 25: both are acrostic psalms that omit the *waw* line and add a line that begins with the Hebrew letter *peh* after the line that begins with the final letter in the Hebrew alphabet, *tav*. Both Pss 25 and 34 also evidence a chiastic structure. It seems, therefore, that Pss 25 and 34 open subunits in Book 1, Pss 25–33 and 34–41, creating groupings of psalms analogous to what we have seen in Pss 3–9, 10–14, and 15–24.

There are several points of contact with preceding psalms, for instance:

> 34:8b (MT 34:9b) "blessed is the man"
> 1:1; 2:12
> 33:12 "blessed is the nation"
> 32:1b, 2 "Blessed is the one. ... Blessed is the man"

Psalm 34 seems to open the final subunit in Book 1. The relationships between these psalms will be explored as we continue through them. My analysis leads me to suggest that these psalms reflect a chiastic structure as follows:

Psalm 34, Salvation
    Psalm 35, Defend Me!
        Psalm 36, Sin and Worship
            Psalm 37, Blessed/Cut Off
            Psalm 38, Save me!
        Psalm 39, Wisdom
    Psalm 40, Delivered
Psalm 41, Blessed

EXPOSITION

**34:1–3 (MT 34:2–4), Praise**

The superscription to Ps 34 (MT 34:1) speaks of David changing his "taste before Abimelech" (CSB, "when he pretended to be insane in the presence of Abimelech"). It goes on to relate that Abimelech "drove him out." Some object to linking this passage to 1 Sam 21:10–15 because the king named there is "Achish," not Abimelech, and in that passage the king only asks if he lacks madmen, in response to which David departs (1 Sam 22:1). It is clear, however, that the king did not welcome David to stay.

As for the difference in the names, some have suggested that Abimelech could have been a title for Philistine kings (cf. Gen 20:2; 26:8). Another possibility—the view I take—is that David refers to Achish by the name of Abimelech to forge an identification between the Philistine kings who caused trouble for both Abraham and Isaac and the Philistine king with whom David had trouble. This move would likewise identify David with Abraham and Isaac. The upshot of these identifications would be that David is like Abraham and Isaac in having the same kinds of problems with the same kinds of Philistine opponents in the land.[138]

The superscription suggests that Ps 34 should be read against the backdrop of the scenario in 1 Sam 21, where Saul's persecution was so vicious that David fled to Gath, of all places, hometown of Goliath. Driven out by his Israelite kinsmen, David was nevertheless feared by the Philistines, but he feigned madness to escape.

Against such a backdrop, the first three verses of Ps 34 are remarkable: David constantly blesses Yahweh (34:1 [MT 34:2]), boasts in him, and summons the humble afflicted to be glad (34:2 [MT 34:3]). David calls on others to join him in magnifying Yahweh and lifting up his name (34:3 [MT 34:4]). Persecuted and afflicted, David responds by praising the Lord and bids others do the same.

### 34:4–7 (MT 34:5–8), Deliverance

David explains why he would praise the Lord though persecuted in 34:4–7 (MT 34:5–8), as he recounts how the Lord heard his prayers, answered, delivered, and saved. The fears from which the Lord delivered David (34:4 [MT 34:5]) are easy to imagine if we locate this psalm as the response to David's flight to Gath in 1 Sam 21. Saul the king of Israel was trying to kill him, and in Gath King Achish was reminded of David's triumphs over the Philistines. Where was David to find safety? At that point he sought the Lord. Along these lines, the shame that threatened David's face (34:5 [MT 34:6]) would be the lot of one whose enemies triumphed over him.

---

[138] Having arrived at this conclusion through my own analysis, prompted by Beckwith's discussion of "homiletical identification," I later found it discussed in Christopher R. Seitz, "Psalm 34: Redaction, Inner-Biblical Exegesis and the Longer Psalm Superscriptions—'Mistake' Making and Theological Significance," in *The Bible as Christian Scripture: The Work of Brevard S. Childs*, ed. Christopher R. Seitz and Kent Harold Richards (Atlanta: Society of Biblical Literature, 2013), 285–87. For Beckwith's discussion of homiletical identification, see "Early History of the Psalter," 18–19.

An interesting feature of Ps 34 is introduced in 34:4 (MT 34:5). The terminology that David uses here to describe his own experience will be redeployed later in the psalm to speak of the experience of the people of God in general:

> 34:4 (MT 34:5) "I sought Yahweh"
> 34:10 (MT 34:11) "those who seek Yahweh"

This happens again with verses 6 (MT 7) and 17 (MT 18):

> 34:6 (MT 34:7), "This poor man called, and Yahweh heard; and from all his distresses he saved him."
> 34:17 (MT 34:18), "They cried, and Yahweh heard. And from all their distresses he delivered them."

It is almost as though those who are aligned with David are to do as he has done, following his example. Then just as the Lord delivers his anointed king he also delivers the people of the king.

David not only praises God (34:1–3 [MT 34:2–4]) for the way God answers prayer and delivers (34:4 [MT 34:5]), he also experiences the favorable results of God's presence. David's description in 34:5 (MT 34:6) evokes the way that the face of Moses shone when he spoke with God (Exod 34:29; cf. Isa 60:5; Jer 31:12). Those who look to God and are radiant (34:5 [MT 34:6]); moreover, experience the fulfillment of the Aaronic blessing of Num 6:24–26. David here seems to put himself in the place of Moses: looking to Yahweh and coming away with a shining face. By using plural forms in Ps 34:5 (MT 34:6), David extends the experience to all who look to Yahweh as he has done, and there is a matching description of what happens to the righteous who are aligned with David in 34:15 (MT 34:16), where the righteous have God's eyes and ears upon them.

Psalm 34:4 and 6 (MT 34:5, 7) present answered prayer. Psalm 34:5 (MT 34:6) depicts the transforming light of God's presence. Psalm 34:7 (MT 34:8) uses language and imagery drawn from Exod 14:19, where the angel of God moved from the front of the camp of Israel to stand between Israel and Egypt. This episode from Israel's history is now applied by David as the kind of the thing the Lord does for his people to protect and deliver them.

The superscription of Ps 34 (MT 34:1) alludes to wicked opposition to the Lord and his anointed. The first three verses of the psalm (34:1–3 [MT 34:2–4]) then present the Lord's anointed summoning God's people to praise, and the following three verses (34:4–7 [MT 34:5–8]) explain why they should: God hears the prayers of those who seek him. He causes their faces to shine when they look to him. He saves them from trouble. His angel surrounds them to protect and deliver them.

As David thinks of the way the Lord delivered him from Abimelech (MT 34:1), he thinks on the way the face of Moses shone after he met with the Lord on Mount Sinai (34:5 [MT 34:6]; cf. Exod 34:29), and he thinks of the way the angel of the Lord circumscribed the camp of Israel protecting them from Egypt at the shore of the Red Sea (Ps 34:7 [MT 34:8]; cf. Exod 14:19–20). As the Lord delivered Israel from Egypt, so the Lord delivered David from the Philistines.

### 34:8–14 (MT 34:9–15), Taste

At this point in the psalm, at the center of its chiastic structure, David invites his audience to join him in the experience of Yahweh's goodness (Ps 34:8 [MT 34:9]). This invitation is to enjoy the Lord's provision (34:9–10 [MT 34:10–11]), to learn to fear the Lord from David (34:11 [MT 34:12]), and to speak and do good not evil (34:12–14 [MT 34:13–15]).

David's call to taste and see that Yahweh is good (34:8 [MT 34:9]) summons his audience to indulge their senses on the discernible delight of knowing God. We neither taste nor see him literally, but we figuratively savor and behold his goodness. Someone who has tasted honey or seen a sunrise knows that words can only do so much to capture the experience. The best thing is to taste, to see, for oneself. David knows that people best experience God first hand, so he calls his audience to enjoy him.

Psalm 32:1 pronounced a blessing on the man whose sins are forgiven. Psalm 33:12 blessed the nation whose God is Yahweh. Now Psalm 34:8 [MT 34:9] proclaims the same blessing on the man who takes refuge in Yahweh (cf. 1:1; 2:12). Driven out of the land of Israel, rejected by the king of Gath, David had no refuge but the Lord.

Whereas exodus from Egypt notes were sounded in 34:5, 7 (MT 34:6, 8), provision in the wilderness keys are struck when David speaks of those who fear the Lord having no lack (34:9 [MT 34:10]; cf. Deut 2:7). He then contrasts the Lord's steady provision for those who fear him with the way that even lions may find themselves famished, while those who seek Yahweh lack no good thing (Ps 34:10 [MT 34:11]). Who can compare to Yahweh as provider for his people? Who can compare to Yahweh's ability to discern good and evil?

Having invited his audience to experience the Lord's goodness and provision (Ps 34:8-10 [MT 34:9-11]), David invites his "sons" to hear him that he might teach them the fear of Yahweh (34:11 [MT 34:12]). The fear of God David seeks to inculcate seems from 34:12 (MT 34:13) to be an awareness that the Lord will give long life and joy to those who keep his commandments (cf. 34:13-14 [MT 34:14-15]), whereas he brings judgment on evildoers (34:16 [MT 34:17]).

The long happy life that David holds out to those who fear God in 34:12 (MT 34:13) reflects the teaching of Moses, and Moses connects such blessings to the instruction on fathers training sons in Deut 6 and the law of the king in Deut 17 (Deut 6:2; 17:20). It is fitting, then, that David, the anointed king, calls his "sons" to hear this instruction as he holds out these blessings (Ps 34:11-12 [MT 34:12-13]).

Fear of God will ensure obedience to the commandments and cash in on the promise of a long and happy life. This is what David holds out to his sons and his audience, and he has particular admonitions regarding speech in 34:13 (MT 34:14) and actions in 34:14 (MT 34:15). David charges his sons to guard their tongues so as not to speak evil, and to keep their lips from speaking what is deceitful (34:13 [MT 34:14]). He then charges his sons to turn away from evil, we might say repent of it, and rather do good; and the opposite of doing evil is seeking and pursuing *shalom*, peace (34:14 [MT 34:15]).

David invites his sons to learn the fear of Yahweh (34:11 [MT 34:12]), references the blessing of long happy life on those who keep the Torah (34:12 [MT 34:13]), then gives instruction on how to speak and act (34:13-14 [MT 34:14-15]). We might have expected the instruction in fearing the Lord to be more cerebral, to press in the knowledge that God is the righteous creator and judge. Here, however, David gives instruction that accords with his invitation to "taste and see" in 34:8 (MT 34:9). He wants people to learn to fear God by living as though they do—by seeking the blessing and working to obey the commandments. It is as though David gives his sons an opportunity to have a healthy respect for the chainsaw by showing them how to use it and putting them to work.

## 34:15-18 (MT 34:16-19), Deliverance

Psalm 34:15-16 (MT 34:16-17) continues the instruction in the fear of the Lord by communicating the fact that God is watching. In 34:15 (MT 34:16) David states that Yahweh's eyes and ears are directed to the righteous, ready to hear their cry for help. This corresponds to the way the righteous look to the Lord and enjoy the light of his face shining upon them in 34:5 (MT 34:6). The wicked have a different experience of God's face: it is against them not only to judge them but to remove all recollection of them (34:16 [MT 34:17]). Those who have rebelled against Yahweh's truth in Yahweh's world will not be remembered as bold and daring heroic figures. They will not be remembered at all.

In keeping with his attentive eyes and ears upon them in Ps 34:15 (MT 34:16), 34:17 (MT 34:18) tells us that the Lord hears when the righteous cry for help, and he delivers them (cf. 34:6 [MT 34:7]). Using the very language he employed in 34:6 (MT 34:7) to describe what the Lord did in his own life, David says the Lord does for all the righteous what he did for him. This connection between David and the congregation of the righteous will be significant as we continue in Ps 34.

David's experience of being afflicted (cf. the superscription, MT 34:1), in the midst of which he experienced the Lord's attention and deliverance (34:1–7 [MT 34:2–8]), leads him to assert that Yahweh is near to the broken hearted, saving the crushed in spirit (34:18 [MT 34:19]). This truth shows us God's character, his tender mercy and fatherly lovingkindness. He does not withdraw from the weak but leans in to be their help. He does not collect the strong as his trophies but shows his compassion by being with the afflicted to save them.

### 34:19–22 (MT 34:20–23), Redemption

David's experience in Ps 34:1–7 (MT 34:2–8) leads him to generalize about the Lord's way with his people. He speaks of the individual righteous man—the role he plays as the Lord's anointed—in 34:19–20 (MT 34:20–21), then speaks of the judgment of the wicked and the salvation of the righteous who align with the Lord's anointed in 34:21–22 (MT 34:22–23).

As David generalizes from his own experience in 34:19–20 (MT 34:20–21), he once again deploys imagery from the Exodus narratives. Having asserted that the Lord delivers the righteous man from all his many afflictions in 34:19 (MT 34:20), David alludes to Exod 12:46 in Ps 34:20 (MT 34:21). Exodus 12:46 is not a predictive prophecy but instructs Israel regarding the Passover lamb: they are not to break any of its bones.

When the blood of the Passover lamb covered the lintels of the homes of the Israelites, God redeemed his people from Egypt. David now seems to place himself, as the individual righteous man, in the place of the Passover lamb. When he is brought through his affliction with unbroken bones, just as the nation was redeemed from Egypt, those aligned with David will be redeemed (34:20, 22 [MT 34:21, 23]). On this understanding, David sees the Passover as a *type* that represents the sort of thing God does when he saves his people. As such, David himself is an installation in an exodus-style pattern of deliverance. This pattern will be fulfilled when Jesus dies as the fulfillment of the Passover lamb with unbroken bones, and John claims fulfillment of Exod 12:46 and Ps 34:20 (MT 34:21).

The point of contact in Ps 34:20 and the Passover lamb in Exod 12:46 is that of unbroken bones, which David takes as an indication that the Lord will preserve him through his trial and bring him through to deliverance. Just as the Egyptians were killed, suffering the plague of the firstborn and being swallowed up by the Red Sea, David asserts in Ps 34:21 (MT 34:22) that the wicked, those who hate the righteous—his own enemies—will be slain and held guilty, condemned.

When God brings David through his afflictions from Saul and Abimelech (cf. superscriptions of Pss 18 and 34) with unbroken bones, everyone aligned with David will be delivered from what threatens them. They will be redeemed (34:22 [MT 34:23]). Moreover, they will take refuge in Yahweh, who redeemed them, and therefore they will not be found guilty. They will not be condemned (34:22 [MT 34:23]). Psalm 32 has outlined the forgiveness available to those who confess and repent, and later revelation will clarify the relationship between what was typified at Passover and will be fulfilled through the seed of David.

BRIDGE

Psalm 34:20 (MT 34:21) stands as a significant bridge text between Exod 12:46 and John 19:36. This passage seems to represent an instance of David placing himself in the role of the Passover lamb in the deliverance that God works for him and all who side with the Lord's anointed. If, as I have repeatedly suggested in working through these psalms, David speaks of himself fully aware that he himself is an installment in a typological pattern that will be fulfilled in the descendant promised to him, here again we can see the way that David writes both of the exodus and his own experience in ways that will find culmination in Jesus. Further, the way that David writes about the exodus and his own life feeds naturally into the way the New Testament authors write about the exodus and Jesus

(1 Cor 5:7; 1 Pet 1:19). What was typified at the exodus was repeated in the life of David and fulfilled in Jesus.

## Psalm 35

OVERVIEW AND STRUCTURE OF PSALM 35

Psalm 35 is a plea for justice. David opens the psalm calling on Yahweh to rise up and fight (35:1–3), and closes it with prayer that Yahweh would cause his allies to shout for joy (35:27–28). A set of imprecations follows in 35:4–8 and another in 35:19–26. David promises to praise the Lord in 35:9–10 and again in 35:17–18. He denounces the wicked for their treachery in 35:11–12 and again in 35:15–16, while his insistence on his faithfulness to the wicked stands at the center of the psalm in 35:13–14.

Psalm 35 thus evidences a chiastic structure as follows:

35:1–3, Plea
    35:4–8, Imprecation
        35:9–10, Praise
            35:11–12, Wicked
                13–14, Faithful
            35:15–16, Wicked
        35:17–18, Praise
    35:19–26, Imprecation
35:27–28, Prayer

In this psalm David calls on the divine warrior to protect him and those aligned with him (35:1–3, 27–28) by giving justice (35:4–8, 19–26) against the treacherous (35:11–12, 15–16) to whom David was faithful (35:13–14), promising to praise the Lord when he is rescued from devastation (35:9–10, 17–18).

We will pursue the exposition of Ps 35 according to its matching sections under the following subheads:

    35:1–3, 27–28, Plea and Prayer
    35:4–8, 19–26, Justice for the Wicked
    35:9–10, 17–18, Praise for Deliverance
    35:11–12, 15–16, Treachery from the Wicked
    35:13–14, David's Genuine Concern

CSB

Author's translation

Of David.

[1] Of David.
Contend, O Yahweh, with those who
    contend with me.
Fight with those who fight me.

[1] Oppose my opponents, Lord;
fight those who fight me.
[2] Take your shields—large and small—
and come to my aid.
[3] Draw the spear and javelin against
    my pursuers,
and assure me, "I am your
    deliverance."

[2] Seize shield and bodyshield, and rise
    to my help.
[3] Even empty the spear and close to
    meet the one who pursues me.
Say to my soul: Your salvation am I.

[4] Let those who intend to take my life
be disgraced and humiliated;
let those who plan to harm me
be turned back and ashamed.
[5] Let them be like chaff in the wind,
with the angel of the Lord driving
    them away.
[6] Let their way be dark and slippery,
with the angel of the Lord pursuing
    them.
[7] They hid their net for me without
    cause;
they dug a pit for me without cause.
[8] Let ruin come on him unexpectedly,
and let the net that he hid ensnare
    him;
let him fall into it—to his ruin.

[4] Let them be ashamed and
    humiliated, those who seek my life.
Let them be turned back and blush,
    those who plot evil of me.
[5] Let them be like chaff before the
    wind,
and the angel of Yahweh driving.
[6] Let their way be darkness and
    slippery places,
and the angel of Yahweh pursuing
    them.
[7] For without cause they hid for me
    the pit of their net,
without cause they dug for my soul.
[8] Let devastation come on him not
    knowing,
and let his net he hid capture him.
In devastation let him fall in it.

[9] Then I will rejoice in the Lord;
I will delight in his deliverance.
[10] All my bones will say,
"Lord, who is like you,
rescuing the poor from one too strong
    for him,
the poor or the needy from one who
    robs him?"

[9] And my soul will rejoice in Yahweh,
it will exult in his salvation.
[10] All my bones will say, "O Yahweh,
    who is like you?
Delivering the afflicted from the one
    stronger than he,
and the afflicted and needy from the
    one who seizes him."

[11] Malicious witnesses come forward;
they question me about things I do
    not know.
[12] They repay me evil for good,

[11] They rise up, witnesses of violence,
what I do not know, they ask me.
[12] They repay me evil for good,
bereavement for my soul.

making me desolate.
[13] Yet when they were sick,
my clothing was sackcloth;
I humbled myself with fasting,
and my prayer was genuine.
[14] I went about mourning as if for my
    friend or brother;
I was bowed down with grief,
like one mourning for a mother.
[15] But when I stumbled, they gathered
    in glee;
they gathered against me.
Assailants I did not know
tore at me and did not stop.
[16] With godless mockery
they gnashed their teeth at me.

[17] LORD, how long will you look on?
Rescue me from their ravages;
rescue my precious life from the
    young lions.
[18] I will praise you in the great
    assembly;
I will exalt you among many people.
[19] Do not let my deceitful enemies
    rejoice over me;
do not let those who hate me without
    cause
wink at me maliciously.
[20] For they do not speak in friendly
    ways,
but contrive fraudulent schemes
against those who live peacefully in
    the land.
[21] They open their mouths wide
    against me and say,
"Aha, aha! We saw it!"

[22] You saw it, LORD; do not be silent.
Lord, do not be far from me.
[23] Wake up and rise to my defense,
to my cause, my God and my Lord!
[24] Vindicate me, LORD my God,
in keeping with your righteousness,
and do not let them rejoice over me.

[13] But I in their weakness my clothing
    was sackcloth.
I humbled with fasting my soul,
And my prayer on my bosom
    returned.
[14] As a friend, as a brother to me,
I went about as mourning a mother,
being dark I bowed down.

[15] But in my stumbling they rejoiced
    and were gathered.
The stricken ones gathered against me,
And I did not know.
They tore me and were not silent,
[16] with profane ones, mockers of cake,
grinding against me their teeth.

[17] O Lord, how long will you watch?
Restore my soul from their
    devastations,
from the young lions my only one.
[18] I will confess you in the great
    assembly,
with numerous people I will give you
    praise.

[19] Let those at enmity with me in
    deception not be glad over me,
those who hate me without cause
    wink the eye,
[20] for they do not speak *shalom*,
but against the quiet of the land,
words of deceits they plot.
[21] And they make wide against me
    their mouths;
they say, "Aha! Aha! Our eyes have
    seen it!"
[22] You have seen, O Yahweh,
be not silent, O Lord, be not far from
    me!
[23] Rise up and awake for my judgment,
my God and my Lord, for my dispute.
[24] Judge me according to your
    righteousness, O Yahweh my God,
and let them not be glad over me.

<sup>25</sup> Do not let them say in their hearts,
"Aha! Just what we wanted."
Do not let them say,
"We have swallowed him up!"
<sup>26</sup> Let those who rejoice at my
     misfortune
be disgraced and humiliated;
let those who exalt themselves over
     me
be clothed with shame and reproach.

<sup>27</sup> Let those who want my vindication
shout for joy and be glad;
let them continually say,
"The LORD be exalted.
He takes pleasure in his servant's
     well-being."
<sup>28</sup> And my tongue will proclaim your
     righteousness,
your praise all day long.

<sup>25</sup> Let them not say in their heart,
"Aha! Our soul!"
Let them not say, "We have
     swallowed him up!"
<sup>26</sup> Let them be ashamed and blush
     together,
those who are glad at evil for me.
Let them be clothed with shame and
     humiliation,
The ones who make themselves great
     over me.

<sup>27</sup> Let them give a ringing cry and be
     glad,
those who delight in my
     righteousness.
And let them say continually,
"May Yahweh be great,
the one who delights in the *shalom* of
     his servant."
<sup>28</sup> And my tongue will mutter [i.e.,
     meditate on] your righteousness,
all the day your praise.

CONTEXT: VERBAL AND THEMATIC LINKS WITH SURROUNDING PSALMS

I have proposed a chiastic structure for Pss 34–41 (see "Context" on Ps 34).
The similarities between Pss 25 and 34 suggest that they stand as opening
psalms of separate subunits of Book 1. David celebrates God's salvation in
Pss 34 and 41, and Pss 35 and 40 have distinct similarities to one another:

### Points of contact between Psalms 35 and 40

| | |
|---|---|
| 35:4, <br>**Let them be ashamed and humiliated,** <br>**those who seek my life.** <br>**Let them be turned back and** blush, <br>**those who** plot **evil** of me. <br>35:26, <br>**Let them be ashamed and** blush <br>**together,** <br>**those who** are glad at **evil** for me. <br>**Let them be** clothed with shame and <br>humiliation, <br>**the ones who** make themselves great <br>over me. | 40:14 (MT 40:15), <br>**Let them be ashamed and** abashed <br>together, <br>**those who seek** to sweep **my life** away. <br>**Let them be turned back and humili-** <br>**ated, the ones who** delight in my **evil.** <br>40:14 (MT 40:15), <br>**Let them be ashamed and** abashed <br>**together,** <br>**those who** seek to sweep my life away. <br>**Let them be** turned back and humiliated, <br>**the ones who** delight in my **evil.** |

| 35:21, And they make wide against me their mouths; they **say**, "**Aha! Aha!** Our eyes have seen it!" 35:25, **Let them** not **say** in their heart, "**Aha!** Our soul!" Let them not say, "We have swallowed him up!" | 40:15 (MT 40:16), Let them be desolate as a consequence of their shame, who **say** to me, "**Aha, Aha!**" 40:15 (MT 40:16), **Let them** be desolate as a consequence of their shame, who **say** to me, "**Aha, Aha!**" |
|---|---|

These connections between Pss 35 and 40 suggest that they stand across from one another in the chiastic structure of Pss 34–41. In both David presents these imprecatory prayers to Yahweh, praising him for past deliverance and pleading for more of the same.

EXPOSITION

### 35:1–3, 27–28, Plea and Praise

David calls on Yahweh to contend and fight for him in 35:1, and he needs the Lord to do this because of those contending with and fighting against him. In 35:2–3 David calls on the Lord to take up arms against his enemies.

David's responds to the challenges he faces by calling on Yahweh. Later statements in the psalm, specifically 35:13–14, reveal that David loved these who have betrayed him and now fight against him. His sympathy for them at an end, he calls on Yahweh to defend him against the traitors. He wants Yahweh to be his salvation (35:3).

David's enemies falsely accuse him in 35:11 and 20, while his allies believe him to be in the right. Thus at 35:27, under the assumption that the Lord will answer his prayer, David summons his allies to celebrate the greatness of Yahweh, who delights in David's shalom.

The following verse, 35:28, reinforces the message of Ps 1, as David declares that when the Lord delivers him he will "mutter" (הגה, CSB "proclaim," ESV "tell") God's righteousness. David uses the same term rendered "meditates" in 1:2 to describe the way that he will rehearse God's righteousness. Promising to praise the Lord all day in 35:28 likewise recalls the reference to meditating "day and night" in 1:2.

David calls on the Lord because he knows God's character from the Scriptures. He promises that when the Lord delivers him he will continue to celebrate God's character.

## 35:4–8, 19–26, Justice for the Wicked

David's statements in 35:4–8 show that he does not expect a physical confrontation between Yahweh and his enemies—one in which Yahweh would use shield, spear, and javelin (35:2–3). In the midst of a cluster of imprecatory prayers in 35:4–8, David explains that those against whom he prays set unjustified traps for him in 35:7.[139] He will speak to what they did to him again in 35:11–12, 15–16, and again in 19–21 and 25–26. David's insistence that he was genuinely concerned for his enemies in 35:13–14 intensifies the sense of how they wronged him.

Four of the terms found in 35:4, the first verse of the first set of imprecations (35:4–8), will be reused in 35:26, the last verse of the second set of imprecations (35:19–26).[140] In 35:4 and 35:26, David wants his enemies shamed. They will be shamed when Yahweh fights against them and overcomes them, vindicating David, whom they accused.

Whereas David's contemplation of the Torah (Ps 1:2) has him calling on Yahweh in 35:1–3, in 35:4 his enemies plot vanity (2:1). Psalm 1:4 declared that the wicked would be like chaff that the wind drives away. Accordingly, in 35:5 David prays that his enemies would be "like chaff before the wind," with the Angel of Yahweh driving them, pursuing them on their dark and slippery paths in 35:6.

In 35:7 David explains why he prays imprecations against his enemies: They had no grounds for opposing him or seeking to ensnare him, but they set unseen traps and dug unjustified pits. David prays in 35:8 that these pits and nets would ensnare those who made them.

Whereas in 35:4–8 David articulates what he wants to happen to his enemies, in 35:19–26 he lists what he does not want them to accomplish. In 35:19 he does not want his enemies, who are deceitful in their enmity with him, who hate him without cause (this line is quoted in John 15:25), and who wink their eyes, to be glad over him. Their gladness would arise from their triumph over David.

David explains why they should not be allowed to triumph in 35:20, as he outlines the way they do not speak peace (שלם). In fact they speak against those who are living quiet lives in the land as they hatch their

---

[139] For sketches of ancient Near Eastern nets and traps, see Keel, *Symbolism of the Biblical World*, 90–91.

[140] The four terms are "ashamed" (בוש), "humiliated" (כלם), "blush" (חפר), and "evil" (רעה).

fraudulent plots (cf. 2:1–3). David recounts the way they taunted him in 35:21, claiming to have seen things that support their cause.

David counters their claims to what they have seen in 35:21 by asserting that Yahweh himself has seen in 35:22. Since Yahweh has seen, he knows that the enemies are in the wrong and David is in the right. Thus, David can call on the Lord to rise up and awaken to do justice for him in 35:23. David has embraced God's standards, while his enemies have created their own canons of right and wrong. For that reason David prays in 35:24 that Yahweh his God would judge him according to his righteous standards, refusing to allow the enemies to be glad over David. David prays against what his enemies would think if they triumphed in 35:25. Then he again calls on the Lord to give them the shame they deserve in 35:26.

### 35:9–10, 17–18, Praise for Deliverance

David's foes have put him in mortal danger. Not only his reputation is at stake, his enemies seek his life (35:4). And everything that David believes hinges on the Lord keeping his promises. David's investment not only in his own life but in Yahweh's purposes informs the soul-deep, bone-felt rejoicing he articulates in 35:9–10. David will exult in Yahweh, and he will repeat words written in response to the exodus (cf. Ps 35:10; Exod 15:11). Indeed, the way that Yahweh rescued Israel from those too mighty for them, Egypt, will correspond to the way that David, who feels afflicted and needy, will be delivered from those who seem to have the advantage.

David's life and soul depend on the Lord answering the prayers David sets forth in this psalm, so it is not surprising that in 35:17 he asks how long, pleading for his soul to be restored (cf. 23:3) from the devastations of his enemies, for his life to be rescued from young lions. When the Lord delivers David, David asserts in 35:18 that he will confess him and praise him in the great assembly of the numerous people. This great assembly would appear to be the congregation of the righteous in which the wicked will not stand (1:5), consisting of those who delight in David's righteousness (CSB, "those who want my vindication").

### 35:11–12, 15–16, Treachery from the Wicked

David's enemies do not "speak peace" (35:20) but rise up as "witnesses of violence" (35:11). Whether this means that they claim to have witnessed some violence they allege David committed, or whether it means that by their testimony they incite violence against him, either way David says that he knows nothing of the matters concerning which they question him (35:11b).

Their treachery can be seen from the fact that David says in 35:12 that he has done good for them, which they have repaid with evil. He even speaks of the loss of their loyalty as a bereavement to his soul.

David gives a bit more insight into the situation, though no specifics, in 35:15–16. He says that in his "stumbling" his enemies "gathered in glee" (35:15, CSB). We do not know whether the mishap referenced was physical (sickness?) or moral (sin?) or political (defeat in battle or swing in public opinion?), but whatever it was his enemies piled onto the misfortune to use it to their advantage against him. Then in 35:16 David characterizes his enemies as profane mockers vicious in their opposition to him.

Everything David has said about his opponents intensifies the contrast between their behavior and his, which he describes in 35:13–14.

### 35:13–14, David's Genuine Concern

David articulates his faithfulness to those now accusing him in 35:13–14. Whereas they pounced on him when he stumbled (35:15), David mourned with them when they were weak, humbling himself, praying, and fasting for their welfare. David's actions betray authentic affection and genuine concern.

In 35:14 David says that his concern for these who have now betrayed him was intimate and familial. He says that he mourned for the traitor as one would for a friend, brother, even a mother. His countenance was dark and he was bowed down.

If we posit someone like Ahithophel as the figure at the center of this group opposing David, we can understand how David has prayed. Second Samuel 16:23 tells us that Ahithophel was a highly esteemed counselor. He was probably close to David in age. His son Eliam was one of David's mighty men (2 Sam 23:34). Eliam had a daughter named Bathsheba (2 Sam 11:3). David sinned with Bathsheba, but he repented. God forgave him (2 Sam 12:13). God visited consequences and pain on David's sin, but the Lord did not remove David from being king of Israel. Thus whatever personal grievance Ahithophel may have felt, he was wrong to join in Absalom's satanic revolt against David, against Israel, and against God (2 Sam 15:31).

This psalm helps us understand the Bible's imprecatory prayers. David felt strong loyalty and affection for whoever it was, perhaps Ahithophel, whose betrayal prompted this psalm. The love David felt is warmly articulated in 35:13–14. The treacherous betrayal, however, alluded to in 35:11–12 and 35:15–16, means that the adversary has joined forces with others gathered together against the Lord and against his anointed. Because the former friend is now in rebellion against the Lord and his king, David prays the imprecations we see in 35:4–8 and 35:19–26, calling on the Lord in 35:1–3 to defend him, and promising to praise the Lord for deliverance in 35:9–10 and 35:17–18 with all those delivered with him in 35:27–28.

Bridge

The events typified in David's life in Ps 35 find ultimate expression and fulfillment in Jesus. David loved and cared for those who betrayed him, but no one more thoroughly loved and cared for those who betrayed him than Jesus, who washed the feet of Judas and wept over Jerusalem. David was wronged by those who engaged in unjustified attacks on him, but no attack was less justified than that lodged against Jesus. David prayed for God's justice against God's enemies; no one was more emotionally aligned with the Father and his justice than Jesus. David promised to praise God for deliverance and relied on the Lord to accomplish it, and Jesus entrusted his soul to him who judges justly and praised God in the midst of his brothers. In Ps 35, David's experience and prayer typifies and anticipates its fulfillment in the life of the one to come.

# Psalm 36

Overview and Structure of Psalm 36

Psalm 36 is about satisfaction and where it can be found. The first four verses (36:1–4 [MT 36:2–5]) discuss the way the wicked seek fullness in sin, and the rest of the psalm celebrates the incomparable delight of knowing God (36:5–12 [MT 36:6–13]). The psalm's chiastic structure can be depicted as follows:[141]

36:1–2 (MT 36:2–3), The Delusion of the Wicked
    36:3–4 (MT 36:4–5), Words and Plots on the Way Not Good
        36:5–6 (MT 36:6–7), Lovingkindness, Righteousness, Justice
        36:7–9 (MT 36:8–10), The Satisfaction of Knowing God

---

[141] Alden proposes a different chiasm, "Chiastic Psalms 1–50," 23–24.

36:10–12 (36:11–13), Prayer for Those Who Know God

We will pursue the exposition of Ps 36 under the following subheads:

36:1–4 (MT 36:2–5), The Way of the Wicked
36:5–12 (MT 36:6–13), The Worship of the Righteous

SCRIPTURE

CSB

For the choir director. Of David, the LORD's servant.

[1] An oracle within my heart
concerning the transgression of the
   wicked person:
Dread of God has no effect on him.
[2] For with his flattering opinion of
   himself,
he does not discover and hate his
   iniquity.
[3] The words from his mouth are
   malicious and deceptive;
he has stopped acting wisely and
   doing good.
[4] Even on his bed he makes malicious
   plans.
He sets himself on a path that is not
   good,
and he does not reject evil.

[5] LORD, your faithful love reaches to
   heaven,
your faithfulness to the clouds.
[6] Your righteousness is like the highest
   mountains,
your judgments like the deepest sea.
LORD, you preserve people and animals.
[7] How priceless your faithful love is,
   God!
People take refuge in the shadow of
   your wings.
[8] They are filled from the abundance
   of your house.

Author's translation

[1] For the Preeminent One.
For the servant of Yahweh.
Of David.

[2] An oracle of the transgression of the
   wicked in the midst of my heart:
there is no dread of God before his
   eyes,
[3] for he makes it smooth for himself in
   his own eyes, to find, to hate his sin.

[4] The words of his mouth are iniquity
   and deceit.
He has ceased to cause wisdom, to
   cause good.
[5] He plots iniquity on his bed.
He takes his stand on the way not
   good.
Evil he does not reject.

[6] O Yahweh, in the heavens your
   lovingkindness,
your truth to the clouds,
[7] your righteousness like the
   mountains of God,
your judgment the great deep,
man and beast you save, O Yahweh.

[8] How precious your lovingkindness,
   O God,
and the sons of man in the shadow of
   your wings take refuge.
[9] They quench thirst from the fatness
   of your house,

You let them drink from your
  refreshing stream.

⁹ For the wellspring of life is with you.
By means of your light we see light.

and the wadi of your edens you cause
  them to drink.

¹⁰ For with you is the fountain of life.
In your light we see light.

¹⁰ Spread your faithful love over those
  who know you,
and your righteousness over the
  upright in heart.

¹¹ Do not let the foot of the arrogant
  come near me
or the hand of the wicked drive me
  away.

¹² There! The evildoers have fallen.
They have been thrown down and
  cannot rise.

¹¹ Draw your lovingkindness to those
  who know you,
and your righteousness to the upright
  of heart.

¹² Let not the foot of majesty come
  on me,
nor the hand of the wicked cause me
  to wander.

¹³ There the workers of iniquity fall.
They are thrust down and not able
  to rise.

Context: Verbal and Thematic Links with Surrounding Psalms

(MT 36:1) "servant"
Compare 35:27

36:1 (MT 36:2) "there is no dread of God before his eyes"
Compare 55:19 (MT 55:20)

36:3 (MT 36:4) "The words of his mouth are iniquity and deceit"
35:20, "words of treachery"
10:7 "treachery"

36:3 (MT 36:4) "He has ceased to cause wisdom"
Compare 2:10; 14:2; 32:8

In the chiastic structure that I have proposed for Pss 34–41, Ps 36 stands across from Ps 39. In Ps 36 David speaks of the differences between those who indulge in sin (who have ceased to cause wisdom) and those who indulge in Yahweh's delights. In the corresponding Ps 39 David contemplates the wisdom that comes from knowing the brevity of life. The message of the two psalms comes together nicely: those who know and enjoy God learn the wisdom that life is short, so sin's temporary pleasures are a bad bargain. Those who learn this lesson impart its wisdom to others.

Exposition

Appearing in the superscription of Ps 36, the phrase "the servant of Yahweh" occurs in only one other psalm superscription, that of Psalm 18

(MT 18:1; see the comments on the phrase there). The use of "servant" in the superscription of Ps 36 also links up with the use of the term in 35:27.

### 36:1-4 (MT 36:2-5), The Way of the Wicked

The translations differ in their rendering of Ps 36:1 (MT 36:2). In my translation I have chosen not to emend the Masoretic Text (MT). The different renderings come down to the question of whose heart is referenced. The MT has David referring to his own heart: "my heart" (לִבִּי), but a few medieval manuscripts (the abbreviation *pc* in *BHS* refers to 3-10 manuscripts) have "his heart" (לִבּוֹ), a reading reflected also in Origen's Hexapla and the Syriac translation. As for the translations, ESV and NAS opt for "his heart," while the CSB, KJV, and NIV go with "my heart."

The difference in meaning is slight. If David is contemplating how the utterance of transgression resonates within the heart of the wicked, Ps 36:1 (MT 36:2) is reminiscent of Pss 10:6, 11, 13; and 14:1, and then the verses that follow elaborate on the workings of the hearts of the wicked. If on the other hand David says, as I have translated this line, "An oracle of the transgression in the midst of my heart," then what follows is David's assessment of the wicked from within David's heart. Either way, then, Ps 36:1-4 (MT 36:2-5) presents a Davidic reflection on the ways of the wicked.

The first observation that David offers about the wicked in 36:1 (MT 36:2)[142] is that they do not fear God (cf. 55:19 [MT 55:20]).[143] David next speaks in 36:2 (MT 36:3) of how the wicked do not adequately deal with their sin. I have rendered the line, "For he makes it smooth for himself in his own eyes, to find, to hate his sin."[144] Taken this way, David describes the sinner speaking smooth things (cf. 5:9; 12:2-3 [MT 5:10; 12:3-4]) to himself, not really probing his heart for the depths of his sin. Rather than experience God and know the purging pain of the exposing, cleansing power of his holiness, the wicked do not fear God and as a result do not recognize the depths of their own sinfulness. David's words assume that when sin is found, it will be hated. For sin to be hated, we have to get past

---

[142] Assuming that he is not referring to transgression speaking to the heart of the wicked, as the ESV renders the line, in which case the first thing he says about them would be that their hearts commune with transgression.

[143] Paul quotes the Greek translation of 36:1 (MT 36:2; LXX 35:2) in Rom 3:18.

[144] Once again the translations differ, though this time the problem is the difficulty of the Hebrew syntax. The CSB's rendering is similar to mine, "For with his flattering opinion of himself, he does not discover and hate his iniquity" (NIV is similar), whereas the ESV takes the Hebrew to mean, "For he flatters himself in his own eyes that his iniquity cannot be found out and hated" (NAS is similar).

the allure of its superficial veneer to see its evil, and the best way to do that is to experience God and fear him.[145]

Psalm 130:4 states a similar connection between the fear of God and sin, bringing in the notion of forgiveness: "for with you there is forgiveness, that you might be feared." The inner logic of these statements seems to go like this: those who fear God have their hearts searched by his holiness, which exposes their sin. Because they fear God, they know they cannot escape his justice, so they hate the sin that robs them of all that matters most, confess it, and experience God's forgiveness. Psalm 36:1–2 indicates that the wicked do not fear God, so they do not have the evil in their hearts exposed, confess their sin, and experience forgiveness. David may be speaking to the joy of the righteous on just this point when he says in 36:9 (MT 36:10), "In your light we see light."

In 36:3 (MT 36:4) David describes the way the wicked speak iniquity and deceit.[146] When we sin we do not act in accord with the truth, and unless we make full confession and repent, our words do not accord with truth. David then says in the second line of 36:3 (MT 36:4) that the wicked have "ceased to cause wisdom, to cause good." The term rendered "cause wisdom" here is the same used in the call to the rebel kings to be wise in Ps 2:10. It is used in 14:2, "Yahweh from the heavens looks down on the sons of Adam, to see if there is anyone causing wisdom, seeking God." And it is used as David urges his audience to confess their sin and find forgiveness in Ps 32:8, "I will cause you to be wise." The wicked man does not kiss the son (2:12), he is a fool (14:1), and he is like a stubborn mule (32:9). He does not submit to Yahweh's king (Ps 2), acknowledge Yahweh as God (Ps 14), or confess his sin to Yahweh (Ps 32).

---

[145] On January 1, 2016, Derek Webb put up a post on Tumblr entitled, "on failure, liturgy, and new years" [sic – in the quotations that follow the punctuation and lack of capitalization are Webb's], http://derekwebb.tumblr.com/post/136376267966/on-failure-liturgy-and-new-years. In the post he discussed his own sin, which led to his divorce, and made these poignant statements: "trust takes years to build and seconds to break. ... i simply cannot change what i've done, nor the consequences. i can only own these despicable actions, which have left me completely devastated and deeply ashamed. Sometimes, no matter how bad you want it or how hard you fight for it, broken things just can't be mended. ... you might be ... seriously considering choices that could destroy your life, your family, and maybe yourself. if that's you please listen to me: what you think you want, what you think you can have, is not real, and you'll lose real things pursuing it."

[146] Webb again (http://derekwebb.tumblr.com/post/136376267966/on-failure-liturgy-and-new-years): "i believed lies, which led me to tell lies."

A progression can be seen in Ps 36:1–4 (MT 36:2–5). The wicked man starts by not fearing God, so he does not recognize the sinful character of his impulses and inclinations in 36:1 (MT 36:2). In keeping with this, his statements are wicked, not wise in 36:2 (MT 36:3), and now David describes what the wicked man does when he is alone in the dark on his bed. When the wicked man is unoccupied, when there is nothing he has to do, his thoughts plot iniquity (36:4 [MT 36:5]). Proverbs 23:7a says, "As he thinketh in his heart, so is he" (KJV). The man who fantasizes about forbidden things in his secret thoughts next "takes his stand on the way not good" (Ps 36:4b [MT 36:5b]). The reference to him taking his stand recalls the wicked kings doing so against Yahweh and his anointed in 2:2, and the reference to the "way not good" recalls the way where the blessed man does not stand in 1:1.

The wicked man does not know God, so he says untrue things that do not give wisdom, and he contemplates evil schemes, takes his stand in wicked ways, and lastly in 36:4 (MT 36:5), "Evil he does not reject." Evil will be rejected by those who look not at what it offers but at what it costs and at what it takes away. Evil will be particularly hated by those who love Jesus, who see that it cost his life, and that it threatens to take their communion with him. Those who do not reject evil will be rejected by God. Once again, the fear of God has a cleansing function. Those who would reject evil must train themselves to look past the momentary pleasure it offers to the lasting pain it causes. They must look past themselves to the impact evil will have on others.

What we contemplate in unoccupied moments, the way of life in which we take our stand, and what we reject and accept, all point to what we regard as sacred and ultimate. For the wicked, God is not sacred and ultimate, sin is. The wicked worship sin or themselves. The righteous, as we will see from Ps 36:5–12 (MT 36:6–13), worship God.

### 36:5–12 (MT 36:6–13), The Worship of the Righteous

Moving from a description of the wicked and what they worship to the object of his own devotion, David's poetry soars to unmatched heights in Ps 36:5–6 (MT 36:6–7). These are the words of a man who knows God, a man practiced in praise, a man whose public paean is rooted in private devotion.

David says in 36:5–6a (MT 36:6–7a), "O Yahweh, in the heavens your lovingkindness, your truth to the clouds, your righteousness like the mountains of God, your judgment the great deep."

What David says here is similar to several other statements in the Psalter (ESV):

"For your steadfast love is great to the heavens, your faithfulness to the clouds" (57:10)

"Your righteousness, O God, reaches the high heavens" (75:19)

"Faithfulness springs up from the ground, and righteousness looks down from the sky" (85:11).

"For as high as the heavens are above the earth, so great is his steadfast love toward those who fear him" (103:11).

"For your steadfast love is great above the heavens; your faithfulness reaches to the clouds" (108:4)

Such sentiments are akin to the way the Lord himself is associated with the transcendent heavens: "There is none like God, O Jeshurun, who rides through the heavens to your help, through the skies in his majesty" (Deut 33:26).

There is no higher place than the heavens, nothing that extends to a greater distance, so this appears to be a way for David to celebrate the all-encompassing steadfast love of the Lord.[147] His *hesed* reaches to the heavens, and his *truth* to the clouds. There is no conflict between the Lord's love and his truth.

Love and truth reach to the skies above, and underneath are the mountains of God's righteousness (36:6 [MT 36:7]). David likens God's righteousness to mighty mountains: the solid, sheer, awesome walls of rock, before which we feel so small.

David employs the extremities of the known world to describe Yahweh's character: the heavens and clouds for *hesed* and truth, the mountains for righteousness, and the great deep for his judgments (36:6 [MT 36:7]). The great deep is the abyss of the sea. This comparison speaks

---

[147] Cf. Keel, *Symbolism of the Biblical World*, 31: "In the psalms, the sky is also perceived to be spatially and temporally endless: 'as the days of the heavens' (Ps 89:29) is parallel to 'for ever' (Ps 89:28). The statement that Yahweh's steadfast love and faithfulness extend to the heavens means that the psalmist considers them to be infinite (Ps 36:5; cf. 57:10–11; 89:2; 103:11)."

to the profound, unsearchable, many-layered decisions God has handed down from his divine seat of justice.

The skies, the mountains, and the seas are perhaps the most mesmerizing features of creation. The sky enchants in its beauty, and the skies of God's steadfast love envelope every mountain of righteousness. You can stand on the shore and get lost in contemplation of the undulating ocean, and the wonders of God's judgments roll in like the waves: rhythmic, powerful, unstoppable, and constant.

At the end of 36:6 (MT 36:7) David moves from the description of God's character to his saving action for man and beast. This shows that God's attributes are not abstract platitudes but personal ways of relating that deliver those who depend on him. Derek Kidner wrote of these verses,

> Here is a whole world to explore, a "broad place" to be brought into (cf. 18:19): unsearchable (*heavens, clouds*), impregnable (*mountains*), inexhaustible (*the great deep*); yet, for all that, welcoming and hospitable (6c–9). It is only man's world that is cramping. Human fickleness makes a drooping contrast to this towering covenant-love and *faithfulness* (5); human standards, where all is relative, are a marshland beside the exacting, exhilarating mountains of his *righteousness* (6); human assessments are shallowness itself in comparison with his *judgments*.[148]

The solid weight of God's glory exposes sin's paltry emptiness.

David's words expose God's exquisite steadfast love as a rare treasure to be prized, thus he says in 36:7a (MT 36:8a), "How precious is your lovingkindness, O God." Those who perceive God as he is take refuge under his wings (36:7b [MT 36:8b]; cf. 2:12; 91:4; Ruth 2:12; Matt 23:37).

Whereas sin never leads to lasting joy, those who worship the Lord are satisfied in him. David articulates this in Ps 36:8 (MT 36:9), "They quench thirst from the fatness of your house, and the wadi of your edens you cause them to drink." The two terms for drinking in this verse ("quench thirst" and "drink") point to the Lord's fullness that he pours out for his parched people. The abundant provision at the Lord's house evokes his amply supplied place of shelter, communion, and refuge. David said he wanted to dwell there forever in 23:5–6, that the one thing he sought was to dwell there to gaze on the Lord's beauty in 27:4, and exclaims that there

---

148 Kidner, *Psalms 1–72*, 165.

his people will be satisfied on his goodness in 65:4 (MT 65:5). Translations typically render the last phrase of this verse, "the river of your delights." The word "delights," however, has the same consonants and pointing as the term that designates the primeval garden, Eden.

The references to the Lord's house and his Eden point to the way that the Lord satisfies his people with his presence, communing with them as their God, their Father. The drinking referenced in Ps 36:8 (MT 36:9) is followed up by the reference to the Lord's "fountain of life" in 36:9 (MT 36:10; cf. Prov 10:11; 13:14; 14:27; 16:22). God spoke light into being, and the light the Lord gives enables all perception experienced by any man: "in your light do we see light" (Ps 36:9 [MT 36:10]; cf. John 1:1–4, 9; 8:12).

Those who have found the fountain of life will want to continue to drink the living water.[149] It is thus no surprise that David prays in 36:10 (MT 36:11) for the Lord to draw his lovingkindness and righteousness over those who know him, those of upright heart (cf. 36:5–6 (MT 36:6–7). He prays in 36:11 (MT 36:12) that the wicked would not tread him underfoot, that their power (hand) would not cause him to "flutter" (cf. 11:1). David does not want to be defeated, and he does not want to be caused to panic.

Psalm 36 closes in verse 12 (MT 13) with David envisioning the wicked fallen, thrust down, and like Ps 1:5, not able to rise. The wicked worship sin with its fleeting pleasure and lasting regret, and in the end they gain eternal destruction. The righteous worship God with his lofty love and rooted righteousness, and in the end they drink from the fountain of life and ever bask in his light.

### Bridge

Jesus offers to shelter his people under his wings (Matt 23:37; Ps 36:7 [MT 36:8]). He offers living water to all who thirst (John 4:10–14; 7:37–39; Ps 36:9 [MT 36:10]). He is the light of the world that gives light to every man (John 1:9; 8:12; Ps 36:9 [MT 36:10]).

---

[149] The targum renders "the fountain of life" in 36:9 (MT 36:10) as "channels of living water" (Stec, *Targum of Psalms*, 78).

## Psalm 37

OVERVIEW AND STRUCTURE OF PSALM 37

Psalm 37 is a chiastic acrostic. In general, every other verse begins with the next letter of the alphabet. The only exception to the alphabetic format comes in the substitution of a *tsade* where the *ayin* should be. In the Aramaic square script, the two letters bear some visual resemblance to one another (ע/צ), and David may have had other reasons for the substitution of which we are not aware.

| | | | | | | | |
|---|---|---|---|---|---|---|---|
| 37:1 | א | 37:12 | ז | 37:23 | מ | 37:34 | ק |
| 37:3 | ב | 37:14 | ח | 37:25 | נ | 37:35 | ר |
| 37:5 | ג | 37:16 | ט | 37:27 | ס | 37:37 | שׁ |
| 37:7 | ד | 37:18 | י | 37:29 | צ | 37:39 | ת |
| 37:8 | ה | 37:20 | כ | 37:30 | פ | | |
| 37:10 | ו | 37:21 | ל | 37:32 | צ | | |

The psalm's chiastic structure can be set forth as follows:[150]

37:1–11, Outcomes
    37:12–15, Violence
        37:16–20, Provision
            37:21–24, Inherit or Cut Off (esp. 37:22)
        37:25–31, Provision
    37:32–33, Violence
37:34–40, Outcomes

The basic teaching of the psalm is that the wicked will be cut off from the land while the righteous will inherit it (37:9, 11, 22, 28–29, 34, 38).

My exposition will discuss the corresponding sections of the psalm, concluding with its central statements as follows:

    37:1–11, 34–40, Outcomes for the Righteous and the Wicked
    37:12–15, 32–33, The Violence of the Wicked
    37:16–20, 25–31, God's Provision for the Righteous
    37:21–24, Blessed to Inherit the Land

---

[150] Cf. Alden, "Chiastic Psalms 1–50," 24–25.

CSB

Of David.

¹ Do not be agitated by evildoers;
do not envy those who do wrong.
² For they wither quickly like grass
and wilt like tender green plants.

³ Trust in the LORD and do what is good;
dwell in the land and live securely.
⁴ Take delight in the LORD,
and he will give you your heart's
    desires.

⁵ Commit your way to the LORD;
trust in him, and he will act,
⁶ making your righteousness shine like
    the dawn,
your justice like the noonday.

⁷ Be silent before the LORD and wait
    expectantly for him;
do not be agitated by one who
    prospers in his way,
by the person who carries out evil
    plans.

⁸ Refrain from anger and give up your
    rage;
do not be agitated—it can only bring
    harm.
⁹ For evildoers will be destroyed,
but those who put their hope in the
    LORD
will inherit the land.
¹⁰ A little while, and the wicked person
    will be no more;
though you look for him, he will not
    be there.
¹¹ But the humble will inherit the land
and will enjoy abundant prosperity.

¹² The wicked person schemes against
    the righteous

Author's translation

¹ Of David
Be not incensed at the ones who
    cause evil.
Be not envious at the ones who do
    malice.
² For like the grass quickly they wilt,
and like green herbs they will wither.
³ Trust in Yahweh and do good.
Settle the land and shepherd fidelity.
⁴ And delight yourself upon Yahweh,
and he will give to you the petitions
    of your heart.
⁵ Roll your way upon Yahweh,
and trust upon him, and he will do it.
⁶ And he will cause your righteousness
    to go forth like the light,
and your justice like the noonday.
⁷ Be quiet in Yahweh, and wait for
    him.
Be not incensed at the one who
    prospers in his way,
at the one who makes schemes.
⁸ Cease from wrath and forsake rage.
Be not incensed, even to do evil.
⁹ For the ones who cause evil will be
    cut off,
but those who wait for Yahweh, they
    will inherit the land.
¹⁰ And yet a little, and there will be no
    wicked;
and you will closely examine his
    place, and he will not be there.
¹¹ And the afflicted [humble/meek]
    will inherit the land,
and they shall delight themselves on
    a multitude of *shalom*.

¹² The wicked plots against the
    righteous,
and grinds against him his teeth.
¹³ Yahweh laughs at him,
for he sees that it comes, his day.

and gnashes his teeth at him.
¹³ The Lord laughs at him
because he sees that his day is coming.

¹⁴ The wicked have drawn the sword
    and strung the bow
to bring down the poor and needy
and to slaughter those whose way is
    upright.
¹⁵ Their swords will enter their own
    hearts,
and their bows will be broken.

¹⁶ The little that the righteous person
    has is better
than the abundance of many wicked
    people.
¹⁷ For the arms of the wicked will be
    broken,
but the Lord supports the righteous.

¹⁸ The Lord watches over the blameless
    all their days,
and their inheritance will last forever.
¹⁹ They will not be disgraced in times
    of adversity;
they will be satisfied in days of
    hunger.

²⁰ But the wicked will perish;
the Lord's enemies, like the glory of
    the pastures,
will fade away—
they will fade away like smoke.

²¹ The wicked person borrows and
    does not repay,
but the righteous one is gracious and
    giving.
²² Those who are blessed by the Lord
    will inherit the land,
but those cursed by him will be
    destroyed.

²³ A person's steps are established by
    the Lord,

¹⁴ The wicked open a sword,
they tread their bow,
to cause the afflicted and needy to
    fall,
to slaughter the upright of way.
¹⁵ Their sword will go into their heart,
and their bows will be shattered.

¹⁶ Better a little for the righteous than
    the crowd of many wicked,
¹⁷ for the arms of the wicked will be
    broken,
but Yahweh supports the righteous.
¹⁸ Yahweh knows the days of those
    who have integrity,
and their inheritance will be to the
    age.
¹⁹ They shall not be ashamed in the
    evil time,
and in days of famine they shall be
    satisfied.
²⁰ But the wicked will perish, along
    with those at enmity with Yahweh:
like splendid pastures,
they are scorched in the smoke; they
    are scorched.

²¹ The wicked borrows but does not
    pay back,
but the righteous graces and gives.
²² For the ones he blesses will inherit
    the land,
but the ones he curses will be cut off.
²³ From Yahweh are the steps of a
    man.
They are established, and in his way
    he delights.
²⁴ If he falls, he will not be hurled,
for Yahweh supports his hand.

²⁵ A young man I was, also I grew old,
and I have not seen the righteous
    forsaken,
or his seed seeking bread.
²⁶ All the day he graces and lends,

and he takes pleasure in his way.
²⁴ Though he falls, he will not be
overwhelmed,
because the Lᴏʀᴅ supports him with
his hand.

²⁵ I have been young and now I am old,
yet I have not seen the righteous
abandoned
or his children begging for bread.
²⁶ He is always generous, always
lending,
and his children are a blessing.

²⁷ Turn away from evil, do what is
good,
and settle permanently.
²⁸ For the Lᴏʀᴅ loves justice
and will not abandon his faithful ones.
They are kept safe forever,
but the children of the wicked will be
destroyed.
²⁹ The righteous will inherit the land
and dwell in it permanently.

³⁰ The mouth of the righteous utters
wisdom;
his tongue speaks what is just.
³¹ The instruction of his God is in his
heart;
his steps do not falter.

³² The wicked one lies in wait for the
righteous
and intends to kill him;
³³ the Lᴏʀᴅ will not leave him
in the power of the wicked one
or allow him to be condemned when
he is judged.

³⁴ Wait for the Lᴏʀᴅ and keep his way,
and he will exalt you to inherit the
land.
You will watch when the wicked are
destroyed.

and his seed a blessing.
²⁷ Turn from evil and do good,
and settle to the age.
²⁸ For Yahweh loves justice,
and he does not forsake his
lovingkind ones:
to the age they are kept,
but the seed of the wicked will be cut
off.
²⁹ The righteous will inherit the land,
and they will settle forever on it.
³⁰ The mouth of the righteous mutters
wisdom,
and his tongue speaks justice.
³¹ The Torah of his God is in his heart,
his steps do not buckle.

³² The wicked keeps watch for the
righteous and seeks to kill him.
³³ Yahweh does not leave him in his
hand,
and he will not consider him wicked
when he is judged.

³⁴ Wait for Yahweh and keep his way,
and he will raise you up to inherit the
land.
When the wicked are cut off, you will
see.
³⁵ I saw the wicked violent
and flaunting himself like a native
luxuriant tree,
³⁶ and he passed by, and behold, he
was not there.
Then I sought him and he could not
be found.
³⁷ Protect the one with integrity and
look at the upright one,
for there is a future for the man of
shalom.
³⁸ But the transgressors will be
destroyed together,
the future of the wicked will be cut
off.

³⁵ I have seen a wicked, violent person
well-rooted, like a flourishing native
tree.
³⁶ Then I passed by and noticed he was
gone;
I searched for him, but he could not
be found.

³⁷ Watch the blameless and observe
the upright,
for the person of peace will have a
future.
³⁸ But transgressors will all be
eliminated;
the future of the wicked will be
destroyed.

³⁹ The salvation of the righteous is
from the LORD,
their refuge in a time of distress.
⁴⁰ The LORD helps and delivers them;
he will deliver them from the wicked
and will save them
because they take refuge in him.

³⁹ And the salvation of the righteous is
from Yahweh,
their stronghold in the time of
distress.
⁴⁰ Yahweh helps them and delivers
them.
He delivers them from the wicked,
and saves them because they take
refuge in him.

CONTEXT: VERBAL AND THEMATIC LINKS WITH SURROUNDING PSALMS

In the flow of thought developing in this section of Book 1, the reflections in Ps 36 on sin and worship find complementary thoughts on the outcomes of the two activities in Ps 37. Those who worship God will inherit the land. Those who give themselves to sin will be cut off from it.

In the chiastic structure of Pss 34–41, Pss 37 and 38 stand in central position announcing that the meek shall inherit the earth (Ps 37) and petitioning to be included in that salvation (Ps 38).

EXPOSITION

**37:1–11, 34–40, Outcomes for the Righteous and the Wicked**
In Ps 37 David sets the two ways before his audience: one leads to being cut off from the land, the other leads to inheriting it. He begins in 37:1–2 by teaching those who heed him neither to be incensed at nor envious of those who do evil and malice, and the reason is that they won't last long. On the one hand, those who do evil can provoke the righteous to feel indignation, and on the other, the righteous can begin to be jealous

of what they perceive to be the pleasures of the wicked. David instructs those who hear him to recognize that the wicked will wilt and wither like the grass of the field. The term "wither" in 37:2 is the same used to describe the way the leaf of the blessed man will not wither in 1:3.

If the wicked will not last, what will? David gives instruction in 37:3-4 as to the kind of life that will be like a tree whose leaf does not wither (Ps 1:3). David urges trust for Yahweh and the practice of good deeds. He calls his audience to dwell in the land and "shepherd fidelity" (ורעה אמונה 37:3; cf. ESV, "befriend faithfulness;" NKJV, "feed on his faithfulness"). To shepherd fidelity is to take care of faithfulness like a shepherd takes care of his sheep—feeding them, watching over them, protecting them, and being always with them. To trust Yahweh, dwell in the land, and shepherd fidelity, David urges finding delight in Yahweh. This simple instruction to enjoy God is a call to satisfy oneself on God the way a nursing child is satisfied by a mother's milk (see Isa 66:11). David calls his audience to relish the refined delicacies enjoyed by those in relationship with God the way that rich people enjoy fine food and drink, luxurious surroundings, and stylish adornment. To delight oneself in God is to find pleasure in him the way that the worldly find pleasure in the satisfaction of their desires. If God becomes our delight, the desires of our hearts become desires for God. Psalm 37:4 says that when we delight ourselves in God, he will give us new desires for himself, desires that he will satisfy. This is the key to life and contentment.

Against the appearances—in which the wicked seem to prosper—David urges entrusting one's way to Yahweh in 37:5-6, trusting him to do justice. David speaks of the way that God will vindicate his own, causing their righteousness to shine, their justice to be like the noonday sun (cf. Matt 5:14-16).

To the frustrated, huffing and puffing, exasperated members of the believing community, David speaks in Ps 37:7-9. He counsels quieting oneself in Yahweh and waiting on him rather than being incensed at the wicked (cf. 37:8, 1), for the irritation the righteous feel could lead them to do evil. The righteous are to find stillness in Yahweh trusting that those who do evil will be cut off from the land, while those who wait for Yahweh will inherit it (37:9).

David reinforces these truths in 37:10-11, saying that the time until the wicked are no more is short, and once it comes the wicked will be nowhere to be found (37:10). The righteous, meanwhile, who have endured affliction in humility will inherit the land and be delighted by God's overflowing *shalom* (37:11).

The threefold command not to be incensed at the wicked (37:1, 7, 8) ties Ps 37:1–11 together, along with the two references to delighting oneself (37:4, 11) and the two references to inheriting the land (37:9, 11).

Psalm 37 closes in the same way it opens. Just as 37:1–11 speaks to the outcome of the righteous and the wicked, 37:34–40 treats the same themes.

In 37:34 David commands his audience to wait for Yahweh to reward the just, when he will exalt, or perhaps raise them up, to inherit the land. This will amount to their vindication, as they will see the wicked cut off.

Psalm 37:35–36 depict the wicked as a flamboyant tree, showing itself off, which suddenly disappears. This image contrasts with the tree imagery used in Ps 1 to describe the blessed man. Psalm 37:36 also corresponds with 37:10 at two points: that the wicked "was no more" and that he "could not be found."

Psalm 37 teaches that the wicked will meet sudden, unexpected destruction, but the righteous will reap the fruit of their good deeds. Whereas the tree of the wicked man vanished in 37:35–36, the next verse (37:37) affirms a future for the man of *shalom*, the man characterized by integrity and uprightness. Whereas there is a future for the righteous in 37:37, the only future for transgressors is to be cut off and destroyed in 37:38. However things may seem in the distribution of powerful posts, elite positions, and in the broader opinion of the public, Ps 37 tells the righteous what the outcomes will be.

The righteous (37:39–40) have Yahweh as their Savior, stronghold, deliverer, and refuge. He will save them.

### 37:12–15, 32–33, The Violence of the Wicked

Whereas the righteous are urged not to be angry and wrathful (37:1, 7–8), the wicked gnash their teeth and plot against the righteous in 37:12. If the plotting hearkens back to Ps 2:1–3, Yahweh's response recalls 2:4. As there so here: in 37:13 Yahweh laughs at the wicked because he knows that the day of reckoning is near.

The wicked ready their weapons, sword and bow, to take advantage of those who seem to have no protector. Too poor to hire defenders, too afflicted to defend themselves, and too upright to engage in violence, the wicked see them as easy prey (37:14). Their defender, however, makes it so that the sword aimed at them strikes the one who wields it and the bows of the wicked are broken (37:15).

David returns to the violent attacks of the murderous wicked in 37:32–33, where though the wicked try to kill the righteous, Yahweh neither abandons them physically nor allows the wicked to condemn them unjustly.

### 37:16–20, 25–31, God's Provision for the Righteous

We must find provision and safety. Once we have our basic needs met, we often look around and compare how we've done with others. Psalm 37 teaches the righteous how to be happy in response to that human tendency.

- 37:1–2, do not to envy the wicked for they'll be judged soon.
- 37:3–4, God can bring true delight to you.
- 37:5–6, to get delight you have to trust him and wait on him.
- 37:7, be still before him, wait, don't be incensed.
- 37:8–9, stop being angry and don't do the evil it would prompt.
- 37:10–11, the meek will inherit the earth.
- 37:12–15, the violent only harm themselves.

If we could take Ps 37:4 and hold it up like a prism, the light that goes in all these different directions with all the various colors would be the different instructions in this psalm. So the prism is, "Delight yourself in the Yahweh, and he will give you the desires of your heart" (37:4). How do we do that? Every varicolored ray of light in this psalm tells us how. All the instructions in Ps 37 tell us how to do 37:4.

So to those who are poor and tempted to envy all that the wicked have, David says in 37:16–20 that God is their Father who will protect and provide for them. Better to have God as your Father than the abundance of the wicked.

David's words in 37:16–17 communicate that it is better to have just what you need and be righteous than have all the plunder the wicked possess because God will break the arm of the wicked but uphold the righteous. These verses apply the truth that those who eat the forbidden fruit will hear the sound of the Lord walking in the garden and have nowhere to hide. Do you want to panic when you hear him coming, or do you want his presence to be a delight? For those who obey and content themselves with what he provides, the sound of his coming is a herald of joy.

In Ps 37:18–20 David again contrasts the outcomes of the righteous and the wicked, this time specifically with reference to provision. As in Ps 1:6, where Yahweh knows the way of the righteous, so in 37:18 he "knows the days of those who have integrity." The heritage mentioned in 37:18 suggests the tribal inheritance of an Israelite, a plot of ground in the land of promise a man would plow and pasture. God blesses the projects and possessions of those who trust him. Trusting him means not taking matters into one's own hands by doing something unlawful to try to bring blessing on oneself. In this way, as 37:19 says, the righteous will not be put to shame in the evil time of famine but have an abundance.

The fate of the wicked, on the other hand, is described in 37:20. If the wicked seem to have a splendid pasture as a result of their disobedience, they will be scorched in the smoke and only a ruin will remain.

David returns to the theme of provision (after the central section of his chiasm, 37:20–24) in 37:25–31. He gives an observation and a testimony in 37:25–26. Whereas the wicked are not content with what they have and are so earnest to get more that they will lie, steal, or kill to have it, the righteous, David says, have a Father who provides for them. That Father, David testifies in 37:25, has never forsaken his children or left them destitute. The righteous are so confident in God as their Father, who provides for them, that in 37:26 David tells of their open-hearted generosity. The righteous have received grace from God, and they give grace to others. They are glad to lend, and the seed of the righteous is a blessing.

David urges his audience in Ps 37:27 to turn from evil and do good that they might inherit the land and dwell there to the age. This is a promise of life in God's presence on God's land in this age and the age to come. David knows it will work because, as he says in 37:28, Yahweh loves justice and will not forsake those marked by his lovingkindness, those who have experienced his *hesed*. God will preserve them forever and make their seed a blessing (37:27), but the seed of the wicked, the seed of the serpent, will be cut off (37:28).

David's message is that sin steals your joy, makes God your enemy, and brings upon you everlasting destruction. Obedience, on the other hand, gives joy, as you trust God as your Father, anticipating everlasting life. Thus 37:29, where David declares that the righteous will inherit the land to enjoy it forever.

If we ask how the righteous become and remain convinced of these realities, and again, how the righteous are to delight themselves in the Lord, it is as though David says to go back and read Ps 1. In 37:30 he employs the same verb used to refer to meditating on the Torah in 1:2 to say that the righteous man meditates on wisdom in 37:30, "the mouth of the righteous mutters wisdom." Wisdom and justice are characteristics of Torah, thus in 37:31 we are shown why the righteous man has wisdom and justice in his mouth: because he has the Torah in his heart. His life will be that of a man whose "steps do not buckle" (37:31). The righteous man will walk securely, and his foot will not slide in due time because he walks with God.

### 37:21–24, Blessed to Inherit the Land

The wicked's disregard for God and neighbor stands in contrast with the regard of the righteous for both in 37:21. The wicked takes out loans that he doesn't pay back because he cares more about himself than the one who made the loan, and he doesn't think God will judge him. The righteous, by contrast, gives and graces others.

Psalm 37:22 functions as the centerpoint of the chiasm in Ps 37 and crystallizes its message: those who enjoy Yahweh's blessing will inherit the land, but those whom Yahweh curses will be cut off from it. Inheriting the land here points beyond this life to the new heaven and new earth.

The blessing of Yahweh is elaborated upon in 37:23–24. The wording of 37:23 is somewhat ambiguous. The first line establishes God's absolute sovereignty over man's life: "From Yahweh are the steps of a man." The second, however, does not specify who does the delighting: "They [the steps] are established, and in his way he delights." Is this the man delighting in Yahweh's way? Or is it Yahweh delighting in the man's way? I am inclined to think that David intended the ambiguity to suggest both. As 37:4 indicates that God gives new desires that he then fulfills, so 37:23 indicates that the righteous man's way is delightful (different term from 37:4) to both God and the righteous man who walks in it.

In Ps 37:24 David speaks to the imperfect way of the righteous. He acknowledges that the righteous may fall, but because the righteous repent, trust God, and walk with God, the sin of the righteous is forgiven. Unlike the unrepentant wicked, the righteous repent, and as a result they are not "cast headlong" but experience the Lord upholding them.

The teaching of David in Ps 37 anticipates the teaching of Jesus in the Sermon on the Mount. David speaks of those who will inherit the land, and this informs the promises of Jesus that the meek will inherit the earth (Matt 5:5). David speaks of how the Lord provides for the righteous, and Jesus says that those who hunger and thirst for righteousness will be satisfied (Matt 5:6). David speaks of the Lord bringing out vindication like the noonday sun, and Jesus says that lamps are not put under a bushel (Matt 5:14–16).

David's teaching finds its culmination, completion, and fulfillment in the teaching of Jesus, for at his coming, Jesus will cut off the wicked from the land and establish the righteous in the new heaven and new earth.

## Psalm 38

Overview and Structure of Psalm 38

Psalm 38 evidences the following chiastic structure:

38:1–2 (MT 38:2–3), Not in Anger Discipline Me
　　38:3–7 (MT 38:4–8), No Soundness because of My Sin
　　　　38:8–10 (MT 38:9–11), Groaning before the Lord
　　　　　　38:11–12 (MT 38:12–13), Left Alone and Betrayed
　　　　　　38:13–14 (MT 38:14–15), Deaf and Mute
　　　　　38:15–16 (MT 38:16–17), Waiting on the Lord
　　　38:17–20 (MT 38:18–21), Weakened by Sin
38:21–22 (MT 38:22–23), Cry for Yahweh's Presence and Salvation

We will exposit the psalm in two parts as follows:

　　38:1–12 (MT 38:2–13), The Rubble of Sin's Destruction
　　38:13–22 (MT 38:14–23), Silently Waiting on the Lord

Scripture

| CSB | Author's translation |
|---|---|
| A psalm of David to bring remembrance. | [1] A Psalm of David. For causing remembrance. |
| [1] Lord, do not punish me in your anger or discipline me in your wrath. | [2] O Yahweh, neither in your anger reprove me, nor in your rage discipline me. |

² For your arrows have sunk into me,
and your hand has pressed down on
    me.

³ There is no soundness in my body
because of your indignation;
there is no health in my bones
because of my sin.
⁴ For my iniquities have flooded over
    my head;
they are a burden too heavy for me
    to bear.
⁵ My wounds are foul and festering
because of my foolishness.
⁶ I am bent over and brought very low;
all day long I go around in mourning.
⁷ For my insides are full of burning
    pain,
and there is no soundness in my body.
⁸ I am faint and severely crushed;
I groan because of the anguish of my
    heart.

⁹ Lord, my every desire is in front of
    you;
my sighing is not hidden from you.
¹⁰ My heart races, my strength leaves
    me,
and even the light of my eyes has
    faded.
¹¹ My loved ones and friends stand
    back from my affliction,
and my relatives stand at a distance.
¹² Those who intend to kill me set
    traps,
and those who want to harm me
    threaten to destroy me;
they plot treachery all day long.

¹³ I am like a deaf person; I do not hear.
I am like a speechless person
who does not open his mouth.
¹⁴ I am like a man who does not hear
and has no arguments in his mouth.

³ For your arrows pierced me,
and your hand came down on me.

⁴ There is no soundness in my flesh
    because of your indignation;
there is no peace in my bones because
    of my sin,
⁵ for my iniquities have passed over
    my head;
like a heavy burden, they are too
    heavy for me.
⁶ They stink, they are festered, my
    wounds, because of my foolishness.
⁷ I am bent and bowed down in
    extremis;
all the day I go about being dark,
⁸ for my loins are filled with
    inflammation,
and there is no soundness in my flesh.

⁹ I am numbed and crushed in
    extremis;
I roar from the groaning of my heart.
¹⁰ O my Lord, before you is all my
    desire,
and my sighing from you is not
    hidden.
¹¹ My heart palpitates; my strength
    has deserted me,
and the light of my eyes, even these
    are not with me.

¹² The ones who love me and my
    friends, from my plague they stand
    aloof,
and those near me, from a distance
    they stand.
¹³ And they set traps, those who seek
    my life,
and those who seek evil for me, they
    speak destructions;
and deceptions all the day they
    mutter [meditate].

¹⁵ For I put my hope in you, Lᴏʀᴅ;
you will answer me, my Lord, my God.
¹⁶ For I said, "Don't let them rejoice
over me—
those who are arrogant toward me
when I stumble."
¹⁷ For I am about to fall,
and my pain is constantly with me.
¹⁸ So I confess my iniquity;
I am anxious because of my sin.
¹⁹ But my enemies are vigorous and
powerful;
many hate me for no reason.
²⁰ Those who repay evil for good
attack me for pursuing good.

²¹ Lᴏʀᴅ, do not abandon me;
my God, do not be far from me.
²² Hurry to help me,
my Lord, my salvation.

¹⁴ But as for me, like a deaf man I do
not hear,
and like a mute man he does not open
his mouth.
¹⁵ And I am like a man who does not
listen,
and there are in his mouth no
reproofs.

¹⁶ But for you, O Yahweh, I wait;
you will answer, O Lord my God.
¹⁷ For I said, "Lest they are glad over
me,
when my foot totters, over me they
magnify themselves.

¹⁸ For I am established to fall [or, for I
am ready to halt/fall]
and my pain is ever before me.
¹⁹ For I declare my iniquity;
I am anxious because of my sin.
²⁰ And those at enmity with me are
alive and strong,
and they multiply—those who hate
me without cause.
²¹ And those who repay me evil in
exchange for good,
they accuse me when I pursue good.

²² Do not forsake me, O Yahweh, my
God do not be far from me.
²³ Make haste to my help, O Lord, my
salvation.

CONTEXT: VERBAL AND THEMATIC LINKS WITH SURROUNDING PSALMS

David celebrated Yahweh's salvation, declaring his need for more of it,
in Ps 34. In Ps 35 he called on Yahweh to defend him against his adversaries, before reflecting on the way sin appeals to the wicked while the
righteous worship Yahweh in Ps 36. David turned his attention to contrasting the outcomes of the righteous and the wicked in Ps 37, and now
in Ps 38 he describes the Lord's discipline and his patient anticipation
of God's salvation.

## 38:1–12 (MT 38:1–13), The Rubble of Sin's Destruction

The superscription of Ps 38 (MT 38:1) is translated "for the memorial offering" by the ESV, but the NKJV has "To bring to remembrance." This is similar to the CSB's "for remembrance." All of these are translations of the *hiphil* infinitive construct of the verb "remember," which I have rendered "For causing remembrance." Perhaps this psalm was composed for David to remember what he describes here, or perhaps he meant it to be used to call on the Lord to remember mercy. Both possibilities work. This psalm teaches sinners what sin produces and the best way to deal with it, and the psalm also supplies language for sinners to use as they call on the Lord for mercy as David did.

### 38:1–2 (MT 38:2–3) Sin Brings Wrath

David opens Ps 38 recognizing the most devastating consequence of sin: God's wrath. David does not aim to avoid the consequences of his sin in 38:1 (MT 38:2), but he does ask that the Lord not bring those consequences in anger and rage. He knows that he will be reproved, but he asks for the reproof not to be visited by the Lord in hot anger. He acknowledges in 38:2 (MT 38:3) that he has already begun to experience the Lord's discipline in the form of the arrows that have sunk into him and the hand that has come down upon him (cf. 32:4). These descriptions speak metaphorically of the way the Lord has convicted David of the guilt of his sin.

Because of God's conviction, David asks for the Lord not to discipline him in anger in 38:1 (MT 38:2). What David requests shows that he understands the difference between the unyielding wrath of an almighty and infinite judge and the loving discipline of his Father.

### 38:3–7 (MT 38:4–8) Sin Weakens Physically

Psalm 38:3–7 (MT 38:4–8) is bracketed by the *inclusio* phrase, "there is no soundness in my flesh" in 38:3 and 7 (MT 38:4, 8). In 38:3 (MT 38:4) David states that his flesh and bones are unsound and without *shalom* because of God's indignation at David's sin. There is a profound connection between our spiritual state and our physical health, and here David notes the way that his sin has made God indignant with him and brought on physical weakness. He feels anxiety in his bones and weakness in his flesh.[151]

---

[151] One of the main characters of Fyodor Dostoevsky's 1866 novel *Crime and Punishment*, Raskolnikov, suffers a severe illness brought on by the horror of the crime he has committed.

David has realized the guilt of his sin, and in 38:4 (MT 38:5) he describes his sins passing over his head, as though his iniquity has gathered and become an overwhelming tide in which he cannot stand and cannot breathe. In the middle of the line he switches the metaphor from something passing over him to something he must carry, but this load is simply too much to bear.

David returns to the physical impact of his sin in 38:5 (MT 38:6). Whether the wounds that have resulted from his sin are literal or metaphorical, their stinking and festering rot communicates the shameful state that David has brought upon himself because of his sin. Sin advertises pleasure and relief only to pay out infection and pus. David acknowledges that he should have known better when he attributes the disgraceful condition to his foolishness at the end of 38:5 (MT 38:6). In addition to the lingering wounds, in 38:6 (MT 38:7) David cannot walk erect, which has him in a brooding, dark mood, and his "bent and bowed down" posture likely results from the fact that his "loins are full of burning pain" (CSB).

### 38:8–10 (MT 38:9–11) Sin Weakens Spiritually

Not only has David been physically weakened by his sin, his transgression has compromised his spiritual condition. Sin steals joy and leaves gloom. David describes the way he feels "numbed and crushed" and moans out the "groaning" of his heart in 38:8 (MT 38:9), "sighing" in 38:9 (MT 38:10). None of this escapes the Lord's sight. The longings that David describes being before the Lord in 38:9 (MT 38:10) probably include the hated desire for sin and the counteracting desire for holiness. David not only sighs in 38:9 (MT 38:10), he describes his heart palpitating, his strength abating, and his eyes not lighting up but going dark in 38:10 (MT 38:11).

Sin has made it so that God will discipline David in 38:1–2 (MT 38:2–3), and as a result of God's discipline, his body is unsound in 38:3–7 (MT 38:4–8) and his spirit groans in 38:8–10 (MT 38:9–11).

---

Raskolnikov's name is built from the root of a Russian word that means something like "split" or "cleave," and his name matches both his crime and what happens to him psychologically as a result of his sin. He splits himself apart. See Fyodor Dostoyevsky, *Crime and Punishment*, trans. Richard Pevear and Larissa Volokhonsky (New York: Knopf, 1993).

*38:11–12 (MT 38:12–13) Sin Alienates Friends and Foes*

David's sin has the theological, physical, and spiritual ramifications we have seen in 38:1–10 (MT 38:2–11), and in 38:11–12 (MT 38:12–13) we see its social ramifications. God's disciplining plague on David has made it so that in 38:11 (MT 38:12) his friends, companions, and those near him, perhaps family members, stand aloof and far off from him. David's allies have withdrawn from him.

At the same time, David's enemies are emboldened. We see in 38:12 (MT 38:13) that they begin to set traps for David, seeking evil for him by talking of destructions, and plotting treacheries. Their plots are their meditations, so they meditate on the opposite of what the blessed man does in Ps 1:3.

The dynamic at work in Ps 38:11–12, abandoned by friends, attacked by enemies, was never more deeply experienced than when every one of the disciples of the king from David's line fled that night in Gethsemane, the night that led to the morning that saw the high priest of Israel urge the Roman prefect to pin him to a cross.

The first half of Ps 38 thus concentrates on how David suffers because of his sin. His relationship with God and others is jeopardized (38:1–2, 11–12 [MT 38:2–3, 12–13]), and the vitality of his body and spirit drains away (38:3–7, 8–10 [MT 38:4–8, 9–11]). The rest of the psalm presents David's response to these woes.

## 38:13–22 (MT 38:14–23), Silently Waiting on the Lord

*38:13–14 (MT 38:14–15) Sin Deadens and Leaves Us without Excuse*

We become what we worship, and all sin results from a failure to worship and be satisfied by the true and living God. When we sin we do obeisance to idols that neither see nor hear nor speak nor smell, and as we worship lifeless things we experience a deadening of our sensory capacities.[152] David's sin has made him like the deaf and dumb idols. He does not hear or speak in 38:13–14 (MT 38:14–15).

This inability to hear or speak also makes David unable to defend himself. He cannot hear the sounds of the attacking enemy, and he cannot speak to marshal forces for his own defense. Nor can he hear the charges

---

[152] See G. K. Beale, *We Become What We Worship: A Biblical Theology of Idolatry* (Downers Grove, IL: InterVarsity Press, 2008).

of the accusers and offer a verbal defense of himself in hope of acquittal. David is guilty. He has sinned. Now he cannot hear and cannot speak.

David's inability to speak or hear in 38:13–14 (MT 38:14–15) is connected to the social ramifications of his sin in 38:11–12 (MT 38:12–13). His friends are far off. His enemies speak evil against him. And he is unable to hear or speak. There is nothing he can do to remedy the societal implications of his sin.

### 38:15–16 (MT 38:16–17) Sin Has One Remedy

Just as David rightly recognized his guilt before God and sought to deal with that first at the beginning of Ps 38 (38:1–2 [MT 38:2–3]), so now David rightly recognizes that only God can deliver him from the guilt of his sin in 38:15–16 (38:16–17). David knows that he can only wait on Yahweh and trust him to answer in 38:15 (MT 38:16), and 38:16 (MT 38:17) shows David mainly concerned for Yahweh's reputation. At first glance David may seem concerned for his own reputation, hoping his enemies won't rejoice at his fall and boast over him, but David is the king of Israel. For Israel's king to be defeated is for Israel's God to be defeated. David now recognizes that his sin has done more than ruin his own life. His sin has jeopardized God's reputation in the world.

David's waiting for the Lord in 38:15–16 (MT 38:16–17) matches his groaning before the Lord in 38:8–10 (MT 38:9–11). All that waiting gives ample time for groaning.

### 38:17–20 (MT 38:18–21) Sin Must Be Hated and Confessed

The first line of Ps 38:17 (MT 38:18) was translated by the King James "ready to halt," giving rise to the character by that name in John Bunyan's *Pilgrim's Progress*. The CSB renders the way David describes himself here as "ready to fall." The idea is that the conditions are now perfect for David to collapse, and with this, in the second half of the line, he says he is constantly aware of his pain.

This devastating situation brings David to the declaration of his iniquity and an acknowledgment of anxiety and sorrow for his sin in 38:18 (MT 38:19). The words "iniquity" and "sin" seem to point to David's sinfulness in general rather than a particular transgression. Though this psalm could very well be a response to one sin in particular, we are given no indication of what that might have been. In 38:18 (MT 38:19) David humbly, forthrightly confesses his sin. He makes no excuses. He offers no explanations. He does not in any way seek sympathy for what led him to sin. He simply confesses it.

The reference to his being ready to fall in 38:17 (MT 38:18) may very well point to a set of circumstances that would result in him being unseated from the throne. This could happen in spite of his confession and repentance in 38:18 (MT 38:19) because, as he says in 38:19–20 (MT 38:20–21), his foes are many, strong, and unreasonable. They hate him without cause. They answer evil for good. They are opposed to him because he seeks what is good.

David's weakened situation in 38:17–20 (MT 38:18–21) reprises his bodily weakness in 38:3–7 (MT 38:4–8).

### 38:21–22 (MT 38:22–23) Sin Separates Us from God

The best thing in David's life was God's presence, and as a sinner his only hope for enjoying God's presence was by experiencing God's salvation. David knows that he has no claims on God's mercy. He knows that his sin compromises his access to God. He also knows, however, that God loves to show mercy to those who confess and repent. Thus in 38:21 (MT 38:22) David pleads that God would neither forsake him nor be far from him, and that plea is complemented by the cry that God would make haste to help him and be his salvation in 38:22 (MT 38:23).

### BRIDGE

Psalm 38 is the prayer of all true believers of all generations. We are all guilty and in danger of God's righteous wrath. We have all experienced not only the theological but the physical, spiritual, and societal fruits of our sin. And the only hope for any of us is the one David acts on in Ps 38. He waits for the Lord, confesses his sin, turns from it, and begs for mercy. David shows how to deal with the rubble of sin's destruction, and the lesson applies to believers under the old covenant as well as the new. The cross of Christ, of course, makes God able to be just and the justifier of those who believe but fall short of his glory (Rom 3:23–26).

George Herbert's poem "Discipline," originally published in 1633, beautifully captures the spirit of Ps 38,

Throw away thy rod,
Throw away thy wrath:
O my God,
Take the gentle path.

For my heart's desire
Unto thine is bent:
I aspire
To a full consent.

Not a word or look
I affect to own,
But by book
And thy book alone.

Though I fail, I weep:
Though I halt in pace,
Yet I creep
To the throne of grace.

Then let wrath remove;
Love will do the deed:
For with love
Stony hearts will bleed.

Love is swift of foot;
Love's a man of war,
And can shoot,
And can hit from far.

Who can scape his bow?
That which wrought on thee,
Brought thee low,
Needs must work on me.

Throw away thy rod;
Though man frailties hath,
Thou art God:
Throw away thy wrath.

## Psalm 39

OVERVIEW AND STRUCTURE OF PSALM 39

The message of Ps 39 is that silence before the Lord in prayer gives perspective on the brevity of life and our biggest problem, sin. The phrase "with my tongue" in 39:1 and 3 (MT 39:2, 4) brackets the focus on David's silence in 39:1–3 (MT 39:2–4). A thematic and stylistic similarity then unites 39:4–6 (MT 39:5–7). The theme is the brevity of life, and the style includes the three "surely" statements in 39:5–6 (MT 39:6–7). The focus shifts slightly to David waiting in hope for the Lord to deliver him from his sin and its consequences in 39:7–11 (MT 39:8–12). David concludes in 39:12–13 (MT 39:13–14) by asking the Lord to hear his prayer and remove his angry gaze, which would amount to the removal of discipline for sin (cf. 39:7–11 [MT 39:8–12]).

The similarity of the final phrases of 39:5 and 11 (MT 39:6 and 12) may serve to mark off 39:6 (MT 39:7) as the centerpoint of the psalm, with matching sections (39:4–5 and 7–11 [MT 39:5–6 and 8–12]) on either side.

> 39:5 (MT 39:6), "Surely every Abel, every Adam stands. *Selah.*"
> 39:11 (MT 39:12), "Surely Abel, every Adam. *Selah.*"

Following this cue, Ps 39 can be seen to reflect a chiastic structure as follows:

39:1–3 (MT 39:2–4), I Am Silent
    39:4–5 (MT 39:5–6), Perspective: Life Is Short
        39:6 (MT 39:7), The Image
    39:7–11 (MT 39:8–12), Perspective: Yahweh Delivers from Sin's
    Consequences
39:12–13 (MT 39:13–14), Be Not Silent

We will exposit Ps 39 according to the following units of thought:

    39:1–3 (MT 39:2–4), Silence
    39:4–6 (MT 39:5–7), Vanity
    39:7–11 (MT 39:8–12), Hope
    39:12–13 (MT 39:13–14), Sojourn

SCRIPTURE

CSB                                    Author's translation

For the choir director, for Jeduthun. A     [1] For the Preeminent One.
psalm of David.                             Of Jeduthun.
                                            A Psalm of David.
[1] I said, "I will guard my ways
so that I may not sin with my tongue;       [2] I said: "I will guard my ways against
I will guard my mouth with a muzzle             sinning with my tongue;
as long as the wicked are in my             I will guard my mouth with a muzzle
    presence."                                  while the wicked are before me."
[2] I was speechless and quiet;             [3] I am mute with silence.
I kept silent, even from speaking good,     I caused silence from good,
and my pain intensified.                    and my pain was stirred up.
[3] My heart grew hot within me;            [4] My heart was warm within me.
as I mused, a fire burned.                  In my musing a fire burned.
I spoke with my tongue:                     I spoke with my tongue.
[4] "LORD, make me aware of my end
and the number of my days                   [5] Cause me to know, O Yahweh, my
so that I will know how short-lived             end,
    I am.                                   and the measure of my days, what
[5] In fact, you have made my days just         it is.
    inches long,                            I would know how transient I am.
and my life span is as nothing to you.      [6] Behold, handbreadths you have
Yes, every human being stands as only           given my days,
    a vapor.                                and my lifespan is as nothing before
Selah                                           you.
                                            Surely every Abel, every Adam stands.
                                                Selah.
[6] Yes, a person goes about like a mere
    shadow.                                 [7] Surely in the image a man will walk.
Indeed, they rush around in vain,           Surely Abel they are in an uproar.
gathering possessions                       He will heap up and not know who
without knowing who will get them.              gathers them.

[7] "Now, Lord, what do I wait for?         [8] And now on what do I wait, O Lord?
My hope is in you.                          My hope is for you.
[8] Rescue me from all my                    [9] From all my transgressions deliver
    transgressions;                             me!
do not make me the taunt of fools.          In the reproach of Nabal do not put
[9] I am speechless; I do not open my           me.
    mouth                                   [10] I am mute.
because of what you have done.              I will not open my mouth.
[10] Remove your torment from me.           For you did it.
Because of the force of your hand I am      [11] Remove from me your plague.
    finished.

¹¹ You discipline a person with
   punishment for iniquity,
consuming like a moth what is
   precious to him;
yes, every human being is only a
   vapor.
*Selah*

¹² "Hear my prayer, LORD,
and listen to my cry for help;
do not be silent at my tears.
For I am here with you as an alien,
a temporary resident like all my
   ancestors.
¹³ Turn your angry gaze from me
so that I may be cheered up
before I die and am gone."

From the blow of your hand I am
   finished.
¹² With reproofs for iniquity you
   discipline a man,
and you cause what he desires to melt
   like a moth.
Surely Abel, every Adam. *Selah.*

¹³ Hear my prayer, O Yahweh,
and to my cry for help give ear.
To my weeping be not silent,
for I am a sojourner with you, a
   pilgrim like all my fathers.
¹⁴ Look away from me, that I may be
   cheerful,
before I walk on and am no more.

CONTEXT: VERBAL AND THEMATIC LINKS WITH SURROUNDING PSALMS

> The wicked in 34, 35, 36:1–4 (MT 36:2-5); 37:1–2, 35
> 39:1 (MT 39:2)
>
> 38:2 hand
> 39:10 (MT 39:11)
>
> 38:11 plague
> 39:10 (MT 39:11)
>
> 38:13 mute
> 39:2, 9 (MT 30:3,10)
>
> 38:15 waiting
> 39:7 (MT 39:8); 40:1 (MT 40:2)

Throughout Pss 34–39, David deals with opposition from the wicked. Also throughout these psalms he waits on the Lord. The waiting continues in Ps 39 but will be resolved in 40:1 (MT 40:2).¹⁵³

In the chiastic structure of this unit of Psalms (see "Context" on Ps 34), Ps 39's focus on the wisdom that comes from knowing the brevity

---

¹⁵³ For the many points of contact between Job and Ps 39, see Kynes, *My Psalm Has Turned into Weeping*, 122–23.

of life balances Ps 36's focus on the wisdom of refusing sin in favor of satisfying oneself on God.

Exposition

### 39:1–3 (MT 39:2–4), Silence

The superscription of Ps 39 mentions "Jeduthun," whose name appears also in the superscriptions to Pss 62 and 77.[154] A Jeduthun is prominent among those who give thanks to Yahweh once David has installed the ark in Jerusalem (1 Chr 16:41–42; 25:1, 3, 6; 2 Chr 5:12; 29:14; 35:15; note that 1 Chr 25:1 refers to Jeduthun as one who prophesied, and cf. the discussion of the superscription of Ps 88). If this psalm is addressed to that Jeduthun, it would appear to have been written after David brought the ark into Jerusalem, perhaps reflecting on the earlier period of his life when he struggled through persecution and opposition while Saul reigned.

David relates in 39:1 (MT 39:2) that he felt the need to guard his ways and words for two reasons: first, he did not want to sin with his speech; and second, the wicked were in his presence. That resolve appears to result in the anguished silence David describes in 39:2 (MT 39:3), where David relates that he even refrained from speaking good things (so CSB, NIV, but ESV takes מטוב as "to no avail"). The pain stirred up by his silence in 39:2 (MT 39:3) also causes David's heart to grow warm and a fire to be kindled by his musing, with the result that he speaks with his tongue in 39:3 (MT 39:4).

Silence is often wise and appropriate, but in these verses David seems to be provoked by the wicked, with the result that he feels he must speak. To the surprise of the psalm's audience, however, David speaks not to the wicked but in prayer to God for wisdom about the brevity of life in 39:4–6 (MT 39:5–7).

### 39:4–6 (MT 39:5–7), Vanity

The three things David wants to know in 39:4 (MT 39:5) are related to one another. Taking them in the order they appear, David asks Yahweh (1) to cause him to know his end, so that (2) he will know the measure of his days. If he knows the endpoint of his life, he will know the distance

---

[154] See David M. Howard, "Psalms Study Notes," in NIV Zondervan Study Bible, ed. D. A. Carson (Grand Rapids: Zondervan, 2015), 1029.

between his present and his end, and thus (3) it will be apparent to him how transient his existence is.

The prayerful contemplation of these realities in 39:4 (MT 39:5) prompts David to reflect in 39:5 (MT 39:6) that the length of his life can be measured in handbreadths, and that before the Lord his span of his life is as nothing. I understand the final line of 39:5 (MT 39:6) to carry over the idea of standing before Yahweh, with David evoking both the way Adam brought sin and death into the world and the brief life of Abel through the words, "Surely every Abel, every Adam stands [before Yahweh]. *Selah.*" English translations universally understand "Adam" as a reference to "mortal man" and "Abel" as "vapor" (CSB). The consonants and pointing of the names Adam and Abel are the same as these nouns, "man" and "vapor," however, and the use of the names ties the concepts of the Psalms to the foundational events in the Torah that bring about the situation David describes. There are several plays on names and terms in Ps 39 (Adam/Abel in 39:5–6, 8, and Nabal in 39:11 [MT 39:6–7, 9; 39:12]). The standard English translations capture an aspect of the meaning of the lines, but the use of these terms that are also names adds a layer to our understanding of what David communicated in his poetry. In my translation I have used the names to bring this out. Life is short because Adam sinned and introduced death into the world, resulting in things like the murder of young Abel well before his time. The selah at the end of 39:5 (MT 39:6) seems to invite reflection on the depths of these tragic realities.

Further indication that David means to evoke Adam and Abel comes in the reference to "the image" (בְּצֶלֶם) in 39:6 (MT 39:7), "Surely in the image a man will walk. Surely Abel they are in an uproar. He will heap up and not know who gathers them." Here again, English translations universally render "image" along the lines of "shadow" (CSB, ESV, NKJV) or "phantom" (NAS, NIV), but here again the consonants and pointing are the same as found with the term rendered "image" in Gen 1:26, where God declares his intention to make man in his own. Those who live these brief lives walk as the image-bearers of their Creator, and David appears to address Abel on the vanity of man's uproarious pursuits and concerns ("Surely Abel they are in an uproar"), only to reflect on the way that all man toils to gather will be left to others at his death (cf. Eccl 2:18–16).

We should not miss the relationship between David's agitated silence in Ps 39:1–3 (MT 39:2–4) and the perspective on the fleeting vanity of life he experiences in prayer in 39:4–6 (MT 39:5–7). When our blood begins to boil under the provocation of the wicked, reflecting on the brevity of our short lives will sober and calm us.

David's contemplation of the end of his life and the short distance to it in 39:4–6 (MT 39:5–7) seems to prompt him to probe the nature of his hopes and the source of his woes in 39:7–11 (MT 39:8–12).

### 39:7–11 (MT 39:8–12), Hope

David continues in prayer in 39:7 (MT 39:8), considering his own hopes as a question posed to the Lord: "And now on what do I wait, O Lord?" His answer asserts that his hope is in the Lord. If we ask what specifically he hopes for as he waits, the answer comes in the plea in 39:8 (MT 39:9) for the Lord to deliver him from all his transgressions and the reproach of Nabal, or, the fool (cf. 1 Sam 25:25).

This plea to be delivered from his transgressions in 39:8 (MT 39:9) seems to arise from David's contemplation of his death in 39:4–6 (MT 39:5–7), driving him to the conclusion that ultimately he will die because he is a sinner. More than the trouble of the wicked he mentioned in 39:1 (MT 39:2), then, David knows that sin is what will kill him.

David also asked not to be put in the reproach of Nabal. Nabal was the man whose name communicated the foolishness of his character (1 Sam 25:25). Here again we find a name that has a meaning: the name Nabal being spelled the same as the word "fool." David's statement is worded such that it can communicate at least two ideas: he neither wants to be a fool, and thus bear the reproach due a fool, nor does he want to be the object of the scorn fools direct at those over whom they rejoice. Either way, David asks the Lord not to put him in the reproach of Nabal. As with the names Adam and Abel, the name Nabal links the words of Ps 39 to biblical narratives that tie into the psalm's message and advances it: Nabal is precisely the kind of man David does not want to be, nor does he want a man like Nabal to reproach him.

Sin puts us in danger of the reproach of the fool. We do not want to be fools bearing reproach, nor do we want fools reproaching us. The only way to avoid that reproach is to have the Lord deliver us from our transgressions.

David's silence in recognition of the fact that God "did it" in 39:9 (MT 39:10) is the response of a man who fears God. David's recognition of his sin (38:8 [MT 39:9]) has wrought in him a silence he could not work in himself (cf. 39:1–3 [MT 39:2–4]). David's prayerful reflection on his short life and inevitable death because he is a sinner has brought him to a place where he offers no excuses, explanations, or arguments. He is silent.

David then asks the Lord to remove his plague, the devastating blow of his hand, in Ps 39:10 (MT 39:11). The "plague" (cf. 38:11 [MT 38:12]) and the "blow" are God's disciplinary response to David's sin, as becomes evident in 39:11 (MT 39:12). David describes the effect of God's reproving discipline against all who are tainted with iniquity in 39:11 (MT 39:12). Rather than enjoy the lasting joy of holy obedience in the splendor of purity that accompanies walking in God's ways, God will cause what they desire "to melt like a moth." The image depicts the way that moths disintegrate, their wings unable to withstand any contact or endure any length of time. So are all the things that make for sinful pleasure: the diminishing joy melts into the shameful rut of addiction, and in the end no happiness remains in the soul-sapping sin. Having captured this in the poetic image of the melting moth, David repeats statements made in 39:5 (MT 39:6) at the end of 39:11 (MT 39:12): "Surely Abel, every Adam. *Selah*." All men will experience life as a vapor, like Abel, because all men descend from Adam.

What can David do in response to such realities but cry out to the Lord as he does in 39:12–13 (MT 39:13–14)?

### 39:12–13 (MT 39:13–14), Sojourn

David asks the Lord to hear his prayer in 39:12 (MT 39:13), then he makes the request he wants heard in 39:13 (MT 39:14).

The request to be heard is stated three different times in three different ways. The repetition communicates urgent desperation. David calls on Yahweh (1) to hear his prayer, (2) to give ear to his cry for help, and (3) not to be silent in response to his weeping. David's emotional pleas in 39:12 (MT 39:13) seem to be prompted by the plague, the blow, the reproofs, and the discipline in 39:10–11 (MT 39:11–12). That discipline caused the insubstantial nature of what he desired to "melt like a moth." The tears David references when he describes himself weeping, then, likely arise from sorrow that he would sin against Yahweh because he desired what has turned out to be worthless.

David feels shame for the folly of his sin, and he wants to be delivered from both his sin and its consequences, such as shame (39:8 [MT 39:9]). The third request to be heard in 39:12 (MT 39:13), for the Lord not to be silent, is a request for him to act.

Having asked the Lord to hear, David continues in 39:12 (MT 39:13) with a reason the Lord should do so. David explains that he is a sojourner with the Lord, a pilgrim like his forefathers. David thus distances himself from those whose portion is in this life (17:14). By describing himself as a sojourning pilgrim David shows that he does not consider this world home. He considers himself to be on the way to the better land, the one that has been promised, where his Lord (110:1) will reign. This amounts to an appeal to the Lord on the basis of the fact that David belongs to the Lord: he is a citizen of God's kingdom, a participant in God's covenant.

David's prayer reveals what he believes, for if he did not believe that the Lord could answer these requests he would not make them. David believes that sin will earn him death, but he believes that God can deliver him from the power of his sin and its consequences. David also believes that life is short for those who bear the image, but that this short life is a pilgrimage to a life that will last.

And Ps 39:13 (MT 39:14) shows that David believes that God himself is visiting justice against him because of his sin. Again, David had spoken of the way the Lord had plagued him and brought down his hand to strike him in 39:10 (MT 39:11). It is in this context that we must understand David's request that the Lord look away from him in 39:13 (MT 39:14). David appeals to the Lord to "turn your angry gaze from me," as the CSB renders the phrase. This, of course, entails the Lord finding some other means of doing justice against transgression. Under the old covenant the sacrificial system provided that means, pointing forward to a better one (Rom 3:24-26).

If the Lord will remove his wrathful look from David (39:13a [MT 39:14a]), then David will be able to enjoy life before his brief sojourn ends (39:13b [MT 39:14b]).[155]

---

[155] Having discussed the use of Ps 39:5-6, 14 in Job 10:20-21; Ps 39:5, 8 in Job 6:8-11 and 7:6-8; and Ps 39:5-6, 14 in Job 13:28-14:6, Kynes concludes, "Through the allusions to this psalm, as well as the other psalms in this study, the book of Job demonstrates how, at least by the postexilic period when Job was likely written, these psalms had gone through a process of moving from their original setting, whether cultic or not, to being considered 'Scripture.' Though we should not read back into their status a modern canonical understanding of that term, the allusions in Job show that the Psalms, freed from the cult, had gained 'a significance in themselves' and could therefore be used in new contexts," Kynes, *My Psalm Has Turned into Weeping*, 122-41 quotation from p. 140.

BRIDGE

In Ps 39:1–3 (MT 39:2–4) David pledges to be vigilant so as neither to sin nor to speak things in the hearing of the wicked. His greater son succeeded in guarding his way against every sin, and he was silent as a sheep before his shearers (Isa 53:7; Matt 26:63; 27:12, 14).

David contemplates the brief walk the sons of Adam who bear the image take before the Lord (39:4–6 [MT 39:5–7]). The eternal one was crucified in his early thirties after a brief public career.

David suffered a plague and blows and the shame of sins he committed (39:7–11 [MT 39:8–12]). The holy one was stricken, smitten, and afflicted for the sins of his people (Isa 53:4).

David cried out to the Lord, asking him to turn his angry gaze away (39:12–13 [MT 39:13–14]). The Father turned his back on Jesus altogether, prompting the God-forsaken cry.

David speaks of his own experience in Ps 39, a pattern of events that finds its fullest expression in the one who fulfilled every good thing David typified.

## Psalm 40

OVERVIEW AND STRUCTURE OF PSALM 40

Psalm 40 stands near the end of Book 1 and seems to mark the moment when David was at last delivered, signaling the end of the period in which David was persecuted by Saul and the beginning of his reign over Israel. This experience in David's life points forward to a similar moment when the seed promised to him would pass from suffering into glory.

David relates how he waited on Yahweh, and Yahweh came through in 40:1–3 (MT 40:2–4). He then pronounces a blessing on the one who trusts the Lord and speaks of how God's wonders are innumerable in 40:4–5 (MT 40:5–6).

David seems to reference the episode in 1 Sam 15:22–23 in Ps 40:6 (MT 40:7), and he then appears to allude to the promises of a coming king in 40:7 (MT 40:8). He announces his desire to please God in 40:8 (MT 40:9), before detailing his proclamation of Yahweh's righteousness, steadfast love, truth, and salvation in 40:9–11 (MT 40:10–12).

Having announced the Lord's saving lovingkindness in 40:9–11 (MT 40:10–12), David reiterates the two problems he has that prompt his need for Yahweh to watch over him: (1) in 40:12–13 (MT 40:13–14) he describes how very sinful he is; and (2) in 40:14–15 (MT 40:15–16) he resumes his call for the shaming of his enemies.

David closes Ps 40 with a prayer in 40:16–17 (MT 40:17–18) that those who love God's salvation might praise him, and he follows that up with a confident assertion that God will be his sure help and swift deliverer.

Psalm 40 reflects the following chiastic structure:

40:1–3 (MT 40:2–4), Deliverance
    40:4–5 (MT 40:5–6), Blessed
        40:6–8 (MT 40:7–9), Delight to Obey
            40:9–11 (40:10–12), Proclaim Righteousness and
                Lovingkindness
        40:12–13 (MT 40:13–14), Save Me from Sin
    40:14–15 (MT 40:15–16), Imprecation
40:16–17 (MT 40:17–18), Praise

We will pursue the exposition of Ps 40 under the following subheads:

    40:1–5 (MT 40:2–6), Delivered at Last
    40:6–11 (MT 40:7–12), The Proclamation of the Prophesied One
    40:12–17 (MT 40:13–18), Deliverance and Dishonor

SCRIPTURE

CSB

For the choir director. A psalm of David.

¹ I waited patiently for the Lord, and he turned to me and heard my cry for help.
² He brought me up from a desolate pit, out of the muddy clay, and set my feet on a rock, making my steps secure.
³ He put a new song in my mouth, a hymn of praise to our God. Many will see and fear, and they will trust in the Lord.

Author's translation

¹ For the Preeminent One.
Of David
A Psalm.

² Waiting I waited for Yahweh, And he inclined to me and heard my cry for help.
³ And he brought me up from the roaring pit, from the muck of the mire. And he made my feet stand on a high ridge; he established my steps.
⁴ And he put in my mouth a new song, praise to our God. Many will see and fear, and they will trust in Yahweh.

⁴ How happy is anyone
who has put his trust in the LORD
and has not turned to the proud
or to those who run after lies!
⁵ LORD my God, you have done many
    things—
your wondrous works and your plans
    for us;
none can compare with you.
If I were to report and speak of them,
they are more than can be told.

⁶ You do not delight in sacrifice and
    offering;
you open my ears to listen.
You do not ask for a whole burnt
    offering or a sin offering.
⁷ Then I said, "See, I have come;
in the scroll it is written about me.
⁸ I delight to do your will, my God,
and your instruction is deep within
    me."

⁹ I proclaim righteousness in the great
    assembly;
see, I do not keep my mouth closed—
as you know, LORD.
¹⁰ I did not hide your righteousness in
    my heart;
I spoke about your faithfulness and
    salvation;
I did not conceal your constant love
    and truth
from the great assembly.

¹¹ LORD, you do not withhold your
    compassion from me.
Your constant love and truth will
    always guard me.
¹² For troubles without number have
    surrounded me;
my iniquities have overtaken me; I am
    unable to see.
They are more than the hairs of my
    head,

⁵ Blessed is the man who puts Yahweh
    as his trust
and does not turn to the proud or
    those who swerve after lies.
⁶ Much you have done, O Yahweh
    my God, your wonders and your
    counsels for us.
There is none comparable to you.
I will declare and speak; they are too
    many to number.

⁷ In sacrifice and offering you do not
    delight. An ear you dug for me.
Burnt offering and sin offering you do
    not request.
⁸ Then I said, "Behold I have come.
In the scroll of the book it is written
    concerning me.
⁹ To do your good pleasure, my God, I
    delight,
and your Torah is in the midst of my
    inner parts."

¹⁰ I proclaim righteousness in the
    great assembly.
Behold, my lips I will not close, O
    Yahweh, you know.
¹¹ Your righteousness I have not
    hidden in the midst of my heart.
Your truth and your salvation I spoke.
I have not concealed your
    lovingkindness and your truth in
    the great assembly.
¹² You, O Yahweh, you will not close
    your womb from me.
Your lovingkindness and your truth
    ever watch over me.

¹³ For evils have encompassed me
    until there is no counting.
My iniquities have overtaken me, and
    I am not able to see.
They are more numerous than the
    hairs of my head, and my heart has
    forsaken me.

and my courage leaves me.
¹³ Lᴏʀᴅ, be pleased to rescue me;
hurry to help me, Lᴏʀᴅ.

¹⁴ Let those who intend to take my life
be disgraced and confounded.
Let those who wish me harm
be turned back and humiliated.
¹⁵ Let those who say to me, "Aha, aha!"
be appalled because of their shame.

¹⁶ Let all who seek you rejoice and be
    glad in you;
let those who love your salvation
    continually say,
"The Lᴏʀᴅ is great!"
¹⁷ I am oppressed and needy;
may the Lord think of me.
You are my helper and my deliverer;
my God, do not delay.

¹⁴ Be pleased, O Yahweh, to deliver
    me! O Yahweh, to my help make
    haste.

¹⁵ Let them be ashamed and abashed
    together, those who seek to sweep
    my life away.
Let them be turned back and
    humiliated, the ones who delight in
    my evil.
¹⁶ Let them be desolate as a
    consequence of their shame, who
    say to me, "Aha, Aha!"

¹⁷ Let them exult and be glad in you,
    all who seek you.
Let them say continually, "May
    Yahweh be great," those who love
    your salvation.
¹⁸ And as for me, afflicted and needy,
    my Lord thinks of me.
My help and the one who delivers me
    are you. My God do not delay.

Cᴏɴᴛᴇxᴛ: Vᴇʀʙᴀʟ ᴀɴᴅ Tʜᴇᴍᴀᴛɪᴄ Lɪɴᴋs ᴡɪᴛʜ Sᴜʀʀᴏᴜɴᴅɪɴɢ Psᴀʟᴍs

40:4 (MT 40:5) "Blessed"
1:1; 32:1; 41:1 (MT 41:2)

See the "Context" discussion at Ps 35 for the similarities between Ps 35:4, 21, 25, and 26 and Ps 40:14–15 (MT 40:15–16). These points of contact suggest that Pss 35 and 40 stand across from one another in the chiastic structure of Pss 34–41. David prays in Ps 35 that God will do justice against his enemies, asking "how long?" In Ps 40 David celebrates the way the Lord put his feet on a rock, and yet the psalm ends with a cry for deliverance against enemies echoing the language of Ps 35. From difficulty to difficulty, delivered from one only to face another, David cries out to Yahweh.

See also the "Context" discussion of Ps 70, which largely repeats Ps 40:13–17 (MT 40:14–18).

**40:1–5 (MT 40:2–6), Delivered at Last**

David has been waiting on Yahweh (39:7 [MT 39:8]; cf. 38:15 [MT 38:16]), and now in 40:1 (MT 40:2) he relates how the Lord inclined to him and heard his cry for help. David metaphorically describes what the Lord did for him in 40:2 (MT 40:3), where he says that Yahweh lifted him out of a roaring pit and set him securely on a high ridge. From the mucky mire to the rock, from the low pit to the ridge, the Lord lifted David up and made him secure. So far as we know, David was never literally in a pit; we never read of him in one in Samuel or Chronicles. The term for "pit" here (בּוֹר) is used repeatedly of Joseph, however (Gen 37:20, 22, 24, 28, 29; 40:15; 41:14).[156] Given the parallels between David and Joseph in Samuel, David may mean to connect himself with Joseph through this description of his difficulties.[157] As Joseph was put in a pit by wicked kinsmen jealous of what God had revealed to him in his dreams, so David was metaphorically put in a pit by Saul's persecutions. As Joseph was lifted out of the pit to reign over Egypt, so David was lifted out of the pit to reign over Israel.

The Lord at last delivers David in Ps 40 at the end of Book 1 of the Psalter. Book 2 opens with a series of psalms by "the sons of Korah" (see Pss 42–49, 43 being the only one without a superscription). David appointed the sons of Korah over the worship in the Yahweh's house after the ark was brought into Jerusalem (1 Chr 6:31, 37). Enemies of course remain, but the Psalter appears to be tracking with David's experience as narrated in Samuel. David continued to have difficulties after Saul's death and his exaltation to the throne, but for the most part he was lifted out of the pit and set on a rock at that point.

If this way of approaching the end of Book 1 and the beginning of Book 2 is correct, the new song the Lord put in David's mouth in 40:3 (MT 40:4) would also be informed by the worship initiatives David undertook once he became king. The Lord's deliverance of David through all his difficulties are what the many will see, and in response they will fear and trust in Yahweh.

Reflecting on the righteous way of life, and echoing the opening of Ps 1, in 40:4 (MT 40:5) David pronounces a blessing (אַשְׁרֵי) on the man who

---

[156] Cf. Keel, *Symbolism of the Biblical World*, 69.

[157] See James M. Hamilton, "Was Joseph a Type of the Messiah? Tracing the Typological Identification between Joseph, David, and Jesus," *SBJT* 12.4 (2008): 52–77.

makes Yahweh his trust rather than turning to the proud or to liars (cf. also 32:1; 41:1 [MT 41:2]). Perhaps reflecting on the way that God preserved him through all Saul's attempts on his life, David speaks in 40:5 (MT 40:6) of the many wonders Yahweh has done and his many thoughts toward his people. David declares that there is none like Yahweh, and that his deeds are too many to number.

### 40:6–11 (MT 40:7–12), The Proclamation of the Prophesied One

Psalm 40:6–8 (MT 40:7–9) seems to reflect Samuel's confrontation of Saul's disobedience in 1 Sam 15:22–23. Samuel had communicated Yahweh's intention for Saul to devote the Amalekites to the ban (1 Sam 15:1–3). Rather than devote them to destruction, Saul and his army spared Agag and the best of the plundered animals (1 Sam 15:9). When Samuel confronted him, Saul protested that the animals were spared to be sacrificed to Yahweh (1 Sam 15:15). Samuel then explained to Saul that Yahweh wanted obedience, not sacrifice.

The table below sets 1 Sam 15:22–23 and Ps 40:6–8 side by side, with common terms in bold (desire, חפץ, the verb in Ps 40, the noun in 1 Sam 15; burnt offering, עלה; sacrifice, זבח; behold, הנה) and with common thematic elements italicized (to obey in 1 Sam 15, to do God's good pleasure in Ps 40; the word of Yahweh in 1 Sam 15, Yahweh's Torah in Ps 40).

**Table 7. Comparison of 1 Samuel 15:22–23 and Psalm 40:6–8.**

| 1 Sam 15:22–23 | Psalm 40:6–8 (MT 40:7–9) |
| --- | --- |
| "Does Yahweh have **desire** for **burnt offerings** and **sacrifices** as much as for obedience to the voice of Yahweh? **Behold**, *to obey* is better than sacrifice, to pay attention than the fat of rams. ... Because you have rejected *the word of Yahweh*, he has rejected you as king." | **Sacrifice** and offering you do not **desire**. An ear you dug for me. **Burnt offering** and sin offering you do not request. Then I said, **Behold** I have come. In the scroll of the book it is written concerning me. *To do your good pleasure*, my God, I desire, and *your Torah* is in the midst of my inner parts. |

Samuel restates Saul's rejection in 1 Sam 15:26, before declaring to Saul that Yahweh has torn the kingdom from him and given it to one better than Saul (1 Sam 15:28). Samuel anoints David king in the very next chapter (1 Sam 16), and the Spirit of Yahweh leaves Saul and rushes upon David (1 Sam 16:13–14).

That turning point in the narrative of 1 Samuel, from Saul to David, seems to be referenced in the penultimate psalm of Book 1 to mark the turn from persecution to enthronement.[158]

Psalms 1–2 introduced the Psalter, then Pss 3–9 respond to Absalom's revolt. What the wicked say in their hearts is the focus of Pss 10–14, and then Pss 15–24 contemplate the coming king. Psalms 25–33 celebrate God's word and glory, and Pss 34–41 sing God's salvation of David through the judgment of his enemies. These groupings of psalms reflect a chiastic structure:

Psalms 3–9, Absalom's Revolt
    Psalms 10–14, The Wicked
        Psalms 15–24, The Coming King
    Psalms 25–33, God's Word and Glory
Psalms 34–41, Salvation through Judgment

The difficulty with enemies that saturates the end of Book 1 resolves into the praises of the Levites David appointed to give thanks at the house of Yahweh in the opening of Book 2 (Pss 42–50).

David's point in Ps 40:6 (MT 40:7) is that Yahweh wants obedience, not sacrifice. Sacrifice makes provision for those unsuccessful at obedience. Obedience is Yahweh's first choice, and sacrifice is provided for those who try to obey and fail. David's statement that Yahweh dug him an ear means that Yahweh has enabled David to hear his word and obey.

In Ps 40:7 (MT 40:8) David indicates that the seed of the woman (Gen 3:15) would be the seed of Abraham (Gen 12:1–3; 17:6), king from Judah (Gen 49:8–12), scepter and star (Num 24:17; cf. 24:9, 19), who would give rest to God's people (cf. Gen 5:29).[159] David understands that a king from Judah has been promised, and because Samuel anointed him king

---

[158] This sequence does not strictly follow the chronology in Samuel, where Saul's persecutions of David come after David is anointed in 1 Sam 16. The Psalter is not pursuing chronological accord with the book of Samuel, as can be seen from the reference to Absalom's revolt in the superscription of Ps 3. Still, the narratives of Samuel provide anchor points and informative background for the Psalter, and the scenes of 1 Sam 15–16 encapsulate the transition from Saul to David in just the way that the Psalter evokes them.

[159] For exposition, see James M. Hamilton, "The Skull Crushing Seed of the Woman: Inner-Biblical Interpretation of Genesis 3:15," *SBJT* 10.2 (2006): 30–54; Hamilton, "Seed of the Woman and the Blessing of Abraham"; and relevant sections of Hamilton, *God's Glory in Salvation through Judgment.*

over Israel (1 Sam 16:13) and Yahweh promised to build him a house (2 Sam 7:8–16), David knew that there was a sense in which he was the prophesied one. In another sense, and David knew this, too (see, e.g., Ps 110:1), the descendant of David promised in 2 Sam 7:12–14 would be *the* prophesied one.

The reading of Ps 40 I am proposing fits nicely with the quotation of these lines in Heb 10:5–7. David speaks in Ps 40 of the way God did not desire Saul's sinful sacrifice but obedience. David comes as the prophesied one who will obey. In fulfillment of this pattern, Jesus comes as the prophesied one in an ultimate sense. With Jesus, too, God did not desire the Old Testament sacrifices but obedience. The sacrifices were only provided for when obedience failed. Jesus did not fail to obey, and his sacrifice accomplished what those outlined in the Old Testament never could. As David replaces Saul, Jesus replaces the failed mediators and provisional sacrifices of a failed covenant. As David came in the line of promise traced all the way back to the seed of the woman, Jesus came as the longed-for culmination of that line of descent.

David explains the origin of three things in 40:8 (MT 40:9): first, of his understanding of what Yahweh desires in 40:6 (MT 40:7); second, of his role in God's purposes in 40:7 (MT 40:8); and third of his desire to obey. In 40:8 (MT 40:9) David explains that these three things spring from the fact that Yahweh's Torah is inside him. This statement at the end of 40:8 (MT 40:9) links up with the allusion to Ps 1 ("Blessed is the man") in 40:4 (MT 40:5) to reinforce David's Torah-informed life and point forward to the way that the king from his line will himself *embody* the word of God.

Having announced his arrival in fulfillment of God's promises in 40:6–8 (MT 40:7–9), David recounts his proclamation of God's character in 40:9–11 (MT 40:10–12; cf. Exod 34:6–7). Using the Hebrew term that will be translated into the Greek with the verb *euangelizo* ("preach good news"), David says that the "glad tidings" (NAS) he has to proclaim in the great assembly is the message of Yahweh's righteousness.

Unlike those who for various selfish reasons refuse to tell the truth about God, David says that he will not close his lips (40:9 [MT 40:10]), he will not hide the message in his own heart (40:10a [MT 40:11a]), nor will he conceal Yahweh's lovingkindness and truth (40:10c [40:11c]). These statements of how David will not suppress the truth of God's character complement his assertions that he articulates the knowledge of God's (1) righteousness, (2) truth, (3) salvation, and (4) lovingkindness for all to hear. David twice references God's "righteousness" (40:9, 10 [MT 40:10, 11]), thrice uses the term "truth" or "faithfulness" (40:10, 11 [MT 40:11, 12]), twice names *hesed* (40:10, 11 [MT 40:11, 12]), and twice locates his proclamation "in the great assembly" (40:9, 10 [MT 40:10, 11]).

The upshot of these verses is as follows: David gathers all those who love Yahweh (the great assembly, cf. 1:5, the congregation of the righteous) to declare how God has kept his promises to deliver the faithful and do justice against the wicked so as to establish his own *righteous* character, uphold the *truth* of his word, showing *lovingkindness* to those in his favor by accomplishing *salvation* on their behalf.

David himself is evidence of the truth of God's character because he is the king from Judah's line, a fulfillment of God's promise, and because he has experienced God's faithful lovingkindness and active righteousness in God's salvation of him from the hands of Saul. And David himself is also a type of the one promised to David, the seed whose throne will be established forever.

### 40:12–17 (MT 40:13–18), Deliverance and Dishonor

Having celebrated God's character in 40:9–11 (MT 40:10–12), David returns to the two reasons he needs God: he needs to be delivered from his own sin in 40:12–13 (MT 40:13–14), and his enemies want to kill him in 40:14–15 (MT 40:15–16).

David speaks of the way that sin surrounds and overwhelms him, catches and blinds him, covering and discouraging him in 40:12 (MT 40:13). His life is pervaded by sin, and as a result he cries out to the Lord for swift deliverance in 40:13 (MT 40:14).

David's statements in Ps 40:14–15 (MT 40:15–16) correspond closely to the words of Ps 35:25–26 (cf. 35:4, 21). This linkage joins with other features of Pss 34–41 to suggest a chiastic structure of this unit of Book 1 (see "Context" discussions at Pss 34, 35, and 40).

David prays that God would shame those who want to kill him in 40:14–15 (MT 40:15–16) and cause those who love God's salvation to rejoice in 40:16–17 (MT 40:17–18). Here again, there is a close correspondence between 40:16 (MT 40:17) and 35:27.

David closes Ps 40 with a confident assertion that though he is poor and needy, his Lord is mindful of him and will be his help and deliverer. Accordingly, David calls on Yahweh not to delay (40:17 [MT 40:18]).

David waited on Yahweh, and eventually the Lord delivered him from Saul. Jesus waited on Yahweh, and he passed through suffering to glory. Enthroned in Jerusalem, David organized worship in Jerusalem. Enthroned at the right hand, Jesus too is about the task of bringing glory to the Father, a task that will be completed in the New Jerusalem. David replaced Saul after Saul's sinful sacrifice. Jesus replaced the old covenant after its mediators and sacrifices proved to be insufficient for the salvation and perfection of God's people. David proclaimed the good news of God's character, a character that would be embodied in Jesus and proclaimed by him like no one else. David spoke of his own sin and enemies. Jesus took the sins of his people and bore the whole burden, those who opposed Jesus being the heirs and fulfillments of those who had opposed David. Like David, Jesus lived for God and his kingdom.

## Psalm 41

Overview and Structure of Psalm 41

Psalm 41 reflects the following chiastic structure:[160]

41:1 (MT 14:2), Blessed Is the One
    41:2 (MT 41:3), Yahweh Protects and Gives Life
        41:3 (MT 41:4), Yahweh Sustains on the Sickbed
            41:4 (MT 41:5), O Yahweh, Be Gracious to Me
                41:5 (MT 41:6), Those at Enmity
                    41:6 (MT 41:7), He Speaks Emptiness
                        41:7 (MT 41:8), Haters United
                    41:8 (MT 41:9), Word of Belial
                41:9 (MT 41:10), The Traitor
            41:10 (MT 41:11), O Yahweh, Be Gracious to Me
        41:11 (MT 41:12), The Enemy Does Not Triumph
    41:12 (MT 41:13), Yahweh Upholds and Causes to Stand
41:13 (MT 41:14), Blessed Be Yahweh

---

[160] For an alternative, unbalanced proposal, see Alden, "Chiastic Psalms 1–50," 25.

We will pursue the exposition of Ps 41 under the following subheads:

41:1–3 (MT 41:2–4), The Blessing of the Lord
41:4–9 (MT 41:5–10), The Curses of the Enemies
41:10–13 (MT 41:11–14), The Blessing of the Lord

SCRIPTURE

CSB

Author's translation

For the choir director. A psalm of David.

For the Preeminent One. A Psalm of David.

¹ Happy is one who is considerate of the poor;
the LORD will save him in a day of adversity.
² The LORD will keep him and preserve him;
he will be blessed in the land.
You will not give him over to the desire of his enemies.
³ The LORD will sustain him on his sickbed;
you will heal him on the bed where he lies.

⁴ I said, "LORD, be gracious to me;
heal me, for I have sinned against you."
⁵ My enemies speak maliciously about me:
"When will he die and be forgotten?"
⁶ When one of them comes to visit, he speaks deceitfully;
he stores up evil in his heart;
he goes out and talks.
⁷ All who hate me whisper together about me;
they plan to harm me.
⁸ "Something awful has overwhelmed him,
and he won't rise again from where he lies!"

¹ For the Preeminent One.
A Psalm of David.

² Blessed is the one who causes wisdom for the poor.
In the day of evil Yahweh will deliver him.

³ Yahweh will protect him and give him life;
he will be blessed in the land.
And you will not give him to the soul of those at enmity with him.

⁴ Yahweh will sustain him on a sickbed;
all his lying down you overturn in his sickness.

⁵ I said, "O Yahweh, be gracious to me;
heal my soul, for I have sinned against you."

⁶ Those at enmity with me speak evil of me,
"When will he die and his name perish?"

⁷ And if he goes to see, emptiness he speaks;
his heart gathers iniquity to it,
he goes to the outside, he speaks.

⁸ United against me they whisper, all my enemies;

<sup>9</sup> Even my friend in whom I trusted,
one who ate my bread,
has raised his heel against me.

<sup>10</sup> But you, Lord, be gracious to me and
raise me up;
then I will repay them.
<sup>11</sup> By this I know that you delight in
me:
my enemy does not shout in triumph
over me.
<sup>12</sup> You supported me because of my
integrity
and set me in your presence forever.

<sup>13</sup> Blessed be the Lord God of Israel,
from everlasting to everlasting.
Amen and amen.

against me they plot evil of me.

<sup>9</sup> "A word of Belial is poured out on
him,
and from where he lies he will not
again rise!"

<sup>10</sup> Even the man at peace with me, in
whom I trusted,
he who ate my bread, he made great
against me the heel.

<sup>11</sup> But you, O Yahweh, be gracious to
me,
and raise me up that I may
make things whole (i.e., make
recompense) with them.

<sup>12</sup> By this I know that you delight in
me:
that the one at enmity with me does
not raise a shout over me.

<sup>13</sup> And as for me, in my integrity you
uphold me,
and you cause me to stand before you
to the age.

<sup>14</sup> Blessed be Yahweh God of Israel!
From the age and unto the age, amen
and amen.

CONTEXT: VERBAL AND THEMATIC LINKS WITH SURROUNDING PSALMS

Psalm 41 closes off the unit that began in Ps 34. Psalm 34 celebrated God's exodus-style salvation of David, and Ps 41 celebrates the blessed man who causes wisdom for the poor (41:1 [MT 41:2]). The use of the term "blessed" (אשרי) in Ps 41:1 (MT 41:2) repeats the opening word of Ps 1, forming an *inclusio* around Book 1 of the Psalter. Psalm 41 confidently asserts that the Ps 2 enemies of the Ps 1 blessed man will not prevail over him (see "Exposition" for development of these ideas).

For the literary and structural relationships between the psalms of Book 1, see the introduction to the commentary and the "Context" section on the commentary to these psalms.

EXPOSITION

### 41:1–3 (MT 41:2–4), The Blessing of the Lord

Psalm 41 is addressed "for the preeminent one," and it is "A Psalm of David" (MT 41:1).

The first word of the body of Ps 41 is the first word of Ps 1, אַשְׁרֵי, "blessed" (41:1 [MT 41:2]; cf. Ps 1:1; 2:12; 32:1, 2; 33:12; 34:8 [MT 34:9]; 40:4 [MT 40:5]). The reuse of this term at the beginning of Ps 41 places bookends around Pss 1–41, points back to the beginning of the Psalter, and joins with other features of the context to mark a turning point in the book. The second term in Ps 41:1 (MT 41:2), מַשְׂכִּיל, rendered "cares for" by the CSB, also points back to the beginning of the Psalter, being the term used when the kings are summoned to "be wise" (CSB) in 2:10, הַשְׂכִּילוּ (cf. 14:2; 32:1; 41:1 [MT 41:2]; 32:8; 36:3 [MT 36:4]). I have rendered this line, "Blessed is the one who causes wisdom for the poor." This could be taken to mean that this blessed man causes the poor to be wise, or that he causes others in society to be wise, or perhaps skillful, toward the poor. Beyond considering or caring for the poor, the idea is that the blessed man causes wisdom as he cares for the poor.

Proverbs 19:17 uses the same term for the "poor" found in Ps 41:1 (MT 41:2) to declare that the one who is generous to the poor lends to Yahweh, and Prov 21:13 uses the term in the statement that the one who closes his ears to the cry of the poor will himself cry and not be heard (cf. Prov 14:31). The opposite is stated in the second line of Ps 41:1–3 (MT 41:2–4), when David describes the blessed man "who causes wisdom for the poor" being delivered by Yahweh in the day of evil, protected and given life, blessed in the land, not given over to those who hate him, sustained on the sickbed, and restored to health.

The one who "causes wisdom for the poor" helps those who cannot bribe him, cannot offer influential protection, and cannot pay back monetary aid. He helps the poor because of his regard for Yahweh. David likely has the same blessed man in view in Ps 41 that he spoke of in Ps 1—the future king the Lord promised to raise up from his line.[161] David speaks

---

[161] The flawed translation philosophy that will not allow third-person singulars ("he," "him," "his") because of an aversion to generic masculine forms in modern American usage of the English language results in the 2011 NIV changing every reference to this blessed man in Ps 41:1–3 (MT 41:2–4) to a third-person plural: "those who," "them," "their." Instead of rendering the text as it reads, leaving open the possibility that David speaks of the future king from his line, this translation philosophy conforms an ancient text to modern

here of that king honoring Yahweh in his wise dealing with the poor, and correspondingly Yahweh protects and delivers the king. David's own life and experiences inform his expectations for the one who is to come, so it is natural for him to speak in the first person in the statements that follow.

### 41:4-9 (MT 41:5-10), The Curses of the Enemies

Whereas in Ps 41:1-3 (MT 41:2-4) David spoke of the blessed man in the third person, in 41:4 (MT 41:5) he switches to speak of himself in the first person. David's expectation for the coming one is based on God's promise to him in 2 Sam 7, and the promise combines with the pattern of his own experience to add color and content to the anticipation.

Thus the Lord's sustenance and restoration of the blessed man from illness (41:1-3 [MT 41:2-4]) seems to spring from David's own experience of sin and sickness and his cry for Yahweh to heal him in 41:4 (MT 41:5).

As we have seen so often in Book 1 of the Psalter, when David is in difficulty he cries out to the Lord. David seems to connect his weakened position to his sin in 41:4 (MT 41:5). Meanwhile, whereas the Lord promised to make David's name great (2 Sam 7:9), his enemies want him to die so that his name will perish (Ps 41:5 [MT 41:6]). David cannot trust those who visit him in his sickness. They speak words that have no substance, their black hearts collect evidence of iniquity in an iniquitous way, and then when they leave David they speak evil of him (41:6 [MT 41:7]). His enemies unite against him, whispering and plotting evil against David (41:7 [MT 41:8]). The term to describe them as "united" is the one used to describe the kings and rulers gathered against Yahweh and his anointed in 2:1-3.

David depicts his enemies saying, "A word of Belial is poured out on him, and from where he lies he will not again rise!" (41:8 [MT 41:9]). The description of what David has suffered reflects a view of the world in which evil spirits are at work, and afflictions, sicknesses, and bad turns are associated with those dark powers in the heavenlies. David is suffering, and his enemies attribute that suffering to the influence of Belial in David's life. Instead of translating the text, which reflects ancient ways of thinking about the world, contemporary translations replace the ancient way of speaking with a modern one. Rather than let David tell

---

standards of political correctness, hiding from its readers the possibility that David speaks of the future king from his line.

us how his ancient enemies thought about things, modern translations put their explanation into modern categories. Thus the 2011 NIV has, "A vile disease has afflicted him" (cf. KJV), the CSB has, "Lethal poison has been poured into him," and the ESV has, "A deadly thing is poured out on him" (cf. NAS).

The animosity toward David extends even to those who owe him loyalty. Showing hospitality to someone, allowing them to eat your bread at your board, created obligations in the ancient world. Fealty and fidelity were owed to the chief who fed his kinsmen, retainers, and fighters. David describes the way that even one obligated on such terms defected to the opposition in 41:9 (MT 41:10). David describes this man making his heel great against him, which vividly depicts one side trying to stomp on the head of the other, recalling the word about the seed of the woman having a bruised heel when the serpent got a bruised head (Gen 3:15).

### 41:10–13 (MT 41:11–14), The Blessing of the Lord

David prefaced his description of the opposition of his enemies with a call for Yahweh to be gracious to him in 41:4 (MT 41:5), and he uses the same language at the beginning of his confession of confidence that God will bless him in 41:10 (MT 41:11).

David calls on Yahweh in Ps 41:10 (MT 41:11) to be gracious to him, and he wants that grace to take the form of Yahweh raising him up from the sickness he suffers (cf. 41:4–5, 8 [MT 41:5–6, 9]). Once raised up, David wants to establish *shalom* by doing justice against those opposed to Yahweh and his messiah, whose plots and thoughts he described in 41:5–9 (MT 41:6–10).

In 41:10 (MT 41:11) David states that the Lord raising him up to repay his enemies will be proof to him that Yahweh delights in him (cf. 40:6, 8 [MT 40:7, 9]). Yahweh's pleasure in David will prevent enemy exultation over the Lord and his anointed.

David is a sinner, and in 41:4 (MT 41:5) he confessed his sin and prayed for God to be gracious to him. That establishes the integrity he claims in 41:12 (MT 41:13), and on the foundation of that integrity he is confident that Yahweh will uphold him, keeping his promise.

At the end of Ps 41:12 (MT 41:13) David speaks of his confidence that the Lord will cause him to stand before himself forever. This is true of David, saved by grace through faith. And it is also true of the king promised to David, whose throne the Lord swore he would establish forever

(2 Sam 7:13). Once again we see an interweaving of David's own experience with his expectation regarding the road his descendant will walk.

David concludes Ps 41 with a benediction that serves as the punctuation mark at the end of Book 1 of the Psalms (41:13 [MT 41:14]; cf. the benedictions that conclude Psalms 72, 89, 106, and Psalms 146–150, and see in the introduction to this commentary, table 2, "The doxologies at the end of each book"). Like the others, this benediction (1) *blesses* (2) *Yahweh* (3) *forever* and (4) concludes with *Amen*.

BRIDGE

Psalm 41 looks forward to the coming king from David's line who will cause wisdom for the poor, against whom the enemies will gather just as they gathered against David, and whom Yahweh will raise up to establish *shalom* by doing justice against the wicked. This way of approaching Ps 41 is validated by the fact that Jesus claimed that Ps 41:9 (MT 41:10) was fulfilled when Judas took the morsel of bread from him at the last supper then departed to betray him (John 13:18, 21–30). Similarly, Zechariah father of the Baptist quotes Ps 41:13 (MT 41:14) as he celebrates the fulfillment of the promises to David (Luke 1:69) in Luke 1:68.

Jesus will cause wisdom for the poor, and he himself is the blessed man who blesses the poor (Luke 6:20). Jesus bruised his heel as he crushed the serpent's head. Jesus has been raised from the dead and will recompense his enemies. Jesus will prompt all God's people to say,

> "Blessed be Yahweh God of Israel!
> From the age and unto the age,
> amen and amen" (41:13 [MT 41:14]).

# BOOK 2

The use of the term "blessed" (אשרי) in Pss 1:1 and 2:12 forms an *ashrey inclusio* around Pss 1 and 2. This term, "blessed" (אשרי), also appears in the first verse of Ps 41, the last psalm of Book 1, forming the *ashrey inclusio* around Book 1 of the Psalter.

The first psalm of Book 2, Ps 42, also hearkens back to Ps 1. In Ps 1, the blessed man is like a tree by streams of water (פלגי מים, 1:3), and in Ps 42 the son of Korah likens himself to a deer longing for streams of water (אפיקי מים, 42:1 [MT 42:2]). The water in Ps 1 is a metaphor for the life-giving Torah of Yahweh, and the water in Ps 42, for which the deer longs, ripples in comparison with the psalmist's longing for the living God himself.

The last psalm in Book 2, Ps 72, also reaches back to Ps 1, as again the term "blessed" (here the verbal form אשר) appears, forming another *ashrey inclusio* with Ps 1, when the nations call the king from David's line blessed in 72:17. This link suggests that the nations herald the Ps 72 king from David's line as the Ps 1 blessed man and kiss the Ps 2 anointed of Yahweh.

As with Book 1, Books 2 and 3 are framed by a literary *inclusio*, as they begin and end with psalms of the sons of Korah (Pss 42–49, 84–89). Within the outer ring of the Korah psalms are psalms of Asaph (Pss 50, 73–83), with Davidic psalms in the middle (Pss 51–72). For further observations on the groupings of the psalms in Books 2 and 3 and the literary structures these groupings form, see the discussions in the introduction to the commentary above and the "Context" sections in the commentary on the individual psalms below.

## Psalms 42–43

OVERVIEW AND STRUCTURE OF PSALMS 42–43

Psalms 42–49 are all superscripted as "of the sons of Korah," Ps 43 being the only exception. Because Ps 43 has no superscription and shares a refrain with Ps 42 (cf. 42:5, 11; 43:5 [MT 42:6, 12]), it appears that they are to be read together.[162] This impression is strengthened by the repetition of 42:9 (MT 42:10) in 43:2. The joining of Pss 42 and 43 at the opening of Book 2 matches the joining of Pss 1 and 2 at the opening of Book 1.

Whereas the name of Yahweh has been in frequent use in Book 1, in the move to Book 2 it is used far less often. It occurs in Ps 42:8 (MT 42:9) but then not again until 46:7 (MT 46:8).[163] The name Yahweh does not appear in Pss 43, 44, or 45.

In Pss 42–43 the psalmist is away from Jerusalem (42:6 [MT 42:7]), taunted by enemies (42:3, 10 [MT 42:4, 11]), oppressed by enemies (42:9 [MT 42:10]; 43:2), depressed of soul (42:5, 11 [MT 42:6, 12]; 43:5), and thirsty for God (42:1 [MT 42:2]). This desperate condition does not prompt the psalmist to abandon God but to grope for him.

We will pursue the exposition of Pss 42–43 under the following subheads:

> 42:1–5 (MT 42:1–6), Longing for God
> 42:6–11 (MT 42:7–12), Why Has God Forgotten?
> 43:1–5, Send Out Light and Truth

SCRIPTURE

CSB

Author's translation

### Psalm 42

### Psalm 42

For the choir director. A *Maskil* of the sons of Korah.

¹ For the Preeminent One.
A *Maskil* of the sons of Korah.
² As a deer longs for streams of water,
so my soul longs for you, O God.
³ My soul thirsts for God, for the God
of the living,
When shall I come and appear before
God?

¹ As a deer longs for flowing streams,
so I long for you, God.
² I thirst for God, the living God.

---

[162] For a chiastic proposal that stretches across the two psalms, see Alden, "Chiastic Psalms 1–50," 25–26.

[163] For discussion, see Wardlaw, *Elohim within the Psalms*.

When can I come and appear before
   God?
³ My tears have been my food day and
   night,
while all day long people say to me,
"Where is your God?"
⁴ I remember this as I pour out my
   heart:
how I walked with many,
leading the festive procession to the
   house of God,
with joyful and thankful shouts.

⁵ Why, my soul, are you so dejected?
Why are you in such turmoil?
Put your hope in God, for I will still
   praise him,
my Savior and my God.
⁶ I am deeply depressed;
therefore I remember you from the
   land of Jordan
and the peaks of Hermon, from Mount
   Mizar.
⁷ Deep calls to deep in the roar of your
   waterfalls;
all your breakers and your billows
   have swept over me.
⁸ The Lᴏʀᴅ will send his faithful love
   by day;
his song will be with me in the night—
a prayer to the God of my life.

⁹ I will say to God, my rock,
"Why have you forgotten me?
Why must I go about in sorrow
because of the enemy's oppression?"
¹⁰ My adversaries taunt me,
as if crushing my bones,
while all day long they say to me,
"Where is your God?"
¹¹ Why, my soul, are you so dejected?
Why are you in such turmoil?
Put your hope in God, for I will still
   praise him,
my Savior and my God.

⁴ My tears were bread to me, day and
   night,
when they said to me all the day,
   "Where is your God?"
⁵ These I will remember and pour out
   my soul upon myself,
that I passed over with the multitude,
as I walked them in procession to the
   house of God,
with the voice of the ringing cry and
   thanksgiving,
a multitude keeping festival.
⁶ Why do you sink down, my soul,
and you are in an uproar within me?
Wait for God, for I shall again praise
   him,
salvations of his presence.

⁷ My God, upon myself my soul sinks
   down,
therefore I remember you
from the land of Jordan and the
   Hermons, from Mount Mizar.
⁸ Deep to deep calls, to the sound of
   your cataracts,
all your breakers and your waves
   have passed over me.
⁹ By day Yahweh commands his
   lovingkindness,
and in the night his song is with me,
a prayer to the God of my life.
¹⁰ I will say to God my high ridge,
   "Why have you forgotten me?
Why do I go being dark, in the
   oppression of the one at enmity?"
¹¹ By a shattering in my bones, my
   adversaries reproach me,
when they say to me all day, "Where
   is your God?"
¹² Why do you sink down, my soul,
and why are you in uproar within
   me?
Wait for God, for I shall again praise
   him,
salvations of my presence and my God.

## Psalm 43 | Psalm 43

| Psalm 43 | Psalm 43 |
|---|---|
| ¹ Vindicate me, God, and champion my cause against an unfaithful nation; rescue me from the deceitful and unjust person. ² For you are the God of my refuge. Why have you rejected me? Why must I go about in sorrow because of the enemy's oppression? | ¹ Judge me, O God, and dispute my dispute against a nation not lovingkind; from a man of deceit and malice deliver me. ² For you, my God, are my stronghold, why have you rejected me? Why being dark do I go about in the oppression of the one at enmity? |

¹ Vindicate me, God, and champion my
  cause
against an unfaithful nation;
rescue me from the deceitful and
  unjust person.
² For you are the God of my refuge.
Why have you rejected me?
Why must I go about in sorrow
because of the enemy's oppression?

³ Send your light and your truth; let
  them lead me.
Let them bring me to your holy
  mountain,
to your dwelling place.
⁴ Then I will come to the altar of God,
to God, my greatest joy.
I will praise you with the lyre,
God, my God.

⁵ Why, my soul, are you so dejected?
Why are you in such turmoil?
Put your hope in God, for I will still
  praise him,
my Savior and my God.

¹ Judge me, O God, and dispute my
  dispute against a nation not
  lovingkind;
from a man of deceit and malice
  deliver me.
² For you, my God, are my stronghold,
  why have you rejected me?
Why being dark do I go about in the
  oppression of the one at enmity?
³ Send your light and your truth.
They will lead me!
They will bring me to the mountain
  of your holiness, and to your
  tabernacles.
⁴ And I will go to the altar of God,
to the God of the gladness of my
  rejoicing,
and I will praise you on the lyre, O
  God, my God.
⁵ Why do you sink down, my soul,
and why are you in uproar within
  me?
Wait for God, for I shall again praise
  him,
salvations of my face and my God.

CONTEXT: VERBAL AND THEMATIC LINKS WITH SURROUNDING PSALMS

Noting the groupings of psalms by superscription, scholars have suggested that Books 2 and 3 of the Psalter reflect the following chiastic structure:[164]

Psalms 42–49, Sons of Korah
    Psalm 50, Asaph
        Psalms 51–72, David
    Psalms 73–83, Asaph
Psalms 84–89, Sons of Korah

---

[164] See, e.g., Mitchell, *Message of the Psalter*, 71; Wardlaw, *Elohim within the Psalms*, 60.

In addition to this, we can observe a balanced movement of thought in Pss 42–49 that reflects a chiastic structure as follows:

Psalms 42–43, Why So Downcast?
    Psalm 44, Remnant
        Psalm 45, King
        Psalm 46, City
    Psalms 47–48, Praise
Psalm 49, Wisdom

At the center of this unit stand celebrations of the wedding of the king from David's line (Ps 45) and the eschatological city (Ps 46). The faithful believing remnant cries out for help in Ps 44, and all nations are summoned to praise in Pss 47–48. The downcast soul of Pss 42–43 stands across from the confident wisdom of Ps 49.

EXPOSITION

### 42:1–5 (MT 42:2–6), Longing for God

Whereas thirty-eight of the forty-one Psalms in Book 1 referenced David (only Pss 1, 2, 10, and 33 lack superscriptions), Book 2 opens with a series of psalms "of the sons of Korah" (42–49, only 43 lacks a superscription). The sons of Korah appear to have been among "the men David put in charge of the music in the LORD's temple after the ark came to rest there" (1 Chr 6:31, 37, CSB [MT 6:16, 22]). At the end of Book 1, particularly in Ps 40, it appeared that David had at last been delivered (40:1 [MT 40:2]). The transition to psalms of the sons of Korah suggests that the Psalter tracks with the narrative of Samuel in an impressionistic sort of way. At the end of Book 1 of the Psalms David has at last been enthroned in Jerusalem, the ark has been brought into the city (cf. 2 Sam 5–6), and now those whom David appointed over the worship at the Lord's house take up their songs in Pss 42–49. Being a psalm of Asaph, Ps 50 is similar (cf. 1 Chr 6:39).

Psalms 42 and 43 are written from the perspective of one who formerly worshiped the Lord in Jerusalem (42:4 [MT 42:5]) but who has now been removed from the city (42:6 [MT 42:7]). That removal would appear to be related to the defeat spoken of in Ps 44, and the remedy will be the coming of the king in Ps 45, followed by the apocalyptic hymn to the eschatological city in Ps 46, prompting the celebrations of Pss 47–49.

The psalmist's removal from Jerusalem causes him to pant for God the way a deer pants for water in a drought (42:1 [MT 42:2]; cf. Joel 1:20). Likening God's presence to water recalls Ps 1, where the mediation of God's presence through the Torah is similarly likened to water (1:3). Here, though, it is not private Bible study but public worship for which the psalmist longs. He wants to "appear before God" (42:2 [MT 42:3]), by rejoining the festal throng (42:4 [MT 42:5]), led by God's light and truth to God's dwelling place to worship at God's altar (43:3–4).

From Ps 42:1–2 (MT 42:2–3) we see that the psalmist recognizes that God is what will satisfy his soul's thirst. He knows that the longings in his heart cry out to be watered from an infinite reservoir. We can compare these longings to the hunger pangs we feel, and put in those terms, the psalmist wants food that will fill his stomach. There are certain foods that, even if I eat a lot of them, I do not find filling. If I eat them for lunch at noon I am going to want a snack at two in the afternoon. Hot dogs are not filling. Pasta is not filling. Soup is not filling. The psalmist doesn't want spiritual food that isn't filling.

This dynamic also works at the level of our loves and pleasures: God created us to be pleased by things he means for us to enjoy in accordance with his instructions. If we try to enjoy one of God's blessings but refuse to follow God's instructions, we will find that the blessing wants to rise up and become a slavemaster.

The psalmist wants God because he knows that only God will satisfy his yearnings, and the details of this psalm indicate that his particular desire is to experience God in public worship (42:4 [MT 42:5]).

The depth of emotion felt is on display in the day and night tears described in Ps 42:3 (MT 42:4). Not experiencing God, longing to be satisfied on God, all the psalmist has are his tears. These tears show his faithfulness. He is neither joining with those who taunt him about God's absence, "Where is your God?" (42:3 [MT 42:4]), nor is he resorting to some sinful or idolatrous source of comfort.

In the midst of his thirsty longing and weeping (42:1–3 [MT 42:2–4]), this son of Korah pours out his soul remembering the way things were in 42:4 (MT 42:5). He relishes the memory of the way he "crossed over with the multitude," the verb "crossed over" (עבר) evoking the exodus. He may have participated in the great worship celebration when the ark was brought into Jerusalem (2 Sam 6), or perhaps he recalls the regularly celebrated feasts as he describes a slow walk with a throng of people "to the house of God," replete "with the voice of the ringing cry and thanksgiving, a multitude keeping festival" (42:4 [MT 42:5]).

The highpoint for the psalmist was that festal procession, being with the people of God, those who shared his view of the world, his approach to life, his values, and lifting his voice with them in celebration of the great king, as instructed, in Jerusalem. The lowpoint is where he is now: far from Jerusalem, with enemies whose voices taunt him about the absence of his God, and with only memories of the time when all was right with the world.

The psalmist's reflections bring him to question and admonish himself in 42:5 (MT 42:6), and this line becomes a refrain as it is revisited in 42:11 (MT 42:12) and 43:5. The psalmist has told us why he is upset, so we know the answer to his question in 42:5 (MT 42:6), which I have rendered, "Why do you sink down, my soul, and you are in an uproar within me?" The answer the psalmist gives to his own question turns his attention away from the reasons he is sad and focuses his gaze on a future hope guaranteed by God himself: "Wait for God, for I shall again praise him, salvations of his presence."

The psalmist admonishes himself to wait for God because he believes that God will keep his promises to judge the wicked, save the righteous, and make the world pervasively blessed. He believes that God will act on his behalf, and he believes that he will again join with all those of like mind in praise of God.

English translations typically smooth the end of 42:5 (MT 42:6), but the MT text as it stands can be understood: the "salvations of his presence" would be exactly what this saint needs: banished from Jerusalem, longing for God, in the midst of enemies asking where his God is. God's presence would guarantee his deliverance, accomplish saving acts, and restore his lost joy.

### 42:6–11 (MT 42:7–12), Why Has God Forgotten?

The psalmist seems to have worked to a resolution in 42:5 (MT 42:6), but his soul has not risen from its sunken state. This is the way life works, and the fact that the psalmist is dealing with it too is tremendously encouraging. Arriving at the right answer, knowing theological truth, as the psalmist obviously does, has neither altered his physical circumstances nor lifted him from the emotional low. So what does he do? He keeps right on praying. He persists. He still does not resort to idolatry or sinful sources of comfort, and he still refuses to join the adversaries who have rejected the Lord.

The same phrase used in 42:5 (MT 42:6) about the soul being sunk down reappears in 42:6 (MT 42:7) because the psalmist's soul is still sunk down. The psalmist models how to respond when the darkness doesn't lift and the circumstances don't change. We see there in 42:6 (MT 42:7) that he still isn't in Jerusalem, he still isn't with the festal throng. Instead, he is in "the land of Jordan and the Hermons, from Mount Mizar." This appears to refer to the source of the river Jordan near the Sea of Galilee. Mount Mizar may be one of the peaks in the range that includes Mount Hermon. He is still there, and his soul is still sunk down. He says to the Lord: "therefore I remember you" (42:6 [MT 42:7]).

If our emotions and circumstances do not change when we have sought the Lord through the Bible and prayer, we can be tempted to conclude that doing so doesn't work, that theology really won't fix our problems, that we need something else, perhaps something more practical. Those conclusions fail to see that the quick fix of the change of circumstance or emotion may not be what God has for us. He may mean to bless us through the long night of yearning, even if that long night lasts years. The question confronting us is whether the one for whom we long is worth the wait.

Psalm 42:7 (MT 42:8) indicates that God met the psalmist in his pain and exile. He does not specify what the deeps are that call to one another in the sound of God's waterfalls, so the statement is tantalizing. It would appear that as the Jordan River rushes through the mountainous region the rolling and tossing of the water prompts the psalmist to reflect on the depths of the waters and the depths of his soul. He then speaks of the breakers and waves passing over him, and it may be that he reflects on God's work in creation seen in the tumultuous waters.[165] The uproar in the waters, with their depths and currents and mysteries, resonates with the depths of his soul and the currents and mysteries there. It may be, too, that in speaking of God's breakers and waves passing over him he

---

[165] Psalm 42:7b (MT 42:8b) is quoted verbatim in Jonah 2:3 (MT 2:4). Assuming that the son of Korah who wrote Ps 42 lived during David's reign (or shortly after), Jonah can be understood to identify with this psalmist who has been separated from Jerusalem.

acknowledges that God's justice has brought upon him the consequences of his own sin.[166]

Such a thought process would lead to the assertions in Ps 42:8 (MT 42:9) about Yahweh commanding his steadfast love through the day resulting in a song to him in the night. Day and night the psalmist weeps in 42:3 (MT 42:4), and day and night he knows God's lovingkindness and worships him in 42:8 (MT 42:9). His circumstances have not changed, his emotions are not soaring, and his enemies have not gone away, and yet he experiences God and can sing to him. God will not abandon us in our deepest woe. The rising of the sun to make day proclaims that he still commands his lovingkindness to order the universe. Thus we sing through the night of weeping.

The psalmist is not, however, merely accepting the way things are. He perseveres. Thus in 42:9 (MT 42:10) he cries out to God, asking why he has been forgotten, why he goes about with a darkened countenance because of the enemy's oppression. From what he has said and will say in this psalm, he knows he is not forgotten. But his circumstances and emotions are not what he wants them to be. In spite of what he knows he feels forgotten, so he cries out honestly to the Lord.

The enemies repeat their question from Ps 42:3 (MT 42:4) "Where is your God?" in 42:10 (MT 42:11), and for the psalmist, hearing it is like having his bones shattered. In 42:11 (MT 42:12) he returns to the question and admonition of 42:5 (MT 42:6): asking himself why he is sunk down in soul and in uproar, and admonishing himself to wait for God, believing that his circumstances and emotions will change when God brings about salvation by his presence.

### 43:1–5, Send Out Light and Truth

In response to his discouragement and removal from Jerusalem, the psalmist has communicated his longing for God as he remembered the way things were (42:1–4 [MT 42:2–5]), he has remembered God, contemplated the waters and the Lord's steadfast love, and asked why he has been forgotten (42:6–10 [MT 42:7–11]), and now in Ps 43 he makes requests. His

---

[166] The psalmist speaking of the waters as God's wrath against his sin would be another point of contact with Jonah's experience, further explaining his quotation of Ps 42:7b (MT 42:8b) in Jonah 2:3 (MT 2:4).

first request in 43:1 is for vindication, and the second in 43:3–4 is for God to send out light and truth that will lead him home.

The psalmist has spoken of God's salvation as his hope in the refrain at 42:5 and 42:11 (MT 42:6, 12), and this hope takes the form of the request for God to judge him in 43:1, which is a plea for vindication. He wants God to take up his dispute and render judgment for him against those not marked by God's lovingkindness but by malice and deceit.

He insists in Ps 43:2 that God is his stronghold, maintaining his rejection of idolatry, and asks why God has rejected him. He then repeats the question asked in 42:9 (MT 42:10) as to why he must go about with a darkened countenance under the enemy's oppression.

If God answers the request made in 43:3 and sends out his light and truth, it will show that God is not absent (42:3, 10 [MT 42:4, 11]), brighten the psalmist's darkened countenance (42:9 [MT 42:10]; 43:2), lift up his sunken soul (42:5, 6, 11 [MT 42:6, 7, 12]), defeat his enemies by vindicating him (43:1), and lead him back to Jerusalem (43:3). This will enable him to ascend the mountain of God's holiness, approach his dwelling places, and worship at God's altar (43:3b–43:4). Doing so is what he longed for when he spoke of appearing before God in 42:2 (MT 42:3).

When this son of Korah describes God as "the deity of the gladness of [his] rejoicing" in 43:4, we understand why his soul longed for God as the deer pants for streams of water (42:1 [MT 42:2]). He desires to praise God in public, in accordance with Mosaic instructions, keeping the feasts (42:4 [MT 42:5]), and he wants to do so with the music of the lyre (43:4).

The return to the refrain from 42:5 and 42:11 (MT 42:6, 12) in 43:5 shows that these requests had not been answered when these psalms were written. The son of Korah had not yet experienced God's intervention to address his physical circumstances, nor had his heavy soul been lightened. He is still waiting on God, still looking forward to praising God as he has in the past, still waiting for God to save him.

The triumph of God for which he longs is yet future in Ps 44, but the one who will bring it about, the king from David's line, is heralded in Ps 45, and then what appears to be the final salvation of Jerusalem is celebrated in Ps 46. It would appear, then, that the resolution of the psalmist's difficulties awaits the coming of the promised king, the salvation he will bring to God's people through the defeat of his enemies, and the kingdom of God he will establish where all God's people will worship.

In Pss 42 and 43 the sons of Korah model how believers should respond when the darkness doesn't lift, and we can enumerate the steps the psalmist takes:

1. He thirsted for God as the source of satisfaction, implicitly rejecting other comforts and allegiances (42:1–2 [MT 42:2–3]).
2. He remembered the joy he experienced in public worship (42:4 [MT 42:5]).
3. He remembered God (42:6 [MT 42:7]).
4. He pondered the depths of the waters and the waves of God's justice (42:7 [MT 42:8]).
5. He recognized God's steadfast love in the day and sang God's praises at night (42:8 [MT 42:9]).
6. He cried out to God asking why? (42:9 [MT 42:10]; 43:2).
7. He cried out to God for vindication (43:1).
8. He asked God to send out his light and truth to lead him home (43:3).
9. He promised to worship God in accordance with the Bible's instructions (43:4).
10. He admonished himself for his sunken soul and called himself to wait, trusting that again he would have the joy of worship (42:5, 11 [MT 42:6, 12]; 43:5).

The psalmist did not resort to sinful sources of comfort. He did not indicate that he needed something other than God. His whole hope was squarely based on what God had promised. God's final salvation would bring the deliverance he sought, and the psalmist resolved to hope for that.

BRIDGE

Psalms 42–43 assume a situation where David the king has brought the ark into Jerusalem, but at the time of writing the psalmist was not enjoying the worship of God in Jerusalem under the Davidic king. In conjunction with Pss 44–46, the psalmist longed for the salvation God would accomplish through his king.

In view of the way that Pss 42–44 resolve in the song of the king in Ps 45, the request for God to send out his light and his truth in Ps 43:3 might partake of the desire for the light that comes after the darkness of God's justice elsewhere (e.g., Isa 8:22–9:7; Mal 4:2; 2 Sam 23:3–4; cf. Luke 1:78).

The request, then, finds its answer in the one who comes as light (John 1:4–5, 9; 8:12) and truth (John 14:6).

Jesus has inaugurated the salvation for which the sons of Korah longed, but that salvation has not yet been consummated. As a result, believers today will find themselves feeling emotions and experiencing circumstances analogous to those described in Pss 42–43. When the darkness does not lift, the psalmist models faithful action steps for God's people: waiting for God, believing we will again praise him.

We follow the example of those who died in faith, not yet having received the promises, but greeting them from afar (Heb 11:13, 39). And James tells us that the prophets set an example of suffering and patience for us to follow (Jas 5:10–11), reminding us of Job's steadfastness while God's hidden purposes are realized in compassion and mercy.

## Psalm 44

Overview and Structure of Psalm 44

Whereas Pss 1–43 have largely reflected the prayers of an individual speaker, first-person plurals dominate Ps 44. The individual speaking in this psalm lifts his voice for the believing community as a whole. The only singulars in Ps 44 appear in 44:6 and 44:15 (MT 44:7; 44:16), the latter standing at the center of the psalm's chiastic structure.

The defeat that resulted in the speaker of Pss 42–43 being separated from Jerusalem (42:4, 6 [MT 42:5, 7]; 43:3), taunted by enemies (42:3, 10 [MT 42:4, 11]), and sunk down in soul (42:5, 11 [MT 42:6, 12]; 43:5) appears to prompt Ps 44 as well. The speaker of Pss 42 and 43 spoke for himself as an individual, and in Ps 44 he speaks for the faithful remnant. The individual's circumstances in Pss 42–43 are shared by the remnant in Ps 44: the community has been scattered among the nations (44:11 [MT 44:12]), is shamed by the taunts of its enemies (44:13–16 [MT 44:14–17]), and the refrain about the cast down soul of the psalmist in Pss 42 and 43 is extended to the community in 44:25 (MT 44:26), "For our soul sinks down to dust." Pss 42–44 all speak of the "soul" (נפש) being "sunk (or cast) down" (שׁיח).

Everything said by the speaker of Ps 44 indicates that he and those aligned with him belong to the believing remnant. He insists that God's mighty deeds of the past have been remembered (44:1–3 [MT 44:2–4]), prompting in turn praise for Yahweh and trust not in their own power but in his might (44:4–8 [MT 44:5–9]). The remembrance and reliance set the stage for the psalmist to object to the way Yahweh has rejected his people, a rejection evidenced both by their defeat before their enemies (44:9–12 [MT 44:10–13]) and the taunts of those enemies (44:13–16 [MT 44:14–17]). The psalmist maintains that the covenant has not been broken (44:17–19 [MT 44:18–20]) and bewails the fact that though they have not committed idolatry the adversary slaughters them like sheep (44:20–22 [MT 44:21–23]). The psalmist's ongoing faith in Yahweh prompts him to cry out for help on the basis of Yahweh's steadfast love (44:23–26 [MT 44:24-27]).

Psalm 44 reflects the following chiastic structure:

44:1–3 (MT 44:2–4), God's Past Help Recounted
    44:4–8 (MT 44:5–9), Trust in and Praise for God
        44:9–12 (MT 44:10–13), Rejected and Sold
            44:13–16 (MT 44:14–17), A Proverb among the Nations
        44:17–19 (MT 44:18–20), Crushed though Faithful
    44:20–22 (MT 44:21–23), Sheep to Slaughter
44:23–26 (MT 44:24–27), God's Present Help Sought

We will pursue the exposition of Ps 44 under the following subheads:

    44:1–8 (MT 44:2–9), Present Trust Based on Past Help
    44:9–16 (MT 44:10–17), Cursed, Rejected, and Mocked
    44:17–26 (MT 44:18–27), Present Faithfulness Based on Future Hope

### SCRIPTURE

| CSB | Author's translation |
|---|---|
| For the choir director. A *Maskil* of the sons of Korah. | [1] For the Preeminent One. Of the sons of Korah. A *Maskil*. |
| [1] God, we have heard with our ears— our ancestors have told us— the work you accomplished in their days, in days long ago: | [2] O God, with our ears we have heard, our fathers have recounted to us the deed you did in their day, in days of old. |
| [2] In order to plant them, you displaced the nations by your hand; in order to settle them, | [3] You, your hand dispossessed the nations, and them you planted; you crushed the peoples, and them you sent out. |

you brought disaster on the peoples.
³ For they did not take the land by
their sword—
their arm did not bring them victory—
but by your right hand, your arm,
and the light of your face,
because you were favorable toward
them.

⁴ You are my King, my God,
who ordains victories for Jacob.
⁵ Through you we drive back our foes;
through your name we trample our
enemies.
⁶ For I do not trust in my bow,
and my sword does not bring me
victory.
⁷ But you give us victory over our foes
and let those who hate us be
disgraced.
⁸ We boast in God all day long;
we will praise your name forever.
*Selah*
⁹ But you have rejected and humiliated
us;
you do not march out with our armies.
¹⁰ You make us retreat from the foe,
and those who hate us
have taken plunder for themselves.
¹¹ You hand us over to be eaten like
sheep
and scatter us among the nations.
¹² You sell your people for nothing;
you make no profit from selling them.
¹³ You make us an object of reproach
to our neighbors,
a source of mockery and ridicule to
those around us.
¹⁴ You make us a joke among the
nations,
a laughingstock among the peoples.
¹⁵ My disgrace is before me all day
long,
and shame has covered my face,

⁴ For by their sword they did not
dispossess the land,
and their arm did not cause them
salvation,
but your right hand and your arm and
the light of your face,
for you were pleased with them.

⁵ You are he, my king, O God:
command salvations for Jacob!
⁶ By you we gore our adversaries;
in your name we trample those who
rise up against us.
⁷ For not in my bow do I trust,
and my sword does not cause
salvation for me.
⁸ For you caused salvation for us from
our adversaries,
and those who hate us you have
caused to be put to shame.
⁹ In God we boast all the day,
and your name to the age we will
thank. *Selah.*

¹⁰ Surely you have rejected us and
humiliated us,
and you will not go out with our
armies.
¹¹ You turned us back from the
adversary,
and those who hate us plunder for
themselves.
¹² You gave us as sheep of food,
and among the nations you have
scattered us.
¹³ You sold your people at no wealth,
and you do not make great their price.

¹⁴ You made us a reproach to our
neighbors,
a derision and mockery to those
around us.
¹⁵ You made us a proverb [a ruler's
phrase] among the nations,
a shaking of the head among the
nations.

¹⁶ because of the taunts of the scorner and reviler,
because of the enemy and avenger.

¹⁷ All this has happened to us,
but we have not forgotten you
or betrayed your covenant.
¹⁸ Our hearts have not turned back;
our steps have not strayed from your path.
¹⁹ But you have crushed us in a haunt of jackals
and have covered us with deepest darkness.
²⁰ If we had forgotten the name of our God
and spread out our hands to a foreign god,
²¹ wouldn't God have found this out,
since he knows the secrets of the heart?
²² Because of you we are being put to death all day long;
we are counted as sheep to be slaughtered.

²³ Wake up, Lord! Why are you sleeping?
Get up! Don't reject us forever!
²⁴ Why do you hide
and forget our affliction and oppression?
²⁵ For we have sunk down to the dust;
our bodies cling to the ground.
²⁶ Rise up! Help us!
Redeem us because of your faithful love.

¹⁶ All the day my humiliation is before me,
and the shame of my face covers me,
¹⁷ from the voice of the one reproaching and the one reviling,
from the presence of the one at enmity and the avenger.

¹⁸ All this has come on us,
and we have neither forgotten you
nor been false to your covenant.
¹⁹ Our heart has not turned back,
nor our steps inclined from your path;
²⁰ but you crushed us in the place of jackals,
and you covered over us with the shadow of death.

²¹ If we have forgotten your name, O our God,
and spread out our hands to a foreign god,
²² would not God search this out?
For he knows the hidden things of the heart.
²³ For because of you we are killed all the day:
we are reckoned as sheep for slaughter.

²⁴ Awake! Why do you sleep, my Lord?
Wake up! Do not reject us to the end.
²⁵ Why do you cause your face to be hidden
and forget our affliction and our oppression?
²⁶ For our soul sinks down to dust;
our belly cleaves to the land.
²⁷ Arise, O help for us,
and redeem us on account of your lovingkindness.

CONTEXT: VERBAL AND THEMATIC LINKS WITH SURROUNDING PSALMS

The desperate situation of the individual in Pss 42–43 becomes the common experience of the faithful remnant in Ps 44. That remnant looks forward to the king who is the subject of Ps 45 and the eschatological Jerusalem God establishes in Ps 46.

Exposition

### 44:1–8 (MT 44:2–9), Present Trust Based on Past Help

In Ps 44:1–3 (MT 44:2–4) the psalmist speaks for those whose fathers have obeyed Deut 6 and taught their children the Torah. These fathers told their sons the story of Yahweh's mighty act of redemption at the exodus (44:1 [MT 44:2]) followed by the conquest of the land. It was Yahweh's outstretched arm and strong hand that accomplished these feats, and like a vine or a tree with well-watered roots, he planted his people in the land (44:2 [MT 44:3]; cf. Exod 15:17; 2 Sam 7:10; Isa 5:1–7; Ps 80:8 [MT 80:9]).

Using language familiar from Deuteronomy and Joshua, the psalmist asserts that the Canaanites were not "dispossessed" by the strong arm or sharp sword of Israel but by Yahweh's: "your right hand and your arm and the light of your face," all powered by Yahweh's delight in his people (Ps 44:3 [MT 44:4]). The mention of the light of Yahweh's face recalls the blessing of Num 6:24–26 and the glory of his life-giving, enemy-conquering, world-blessing presence.

The words of Torah on the heart of God's people in Deut 6:6 would found and buttress the monotheistic theology and covenant love for Yahweh in Deut 6:4–5, and that is exactly how the rehearsal of Yahweh's saving power in Ps 44:1–3 (MT 44:2–4) functions in 44:4–8 (MT 44:5–9). God's acts for his people prompt the devoted confession of allegiance and cry for help in 44:4 (MT 44:5). This psalmist is confident that what Yahweh commands comes to pass, so he calls on him to "command salvation for Jacob" (44:4 [MT 44:5]).

Often in the Old Testament military prowess will be spoken of in terms of wild oxen who establish dominance by means of their horns (Num 23:22; 24:8), and in Daniel a king is depicted as a ram with a strong horn and the ability to trample foes underhoof (Dan 8:5–7). Such imagery appears in Ps 44:5 (MT 44:6) as the psalmist sings, "By you we gore our adversaries; in your name we trample those who rise up against us." The psalmist here uses the image of the alpha male establishing dominance in the herd to say that by God's power Israel defeats and subjugates her enemies. It is noteworthy that whereas the psalmist speaks of God's "name" at several points in Ps 44 (44:5, 7, 20 [MT 44:6, 8, 21]), neither Pss 44 nor 45 use the divine name "Yahweh."

The corollary to relying on God is stated in 44:6 (MT 44:7), where the psalmist declares that he does not trust in his own weapons because he knows they cannot save him. God has saved his people and shamed the wicked (44:7 [MT 44:8]), and the people therefore boast in God and give thanks to his name, pledging to do so forever (44:8 [MT 44:9]).

The piety in Ps 44:1–8 (MT 44:2–9) sets up the jarring and unexpected complaint about God rejecting his people and allowing them to be defeated in 44:9–19 (MT 44:10–20). This pattern of the believing remnant's experience matches the pattern experienced by the righteous sufferer in the Psalms—the man who in spite of his piety is opposed by the wicked as we have seen throughout Book 1 of the Psalter. The experience of the righteous man has now become the experience of the righteous remnant, partaking of the dynamic between the one and the many seen so often in the Old Testament, setting up the relationship between Christ the covenant head and his covenant people.

## 44:9–16 (MT 44:10–17), Cursed, Rejected, and Mocked

The blessings of the covenant (Lev 26; Deut 28) promise blessings for obedience and curses on disobedience. The psalmist has described trusting devotion in Ps 44:1–8 (MT 44:2–9], and so the blessings of the covenant should follow. Because the psalmist and the remnant he represents have experienced the curses rather than the blessings of the covenant, he brings his complaints to the Lord. The psalmist in 44 is responding along the same lines of what we saw in Pss 42 and 43. He does not seek sinful comfort, resort to idolatry, or defect to the enemy. He takes his complaint to the Lord.

Perhaps the explanation for what has happened to God's people lies in the fact that the believing remnant is but a small fraction of the population, with the majority having broken the covenant and incurred God's wrath. Or perhaps there is some other explanation in the hidden purposes of God (cf. Deut 29:29). Such considerations are not the psalmist's concern.

For him, he sees that whereas God's people should have been blessed with God's presence and victory in battle, God has rejected them; they have experienced disgrace; and God has not gone out with their army (Ps 44:9 [MT 44:10]). Rather than triumphing over other nations, they have fled before them and been plundered (44:10 [MT 44:11]; cf. Lev 26:8, Deut 28:7, 25; 32:30). They have been devoured like sheep before ravenous wild beasts and scattered from the land of life into the unclean realm of the dead (Ps 44:11 [MT 44:12]; cf. Deut 4:27; 28:64). They have been sold to their enemies on the cheap, commanding no high price (Ps 44:12 [MT 44:13]; cf. Deut 32:30; Judg 2:14; 3:8).

Instead of a praise and glory in the earth (cf. Jer 33:9), God's people have become a reproach, receiving only derision and mockery, a proverbial byword about what happens to the wicked who deserve destruction, while their enemies shake their heads about the bad end to which they've come (Ps 44:13–14 [MT 44:14–15]). The psalmist states that this humiliation haunts him all day, that the shame of it has covered his face, and that the reproachers and revilers and enemy and avenger will give him no rest (44:15–16 [MT 44:16–17]). The phrase, "the enemy and avenger" (CSB) is the same found in Ps 8:2 (MT 8:3).

## 44:17–26 (MT 44:18–27), Present Faithfulness Based on Future Hope

Having recounted the curse of defeat in 44:9–16 (MT 44:10–17), the psalmist returns to the faithfulness of the remnant in 44:17–22 (MT 44:18–23) before crying out for deliverance in 44:23–26 (MT 44:24–27).

The wretchedness described in Ps 44:9–16 (MT 44:10–17) is due to those who forget God, but the psalmist protests in 44:17 (MT 44:18) that he and the remnant for which he speaks have neither forgotten God nor been false to his covenant. He continues in 44:18 (MT 44:19) by saying that in both heart and way of life they have been true to Yahweh, and yet, as he says in 44:19 (MT 44:20), they have been crushed like jackals and covered with the shadow of death as though they were God's enemies.

The logic of this complaint is that the punishment has been unjust: righteous people are suffering unduly as though they have been unrighteous. The psalmist is not pursuing a theological explanation but presenting his complaint to the God whom he knows on a personal level. Nor does he make threats or offer to cut deals with God but simply makes known his plight and perspective.

The assumption behind these statements is that God is just. The conviction here is that God will make things right. There is a bedrock, gut-level belief that God's steadfast love is on his people, so he will defend them when he sees their strength is gone (cf. Deut 32:36).

Again in Ps 44:20–21 (MT 44:21–22) the psalmist protests that he and his people have not forgotten God and resorted to idolatrous appeals to foreign gods precisely because they knew that God would see and know and judge them. His complaint is that they experience judgment they do not deserve in 44:22 (MT 44:23), noting that though they have not been unfaithful they are being killed for God's sake, regarded as sheep to the slaughter.

This awful reality does not cause the remnant to abandon God but to cry out to him, and that faithfulness makes Paul's citation of this text in Rom 8:36 so profoundly appropriate. Paul is explaining that God's steadfast love to his people makes it so that no power in heaven or on earth can separate them from him, certainly not by prompting his people to abandon him, even if they are killed, treated like sheep at slaughter. That same dynamic is at work in Ps 44, where God's faithful remnant continue to trust him and hope in him even as they experience undue suffering unto death.

The visceral confidence in God's character and belief in God's promises prompt the response to undue suffering we see in Ps 44:23–26 (MT 44:24–27). In a daring anthropomorphism, the psalmist summons God to wake, asking him why he sleeps (44:23 [MT 44:24]). This urgent petition in the form of a command reveals a conviction that things are not the way God wants them to be. Such a conviction is thoroughly true, even if in the mystery of God's purposes and will he means for things to be exactly as they are. The second command in 44:23 (MT 44:24) is like the first, a call for God to wake up, and an imperatival petition that he not reject his people forever (cf. 44:9 [MT 44:10]).[167]

It was God's presence that gave victory in 44:3 (MT 44:4), and God's absence that resulted in defeat in 44:9 (MT 44:10). Accordingly, the psalmist asks God why he hides his face in 44:24 (MT 44:25), and he proceeds, correctly assuming that God loves his people, to ask why God is acting as though he has forgotten that his beloved are suffering affliction and oppression.

The psalmist neither consoles himself with complicated theological explanations nor resorts to sinful anger. He responds to his pain by fleeing

---

[167] The psalmist does not mean to indicate that God has literally gone to sleep. Cf. Saint Gregory of Nazianzus, *On God and Christ: The Five Theological Orations and Two Letters to Cledonius*, trans. Frederick Williams and Lionel Wickham (Crestwood, NY: St Vladimirs Seminary Press, 2002), 133–34: "In the Bible, God 'sleeps,' 'wakes up,' ... and has a 'throne of cherubim.'... This is a nonfactual, mental picture. We have used names derived from human experience and applied them, so far as we could, to aspects of God. His retirement from us, for reasons known to himself into an almost unconcerned inactivity, is his 'sleeping.'"

to the Father because he knows God's love. This accords with the pitiable description of the remnant in Ps 44:25 (MT 44:26). Like the individual whose soul is cast down in 42:5; 42:11; and 43:5 (MT 42:6, 12), the psalmist says that the soul of the people is sunk down to dust, their belly cleaving to the earth (44:25 [MT 44:26]).

This sad state prompts the final plea for God to "Arise!" and be his people's help, to redeem them because of his *hesed*, his lovingkindness (44:26 [MT 44:27]).

This psalmist speaks for a remnant that knows the Bible and has been faithful to trust, love, and praise God. That same remnant has suffered grinding defeat and humiliation, in response to which they cry out to the God whose justice they trust, whose promises they believe, whose steadfast love they have experienced. They cry out believing that God cares for them and will act to set things right.

### Bridge

To this point in the Psalter we have seen David in the pattern of the righteous sufferer, but at the end of Book 1 we seem to have arrived at the moment when having passed through suffering he was enthroned and entered into his kingdom. Now in Ps 44 we see a psalmist speak on behalf of a believing remnant who, like their individual representative, is righteous and yet suffers.

David suffers through much of Book 1 and enters his kingdom in Book 2. As Book 2 opens, however, the righteous community suffers on the way to entering the kingdom—the city of God described in Ps 46. Such a sequence matches the way that Jesus first suffered before entering into his glory, and now the church suffers on the way to entering the new Jerusalem. The flow of thought in this section of the Psalter, and particularly the function of Ps 44, fits hand in glove with the way that Paul quotes Ps 44:22 (MT 44:23) in Rom 8:36.

## Psalm 45

### Overview and Structure of Psalm 45

Psalm 45 has a literary ring structure, where the first and last statements match, then second and second-to-last do as well, and so forth to the central statement about the anointing of the king in 45:7 (MT 45:8). The psalm opens and closes with the psalmist describing what he is doing in the psalm: he writes of the king (45:1 [MT 45:2]) and will thereby cause his name to be remembered and praised forever (45:17 [MT 45:18]). Within that outer frame where he speaks of his own intentions, the psalmist makes matching statements about the handsome king and the glorious queen, and in both cases "sons" are referenced (45:2, 13–16 [MT 45:3, 14–17]). The psalmist next addresses a series of commands to the king and speaks of what will result from the proposed action (45:3–4 [MT 45:4–5]), and the commands and result addressed to the king are balanced by the psalmist likewise addressing the queen with a series of commands and a statement of what will result from the proposed action (45:10–12 [MT 45:11–13]). The psalmist celebrates the way enemy peoples will fall under the king in 45:5 (MT 45:6), resulting in the presence of daughters of conquered kings in his court, from the ranks of whom he takes his glorious bride (45:9 [MT 45:10]).

The chiastic structure of Ps 45 can be depicted as follows:[168]

45:1 (MT 45:2), The Psalmist Speaks
   45:2 (MT 45:3), The King More Handsome Than Sons of Adam
      45:3–4 (MT 45:4–5), Commands for the King
         45:5 (MT 45:6), Conquest of the Peoples
            45:6 (MT 45:7), God's Throne and Scepter
               45:7 (MT 45:8), Anointed
            45:8 (MT 45:9), Ointments, Palaces, Instruments
         45:9 (MT 45:10), Daughters of Conquered Kings
      45:10–12 (MT 45:11–13), Commands for the Queen
   45:13–16 (MT 45:14–17), The Glorious Queen and Her Sons
45:17 (MT 45:18), The Psalmist Speaks

We will pursue the exposition of Ps 45 under the following subheads:

     45:1–5 (MT 45:2–6), The King's Conquest
     45:6–8 (MT 45:7–9), The King's Throne
     45:9–17 (MT 45:10–18), The King's Wedding

---

[168] For a different chiastic proposal, see Alden, "Chiastic Psalms 1–50," 26.

SCRIPTURE

| CSB | Author's translation |
|---|---|
| | |

For the choir director: according to "The Lilies." A *Maskil* of the sons of Korah. A love song.

¹ My heart is moved by a noble theme as I recite my verses to the king; my tongue is the pen of a skillful writer.
² You are the most handsome of men; grace flows from your lips. Therefore God has blessed you forever.
³ Mighty warrior, strap your sword at your side. In your majesty and splendor—
⁴ in your splendor ride triumphantly in the cause of truth, humility, and justice. May your right hand show your awe-inspiring acts.
⁵ Your sharpened arrows pierce the hearts of the king's enemies; the peoples fall under you.

⁶ Your throne, God, is forever and ever; the scepter of your kingdom is a scepter of justice.
⁷ You love righteousness and hate wickedness; therefore God, your God, has anointed you with the oil of joy more than your companions.
⁸ Myrrh, aloes, and cassia perfume all your garments; from ivory palaces harps bring you joy.
⁹ Kings' daughters are among your honored women; the queen, adorned with gold from Ophir, stands at your right hand.

¹ For the Preeminent One.
On Lilies.
Of the sons of Korah.
A *Maskil*.
A Song of Beloveds.

² My heart stews on a good word, saying,
as for me, my works are for the king; my tongue is the stylus of a swift scribe.

³ You are more handsome than the sons of Adam,
grace is poured out on your lips, therefore God has blessed you to the age.

⁴ Gird your sword upon your thigh, O mighty man,
your splendor and your majesty!
⁵ And your majesty, prosper!
Ride on the word of truth and the humility of righteousness!
And your right hand will teach you fearsome things.

⁶ Your arrows are sharp—peoples fall under you—
in the heart of those at enmity with the king.

⁷ Your throne, O God, the age and on!
The scepter of uprightness is the scepter of your kingdom.

⁸ You loved righteousness and hated wickedness,
therefore God your God anointed [*messiahed*] you,
oil of exultation beyond your companions.

¹⁰ Listen, daughter, pay attention and
    consider:
Forget your people and your father's
    house,
¹¹ and the king will desire your beauty.
Bow down to him, for he is your lord.
¹² The daughter of Tyre, the wealthy
    people,
will seek your favor with gifts.

¹³ In her chamber, the royal daughter
    is all glorious,
her clothing embroidered with gold.
¹⁴ In colorful garments she is led to the
    king;
after her, the virgins, her companions,
    are brought to you.
¹⁵ They are led in with gladness and
    rejoicing;
they enter the king's palace.
¹⁶ Your sons will succeed your
    ancestors;
you will make them princes
    throughout the land.
¹⁷ I will cause your name to be
    remembered for all generations;
therefore the peoples will praise you
    forever and ever.

⁹ Myrrh and aloes, cassias, all your
    garments,
from palaces of ivory instruments of
    string gladden you.

¹⁰ Daughters of kings are among your
    noble ladies,
the queen stands at your right hand
    in gold of Ophir.

¹¹ Hear, o daughter, and see, and
    incline your ear,
and forget your people and the house
    of your father.
¹² Then the king will desire your
    beauty;
because he is your lord, you must bow
    down to him.
¹³ And the daughter of Tyre with a gift
    in your presence,
the rich of the people will appease
    you.

¹⁴ All glorious is the daughter of the
    king within,
from woven things of gold her
    raiment.
¹⁵ In embroideries she is borne along
    to the king,
her virgin companions after her,
    being brought to you.
¹⁶ They are led in gladnesses and
    rejoicing;
they come to the palace of the king.
¹⁷ In place of your fathers shall be
    your sons.
You shall appoint them chieftains in
    all the land.

¹⁸ I will cause your name to be
    remembered in every generation
    and generation,
therefore peoples shall praise you to
    the age and on.

The longing of the individual psalmist (Pss 42–43) and that of the believing remnant (Ps 44) resolves in the celebrated king from David's line in Ps 45. Two terms in the superscription of this wedding song also appear in the Song of Songs: "lilies" occurs eight times in Song of Songs (e.g., 2:1, 2) and "beloveds" (ידידות) is related to "my beloved" in the Song (דודי, e.g., Song 1:13, 14, 16). Other points of contact with the Song include "lips" in Ps 45:2 (MT 45:3; cf., e.g., Song 4:3, 11) and "myrrh and aloes" in Ps 45:8 (MT 45:9; Song 4:14). These linguistic points of contact with the Song of Songs join with the thematic similarity between the two—both Ps 45 and the Song of Songs celebrate the wedding of the king from David's line—to make the two pieces of poetry uniquely similar to one another.

Exposition

**45:1–5 (MT 45:2–6), The King's Conquest**

As noted above, Ps 45 opens and closes with the psalmist describing what he himself is doing. In 45:1 (MT 45:2) he speaks of himself stewing on a good word, as though the thoughts within him are simmering, being stirred, as he reflects. The terms used to speak of this "good word" (דבר טוב) indicate that the psalmist is meditating on scriptural promises. He then elaborates that his "works," probably referring to the poetry in this psalm (and perhaps others), are "for the king" (מעשי למלך). The psalmist seems to be reflecting on God's promises about the king from David's line, then declaring that he writes for that king. God promised to make David's name great (2 Sam 7:9) and that the throne of his seed would be established forever, so the psalmist's statement about causing the king's name (the "your" is masculine) to be remembered and praised forever in 45:17 (MT 45:18) would appear to confirm this.

When the psalmist says in 45:1 (MT 45:2), "my tongue is the stylus of a swift scribe," he uses the same phrase employed in Ezra 7:6 to describe Ezra (the only difference is the inclusion of a *holem-waw* in the psalmist's phrase: סופר מהיר). A "ready" or "swift" scribe is one so familiar with the texts that he knows his way around in them, finds exactly what he seeks quickly, and shows evident skill in their navigation. This psalmist, like Ezra, is a man of the book, and that has him contemplating the book's hope. Such hope flows from promises found in earlier Scripture, promises about the king from David's line who will actualize the blessing of

Abraham, in fulfillment of the Gen 3:15 word about the seed of the woman who will triumph over the serpent and his seed.

The hopes vested in this king prompt the psalmist to long for his coming and see him as beautiful. This is why he speaks of him as "more handsome than the sons of Adam" in Ps 45:2 (MT 45:3). The reference to the sons of Adam also recalls both Adam's fall and the word about the seed of the woman. The wording of the description of the king as handsome also recalls the description of David in 1 Sam 16:12.

The psalmist's expectation for the seed of David seems to be informed by the pattern of David's life when he writes of the future king in Ps 45:2 (MT 45:3): "grace is poured out on your lips." This statement recalls the words of David in 2 Sam 23:2, "The Spirit of Yahweh speaks by me, and his utterance is upon my tongue." That the future king is the fulfillment of what was *promised* to David and the fullest expression of the *pattern* seen in David (here, a king who speaks as an inspired prophet) means ("therefore") that this king is the one whom God will bless forever, in fulfillment of 2 Sam 7:13.

The reflection on the promises and their fulfillment that has the psalmist's heart stewing now gathers to a boil and overflows in the laudatory cheers that take the form of commands addressed to the king in Ps 45:3–4 (MT 45:4–5).

The psalmist calls his king to arm himself for war. His hope is for the king to come, and once come, to conquer. Thus he longs for the mighty man to come in splendor and majesty (cf. 8:5; 21:5 [MT 8:6; 21:6]). He next commands the king to "prosper" using the verb from 1:3 (צלח), then follows with an exhortation to him that he ride forth on the word of truth and in the humility of righteousness. The psalmist wants a king who obeys Deut 17:14–20, whose power flows from God's promises, who humbly embraces God's commands such that his heart is not lifted up over the Torah with the result that he oppresses God's people. Righteousness is humble because it accepts God's boundaries, and humility results in righteousness.

I take the last line of 45:4 (MT 45:5) to state the result of the king carrying out the psalmist's commands (as opposed to this being another command, as in CSB and ESV). When the king straps his sword to his thigh and rides out to prosper, his right hand will do fearsome deeds. Taking the grammar this way results in a structural parallel with the commands addressed to the queen in 45:10 (MT 45:11), followed by what will result when she does as the psalmist commands in 45:11–12 (MT 45:12–13).

The Hebrew word order of Ps 45:5 (MT 45:6) communicates the psalmist's enthusiasm. He starts into the phrase about the arrows being sharp in the hearts of the king's enemies, but he interrupts it with the exclamation that the peoples fall under the king: "Your arrows are sharp—peoples fall under you—in the heart of the king's enemies." That the peoples fall under the king in 45:5 (MT 45:6) results in the daughters of conquered kings in his court, from whom he chooses a bride, in 45:9 (MT 45:10).

The longed for king has come, banishing the anguished despair in Pss 42–44, and he is a welcome sight whom his people cheer on to victory.

## 45:6–8 (MT 45:7–9), The King's Throne

Every statement in Ps 45:6–9 (MT 45:7–10) pertains to the king's royal position in fulfillment of the promises to David.

In Ps 45:6 (MT 45:7) the psalmist appears to address the expected king from David's line as God. To identify a people's king with their God was not unprecedented but common in the world of ancient Israel. The surprise at the fact that Jesus came as the incarnation of the God of Israel (e.g., Mark 4:41) shows, however, that such identification did not imply everything that Jesus embodied. Adam was God's visible image and likeness, and something along those lines probably informs other nations who identified their king as the representative of their god(s). So it would likely be a mistake to assume that the psalmist understood the Christology of Chalcedon, but it would also be a mistake *not* to see Jesus as the fulfillment of what the psalmist says (see Heb 1:8–9).[169]

As the psalmist speaks of the everlasting (עולם ועד) throne (כסא) in Ps 45:6 (MT 45:7), he puts in poetic form the promise of 2 Sam 7:13, "And I will establish the throne [כסא] of his kingdom forever [עד עולם]." When he references the power of the king's uprightness in the phrase "scepter of uprightness" being the "scepter of your kingdom," he speaks both to the hope for a righteous king, growing out of Deut 17's instructions for the king to be a man who keeps and enforces Torah, and also of the "scepter" that would be between the feet of the lion of Judah (Gen 49:10). The one Num 24:17 declares would arise and smash the forehead of the enemies trying to curse God's people, shattering those conspiring against him (Ps 2:9; cf. Isa 11:4).

---

[169] For discussion of Origen's remarks that reflect early Jewish-Christian debate over this passage, see Edwards, *Exegesis in the Targum of Psalms*, 185–92.

The character of the king was reflected in the reference to God's grace on his lips in Ps 45:2 (MT 45:3), in the command for him to "ride on the word of truth and the humility of righteousness" in 45:4 (MT 45:5), and in the reference to the "scepter of uprightness" in 45:6 (MT 45:7). The king's rejection of the lure of sin and his volitional choice to do right is articulated in 45:7 (MT 45:8). The king did not disqualify himself by wickedness, so God anointed him with the "oil of exultation beyond your companions." The description of the anointing of the king recalls Samuel anointing David in 1 Sam 16:13 and employs the verb from which we derive the term, messiah (משׁח). This king is without peer in his obedience, and in keeping with his character he receives unparalleled status and joy from God himself.

Standing at the center of the psalm's chiastic structure, Ps 45:7 (MT 45:8) states the king's choice of righteousness not wickedness, God's anointing of him, and the unmatched gladness he enjoys.

Corresponding to the description of the king's scepter and throne in 45:6 (MT 45:7) is the description of his fragrant robes and the ivory palaces from which his instruments cause gladness in 45:8 (MT 45:9). The phrase that opens this verse also occurs in Songs 4:14, as the wedding in that book nears its consummation.[170] The king's throne is established, his garments are fragrant, and music fills the air. He has triumphed, and in his reign the joy of peace rings forth.

### 45:9–17 (MT 45:10–18), The King's Wedding

The psalmist now turns his attention to the king's new bride. In the psalm's chiastic structure, the reference in 45:9 (MT 45:10) to the daughters of kings stands across from the description of the Israelite king's conquest of peoples (45:5 [MT 45:6]). The queen in 45:9 (MT 45:10) is drawn from the ranks of these foreign ladies of nobility. She is addressed as a "daughter" and commanded to forget her people and her father's house in 45:10 (MT 45:11). When she obeys, the king will desire her, and as he is her new lord she should bow to him (45:11 [MT 45:12]). This reference to the queen bowing to the king recalls the way that Joseph dreamed his family would bow to him in Gen 37:7, 9, and 10, then Judah was told his brothers would bow to him in Gen 49:8. The king will desire her, and the

---

[170] For discussion, see James M. Hamilton, *Song of Songs: A Biblical-Theological, Allegorical, Christological Interpretation*, Focus on the Bible (Fearn: Christian Focus, 2015).

daughter of Tyre and the richest of the people will bring her tribute (Ps 45:12 [MT 45:13]). This sequence of commands to the queen ("hear ... see ... incline ... forget") followed by a description of the results of her obedience in 45:10–12 (MT 45:11–13) is the chiastic complement to a similar series of statements addressed to the king in 45:3–4 (MT 45:4–5).

Just as the king's appearance and character was celebrated in 45:2 (MT 45:3), so is the queen's in 45:13–16 (MT 45:14–17). The splendor of the queen's raiment and the young ladies who accompany her add the glory of feminine beauty and refinement to the celebration of the reign of the king. Far from being mere decoration, however, this is the queen with whom the king will be fruitful and multiply in 45:16 (MT 45:17). Though the pronouns and verb forms in 45:16 (MT 45:17) are masculine (prompting some to conclude that these statements are addressed to the king), the statement that the sons will replace the fathers in 45:16 (MT 45:17) seems to recall the way the queen was exhorted to forget her father in 45:10 (MT 45:11).[171] This inclines me to think the words of 45:16 (MT 45:17) are addressed to the queen.

The psalmist again describes what he himself is doing in the psalm in 45:17 (MT 45:18; cf. 45:1 [MT 45:2]). Here he seems to turn from speaking to the queen to addressing the king. Just as God had promised David a great name (2 Sam 7:9), the psalmist says he will cause the king's name to be remembered forever. Just as all nations will be blessed in Abraham and his seed (Gen 12:3; 22:18), so the psalmist says that the peoples will praise Israel's future king forever.

BRIDGE

Craigie writes of Ps 45, "In its original sense and context, it is not in any sense a messianic psalm. And yet within the context of early Christianity (and in Judaism before that), it becomes a messianic psalm par excellence."[172] Against this kind of conclusion, which holds that both Judaism and Christianity have departed from the "original sense and context" of Ps 45 to give it new meaning, I contend that approaching Ps 45 within

---

[171] These scholars, e.g., Craigie, *Psalms 1–50*, 340; Kidner, *Psalms 1–72*, 191, could be correct that 45:16 (MT 45:17) is addressed to the king, but consider the words of Paul Joüon, *A Grammar of Biblical Hebrew*, trans. and rev. T. Muraoka, 2 vols., SubBi 14 (Rome: Pontifical Biblical Institute, 1996) § 89 a: "a feminine verb form can indicate that the subject noun is feminine, but nothing certain can be inferred from a masculine form."

[172] Craigie, *Psalms 1–50*, 340.

the wider context of both the book of Psalms and the Old Testament allows it to be situated firmly within the developing hope for the future king from David's line. Psalm 2 refers to that future king as the Lord's anointed, his messiah (2:2).

Psalm 45 anticipates a king whose coming will resolve the emotional and spiritual pain of individual Israelites and the nation's faithful remnant (Pss 42–44), who will fulfill the blessing of Abraham by conquering the seed of the serpent and overcoming all who curse God and his people, thereby blessing all the families of the earth and rolling back the words of judgment God spoke in response to sin (Gen 3:14–19; 5:29; 12:1–3). This king will be the seed promised to David (2 Sam 7:13–14). His reign will be as glorious as his gentile bride will be beautiful. He will conquer the world and fill it with the aroma of his glorious humility and the joy of his reign.[173]

## Psalm 46

OVERVIEW AND STRUCTURE OF PSALM 46

The literary structure of Ps 46 seems to be marked by the three instances of selah that are found at the end of verses 3, 7, and 11 (MT 4, 8, 12), and the use of selah marks the end of the psalm's three thought units. In all three sections God is present "for us" (לָנוּ, CSB "our" in 46:1, 7, 11 [MT 46:2, 8, 12]) as their refuge and stronghold. The first of these three sections (46:1–3 [MT 46:2–4]) envision a time when all creation—land, mountains, seas—experience an apocalyptic uproar. As creation is unmade, God's people find refuge and help in him. The second section (46:4–7 [MT 46:5–8]) depicts the city of God strong and secure because of God's presence and protection as nations crumble, kingdoms totter, and the earth melts. The third and final section (46:8–11 [MT 46:9–12]) calls the psalm's audience to behold Yahweh's wondrous works: his judgment has put an end to war, destroyed its implements, and filled the world with his glory.[174]

Psalm 46 teaches that God is our refuge when:

---

[173] For the quotation of Ps 45:6 (MT 45:7) in Heb 1:8, the flow of thought in Heb 1, and for reflection on the identity of Christ, see Thomas R. Schreiner, *Commentary on Hebrews*, Evangelical Biblical Theology Commentary (Bellingham, WA: Lexham Press, 2020), 70–72; and Stephen J. Wellum, *God the Son Incarnate: The Doctrine of Christ*, Foundations of Evangelical Theology (Wheaton, IL: Crossway, 2016), 201, 206.

[174] Alden proposes a chiasm for Ps 46, "Chiastic Psalms 1–50," 26–27.

46:1–3 (MT 46:2–4), The Creation Is Unmade
46:4–7 (MT 46:5–8), The City Is Made Glad
46:8–11 (MT 46:9–12), The Peace Is Established

SCRIPTURE

CSB

For the choir director. A song of the
sons of Korah. According to *Alamoth.*

¹God is our refuge and strength,
a helper who is always found
in times of trouble.
²Therefore we will not be afraid,
though the earth trembles
and the mountains topple
into the depths of the seas,
³though its water roars and foams
and the mountains quake with its
turmoil.
*Selah*

⁴There is a river—
its streams delight the city of God,
the holy dwelling place of the Most
High.
⁵God is within her; she will not be
toppled.
God will help her when the morning
dawns.
⁶Nations rage, kingdoms topple;
the earth melts when he lifts his voice.
⁷The LORD of Armies is with us;
the God of Jacob is our stronghold.
*Selah*

⁸Come, see the works of the LORD,
who brings devastation on the earth.
⁹He makes wars cease throughout the
earth.
He shatters bows and cuts spears to
pieces;
he sets wagons ablaze.

Author's translation

¹ For the Preeminent One.
Of the sons of Korah.
On *Alamoth.*
A Song.

² God is for us refuge and strength:
a help in straits is found for sure.
³ Therefore we will not fear when
changed is the earth,
and when totter the mountains in the
heart of the seas.
⁴ They are in uproar, they foam—the
waters of it.
The mountains quake at the majesty
of it. *Selah.*

⁵ A river. The streams of it gladden
the city of God,
the holy tabernacles of the Most High.
⁶ God is in the midst of her.
She will not totter.
God will help her at the turn of the
morning.
⁷ The nations are in uproar.
The kingdoms totter.
He lifts his voice.
The earth melts.
⁸ Yahweh of hosts is with us.
A stronghold for us is the God of
Jacob. *Selah.*

⁹ Come! See the works of Yahweh,
who put desolations on the earth.
¹⁰ He makes wars *sabbath* to the end of
the earth.
The bow he shatters and hews the
spear.

¹⁰ "Stop fighting, and know that I am
God,
exalted among the nations, exalted on
the earth."
¹¹ The LORD of Armies is with us;
the God of Jacob is our stronghold.
*Selah*

He burns the wagons in the fire.
¹¹ Be still and know that I am God.
I will be exalted among the nations.
I will be exalted in the earth.
¹² Yahweh of hosts is with us.
A stronghold for us is the God of
Jacob. *Selah.*

CONTEXT: VERBAL AND THEMATIC LINKS WITH SURROUNDING PSALMS

We have seen the individual psalmist sunk down in soul in Pss 42–43, then the psalmist speaks for the faithful old covenant remnant that is likewise sunk down in soul in Ps 44. The despair of the individual and the community arises from the absence of the king, whose conquest, kingdom, and marriage are celebrated in Ps 45. With the arrival of the king and the covenant of marriage he makes in Ps 45, Ps 46 celebrates an apocalyptic destruction of the earth and its nations, as the city of God enjoys unmoved stability because of God's presence and protection, which brings the longed for lasting peace and worldwide weal.

Psalm 46 was written before the cross, but its fulfillment depends upon the cross and resurrection.

EXPOSITION

### 46:1–3 (MT 46:2–4), The Creation Is Unmade

The superscription of Ps 46 is like the others on Pss 42–49, with the addition of the cryptic "On *Alamoth*." We do not know what this phrase means.

Psalm 46:1 (MT 46:2) confesses that in times of great difficulty Yahweh himself is a place of refuge and strength, a help for the people of God. Because God's people have found help, refuge, and strength in God in ordinary times, 46:2 (MT 46:3) states that they will not fear in *extra*ordinary times. The scene in Ps 46:2–3 (MT 46:3–4) depicts the unmaking of the world. The earth is changed as the mountains totter off its surface into the heart of the seas, tsunamis result, and earthquakes follow (cf. Rev 8:8; 11:19; 16:18).

These verses declare that the people of God will find him to be a strong refuge and an ever present help when the world as we know it comes to an end. The cosmic disruption described here points to the final end of history, when the just displeasure of God purges creation of everything that has defiled the world he made pure.

If God's people themselves have been impure, if they too have defiled his holy creation, how are they able to take refuge in God? Does not God's justice demand that their iniquity also receive its due consequence? The psalmist does not describe it here, but we have seen hints of the answer in places like Ps 34:17–22 (MT 34:18–23), and the patterns of the flood and the exodus point to judgment on God's enemies and mercy to those who repent of sin and trust in God. The ultimate answer, however, that will make possible the fulfillment of what this psalm describes is the death and resurrection of Jesus (see esp. Rom 3:24–26).

### 46:4–7 (MT 46:5–8), The City Is Made Glad

There is no river through the present city of Jerusalem. Several passages in the prophets, however, describe a river running through the new Jerusalem, the one that God will make new after the purging apocalypse that precedes the new heavens and new earth (see Ezek 47:1–14; Joel 3:18 [MT 4:18]; Zech 13:1; 14:8–9; Rev 22:1–2). This is the river in view in Ps 46:4 (MT 46:5).

After the apocalyptic destruction of the world, in the new creation (Isa 65:17), which will be a cosmic temple (Ezek 40–48; Dan 9:24), the new Jerusalem will enjoy the waters of a life-giving river. The term rendered "streams" in Ps 46:4 (MT 46:5) is the same used in 1:3 where the blessed man is likened to a tree planted by streams of water. God's word and presence are the delight of God's people now, and God's word and presence will be our delight when all is made new.

The Jerusalem of old was the place of God's temple, and this new Jerusalem will be his city, "the holy tabernacles of the Most High" (46:4 [MT 46:5]). This psalm anticipates the day when it will be declared, "Behold, the dwelling place of God is with man. He will dwell with them, and they will be his people, and God himself will be with them as their God" (Rev 21:3, ESV). In view of the wedding scene in Ps 45, it is interesting that Rev 21:2 describes "the holy city, new Jerusalem, coming down out of heaven from God, prepared as a bride adorned for her husband."

The mountains were described as "tottering" into the heart of the sea in Ps 46:2 (MT 46:3), and this is precisely what God's city will not do: "She will not totter" (46:5 [MT 46:6]). And the reason she will not totter is in the first line of 46:5 (MT 46:6), "God is in the midst of her." God's presence stabilizes his people even when the ground beneath their feet gives way.

The third line of Ps 46:5 (MT 46:6) states, "God will help her at the turn of the morning." Sunrise is a powerful image of hope (Isa 8:20; 9:2; Mal 4:2; Luke 1:78), connoting a coming awake after sleep, which likewise suggests resurrection from the dead (Ps 17:15; Isa 26:19; Dan 12:2). This reference in Ps 46:5 (MT 46:6) to God helping Jerusalem when morning dawns, then, hints at the dawning of life on the morning of the new creation when the sleepers in death will be raised to life.

On that day the wicked will be judged and the repenters will be hidden from God's justice in God's mercy. Psalm 46:6 (MT 46:7) puts the camera on the rebellious of the world, who are in uproar as the world comes to an end, as the kingdoms "totter" with the mountains. The mountains totter (46:2 [MT 46:3]). God's city will not totter (46:5 [MT 46:6]). The kingdoms will totter (46:6 [MT 46:7]).

The last line of Ps 46:6 (MT 46:7) employs a term used to describe the Canaanites melting away before Israel in Exod 15:15 (so also Josh 2:9, 24), and Amos 9:5 describes Yahweh touching the earth with the result that it melts (cf. Nah 1:5). When the Lord rises to judge the earth, the same word that made the world will melt it.

God's vowels, consonants, syllables, lexemes, phrases, syntactical constructions, and sentences cause things like protons and neutrons to form atoms, atoms to form molecules, and on the power of God's almighty utterance the earth and the universe spring into being. The same utterance that caused them to congeal will cause them to dissolve.

When the sky falls and the sun explodes and the earth melts, the only safe place will be the one had by the people of God, who confess in 46:7 (MT 46:8) that Yahweh is with them. The God who revealed himself to Abraham and changed Jacob's name to Israel is their fortress.

### 46:8–11 (MT 46:9–12), The Peace Is Established

In Ps 46:8 (MT 46:9) an invitation is sounded to all who can hear. This invitation envisions the time described in the psalm, when the earth has been destroyed under the wrath of God. The survivors would be those who belong to the city of God, those who found refuge in him, making what the psalm envisions similar to passages like Rev 19:1–5, where the redeemed worship God in response to the destruction of Babylon. That future destruction is still to take place, and yet the psalm speaks to its original audience and to us. By the eye of faith—believing that God will destroy his enemies and purge creation—we behold what God has done, what he will do.

We are thus invited by Ps 46:8–9 (MT 46:9–10) to inspect the way that God will destroy the works of evildoers, putting "desolations on the earth." A day will come when those who refuse to turn from evil impulses will no longer be permitted to do evil. The long rebellion will be over, when kings gathered armies to conquer other nations for plunder, so they could enslave enemy peoples. All who will not repent will be consigned to their place of punishment. Only those who repented, trusted, and are now glorified like Christ himself will be loose in the land. Thus there will be no further need for locks or weapons or gates.

What will have ended the possibilities of the rebels? The psalmist speaks in 46:9 of the way that Yahweh will have put war on permanent sabbatical. The bow will be shattered, the spear hewn, the oxcart used to transport men and munitions burned in the fire.

Having destroyed his enemies and the material with which they engaged in their revolt, Yahweh issues a call for all other efforts to cease, that he might be acknowledged as God. Never again will God's people be worried by persecutors and oppressors. Never again will they need to defend themselves in word or deed. Never again will they offer anxious prayers for the safety of their children. Never again will they endure insufferable campaign cycles where flawed men vie for the most powerful office in the world.

When the Lord unmakes the world, protecting his city, ending war, throwing down all rival kingdoms, God's people will be still and know him.[175] He is God. There is none like him.

His purpose at creation was to fill the earth with his image bearers, that his character might be reflected in them everywhere (Gen 1:28). Instead of filling the world with God's glory, men filled the earth with violence (Gen 6:11). When God puts an end at last to the violence, he will indeed be exalted among the nations and in all the earth, just as Ps 46:10 (MT 46:11) describes (cf. Isa 2:1–4, 11, 17).

---

[175] Dan Phillips related the following helpful note to me (pers. comm.): James L. Kugel (*The Idea of Biblical Poetry* [Baltimore: Johns Hopkins University Press 1981], 9) notes (re: Isa 1:3): "In Near Eastern treaty language, 'know' was regularly used in the sense of 'acknowledge as sovereign'," citing Herbert B. Huffmon, "The Treaty Background of Hebrew *Yāda'*," BASOR 181 (1966): 31–37.

Psalm 46 concludes in verse 11 with a repetition of verse 7 (MT 46:8, 12). God's people confess that Yahweh is with them, that the God of Jacob is their fortress.

In the flow of thought reflected in the juxtaposition of these psalms, the longing of the psalmist and his community in Pss 42–44 reaches for the coming of the king from David's line in Ps 45. The coming of the king ends the psalmist's separation from Jerusalem. Psalm 46 sings of the day when Daniel's statue (cf. Dan 2) will have been struck by the small stone that becomes a great mountain to fill the whole earth, when the four beasts will have been stripped of dominion (Dan 7), and the one like a son of man will have received the kingdom that cannot be shaken. The destruction of the kingdoms and the purging of the defiled world in Ps 46 is accompanied by the depiction of the river that gladdens God's city with foundations, where the things that cannot be shaken remain.

Sin's warrant has been canceled, death's power defeated, the dragon dethroned, the serpent's head crushed, all because the king died and rose. And Ps 46 sings the day when he will establish his reign, put an end to war, burn its implements, remake the world, wipe away every tear, restore his people to life, glorify their bodies like his own, bring them to the river, and let them eat from the tree of life that stands on its shores.

## Psalm 47

OVERVIEW AND STRUCTURE OF PSALM 47

The impressionistic flow of thought in the Psalms broadly corresponds to the narrative in Samuel. At the end of Book 1 of the Psalter, we seem to see David finally delivered from the danger posed by Saul's persecution. Psalm 45 can be seen to correspond to David being anointed king over both Israel and Judah in 2 Sam 5, and the superscription of Ps 51 ties that text to David's sin with Bathsheba in 2 Sam 11. Along these lines, there is correspondence of language between to 2 Sam 6:15 and Ps 47:5 (MT 47:6). This would seem to place Ps 47 at the point where the ark has been brought into Jerusalem, and the praises and triumphs of Pss 47–50 would match that triumphant section of narrative when after God made his covenant with David in 2 Sam 7 David expanded the borders of Israel through conquest in 2 Sam 8–10.

Psalm 47 reflects a chiastic structure as follows:

47:1 (MT 47:2), Praise of the Peoples
  47:2–3 (MT 47:3–4), The Conquering King
    47:4 (MT 47:5), Inheritance
      47:5 (MT 47:6), Triumph
    47:6 (MT 47:7), Praise
  47:7–8 (MT 47:8–9), The King of the Nations
47:9 (MT 47:10), Peoples Assemble to Praise

SCRIPTURE

CSB

For the choir director. A psalm of the sons of Korah.

[1] Clap your hands, all you peoples;
shout to God with a jubilant cry.
[2] For the LORD, the Most High, is awe-inspiring,
a great King over the whole earth.
[3] He subdues peoples under us
and nations under our feet.
[4] He chooses for us our inheritance—
the pride of Jacob, whom he loves.
*Selah*

[5] God ascends among shouts of joy,
the LORD, with the sound of a ram's horn.
[6] Sing praise to God, sing praise;
sing praise to our King, sing praise!
[7] Sing a song of wisdom,
for God is King of the whole earth.

[8] God reigns over the nations;
God is seated on his holy throne.
[9] The nobles of the peoples have assembled
with the people of the God of Abraham.

Author's translation

[1] For the Preeminent One.
Of the sons of Korah.
A Psalm.

[2] All peoples clap your hands!
Shout to God with the voice of a ringing cry!

[3] For Yahweh Most High is fearsome,
the great King over all the earth.
[4] He causes peoples to be spoken under us,
and the nations under our feet.

[5] He chose our inheritance for us,
the majesty of Jacob, whom he loves.
*Selah.*

[6] God has gone up with a shout,
Yahweh with the voice of the shofar.

[7] All of you psalm God, psalm!
All of you psalm our King, psalm!

[8] For King of all the earth is God,
all of you psalm a *maskil* [causer of wisdom].
[9] God reigns as king over the nations.
God sits on the throne of his holiness.

For the leaders of the earth belong to
   God;
he is greatly exalted.

[10] The nobles of the peoples are
   gathered,
people of the God of Abraham,
for to God belong the shields of the
   earth.
Exceedingly he is lifted up.

CONTEXT: VERBAL AND THEMATIC LINKS WITH SURROUNDING PSALMS

The individual discouragement in Pss 42–43 resonated with the anguish of the believing community in Ps 44. The longings of those psalms were met with the coming of the king in Ps 45, who established the apocalyptic city in Ps 46, and now in Ps 47 the peoples of the nations praise the conquering king.

EXPOSITION

Psalm 47 opens and closes with the praise of Yahweh from the peoples: in 47:1 (MT 47:2) the peoples are summoned to clap and shout to God, and in 47:9 (MT 47:10) the nobles of all nations have been incorporated into the people of God and gather to exalt Yahweh.

Psalm 47:1 (MT 47:2) seems to build on the summons to behold Yahweh's works in 46:8 (MT 46:9). Staying with that flow of thought, for Yahweh to be described as the fearsome high King over all the earth in 47:2 (MT 47:3) makes perfect sense in light of the way he unmade creation in 46:2–3 (MT 46:3–4) and put an end to war so that he alone would be exalted in 46:9–10 (MT 46:10–11). He is the only power that stands after the apocalyptic purging of the earth, so he alone is to be praised and feared (47:1–2 [MT 47:2–3]).

The ESV renders Ps 47:3 (MT 47:4) in the past tense, but the CSB and NAS put it in the present tense. The verse describes what God did when Israel conquered the land of promise, but rendering the verbs in the present tense is preferable because of the wider context of Ps 47. As present-tense statements, this describes the way God acts for his people, in the past, present, and future. What God did for Israel at the exodus from Egypt, at the conquest of the land, and when King David conquered surrounding nations is what God will do for his people when the King comes and the new Jerusalem is established. The description of God as the fearsome, conquering King in 47:2–3 (MT 47:3–4) matches the description of God as the King of the nations in 47:7–8 (MT 47:8–9).

The historical background of the "inheritance" in 47:4 (MT 47:5) is the land of promise. That land of promise is the pride of God's people, referenced here as Jacob, and Jacob is a poetic way of referring to the people of Israel, on whom the Lord set his love (cf. Deut 7:8). The psalmist here uses the sequence of exodus and conquest to point forward to the eschatological conquest. God's choice and love in Ps 47:4 (MT 47:5) are matched by the call for all to sing psalms to him in 47:6 (MT 47:7).

The centerpoint of the chiastic structure of Ps 47 is the description of Yahweh going up with a shout, with the blast of the shofar in 47:5 (MT 47:6).[176] This short description captures the moment when Yahweh rises to triumph for his people. It likely has in view the sending of the king who represents Yahweh and fights his battles in Ps 45, and the way Yahweh thereby puts an end to war and brings about the worldwide dominion of his king in Ps 46.

The triumph of God under discussion provokes the fourfold call to sing praise to God our king in 47:6 (MT 47:7). The repetition of the verb that calls for Yahweh to be "psalmed" communicates urgent enthusiasm. The psalmist's joyous celebration overflows in staccato second-person plural imperatives: "Psalm God, psalm! Psalm our King, psalm!"

Psalm 47:7 (MT 47:8) shows that the second-person plurals ("you all") in 47:6 (MT 47:7) are addressed to everyone, because 47:7 (MT 47:8) declares that God is King of all the earth. Therefore everyone should psalm a *maskil*, that is, sing psalms that cause wisdom. This term *maskil* occurs in a number of psalm superscriptions, indicating that the psalmist wants everyone in the world to declare the truths about Yahweh in poetic songlike form along the lines of what is being done in the Psalms.

Psalm 47:8 (MT 47:9) declares that God is the true king of the nations. He is the worldwide ruler, and holiness is his throne. This means that his separate purity, the way that he is distinguished from all other things by his utter devotion to righteousness and love, to his own character, is the seat of his power, the throne of his judgment, and the wisdom of his governing authority.

Psalm 47:9 (MT 47:10) consummates the celebration of God's conquest and the call to praise with a description of nobles from the nations

---

[176] Rightly William S. Plumer, *Psalms: A Critical and Expository Commentary with Doctrinal and Practical Remarks* (Philadelphia: Lippincott, 1867; repr. Carlisle, PA: Banner of Truth, 2016), 528: "This verse is the key to the right understanding of the whole Psalm."

gathering together, and these foreigners seem to be described as the people of the God of Abraham. Against the CSB and NET ("assembled with the people of the God of Abraham"), the two phrases seem to be in apposition to one another: "the nobles of the peoples gathered, people of the God of Abraham." This relationship is interpreted to mean that the nations are gathered "as the people of the God of Abraham" by the ESV, KJV, NAS, and NIV. God promised Abraham that all the families of the earth would be blessed in him (Gen 12:3), and Ps 47:9 (MT 47:10) heralds the fulfillment of that promise.

The nations have been subdued (47:3 [MT 47:4]), and with all other powers defeated, it is clear that all people belong to Yahweh. This would explain why the next phrase in 47:9 (MT 47:10) explains that the shields of the earth belong to God: he has defeated all rival powers, and he is now the only source of protection—symbolically referenced here as "shields"—for anyone anywhere. The last line of the verse declares that God is "greatly exalted" (CSB). As Kidner notes, "This was, in different words, the climax of 46:10, above and beyond 46:9. It is the point to which everything is moving."[177]

BRIDGE

We exist for God's glory. Our problem is that we keep wanting to exist for ourselves, for our own pleasure and renown rather than God's. Psalm 47 celebrates the day when Yahweh's King (Ps 45) will have established Yahweh's new city (Ps 46) and all the nations will celebrate him as the world's only true Lord. He is triumphant, resplendent, and worthy.

If we survey the news, we will see that the world is currently ruled by human beings who tend to be corrupt, unrighteous, malevolent, foolish, misguided, and deceitful. Psalm 47 calls all the world's inhabitants to erupt in praise because Yahweh has gone up with a shout, the shofar has sounded, and the faith has become sight.

## Psalm 48

OVERVIEW AND STRUCTURE OF PSALM 48

Psalm 48 reflects the following chiastic structure:

---

[177] Kidner, Psalms 1-72, 196.

48:1–3 (MT 48:2–4), God's Glory in Zion's Splendid Citadels
　48:4–7 (MT 48:5–8), Kings Astounded, Ships Shattered
　　48:8 (MT 48:9), God Establishes His City
　48:9–11 (MT 48:10–12), God's Lovingkindness, Righteousness, and
　　Judgments
48:12–14 (MT 48:13–15), God's Glory in Zion's Towers, Ramparts, and
　Citadels

Scripture

CSB

Author's translation

A song. A psalm of the sons of Korah.

¹ The Lord is great and highly praised
in the city of our God.
His holy mountain, ² rising splendidly,
is the joy of the whole earth.
Mount Zion—the summit of Zaphon—
is the city of the great King.
³ God is known as a stronghold
in its citadels.

⁴ Look! The kings assembled;
they advanced together.
⁵ They looked and froze with fear;
they fled in terror.
⁶ Trembling seized them there,
agony like that of a woman in labor,
⁷ as you wrecked the ships of Tarshish
with the east wind.
⁸ Just as we heard, so we have seen
in the city of the Lord of Armies,
in the city of our God;
God will establish it forever.
*Selah*

⁹ God, within your temple,
we contemplate your faithful love.
¹⁰ Like your name, God, so your praise
reaches to the ends of the earth;
your right hand is filled with justice.
¹¹ Mount Zion is glad.

¹ A Song.
A Psalm.
Of the sons of Korah.

² Great is Yahweh,
and being praised exceedingly,
in the city of our God,
the mountain of his holiness.
³ Beautiful in elevation,
the rejoicing of the whole earth,
Mount Zion, the remotest parts of the
north,
city of the great King.
⁴ God in her palaces is known as a
stronghold.

⁵ For behold, the kings are met;
they cross over together;
⁶ they saw, thus they were astounded;
they were terrified: they were put to
flight.
⁷ Trembling seized them there,
writhing as a woman giving birth.
⁸ With a wind of the east
you will shatter the ships of Tarshish.

⁹ As we have heard, thus we have seen,
in the city of Yahweh of hosts,
in the city of our God:
God establishes her unto the age.
*Selah.*

Judah's villages rejoice
because of your judgments.

<sup>12</sup> Go around Zion, encircle it;
count its towers,
<sup>13</sup> note its ramparts; tour its citadels
so that you can tell a future
  generation:
<sup>14</sup> "This God, our God forever and
  ever—
he will always lead us."

<sup>10</sup> We ponder, O God, your
  lovingkindness, in the midst of
  your temple,
<sup>11</sup> as your name, O God, thus your
  praise,
to the ends of the earth, your right
  hand fills righteousness.
<sup>12</sup> Let Mount Zion be glad,
the daughters of Judah rejoice,
because of your judgments.

<sup>13</sup> Go around Zion, and encircle her;
count her towers.
<sup>14</sup> Put her ramparts to your heart;
pass between her palaces,
that you may recount to the
  generation afterward,
<sup>15</sup> that this is God, our God of the age
  and on;
he will lead us over death.

CONTEXT: VERBAL AND THEMATIC LINKS WITH SURROUNDING PSALMS

Psalm 45 celebrates the king, and Ps 46 speaks of the hope for the city that will stand after the earth gives way. In Ps 47 the nations of the earth praise God as the great King over all the earth, and in Ps 48 the sons of Korah sing the presence of God in the city of God.

EXPOSITION

Psalm 48 opens and closes with statements that glorify God by celebrating his city (48:1–3, 12–14 [MT 48:2–4, 13–15]).[178] The psalmist then describes the way enemy kings were overcome—apparently by the imposing fortifications of the city—and ships were shattered by the wind, and across from this stands a meditation on the way God's lovingkindness (*hesed*), righteousness (*tsedek*), and judgment (*mishpat*) mark his dwelling place (48:4–7, 9–11 [MT 48:5–8, 10–12]). The chiastic structure frames the central statement of 48:8 (MT 48:9), which declares that what the people of God have heard corresponds to what they see in the city that God will establish forever.

---

<sup>178</sup> Cf. Keel, *Symbolism of the Biblical World*, 17–18, for other ancient Near Eastern instances of the glory of the gods being reflected in buildings and cities.

Psalm 48:1 (MT 48:2) picks up right where Ps 47 left off. Psalm 47:9 (MT 47:10) noted the way the nations "are gathered" and described Yahweh being praised "exceedingly." Those gathered nations praise the greatness of Yahweh "exceedingly" in his city in 48:1 (MT 48:2). Just as Yahweh was seated "on the throne of his holiness" in 47:8 (MT 47:9), so Zion is referenced as "the mountain of his holiness" in 48:1 (MT 48:2).

That mountain is the fulfillment of the primal mountain of Eden (cf. Ezek 28:13–14). It is the mountain that will be high and exalted, to which the nations will stream to praise Yahweh (cf. Isa 2:1–5). Psalm 48:2 (MT 48:3) says that its elevation—if not in physical altitude then in significance—is lovely, causing joy for all inhabitants of the earth.[179] This Mount Zion is the city of the great king, the city of the Davidic king, and the phrase "the remotest parts of the north" seems to indicate the place of the great king's throne—where Lucifer sought to seat himself (Isa 14:12–13), whence the eschatological enemy Gog of Magog will draw his peoples (Ezek 38:6; 39:2). There seems to be a polemic against the idolatry of Israel's neighbors here as well. David Howard writes,

> The term [north] is also the name of a mountain marking the boundary between the Holy Land and Syria. The Canaanites believed that Baal resided there. ... Canaanite texts refer to this mountain as Baal's "beautiful hill," his "inheritance," his "holy mountain," and a "lovely, mighty mountain." So by affirming these things about Mount Zion, Ps 48 deliberately argues that Yahweh is greater than Baal and that his dwelling place is greater than Baal's.[180]

Psalm 48:4 (MT 48:5) declares that God is known as a stronghold in the strong houses, palaces or citadels, of Mount Zion. The upshot of this statement is that God, rather than the castle, is the stronghold.

From the description of the city in 48:1–3 (MT 48:2–4), the psalmist turns to the impression it makes on God's enemies in 48:4–7 (MT 48:5–8). The kings marched on the city to attack in 48:4 (MT 48:5), but in 48:5 (MT 48:6) as soon as they saw the imposing and impenetrable city of God they were overawed and fled, writhing in 48:6 (MT 48:7) as a woman in

---

[179] Keel, *Symbolism of the Biblical World*, 114, discusses the fact that because of the temple "Zion could bear the title 'mountain' even though there is no appreciable rise of terrain in the area."

[180] Howard, "Psalms Study Notes," 1042.

childbirth—a common Old Testament way of describing those suffering God's eschatological wrath. Continuing to describe the destruction of God's enemies, the psalmist speaks of the ships of Tarshish shattered by the east wind. This is similar to the way Jonah took a ship bound for Tarshish, in response to which Yahweh hurled a wind on the water, and the ship thought to be shattered (Jonah 1:4).

In Ps 48:8 (MT 48:9) the psalmist arrives at what appears to be his overarching point: That the report of Yahweh's mighty deeds heard by the people is matched by the manifestation of Yahweh's glory in his city. God establishes this city forever. The awesome power whereby God made the world, brought Israel out of Egypt, and gave Israel the land will be on display when God does the new creation work of the new exodus, new conquest, and establishment of the new Jerusalem through the new David.[181]

The psalmist relates how the temple, God's dwelling place, provokes thoughts of the Lord's lovingkindness (*hesed*) in 48:9 (MT 48:10). In 48:10 (MT 48:11) he confesses that God's purpose of filling the earth with his glory has been realized, as Yahweh's name and praise extend to the ends of the earth because his "right hand fills righteousness." The idea seems to be that the Lord's right hand, his power and skill, establish and execute the meaning of righteousness.[182] What the Lord does defines righteousness, and what the Lord does upholds the righteousness that derives its meaning from his character. In 48:11 (MT 48:12) the psalmist calls Mount Zion, populated by the daughters of Judah, to rejoice in response to God's judgments. Just judgment wins God praise. Righteous character results in a good exercise of power. And steadfast love surrounds the presence of the Lord in his dwelling place.

All of this declares that God's presence makes God's character visible to God's people. In response to the revelation of God in the city, the psalmist invites his audience to explore Zion, to travel its circumference, counting

---

[181] On the targum of Ps 48, Edwards, *Exegesis in the Targum of Psalms*, 143, writes: "Through the stimulus of other midrashic connections, therefore, [the targum of Ps 48] has become a means of encouragement to its readers to both remember God's historic redemption of his people and look forward to his future redemption." My analysis of Ps 48 arrives at the same conclusion by different means.

[182] Rightly Keel, *Symbolism of the Biblical World*, 27: "The psalms repeatedly assert that the whole earth is full of the glory of the divine name (Pss 8:1, 9; 48:10; 72:19; cf. 57:11). God's action and order dominate the space between heaven and earth."

the towers in Ps 48:12 (MT 48:13), in 48:13 (MT 48:14) contemplating the ramparts, moving between the citadels and palaces, all so that the fathers can give a full accounting of the visible glory of God to their children (cf. Deut 6:7). What is told is not ultimately about the glory of the city but about the glory of God, as 48:14 (MT 48:15) makes clear. The point is not that the city is to be equated with God but that the glory of God is revealed in the city. The city is made possible only because of God's power. The people were brought out of Egypt by God's power, conquered Canaan by God's power, defeated the nations by God's power, and their lives are sustained in the land by God's power as well.

The last phrase of 48:14 (MT 48:15) in *BHS* can be rendered, "he will lead us over death," a translation reflected in a footnote in the ESV, which is also similar to the rendering found in the KJV and NAS. God's power will not be stymied by old age, nor will death bring it to an end.

### Bridge

Those made in the image of their creator will never build a grander city than the one built by the one whose image they bear. What God will do in the new Jerusalem surpasses any city ever built for glory. Not Rome with its Coliseum, not Beijing with its Forbidden City, not Paris with its Louvre, nor Washington DC with its mall will surpass the splendor of the city of God.

The flight of the gathered kings in 48:4–5 (MT 48:5–6) will be fulfilled when the nations gather as a result of satanic deception to surround the beloved city only to be consumed when fire falls from heaven (Rev 20:7–10).

The Lord Jesus will come (Ps 45). The creation will be unmade and made new (Ps 46). The nations will praise the Lord (Ps 47). And the new Jerusalem will shine forth the glory of God (Ps 48; Rev 21–22).

## Psalm 49

### Overview and Structure of Psalm 49

Psalm 49:1–4 (MT 49:2–5) summons everyone in the world to listen to its message. The psalmist then responds in verses 5–6 (MT 6–7) to the intimidating wicked who boast in their wealth by asking why he should fear them. He asserts in 49:7–9 (MT 49:8–10) that no man can redeem another, and follows that in verses 10–12 (MT 11–13) with the assertion that *everyone* dies. The psalmist then reflects in 49:13–15 (MT 49:14–16) on the way that the wealthy wicked are not intimidating but stupid. Though many celebrate what they say, they will die and the upright will be rewarded when this life is over and the new day dawns. Whereas the wealthy cannot pay for their redemption, the psalmist is confident that God will redeem him. He then urges his audience not to fear in 49:16–17 (MT 49:17–18) and closes the psalm in 49:18–20 (MT 49:19–21) with a reflection on the finality of death and the futility of all that ends when this life is over.

This material forms a chiasm as follows:

49:1–4 (MT 49:2–5), Hear This, All Peoples
   49:5–6 (MT 49:6–7), Why Should I Fear?
      49:7–9 (MT 49:8–10), No Redemption
         49:10–12 (MT 49:11–13), All Die
      49:13–15 (MT 49:14–16), My Redemption
   49:16–17 (MT 49:17–18), Do Not Fear
49:18–20 (MT 49:19–21), All Die

We will pursue the exposition of this psalm under the following subheads:

   49:1–4 (MT 49:2–5), Wisdom for Everyone
   49:5–17 (MT 49:6–18), Don't Fear the Rich Who Can't Redeem
   49:18–20 (MT 49:19–21), Man in His Pomp Will Not Endure

| SCRIPTURE | Author's translation |
|---|---|
| CSB | |
| For the choir director. A psalm of the sons of Korah. | [1] For the Preeminent One. Of the sons of Korah. A Psalm. |
| [1] Hear this, all you peoples; listen, all who inhabit the world, [2] both low and high, rich and poor together. [3] My mouth speaks wisdom; my heart's meditation brings understanding. [4] I turn my ear to a proverb; I explain my riddle with a lyre. | [2] Hear this, all the peoples! Give ear, all inhabitants of the world, [3] even the sons of Adam, even the sons of man, together rich and poor: [4] my mouth will speak wisdoms, and the meditation of my heart is understandings. [5] I will incline my ear to a proverb [a ruler's phrase], I will open my riddle on a lyre. |

⁵ Why should I fear in times of
   trouble?
The iniquity of my foes surrounds me.
⁶ They trust in their wealth
and boast of their abundant riches.
⁷ Yet these cannot redeem a person
or pay his ransom to God—
⁸ since the price of redeeming him is
   too costly,
one should forever stop trying—
⁹ so that he may live forever
and not see the Pit.

¹⁰ For one can see that the wise die;
the foolish and stupid also pass away.
Then they leave their wealth to others.
¹¹ Their graves are their permanent
   homes,
their dwellings from generation to
   generation,
though they have named estates after
   themselves.
¹² But despite his assets, mankind will
   not last;
he is like the animals that perish.

¹³ This is the way of those who are
   arrogant,
and of their followers,
who approve of their words.
*Selah*

¹⁴ Like sheep they are headed for Sheol;
Death will shepherd them.
The upright will rule over them in the
   morning,
and their form will waste away in
   Sheol,
far from their lofty abode.
¹⁵ But God will redeem me
from the power of Sheol,
for he will take me.
*Selah*

⁶ Why should I fear in the days of evil?
   The iniquity of my heels surrounds
   me.
⁷ Those who trust in their wealth and
   in the abundance of their riches,
   they boast.
⁸ A brother will not redeeming
   redeem a man, he will not give to
   God his ransom.
⁹ The redemption price of their soul
   is exorbitant, and it ceases to the
   age,[183]
¹⁰ that he might live everlasting: he
   will not see the pit.

¹¹ For he will see wise ones die;
   together the stupid and the
   senseless perish,
and they leave their wealth to others.
¹² Within them their houses are to the
   age,
their tabernacles to generation and
   generation: they called their names
   over the lands.
¹³ But man with his exorbitance will
   not endure.
He is ruled like the beasts: they are
   destroyed.

¹⁴ This is their way, the stupidity of
   them;
and after them, in their mouth they
   delight. *Selah.*
¹⁵ Like the flock, for Sheol they are
   set. Death will shepherd them,
and the upright will rule over them in
   the morning.
And their form will wear out Sheol,
   away from his lofty abode.[184]
¹⁶ Surely God will redeem my soul
   from the hand of Sheol, for he will
   take me. *Selah.*

---

[183] ESV, "For the ransom of their life is costly and can never suffice."
[184] ESV, "Their form shall be consumed in Sheol, with no place to dwell." NIV, "Their forms will decay in the grave, far from their princely mansions."

16 Do not be afraid when a person gets
  rich,
when the wealth of his house
  increases.
17 For when he dies, he will take
  nothing at all;
his wealth will not follow him down.
18 Though he blesses himself during
  his lifetime—
and you are acclaimed when you do
  well for yourself—
19 he will go to the generation of his
  ancestors;
they will never see the light.
20 Mankind, with his assets
but without understanding,
is like the animals that perish.

17 Do not fear when he causes a man
  wealth, when he multiplies the
  glory of his house,
18 for when he dies he will not take
  the whole.
His glory will not go down after him.
19 Though his soul in his life he
  blesses:
"May they praise you because you
  have done well for yourself!"
20 It [his soul] will go to the generation
  of his fathers, until the end they
  will not see light.
21 Man with his exorbitance, but he
  will not understand.
He is ruled like the beasts: they are
  destroyed.

CONTEXT: VERBAL AND THEMATIC LINKS WITH SURROUNDING PSALMS

In Pss 42–43 the psalmist was cast down in soul, taunted by the wicked and unjust about where his God had gone. That individual plea was extended to the believing remnant in Ps 44, and their relief came in the celebration of the king in Ps 45, followed by the establishment of the eschatological city in Ps 46. The peoples were called to celebrate in Ps 47, and Ps 48 sang the glory of God in the beauty of the city. Ps 49 now compares the worthless wealth of the nations, wealth that cannot redeem them or continue with them after death, with the lasting treasures of those who know God. Psalms 42–49 are "of the sons of Korah," and Ps 50, "of Asaph," will complement the Korah-cycle with a depiction of Yahweh coming forth for final judgment, demanding the worship due his name.

This set of non-Davidic psalms that open Book 2 of the Psalter reflects a recursive, ring structure chiastic arrangement as follows:

Psalms 42–43, The Cast Down Soul of the Believer
    Psalm 44, The Believing Community Waits for the Lord
        Psalm 45, The Conquering King and His Covenant Marriage
        Psalm 46, The City Stands When the Earth Gives Way
    Psalm 47–48, International Celebration of the Conqueror and His City
Psalms 49–50, The Vanity of Worldly Wealth at the Final Judgment

### 49:1–4 (MT 49:2-5), Wisdom for Everyone

Psalm 49:1–2 (MT 49:2–3) summons all peoples, all the world's inhabitants, sons of Adam and sons of man, rich and poor together to hear the message of the psalm. No one anywhere is exempt from the truth of the urgent message of Ps 49.

Having summoned his audience and stated its scope, the psalmist announces what he plans to do in 49:3–4 (MT 49:4–5). Using a cluster of terms that appear prominently in Prov 1:1–7, he declares that his mouth will speak *wisdom*. Flowing from the meditation of his heart (cf. Ps 1:2) is *understanding*, and because he pays attention to the *proverb*, he can open the meaning of the *riddle* on the lyre. This language indicates that Ps 49 will present biblical wisdom that teaches skill for living well. This wisdom enables those who contemplate it by meditating on it in their hearts and chewing on its deep truth, being shaped by its promises and warnings, to understand how God made the world to work. The word for "proverb," *mashal*, is homonyimic with a verb that means "rule." There may be an etymological connection indicating that proverbs communicate the truths that rule the world, truths that kings should embrace. Referring to these as "riddles" (cf. Prov 1:6) points to the surprising conundrums and mysteries that characterize the appearance of God's truth in God's world.

### 49:5–17 (MT 49:6-18), Don't Fear the Rich Who Can't Redeem

The body of Ps 49 opens with the psalmist's question why he should fear in verse 5 (MT 6) and concludes with the psalmist's instruction to his audience that they should not fear in verse 16 (MT 17). There seem to be five thought units in this section: (1) why fear? (49:5–6 [MT 49:6–7]); (2) the rich cannot ransom themselves (49:7–9 [MT 49:8–10]); (3) everyone dies (49:10–12 [MT 49:11–13]); (4) God ransoms the upright (49:13–15 [MT 49:14–16]); and (5) a command not to fear (49:16–17 [MT 49:17–18]).

The question in Ps 49:5 (MT 49:6) as to why the psalmist should fear is informed by what he goes on to say in the rest of verse 5 and into verse 6 (MT 6–7). The psalmist's fear would be prompted by, literally, "the iniquity of my heels" (49:5 [MT 49:6]) The CSB renders this, "The iniquity of my foes surrounds me," and the ESV, "the iniquity of those who cheat me surrounds me." Rashi took this as a reference to "iniquities, which

I trample with my heels."[185] The psalmist appears to be surrounded by iniquitous people sniping at his heels (cf. Gen 3:15), and he explains in 49:6 (MT 49:7) that these people trust in their wealth. People boast about what they trust, so naturally these enemies boast in their riches.

Wealthy enemies with wicked intent surround the psalmist, and he does not respond as the world would expect. The resources and influence of the rich should make them intimidating, but having asked why he should fear them, the psalmist explains the perspective that enables his confidence.

The psalmist asserts that the wealth in which the wicked trust in 49:6 (MT 49:7) can't redeem their souls in 49:7–9 (MT 49:8–10). The ransom price would be paid to God in 49:7 (MT 49:8), but such price could never be paid by a brother for a man. The ransom to God (49:7 [MT 49:8]) cannot be paid because, 49:8 (MT 49:9) explains, the price is too high and the money will simply run out. The "redemption price" is the subject of both verbs in 49:8 (MT 49:9): the price is exorbitant, and the amount fails forever. What the price would accomplish is stated in 49:9 (MT 49:10): the price under discussion would enable everlasting life, buying deliverance from the pit, that place of destruction where the dead are punished. Humanity has despoiled God's world. Mere money, of which God has no need, will not satisfy his justice.

Having explained that he does not fear the wealthy wicked (49:5–6 [MT 49:6–7]) because they cannot redeem themselves from God's justice (49:7–9 [MT 49:8–10]), the psalmist explains in 49:10–12 (MT 49:11–13) that everyone dies and that earthly wealth cannot be taken into the afterworld.

Psalm 49:10 (MT 49:11) asserts that the wise and the foolish, the stupid and the brutish all perish. When they perish, moreover, their money stays in this world while they go to the next. All that wealth, foundation of their confidence and theme of their boast, will fall into the hands of others. As Timothy Keller writes, "Only God can give you things of value that death cannot touch but only enhance."[186]

The Hebrew text of Ps 49:11 (MT 49:12) reads, "Within them their houses are forever," which the NAS rightly takes to mean, "Their inner thought is that their houses are forever" (so also KJV). The CSB, ESV, and

---

[185] Rashi, *Commentary on Psalms*, trans. Mayer I. Gruber (Philadelphia: Jewish Publication Society, 2008), 371.

[186] Timothy Keller and Kathy Keller, *The Songs of Jesus: A Year of Daily Devotions in the Psalms* (New York: Viking, 2015), 103.

NIV, however, follow the Greek and Syriac translations and the targum in reading "within" (קרב) as a scribal error for "grave" (קבר), terms that have the same consonants but put the final two in different order. If we read the text as it stands in the MT, the three lines of 49:11 (MT 49:12) all refer to the way the wicked expect to live and enjoy their homes and lands forever. The other reading would link the first line of verse 11 (MT 12) with the sentiment of verse 10 (MT 11). Either way the psalmist reflects on the way the expectation of the wicked expect does not match reality: they think they will remain forever, but they will die and their influence will end. The reference in Ps 49:12 (MT 49:13) to man with his "exorbitance" (CSB "assets," ESV "pomp") employs the noun that is cognate with the verb used in 49:8 (MT 49:9) to speak of the "exorbitant" redemption price of a man. Those who try to amass the exorbitant, costly price of redemption will not succeed. They will not achieve life. They will be like beasts that perish.

Everyone dies, including the very rich. The psalmist wants all the world's inhabitants to learn the wisdom that no one will be able to buy off God's justice. The debt is too great to be repaid, and when the debt comes due, those cast into God's debtor's prison will retain neither cash nor real estate. They will die and pay the penalty.

Psalm 49:13 (MT 49:14) marvels at the stupidity of the way of the wicked. Not only do they live for all they can get, without regard for life after death, without regard for God, without regard for hell, they celebrate one another for the things they say. These are people who have failed at life. They will incur God's judgment. They are fools. And yet they treat one another as champions of wisdom who have succeeded in life.

In 49:14 (MT 49:15) the psalmist likens these people to sheep appointed for Sheol. If the righteous are like sheep to the slaughter, martyred for their faithfulness to Yahweh (44:11, 22 [MT 44:12, 23]), the wicked are like sheep set for Sheol. Whereas the righteous have the Yahweh as their shepherd (23:1), Death (personified) will shepherd the wicked. And when the day of the new creation dawns, the wicked wealthy who have taunted and intimidated the righteous will find the upright ruling over them in the morning (49:14 [MT 49:15]). After the reference to Sheol and Death, this mention of "the morning" would seem to be the dawning of a new day after death: the resurrection morning. The last line of 49:14 (MT 49:15) indicates that whereas the unrighteous rich formerly enjoyed luxurious dwelling places, their forms will have a new abode in Sheol. It is unclear whether "Sheol" or "their form" is the subject of the infinitive "to wear out." Either Sheol will wear out the wicked, or the wicked will be in Sheol so long, forever, that they will wear it out. Either way, those who formerly lived in luxury will now inhabit misery in Sheol.

The rich who rely on money will have no redemption, but the psalmist knows where redemption can be found. He asserts in 49:15 (MT 49:16) that God will surely redeem him from the hand, or power, of Sheol.[187] God will take him, receive him, and free him from the power of his debt to God's own righteousness.

Money cannot redeem, but God can and does. The psalmist's confidence in God's justice frees him from fear of the wicked and their wealth. Not only is the psalmist himself freed from such fear, in 49:16 (MT 49:17) he calls his audience not to fear when men indulge in wealth, when the glory of their holdings multiplies. To establish the reason for this admonition not to fear he once again asserts in 49:17 (MT 49:18) that the wicked cannot take it with them: when he dies he cannot take his treasures to Sheol, and his glory will not go there with him.

### 49:18–20 (MT 49:19-21), Man in His Pomp Will Not Endure

The psalmist rounds out the psalm with a response to what appears to be a representation of what the wicked says to himself in 49:18 (MT 49:19). The wicked assures himself that he is blessed (his money proves it), and the second line of 49:18 (MT 49:19) reads, "May they praise you because you have done well for yourself!" This would indicate that the wicked expects others to be impressed with the wealth he has gained.

The psalmist's response in 49:19 (MT 49:20) is that the soul of the wicked will go to the generation of his fathers. That is: he will join them in Sheol. And whereas the wealthy sought to buy redemption that they might not see the pit (49:9 [MT 49:10]), they will never see the light (49:19 [MT 49:20]). This light likely comes with the "morning" when the upright will rule over the wicked (49:14 [MT 49:15]). In the resurrection they will not enjoy God's light.

The psalm concludes in 49:20 (MT 49:21) with a variation of the statement made in 49:12 (MT 49:13). For all his wealth with which he seeks

---

[187] For the argument that these statements contribute to resurrection hope, see Mitchell L. Chase, "From Dust You Shall Arise: Resurrection Hope in the Old Testament," *SBJT* 18.4 (2014): 9–29.

to do his own will, man will not be able to buy his redemption from God, nor will his wealth justify him before God. These wicked will not hear the wisdom the psalmist communicates in Ps 49, so 49:20 (MT 49:21) asserts that they will remain without understanding (cf. 49:3–4 [MT 49:4–5]), like beasts, and their end will be worthy of an uncomprehending animal.

BRIDGE

Psalm 49, like the books of Proverbs and Ecclesiastes, teaches the vanity of wealth. Timothy and Kathy Keller penned a prayer in response to Ps 49 that reads in part, "Lord, I often catch myself imagining how much greater life would be if I had more. I also quietly 'boast' in my heart when I see myself able to afford certain goods and inhabit certain places. Save my heart from such shallowness and foolishness."[188]

In addition to the vanity of trust in money, the psalmist is also confident that God will redeem and receive him. The language of redemption used in this psalm recalls the way God delivered Israel at the exodus from Egypt. The verb used in 49:15 (MT 49:16) to describe the way that God will take/receive the psalmist is the same used to describe the Lord taking Enoch in Gen 5:24.[189] The fact that Enoch did not die shows that God's power transcends death, and the fact that God redeemed his people at the exodus points forward to the way he will redeem them again. There is also the reference to the enemies being at the psalmist's heels in 49:5 (MT 49:6), which seems to employ imagery that springs from Gen 3:15. As the progress of revelation continues through the pages of the Bible, we see the seed of the woman come and accomplish the new exodus redemption, which grounds the resurrection/new creation hope for God's people. Jesus also taught the vanity of trusting in wealth (e.g., Luke 12:13–34), even as he proved himself to be, in every way, a sure foundation for the hopes of God's people.

## Psalm 50

OVERVIEW AND STRUCTURE OF PSALM 50

The content of Ps 50 breaks down in a straightforward way:

---

[188] Keller and Keller, *Songs of Jesus*, 103.

[189] Kidner, *Psalms 1-72*, 202.

50:1–6, God Comes for Judgment
50:7–15, A Rebuke for Covenant Keepers: Give Thanks and
    Praise
50:16–23, A Rebuke for Covenant Breakers: Give Thanks and
    Praise

These contents may reflect a chiastic structure along the following
lines:

50:1–3, God Comes
    50:4–6, Summons to Judgment
        50:7–11, Sacrifice Misunderstood
        50:12–15, Thanks and Praise as Sacrifice
    50:16–21, Judgment of the Wicked
50:22–23, Fear, Repentance, Thanks, and Praise

SCRIPTURE

**CSB**

A psalm of Asaph.

¹ The Mighty One, God, the LORD, speaks;
he summons the earth
from the rising of the sun to its
    setting.
² From Zion, the perfection of beauty,
God appears in radiance.
³ Our God is coming; he will not be
    silent!
Devouring fire precedes him,
and a storm rages around him.
⁴ On high, he summons heaven and
    earth
in order to judge his people:
⁵ "Gather my faithful ones to me,
those who made a covenant with me
    by sacrifice."
⁶ The heavens proclaim his
    righteousness,
for God is the Judge.
*Selah*

**Author's translation**

¹ A Psalm of Asaph.
The Deity, God, Yahweh speaks and
    calls the earth
from the rising of the sun to the place
    of its setting.
² Out of Zion, the perfection of beauty,
    God shines forth.
³ Our God will come, and he will not
    keep silence.
A fire before him will devour, and
    around him it storms to excess.

⁴ He calls to the heavens above, and to
    the earth, to judge his people.
⁵ Gather to me those of my
    lovingkindness, the ones who cut
    my covenant by sacrifice.
⁶ And the heavens will declare his
    righteousness, for God himself is
    the judge. *Selah*.

⁷ Hear, my people, and I will speak;
O Israel, and I will bear witness
    against you.

7 "Listen, my people, and I will speak;
I will testify against you, Israel.
I am God, your God.
8 I do not rebuke you for your
    sacrifices
or for your burnt offerings,
which are continually before me.
9 I will not take a bull from your
    household
or male goats from your pens,
10 for every animal of the forest is
    mine,
the cattle on a thousand hills.
11 I know every bird of the mountains,
and the creatures of the field are mine.
12 If I were hungry, I would not tell
    you,
for the world and everything in it is
    mine.
13 Do I eat the flesh of bulls
or drink the blood of goats?
14 Offer a thanksgiving sacrifice to God,
and pay your vows to the Most High.
15 Call on me in a day of trouble;
I will rescue you, and you will honor
    me."

16 But God says to the wicked:
"What right do you have to recite my
    statutes
and to take my covenant on your lips?
17 You hate instruction
and fling my words behind you.
18 When you see a thief,
you make friends with him,
and you associate with adulterers.
19 You unleash your mouth for evil
and harness your tongue for deceit.
20 You sit, maligning your brother,
slandering your mother's son.
21 You have done these things, and I
    kept silent;
you thought I was just like you.
But I will rebuke you
and lay out the case before you.

God, your God, am I.
8 Not for your sacrifices do I rebuke
    you,
while your burnt offerings are before
    me continually.
9 I will not receive from your house
    a bull, from your sheepfolds male
    goats;
10 for every beast of the forest is mine,
    the cattle on a thousand hills.
11 I know every bird of the mountains,
    and the zyzzyva of the field are
    with me.

12 If I was hungry, I would not tell you,
    for the world and its fullness are
    for me.
13 Do I eat the flesh of the mighty ones
    or the blood of male goats drink?
14 Sacrifice to God thanksgiving, and
    fulfill to the Most High your vows.
15 And call upon me in the day of
    distress: I will deliver you, and you
    will glorify me.

16 But to the wicked, God says:
What to you to recount my statutes,
and to take my covenant upon your
    lips?
17 But you hate discipline and cast my
    words behind you.
18 If you see a thief, you are pleased
    with him!
And with those who commit adultery
    is your portion.
19 You send out your mouth in evil,
    and your tongue causes webs of
    deceit.
20 You sit, against your brother you
    speak, on the son of your mother
    you place blame.
21 These you do, and I kept silent.
You thought I would be like you.
I rebuke you and will set it out before
    your eyes.

<sup>22</sup> "Understand this, you who forget God,
 or I will tear you apart,
and there will be no one to rescue you.
<sup>23</sup> Whoever offers a thanksgiving sacrifice honors me,
and whoever orders his conduct,
I will show him the salvation of God."

<sup>22</sup> Please understand this, those who forget the Divine One,
lest I tear, and there will be none who causes deliverance:
<sup>23</sup> the one who sacrifices thanksgiving glorifies me,
and the one who sets the way, I will show him the salvation of God.

CONTEXT: VERBAL AND THEMATIC LINKS WITH SURROUNDING PSALMS

The individual psalmist's woe in Pss 42 and 43 was shared by the believing community in Ps 44, but then the king came in Ps 45 and established his city in 46. All peoples were summoned to celebrate the great king in Ps 47, then the glory of God in the city was extolled in 48. The wealth of the nations was exposed as a false hope of redemption in Ps 49, and now in Ps 50 Yahweh comes forth for judgment.

EXPOSITION

**50:1–6, God Comes for Judgment**

Psalm 50 is a psalm of Asaph. He was among those whom David placed over the service of song at the house of Yahweh after the ark was brought into Jerusalem (1 Chr 6:31, 39; 15:16–17). In 1 Chr 16:5 Asaph is referred to as the chief of these ministers (cf. 1 Chr 25:2). In 2 Chr 29:30 Hezekiah ordered the Levites and singers of his day "to praise Yahweh with the words of David and of Asaph the seer." Here the author of Chronicles seems to present Hezekiah interpreting the psalm superscriptions as indicating authorship of the psalms. Psalms 50 and 73–83 have "Of Asaph" in their superscriptions, and 2 Chr 29:30 appears to interpret this to mean that these psalms constitute "the words of ... Asaph."

Psalm 50:1–3 describes God coming in majesty, and 50:4–6 presents him summoning both the witnesses to the covenant (Deut 4:26) and his covenant-partners to judgment.

The psalmist solemnly begins with three different ways of referring to God: "The Deity, God, Yahweh" (50:1). This piling up of references to the one who "speaks and calls the earth from the rising of the sun to the place of its setting" emphasizes the Lord's authority and majesty. The extended introduction impresses the gravity and sobriety of the one who now calls the earth to account. The comprehensive summons to all people everywhere functions the same way. Though the psalm seems to focus its attention and judgment on the people of Israel, its warning and message extend to all people: if Israel will be judged on these terms, how much more the rest of the nations? The God of the Bible does not summon merely one local tribe but anyone on whom the sun's rays fall—which is to say, everyone everywhere.

Psalm 50:2 seems to assume the apocalyptic upheaval of Ps 46 and the establishment of Zion as the radiance of God's glory in Ps 48, as God is described shining forth from Zion, the completion of beauty. Asaph appears to envision something along the lines of what Isa 2:1–4 depicts, when Yahweh's throne will be established in Zion, and now he shines forth from his city, summoning all to the eschatological assize.

In "Sinners in the Hands of an Angry God," Jonathan Edwards wrote,

> 'Tis true, that judgment against your evil works has not been executed hitherto; the floods of God's vengeance have been withheld; but your guilt in the meantime is constantly increasing, and you are every day treasuring up more wrath; the waters are continually rising and waxing more and more mighty; and there is nothing but the mere pleasure of God that holds the waters back that are unwilling to be stopped, and press hard to go forward; if God should only withdraw his hand from the floodgate, it would immediately fly open, and the fiery floods of the fierceness and wrath of God would rush forth with inconceivable fury, and would come upon you with omnipotent power; and if your strength were ten thousand times greater than it is, yea, ten thousand times greater than the strength of the stoutest, sturdiest devil in hell, it would be nothing to withstand or endure it.

In Ps 50:21, the Lord speaks of the way sinners continue in their sin and he kept silent, but 50:3 speaks of that future moment when the silence of God will end: when he comes forth. The one who is beyond compare, whose worth and glory are matchless, will at last come forth in his radiant purity. His voice will reach to the ends of the earth, all will be summoned before him, and the silence of the ages will end. The Lord's coming forth in 50:3 is reminiscent of the way that he came at Sinai, in flame and thick darkness of thundercloud. The psalmist describes a consuming fire going before him, a tempest raging around him.

Beginning in Deut 4:26 the Lord summoned heaven and earth to be witnesses against Israel in the covenant he entered into with them. These witnesses are invoked repeatedly after that (cf., e.g., Deut 30:19; 31:28; 32:1; Isa 1:2; Mic 6:1–2). Along these lines, Ps 50:4 presents Yahweh calling the heavens and the earth together for the judgment of his people, whom he refers to in 50:5 as those who are marked by his lovingkindness (pl. form of חסיד), who have entered into covenant with him by sacrifice (cf. Exod 24). Psalm 50:5 indicates that Yahweh set his steadfast love on Israel and thereby allowed them to enter into covenant with him by sacrifice. People to whom Yahweh has been gracious, to whom he has given privileges and unique access to himself, are now called to account for their stewardship of God's grace.

By calling the heavens and earth as the witnesses to the covenant, Yahweh invokes the testimony of witnesses who never avert their gaze, whose constant presence cannot be escaped, and whose reliability is as solid as the earth beneath, all-encompassing as the atmosphere around. These witnesses will know Israel's conduct in exacting detail, and they will have as full a reckoning of Yahweh's righteousness. The heavens thus declare God's righteousness in 50:6, and God himself is the judge in this dispute. God sits on the throne as the judge. The partners in his covenant, the people of Israel, stand before him, and the witnesses to the covenant, the heavens and the earth, give testimony.

### 50:7–15, A Rebuke for Covenant Keepers: Give Thanks and Praise

Psalm 50:7–15 seems to fall into two parts. In 50:7–11 the Lord explains why he does not rebuke Israel for their sacrifices, though he does correct their misunderstanding. Then in 50:12–15 he continues the correction while calling for the kind of sacrifice he seeks: that of thanks and praise.

God summoned the partners to the covenant in 50:5, and he addresses his people Israel in 50:7. Here the psalmist presents Yahweh himself speaking, which is an astonishing claim: the psalmist presents a direct message from the Lord of all. He presents God not only *speaking* but *bearing witness*, that is, giving testimony, against Israel, concluding with the solemn pronouncement, "God, your God, am I."

The upshot of Ps 50:8 seems to be that God does not rebuke Israel for failing to offer required sacrifices, since the burnt offerings are continually before him. God rebukes Israel not for failing to offer sacrifices in 50:8–15 but for their mistaken assumptions about those sacrifices.

The first mistaken assumption appears in 50:9–11 and concerns the *source* and *ownership* of the animals to be sacrificed. In 50:9 the Lord declares that he is not taking/receiving animals from Israel: neither bulls from their houses nor goats from their sheepfolds. Verse 10 asserts the reason this is so, namely, that every animal in the world already belongs to God. Psalm 50:10–11 declare that every beast of the field, the cattle on a thousand hills, every bird of the mountains, and the zyzzyva of the fields all belong to God. They are his creatures. He made them. This counters the mistaken notion that by offering sacrifices Israel provides for God's needs.

Supplying provender for God was never the point of the sacrifices. God did not need them; Israel did. The sacrifices did not bring God something he lacked but satisfied his justice against sin by making atonement. God prefers holy obedience over sacrifice. When those aiming at holy obedience failed to accomplish it, the sacrifices were provided so that those who failed in their attempt to obey could avoid the death due transgressors. Israel was not enriching Yahweh from their flocks and herds. He had no lack but an overflowing abundance. It was not Yahweh who needed the sacrifices but Israel.

The refutation of the false assumption about the source and ownership of the sacrificial animals—they already belonged to Yahweh before Israel offered them—is extended into a second related false assumption in 50:12–13. This second mistaken notion holds that Yahweh somehow depends upon the sacrificial animals for his sustenance. He repudiates this idea in 50:12 with the declaration that if he were in need of food he would not tell Israel of his need, for the world and all its fullness exist for him. He has everything. Why would he need Israel to provide his food? Then to guard against the idea that his ownership of all things might imply that he does need to eat and drink to be sustained, he scornfully asks whether he eats flesh and drinks blood—the question obviously expecting a negative answer. Yahweh is the creator. His creation does not in any way sustain him. He did not create to meet some need he had, nor did he ordain sacrifices for Israel to meet some need he had.

When he tells Israel what he wants from them in 50:14–15, moreover, he is not declaring what his real need is. Yahweh does not need the thanks and praise of men, but if his people want to please him, their hearts must feel gratitude, fidelity, and wonder at his deliverance. Thus in 50:14 the Lord commands his people to offer thanksgiving as their sacrifice. Such a sacrifice reflects the reality that every good thing comes from him. He also commands them to fulfill the vows they have made to the Most High. He wants his people to have the integrity to follow through on their commitments. And then he wants them to rely on him, to cry out to him in distress, to experience his deliverance, and to glorify him for his mercy.

God's people do not put him in their debt by meeting his needs out of their abundance. Rather, they are to feel gratitude in response to all his beneficent bounty, follow through on the fulfillment of their vows, call on the Lord as their Savior, and glorify him for his deliverance.

The fact that 50:16 addresses the wicked creates the impression that in 50:7–15 Yahweh has addressed those trying to keep the covenant by offering sacrifices. What the Lord says to those offering sacrifice indicates that their understanding of him is insufficient. Similarly, what the Lord says to the wicked indicates that they too have a deficient understanding of the true and living one.

### 50:16–23, A Rebuke for Covenant Breakers: Give Thanks and Praise

Those rebuked in 50:7–15 seem to have assumed that, like themselves, God needed others to enrich him by animals, by which his hunger would be assuaged and his life sustained. Similarly, those rebuked in 50:16–23 make the wrong assumption that God is like them. They are unholy and do not rebuke sinners, and they assume that God will be unholy and unwilling to uphold righteousness.

God asks the wicked in Ps 50:16 what business they have recounting his statutes or speaking of his covenant. It seems from 50:18–20 that the statutes in view are the Ten Commandments. Before specifying their sins, in 50:17 the Lord asserts that the wicked hate discipline, which is evident from the way they continue in unrepentant sin. By their ongoing misbehavior they also put God's words behind them rather than before their faces as guidelights for the way they will walk. Thus in 50:18 they are pleased by those who break the commandment not to steal, and they do not separate themselves from those who commit adultery. Delighting in those who do evil is the opposite of holiness, which separates from sin to pursue devotion to Yahweh.

The evil deeds of Ps 50:18 are accompanied by the evil speech of 50:19–20. The wicked send out their mouths to do evil, and their tongues weave webs of lies (50:19). Like Cain they do not play the role of a brother's keeper, but, bearers of false witness, they speak against their own brothers and fail to honor father and mother as they place blame on their own brothers (50:20).

The wicked have misinterpreted the Lord's longsuffering patience. God announces in 50:21 that as he kept silence about the evil of their actions and words, they concluded that God would be like them. Sin does not bother them. They assume it will not bother God. They do not rebuke or punish sinners. They assume God won't either. God, however, now announces his rebuke, setting the case out before their eyes. Their guilt is evident and inescapable.

Having indicted both those whose deficient theology keeps them from worshiping in truth and those whose deficient theology keeps them from repentance and purity, an appeal for repentance is made in 50:22–23. In 50:22 God pleads with those who forget him to understand lest he tear them with none to deliver. What exactly he wants them to understand is articulated in 50:23. God wants the sacrifice of thanksgiving, and he announces that the one who offers it glorifies him. God wants thanks and praise. Moreover, those who are thankful and who praise him will order their way in accordance with his revelation of his own character. He is a holy God. Those who believe what God reveals of himself will repent, and God will reveal his salvation to them.

### Bridge

The wrong approaches to worship and life rebuked in Ps 50 grow from wrong theology. The psalmist first repudiates the idea that God will not come, then the idea that God is needy, and finally the idea that God is unconcerned for holiness.

The rebuke of those worshiping the Lord as though he is needy can be considered by those of us seeking to worship God in the new covenant context. Just as God did not need the old covenant sacrifices because he lacked resources or felt physical hunger, God does not need us to accomplish his purposes. Just as the sacrifices were needed by Israel, so today we are the beneficiaries of our new covenant offering of ourselves as living sacrifices.

In Ps 50:14–15 and again in 50:23 the Lord declares that he wants thanks and praise. Paul indicted sinners in Rom 1:21 for failing to honor God as God and give thanks to him. We were made to enjoy God's goodness. Thanking God for his goodness and celebrating it increases and completes our enjoyment of God's goodness.

## Psalm 51

OVERVIEW AND STRUCTURE OF PSALM 51

Psalm 51 reflects a chiastic structure that includes the superscription and centers on the requests in 51:9 (MT 51:11) that God hide his face from David's sin and blot out all his iniquities as follows:

51:superscription–1 (MT 51:1–2), David's Sin
  51:1–2 (MT 51:3–4), Mercy and Cleansing
    51:3–4 (MT 51:5–6), Sin against God's Righteousness
      51:5–6 (MT 51:7–8), Born in Sin, God Delights in Truth
        51:7–8 (MT 51:9–10), Purified and Rejoiced
          51:9 (MT 51:11), Forgiveness
        51:10–11 (MT 51:12–13), New Heart and God's Presence
      51:12–13 (MT 51:14–15), Restored to Teach Repentance
    51:14–15 (MT 51:16–17), Justified and Celebrating God's Righteousness
  51:16–17 (MT 51:18–19), Sacrifice of Contrition
51:18–19 (MT 51:20–21), Jerusalem Restored and Sacrificing

For the purposes of exposition, we will approach the psalm in three sections:

    51:1–4 (MT 51:2–6), Have Mercy
    51:5–13 (MT 51:7–15), Fix Me
    51:14–19 (MT 51:16–21), Get Glory

SCRIPTURE

| CSB | Author's translation |
| --- | --- |
| For the choir director. A psalm of David, when the prophet Nathan came to him after he had gone to Bathsheba. | [1] For the Preeminent One. A Psalm of David. [2] When Nathan the prophet went to him, just as he had gone to Bathsheba. |
| [1] Be gracious to me, God, according to your faithful love; according to your abundant compassion, blot out my rebellion. | [3] Be gracious to me, O God, according to your lovingkindness. According to your great mercy blot out my transgressions. |

² Completely wash away my guilt
and cleanse me from my sin.
³ For I am conscious of my rebellion,
and my sin is always before me.
⁴ Against you—you alone—I have
    sinned
and done this evil in your sight.
So you are right when you pass
    sentence;
you are blameless when you judge.
⁵ Indeed, I was guilty when I was born;
I was sinful when my mother
    conceived me.

⁶ Surely you desire integrity in the
    inner self,
and you teach me wisdom deep
    within.
⁷ Purify me with hyssop, and I will be
    clean;
wash me, and I will be whiter than
    snow.
⁸ Let me hear joy and gladness;
let the bones you have crushed rejoice.
⁹ Turn your face away from my sins
and blot out all my guilt.
¹⁰ God, create a clean heart for me
and renew a steadfast spirit within me.
¹¹ Do not banish me from your
    presence
or take your Holy Spirit from me.
¹² Restore the joy of your salvation to
    me,
and sustain me by giving me a willing
    spirit.
¹³ Then I will teach the rebellious your
    ways,
and sinners will return to you.

¹⁴ Save me from the guilt of bloodshed,
    God—
God of my salvation—
and my tongue will sing of your
    righteousness.
¹⁵ Lord, open my lips,

⁴ Wash me thoroughly from my
    iniquity,
and from my sin cleanse me.

⁵ For my transgressions I know,
and my sin is before me continually.
⁶ Against you, you only, I sinned,
and what was evil in your eyes I did,
so that you are righteous when you
    speak, pure when you judge.

⁷ Behold, in iniquity I was born,
and in sin my mother conceived me.
⁸ Behold, you delight in truth in the
    inner parts,
and in the secret place wisdom you
    cause me to know.

⁹ Purify me with hyssop, and I will be
    clean.
Wash me, and I will be whiter than
    snow.
¹⁰ Cause me to hear joy and gladness.
Make the bones you crushed rejoice.

¹¹ Hide your face from my sins,
and all my iniquities blot out.

¹² A heart clean create for me, O God,
and a spirit established renew within
    me.
¹³ Do not cast me from your presence,
and do not take your Holy Spirit from
    me.

¹⁴ Restore to me the joy of your
    salvation,
and support me with a willing spirit.
¹⁵ I will teach transgressors your ways,
and sinners to you will return.

¹⁶ Deliver me from bloods, O God, God
    of my salvation.
My tongue will give a ringing cry of
    your righteousness.
¹⁷ O Lord, my lips you will open,

and my mouth will declare your praise.

¹⁶ You do not want a sacrifice, or I would give it;
you are not pleased with a burnt offering.

¹⁷ The sacrifice pleasing to God is a broken spirit.
You will not despise a broken and humbled heart, God.

¹⁸ In your good pleasure, cause Zion to prosper;
build the walls of Jerusalem.

¹⁹ Then you will delight in righteous sacrifices,
whole burnt offerings;
then bulls will be offered on your altar.

and my mouth will declare your praise.

¹⁸ For you do not desire sacrifice, or I would give.
With a burnt offering you are not pleased.

¹⁹ The sacrifices of God are a broken spirit,
a heart broken and crushed, O God, you will not despise.

²⁰ Do Zion good in your good pleasure.
You will build the walls of Jerusalem.

²¹ Then you will delight in sacrifices of righteousness, burnt offering and holocaust.
Then bulls will be offered up on your altar.

CONTEXT: VERBAL AND THEMATIC LINKS WITH SURROUNDING PSALMS

In Ps 50:7–13 God asserted that he needed neither a supply of sacrificial animals nor to eat their flesh for sustenance, then in 50:14 he called his people to make thanksgiving their sacrifice. In keeping with this emphasis on the state of the worshiper's heart, in Ps 51:16–17 (MT 51:18–19) David asserts that God wants a repentant and contrite heart not mere sacrifices.

Psalms 50 and 51 are connected not merely on the point of God's concern for the heart of the one offering sacrifice but also at a deeper level. It is as though the warning of judgment in Ps 50 prompts the sincere repentance in Ps 51. Psalm 50:18 denounced adulterers, and the wider context of Ps 50 presents the Lord coming in judgment (cf. 50:1–6). The terrible prospect of judgment crushes David's rebellion and puts him on his knees in Ps 51, crying out for mercy from the one whose righteousness his sin offended.

EXPOSITION

### 51:1–4 (MT 51:3–6), Have Mercy

The superscription of Ps 51 (MT 51:1–2) places this as David's response to the way that Nathan confronted him after his sin with Bathsheba (cf. 2 Sam 12). The psalm's closing verses (51:18–19 [MT 51:20–21) match the context of David's sin with an appeal for God to do good to Zion and rebuild Jerusalem that sacrifices might be offered to him. These appeals are necessitated by the way that David's sin could result in wrath on God's people and place.

In Ps 51:1–2 (MT 51:3–4) David cries out to God for forgiveness and cleansing. The corresponding two verses at the end of the psalm, 51:16–17 (MT 51:18–19), assert that God is not pleased by sacrifices but by genuine repentance. David makes two requests in 51:1 (MT 51:3), each grounded in an appeal for God to act in accordance with his own self-description in Exod 34:6–7. In Ps 51:1 (MT 51:3) David asks God to be gracious to him (חנן) and to blot out his transgressions. He does not appeal to anything in himself, whether his inherent worth or diligent effort, but to something in God. David appeals to God's lovingkindness (חסד) and mercy (רחם), for Yahweh describes himself as a God *merciful* (רחם) and *gracious* (חנן), abounding in *lovingkindness* (חסד) and *truth* (אמת) in Exod 34:6.

In Ps 51:1 (MT 51:3) David appeals to God's own character to ask for forgiveness, and in 51:2 (MT 51:4) he cries out for cleansing from the defiling effect of sin. For this, David asks the Lord to wash him thoroughly and cleanse him from his iniquity and sin. These verbs "wash" and "cleanse" appear frequently in Leviticus to describe ritual purification.

In Ps 51:3–4 (MT 51:5–6) David explains why he needs the forgiveness of 51:1 (MT 51:3) and the cleansing of 51:2 (MT 51:4): David is painfully aware of his sin (51:3 [MT 51:5]), and he knows that he has transgressed God's own holiness, which will be manifested when God speaks in righteousness and judges in purity (51:4 [MT 51:6]). The corresponding statements in 51:14–15 (MT 51:16–17) present David appealing for deliverance from "bloods" (CSB "the guilt of bloodshed"), likely a reference to Uriah, and this is accompanied by a reference to God's righteousness. In both 51:3–4 (MT 51:5–6) and 51:14–15 (MT 51:16–17) David confesses that God is in the right.

David speaks in 51:3 (MT 51:5) of knowing his transgression because his sin is ever before him. This statement reflects an acute awareness of sins large and small. It may also speak to the way that the woman with whom David had committed adultery, whose husband he murdered, became his wife (compare the way that Hamlet's uncle considers the propriety of retaining Gertrude as his wife should he repent of murdering Hamlet's father in Shakespeare's play). Once convicted of his sin, Bathsheba's presence would be for David a constant reminder of it.

David does not deny in 51:4 (MT 51:6) that he sinned against Bathsheba, Uriah, or anyone else harmed by what he did. He does, however, confess his sin as a personal affront to Yahweh.

What David says here corresponds to the text of Samuel in two ways. First, David had told Joab not to allow the death of Uriah to be evil in his sight (2 Sam 11:25), the narrator countering that what David did was evil in Yahweh's eyes (2 Sam 11:27). In Ps 51:4 (MT 51:6) David confesses that what he did was evil in the Lord's eyes. Second, Nathan the prophet told David that by his sin he had despised the word of Yahweh and Yahweh himself (2 Sam 12:9, 10). Those statements likely prompt David's confession that his sin was against the Lord. David confesses the most grievous reality of his sin: his action defiled God's holy word. The fact of David's guilt means that anything God says in condemnation of him is righteous. God is pure in his judgment, holy in his wrath, and justified in all judgment.

### 51:5–13 (MT 51:7–15), Fix Me

Encountering God's holiness exposes the depths of our problem, depths David plumbs in an unparalleled way in Ps 51:5 (MT 51:7). Here David states the problem faced by every descendant of Adam. We did not come into the world innocent and sinless, finding ourselves freshly placed in a pristine world. We were born in sin, having been conceived by sinners, and we live in a world pervaded by sin.[190] How then are we to do what is holy?

The circumstances of our conception and birth do not excuse us, as David makes clear in 51:6 (MT 51:8), where he confesses that God delights in truth in the inner parts of man and teaches wisdom in the secret heart. What man has become as a consequence of sin in 51:5 (MT 51:7) calls into question whether he can please God (51:6 [MT 51:8]). The solution to this dilemma is not to attempt to scale back God's standard, a project less likely of success than attempting to live in an imaginary castle in the skies. God's standard will not be changed.

---

[190] Discussing "original sin," Alter, *Book of Psalms*, 181, suggests "there is not much here to support the idea that this is the case of every human born." Against this, and for the wider biblical context that reveals original sin to be a feature of the biblical authors' worldview, see James M. Hamilton, "Original Sin in Biblical Theology," in *Adam, the Fall, and Original Sin: Theological, Biblical, and Scientific Perspectives*, ed. Hans Madueme and Michael Reeves (Grand Rapids: Baker Academic, 2014), 189–208.

If God's standard cannot be changed, the man who would enjoy God's holiness must be. This is why David prays as he does in the following verses. David desires more than forgiveness in this psalm. He prays to be transformed into a man who loves holiness and acts on that love.

For this to happen the stains of his sin must be cleansed, and the inclinations of his heart must be redirected. Addressing the way the idol factory of his heart has polluted and blighted the landscape of his whole being, David again employs terminology from the Levitical rituals as he calls on the Lord to purify him with hyssop that he might be clean, to wash him that he might be whiter than snow in 51:7 (MT 51:9). David has sinned against God, and David is confident that God can wash away the stain.

There is a profound connection between our sin and our moods. Holiness really does work happiness, and sin spoils everything. David's words in 51:8 (MT 51:10) reflect these truths. The cry that God would cause him to hear joy and gladness shows that he experiences the woes of sorrow from sin. The request that bones God has crushed might rejoice reveals that God's heavy hand of discipline has come down on him, crushing his bones. But again, David believes that repentance and confession and petition can result in mercy that cleanses, heals, restores, and rejoices.

The statements in Ps 51 tend to come in two-verse sections, the one exception being Ps 51:9 (MT 51:11), which stands at the center of the psalm's chiastic structure. This is the essence of the psalm's message, where David makes two requests: first, for God to hide his face from his sin, and second, for God to blot out all his iniquities. David's sin is against God and would separate him from God, and David asks God to apply his almighty power to the task of making it so that he does not see David's sin. The second request for God to blot out David's iniquities would bring about the cleansing for which he has been asking since 51:1 (MT 51:3).

If God grants these requests, David will be cleansed and forgiven, and neither his actions nor their consequences will cause separation between himself and God.

As David continues to speak in 51:10 (MT 51:12), he seems to turn his attention from the past to the future. So that his future actions will be pleasing to God, he prays in 51:10 (MT 51:12) for a newly created clean heart. The term for create (ברא) is the term from Gen 1, the verb of which Yahweh alone is the subject in the Old Testament. David asks God to create something fresh and new in him: a heart that loves God and obeys his commandments. With this David asks God to renew an "established spirit" in him. He seems to be asking for a new heart and a firm spirit that will continue in willing obedience and holiness.

In Ps 51:11 (MT 51:13) David asks the Lord not to do to him what he did to Saul: take the Holy Spirit and banish him from his presence. David boldly asks that rather than being removed from his station as the Lord's anointed, king of Israel, he be allowed to continue in God's presence, enjoying the Spirit as King.

These requests to go forward as God's new-hearted king in Ps 51:10–11 (MT 51:12–13) stand across from the requests for cleansing and restoration of joy in 51:7–8 (MT 51:9–10). See further the "Bridge" discussion below.

Psalm 51:12 (MT 51:14) summarizes the backward- and forward-looking statements made to this point. The requests to be cleansed, forgiven, and created anew are requests to have the joy of God's salvation restored in him, and the request for a willing spirit that he might be supported is a plea that God would enable him to continue in his resolve to obey. David declares what he will do if God grants these requests in 51:13 (MT 51:15), where he says he will teach God's ways to transgressors that they might repent and return to the Lord. Psalm 51 is a realization of David's purpose. This text has taught countless transgressors God's ways, leading untold numbers of souls back to the Lord. David's request that he be restored to the joy of salvation that he might teach sinners God's ways in Ps 51:12–13 (MT 51:14–15) stands across from the statements in 51:5–6 (MT 51:7–8) to the effect that he was born in sin but God desires truth and teaches wisdom. The matching of these statements indicates that the truth that delights God and the wisdom he teaches (51:6 [MT 51:8]) will be mediated through God's restoration of David to the joy of salvation that he might teach transgressors God's ways (51:12–13 [MT 51:14–15]).

### 51:14–19 (MT 51:16–21), Get Glory

In 51:14–15 (MT 51:16–17) David appeals to the Lord for deliverance from the bloodguilt of his sin, promising to celebrate God's righteousness. What is remarkable is that those who do not know God would expect his righteousness to demand David's bloodguilt. Those who know God's character as he himself revealed it in Exod 34:6–7, however, know that God righteously forgives those who repent and seek his mercy. This is a righteousness unique to the God of the Bible, a righteousness that upholds the standard of truth while forgiving those who transgress but turn. This is a righteousness that is not bad news to sinners but good news, a righteousness that produces what David describes in 51:15 (MT 51:17), lips opened that the mouth might declare God's praise.

God's desire is not sacrifice but obedience, and this David articulates in 51:16–17 (MT 51:18–19). David knows that God wants what he brings: repentance. These assertions stand across from the appeal for forgiveness and cleansing in 51:1–2 (MT 51:3–4).

The final statements of Ps 51 communicate the societal ramifications of David's behavior. If David incurs God's wrath, that wrath falls on all under David's reign. But if David experiences God's favor, all Israel will enjoy the good pleasure of God. David prays for just this in 51:18 (MT 51:20), promising that God's good favor on Israel will result in worship that is pleasing to God in 51:19 (MT 51:21). These words about the public results of David's repentance function as the outer ring brackets of the psalm with the description of David's public sin and Nathan's rebuke in the psalm's superscription (MT 51:1–2).

### Bridge

Across the Testaments Old and New God's righteousness is a sheer precipice of holiness. Since Adam's fall into sin, that righteousness of God has been a crushing force of judgment. In the mystery of God's mercy, however, God is pleased to show the power of his creativity, love, and grace in the righteous forgiveness of the guilty. For the forgiveness to be righteous, the guilty must repent and return to the Lord. The Lord put Jesus forward as a sacrifice of propitiation because of the passing over of sins formerly committed, establishing himself as righteous and the one who makes the guilty righteous (Rom 3:24–26). Psalm 51 is a prayer that every sinner needs.

What David says about the Holy Spirit in 51:11 (MT 51:13) has to be understood in the unfolding of biblical theology. Under the old covenant, David enjoyed the anointing of the Spirit as Israel's king. Saul had previously enjoyed the same, but when he sinned the Spirit was taken from him. When David was anointed, the Spirit came on David. Saul was rejected, and David was established as his replacement (see esp. 1 Sam 16:13–14 and the wider context). David, then, asks the Lord not do to him what he did to Saul: remove the Spirit, end his reign as king, and banish him from God's presence.[191]

Under the new covenant, believers experience not only the new heart for which David prays, believers are also the temple of the Holy Spirit (1 Cor 3:16). David's words easily translate into a new covenant context for those who seek the renewal only God can provide and the presence that will be enjoyed only by those who have experienced the transforming power of God's holiness.

## Psalm 52

OVERVIEW AND STRUCTURE OF PSALM 52

The superscription of Ps 52 locates this psalm as David's response to the way that Doeg the Edomite reported to Saul that David had gone to the house of Ahimelech when he fled from Saul. On learning the news, Saul commissioned Doeg to slaughter the priests (1 Sam 21–22). In Ps 53, then, David responds to the atrocities of a war criminal who put priests and their families—man, woman, child, infant—under a wicked ban, murdering them all on the orders of the renegade king. Saul's reign had become satanic, and he commissioned Doeg to kill and destroy. Since the superscription names Doeg, David seems to address him in the psalm.

David first asks Doeg why he boasts in evil, then describes the wickedness and destruction Doeg speaks (52:1–4 [MT 52:3–6]). David warns of God's judgment (52:5 [MT 52:7]), before describing the way the righteous will respond to God's judgment (52:6–7 [MT 52:8–9]). David then closes with a description of his Ps 1 status as a blessed tree in God's presence, trusting and praising the Lord (52:8–9 [MT 52:10–11]).

There may be a thematic chiasm here, with the references to the "house" in the superscription (MT 52:2) and at the end (52:8 [MT 52:10]). There is also a contrast between the evil intrigue between Saul and Doeg at the beginning and David's trust and praise at the end. David then contemplates the evil speech of the wicked (52:1–4 [MT 52:3–6]), which is matched by his contemplation of the boastful celebration of the righteous

---

[191] For further discussion, see James M. Hamilton, *God's Indwelling Presence: The Holy Spirit in the Old and New Testaments*, NAC Studies in Bible and Theology (Nashville: Broadman & Holman, 2006).

(52:6–7 [MT 52:8–9]), and the whole psalm would then center on the warning of God's coming judgment in 52:5 (MT 52:7).[192]

52 superscription (MT 52:1–2), Evil Intrigue (House)
   52:1–4 (MT 52:3–6), Wicked Boasts and Wicked Speech
      52:5 (MT 52:7), God's Judgment
   52:6–7 (MT 52:8–9), Righteous Taunts
52:8–9 (MT 52:10–11), Trust and Praise (House)

This chiastic structure will provide the framework for the exposition below.

## Scripture

### CSB

For the choir director. A *Maskil* of David. When Doeg the Edomite went and reported to Saul, telling him, "David went to Ahimelech's house."

¹ Why boast about evil, you hero! God's faithful love is constant.
² Like a sharpened razor, your tongue devises destruction, working treachery.
³ You love evil instead of good, lying instead of speaking truthfully. *Selah*

⁴ You love any words that destroy, you treacherous tongue!
⁵ This is why God will bring you down forever.
He will take you, ripping you out of your tent;
he will uproot you from the land of the living. *Selah*

⁶ The righteous will see and fear,

### Author's translation

¹ For the Preeminent One. A *Maskil* of David.
² When Doeg the Edomite went and declared to Saul, and he said to him, "David went to the house of Ahimelech."

³ Why do you boast in evil, O mighty man? The lovingkindness of God is all day long.
⁴ Your tongue plots destruction, like a sharpened razor working deceit.
⁵ You loved evil rather than good, falsehood rather than speaking righteousness. *Selah.*
⁶ You loved all words of devouring, O tongue of deception.

⁷ Surely God will break you down forever.
He will snatch you up and tear you away from your tent
and uproot you from the land of the living. *Selah.*

[192] For a slightly different proposal, see Willem A. VanGemeren, *Psalms*, EBC 5 (Grand Rapids: Zondervan, 2008), 440.

and they will derisively say about that hero,

⁷"Here is the man
who would not make God his refuge,
but trusted in the abundance of his riches,
taking refuge in his destructive behavior."

⁸But I am like a flourishing olive tree
in the house of God;
I trust in God's faithful love forever and ever.
⁹I will praise you forever for what you have done.
In the presence of your faithful people,
I will put my hope in your name, for it is good.

⁸And the righteous will see and fear,
and they will laugh at him:
⁹Behold the man who does not put
God as his strength,
and he trusted in the abundance of his wealth.
He will be strong in his destruction.

¹⁰But I am like a luxuriant olive tree
in the house of God.
I trust in the lovingkindness of God to the age and on.
¹¹I will praise you to the age, for you have done it.
And I will wait for your name, for it is good,
before those of your lovingkindness.

### CONTEXT: VERBAL AND THEMATIC LINKS WITH SURROUNDING PSALMS

After the prayer of repentance in Ps 51, the superscriptions of the following psalms present David plunged back into difficulty. These psalms revert to the period in David's life after he had been anointed but before Saul's death, while Saul was trying to kill him. The superscription of Ps 52 recalls the way Doeg the Edomite reported on David and then slaughtered the priests (1 Sam 21–22). That of Ps 54 evokes the way the Ziphites twice alerted Saul to David's whereabouts (1 Sam 23:19; 26:1). Both Kidner and Willem VanGemeren note that the term "fool" (נבל) in 53:1 (MT 53:2) recalls Nabal, whom David encountered in 1 Sam 25, making this psalm also one that relates to that section of the Samuel narrative.[193] The superscription of Ps 56 pins it to one of David's attempts to flee into Philistia (1 Sam 21:10–15; cf. 27:1–12), and that of Ps 57 locates the psalm when David hid from Saul in a cave (1 Sam 22:1; 24:1–3). The last of this sort is the superscription of Ps 59, which places it at the time Saul sent men to watch David's house to kill him (1 Sam 19:11).

It is as though the Psalms are arranged to correspond to the narrative of Samuel with an interesting twist. In the narrative of Samuel, David was first persecuted by Saul. Then he was established as king, sinned with Bathsheba, and afterward was persecuted by Absalom. The book of

---

193 Kidner, *Psalms 1–72*, 214; VanGemeren, *Psalms*, 444.

Psalms opens with the blessed man in Ps 1, who is God's appointed king in Ps 2. Then follows a series of psalms that reflect David persevering through persecution, but the superscription of Ps 3 identifies the persecutor as Absalom. Eventually, near the end of Book 1 of the Psalms, David is delivered from persecution and apparently established as king. Then Ps 51 mentions David's sin with Bathsheba, after which follow a series of psalms reflecting Saul's persecution of David. The sequences can be depicted as follows:

| Narrative sequence in Samuel | | | | |
|---|---|---|---|---|
| David Anointed 1 Sam 16 | Persecuted by Saul 1 Sam 18–31 | David Enthroned 2 Sam 5 | Sin with Bathsheba 2 Sam 11 | Persecuted by Absalom 2 Sam 15–18 |
| Narrative sequence in Psalms | | | | |
| David(ide) Anointed Ps 2 | Persecuted by Absalom Ps 3–14 | David(ide) Enthroned Ps 40–41 | Sin with Bathsheba Ps 51 | Persecuted by Saul Ps 52–59 |

The sequence in Book 1 of the Psalter (David anointed then persecuted) is repeated theme and variation style in Book 2 (David enthroned then persecuted after his sin with Bathsheba). This impression is strengthened by the reproduction of much of Ps 14 in Ps 53.[194] What would be the interpretive payoff of these repetitions? They show that a repeated pattern was noted in David's own life, a pattern similar to what could also be found in the lives of Joseph and Moses. The repetitions increase significance, leading to the expectation of a fulfillment of these patterns in the life of the seed promised to David. The patterning would also lead people to see Saul and Absalom as being the same *type* of character, cut from the same cloth. Both are impressive in worldly ways, and both oppose God's anointed, trying to be king in place of David, the one God chose.

---

[194] Along these lines, Hossfeld notes that Ps 52 is similar in structure to Pss 4 and 11–14 (Hossfeld and Zenger, *Psalms 2*, 28).

## 52 superscription (MT 52:1–2), Evil Intrigue (House)

The superscription of Ps 52 locates this prayer in the events narrated in 1 Sam 21–22. David was the anointed of the Lord, and though Saul was trying to kill him, David was avoiding open conflict. Doeg knew that Saul wanted to kill David, so to inform Saul of David's actions was to declare allegiance to Saul against the Lord and his anointed, David.

## 52:1–4 (MT 52:3–6), Wicked Boasts and Wicked Speech

References to what the wicked man says pervade 52:1–4. His "boast" is in evil (52:1 [MT 52:3]), his "tongue plots destruction" (52:2 [MT 52:4]), he loves "falsehood rather than speaking righteousness" (52:3 [MT 52:5]) and "words of devouring" (52:4 [MT 52:6]). The section is closed off with the wicked man being addressed as the "tongue of deception" (52:4 [MT 52:6]).

David opens by addressing his adversary, likely Doeg, with an aggressive question. He asks why he boasts in evil, and with what appears to be sarcastic scorn he addresses his adversary as, "O mighty man" (CSB, "you hero!"). Kidner captures the irony of the idea of the criminal being described as valiant, "as if earned by Doeg's exploit in butchery."[195] David diagnoses Doeg's hope to prosper by showing loyalty to Saul against David as boasting in evil, and David denounces the false confidence in worldly prowess that leads Doeg and Saul to think that they can triumph over Yahweh and David. David's reply to Doeg's action is in the second line of 52:1 (MT 52:3), where he declares that God's lovingkindness lasts all day long. At no point in the day will Yahweh's character change, so at no point in the day will Doeg be able to escape the Lord's faithful love to David.

Doeg's words to Saul would bring about David's death, as David makes plain in 52:2 (MT 52:4), where he describes Doeg's tongue plotting destruction. The mention of plots recalls the plans of the enemies of Yahweh and his anointed in 2:1–3. The deadly power of Doeg's words—which did bring about the death of eighty-five priests and the city of Nob put under the ban—is captured by David likening his tongue to a "sharpened razor." And the cause of Doeg is not the cause of truth, so in his protestations of loyalty to Saul that brought about so many murders he was "working deceit" (52:2 [MT 52:4]).

---

[195] Kidner, *Psalms 1–72*, 213.

The mouth speaks out of the overflow of the heart (Matt 12:34). David shows his awareness that the tongue speaks what the heart loves when he indicts the wicked for loving evil rather than good, and as a result loving falsehood rather than speaking righteousness in 52:3 (MT 52:5). Our words are inevitably consistent with our hearts. One way to gauge the state of the heart is to listen to the work of the tongue.

What Doeg loved was revealed by what Doeg said. David says as much in Ps 52:4 (MT 52:6). Doeg loved words that devoured lives. He was a man of deception. His tongue revealed the state of his heart.

### 52:5 (MT 52:7), God's Judgment

David warns of the wrath Doeg faces in 52:5 (MT 52:7). Mighty as he may be, he will not stand when God breaks him down. God's destruction of the wicked will never stop. Protected as a wicked man may feel, the Lord is able to snatch him up. His tent will not keep God from tearing him away. And no roots will withstand the one who will uproot the weeds and burn the chaff. Unlike the blessed man, who is like a tree planted by streams of water, the wicked man will be uprooted from the land of life. He will not flourish.

### 52:6–7 (MT 52:8–9), Righteous Taunts

David details the response of the righteous in Ps 52:6–7 (MT 52:8–9). Just as the Lord laughed at his enemies in 2:4 (cf. also 37:13; 59:8), the righteous will laugh at the wicked when they are destroyed. The righteous will then talk with one another about the folly of the destroyed wicked, those who refused to trust God and instead trusted their wealth. Their destruction will be impressive.

It is important to recognize that the response of the righteous is being described before the destruction of the wicked has come to pass. This is to be understood, then, as a warning of the coming destruction. That destruction is certain. It is inexorable. It will be remarkable. And it will generate celebration in the hearts of those delivered, vindicated, avenged, and satisfied by it.[196] Doeg, remember, is a man whose treachery brought about the murder of children and infants in the city of Nob. Those he wronged will be satisfied when justice is done upon him.

---

[196] So also Hossfeld and Zenger, *Psalms 2*, 32: "Laughing over the crushed 'hero' is thus not an expression of cheap smugness, but unchallenged satisfaction at the victory of God's righteousness."

Returning, however, to the fact that this description of the way the righteous will respond is being given before the judgment falls, we must recognize that the description of the way the righteous will respond affords the wicked an opportunity to repent. It does kindness to the wicked to confront them with the fact that if they do not repent they will not be mourned. Rather, their demise will be a cause for celebration. No one will lament their end.

### 52:8–9 (MT 52:10–11), Trust and Praise (House)

Unlike the wicked man who was uprooted from the land of the living, David describes himself in Ps 1 terms as a flourishing tree in God's house (52:8 [MT 52:10]; cf. Prov 11:28). The luxuriant tree no doubt thrives on the rich soil that enjoys ample water. The reference to God's house connotes not only the temple but the cosmos. A tree in the land of the living is a tree in the presence of God, and David goes on to describe his everlasting trust in God's steadfast love. That faith in God's character is saving faith that transforms and enables obedience.

In Ps 52:9 (MT 52:11) David says that he will praise God forever because of what God has accomplished. God has defeated the wicked and established the right. That final triumph has not yet come to pass, so David asserts that he will wait for God's name to be exalted because he believes that God is good, and he surrounds himself with those marked by the Lord's own lovingkindness.

BRIDGE

The righteous taunt against the wicked in Ps 52 is not unlike the scene in Rev 18–19, where the fall of Babylon is announced and the righteous praise God when they see the smoke going up from her forever and ever (Rev 19:1–3). The promised son of David is the epitome of the blessed man, the tree planted by streams of water, the true vine whose Father is the gardener, and his enemies will experience everlasting defeat.

## Psalm 53

OVERVIEW AND STRUCTURE OF PSALM 53

As noted in the discussion of the "Context" of Ps 52, Ps 53 largely reproduces the content of Ps 14. There are differences between the two psalms in the following statements:

| Psalm 14 | Psalm 53 |
|---|---|
| | The superscription to Ps 53 adds "On Mahalat. A Maskil." |
| 14:1 "They despoil. They do abominable work." | 53:1 (MT 53:2) "They despoil and do abominable perversity." |
| 14:2 "Yahweh from the heavens looks down" | 53:2 (MT 53:3) "God from the heavens looks down" |
| 14:3 "The whole have turned aside." | 53:3 (MT 53:4) "All of it turns away." |
| 14:4 "Do they not know, all workers of iniquity" | 53:4 (MT 53:5) "Do they not know, workers of iniquity" |
| 14:4 "On Yahweh they do not call." | 15:4 (MT 15:5) "On God they do not call." |
| 14:5–6 ⁵There they dread with dread, for God is with the generation of the righteous. ⁶The counsel of the afflicted you all put to shame, but Yahweh is his refuge. | 53:5 (MT 53:6) ⁶There they dread with dread, there is no dread, because God scatters the bones of those who camp against you. You put them to shame because God rejected them. |

Aside from these points of distinction, every other word, phrase, and sentence is exactly the same from Ps 14 in Ps 53. Hossfeld and Zenger summarize four ways this similarity has been explained: (1) variations derived from a primitive original; (2) the same text corrupted by errors in transmission; (3) alterations made because of new use in a new life-situation; and (4) redaction critical adjustment according to literary context.[197]

Hossfeld and Zenger argue for the fourth explanation, and they offer explanations of the differences in detail between the two psalms. I want to suggest an analogous artistic reprise that provides a more wide-angle function of the repetition, which will also account for the minor changes. Consider the way that repetitions of melodies, rhythms, and phrases work in modern musicals. For instance, the rhythm and melody of the "Prologue: Work Song" ("Look Down") of *Les Miserables*, with its interchange between Inspector Javert and Jean Valjean, will be reprised later in "Fantine's Death: Confrontation" as Javert and Valjean struggle at cross

---

[197] Hossfeld and Zenger, *Psalms 2*, 36–39.

purposes.[198] The repetitions are intentional, and the changes develop the storyline and fit the new context.

Similarly, the repetitions across the Psalter are intentional artistic reprises of earlier material that function to forge and tighten connections intended by those who put the Psalter together. So I have argued that after the anointing of the Davidic king in Ps 2, Pss 3–14 present David's difficulties caused by Absalom's revolt. Then after the sin with Bathsheba in Ps 51, Pss 52–64 present David's difficulties caused by Saul's persecution. The reprise of Ps 14 in Ps 53 strengthens these associations, as does the reprise of Ps 40 (near the end of Book 1) in Ps 70 (near the end of Book 2). In the same way that repeated lyrical lines, melodic movements, and rhythmic patterns exposit characters and enrich meaning in musicals, so the repetitions serve to bring out meaning in the Psalms.

For the structure of Ps 53, see the discussion of Ps 14.

SCRIPTURE

CSB

Author's translation

For the choir director: on *Mahalath*. A *Maskil* of David.

[1] For the Preeminent One.
On *Mahalat*.
A *Maskil* of David.

[1] The fool says in his heart, "There's no God."
They are corrupt, and they do vile deeds.
There is no one who does good.
[2] God looks down from heaven on the human race
to see if there is one who is wise, one who seeks God.
[3] All have turned away; all alike have become corrupt.
There is no one who does good, not even one.

[2] The fool says in his heart, "There is no God."
They despoil and do abominable perversity.
There is no one who does good.

[3] God from the heavens looks down on the sons of Adam,
to see if there is anyone causing wisdom, seeking God.

[4] All of it turns away.
Together they are corrupted.
There is no one who does good, not even one.

[4] Will evildoers never understand?
They consume my people as they consume bread;
they do not call on God.

[5] Do they not know, workers of iniquity,

---

[198] For Herbert Kretzmer's English language lyrics to *Les Miserables*, see "Les Miserables Lyrics," https://www.allmusicals.com/l/lesmiserables.htm.

<sup>5</sup>Then they will be filled with dread—
dread like no other—
because God will scatter
the bones of those who besiege you.
You will put them to shame,
for God has rejected them.

<sup>6</sup>Oh, that Israel's deliverance would
come from Zion!
When God restores the fortunes of his
people,
let Jacob rejoice, let Israel be glad.

the ones who eat my people like they
eat bread?
On God they do not call.

<sup>6</sup>There they dread with dread—there
is no dread—
because God scatters the bones of
those who camp against you.
You put them to shame because God
rejected them.

<sup>7</sup>Who will give from Zion salvation
for Israel?
When God restores the captivity of
his people,
Jacob will rejoice.
Israel will be glad.

CONTEXT: VERBAL AND THEMATIC LINKS WITH SURROUNDING PSALMS

For the function of Ps 53 in Book 2 of the Psalter, see the discussion of "Context" on Psalm 52 and the "Overview" directly above.

EXPOSITION

For the exposition of Ps 53:1–4, 6 (MT 53:2–5, 7), see the corresponding exposition of Ps 14.

At Ps 53:5 (MT 53:6) it becomes clear that the psalmist addresses either the people of God, referenced here as a collective singular, or perhaps the descendant promised to David. The psalmist seems to describe the enemy frightened though there is nothing to make them afraid (cf. Prov 28:1), explaining that God is at work against them. The image of God scattering the bones of those who encamp against Israel implies that the enemy had besieged God's people, God killed them, and their remains were driven away like chaff before the wind. The last line of 53:5 (MT 53:6) speaks of the "you," whom I am inclined to understand as the future king from David's line, putting the enemies to shame. This would indicate that God works for Israel through the triumphant Davidic king. God rejected the enemies of the son of David, and the son of David thereby put those enemies to shame.

Understanding 53:5 (MT 53:6) as being addressed to the future king from David's line would also affect the question in 53:6 (MT 53:7), literally, "Who will give from Zion salvation for Israel?" This question reflects an expectant longing for the scion of David to come. When he does, God will restore the captivity of his people, and Jacob and Israel will rejoice and be glad.

BRIDGE

The reprise of Ps 14 in Ps 53 suggests that at different points in his life David faced similar godless opposition. Those who opposed him after his Ps 2 anointing in Ps 14 were fools, convincing themselves in their hearts that there would be no God who would keep his promises to David. Thus, according to their reasoning, they could oppose David and hope to triumph over him. Psalm 53 presents the same kinds of fools thinking the same kinds of thoughts as they opposed David after his Ps 51 sin with Bathsheba.

The repetition of Ps 14 in Ps 53 suggests that David's enemies can be identified with one another, that they think the same way and pursue the same course: setting themselves against Yahweh and his messiah (Ps 2:1–3). The seed of the serpent are at enmity with the seed of the woman.

Paul's quotation of the words of Ps 14/53:1–3 in Rom 3:10–12 buttresses his argument that Jews and gentiles are all under sin (3:9).[199] He supports that claim by quoting Scripture, and the Scriptures he quotes fit the context. Absalom (Pss 3–14) and Saul (Pss 52–64) were Jews who rejected David, persecuted David, and sought to kill David, Yahweh's anointed. Their actions were foolish, and Pss 14 and 53 indicate that they and their henchmen were convincing themselves that "there is no God" who would protect David against them. Similarly, all who reject Yahweh's anointed, his Messiah, all who refuse to acknowledge Jesus as Savior and Lord, are setting themselves against Yahweh and his Messiah (Ps 2:2). As in David's day, the seed of the serpent foolishly think they can triumph over Yahweh's king, Jesus. They think no God will vindicate Jesus, so they reject him, crucifying him for themselves—agreeing with the rebels who did so. Their actions are abominable. They do not do good. Paul seems to understand the reprise of Ps 14 in Ps 53, and he writes the lyrics into his

---

[199] For the literary structure of the case against the Jews in Rom 2:1–3:20, see David G. Peterson, *Commentary on Romans*, Biblical Theology for Christian Proclamation (Nashville: Broadman & Holman, 2017), 132.

own musical the way that Lin Manuel-Miranda echoes "Drink with Me" from *Les Miserables* in "The Story of Tonight" in his Hamilton musical.[200]

## Psalm 54

OVERVIEW AND STRUCTURE OF PSALM 54

The superscription of Ps 54 (MT 54:1–2) places this prayer as a response to the way the Ziphites betrayed David to Saul. In response to the treachery of the Ziphites, David calls on God to hear his prayer and save him in 54:1–2 (MT 54:3–4), explains that strangers seek to kill him in 54:3 (MT 54:5) but relies on God as his helper and deliverer in 54:4–5 (MT 54:6–7), and closes with praise for God upon deliverance in 54:6–7 (MT 54:8–9).

Psalm 54 reflects a chiastic structure as follows:[201]

54:1–2 (MT 54:3–4), Prayer
    54:3 (MT 54:5), Enemies
        54:4 (MT 54:6), God David's Helper
    54:5 (MT 54:7), Enemies Annihilated
54:6–7 (MT 54:8–9), Praise

This breakdown will inform the exposition below.

SCRIPTURE

| CSB | Author's translation |
|---|---|
| For the choir director: with stringed instruments. A *Maskil* of David. When the Ziphites went and said to Saul, "Is David not hiding among us?" | [1] For the Preeminent One. With stringed instruments. A *Maskil* of David. [2] When the Ziphites went and said to Saul, "Is not David hiding with us?" |
| [1] God, save me by your name, and vindicate me by your might! [2] God, hear my prayer; listen to the words from my mouth. [3] For strangers rise up against me, and violent men intend to kill me. | [3] O God, in your name cause salvation for me, and in your might judge for me. [4] O God, hear my prayer. Give ear to the words of my mouth. |

---

[200] See Lin-Manuel Miranda and Jeremy McCarter, *Hamilton: The Revolution* (New York: Grand Central Publishing, 2016).

[201] Similarly VanGemeren, *Psalms*, 447.

They do not let God guide them.
*Selah*

⁴ God is my helper;
the Lord is the sustainer of my life.
⁵ He will repay my adversaries for
their evil.
Because of your faithfulness,
annihilate them.

⁶ I will sacrifice a freewill offering to
you.
I will praise your name, LORD,
because it is good.
⁷ For he has rescued me from every
trouble,
and my eye has looked down on my
enemies.

⁵ For strangers rose against me;
violent men seek my life.
They do not put God before them.
*Selah.*

⁶ Behold, God is the one who helps
me.
My Lord is among the ones who
support my soul.

⁷ He will return the evil to the ones
who watch me;
in your truth cause their annihilation.

⁸ With a freewill offering I will
sacrifice to you.
I will praise your name, O Yahweh, for
it is good.
⁹ For from every distress he delivered
me,
and on those at enmity with me my
eye looks.

CONTEXT: VERBAL AND THEMATIC LINKS WITH SURROUNDING PSALMS

As noted in the "Context" section at Ps 52, the impressionistic narrative in the Psalms is tracking with the narrative of Samuel. David was anointed, then persecuted, enthroned, sinned with Bathsheba, then was persecuted again before being reestablished. In keeping with the return to persecution, the superscription of Ps 54 locates this prayer at 1 Sam 23:19 and 26:1, two episodes when the Ziphites alerted Saul to David's whereabouts. We know little else about the identity of the Ziphites.

EXPOSITION

### 54:1–2 (MT 54:3–4), Prayer

As with Ps 52, David again faces mortal danger because people have betrayed him to Saul. David's confidence is not in his own strength, savvy, mobility, or henchmen. His confidence is in the character of Yahweh who has anointed him king. This can be seen from the way that he appeals to God for salvation in God's own name (54:1 [MT 54:3]). Because of the way that God has identified himself in Exod 34:6–7, David can appeal to God's name for deliverance. When David appeals for God to judge him in Ps 54:1 (MT 54:4), he is asking for vindication, and he wants the Lord to do this in his own might, by his own power. In 54:2 (MT 54:4) David beseeches the Lord to hear his prayer.

### 54:3 (MT 54:5), Enemies

David explains his need in 54:3 (MT 54:5). The "strangers" would appear to be the Ziphites mentioned in the superscription, perhaps indicating that they are non-Israelites. The violent who seek his life would include Saul and those like Doeg (cf. Ps 52). These are men whose thoughts and actions are not regulated by the knowledge of God, thus David declares that they do not set God before themselves.

### 54:4 (MT 54:6), God David's Helper

Again and again David returns to this reality: However strong and impressive and strategic his enemies may be, they are no match for the world's maker. David declares in 54:4 (MT 54:6) that God is the one who helps him, that the Lord is among those who support him. To be on God's side is to be on the side of truth and righteousness. To be on God's side is to be with the one who will prevail.

### 54:5 (MT 54:7), Enemies Annihilated

The enemies have arisen, but God is David's helper, and he will surely return the evil of the opponents onto their own heads. Those watching for David's life will fall into the pit they dug, be snared in the net they laid, and have the arrows they shot backfire. VanGemeren calls this "the boomerang effect of sin."[202] The Lord will insure that evil will always be self-defeating. God's truth annihilates his enemies. God is faithful to his own truth, so the enemies will be destroyed.

### 54:6–7 (MT 54:8–9), Praise

David is confident of the Lord's deliverance, so he asserts that he will sacrifice a freewill offering and praise the good name of Yahweh on which he has relied (54:6 [MT 54:8], cf. 54:1 [MT 54:3]). David's confidence in God's promises and certainty that God will always do what is in keeping with his own character leads him to say in 54:7 (MT 54:9) that the Lord has delivered him from every distress—as though it has already happened!

---

[202] VanGemeren, *Psalms*, 449.

And David knows that if his enemies are God's enemies, they will all be defeated. Thus his eye will look in triumph upon them.

BRIDGE

Psalms like these pray in response to the reality articulated in Rom 12:19, "Vengeance belongs to me; I will repay, says the Lord," in which Paul cites Deut 32:35.

## Psalm 55

OVERVIEW AND STRUCTURE OF PSALM 55

Psalm 55 reflects a chiastic structure that can be depicted as follows:

55:1–3 (MT 55:2–4), Prayer
    55:4–8 (MT 55:5–9), Fear
        55:9–11 (MT 55:10–12), Plea for Justice
            55:12–15 (MT 55:13–16), The Traitor
        55:16–19 (MT 55:17–20), Faith in God
    55:20–21 (MT 55:21–22), Unrepentant Sin
55:22–23 (MT 55:23–24), Outcomes

This understanding of the psalm's flow of thought places central emphasis on the one who betrayed David (55:12–15 [MT 55:13–16]). It also shows that David has faith that God will administer the justice for which he pleads (55:9–11, 16–19 [MT 55:10–12, 17–20]), and that David's fear arises from the unrepentant wickedness of his adversaries: he fears them because they don't fear God (55:4–8, 20–21 [MT 55:5–9, 21–22]). Finally, David prays knowing what God will do (55:1–3, 22–23 [MT 55:2–4, 23–24]).

For the purposes of this exposition, we will approach the psalm under the following three subheads:

      55:1–8 (MT 55:2–9), Terrified Prayer
      55:9–15 (MT 55:10–16), Betrayed Trust
      55:16–23 (MT 55:17–24), Steadfast Confidence

SCRIPTURE

| CSB | Author's translation |
|---|---|
| For the choir director: with stringed instruments. A *Maskil* of David. | [1] For the Preeminent One.<br>With stringed instruments.<br>A *Maskil* of David. |

[1] God, listen to my prayer
and do not hide from my plea for help.
[2] Pay attention to me and answer me.
I am restless and in turmoil with my
    complaint,
[3] because of the enemy's words,
because of the pressure of the wicked.
For they bring down disaster on me
and harass me in anger.

[4] My heart shudders within me;
terrors of death sweep over me.
[5] Fear and trembling grip me;
horror has overwhelmed me.
[6] I said, "If only I had wings like a
    dove!
I would fly away and find rest.
[7] How far away I would flee;
I would stay in the wilderness.
*Selah*

[8] I would hurry to my shelter
from the raging wind and the storm."

[9] Lord, confuse and confound their
    speech,
for I see violence and strife in the city;
[10] day and night they make the rounds
    on its walls.
Crime and trouble are within it;
[11] destruction is inside it;
oppression and deceit never leave its
    marketplace.

[12] Now it is not an enemy who insults
    me—
otherwise I could bear it;
it is not a foe who rises up against
    me—

[2] Give ear, O God, to my prayer, and
    do not hide yourself from my
    supplication.
[3] Give attention to me and answer
    me: I rove in my complaint and am
    noisy,
[4] because of the sound of the one at
    enmity,
because of the presence of the
    pressure of the wicked,
for they cause iniquity to totter upon
    me,
and in anger they bear a grudge
    against me.

[5] My heart writhes within me,
and the terrors of death fall upon me.
[6] Fear and trembling come upon me,
and shuddering covers me.
[7] And I say, who will give to me
    pinions like a dove?
I would fly away and alight.
[8] Behold, I would cause distance by
    retreating.
I would lodge in the wilderness. *Selah.*
[9] I would hasten my escape from the
    rushing wind, from the tempest.

[10] Swallow up, my Lord, divide their
    tongues,
for I see violence and strife in the city.
[11] Day and night they surround her,
    on her walls,
and iniquity and trouble in her midst.
[12] Destruction in her midst,
and oppression and deceit do not
    depart from her plaza.

otherwise I could hide from him.
¹³ But it is you, a man who is my peer,
my companion and good friend!
¹⁴ We used to have close fellowship;
we walked with the crowd into the
    house of God.

¹⁵ Let death take them by surprise;
let them go down to Sheol alive,
because evil is in their homes and
    within them.
¹⁶ But I call to God,
and the Lord will save me.
¹⁷ I complain and groan morning, noon,
    and night,
and he hears my voice.
¹⁸ Though many are against me,
he will redeem me from my battle
    unharmed.
¹⁹ God, the one enthroned from long
    ago,
will hear and will humiliate them
*Selah*

because they do not change
and do not fear God.

²⁰ My friend acts violently
against those at peace with him;
he violates his covenant.
²¹ His buttery words are smooth,
but war is in his heart.
His words are softer than oil,
but they are drawn swords.

²² Cast your burden on the Lord,
and he will sustain you;
he will never allow the righteous to
    be shaken.

²³ God, you will bring them down
to the Pit of destruction;
men of bloodshed and treachery
will not live out half their days.
But I will trust in you.

¹³ For it is not one at enmity who
    reproaches me, or I would bear it;
not one who hates me magnifies
    himself against me, or I would be
    hid from him.
¹⁴ But you, a man of my order, my
    friend and one known to me,
¹⁵ with whom together we took sweet
    counsel,
in the house of God we walked in the
    throng.
¹⁶ Let death seize upon them; let them
    go down to Sheol alive,
for evils are in their dwelling place, in
    their midst.

¹⁷ I to God will cry, and Yahweh will
    cause salvation for me.
¹⁸ Evening and morning and at noon I
    complain and make noise,
and he hears my voice.
¹⁹ He redeems my soul in peace from
    the battle against me,
for in multitudes they were with me.
²⁰ God will hear, and he will answer
    them, even the one who sits of old.
    *Selah.*
Because there are no changes to
    them, and they do not fear God.

²¹ He sends his hands against those of
    his peace. He pollutes his covenant.
²² Smooth are the curds of his mouth,
    but war is in his heart.
More tender his words than oil, but
    they are drawn swords.

²³ Cast what is given to you on
    Yahweh, and he will sustain you.
He will not give to the age stumbling
    to the righteous.
²⁴ And you, O God, will cause them to
    go down to the well of the pit.
Men of bloods and deceit, they will
    not half their days.
But as for me, I trust in you.

As will be seen from verses 12–14 (MT 13–15), David has been betrayed by someone he trusted. From the narrative of Samuel, the most likely candidate would be Ahithophel, Bathsheba's grandfather. The fact that Ps 55 has been grouped with a series of psalms that follow the reference to David's sin with Bathsheba in the superscription of Ps 51 would seem to strengthen this identification. As noted in the discussion of the context of Ps 52, several of these psalms reference David's difficulties with Saul. There may have been an unnamed traitor from that period who prompted the prayer of Ps 55, or perhaps the psalms have been arranged such that difficulties from Saul and Absalom have been intermingled here.

### EXPOSITION

#### 55:1–8 (MT 55:2–9), Terrified Prayer

Psalms 52, 53, 54, and 55 all have "maskil" in the superscription. On this term in the superscriptions, see "The Superscriptions of the Psalms" in the Introduction, and on its meaning see the exposition of 47:7.

In Ps 55:1–3 (MT 55:2–4) David calls on the Lord to hear him and explains his need. Then in 55:4–8 (MT 55:5–9) David frankly details the bodily terror he feels that makes him want to flee the scene.

David beseeches the Lord to hear his prayer, urging him not to be hidden from his supplication for God's grace in 55:1 (MT 55:2). He explains his need for God's attention in 55:2, describing himself as one who is restless, unable to sit still and quiet, roving about with anxious groans and complaints. David's anxiety is caused by men, but he knows that the answer he needs is from God. Those at enmity with him are making noise, causing pressure on David, threatening his stability, and bearing a grudge against him (55:3 [MT 55:4]), and David addresses the situation by praying to God. The Psalms abundantly demonstrate David's faith as they show him seeking solutions to his problems by means of prayer to the one who can answer.

We see the authentic humanity of David in his description of himself in 55:4–8 (MT 55:5–9). David does not hide his feelings from the Lord under an undaunted appearance but declares in vivid terms how troubled he is. He speaks of his heart in anguish and death's terrors falling on him (55:4 [MT 55:5]), of the feeling of fear and his body shaking and shuddering (55:5 [MT 55:6]), and then he describes how he would like to respond. He asks who will provide the pinions of a dove for him that he might flee the situation and find a safe place to alight far from danger, in the wilderness away from the city, speaking of the difficulty caused by his enemies as a rushing wind and a tempest (55:6–8 [MT 55:7–9]).

It is interesting to observe that the wings of a dove are not the only way for David to flee. He could flee danger in other ways. Though he abandoned Jerusalem when Absalom revolted in the narrative of Samuel, he did not abdicate his throne and go into exile but fought to regain his position, eventually defeating Absalom and Ahithophel. On this basis, then, it seems that we can say that though David wanted to avoid conflict and flee the situation altogether, instead of doing that he prayed to the Lord, explained his desire to flee, but then called on the Lord for justice, standing fast to see the Lord act on his behalf.

### 55:9–15 (MT 55:10–16), Betrayed Trust

Having articulated a desire to flee but, so far as we can tell, not acted on it, David now calls on the Lord to do justice. He first asks the Lord for justice against his enemies in 55:9–11 (MT 55:10–12), then explains how he has been personally betrayed in 55:12–15 (MT 55:13–16).

David wants the Lord to swallow his enemies up, and he uses the term employed to describe the earth swallowing Korah and the men of his rebellion in Num 16:32 (Ps 55:9 [MT 55:10]). His next request is for the Lord to divide their tongues, and here he seems to allude to the division of the languages in Gen 11. The verb is related to the name Peleg in Gen 10:25, "for in his days the earth was divided." David then moves into support for his argument that God should judge as he explains that violence and strife are loose in the city, going around on its walls day and night, with iniquity and trouble also present, ruin in the midst, and the marketplace ever haunted by oppression and deceit (Ps 55:9–11 [MT 55:10–12]). Here David personifies Violence, Strife, Iniquity, Trouble, Oppression, and Deceit. These characters stalk the scene, and their activity warrants God opening up the earth to swallow them, confusing their tongues to stymy their communications.

As noted above, Ps 55 is chiastically structured to center on the description of the traitor in 55:12–15 (MT 55:13–16). This figure was evidently instrumental in the wider difficulties David alludes to in the psalm. David speaks in 55:12 (MT 55:13) of how this man was not at enmity with him, not one who hated him—saying that if it were an inveterate enemy of that sort, he would be more able to deal with the situation. In

55:13 (MT 55:14) David says that this man was of his order, his row, which seems to mean that he was a peer or equal of David, a companion well known to him. David then reminisces in 55:14 (MT 55:15) about the way he formerly enjoyed mutual confidences with this man, taking counsel with him, even participating in the worship of Yahweh together with the crowds at the house of God.

To be betrayed by a trusted ally, a friend, is more painful than to be opposed by an outright foe. In response to the treachery, David calls on the Lord in 55:15 (MT 55:16) to cause personified Death to capture this traitor, to cause him to descend alive into Sheol because he has cultivated the cause of evil. Not only is David personally betrayed by a former friend, by opposing David this former friend opposes Yahweh's cause in the earth. Justice demands that righteousness be done upon him.

### 55:16–23 (MT 55:17–24), Steadfast Confidence

All through this psalm we see evidence that David believes the Lord is the one who solves problems, so when David is confronted with personal betrayal he takes the matter to the Lord. In direct response to his description of the traitor in 55:12–15 (MT 55:13–16), David asserts in 55:16 (MT 55:17) that he calls to God and that Yahweh will save him. Resuming the language of 55:2 (MT 55:3) in 55:17 (MT 55:18), David asserts that all through the day—evening and morning and at noon—he complains and makes noise, and God hears him. God not only hears, in 55:18 (MT 55:19) David celebrates the fact that the Lord redeems him from the heavy fighting with his numerous enemies. God gives David peace.

In 55:19 (MT 55:20) David articulates his confidence that God, who sits on the throne of justice from eternity past, will hear his prayer and humble his unrepentant adversaries, those who neither change their actions nor fear God himself.

Giving further evidence of the justice of his cause, David details the actions of the one who betrayed him in Ps 55:20–21 (MT 55:21–22). This is a man who profaned a sacred compact into which he had entered, a covenant, by lifting his hand against the ones who were at peace with him. He spoke words that are described as buttery smooth and softer than oil, words of assurance and reassurance and fidelity and loyalty, but in his heart he meant to make war on David. His kind statements were in reality hostile weapons, opened swords, loosed from the sheath, ready to strike.

This outrageous treachery provides David an opportunity to instruct others to do as he has done in 55:22 (MT 55:23), so he gives the command to cast what one encounters on the Lord, who will sustain those who trust him, not allowing the righteous to stumble, even to the end of the age. The wicked, meanwhile, will have what David describes in 55:23 (MT 55:24). God will sink them in the deepest well of the darkest pit. Those who are characterized by deceit and bloodshed "will not half their days," which apparently means that they will not live out half their days. David describes himself at the end of 55:23 (MT 55:24), saying that in contrast to the judgment that awaits the wicked, his trust is in God.

Bridge

The betrayal that David describes in Ps 55 shadows and typifies what Jesus would endure from Judas. The contemplation of such treachery affords us the opportunity to ask ourselves if we have been loyal to our covenant Lord. No king has more right to the loyalty of his people, and no father has more claim on the fidelity of his children. We must repent of our infidelity and treachery.

As with Ps 55, however, our hope is not in our ability to keep the covenant, but in the fact that Jesus kept it and keeps us in spite of our failures because he loves to show mercy to the repentant. If we are faithless, he remains faithful. He cannot deny himself (2 Tim 2:13).

## Psalm 56

Overview and Structure of Psalm 56

Psalm 56 centers on the prayer in 56:7 (MT 56:8), where David calls on Yahweh to throw down the nations. The chiastic structure surrounding that statement can be depicted as follows:

56:1–3 (MT 56:2–4), Prayer and Trust in Fear
   56:4 (MT 56:5), In God I Trust
      56:5–6 (MT 56:6–7), The Enemies Scheming
         56:7 (MT 56:8), Bring Down the Nations
      56:8–9 (MT 56:9–10), The Righteous Remembered
   56:10–11 (MT 56:11–12), In God I Trust
56:12–13 (MT 56:13–14), Vows and Thanksgivings in Deliverance

SCRIPTURE

| CSB | Author's translation |
|---|---|

For the choir director: according to "A Silent Dove Far Away." A *Miktam* of David. When the Philistines seized him in Gath.

¹ Be gracious to me, God, for a man is trampling me;
he fights and oppresses me all day long.
² My adversaries trample me all day, for many arrogantly fight against me.

³ When I am afraid,
I will trust in you.
⁴ In God, whose word I praise,
in God I trust; I will not be afraid.
What can mere mortals do to me?

⁵ They twist my words all day long;
all their thoughts against me are evil.
⁶ They stir up strife, they lurk,
they watch my steps
while they wait to take my life.
⁷ Will they escape in spite of such sin?
God, bring down the nations in wrath.

⁸ You yourself have recorded my wanderings.
Put my tears in your bottle.
Are they not in your book?
⁹ Then my enemies will retreat on the day when I call.
This I know: God is for me.

¹⁰ In God, whose word I praise,
in the LORD, whose word I praise,
¹¹ in God I trust; I will not be afraid.
What can mere humans do to me?

¹² I am obligated by vows to you, God;
I will make my thanksgiving sacrifices to you.
¹³ For you rescued me from death,

---

¹ For the Preeminent One.
On Dove of Silence, Distances.
Of David.
A *Miktam*.
When the Philistines seized him in Gath.

² Be gracious to me, O God, for men trample me.
All the day the fighter presses me.
³ Those who watch me trample all the day,
for many are the fighters against me on high.
⁴ In the day I fear; I will trust in you.

⁵ In God, I will praise his word.
In God I trust.
I will not fear.
What will flesh do to me?

⁶ All the day my words they twist.
Against me are all their counsels for evil.
⁷ They stir up strife.
They hide.
They watch my heels while they wait for my soul.

⁸ Concerning iniquity, deliver them!
In wrath, bring down the peoples, O God.

⁹ My wanderings you counted.
Put my tears in your bottle.
Are they not in your book?
¹⁰ Then they will turn back, those at enmity with me, on the day I call.
This I know: that God is for me.

¹¹ In God, I will praise the word.
In Yahweh, I will praise the word.
¹² In God I trust.

| even my feet from stumbling,<br>to walk before God in the light of life. | I will not fear.<br>What will man do to me? |

<sup>13</sup> Upon me, O God, are your vows.
I will complete thanksgivings to you.
<sup>14</sup> For you deliver my soul from death.
Are not my feet from stumbling,
to walk before God in the light of life?

CONTEXT: VERBAL AND THEMATIC LINKS WITH SURROUNDING PSALMS

Psalms 56–60 all have the term "Miktam" in their superscriptions, as does Ps 16:1. *HALOT* provides "inscription" as a proposed gloss. The superscription of Ps 56 locates this as a prayer David prayed on what appears to be the occasion narrated in 1 Sam 21:10–15 (cf. also the superscription of Ps 34). Fleeing Saul, David went among the Philistines in Gath. He was brought before Achish their king, where report was made of David's prowess. To escape the dangerous situation, David feigned insanity and escaped to the cave of Adullam (1 Sam 22:1).

Psalm 56, then, appears to be one of David's prayers in the midst of Saul's persecutions, which resulted in him being endangered by the Philistines. This continues the way that the superscriptions of Pss 52 and 54 tie those psalms to the period when Saul sought to kill David, and we find the same in Pss 57, 59, and 63. The whole series of psalms following 51, from 52–71, seem tinged with that tale.

EXPOSITION

After the phrase "For the preeminent one" in the superscription of Ps 56, we find a phrase that the CSB renders "according to 'A Silent Dove Far Away.'" This rendering is preferable to the ESV's "according to the Dove on Far-off Terebinths." The KJV and NAS transliterate the phrase ("Jonath elem rehokim"), putting the Hebrew words into English letters. The CSB, ESV, NAS, and NIV all treat the phrase as the name of a tune. It could be a tune, a kind of instrument, or a phrase meant to set the mood in which the psalm was to be read. Images of a dove silently floating in the distance may be intended.

In 56:1–3 (MT 56:2–4) David calls on God to be gracious to him because of those who trample on and attack him. Though this causes him fear, David asserts that he will trust God. In 56:1–2 (MT 56:2-3), the first line of each verse refers to those who "trample" David, and the second line refers to the individual and the many who "fight" him. In 56:1 (MT 56:2), the fighter is pressing David, and he says it is happening "all the day"—a phrase that appears in 56:1, 2, and 5 (MT 56:2, 3, and 6).

David appeals to God to be gracious to him in Ps 56:1 (MT 56:2). He explains the reason he needs God's grace, what causes him fear, in 56:1b–56:2 (MT 56:2b–56:3), and in 56:3 he asserts his trust in God (MT 56:4). Dan Phillips called my attention to Kidner's remark: "The Hebrew expression here for 'When' is '(In) the day (when)', much as in verse 9. Cf. the old translation 'What time I am afraid'—which brings a certain vividness to the phrase. *Faith is seen here as a deliberate act, in defiance of one's emotional state.*"[203]

Laying out the reason he trusts God in Ps 56:4 (MT 56:5), repeating himself almost verbatim in 56:10–11 (MT 56:11–12), David explains in 56:4 (MT 56:5) that he trusts God and praises his word. The word in view likely includes not only all the Scripture available to David but also the promise of God made to him by the prophet Samuel—the promise that he would be king. David's logic here is simple: If God has said he will be king, there is nothing any human can do to prevent that from happening. Thus David's rhetorical question as to what flesh can accomplish against him is based squarely on the fact of God's promise to him and his confidence in God's character. God will keep his word, and no man will prevail against him.

Having stated his praise for God's word in 56:4 (MT 56:5), David describes what the wicked do with his words and their own in 56:5 (MT 56:6). They do harm against David's words, probably twisting, distorting, and misrepresenting what he has said, and they use their own words to make plots against him. In 56:6 (MT 56:7) David describes the way his enemies foment trouble then try to hide themselves, keeping close watch on him to take his life. The reference to the enemies watching David's "heels" may allude to the bruised heel of the seed of the woman in Gen 3:15.

As noted above, Ps 56:7 (MT 56:8) stands at the center of the chiastic structure of the psalm. Here David prays that God would bring down the peoples. The first line of 56:7 (MT 56:8) is difficult and has been rendered as a question by CSB and ESV, "Will they escape in spite of such sin?" (CSB). The problem is that the MT as it stands is an imperative and not a question. It can be literally rendered, "Concerning iniquity, deliver them!" The "them" in view could be the godly, and on this understanding David would be praying for the wicked to be destroyed so that the godly would be thereby delivered. Alternatively, David could be calling on God to

---

[203] Kidner, *Psalms 1–72*, 221 (emphasis added). Phillips, pers. comm.

deliver the wicked from their iniquity by bringing them down. Whatever the case, in view of the superscription, David clearly calls on God to keep his word by destroying those opposed to David and his kingdom.

Seeking to motivate God to act on his behalf, David describes his suffering in 56:8 (MT 56:9). He speaks of the way the Lord has kept a full account of his wanderings, and he gives a prayer-wish command to the Lord, calling on God to put all the tears he (David) has cried in his bottle. He knows God's concern for him, so he asks rhetorically whether all this is not in God's book. Psalm 56:8 (MT 56:9) amounts to a Davidic meditation on God's concern for his people manifested in his awareness of all their pain and discomfort.

God's attention to the tears and wanderings of his own will result in him hearing when they call on him, and this David articulates in Ps 56:9 (MT 56:10). David confidently asserts that when he calls on God, because God is for him, those at enmity with him will be turned back. David's righteous suffering and confidence that God is for him in 56:8–9 (MT 56:9–10) stand across from the schemes and strife of the wicked in 56:5–6 (MT 56:6–7). All the efforts of the wicked cause David pain, but God will turn them back.

In a repetition of 56:4 (MT 56:5), in 56:10–11 (MT 56:11–12) David again asserts his praise for God's word, his trust in God, and the fearlessness this gives him because no human power can overcome God. One sometimes hears references to "bibliolatry." Given the sad state of our idol-making hearts, such a perversion is of course possible. But those who love God and want to worship him find him in the special self-revelation he has made of himself in the word. David clearly has no qualms about rightly trusting in and praising the goodness of God's word.

Because of God's word and character, because of God's concern for David, David knows that whatever his difficulties, however impossible his circumstances, God will bring him through the suffering to glory. Thus in 56:12 (MT 56:13) David states his obligation to God by saying that he must keep the vows he has made to worship the Lord. In addition to the vows, David asserts his intention to make good on all the thanksgivings he owes the Lord. In 56:13 (MT 56:12) David connects his worship and gratitude to the way the Lord has delivered him, kept his feet from stumbling, and made him able to walk before God in the light of life.

David's distress and fear in 56:1–3 (MT 56:2–4) is matched in the chiastic structure of the psalm by his confidence in 56:12–13 (MT 56:13–14) that

God will deliver him, prompting him to make vows to worship the Lord and promise to render all the thanks due. Whereas at the beginning of the psalm David's enemies seek to trample him, at the end David confidently states that he will walk before God in the light of life.

BRIDGE

David fled the land of promise and the people of God to go to the Philistines because Israel's king was trying to kill him. The persecution of the true king by the establishment typifies the one who would come as Israel's ultimate king, only to be rejected by the establishment. Just as David fled to the Philistines, at various points in his ministry Jesus went outside the borders of Israel. And the opposition to David found its typological fulfillment in the opposition to Jesus. David's suffering was fulfilled in Jesus, and the type made it necessary that the fulfillment would pass through suffering on the way to glory.

Both David and Jesus knew that God would deliver them because they knew what God had promised them. Followers of Jesus today can believe that because God has promised to complete what he began (Phil 1:6), God will preserve and perfect us, even if the path to that goes through our death. God will keep his word, and we can join King David and the Lord Jesus in celebrating that fact.

## Psalm 57

OVERVIEW AND STRUCTURE OF PSALM 57

In the midst of his difficulties, in Ps 57 David calls on God to exalt himself and cover the earth with his glory through the destruction of his enemies and the establishment of his kingdom. The chiastic structure of Ps 57 can be depicted as follows:

57:1 (MT 57:2), Be Gracious
    57:2–3 (MT 57:3–4), I Call, He Saves (Lovingkindness and Truth)
        57:4 (MT 57:5), Lions
            57:5 (MT 57:6), Be Exalted
        57:6 (MT 57:7), They Fall in Their Own Pit
    57:7–10 (MT 57:8–11), Praise (Lovingkindness and Truth)
57:11 (MT 57:12), Be Exalted

CSB

Author's translation

For the choir director: "Do Not Destroy." A *Miktam* of David. When he fled before Saul into the cave.

¹ Be gracious to me, God, be gracious to me,
for I take refuge in you.
I will seek refuge in the shadow of your wings
until danger passes.
² I call to God Most High,
to God who fulfills his purpose for me.
³ He reaches down from heaven and saves me,
challenging the one who tramples me.
*Selah*

God sends his faithful love and truth.
⁴ I am surrounded by lions;
I lie down among devouring lions—
people whose teeth are spears and arrows,
whose tongues are sharp swords.
⁵ God, be exalted above the heavens;
let your glory be over the whole earth.
⁶ They prepared a net for my steps;
I was despondent.
They dug a pit ahead of me,
but they fell into it!
*Selah*

⁷ My heart is confident, God, my heart is confident.
I will sing; I will sing praises.
⁸ Wake up, my soul!
Wake up, harp and lyre!
I will wake up the dawn.
⁹ I will praise you, Lord, among the peoples;
I will sing praises to you among the nations.

¹ For the Preeminent One.
Do Not Destroy.
Of David.
A *Miktam*.
When he fled from before Saul, in the cave.

² Be gracious to me, O God.
Be gracious to me,
for in you my soul takes refuge,
and in the shadow of your wings I will take refuge,
until destructions pass by.

³ I call to God Most High,
to God the one who completes for me.
⁴ He will send from heaven and cause salvation for me.
He reproaches the one who tramples me. *Selah*.
God will send his lovingkindness and his truth.

⁵ My soul is in the midst of lions.
I will lie down.
Burning ones, sons of Adam, their teeth spear and swords,
and their tongue a sharp sword.

⁶ Be exalted above the heavens, O God,
over all the earth your glory.

⁷ A net they prepared for my steps.
My soul was bent.
They dug a pit before me.
They fell into it. *Selah*.

⁸ Established is my heart, O God.
Established is my heart.
I will sing, and I will psalm.
⁹ Awake, my glory!
Awake the harp and the lyre!
I will awaken the dawn.

<sup>10</sup> For your faithful love is as high as
   the heavens;
your faithfulness reaches the clouds.
<sup>11</sup> God, be exalted above the heavens;
let your glory be over the whole earth.

<sup>10</sup> I will praise you among the peoples,
   my Lord.
I will psalm you among the nations,
<sup>11</sup> for great to the heavens is your
   lovingkindness, and to the clouds
   your truth.

<sup>12</sup> Be exalted above the heavens, O God,
over all the earth your glory.

## Context: Verbal and Thematic Links with Surrounding Psalms

There are a number of points of contact between Pss 56 and 57. Both open with the plea, "Be gracious to me." In both David speaks of enemies "trampling" on him.

These links tie the two psalms together, as does the fact that both have "*Miktam*" in the superscription, where both also mention historical events relating to Saul's persecution of David. Psalm 57 continues the series of psalms following 51 that deal with the difficulties Saul caused for David.

## Exposition

The superscription of Ps 57 follows "For the preeminent one" with the phrase "Do not destroy." There is no preposition "on" or "according to" preceding this phrase, so the translations that supply that seem to be assuming that "Do not destroy" is the name of a tune or style. It could just as well be a kind of subheading that states the psalm's theme and sets its tone.

The phrase "in the cave" in the superscription could refer to the episode in 1 Sam 24, when David refused to kill Saul when they were together in a cave. Because the superscription of Ps 56, however, locates that psalm at the end of 1 Sam 21, it seems that the reference to "the cave" in the superscription of Ps 57 more likely refers to the "cave of Adullam" to which David escaped at the beginning of 1 Sam 22 (1 Sam 22:1).

Once again David calls out to God to be gracious to him in Ps 57:1 (MT 57:2), and the repetition of the plea adds urgency. David has taken refuge from all the dangers posed him by Saul and the Philistines in a cave, but he is really taking refuge in God. Physically underground, David figuratively speaks of himself as being overshadowed by the wings of Yahweh, hiding in the Lord until the destructions have passed over.

David identifies God as the Most High in 57:2 (MT 57:3), asserting that there is none higher in dignity, authority, or power. No principality outranks him, none were before him, and none supersede him. This God who is the greatest of all is the one who has purposes for David that he will bring to fruition. As in Ps 56, where David's praise for God's word in 56:4 and 10 (MT 56:5 and 11) celebrated God's promise that David's throne would be established, so here in 57:2 (MT 57:3) the purpose God will fulfill for David is that David will be established as king of Israel. In danger, God's promises of good for David give David confidence that God will deliver him.

In Ps 57:3 (MT 57:4) David states that God's character will mean salvation for him and destruction for his enemies. David is confident, first, that God will send from heaven and save him because of God's promise. This means that those seeking to trample David underfoot will be reproached. David mentions God's "lovingkindness" and his "truth" because it is God's commitment to be loyal to David and his faithfulness to his own word that guarantees David's deliverance.

David knows God will deliver him in spite of the situation he finds himself in as described in 57:4 (MT 57:5). Fleeing from Saul and the Philistines is like lying down in the midst of lions. The beastly killers would eat him alive, and David describes them as inflammatory "burning ones," these sons of Adam have teeth like spear and blade, and their tongues are a sharp sword. The words these men speak are weapons of war used in attacks.

David's next words in this psalm are most surprising. In the midst of killers threatening his life, he praises God. David calls on the Lord to exalt himself above the heavens and to cover the earth with his glory in 57:5 (MT 57:6), a refrain that will be repeated almost word for word in 57:11 (MT 57:12). This Davidic exhortation to the Lord for God to show himself to be the Most High (cf. 57:2 [MT 57:3]) stands at the center of the psalm's chiastic structure. David knows that when God defends him and delivers him, it will show God to be more powerful than the forces aligned together against the Lord and his anointed. David wants God to exalt himself that way, and he wants the goodness of the reign of God's king to extend to the ends of the earth, filling it with God's glory.

The statement of God's exaltation in 57:5 (MT 57:6) is at the center of the psalm, preceded and followed by words about the wicked. They are likened to lions in 57:4 (MT 57:5), and the rebound effect of their schemes is described in 57:6 (MT 57:7). David's enemies have set snares in his way: they prepared a net to entrap his feet as he walked, and they dug a pit hoping he would fall into it. These schemes caused David's soul to be bowed down, but God made the enemies fall into the pit they dug.

David had earlier called on God, confident that he would fulfill his purpose in keeping with his character, delivering David and reproaching his enemies (57:2–3 [MT 57:3–4]), and now in 57:7–10 (MT 57:8–11) David speaks of how his heart is established and he will praise the Lord because of the Lord's lovingkindness and truth.

David twice asserts that his heart is established in Ps 57:7 (MT 57:8), repeating the phrase to emphasize the point. Beset with difficulty, threatened by killers, with no place to lay his head but a cave, David's heart is strong because of God's promises and God's character. In the midst of his difficulties David sings and psalms God's greatness.

In 57:8 (MT 57:9) David calls his glory to awake, along with the harp and lyre, stating that he will awaken the dawn. The reference to the dawn perhaps points to the light rising on the new day of David's reign, which David seems to be praising into existence here. This flows naturally into his intention to praise the Lord among the peoples, psalming him among the nations in 57:9 (MT 57:10). When David reigns over Israel, all the nations will see God's glory in the goodness of the reign of the new Adam. The one made in God's image and likeness will reign like the one whose image he bears, thus God's lovingkindness and truth will be made manifest in the reign of his king. God's lovingkindness saturates the atmosphere, reaching to the heavens, and his truth does likewise to the clouds. All creation is pervaded with the glory of God's character.

In keeping with the flooding of the atmosphere with God's lovingkindness and truth, David prays in 57:11 (MT 57:12) that God would be exalted above the heavens, covering the earth with his glory (cf. 57:5 [MT 57:6]). This will result from God answering David's prayer at the beginning of the psalm (57:1 [MT 57:2]). When God is gracious to David, David's enemies will be defeated, his throne will be established, and the knowledge of God's character and glory will spread over all the earth. If not in David's life, then in the life of the king God promised to raise up from his line.

Bridge

David demonstrates in Ps 57 that he had a clear idea of the connection between God's purposes for him personally and God's intention to make his name great in all the earth. David's prayers for himself are thereby prayers for God to exalt himself above the heavens and fill the world with his glory.

The scion of David, the everlasting King God promised to raise up from his line, also had a clear understanding of the connection between God's purposes for him personally and God's commitment to his own glory. Jesus prayed repeatedly in John 12–17 for God to glorify himself through what Jesus himself was facing. Nowhere is the glory of God more clearly seen than in the death and resurrection of Jesus the Messiah (see John 12:23–33; 13:31–32).

Along these lines, believers today should think through their lives and God's purposes. As we pray, we should beseech God to make his name great in our lives in accordance with the way the New Testament says that he will do just that: by keeping us faithful through our sufferings, by completing the good work he began in us, and by presenting us blameless before himself because of our faith in Christ (see esp. 2 Thess 1:11–12; Jude 24–25).

## Psalm 58

OVERVIEW AND STRUCTURE OF PSALM 58

Psalm 58 opens and closes with statements about righteous judgment: It isn't happening in 58:1–2 (MT 58:2–3), but God will establish it in 58:10–11 (MT 58:11–12). The wicked "turn aside from the womb; they go astray from the belly" in 58:3 (MT 58:4), and they "wander" and are likened to a "miscarriage" in 58:7–9 (MT 58:8–10). These wicked are compared to venomous snakes in 58:4–5 (MT 58:5–6), and David calls on God to break their teeth in their mouths in 58:6 (MT 58:7). The psalm reflects the following chiastic structure:[204]

58:1–2 (MT 58:2–3), Righteous Judgment Not Executed
    58:3 (MT 58:4), They Go Astray from the Womb
        58:4–5 (MT 58:5–6), Uncharmed Venomous Snakes
        58:6 (MT 58:7), Break Their Teeth
    58:7–9 (MT 58:8–10), Wander, Miscarriage
58:10–11 (MT 58:11–12), Righteous Judgment Executed by God

---

[204] Similarly Robert L. Alden, "Chiastic Psalms (II): A Study in the Mechanics of Semitic Poetry in Psalms 51–100," *JETS* 19 (1976): 192–93.

We will pursue the exposition of Ps 58 under the following subheads:

58:1–5 (MT 58:2–6), The Injustice of the Wicked
58:6–9 (MT 58:7–10), Prayer for God to Thwart the Wicked
58:10–11 (MT 58:11–12), The Response to God's Justice

SCRIPTURE

CSB                                          Author's translation

For the choir director: "Do Not            [1] For the Preeminent One.
Destroy." A *Miktam* of David.             Do Not Destroy.
                                           Of David.
[1] Do you really speak righteously, you   A *Miktam*.
    mighty ones?
Do you judge people fairly?                [2] Really in silence do you all speak
[2] No, you practice injustice in your         righteousness,
    hearts;                                uprightly do you judge, O sons of
with your hands you weigh out                  Adam?
    violence in the land.                  [3] Indeed in heart injustices you all
                                               perform.
[3] The wicked go astray from the          In the earth the violence of your
    womb;                                      hands you weigh out.
liars wander about from birth.
[4] They have venom like the venom of      [4] The wicked turn aside from the
    a snake,                                   womb;
like the deaf cobra that stops up its      they go astray from the belly, those
    ears,                                      who speak falsehood.
[5] that does not listen to the sound of
    the charmers                           [5] Their venom is like the venom of a
who skillfully weave spells.                   serpent,
                                           like the deaf viper he shuts his ear;
[6] God, knock the teeth out of their      [6] whereas he will not listen to the
    mouths;                                    voice of the charmer,
LORD, tear out the young lions' fangs.     the wizened speller of spells.
[7] May they vanish like water that
    flows by;                              [7] O God, break their teeth in their
may they aim their blunted arrows.             mouth;
[8] Like a slug that moves along in slime, the fangs of the young lions pull out,
like a woman's miscarried child,               O Yahweh.
may they not see the sun.
                                           [8] Let them wander about like water:
                                               they go about for themselves.

⁹ Before your pots can feel the heat of
the thorns—
whether green or burning—
he will sweep them away.
¹⁰ The righteous one will rejoice
when he sees the retribution;
he will wash his feet in the blood of
the wicked.
¹¹ Then people will say,
"Yes, there is a reward for the
righteous!
There is a God who judges on earth!"

He treads his arrows, let them be as
those that wither.
⁹ Like the snail of slime he walks.
The miscarriage of a woman that sees
not the sun.
¹⁰ Before your pots discern the
bramble,
like living, like burning, may he
sweep him away.

¹¹ The righteous will be glad when he
sees vengeance.
His steps he will bathe in the blood of
the wicked.
¹² And man will say, "Surely the fruit
for the righteous!
Surely there is a God who judges in
the earth."

CONTEXT: VERBAL AND THEMATIC LINKS WITH SURROUNDING PSALMS

Psalm 58 sits in a series of psalms that carry the superscription "Do not destroy" (57, 58, 59, cf. 75) accompanied by the word "*Miktam*" (56, 57, 58, 59, 60, cf. 16). David responds to persecution and opposition in these psalms, and several mention Saul's name (52, 54, 57, 59, with 56 referencing circumstances relating to Saul's persecution). Though the superscription of Ps 58 does not directly mention Saul, its placement in the Psalter makes that period of David's life when Saul was trying to kill him the likeliest context for its composition.

EXPOSITION

### 58:1–5 (MT 58:2–6), The Injustice of the Wicked

As pointed in *BHS* the Hebrew text of Ps 58:1 (MT 58:2) reads as follows: "Really in silence do you all speak righteousness ... ?" The term rendered "in silence" can be re-pointed (i.e., given different vowels, revocalized) to mean either "gods" (ESV, NAS) or "mighty ones/rulers" (CSB, NIV). The Greek translation leaves the term in question untranslated (cf. NETS), and the targum renders it "silent."[205]

I have stayed with the *BHS* to render the term in question "in silence" (with the footnote/marginal reading in the CSB and ESV) and, assuming

---

[205] Stec, *Targum of Psalms*, 116.

the context of Saul's persecution of David, take the phrase to articulate David's objection to the way that influential people are silent in response to Saul's wickedness. Those who should stand for righteousness and justice, using their influence and authority for truth and goodness, instead passively allow Saul to continue in his murderous wickedness. Whereas those who keep the Torah strive against the wicked, those who do not stand against the wicked join their cause against the truth of God's word (cf. Prov 28:4, 23; 24:25).

David raises his objection to the silence that results in ongoing injustice as a question in 58:1 (MT 58:2), and he proceeds to answer his own question in 58:2 (MT 58:3). Rather than speak righteousness against Saul's wickedness, those who have failed to uphold the standards of God's word have aided the cause of those who seek its overthrow. This, at least, explains how those with influence to judge uprightly (58:1 [MT 58:2]) are instead performing injustices in their hearts and weighing out violence in the land (58:2 [MT 58:3]).

In Ps 58:3–5 (MT 58:4–6) David characterizes the actions of the wicked. Doing so establishes the indisputable truth: They have no redeeming characteristics. Those who support them and those who fail to oppose them are wrong. By stating these truths, David asserts the rightness of his own cause and indicts those who aid and abet the wicked by failing to resist their injustice.

Just as David knows that he himself was born in sin (51:5 [MT 51:6]), he knows that the wicked have been going astray, speaking lies, since birth (58:3 [MT 58:4]). This is the inexorable tendency of every human unless the Lord intervenes in their lives to circumcise their hearts, prompt them to repent, and give them a life-giving love for God's word (cf. Lev 26:41; Deut 10:16; 6:4–6; Ps 19:7–11).

Apart from God's work to give life to the sinner's dead heart and light to spiritual eyes by his word, what David says in Ps 58:3 (MT 58:4) of the wicked is true of every human who has ever lived. David's brilliant poetic statement in 58:3–5 (MT 58:4–6) characterizes his enemies in biblical, behavioral, and visceral terms.

Biblically speaking, by likening his enemies to snakes David labels them seed of the serpent, links them with their father the devil, and lays claim to his own identity as seed of the woman (Gen 3:15). Behaviorally speaking, his enemies are like venomous vipers with whom skilled snake charmers have no success. This captures the way that David's enemies intend to kill him and will not listen to reason. People do not cozy up to poisonous snakes that cannot be charmed, and therein lies the primeval power of David's poetry. The wicked are dangerous, and David communicates that in a way that removes all sentiment for them personally, all sympathy for their cause, and all suggestion that they might be peacefully appeased. There is only one way to ensure safety when dealing with venomous snakes.

### 58:6–9 (MT 58:7–10), Prayer for God to Thwart the Wicked

David prays that God would do what is necessary with the snakes that safety might be established in 58:6 (MT 58:7). By also characterizing his enemies as fanged lions, David links the enemies of Ps 58 with those of 57:4 (MT 57:5). David wants the teeth of the snakes broken and those of lions pulled (58:6 [MT 58:7]). In 58:7 (MT 58:8) David prays that their cause would dissipate like water poured out on the ground, which does not stay puddled and stand strong but flows away and is gone. He also wants his enemies to tread the bow only to have their arrows be withered shafts, ineffectual against their targets.

In Ps 58:8 (MT 58:9) David says his enemies are like snails that leave a trail of slime, contaminating and defiling every place they have been. He does not want them to have the sun rise upon them but rather desires that they perish like a baby born already dead. David wants the Lord to keep the cause of his enemies from growing and flourishing. He wants the cause of wickedness to be seen for what it is and to experience its own rightful outcome. In 58:9 (MT 58:10) David prays that the sweeping away of his enemies might be swift—faster than a pot can heat up when the fire is lit beneath it.

### 58:10–11 (MT 58:11–12), The Response to God's Justice

The rejoicing righteous in Ps 58:10 (MT 58:11) are those who love God and love God's word. Those who love God and God's word love God's people. Thus those who love God, his word, and his people, cannot be reconciled to the unjust and unrighteous wickedness of those who set aside God's word, exploit God's people, and make war on God's kingdom. They love justice, and they rejoice when God executes it. They love to see the afflicted liberated from oppressors.

There may be a poetic interpretation of Gen 3:15 in Ps 58:10 (MT 58:11) as David depicts the righteous bathing his feet in the blood of the wicked.

This may result from the seed of the woman bruising their heels as they bruise the head of the seed of the serpent by stomping them underfoot, with the result that their feet are bathed in the blood of the wicked. If this is indeed the meaning of the imagery, it points to the way that God's justice will be visited by means of God's people (cf. Rom 16:20). The statement is made with singular rather than plural forms, as in Gen 3:15. These singulars can be taken to refer to the way that God's people in general will visit his justice, or they could also point to the way the singular seed of the woman will wear garments sprinkled by the blood of his enemies (Isa 63:1–6; Rev 19:13).

Psalm 58:11 (MT 58:12) speaks to the more general response to the execution of God's justice. People will be convinced that God exists, that he is just, and that he rewards the righteous and punishes the guilty when the debts come due.

### Bridge

David knew that his enemies were God's enemies and that those not for the Lord were against him, even if only passively. Does this moral clarity mark your disposition toward your fellow man? Jesus said that those who were not for him were against him (Matt 12:30). Are you actively supporting the cause of God's word or passively aiding the enemies of God?

David also knew that his enemies were the seed of the serpent, pursuing the kingdom of the archenemy of God. Jesus shared this biblical assessment of those opposed to him (John 8:39–47). Do you think about the wicked in biblical terms? Are you able to identify the seed of the serpent, those who seek Satan's triumph over the kingdom of God?

Jesus will come and crush the head of the serpent and all his seed. Will you rejoice when he liberates creation from the power of evil, or will your blood be spattered on his robes (Isa 63:3)?

## Psalm 59

### Overview and Structure of Psalm 59

VanGemeren proposes a chiastic structure for Ps 59, but I neither find it persuasive nor see an alternative to propose. The psalm seems to have two turning points, each at an occurrence of selah. The selah at the end of 59:5 (MT 59:6) is followed by a description of the wicked in 59:6 (MT 59:7), "They return at evening. They growl like a dog. And they go about the city." This sequence is repeated when the selah that ends 59:13 (MT 59:14) is followed by the same description of the wicked in 59:14 (MT 59:15), "And they return at evening. They growl like a dog. And they go about the city."

The psalm thus appears to fall into three sections:[206]

> 59:1–5 (MT 59:2–6), Deliver Me
> 59:6–13 (MT 59:7–14), That They May Know
> 59:14–17 (MT 59:15–18), Your Lovingkindness

SCRIPTURE

| CSB | Author's translation |
|---|---|
| For the choir director: "Do Not Destroy." A *Miktam* of David. When Saul sent agents to watch the house and kill him. | [1] For the Preeminent One.<br>Do Not Destroy.<br>Of David.<br>A *Miktam*.<br>When Saul sent, and they watched the house to kill him. |
| [1] Rescue me from my enemies, my God; protect me from those who rise up against me.<br>[2] Rescue me from evildoers, and save me from men of bloodshed.<br>[3] Because look, LORD, they set an ambush for me.<br>Powerful men attack me, but not because of any sin or rebellion of mine.<br>[4] For no fault of mine, they run and take up a position.<br>Awake to help me, and take notice.<br>[5] LORD God of Armies, you are the God of Israel.<br>Rise up to punish all the nations; do not show favor to any wicked traitors.<br>*Selah* | [2] Deliver me from those at enmity with me, O God!<br>Make me higher than those who rise against me.<br>[3] Deliver me from those who work iniquity, and from men of bloods save me.<br>[4] For behold they lie in wait for my soul, fierce men sojourn against me—<br>not my transgression and not my sin, O Yahweh.<br>[5] Unprovoked by sin they run and make themselves ready.<br>Awake to my cry and see!<br>[6] Even you, O Yahweh, God of Hosts, God of Israel,<br>wake up to visit all the nations!<br>Do not be gracious to any who deal treacherously of iniquity. *Selah*. |
| [6] They return at evening, snarling like dogs<br>and prowling around the city. | |

---

[206] Alden, "Chiastic Psalms (II)," 193, also proposes a chiasm.

⁷Look, they spew from their mouths—
sharp words from their lips.
"For who," they say, "will hear?"
⁸But you laugh at them, Lᴏʀᴅ;
you ridicule all the nations.
⁹I will keep watch for you, my
strength,
because God is my stronghold.
¹⁰My faithful God will come to meet
me;
God will let me look down on my
adversaries.

¹¹Do not kill them; otherwise, my
people will forget.
By your power, make them homeless
wanderers
and bring them down,
Lord, our shield.
¹²For the sin of their mouths and the
words of their lips,
let them be caught in their pride.
They utter curses and lies.
¹³Consume them in fury;
consume them until they are gone.
Then people will know throughout
the earth
that God rules over Jacob.
Selah

¹⁴And they return at evening, snarling
like dogs
and prowling around the city.
¹⁵They scavenge for food;
they growl if they are not satisfied.

¹⁶But I will sing of your strength
and will joyfully proclaim
your faithful love in the morning.
For you have been a stronghold for
me,
a refuge in my day of trouble.
¹⁷To you, my strength, I sing praises,
because God is my stronghold—
my faithful God.

⁷ They return at evening. They growl
like a dog. And they go about the
city.
⁸ Behold their mouths gush forth,
swords on their lips, for "who
hears?"
⁹ But you, O Yahweh, laugh at them.
You mock all the nations.
¹⁰ His strength. For you I will watch,
for God is my high place.
¹¹ The God of my lovingkindness will
meet me.
God will cause me to look at my
watchers.
¹² Do not kill them, lest my people
forget.
Cause them to totter by your power.
Bring them down, O Lord our shield.
¹³ The sin of their mouth, the word of
their lips,
so let them be taken in their
exaltation,
and for the oath and lying they
recount.
¹⁴ Consume in wrath, consume, that
they may be no more,
and they will know that God rules in
Jacob to the ends of the earth. Selah.

¹⁵ And they return at evening. They
growl like a dog. And they go about
the city.
¹⁶ They roam to eat; if they are not
satisfied, then they spend the
night.
¹⁷ But as for me, I will sing of your
strength
and give a ringing cry in the morning
of your lovingkindness,
for you are a high place for me, and
a place of refuge on the day of my
distress.
¹⁸ My strength, to you I will psalm,
for God is my high place, the God of
the lovingkindness of me.

See the observations about the superscriptions of this string of psalms in the context section of the commentary on Ps 58. The additional information in the superscription of Ps 59 locates the setting of this psalm at 1 Sam 19:11–17 by the phrase, "When Saul sent and they watched the house to kill him" (Ps 59 superscription [MT 59:1]).

In a series of psalms dealing with Saul's persecution of David, Ps 59 responds to the lackeys of Saul prowling the city in the dark to spy out David's dwelling and movements in an attempt to bring about his demise.

EXPOSITION

**59:1–5 (MT 59:2–6), Deliver Me**

David's immediate response to Saul's spies comes in the twofold cry for deliverance in 59:1–2 (MT 59:2–3). David needs deliverance because those who are at enmity with him have risen against him, workers of iniquity whose violent ways prompt David to describe them as "men of bloods."

The injustice of Saul's attempts on David's life is articulated in 59:3–4 (MT 59:4–5). David repeatedly asserts that Saul and his assassins are not opposed to him because of his sin. David is not a wicked enemy of the state. He is not being justly executed or persecuted as an evildoer. He is innocent. In spite of his upstanding character and good standing in Israel, Saul's lackeys lie in wait to kill him, sojourning at his home through the night hoping for an opportunity against him. They have hastened to ready themselves, but David calls on the Lord to wake to his defense.

In Ps 59:5 (MT 59:6) David asserts the identity of his defender: Yahweh, God of hosts. The God of Israel is for him, and David calls on the Lord to rise up to bring a visitation against all the nations. David calls on the Lord, urging him not to be gracious to those whose iniquity shows itself in their treacherous conduct. David's prayer here is reformulated in Prov 17:15, where Solomon asserts that it is an abomination to Yahweh to justify the wicked and condemn the righteous. In Ps 59:5 (MT 59:6) David calls on the Lord to be consistent with himself.

**59:6–13 (MT 59:7–14), That They May Know**

In Ps 59:6 and 59:14 (MT 59:7 and 15) David likens the killers haunting his home to growling dogs, prowling the city by night. In 59:7 (MT 59:8) he depicts them gushing out arrogant and dangerous words that they think will not be heard and judged by God—the upshot of their asking "who hears?"

David bases his reply squarely on Ps 2:4, which asserts that the Lord laughs at those who join together against him and his anointed (cf. 37:13 and 52:6). The Lord mocks all who think to overthrow his almighty power. Only laughable fools would attempt to overcome the omnipotent.

The Hebrew text has "His strength" as the opening phrase of 59:9 (MT 59:10), and I take this to be David's brief contemplation of the strength of his enemies (so also the NAS). CSB, ESV, and NIV emend the text to "my strength" and understand David to be speaking of the Lord as his strength.

In response to the strength of his foes who watch for him (59:9, superscription [MT 59:10, 1]), David asserts that he will watch for God, who is his high place (a term related to the plea "make me higher" in 59:1, cf. 59:16 [MT 59:2, 17]). So confident in God's lovingkindness, he knows the Lord will keep his word and give him triumph over those who watch for his life (59:10 [MT 59:11]).

Whereas David prayed swift destruction for his enemies in Ps 58:9 (MT 58:10), the different circumstances have him calling for the Lord not to put his enemies immediately to death in 59:11 (MT 59:12). Captured foes are sometimes useful for the testimony they provide, and here David does not want his people to forget because the enemies have been so quickly defeated. He wants them to totter, to be brought down, such that their demise will be an ongoing testimony to the righteousness of David's cause and the shielding power of God (59:11 [MT 59:12]).

And whereas David himself is innocent (59:3–4 [MT 59:4–5]), the words of his enemies show that they are guilty (59:12 [MT 59:13]). Because they make oaths that they break, David wants his enemies trapped in 59:12 (MT 59:13) and consumed in 59:13 (MT 59:14). And David wants this for God's glory: just as people would know that there is a God who judges in 58:11 (MT 58:12), in 59:13 (MT 59:14) God's justice will show that God rules over his people, Jacob, to the ends of the earth. There is no place or realm in all creation that is not subject to Yahweh's standards, Yahweh's evaluation, and Yahweh's reward.

### 59:14–17 (MT 59:15–18), Your Lovingkindness

The restatement of 59:6 (MT 59:7) in 59:14 (MT 59:15) indicates that David is yet to be delivered from Saul's lurking assassins. He describes their ravenous hunger to devour him in 59:15 (MT 59:16) before asserting his own confidence and praise for God in 59:16–17 (MT 59:17–18).

In spite of the fact that killers are spending the night at his home seeking to extinguish him, David declares in 59:16 (MT 59:17) that he will sing of Yahweh's strength, which will protect him through the night so that he can "give a ringing cry" about the Lord's lovingkindness "in the morning." The Lord's strength and lovingkindness are manifested here as David takes refuge in the Lord in his distress and finds the Lord to be a high place, removing him from the reach of the men of blood.

In 59:17 (MT 59:18) David again asserts that Yahweh is his strength, and he states his intention to do the very thing he does in all his psalms: psalm to the Lord, because God is his high place of refuge, the God whose lovingkindness is for him.

BRIDGE

One greater than David arose who was more innocent than David could ever claim to be, for whom enemies prowled about seeking his life. David's enemies gathered together against the Lord and him, the Lord's anointed, just as they would gather against Yahweh and Jesus, *the* anointed of the Lord. And as Pss 2:4, 37:13, and 59:8 (MT 59:9) assert, the Lord laughs and mocks at those with the audacity to seek to kill the one who has life in himself (cf. John 5:26).

The destruction of God's enemies is both fast and slow: it often happens swiftly, but the Bible indicates that the everlasting torment of the wicked will be an ongoing testimony of God's justice (cf. Rev 19:3). God rules not only over his people but to the ends of the earth. His people will psalm the praise of his lovingkindness forever.

## Psalm 60

OVERVIEW AND STRUCTURE OF PSALM 60

The superscription of Ps 60 sets the historical context for the psalm, and it seems to allude to the events narrated in 2 Sam 8–10 and 1 Chr 18–19. The psalm presents an ABA structured response to an occasion when Israel was attacked by intimidating forces.

The onslaught prompts David to cry out to God asking why his rejection has resulted in an earth-rending and destabilizing defeat of Israel

(60:1–5 [MT 60:3–7]). The Lord's response, in which he declares his absolute sovereignty over lands and peoples, follows (60:6–8 [MT 60:8–10]). That response prompts David to cry out to the Lord to bring his sovereignty to bear on the battle at hand (60:9–12 [MT 60:11–14]).

David here calls on the Lord to restore his people from their experience of his rejection, and the superscription seems to record the victory brought about on the occasion in question:

60:1–5 (MT 60:3–7), Israel's Rejected Distress
60:6–8 (MT 60:8–10), God's Sovereign Authority
60:9–12 (MT 60:11–14), David's Cry for Help

SCRIPTURE

| CSB | Author's translation |
|---|---|
| For the choir director: according to "The Lily of Testimony." A *Miktam* of David for teaching. When he fought with Aram-naharaim and Aram-zobah, and Joab returned and struck Edom in Salt Valley, killing twelve thousand. | [1] For the Preeminent One. On *Shushan Edut* [On the Lily of Testimony] A *Miktam* of David. For teaching. |
| [1] God, you have rejected us; you have broken us down; you have been angry. Restore us! [2] You have shaken the land and split it open. Heal its fissures, for it shudders. [3] You have made your people suffer hardship; you have given us wine to drink that made us stagger. [4] You have given a signal flag to those who fear you, so that they can flee before the archers. *Selah* | [2] In his struggle with Aram Naharaim [Aram of the two rivers, i.e., Mesopotamia] and with Aram Zobah, and Joab returned and struck Edom in the Valley of Salt— twelve thousand. [3] O God, you have rejected us. You have broken us. You were angry. You must restore us. [4] You caused the earth to quake. You split it open. Heal its breaches, for it totters. [5] You caused your people to see difficulty. You caused us to drink the wine of staggering. [6] You gave to those who fear you a banner to blazon from before the bow. *Selah*. |
| [5] Save with your right hand, and answer me, so that those you love may be rescued. | |

⁶God has spoken in his sanctuary:
"I will celebrate!
I will divide up Shechem.
I will apportion the Valley of Succoth.
⁷Gilead is mine, Manasseh is mine,
and Ephraim is my helmet;
Judah is my scepter.
⁸Moab is my washbasin.
I throw my sandal on Edom;
I shout in triumph over Philistia."

⁹Who will bring me to the fortified
city?
Who will lead me to Edom?
¹⁰God, haven't you rejected us?
God, you do not march out with our
armies.
¹¹Give us aid against the foe,
for human help is worthless.
¹²With God we will perform valiantly;
he will trample our foes.

⁷ So that your beloved ones might be
delivered,
cause salvation by your right hand
and answer us.

⁸ God has spoken in his holiness.
"I will exult!
I will apportion Shechem,
and the valley of Succoth I will
measure.
⁹ For me is Gilead,
and for me is Manasseh.
Ephraim is the protection for my
head.
Judah is my ruler's staff.
¹⁰ Moab is the pot for my washing.
Over Edom I cast my sandal.
Over me, O Philistia, shout in
triumph!"

¹¹ Who will bring me to the besieged
city?
Who will lead me to Edom?
¹² Have you not rejected us, O God?
And you do not go out, O God, with
our armies.
¹³ Give us help from distress,
for vain is the salvation of man.
¹⁴ In God we will do what is mighty,
and he will trample our adversaries.

CONTEXT: VERBAL AND THEMATIC LINKS WITH SURROUNDING PSALMS

The superscription of Ps 60 (MT 60:1–2), the longest in the Psalter, presents this as a psalm "for the preeminent one," adding that it is "On *shushan edut*" (cf. ESV) or as that phrase might be translated, "on the lily of testimony" (cf. CSB). It is interesting to note that the term "lilies" also occurs in the superscription of Ps 45, as does the term rendered "beloved ones" in 60:5 (MT 60:7). Both these terms, "lilies" and "beloved ones," occur in the Song of Songs as well. Psalm 60 uses phrases familiar from Ps 44:10 in 60:1 and 10 (MT 60:3, 12), and in Ps 61 David prays for the future king in 61:6–7 (MT 61:7–8). This creates a matching progression from Psalms 44–45 in Psalms 60–61:

Psalms 44, 60, The people in distress
Psalms 45, 61, The future king

This progression indicates that the Psalter repeatedly presents the promised king as the ultimate resolution to the difficulties experienced by the people of God. This progression might explain Ps 60's placement as the last of the "Miktams" (Pss 57, 58, 59, and 60). At this point the psalms of David numbered 51–72 seem to take a turn from difficulty to triumph and growing confidence. Even Ps 63, superscripted "When he was in the wilderness of Judah," apparently fleeing Saul, is remarkably upbeat.

Psalm 60, like Pss 56–59, is a "Miktam," but whereas Pss 56–59 respond to Saul's persecution of David, the rest of the superscription of Ps 60 (MT 60:2) refers to a conflict during David's reign with Joab as his general. The psalm is "For teaching," indicating that God's people are to learn from the crisis, the prayer, and the outcome reflected in this psalm. It is interesting to reflect on the fact that psalms dealing with David in difficulty during the reign of King Saul (52–59) are set in context with a psalm from David's reign (60)—the old difficulties passed to be replaced by new ones.

The crisis is presented in the information in the superscription (MT 60:2) which keys the psalm to 2 Sam 10 and 1 Chr 19. On the occasion narrated there, David was confronted with enemies allied with "Aram Nahariam" and "Aram Zobah." Translations of Chronicles and Samuel render references to "Aram" as "Syrians," and "Naharaim" refers to "the two rivers," that is, the Tigris and the Euphrates, or Mesopotamia. Zobah is yet another geographic place name. The occasion, then, is one when David was faced with powerful enemies. The last line of the superscription (MT 60:2), however, indicates that Joab was successful against the enemy forces.

The superscription thus intends to instruct us by relating the crisis and the victory before presenting to us the cry of distress in the body of the psalm. We approach the psalm knowing the outcome of the prayer. God granted David's request and gave him the victory. Knowing that, we then work through David's fears, anxieties, and theological questions.

Reading this psalm invites us to reflect on what it would be like to reenter the moments of crisis in our own lives having been shown our final outcome, like being shown the end, our enjoyment of God's heavenly new kingdom, then reliving the journey toward it. That seems to be the perspective Ps 60 intends to give.

### 60:1–5 (MT 60:3–7), Israel's Rejected Distress

Knowing the outcome announced in the superscription (MT 60:2) takes nothing away from the reality of divine displeasure and the uncertainty created by it in 60:1 (MT 60:3). Here David presents a theological interpretation of Israel's historical experience: David interprets the fact that Israel is embattled and looks to be defeated as evidence that God has rejected and broken Israel because he was angry with them. David does not respond to this by charging God with unfaithfulness; he knows God is faithful even when his people are not. Instead, David calls on the Lord for restoration.

Whereas Ps 60:1 (MT 60:3) betrays the truth that Israel can only be defeated if God becomes angry with them and hands them over to be disciplined, 60:2–3 (MT 60:4–5) betray the truth that the fate of the world hangs in the balance of what happens with Israel. Israel's sin endangers all creation. In 60:2 (MT 60:4), the earth quakes and Yahweh splits it open in his displeasure against his people, prompting David to plead with God to heal the earth's gashes because it totters unsteadily. Then in 60:3 (MT 60:5) David appeals to the Lord's compassion for his people, complaining of the discipline they have experienced, noting that it is as though they have been made to drink the wine of God's wrath to the point of staggering drunkenness. The flourishing of the world and the people who inhabit it depends on God's favor to his people. The obedience of God's people has cosmic ramifications. The stability of all the world is jeopardized by the sin of God's people.

Perhaps recalling the way Moses celebrated Yahweh as his people's banner after he gave them victory in Exod 17:14–16, in Ps 60:4 (MT 60:6) David rehearses the way God gave those who fear him a banner to which they could rally in danger. Then in 60:5 (MT 60:7) he calls on the Lord to cause salvation by his right hand, answering David's prayer, so that the Lord's beloved ones might be delivered. This takes for granted the fact that God loves his people and has made promises to them. David appeals to God to act in accordance with his own word and heart.

These statements also recognize that God's people suffer God's discipline and displeasure, and acknowledging their difficulties as such confesses that they are in the wrong and God is in the right. The appeal for help, then, is an appeal for mercy.

## 60:6–8 (MT 60:8–10), God's Sovereign Authority

David's next words bring out the paradox that while God is altogether sovereign, his people are often lowly and afflicted. In Ps 60:6–8 (MT 60:8–10), God makes an announcement that flows from his holiness. He is altogether set apart and distinct, and the realities he declares in these verses comport with his unique status as the holy one.

In 60:6 (MT 60:8) God declares that he will exult. His is a happy existence as the holy one. If what is good is what is holy, then God has the uniquely happy experience of the fullness of goodness uncontaminated by anything that would defile or take away life. God exults. The Lord goes on to announce that authority over the lands east and west of the Jordan River, moving from north to south, is his alone. He will do with them as he pleases and dispose of them as he wills.

God apportions and measures Shechem and Succoth, Gilead and Manasseh belong to him, and he uses Ephraim and Judah for his own exalted purposes (60:7 [MT 60:9]), while he uses Moab and Edom for more menial needs (60:8 [MT 60:10]). The CSB, ESV, and NIV all understand the last line as a statement that God shouts in triumph over Philistia, but the Hebrew text as it stands in *BHS* seems to present a sarcastic challenge to the Philistines, with God daring them to shout in triumph. Taunting them to "bring it on," the Lord says, "Over me, O Philistia, shout in triumph!"

Yahweh triumphs over nine place names in Ps 60:6–8 (MT 60:8–10). Keel has two ancient pictures from Egypt that depict relevant scenes. In the first, an enthroned king holds his son on his lap, and under the son's feet are nine defeated enemies. In the second, nine bows—symbolizing hostile powers—lie under the feet of the conqueror. Keel comments, "three times three denotes a totality."[207]

These statements declare the reality that God rules over the nations. God rules over all lands and peoples. The context forces the issue, then, of why God's people do not experience total victory. If God is so powerful, why are his people so weak?

The resolution to that question comes in the final verses of the psalm, having already been announced in its superscription (MT 60:2).

---

[207] Keel, *Symbolism of the Biblical World*, 255.

## 60:9–12 (MT 60:11–14), David's Cry for Help

David's rhetorical question in 60:9 (MT 60:11) has an obvious answer that will be made explicit in 60:11–12 (MT 60:13–14), being implied from 60:6–8 (MT 60:8–10). God is the one who will lead David to victory over the besieged city, and God is the one who will give him the battle against Edom.

The problem, articulated already in 60:1 (MT 60:3), is that Israel's beleaguered situation indicates that God has rejected his people. Believing that God has not rejected his people, but forcing the issue, David asks the question outright in 60:10 (MT 60:12), "Have you not rejected us, O God?" The evidence that would lead to that conclusion is articulated in the next line of the verse, where David asserts that God does not go out with Israel's armies. Israel's lack of success in battle is a direct reflection of their lack of God's favor. How they do in battle shows where they stand with God.

At 60:11 (MT 60:13) David calls on the Lord for help from distress, declaring the vanity of any help they might get from other humans. He then asserts in 60:12 (MT 60:14) that by God's help God's people will do valiant deeds and trample down their foes.

BRIDGE

God's people live in the tension between their knowledge of God's absolute power and sovereignty and their experience of humiliation and defeat. Psalm 60 models a way to wrestle with this tension from a position of faith. God's character, justice, and concern are never challenged. God's righteous indignation is assumed and articulated. The sin of God's people implicitly prompts the divine displeasure, but David nevertheless calls on the sovereign one to show mercy and save.

David does not accept the disconnect between God's power and the defeat of God's people but calls on the Lord to bring his power to bear that his people might gain the victory.

## Psalm 61

OVERVIEW AND STRUCTURE OF PSALM 61

Psalm 61 is a briefly stated ABA prayer. In 61:1–3 (MT 61:2–4) David cries out to be heard by God because God is his refuge and tower of strength. In 61:4–5 (MT 61:5–6) David communicates his hope ever to dwell in the Lord's presence, thereby receiving what those who fear God inherit. David then makes a smooth transition from prayer for himself in response to his own experience to prayer for the king God promised to raise up from his line in 61:6–8 (MT 61:7–9), where he calls on God to keep his promises that he himself might praise God's name forever.

61:1–3 (MT 61:2–4), Prayer to Be Heard
    61:4–5 (MT 61:5–6), Hope and Heritage
61:6–8 (MT 61:7–9), King of Praise

SCRIPTURE

CSB

Author's translation

For the choir director: on stringed instruments. Of David.

¹God, hear my cry;
pay attention to my prayer.
²I call to you from the ends of the earth
when my heart is without strength.
Lead me to a rock that is high above me,
³for you have been a refuge for me,
a strong tower in the face of the enemy.
⁴I will dwell in your tent forever
and take refuge under the shelter of your wings.
*Selah*

⁵God, you have heard my vows;
you have given a heritage
to those who fear your name.
⁶Add days to the king's life;
may his years span many generations.
⁷May he sit enthroned before God forever.
Appoint faithful love and truth to guard him.
⁸Then I will continually sing of your name,
fulfilling my vows day by day.

¹ For the Preeminent One.
On the string.
Of David.

² Hear, O God, my ringing cry!
Attend to my prayer.
³ From the end of the earth, to you I cry when faint is my heart.
To the rock higher than I, lead me,
⁴ for you are a refuge to me,
a tower of strength before the one at enmity.
⁵ I will sojourn in your tent for ages.
I will take refuge in the hiding place of your wings. *Selah.*
⁶ For you, O God, listened to my vows.
You gave me the possession of those who fear your name.

⁷ Days upon the days of the king you will add.
His years like generation and generation.
⁸ May he sit to the age before God.
Lovingkindness and truth appoint that they may keep him.
⁹ Thus I will psalm your name forever,
that I may fulfill my vows day by day.

The psalms of the sons of Korah (Pss 42–49) seem to mark the beginning of David's reign, for he appointed the Levites, including a son of Korah and his brother Asaph (Ps 50) over the worship of God after the ark rested there (1 Chr 6:31, 37, 39; 2 Sam 6). David then sinned with Bathsheba (Ps 51), and the psalms that follow present him in difficulty (Pss 52–59). Psalm 60 seems to present David back in command, with Yahweh proclaiming his sovereign authority over the land. In Ps 61 David again calls on the Lord for deliverance, and his prayer for the king (61:6–8 [MT 61:7–9]) appears to reflect his confidence that God will not cast him away but keep his 2 Sam 7 promise.

The opening two words of Ps 61, "Hear, O God" (שמעה אלהים, MT 61:2) will be repeated at the beginning of Ps 64 (64:1 [MT 64:2]). Hossfeld and Zenger suggest that the repetition of the phrase forms an *inclusio* around Pss 61–64, marking them out as a subunit within the wider Book 2 collection.[208] Longing for God dominates Pss 61–64, which comprise a chiasm as follows:

Psalm 61, Hear, O God
　　Psalm 62, For God Alone
　　Psalm 63, My Soul Thirsts for You
Psalm 64, Hear, O God

EXPOSITION

**61:1-3 (MT 61:2-4), Prayer to Be Heard**

David calls on God to hear his ringing cry and attend to his distress in 61:1 (MT 61:2), explaining his plea in 61:2–3 (MT 61:3–4). He calls on God from the end of the earth, which is probably more a description of his spiritual sense of separation from God than a geographical statement of his physical location. David's prayer is prompted not only by his location but by his faintness of heart, as he calls on the Lord to lead him to a rock higher than himself. Against the backdrop of ancient iconography, Keel proposes, "Ps 61:2–4 may be understood in a cosmic frame of reference: the ends of the earth represent the realm of death; the rock to which the suppliant desires to be led is the earth and temple-mountain.

---

[208] Hossfeld and Zenger, *Psalms 2*, 109.

There he finds shelter under the wings of God, signifying the (near) sky."[209] Whether or not these identifications are correct, David knows that God can give him safety and stability, and he looks to God to do it.

Having explained the reason for his prayer in Ps 60:2 (MT 60:3), David adds justification for his prayer in 60:3 (MT 60:4): He has known God as a refuge and tower of strength in the face of enemies. David's experience of God's power and protection prompts him to call on God to hear his prayer and lead him to a place that is out of enemy reach.

### 61:4–5 (MT 61:5–6), Hope and Heritage

Though in difficulty, David's hope is that he will enjoy God's presence in God's place. In 61:4 (MT 61:5) David asserts his confident intention to sojourn in God's own tent for ages. This statement indicates that David expects an ongoing experience of God's presence and goodness that will not be extinguished by death. He then speaks of his intention to take refuge under God's protection, vividly describing the hiding place under God's metaphorical wings.

He references the commitments he made to the Lord in the form of vows in 61:5 (MT 61:6), and these vows were apparently provoked by David's experience of God's submission-inducing greatness, for David speaks of God giving him "the possession of those who fear your name." God revealed himself to David in such a way that David knew that he had to submit to God, indeed he feared not doing so, and in reward of the homage David duly rendered, God granted David the blessing of access to his presence (60:4 [MT 60:5]).

### 61:6–8 (MT 61:7–9), King of Praise

Having called on the Lord to hear him in his need and stated his hope and heritage of enjoyment of God's presence, David turns to the realization of what God has promised in 61:6–8 (MT 61:7–9). He calls on the Lord to keep the promise that one of his descendants would reign forever in 61:6 (MT 61:7). The request that God would add days to the days of the king, and make his years from generation to generation are poetic ways to call on the Lord to make the king reign forever. David here asks God to do what he promised in 2 Sam 7:13. Similarly, in Ps 61:7 (MT 61:8) David asks the Lord to allow the king to remain enthroned before God unto the

---

[209] Keel, *Symbolism of the Biblical World*, 28.

age (cf. 110:1). To accomplish this, David calls on the Lord to protect the king with his own character, the upshot of David requesting that God appoint lovingkindness and truth to keep the king.

The granting of these requests, David declares in 61:8 (MT 61:9), will result in David psalming God's name forever, fulfilling his vows daily. David calls on God to keep his promises and act in keeping with his character, and David declares that God being God in this way will ensure that he, David, will ever praise the Lord.

BRIDGE

The fact that Ps 61:6–7 (MT 61:7–8) could be read as David's request that God extend his own (David's) reign as king reinforces a point made repeatedly in these pages: the pattern of David's experience foreshadows and typifies that of the one God promised to raise up from David's line.

And as with Pss 42–45, where the difficulties of God's people were answered by the coming of the Davidic king, so here the difficulties of God's people in Ps 60 meet with reminders of God's promise to establish his purpose through the scion of David in Ps 61.

## Psalm 62

OVERVIEW AND STRUCTURE OF PSALM 62

Psalm 62 seems to reflect a chiastic structure that can be reflected as follows:[210]

62:1–2 (MT 62:2–3), Waiting for God
    62:3–4 (MT 62:4–5), Enemies
        62:5–6 (MT 62:6–7), Waiting for God
        62:7–8 (MT 62:8–9), Call for Trust
    62:9–10 (MT 62:10–11), Vanity of Human Solutions
62:11–12 (MT 62:12–13), God's Strength and Steadfast Love

The statements of Ps 62 appear to fall into two verse units: David's description of himself waiting on God in 62:1–2 (MT 62:2–3) seems to set up a warning to his enemies in 62:3–4 (MT 62:4–5). He then restates 62:1–2 (MT 62:2–3) in 62:5–6 (MT 62:6–7), this time commanding himself

---

[210] Cf. Alden, "Chiastic Psalms (II)," 194.

to wait for God, which in turn sets up a call for those aligned with him to trust God (62:7–8 (MT 62:8–9). Reinforcing the call to wait for God and trust him, David describes the vanity of human solutions in 62:9–10 (MT 62:10–11), before heralding God's strength, lovingkindness, and justice in 62:11–12 (MT 62:12–13).

We will pursue the exposition of Ps 62 in accordance with these two-verse units.

SCRIPTURE

CSB

For the choir director: according to Jeduthun. A psalm of David.

¹ I am at rest in God alone;
my salvation comes from him.
² He alone is my rock and my
salvation,
my stronghold; I will never be
shaken.

³ How long will you threaten a man?
Will all of you attack
as if he were a leaning wall
or a tottering fence?
⁴ They only plan to bring him down
from his high position.
They take pleasure in lying;
they bless with their mouths,
but they curse inwardly.
Selah

⁵ Rest in God alone, my soul,
for my hope comes from him.
⁶ He alone is my rock and my
salvation,
my stronghold; I will not be shaken.
⁷ My salvation and glory depend on
God, my strong rock.
My refuge is in God.
⁸ Trust in him at all times, you people;
pour out your hearts before him.
God is our refuge.
Selah

Author's translation

¹ For the Preeminent One.
On Jeduthun.
A Psalm of David.

² Surely for God is the still waiting of
my soul.
From him is my salvation.
³ Surely he is my rock and my
salvation, my stronghold;
I will not greatly totter.

⁴ How long will you shout at a man?
You will all be shattered, like a
stretched wall, a breached wall.
⁵ Surely from his exaltation they take
counsel to thrust him down.
They are pleased with a lie:
To his face they bless, but in their
midst they curse. Selah.

⁶ Surely for God wait still, O my soul,
for from him is my hope.
⁷ Surely he is my rock and my
salvation, my stronghold;
I will not totter.

⁸ Upon God is my salvation and my
glory;
rock of my strength, my refuge is in
God.
⁹ Trust in him at all times, people,
pour out your heart before him.
God is a refuge for us. Selah.

⁹ Common people are only a vapor;
important people, an illusion.
Together on a scale,
they weigh less than a vapor.
¹⁰ Place no trust in oppression
or false hope in robbery.
If wealth increases,
don't set your heart on it.

¹¹ God has spoken once;
I have heard this twice:
strength belongs to God,
¹² and faithful love belongs to you,
Lord.
For you repay each according to his
works.

¹⁰ Surely a vapor [Abel] are sons of
Adam,
a lie are sons of man, in the balances
to go up.
They are less than a vapor [Abel]
together.
¹¹ Do not trust in oppression and in
robbery.
Do not be vapor [Abel] of might
because it bears fruit.
Do not put it to heart.

¹² One, God spoke; two, this I heard:
that strength is of God.
¹³ And to you, my Lord, is
lovingkindness,
for you recompense to a man
according to his work.

CONTEXT: VERBAL AND THEMATIC LINKS WITH SURROUNDING PSALMS

Psalms 61 and 62 are tied together by the references to God as "rock" (61:2;
62:2, 6 [MT 61:3; 62:3, 7]) and "refuge" (61:3, 4; 62:7 [MT 61:4, 5; 62:8]).[211]
God's announcement of his sovereign reign in 60:6–8 (MT 60:8–10) seems
to prompt the growing confidence that leads to David's prayer for the
future king in 61:6–7 (MT 61:7–8). That confidence in turn has David
declaring his trust in Yahweh alone in Ps 62. The particle אַךְ, which can
be rendered "alone," "surely," or "only" (so KJV) occurs six times in Ps
62, prompting Charles Spurgeon to refer to it as the "only" psalm.[212]

EXPOSITION

### 62:1–2 (MT 62:2–3), Waiting for God

On the mention of "Jeduthun" see the comments in the exposition of Ps
39:1–3 above.

We cannot be certain about the circumstances that prompted Ps 62, but
it is positioned in a series of psalms in which David communicates his need
for God. The contribution that Ps 62 makes is in David's resolute intention
to wait for God. He waits not for a change in circumstances—whether an

---

²¹¹ Hossfeld and Zenger, *Psalms 2*, 117.
²¹² Charles Haddon Spurgeon, *The Treasury of David*, 3 vols. (Peabody, MA: Hendrickson,
2008), ad loc. I owe this reference to Dan Phillips.

end to the persecution visited by Saul or Absalom or some other alter-
ation—but for God. David knows that God is what he needs. Accordingly,
in 62:1–2 (MT 62:2–3) David describes himself waiting for God because
God is the source of his salvation, his place of security, and his defense
against enemies, resulting in confidence that he will not be toppled.

## 62:3–4 (MT 62:4–5), Enemies

English translations typically render the second verb in Ps 62:3 (תרצחו, MT
62:4) not as it appears in BHS, as a *pual* (passive: "you will all be shattered"),
but translate it instead repointed as an active *piel* form (CSB "Will all of
you attack?" ESV "to batter him," NAS "that you may murder *him*"). My
translation stays with the text as presented in BHS: "How long will you
shout at a man? You will all be shattered, like a stretched wall, a breached
wall." The man being shouted at here is David, with David fully aware that
the pattern of his experience will be fulfilled in that of his descendant.
This understanding makes better sense of the end of the line. On this
reading, David asks his enemies how long they will oppose him, then
warns them of their inevitable fate, saying they will be shattered like a
wall built too long of too little. His enemies are like a wall built without
enough stone to cover the distance, so the material has been spaced out
("stretched"), weakening the barrier, making it easy to breach.

This way of understanding 62:3 (MT 62:4) also makes sense of 62:4 (MT
62:5), where the plotters familiar from Ps 2 are once again scheming to
overcome the Lord and his anointed. These who take counsel to throw
down the one the Lord has exalted are pleased with falsehoods, and they
say one thing in the presence of the king, something else entirely when
they are alone with each other. They bless the king to his face, but when
they are among themselves they curse him.

## 62:5–6 (MT 62:6–7), Waiting for God

David described himself as waiting on God in 62:1–2 (MT 62:2–3), but in
62:5–6 (MT 62:6–7) he must command himself to do so, reminding himself
of all the things that made him confident and secure. Spiritual equilib-
rium is not something we achieve and then never have to reestablish. We
often find a place of balance and rest in the Lord, only to be thrown into
turmoil by a new development. That seems to be David's experience here.

His own experience of waiting for God, then urging himself to do so
and reminding himself that God is his rock, salvation, stronghold, and

confidence (62:5–6 [MT 62:6–7]), prompts him to address those aligned with him in 62:7–8 (MT 62:8–9).

### 62:7–8 (MT 62:8–9), Call for Trust

David testifies in 62:7 (MT 62:8), and he commands in 62:8 (MT 62:9). His testimony is that his salvation and glory depend upon God. The glory in view here is likely David's exaltation to the throne and ongoing rule. For him to be delivered from danger and established as king, God will have to act. David's protection, power, and place of safety are all in God.

Having asserted these things in 62:7 (MT 62:8), David issues a call to the people to trust God at all times, to pour out their hearts to him, because he is a refuge for his people.

The selahs at the end of 62:4 and 8 (MT 62:5 and 9) seem to mark out the stanzas of the psalm.

### 62:9–10 (MT 62:10–11), Vanity of Human Solutions

Some translations treat the statements in 62:9 (MT 62:10) as a merism describing the rich and the poor. Unconvinced of this interpretation, I have rendered the text as it appears in *BHS*. I take the expressions to indicate that people are a meaningless delusion, the sons of man are a vapor and a lie that will be weighed in God's scales. They will go up in those balances as nothing. This statement in 62:9 (MT 62:10) sets up the evaluation of human means of exercising influence and gathering wealth in 62:10 (MT 62:11). The extortion and robbery in view are wicked ways of acquiring power and means, and David urges his audience not to put their trust in such wicked and worldly methods.

David's enemies are opposing God's king, David, and thereby God's kingdom. They align themselves with another kingdom, one opposed to God's. So why would they follow God's instructions and ways as they oppose God's kingdom? Their ways will be in keeping with the kingdom that has their allegiance. Thus, rather than seek God's righteous ways of exercising influence or gathering wealth they practice extortion and robbery.

David says in the second line of Ps 62:10 (MT 62:11), "Do not be vapor of might because it bears fruit. Do not put it to heart."[213] He means that

---

[213] This translation follows the Masoretic accentuation and groups the phrases differently than the ESV and CSB.

worldly power and wealth can seem impressive and effective ("it bears fruit"), but to trust in them is to make oneself vapor. David urges his audience not to be deceived. He tells his people not to "put to heart" the apparent success of the wicked, for as he has asserted, it is a lie, a delusion, a vapor. It will not last.

## 62:11–12 (MT 62:12–13), God's Strength and Steadfast Love

Having urged his audience not to trust in human solutions in 62:9–10 (MT 62:10–11), David asserts that God alone has true power, lovingkindness, and justice in 62:11–12 (MT 62:12–13). He plainly states that God himself has revealed his strength in what he has spoken in 62:11 (MT 62:12). This power is then balanced with the Lord's lovingkindness in 62:12 (MT 62:13). Raw power is a frightful thing, but God's power accompanied by his lovingkindness makes him a safe refuge, as David has described the Lord to be throughout this psalm. Finally, at the end of 62:12 (MT 62:13) David asserts that the Lord will judge justly, recompensing people in accordance with their deeds. God alone thus establishes the kind of government for which all people long: powerful, good, loving, and just.

Bridge

David both waits and commands himself to wait in Ps 62. He warns his enemies of their certain destruction, and he urges his allies to trust God. He asserts the vanity of human solutions, and he proclaims the strength, steadfast love, and justice that belong to God alone. The kingdom of which David speaks, for which he waits, would be anticipated in his own reign, to be realized when his Lord, seated at the right hand, sees the Father put all enemies underfoot (Ps 110:1). King Jesus will establish the reign of loving power in justice. Just as Ps 62 describes, we all wait for God to establish salvation and safety through his return. Psalm 63 represents David's description of how he is enabled to wait on the Lord.

Psalm 62 references earlier Scripture and is itself quoted later in the Bible. David speaks of the brevity of life in 62:9–10 (MT 62:10–11) using a term that is homonymic with the name Abel (הבל), evoking his early death in Gen 4. Then Paul cites Ps 62:12 (MT 62:13) in Rom 2:6 and 2 Tim 4:14, communicating the same confidence in God's justice that David articulates.

## Psalm 63

OVERVIEW AND STRUCTURE OF PSALM 63

In Psalm 63:1–2 (MT 63:2–3) David speaks to the situation described by the psalm's superscription: in the wilderness, "in a land dry and weary without water," he thirsts for the Lord (63:1 [MT 63:2]) precisely because he has seen God's power and glory in the holy place (63:2 [MT 63:3]).

References to his lips praising God bracket the next section of the psalm (63:3–5 [MT 63:4–6]), where David responds to the fact that God's love is better than life, with a mouth full of praise and hands lifted high. His soul thirsts for God (63:1 [MT 63:2]), and the experience of God's love (63:3 [MT 63:4]), which prompts David's praise, also leaves his soul satisfied as from a sumptuous feast (63:5 [MT 63:6]).

David describes the way he meditates on Yahweh as he lies in bed at night in 63:6–8 (MT 63:7–9). He thinks on the way the Lord has helped him in the past, the way the shadow of God's wings makes him sing for joy, and the way his soul clings to the Lord as God's right hand upholds him (63:7–8 [MT 63:8–9]).

David was in the wilderness (superscription [MT 63:1]) because people were trying to kill him, whether Saul at the beginning or Absalom at the end. David's desire for God (63:1–2 [MT 63:2–3]), praise of God (63:3–5 [MT 63:4–6]), and meditation on God's past help (63:6–8 [MT 63:7–9]) make him confident that the wicked will be punished and the righteous rewarded (63:9–11 [MT 63:10–12]).

The movement of thought in Ps 63 can be depicted as a chiastic structure:

63:1–2 (MT 63:2–3), Thirsty
    63:3–5 (MT 63:4–6), Better
    63:6–8 (MT 63:7–9), Help
63:9–11 (MT 63:10–12), Stopped

SCRIPTURE

| CSB | Author's translation |
|---|---|
| A psalm of David. When he was in the Wilderness of Judah. | [1] A Psalm of David. When he was in the wilderness of Judah. |

¹ God, you are my God; I eagerly seek
you.
I thirst for you;
my body faints for you
in a land that is dry, desolate, and
without water.
² So I gaze on you in the sanctuary
to see your strength and your glory.

³ My lips will glorify you
because your faithful love is better
than life.
⁴ So I will bless you as long as I live;
at your name, I will lift up my hands.
⁵ You satisfy me as with rich food;
my mouth will praise you with joyful
lips.

⁶ When I think of you as I lie on my
bed,
I meditate on you during the night
watches
⁷ because you are my helper;
I will rejoice in the shadow of your
wings.
⁸ I follow close to you;
your right hand holds on to me.

⁹ But those who intend to destroy my
life
will go into the depths of the earth.
¹⁰ They will be given over to the power
of the sword;
they will become a meal for jackals.
¹¹ But the king will rejoice in God;
all who swear by him will boast,
for the mouths of liars will be shut.

² O God, my Deity you are.
I long for you.
My soul thirsts for you;
my flesh faints for you,
in a land dry and weary without
water.
³ Thus I have seen you in the holy
place:
to see your strength and your glory!

⁴ Because your lovingkindness is
better than life
my lips will laud you.
⁵ Thus I will bless you in my life.
In your name I will lift up my hands.
⁶ As with lard and fatness you satisfy
my soul,
and with lips of ringing cries my
mouth will praise you.

⁷ When I remember you on my couch,
in the night watches I will meditate
on you.
⁸ For you are a help to me,
and in the shadow of your wings I will
shout for joy.
⁹ My soul cleaves after you.
Your right hand upholds me.

¹⁰ While they for devastation seek my
soul,
they will go to the lowest parts of the
earth.
¹¹ They will hand him over on the
hands of the sword.
A portion of jackals they shall be.
¹² And the king will be glad in God.
Everyone who takes oaths by him will
exult,
for the mouth of those who speak
deception has been stopped.

CONTEXT: VERBAL AND THEMATIC LINKS WITH SURROUNDING PSALMS

The superscription of Ps 63 sets it "When he was in the wilderness of
Judah." David was in the wilderness early in his life when he fled from

Saul, and he was in the wilderness late in his life when he fled from
Absalom. Either situation informs the interpretation of Ps 63, for David
is seeking *God* in his distress rather than a change of circumstances
(63:1 [MT 63:2]), and he is confident that those who seek his life will be
destroyed (63:9–10 [MT 63:10–11]). Given the many references to Saul's
persecution of David in Pss 52–59, Ps 63 likely continues in the same
vein. Psalm 63 resonates strongly with Ps 62, where David waited for
God alone. In Ps 63 David earnestly seeks and thirsts for God. The two
psalms are also linked by the references to God's "strength" and "lovingkindness" that close the one (62:11 [MT 62:12]) and open the other
(63:2–3 [MT 63:3–4]).

EXPOSITION
### 63:1–2 (MT 63:2–3), Thirsty
David's identification of God as his deity results in him earnestly seeking
God in Ps 63:1 (MT 63:2). David does not seek relief in the end of his difficulties but in God. His body and soul yearn for the Lord: soul thirsting,
body fainting, as in a waterless, restless land in 63:2 (MT 63:3). We sometimes feel a craving for the satisfaction of our desires that has our souls
panting like winded dogs, our bodies trembling like deprived addicts.
David feels that way for God. He must have him.

David's experience of God *as* God has him yearning for God as the
alone satisfaction for his deepest longing.

The word "thus" at the beginning of 63:2 (כֵּן, MT 63:3, CSB, ESV: "so"),
indicates that David's past yearning for God resulted in him going to
the holy place to behold God's power and glory. We seek what we think
will satisfy us. God's identity as the deity convinced David that what he
needed was God himself. Because David longed for God, he went to the
holy place. In David's day, prior to Solomon's building of the temple, this
was evidently a tent or tabernacle structure (2 Sam 7:2) where God had
revealed himself and taken up residence (cf. 1 Sam 3:1–14, esp. 3:3). As a
symbol of the cosmos and a preview of the new heaven and new earth,
the tabernacle and later the temple portrayed God's power in creation
and glory in redemption.

David's longing for God (Ps 63:1 [MT 63:2]) prompted him to seek
God by visiting the temple (63:2 [MT 63:3]) where he saw the symbolic
depiction of God's glory in redemption in the sacrificial system and the

symbolic depiction of God's awesome creative power in the architecture and decor of the temple.

The symbolic display of God's accomplishments in creation and redemption at the temple prompt David to consider God's character, to which he responds in praise in 63:3–5 (MT 63:4–6).

### 63:3–5 (MT 63:4–6), Better

David knows that only God is God, that only God will satisfy his soul, so he seeks him (63:1–2 [MT 63:2–3]). David also knows that God's love is not just better than some *aspects* of life. God's love is better than life *itself*. This profound way of asserting that nothing is better than God's lovingkindness, his *hesed*, is followed by its natural corollary: because God's lovingkindness is the most superior thing in David's experience, David's lips will praise God.

We choose what we want, seek what we love, and praise what we enjoy. For David, his experience of God convinces him that he must have God: he longs for him above all else. And the incomparable love of God has David's lips doing what they should.

David's experience of God's love as better than life in 63:3 (MT 63:4) results in the logical conclusion of 63:4 (כֵּן, MT 63:5, "thus") that David will bless God with his life. If God is better than life, the best thing to do with one's life is bless God with it. To this David commits himself, asserting also that he will lift up his hands in God's name.

In Ps 63:1 (MT 63:2) David's soul was thirsting and his flesh was fainting for God, and as he celebrates God's love (63:3 [MT 63:4]) he comes to a place in 63:5 (MT 63:6) where his soul is as satisfied as his body would be by a rich feast. He declares his soul satisfied "as with lard and fatness" because God has met his need. David's description of God satisfying his soul in 63:5 (MT 63:6) is accompanied by another assertion that his lips will praise God, the references to lips praising forming an *inclusio* around 63:3–5 (MT 63:4–6).

David has experienced the one who is more satisfying than sex, money, power, acclaim, popularity, luxury, or even life itself. David knows God, sees his power in creation and redemption, and feels the visceral truth that God's character, his steadfast love, is better than life itself. No wonder he states in four different ways that he will praise God in 63:3–5 (MT 63:4–6), the descriptions of praise forming a chiastic structure of their own (italics added to highlight the different aspects of his person that David employs to praise God):

63:3 (MT 63:4), "my *lips* will laud you"
    63:4a (MT 63:5a), "I will bless you in my *life*"
    63:4b (MT 63:5b), "In your name I will lift up my *hands*"
63:5 (MT 63:6), "with *lips* of ringing cries my *mouth* will praise you"

### 63:6–8 (MT 63:7–9), Help

David describes himself in Ps 63:6–8 (MT 63:7–9) as a man consumed with God. In verses 6 and 8 (MT 7 and 9) David describes how he remembers God, meditates on him, and cleaves his soul to him. In verse 7 (MT 8) David explains why: because the Lord has been his help, and because he took refuge in the shadow of God's wings.

When David says that he remembers God on his couch and meditates on him in the night watches in 63:6 (MT 63:7), his use of the term "meditate" (אהגה) recalls the blessed man meditating on Torah day and night in Ps 1. This indicates that David's remembrance of and meditation on God is meditation on Scripture.

In addition to Scripture, David contemplates his personal experience of God's help in 63:7 (MT 63:8). God has helped David in the past and established himself as David's help. Thus David states that he will go on taking refuge under God's wings, where he will sing God's praise in spite of the difficult circumstances that drove him to seek shelter. God's great power and steadfast love eclipse David's difficulties and summon him to worship.

Moses called Israel to cleave to Yahweh (Deut 10:20), and David asserts in Ps 63:8 (MT 63:9) that his soul cleaves to the Lord. He then adds that the Lord's right hand upholds him. God thus blesses David as shelter (63:7 [MT 63:8]) and sustainer (63:8 [MT 63:9]). These truths David savors as he meditates on the Lord, remembering God as he lies in bed at night.

We are what we contemplate. David's thoughts are of God, of his desirability, of his incomparable love, of the way he satisfies the soul, of his protection, and of his upholding right hand. What we think about bears fruit in what we do. David's heart is high on God, and his pen declares God's praise.

## 63:9–11 (MT 63:10–12), Stopped

As noted above, the wilderness setting of this psalm (superscription, MT 63:1) likely resulted from the persecution of Saul. David is confident in 63:9 (MT 63:10) that those who seek to kill him "will go to the lowest parts of the earth." He has been convinced of this by the display of God's power and glory in the holy place (63:2 [MT 63:3]) and by the lovingkindness that God has placed upon his beloved (63:3 [MT 63:4]), guaranteeing that he will defend. David's nightly meditation on the Lord (63:6–8 [MT 63:7–9]) has convinced him to the point of confidence. Those who set themselves against the Lord and his anointed will not prosper but be blasted by the scorching wind (cf. Pss 1–2). The wicked will be given over to the "hands of the sword" (63:10a [MT 63:11a]), which is to say they will die violent deaths. And they will be "a portion of jackals" (63:10b [MT 63:11b]), which seems to mean that their dead bodies will be eaten by the beasts of the wilderness.

The wicked have afflicted, persecuted, and sought the life of the king, who took refuge in God. When God destroys the wicked, then, the king who took refuge in God will be glad in him (63:11a [MT 63:12a]).

Moses called Israel to swear by God's name in Deut 10:20, so the reference to those who "swear by him" in Ps 63:11b (MT 63:12b) probably points to those who swear by God. David says they will exult. The ambiguity (could they be swearing by the king?), however, highlights the close connection between Israel's king and Israel's God.

The identification of those who sought the king's life as those who speak deception in 63:11c (MT 63:12c) connects them to those raging and plotting vanity in Ps 2:1–3. The fact that their mouths will be stopped creates a contrast between them and David, whose mouth is full of praise.

### Bridge

Contemplate the Scriptures and your mouth will be full of praise for God. Contemplate how you will overthrow the God of the Bible and rebel against his king and your mouth will be stopped.

Know the Lord as God, look to him to meet your needs, and you will experience his love, which is better than life, satisfying your soul and sheltering you from harm, upholding you with a righteous right arm. Put some idol in his place and look to it for satisfaction, and you will be left empty and alone, with the wrath of God remaining upon you.

David, of course, was not fully consistent in blessing God with his life (see 2 Sam 11). No one, however, could convict his greater son of sin (John 8:46). Jesus lived the words of Ps 63 more perfectly than David himself, modeling for us a life of steadfast love and satisfaction in God.

## Psalm 64

Overview and Structure of Psalm 64

Psalm 64 reflects a chiastic structure as follows:[214]

64:1 (MT 64:2), Prayer
  64:2 (MT 64:3), Refuge
    64:3 (MT 64:4), Tongue, Arrow
      64:4 (MT 64:5), Shoot
        64:5 (MT 64:6), Evil
        64:6 (MT 64:7), Injustice
      64:7 (MT 64:8), Shot, Arrow
    64:8 (MT 64:9), Tongue
  64:9 (MT 64:10), Fear of God
64:10 (MT 64:11), Exultation

In this psalm David cries out to the Lord to hear him, confident that God will hide him from the wicked plots of those who would shoot him with their words (64:1–4 [MT 64:2–5]). He then explains that these wicked schemers have thoroughly investigated injustice and set out their snares (64:5–6 [MT 64:6–7]). What they do not expect is for God to bring their injustice and wickedness back on their own heads, which he will do, bringing on them what they have plotted for others (64:7–8 [MT 64:8–9]). People will see God's justice and ponder it, and the righteous will exult in Yahweh (64:9–10 [MT 64:10–11]).

The exposition will proceed according to the following subheads:

    64:1–4 (MT 64:2–5), Deliver Me from Weaponized Tongues
    64:5–6 (MT 64:6–7), Deep Evil and Injustice
    64:7–8 (MT 64:8–9), Sudden Defeat of Evil
    64:9–10 (MT 64:10–11), Fear and Exultation

---

[214] Similarly Alden, "Chiastic Psalms (II)," 194.

SCRIPTURE

CSB                                           Author's translation

For the choir director. A psalm of            [1] For the Preeminent One.
David.                                        A Psalm of David.

[1] God, hear my voice when I am in           [2] Hear, O God, my voice in my
    anguish.                                      complaint,
Protect my life from the terror of the        from the dread of the one at enmity
    enemy.                                        you will deliver my life.
[2] Hide me from the scheming of
    wicked people,                            [3] You will cause me to be hidden from
from the mob of evildoers,                        the counsel of those who cause evil,
[3] who sharpen their tongues like            from the throng of workers of iniquity,
    swords
and aim bitter words like arrows,             [4] who sharpen like the sword their
[4] shooting from concealed places at             tongue;
    the blameless.                            they tread their arrow, a bitter word,
They shoot at him suddenly and are
    not afraid.                               [5] to shoot in the hiding places the
[5] They adopt an evil plan;                      man of integrity.
they talk about hiding traps and say,         Suddenly they shoot him and do not
"Who will see them?"                              fear.
[6] They devise crimes and say,
"We have perfected a secret plan."            [6] They hold fast for themselves an evil
The inner man and the heart are                   word.
    mysterious.                               They recount to hide snares.
                                              They say, "Who will see them?"
[7] But God will shoot them with arrows;
suddenly, they will be wounded.               [7] They search out injustices:
[8] They will be made to stumble;             "We completed a searched out
their own tongues work against them.              search!"
All who see them will shake their             Surely the midst of a man, and the
    heads.                                        heart is deep.
[9] Then everyone will fear
and will tell about God's work,               [8] And God shot them with an arrow
for they will understand what he has              suddenly.
    done.                                     They became their wounds.

[10] The righteous one rejoices in the        [9] And they caused him to stumble,
    LORD                                          upon them their tongue.
and takes refuge in him;                      They will flee, all who see them.
all those who are upright in heart
will offer praise.                            [10] And all men feared,
                                              and they declared the work of God,
                                              and his achievement they pondered
                                                  unto wisdom.

> [11] The righteous will be glad in
> Yahweh and seek refuge in him,
> and all the upright of heart will exult.

### Context: Verbal and Thematic Links with Surrounding Psalms

As noted in the "Context" section to Ps 61, Pss 61 and 64 open with the same phrase, "Hear, O God." David called for the fulfillment of God's 2 Sam 7:13 promise in Ps 61, waited for God alone in Ps 62, thirsting for him earnestly in Ps 63, and now he spells out what God will do to his enemies in Ps 64. Given the way the psalms in the near context respond to Saul's persecutions (Pss 52–63), this psalm likely responds to the wicked who joined Saul in his attempt to destroy David, the Lord's anointed.

See the exposition of 64:10 (MT 64:11) for its significant verbal connections with 63:11 (MT 63:12).

### Exposition

#### 64:1–4 (MT 64:2–5), Deliver Me from Weaponized Tongues

In language reminiscent of 61:1 (MT 61:2), David cries out to God to hear his voice in 64:1 (MT 64:2), calling on the Lord to preserve his life from fearsome enemies. Translations rightly render the verb in 64:2 (MT 64:3) as a prayer-imperative. David calls on God to hide him from those who plot together against Yahweh and his anointed (cf. 2:1–3). At this point the assault of the workers of iniquity seems to be verbal: they sharpen their tongue like a sword and prepare their bitter words the way an archer readies the bow to shoot his arrows (64:3 [MT 64:4]). That done, from hidden places, like snipers they take fearless surprise shots at the one who has integrity (64:4 [MT 64:5]).

David himself is the man of integrity, here, and those opposed to him and his kingdom are the enemies.

#### 64:5–6 (MT 64:6–7), Deep Evil and Injustice

David meditates on the deep evil of his enemies in 64:5–6 (MT 64:6–7). He describes them clinging to an "evil word," that is, a wicked plot, and rehearsing for themselves how they can set traps. In their blindness, they think no one sees them. David clearly implies that God sees everything they are doing, and by his description of their deeds, it is evident that David is also fully apprised of their actions. Sin has a blinding, stupefying effect upon us, but our folly is all too apparent to the one who sees all.

In Ps 64:6 (MT 64:7) David brings out the implications of the way of the wicked. They probably do not consciously think of themselves as diligently searching out how to accomplish injustice, but that is what their plots add up to. In the depths of their souls, in their inner hearts, they are conniving and scheming and trying to account for all contingencies in their steadfast opposition to David and all he represents. This is indeed an attempt at comprehensive research into injustice.

### 64:7–8 (MT 64:8–9), Sudden Defeat of Evil

David cried out to the Lord in confidence in 64:1–2 (MT 64:2–3), and the Lord's answer is described as though it has already taken place in 64:7–8 (MT 64:8–9). The CSB renders 64:7 (MT 64:8) as a statement about the future, ESV as a present, but the Hebrew text has an imperfect with a *waw*-consecutive (*wayyiqtol*), as though the event has already taken place, likely communicating David's confidence in the Lord's justice.

David describes God doing to the wicked in 64:7–8 (MT 64:8–9) what they planned to do to the man of integrity in 64:3–4 (MT 64:4–5): shooting them with an arrow. David's words poetically describe the way that God will enforce his decree—those who speak evil against God's king will suffer for the wickedness their own tongues perpetrated. Their weapons and ammunition will be turned against them. They will ultimately harm only themselves. God suddenly shoots them, and the result of his justice so thoroughly defeats them that they can be described as a wound entire. The Hebrew phrasing of 64:7b (MT 64:8b) can be rendered, "They became their wounds."

The enemies stumble as what their own tongues spoke comes down upon them, and all who see their staggering flee from them (64:8 [MT 64:9]).

### 64:9–10 (MT 64:10–11), Fear and Exultation

David describes the response to God's justice against the wicked in 64:9–10 (MT 64:10–11). Everyone will fear God and be so impressed with the downfall of the evildoers that they will talk about it with enthusiasm and amazement. They will then do what the rebel kings were commanded to do in Ps 2:10, namely, ponder what they have seen and gain wisdom from it.

The first part of the description in 64:10 (MT 64:11) is in the singular: the individual righteous man will be relieved, delivered, and made happy by the visitation of God's justice, and he will take refuge in Yahweh. The second half of the verse is in the plural: all the upright of heart will exult in Yahweh. They will rejoice over the deliverance of the righteous one. Here again we have statements that seem to point to the deliverance of the Davidic king and its implications for all who are aligned with him. This interpretation of the individual righteous one as the king, and the upright in heart who rejoice with him as his people, is strengthened by the paralleling of the singulars and plurals with the same verbs from 63:11 (MT 63:12) in 64:10 (MT 64:11), and in Ps 63 the singular is explicitly named the king:

| 63:11 (MT 63:12) | 64:10 (MT 64:11) |
|---|---|
| "And the king will be glad in God. Everyone who swears by him will exult" | "The righteous will be glad in Yahweh ... and all the upright of heart will exult" |

This parallel indicates that the king is the righteous one, and those who swear by him—with perhaps intended ambiguity as to whether the swearing is by the king or by God—are the upright in heart who exult.

### Bridge

The fear of God produces wisdom because it results from vivid apprehension of God's awesome justice. Those who see his powerful righteousness are too afraid of God's wrath to transgress his commands. That is the beginning of wisdom.

We see a confident faith in this prayer of David. Though his enemies surround him with all the depths of their evil, he believes that God will hide his people and speaks of God's justice upon the wicked as though it has already happened, fully confident that his descendant will be righteous and that he will rejoice in Yahweh and take refuge in him.

## Psalm 65

### Overview and Structure of Psalm 65

Psalm 65 seems to fall into three parts. In 65:1–4 (MT 65:2–5) David praises God because the Lord hears prayer, atones for sin, and draws his chosen near.[215] In 65:5–8 (MT 65:6–9) David celebrates the fact that God answers prayer in creation-dominating righteousness. Finally, in 65:9–13 (MT 65:10–14) David hymns the way God blesses the land.

The exposition will follow this threefold movement:

> 65:1–4 (MT 65:2–5), Praise for God
> 65:5–8 (MT 65:6–9), Who Answers Prayer
> 65:9–13 (MT 65:10–14), And Blesses the Land

SCRIPTURE

| CSB | Author's translation |
|---|---|
| For the choir director. A psalm of David. A song. | [1] For the Preeminent One. A Psalm of David. A Song. |
| [1] Praise is rightfully yours, God, in Zion; vows to you will be fulfilled. | [2] For you the silence of praise, O God, in Zion, and for you the vow will be fulfilled. |
| [2] All humanity will come to you, the one who hears prayer. | [3] Hearing prayer, to you all flesh will come. |
| [3] Iniquities overwhelm me; only you can atone for our rebellions. | [4] Matters of iniquities are too strong for me. |
| [4] How happy is the one you choose and bring near to live in your courts! We will be satisfied with the goodness of your house, the holiness of your temple. | As for our transgressions, you cover them. [5] Blessed is the one you choose and bring near. He will dwell in your courts. We will be satisfied by the good things of your house, your holy temple. |
| [5] You answer us in righteousness, with awe-inspiring works, God of our salvation, the hope of all the ends of the earth and of the distant seas. | [6] With fearsome things in righteousness you answer us, O God of our salvation, trust of all the ends of the earth and the sea of distances, |
| [6] You establish the mountains by your power; you are robed with strength. | |
| [7] You silence the roar of the seas, | |

---

[215] In his critical edition of the Greek translation of Psalms, Alfred Rahlfs includes a reference to Jeremiah and Ezekiel in the superscription of Ps 65 (LXX Ps 64). See Alfred Rahlfs, *Psalmi cum Odis*, SVTG 10 (Göttingen: Vandenhoeck & Ruprecht, 1979), ad loc. Pietersma, however, argues convincingly that the mention of Jeremiah and Ezekiel is a later development and excludes it from his NETS translation of Psalms. See Pietersma, "Superscriptions of the Greek Psalter," 118–20.

the roar of their waves,
and the tumult of the nations.
⁸ Those who live far away are awed by
    your signs;
you make east and west shout for joy.

⁹ You visit the earth and water it
    abundantly,
enriching it greatly.
God's stream is filled with water,
for you prepare the earth in this way,
providing people with grain.
¹⁰ You soften it with showers and bless
    its growth,
soaking its furrows and leveling its
    ridges.
¹¹ You crown the year with your
    goodness;
your carts overflow with plenty.
¹² The wilderness pastures overflow,
and the hills are robed with joy.
¹³ The pastures are clothed with flocks
and the valleys covered with grain.
They shout in triumph; indeed, they
    sing.

⁷ establishing the mountains by his
    strength, girded with might,
⁸ stilling the roar of the seas, the roar
    of their waves and the tumult of
    the peoples.
⁹ And they feared, the inhabitants of
    the ends, from your signs.
The goings forth of the morning and
    the evening you cause to give a
    ringing cry.

¹⁰ You visit the earth and cause it to
    overflow.
You cause it to be rich in much.
The stream of God is full of water.
You establish their grain, for thus you
    establish it.
¹¹ Its furrows saturating, pressing
    down its cuts,
with abundant showers you soften it.
Its growth you bless.
¹² You crown the year with your
    bounty,
and your wagon tracks drip fat.
¹³ They drip, the pastures of the
    wilderness,
and the hills are girded with rejoicing.
¹⁴ The meadows are clothed with the
    flock,
and the valleys cover themselves with
    grain.
They shout for joy, yes, they sing.

CONTEXT: VERBAL AND THEMATIC LINKS WITH SURROUNDING PSALMS

Psalms 52–59 dealt with Saul's persecution of David. Yahweh proclaimed his sovereignty over the land in Ps 60, and then Pss 61–64 are marked off by the opening phrase, "Hear, O God," at the beginning of Pss 61 and 64, each yearning for God.

Psalms 65, 66, 67, and 68 all have "A song" in their superscriptions. Whereas 65 and 68 are psalms of David, neither 66 nor 67 mentions David in the superscription.

These superscriptions suggest a chiastic structure for Pss 65–68 as follows:

65, For the Preeminent One. A Psalm of David. A Song.

66, For the Preeminent One. A Song. A Psalm.

67, For the Preeminent One. With stringed instruments. A Psalm.
A Song.

68, For the Preeminent One. Of David. A Psalm. A Song.

Some observations: First, as noted above, Pss 65 and 68 mention David in the superscription, while 66 and 67 do not. Second, 65 and 68 vary the placement of "A psalm." Psalm 65 has it in slot 3 prior to David's name in slot 4, while Ps 68 has it after David's name in slot 5.[216] Third, just as the outer two (65 and 68) vary their elements, so the inner two (66 and 67) vary theirs: 66 has "A song" first, then "A psalm," while 67 reverses this.

These intricate variations are significant for seeing the way the praises of Pss 65–68 are interconnected and respond to the longing for God in Pss 61–64. After the yearning for God in Pss 61–64, Pss 65–68 joyfully shout his triumphant worldwide conquest.

The praise and celebration of Yahweh in Ps 65 responds to the fact that he has defeated David's enemies in 64:7–8 (MT 64:8–9). That triumph leads to praise for God because he has heard prayer, atoned for the sins of his people, brought them near to himself, and blessed their land. This psalm of celebration seems to mark the establishment of David and his kingdom after the long endurance of Saul's persecutions (Pss 52–59), the proclamation of Yahweh's sovereignty over the land (Ps 60), the prayer for the future king (Ps 61), the waiting for God alone (Ps 62) because his love is better than life (Ps 63), and the confidence arising from the fact that God has defeated all enemies (Ps 64, esp. 64:7 [MT 64:8]).

Exposition

### 65:1–4 (MT 65:2–5), Praise for God

David opens Ps 65 declaring the "silence of praise" is for God in Zion (65:1 [MT 65:2]). This "silence of praise" likely refers to a reverential hush, in which those who have experienced God's just vindication are speechless before him. The silence is not permanent, however, and the verse goes

---

[216] On the "information slots" in the psalm superscriptions, see "The Superscriptions of the Psalms" in the introduction, where the discussion includes table 5, "Superscription information slots."

on to speak of how those to whom Yahweh has made himself known will make vows to worship him, vows they then fulfill.

The implications of God's work on behalf of his people are stated in 65:2 (MT 65:3). Because he hears prayer, all flesh will come to him. God's people are a magnetic force, and God's evident goodness to them draws all people to him.

In Ps 65:3 (MT 65:4), David states plainly that sin is too much for him. He cannot overcome iniquity. He cannot deal with it. And he cannot make atonement for himself. Thus he praises God in the second line of this verse because God is the one who "covers," as in, "makes atonement for" the transgressions of his people. God hears prayer, and God is able to deal with sin.

David next praises God by speaking of how "blessed"—using the same term that appears in Ps 1:1—the man is whom God chooses and draws to himself. Just as there was a statement about a singular person followed by statements about those aligned with him in 63:11 (MT 63:12) and 64:10 (MT 64:11), so the statement about the singular blessed man in 65:4 (MT 65:5) is followed by a statement from those who will enjoy God's goodness with him. The blessed man is chosen by God, brought near to God, and then dwells in God's courts. The people of the blessed man then assert that they will be satisfied by the good things of God's house, his holy temple. David spoke of atonement for sin (65:3 [MT 65:4]), of the chosen one being brought into God's courts to dwell there (65:4 [MT 65:5]), and as if in response, the people of the chosen one speak of how they too will enjoy the blessings of God's dwelling place at the end of 65:4 (MT 65:5).

### 65:5–8 (MT 65:6–9), Who Answers Prayer

David spoke of God hearing prayer in 65:2 (MT 65:3), and now in 65:5 (MT 65:6) he speaks of the way God answers his people. Specifically, God answers "with fearsome things in righteousness." God does awe-inspiring deeds of justice and mercy on behalf of his people, and he does them all flawlessly, with no moral failure, no transgression of any boundary, and no unjust omission of rightful claims. David then identifies God as the trust of all creation using the merismic reference to the ends of the earth and the farthest seas. God is basic to all life in all creation.

Having spoken of the way that God answers his people, David continues describing the Lord in 65:6–8 (MT 65:7–9). He first notes in 65:6 (MT 65:7) that the Lord is the one who established those massive, seemingly immovable mountains. The granitic roots were put in place by the one girded with might. And it isn't only the dry land where he holds sway. He it is in 65:7 (MT 65:8) who stills the roaring waves of the seas. And lest anyone think that the one sovereign over creation might not rule among the peoples of the earth, David also asserts that God stills the tumult of the peoples.

All the inhabitants of the earth fear the Lord because of the signs he does in 65:8 (MT 65:9), and the rising and setting of the sun join together to sing his praise.

### 65:9-13 (MT 65:10-14), And Blesses the Land

The final section of Ps 65 is one of the most beautiful portraits of God's blessing on the land in all the Bible. God is the source of all life and blessing, and where he is present all things thrive and flourish. Thus when he visits the earth in 65:9 (MT 65:10), it abounds, overflows, and is rich in many and manifold ways. The created order is brought into perfect balance by the presence of the creator. His streams never run dry. There is no lack of replenishing water in his stream, and the grain he plants, waters, and causes to grow will always flourish.

Even the efforts of God's people are made prosperous only by God's blessing. Psalm 65:10 (MT 65:11) describes how the furrows in the land cut by man's harrowing farm implements are made fruitful by God's saturating rain. The soil turned up by the plow is softened and pressed back into place around the planted seeds by the abundant showers God gives, blessing the growth, the sprouts and shoots, giving life.

In 65:11 (MT 65:12) David personifies the year. It is as though the year is a young prince to be crowned, and the headgear that rests on his temples is God's bounty. David then switches the image to God driving a wagon through a field over and over until tracks are made on his path, and those tracks, he says, drip with fat. Where God goes blessings and plenty multiply and overflow.

The imagery in this section of Ps 65 is positively Edenic. Like a land undefiled and uncursed, the pastures of the wilderness in 65:12 (MT 65:13) drip with goodness. Having stated this, David once again personifies creation. It is as though the hills are a man who gathers up his robes with a girdle of joy. The point here is that all creation is happy because God is there. Everything works as it should. The world cooperates with God's viceregent, and all things flourish in God's blessed presence.

The meadows and valleys are likewise personified in Ps 65:13 (MT 65:14). The meadows are like a man who puts on his robe, but the attire with which he clothes himself is the flock. The meaning of this imagery is that the pasturage in the meadows more than supports the animal life that grazes there. Similarly, the valleys are like a man who puts on his covering, and the clothes the valleys wear is grain. The soil is well watered and richly nourishes the plant life. Then the meadows and valleys join together to shout and sing for joy.

God's presence creates the realm of life so poetically described here by the sweet psalmist of Israel.

### Bridge

The movement of thought from Ps 64 to Ps 65 exactly matches the movement from the end of Rev 20 to the beginning of Rev 21. At the end of Ps 64 God shoots his enemies and gives joy to the righteous (64:7–10 [MT 64:8–11]). That triumph is followed by a comprehensive celebration of God's salvation and the way that God's people enjoy God's presence in a renewed creation because the chosen one has been drawn near to God in Ps 65. This sequence has also been seen in the movement from Ps 45 to 46, where the king and his marriage are the theme of 45, followed by the eschatological city in 46.[217] These things will be fulfilled when God takes his seat on the great white throne of judgment, as described in Rev 20:11–15, then brings about the new creation in 21:1–4. And blessed are those invited to the wedding feast of the Lamb (Rev 19:9).[218]

## Psalm 66

### Overview and Structure of Psalm 66

Psalm 66 is divided by three instances of the term selah, each of which seems to mark a movement of thought (66:4, 7, 15). The change from addressing the Lord to speaking in the first person at 66:12–13 also seems

---

[217] The connection to Pss 45 and 46 grows stronger by the fact that prior to Ps 65, only those two psalms also have "A song" in slot 5 of their superscriptions. See table 6 in the introduction.

[218] Hossfeld suggests linguistic points of contact between "your holy temple" in 65:4 (MT 65:5) and 1 Cor 3:17. He also suggests that Ps 65:7 [MT 65:8] has influenced the stilling of the storm in Mark 4:39 and parallels, and that "the treatment of the coming of the Son of Man in Luke 21:25 reflects" LXX Ps 64:8 (CSB Ps 65:7 [MT 65:8]).

to mark a shift, and as a result the psalm can be divided into the following five sections:

> 66:1–4, Commands to Praise
> 66:5–7, Call to See God's Work
> 66:8–12, Rehearsal of Purifying Suffering
> 66:13–15, Commitment to Sacrifice
> 66:16–20, Testimony

These five sections naturally fall into a chiastic structure with the refining suffering at the center, bracketed by the response of sacrifice to God's work, with the command to praise answered by testimony to the benefit of doing so:

66:1–4, Commands to Praise
   66:5–7, Call to See God's Work
      66:8–12, Rehearsal of Purifying Suffering
   66:13–15, Commitment to Sacrifice
66:16–20, Testimony

SCRIPTURE

| CSB | Author's translation |
|---|---|
| For the choir director. A song. A psalm. | [1] For the Preeminent One. A Song. A Psalm. |
| [1] Let the whole earth shout joyfully to God! | Shout to God, all the earth! |
| [2] Sing about the glory of his name; make his praise glorious. | [2] Psalm the glory of his name. Place the glory of his praise. |
| [3] Say to God, "How awe-inspiring are your works! Your enemies will cringe before you because of your great strength. | [3] Say to God: How fearsome your deeds! In the abundance of your strength those at enmity feign obedience to you. |
| [4] The whole earth will worship you and sing praise to you. They will sing praise to your name." *Selah* | [4] All the earth bows down to you, and they psalm you: they psalm your name. *Selah.* |
| [5] Come and see the wonders of God; his acts for humanity are awe-inspiring. | [5] Come and see the deeds of God! Fearsome work for the sons of Adam. |

⁶ He turned the sea into dry land,
and they crossed the river on foot.
There we rejoiced in him.
⁷ He rules forever by his might;
he keeps his eye on the nations.
The rebellious should not exalt
    themselves.
*Selah*

⁸ Bless our God, you peoples;
let the sound of his praise be heard.
⁹ He keeps us alive
and does not allow our feet to slip.

¹⁰ For you, God, tested us;
you refined us as silver is refined.
¹¹ You lured us into a trap;
you placed burdens on our backs.
¹² You let men ride over our heads;
we went through fire and water,
but you brought us out to abundance.

¹³ I will enter your house with burnt
    offerings;
I will pay you my vows
¹⁴ that my lips promised
and my mouth spoke during my
    distress.
¹⁵ I will offer you fattened sheep as
    burnt offerings,
with the fragrant smoke of rams;
I will sacrifice bulls with goats.
*Selah*

¹⁶ Come and listen, all who fear God,
and I will tell what he has done for me.
¹⁷ I cried out to him with my mouth,
and praise was on my tongue.
¹⁸ If I had been aware of malice in my
    heart,
the Lord would not have listened.
¹⁹ However, God has listened;
he has paid attention to the sound of
    my prayer.

⁶ He turns the sea to dry land; in the
    river they cross over on foot.
There we are glad in him.
⁷ Ruling in his might forever, his eyes
    keep watch on the nations.
The stubborn ones, let them not exalt
    themselves. *Selah.*

⁸ Bless, O peoples, our God, and cause
    the voice of his praise to be heard.
⁹ The one who puts our soul among
    the living and does not give our
    foot to tottering,
¹⁰ for you tested us, O God, you refined
    us as silver is refined.
¹¹ You brought us into the net; you
    put affliction on our loins.
¹² You caused men to ride over our
    heads; we went into the fire and
    the water,
and you brought us out to the lush
    place.

¹³ I will go to your house with burnt
    offerings. I will fulfill for you my
    vows,
¹⁴ which my lips opened and my
    mouth spoke in my distress.
¹⁵ Burnt offerings of fatlings I will
    cause to go up to you, with the
    smoke of rams;
I will make an offering of the herd
    with goats. *Selah.*

¹⁶ Come! Hear! And I will recount, all
    who fear God, what he has done for
    my soul.
¹⁷ To him my mouth called, and
    extolling praise was under my
    tongue.
¹⁸ If I see iniquity in my heart, my
    Lord will not hear.
¹⁹ Surely God hears. He gives attention
    to the voice of my prayer.

<sup>20</sup> Blessed be God!
He has not turned away my prayer
or turned his faithful love from me.

<sup>20</sup> Blessed be God, who has caused
neither my prayer nor his
lovingkindness to turn aside from
me.

CONTEXT: VERBAL AND THEMATIC LINKS WITH SURROUNDING PSALMS

After God shoots his enemies in Ps 64:7 (MT 64:8), David praises the Lord in Ps 65, and that praise continues in Pss 66 and 67. Hossfeld and Zenger catalogue numerous instances of common terminology and theme between Pss 65 and 66: praise from the whole earth; abundance; divine power; awesome deeds; the sea; the temple; and blessing.[219]

In this set of four songs (Pss 65, 66, 67, and 68 all have "A Song" in their superscriptions), the first and last (65 and 68) are Davidic, whereas the middle two (66, 67) do not have a name in their superscriptions.

See further the "Context" discussion on Psalm 65.

EXPOSITION

**66:1-4, Commands to Praise**

The first three verses of Ps 66 issue four plural commands to praise God: (1) all the earth is summoned to shout to him (66:1), (2) then follow plural imperatives to psalm the glory of his name, (3) place the glory of his praise (66:2), and (4) exclaim to God how fearsome his deeds are (66:3a).

The middle of 66:3 switches to description, as God's enemies are described feigning obedience to him, before the opening unit of the psalm concludes in verse 4 with a description of all the earth bowing down and psalming God's name.

The repetition of "all the earth" in verses 1 and 4 joins the use of the verb "psalm" (CSB and ESV, "sing") once in verse 2 and twice in verse 4 to bracket this unit as a call to praise.

**66:5-7, Call to See God's Work**

The psalmist motivates his audience to obey his call to praise in Ps 66:1-4 by his call to consider God's fearsome work in 66:5-7. What God does puts on display his overwhelming power and holiness and freedom. In response, people feel small, powerless, and intimidated.

Psalm 66:5 declares that God does this fearsome work for the sons of Adam, and in 66:6 it becomes clear that the sons of Adam in view are

---

[219] Hossfeld and Zenger, *Psalms 2*, 147-48.

the Israelites who saw God's unparalleled greatness at the Red Sea and the Jordan River. The crossing of the waters on foot made God's people glad in him.

Psalm 66:7 declares God's reign to be eternal and his oversight vigilant, adding a petition that those who resist the display of God's power might not succeed in their self-exaltation.

God deserves praise, and the narratives of the Bible inspire and motivate the praise he deserves.

### 66:8–12, Rehearsal of Purifying Suffering

Psalm 66:8 resumes the theme of 66:1–4 by again commanding the peoples to bless the God of Israel and cause his praise to be heard. The idea of blessing God seems to communicate a bowing down before him to do homage. In 66:9 the psalmist adds reasons to praise God: he put the souls of his people among the living and established their footsteps before him. The idea that God gave their souls life may point beyond the sustenance of physical life to a restoration of the souls of God's people to spiritual life.

The psalmist turns in 66:10 to the purifying testing through which God brought his people. He relates how God has refined his people the way that dross is smelted out of silver. Then in 66:11–12 he details what this looked like: the people were taken captive, afflicted, and defeated in battle, suffering through flame and flood. These statements seem to point back to various difficulties in Israel's history: slavery in Egypt, experience of the curses of the covenant, defeat in battle, but then at the end of 66:12 the psalmist proclaims that God has brought his people "out to the lush place." Here he seems to speak of the way God brought his people into the land of promise after the exodus from Egypt and the wilderness wandering, anticipating also a restoration to the land of blessing after the yet future new exodus.

The psalmist's perspective is that God had a good purpose for afflicting his people. He meant to refine them through suffering, and the psalmist recognizes that God has brought the suffering to the end.

### 66:13–15, Commitment to Sacrifice

The psalmist speaks as one who has been liberated from captivity and brought into the land of life in 66:12, and in 66:13–15 he declares his intention to go to the house of God to offer sacrifice. He twice speaks of offering burnt offerings (66:13, 15), as he relates his intention to fulfill the vows he made while in distress (66:13b–14). His lavish description of the sacrifices he will make in 66:15 reveals the psalmist is in earnest to act out his devotion to the Lord who has brought about his deliverance.

The suffering described in 66:10–12 appears to have been the distress that prompted the psalmist to make vows in 66:13–14. Delivered from distress, the psalmist will keep the vows he made to the one who is worthy of praise.

### 66:16–20, Testimony

Having summoned his audience to "come and see" in 66:5, the psalmist now calls them to "come and hear" in 66:16. The psalmist both shows God's greatness and testifies to its significance. He asserts in 66:16 that he will recount what God has done for him personally. In 66:17 he details how he called on the Lord, apparently in the midst of the refining affliction of 66:10–12, with extolling praise for God. Though he was suffering, the psalmist trusted God, made vows to God, and offered up praises to God.

He seems to address alternative attitudes in 66:18, where he relates that the Lord would not have heard him if he had held iniquity in his heart. That is to say, if the psalmist had held onto evil thoughts or sought wicked comforts in the midst of his affliction, the Lord would not have heard his prayer (cf. John 9:31). This makes sense, as typically those who harbor and cultivate evil in their hearts are not mindful of the Lord, and if they do call on him, if they are unrepentant, they do not pray in a way that pleases God. Only by repenting of all known sin and setting our hearts on what God himself intends to do can we offer the kinds of prayers that please God, the kinds that accord with his purposes, the kinds that he answers.

If we offer such prayers, the psalmist declares in Ps 66:19 that God surely hears and attends, prompting the concluding blessing in 66:20, where the psalmist celebrates the fact that God has neither rejected his prayer nor removed his lovingkindness.

### Bridge

Psalm 66 is a testimony of faith (esp. 66:16–19). It is the testimony of a man who praised God by trusting him in the midst of affliction, refusing to cultivate wicked sources of comfort, faithless explanations of his circumstances, or godless hopes for his future. Having experienced God's deliverance from his affliction, the psalmist recognizes that the Lord was using his difficulties to refine, purify, and perfect him. To all this the psalmist responds by summoning all the earth (66:1) and all peoples (66:8) to hear his testimony, see the greatness of what God has done, and join him in praising God.

Psalm 66 is another example of a psalm that deals with the experience of one who passed through suffering trusting God, experienced God's deliverance, and praised him among the peoples. The psalm also employs imagery reminiscent of the exodus and conquest, again suggesting that those patterns of events are relevant not only for interpreting how God delivers his people in the psalmist's own day but also point forward to more deliverance along those lines in the future.

What the psalmist says about when God does not hear in 66:18 over against the way he does in 66:19 can be traced through to Jesus teaching his disciples to pray in his own name. Peter seems to have recognized, from the Scriptures and the teaching of Jesus, that the prayers of un-Christlike husbands would be hindered (1 Pet 3:7). The psalmist's 66:19 prayer is in accord with the Lord's purpose and promise. To pray in the name of Jesus is to pray in accordance with Jesus' own mission and purpose, which he will certainly accomplish. God will hear, and answer, such prayers.

## Psalm 67

Overview and Structure of Psalm 67

Psalm 67 has a notable repetition of 67:3 in 67:5 (MT 67:4 and 67:6), and this refrain keys us to the psalm's matching chiastic structure:[220]

67:1 (MT 67:2), Blessing
    67:2 (MT 67:3), Salvation
        67:3 (MT 67:4), Praise
            67:4 (MT 67:5), Gladness
        67:5 (MT 67:6), Praise
    67:6 (MT 67:7), Fruitbearing
67:7 (MT 67:8), Blessing

---

[220] Cf. Alden, "Chiastic Psalms (II)," 194–95.

| CSB | Author's translation |
|---|---|
| For the choir director: with stringed instruments. A psalm. A song. | [1] For the Preeminent One. With stringed instruments. A Psalm. A Song. |
| [1] May God be gracious to us and bless us; may he make his face shine upon us *Selah* | [2] May God be gracious to us. May he bless us. May he cause the light of his face to be with us. *Selah*. |
| [2] so that your way may be known on earth, your salvation among all nations. | [3] That your way may be known on the earth, among all nations your salvation. |
| [3] Let the peoples praise you, God; let all the peoples praise you. [4] Let the nations rejoice and shout for joy, for you judge the peoples with fairness and lead the nations on earth. *Selah* | [4] May the peoples praise you, O God. May the peoples praise you, all of them. [5] May they be glad. May the nations give a ringing cry. For he judges the people with uprightness, and the nations on the earth, he guides them. *Selah*. |
| [5] Let the peoples praise you, God, let all the peoples praise you. | [6] May the peoples praise you, O God. May the peoples praise you, all of them. |
| [6] The earth has produced its harvest; God, our God, blesses us. [7] God will bless us, and all the ends of the earth will fear him. | [7] The earth gives her produce. God our God will bless us. [8] May God bless us, and may they fear him, all the ends of the earth. |

CONTEXT: VERBAL AND THEMATIC LINKS WITH SURROUNDING PSALMS

Zenger provides an excellent summary of the connections between Ps 67 and its neighbors:

The motif of blessing formulated with ברך (cf. 65:11; 66:8, 20; 67:2, 7, 8; cf. also 68:20, 27, 36), the (peace-bringing) judgment

of the nations (cf. 66:7; 67:5; cf. also 68:2), the fruitfulness of
earth/land (cf. 65:10–14; 66:6; 67:7), the praise of the peoples
(cf. 65:9; 66:8; 67:4–6), the experience of salvation/rescue (cf.
65:6; 67:3; cf. also 68:20–21), and in general the cultic saturation
or Temple perspective (cf. 65:2–5; 66:1–4, 13–20 ... ).[221]

The Lord's conquest of his enemies in 64:7–9 (MT 64:8–10) results in praise
and the flourishing of the land in Ps 65, all the earth psalming the Lord
in 66, and the gladness of the nations in 67. This builds to Ps 68, which
reprises the building of the tabernacle in anticipation of David's son
building the temple.

EXPOSITION

Psalm 67 opens with a prayer that God would be gracious, bless, and
cause the light of his face to shine on his people (67:1 [MT 67:2]; cf. Num
6:24–26). As Nissim Amzallag notes, "Three of the six verbs of the Aaronic
benediction (Num 6:24–26) are also found in Ps 67:2."[222] This prayer recognizes that the well-being of God's people depends upon God's favor
toward them.

In Ps 67:2 (MT 67:3) the psalmist states the reason he asks for God's
blessing: He wants God's goodness to resound through Israel that its echo
might be heard in all nations, that they too might relish the music. In
other words, if God is present with his people, causing his face to shine
upon them as he blesses them (67:1 [MT 67:2]), Israel will prosper, succeed,
and their borders will expand as their influence grows. This will all result
in other nations experiencing the goodness of God's ways as they come
in contact with the way that God has revealed himself in Israel. Not only
will God's *ways* be known, his salvation will be known.

---

[221] Hossfeld and Zenger, *Psalms 2*, 157.

[222] Nissim Amzallag, "Psalm 67 and the Cosmopolite Musical Worship of YHWH," *BBR*
25 (2015): 174. Rather than focus on the intent of the psalm's author, Amzallag proposes a
speculative, hypothetical reconstruction of how Ps 67 was sung, replete with the suggestion
that "these considerations point to substantial differences between the so-called official theology and the beliefs specifically related to the singers, defined here as a 'musical theology'
of YHWH" (187). Such claims cannot be sustained from the words of the text of the psalm,
which gives no indication of "substantial differences" with the theology communicated
throughout the rest of the Psalter, the OT, and indeed the whole Bible.

The reference to God's way points to God's character reflected in God's actions and commandments. God is good, all he does is good, and he has set out good instructions by which people should live.

God's salvation being made known points not merely to physical deliverance from wicked oppressors but to the kind of deliverance experienced by Noah at the flood and by Lot at the destruction of Sodom—that is to say, deliverance from the wrath of God against human sin. Like the making known of God's ways, the making known of God's salvation reveals his character. He declared himself to be one who forgives iniquity, transgression, and sin, even as he also upholds justice (Exod 34:6–7).

There is a clear progression of thought in Ps 67: God's grace to Israel (67:1 [MT 67:2]) will cause his way and salvation to be known (67:2 [MT 67:3]), and that in turn will cause all peoples to praise God, as the psalmist prays they will in 67:3 (MT 67:4). The repetition of the request that the peoples might praise God in 67:3 (MT 67:4) emphasizes the fervor the psalmist feels about God's praise resounding from all peoples.

The psalmist wants God to be glorified by the praise, and in 67:4 (MT 67:5) he makes it clear that he also wants the nations to be made glad in God. The gladness that gives rise to the ringing cry comes from knowing God, and it is this the psalmist prays the nations might experience.

Why would the nations be glad and rejoice in God? Because no one could be more satisfying than God, but the psalmist also states here in 67:4 (MT 67:5) that God's justice is upright and his guidance reliable. God will deliver from injustice, oppression, and lostness in the trackless waste of a world that has no meaning apart from him.

Gladness comes from praise. The psalmist makes the point that worship satisfies and gladdens as he brackets the prayer for the gladness of the nations in 67:4 (MT 67:5) with the refrain of the peoples praising God in 67:3 and 67:5 (MT 67:4 and 67:6). Praise is the purifying purpose for which we were made. Praise is our response to God's unmatched greatness.

We long to be impressed with jaw-dropping feats of greatness that flow from unique ability and peerless power. This is why so many around the world are intoxicated by the prowess of elite athletes. It is why we love to see the majesties of creation—the ocean, the Grand Canyon, Niagara Falls, and the starry heavens. We love these indescribable glories because there is a yearning in us for the one who alone could create them. Praise completes our enjoyment, and there is nothing we were made to enjoy more than God.

When we experience God we encounter one more satisfying, more compelling, more capable, and more impressive than anything else in all creation. There is no greater source of gladness than God, and no one has elicited more praise than God. Gladness gives rise to praise (67:3–5 [MT 67:4–6]), and gladness comes from knowing God's way and God's salvation (67:2 [MT 67:3]). These in turn come from God's gracious good pleasure to bless those on whom he makes his face to shine (67:1 [MT 67:2]).

God's presence with people who are glad in him and praise him will lead to the blessings of the covenant, and those blessings are epitomized in 67:6 (MT 67:7), where the earth is like the garden of Eden. It gives its produce under the blessing of God.

Psalm 67:7 (MT 67:8) is a summary of the message of the whole psalm: when God blesses his people, he will be feared to the ends of the earth in just the way that Ps 67 has described.

### BRIDGE

Psalm 67 captures God's purpose for the world when he created it and placed Adam and Eve in the garden. After their expulsion from Eden, God set about accomplishing the same purpose when he redeemed Israel from Egypt and put them in the land of promise. He meant to cause his glory to cover the dry lands as the waters cover the sea, as those who reflected his character exercised dominion over all he had made.

God means to bless the nations with the knowledge of his character and salvation that they might be glad in him, that they might praise him, that they might dwell in his presence and enjoy his blessing on the totality of their lives. He is pursuing this purpose now through the church, and when Jesus returns that purpose will be realized. The light of his presence will shine everywhere, replacing the sun as the source of radiance in all creation, and all will be glad in him, praise him, and enjoy his all-saturating goodness.

## Psalm 68

### OVERVIEW AND STRUCTURE OF PSALM 68

Psalm 68 seems to reflect a chiastic structure that can be depicted as follows:[223]

---

[223] For a more complicated proposal, see Alden, "Chiastic Psalms (II)," 195–96.

68:1–4 (MT 68:1–5), Desert Rider
  68:5–10 (MT 68:6–11), Home Giver
    68:11–14 (MT 68:12–15), Triumphant Procession
      68:15–18 (MT 68:16–19), Sinai in the Sanctuary
        68:19–20 (MT 68:20–21), Life Giver
      68:21–23 (MT 68:22–24), Head Crusher
    68:24–27 (MT 68:25–28), Triumphant Procession
  68:28–31 (MT 68:29–32), Land Giver
68:32–35 (MT 68:33–36), Sky Rider


    68:1–14 (MT 68:2–15), He Leads the Procession
    68:15–23 (MT 68:16–24), To the Holy Mountain
    68:24–35 (MT 68:25–36), To Which the Nations Stream

SCRIPTURE

**CSB**

**Author's translation**

For the choir director. A psalm of David. A song.

[1] For the Preeminent One.
Of David.
A Psalm.
A Song.

[1] God arises. His enemies scatter, and those who hate him flee from his presence.
[2] As smoke is blown away, so you blow them away. as wax melts before the fire, so the wicked are destroyed before God.
[3] But the righteous are glad; they rejoice before God and celebrate with joy.

[2] God will arise, and those at enmity with him will be scattered. Those who hate him will flee before him.
[3] As smoke is driven you will drive them; As wax melts before fire, the wicked will perish before God.
[4] And the righteous will be glad. They will rejoice before God, and they will exult in gladness.
[5] Sing to God! Psalm his name. Lift up a song to the one who rides on the deserts, in Yah, his name, and exult before him.

[4] Sing to God! Sing praises to his name. Exalt him who rides on the clouds— his name is the Lord—and celebrate before him.
[5] God in his holy dwelling is a father of the fatherless and a champion of widows.
[6] God provides homes for those who are deserted. He leads out the prisoners to prosperity,

[6] Father of orphans and judge for widows is God in the habitation of his holiness.

but the rebellious live in a scorched
   land.

⁷ God, when you went out before your
   people,
when you marched through the
   desert,
*Selah*

⁸ the earth trembled and the skies
   poured rain
before God, the God of Sinai,
before God, the God of Israel.
⁹ You, God, showered abundant rain;
you revived your inheritance when it
   languished.
¹⁰ Your people settled in it;
God, you provided for the poor by
   your goodness.

¹¹ The Lord gave the command;
a great company of women brought
   the good news:
¹² "The kings of the armies flee—they
   flee!"
She who stays at home divides the
   spoil.
¹³ While you lie among the sheep pens,
the wings of a dove are covered with
   silver,
and its feathers with glistening gold.
¹⁴ When the Almighty scattered kings
   in the land,
it snowed on Zalmon.

¹⁵ Mount Bashan is God's towering
   mountain;
Mount Bashan is a mountain of many
   peaks.
¹⁶ Why gaze with envy, you mountain
   peaks,
at the mountain God desired for his
   abode?
The Lᴏʀᴅ will dwell there forever!
¹⁷ God's chariots are tens of thousands,

⁷ God causes the solitary to dwell in a
   house;
he causes prisoners to go out in the
   prosperities;
surely the rebellious dwell in a
   scorched land.
⁸ O God, when you went out before
   your people,
when you strode through the
   wilderness. *Selah.*
⁹ The land quaked, even the heavens
   dripped,
before God, the one of Sinai,
before God, the God of Israel.
¹⁰ Showers of freewill offerings you
   cause to fall, O God.
As for your inheritance, when it was
   weary you established it.
¹¹ Your living things, they dwell in it.
You established in your goodness for
   the afflicted, O God.

¹² My Lord will give the word:
the women who announce good news
   are a great host.
¹³ The kings of the hosts, they flee!
   They flee.
The pasture of the house divides the
   plunder.
¹⁴ If you all lie between the sheepfolds,
the wings of the dove are covered
   with the silver,
and her pinions with shimmering
   gold.
¹⁵ When the Almighty spread out
   kings in it,
you caused snow in Zalmon.

¹⁶ Mountain of God, mountain of
   Bashan,
mountain of peaks, mountain of
   Bashan:
¹⁷ Why do you look with envy, many-
   peaked mountains,

thousands and thousands;
the Lord is among them in the
  sanctuary
as he was at Sinai.
¹⁸ You ascended to the heights, taking
  away captives;
you received gifts from people,
even from the rebellious,
so that the Lᴏʀᴅ God might dwell there.

¹⁹ Blessed be the Lord!
Day after day he bears our burdens;
God is our salvation.
*Selah*

²⁰ Our God is a God of salvation,
and escape from death belongs to the
  Lᴏʀᴅ my Lord.
²¹ Surely God crushes the heads of his
  enemies,
the hairy brow of one who goes on in
  his guilty acts.
²² The Lord said, "I will bring them
  back from Bashan;
I will bring them back from the
  depths of the sea
²³ so that your foot may wade in blood
and your dogs' tongues may have
  their share
from the enemies."
²⁴ People have seen your procession,
  God,
the procession of my God,
my King, in the sanctuary.
²⁵ Singers lead the way,
with musicians following;
among them are young women
playing tambourines.
²⁶ Bless God in the assemblies;
bless the Lᴏʀᴅ from the fountain of
  Israel.
²⁷ There is Benjamin, the youngest,
  leading them,

at the mountain God desired as his
  seat?
Surely Yahweh will dwell forever.
¹⁸ The chariot of God with twice ten
  thousand,
thousands of repetition:
my Lord among them.
Sinai is in the holy place.
¹⁹ You went up to the height.
You took captivity captive.
You received gifts among men,
and even the rebellious, for Yah God
  to dwell.

²⁰ Blessed be my Lord:
day by day he bears for us,
the God of our salvation. *Selah.*
²¹ The God who is for us:
God of our salvations,
and to Yahweh, my Lord,
to the death, goings out [i.e., belong
  ways of escape from death].

²² Surely God will smash the head of
  those at enmity with him,
the hairy crown of the one who walks
  in his culpabilities.
²³ My Lord said, "From Bashan I will
  cause to return,
I will cause to return from the depths
  of the sea
²⁴ that you might smash your foot in
  blood,
the tongue of your dogs from those at
  enmity its portion."²²⁴

²⁵ They see your processions, O God,
the processions of my God, my King,
into the holy place:
²⁶ the singers go before,
the string players after,
in the midst the young women who
  beat the timbrels.
²⁷ Bless God in the assemblies,

---

²²⁴ ESV: "that the tongue of your dogs may have their portion from the foe."

the rulers of Judah in their assembly,
the rulers of Zebulun, the rulers of
  Naphtali.

²⁸ Your God has decreed your strength.
Show your strength, God,
you who have acted on our behalf.
²⁹ Because of your temple at Jerusalem,
kings will bring tribute to you.
³⁰ Rebuke the beast in the reeds,
the herd of bulls with the calves of the
  peoples.
Trample underfoot those with bars of
  silver.
Scatter the peoples who take pleasure
  in war.
³¹ Ambassadors will come from Egypt;
Cush will stretch out its hands to God.

³² Sing to God, you kingdoms of the
  earth;
sing praise to the Lord,
*Selah*

³³ to him who rides in the ancient,
  highest heavens.
Look, he thunders with his powerful
  voice!
³⁴ Ascribe power to God.
His majesty is over Israel;
his power is among the clouds.
³⁵ God, you are awe-inspiring in your
  sanctuaries.
The God of Israel gives power and
  strength to his people.
Blessed be God!

Yahweh from the fountain of Israel!
²⁸ There is Benjamin, the youngest,
  ruling them;
the chieftains of Judah in their heaps;
chieftains of Zebulun;
chieftains of Naphtali.

²⁹ Your God commanded your strength.
Be strong, O God, in this you have
  done for us.
³⁰ Because of your temple at
  Jerusalem, kings bring gifts to you.
³¹ Rebuke the living things of the reed,
the congregation of bulls in the calves
  of the peoples,
trampling themselves in the bars of
  silver:
he scattered the peoples;
they delighted in wars.
³² Ambassadors will come from Egypt;
Cush causes his hands to run to God.

³³ The kingdoms of the earth sing to
  God;
they psalm my Lord. *Selah.*
³⁴ To the one who rides the heavens,
  the ancient heavens:
behold, he will give his voice, the
  voice of might.
³⁵ Ascribe strength to God.
His majesty is over Israel,
and his strength among the clouds.
³⁶ Fearsome, O God, from your holy
  places.
God of Israel is he,
giving strength and fullness of might
  to the people.
Blessed be God.

CONTEXT: VERBAL AND THEMATIC LINKS WITH SURROUNDING PSALMS

For the way the superscriptions link the four-psalm set of 65–68, see
"Context" on Ps 65. These psalms bless God (ברך in 65:10 [MT 65:11]; 66:8,
20; 67:1, 6, 7 [MT 67:2, 7, 8]; 68:19, 26, 35 [MT 68:20, 27, 36]) in response to
the need for him in Pss 61–64 prompted by Saul's persecutions in 52–59.

Yahweh declared his sovereignty in Ps 60, shot his enemies in Ps 64, prompting the praises of Pss 65-68. In Ps 68, Yahweh's triumphant procession through the wilderness is evoked (cf. Ps 68:1 [MT 68:2] and Num 10:35-36), as is the plunder of the Egyptians used to build the tabernacle (Ps 68:18 [MT 68:19]). Psalm 68 indicates that Yahweh has done for David what he did for Israel at the exodus, and that just as Israel plundered Egypt and built the tabernacle, David has plundered his enemies to set Solomon up to build the temple. The construction of the temple, of course, celebrates the way Yahweh has given rest to the land through the Davidic king (cf. 2 Sam 7:1-5), pointing forward to the final conquest and the building of Yahweh's cosmic new heaven and new earth temple.

EXPOSITION

### 68:1-14 (MT 68:2-15), He Leads the Procession

Psalm 68 opens with a slight adaptation of Num 10:34-35 in Ps 68:1 (MT 68:2), and the reference to the "thousands of Israel" in Num 10:35 may be reflected in the "thousands" of Ps 68:17 (MT 68:18). The evocation of the words that Moses proclaimed "whenever the ark set out" (Num 10:35) colors Ps 68 with the processional imagery of Israel setting out from Sinai for the march on the land of promise after the exodus from Egypt. By placing these words from the past in the future tense, David indicates that God will do in the future what he did in the past: as he acted when Israel left Sinai for the land of promise, so he will act when salvation is consummated and the people of God follow in the train of the triumphant divine warrior to claim the land he will cause them to inherit.

The enemies will be scattered and flee, driven away like smoke (Ps 68:1-2 [MT 68:2-3]). Just as God led Israel into the land and the hearts of its inhabitants melted (Josh 5:1), so when the Lord leads his people on the march in the future the wicked will melt like wax and perish before God (Ps 68:2 [MT 68:3]). The defeat of the wicked means triumph for the righteous, thus their gladness and exultation in 68:3 (MT 68:4), and the call to sing a psalm to the God who "rides on the deserts" in 68:4 (MT 68:5) further celebrates the way the Lord led Israel through the wilderness to the land of promise.

The Desert Rider is also a home giver: the Lord who led Israel from Sinai to the land by pillar of fire and cloud also made them a home in that land, and the Lord's provision for orphans, widows, and the lonely is commemorated in 68:5–6 (MT 68:6–7; cf. Deut 10:18–19). These verses say that the people of God who have no protector—no father, husband, or family—find what they need in the Lord who leads, guides, protects, and provides.

The end of Ps 68:6 (MT 68:7) speaks of the rebellious dwelling in a scorched land. The land of Egypt aptly illustrates the truth of this statement. God mercifully gave the Egyptians all they had, but they rebelled against him and refused to obey his prophet, Moses. God visited plagues upon them that left their land parched.

Psalm 68:7–10 (MT 68:8–11) returns to the forward-looking commemoration of the way God led his people through the wilderness after the exodus. Psalm 68:7 (MT 68:8) evokes the Lord leading Israel from Egypt to Sinai to the land, with the description of the land quaking (68:8 [MT 68:9]) calling to mind the earthquake at Sinai narrated in Exod 19. The references to the heavens pouring down rain could point to thunderstorms from thick clouds on that third day. Alternatively, the thick clouds might not have rained but caused deep humidity and moisture, which might fit better with my rendering of this phrase in Ps 68:8 (MT 68:9), "even the heavens dripped." The language of Ps 68:8 (MT 68:9) is almost an exact quotation of Judg 5:4, and Judg 5:5—which explicitly mentions Sinai—has similar phraseology as well.

The CSB and ESV understand Ps 68:9 (MT 68:10) to refer to plentiful rain, but I have rendered the line, "Showers of freewill offerings you cause to fall, O God," and this could point to the freewill offerings given at Mount Sinai and used for the construction of the tabernacle.

The "inheritance" that God established in 68:9b (MT 68:10b) is the land where his "living things" dwell in 69:10 (MT 69:11). The weariness of the inheritance in 68:9b (MT 68:10b; CSB, ESV, "languishing") was likely prompted by the sin of the inhabitants of Canaan. God brought judgment on those inhabitants of the land and established a home for his people.

In Ps 68:11–14 (MT 68:12–15) David juxtaposes imagery from the exodus from Egypt with imagery from the conquest of the land. The description of the great host of women announcing the good news in 68:11 (MT 68:12) recalls the scene in Exod 15:20–21, where Miriam and all the women sang of God's victory over Egypt at the Red Sea with tambourines and dancing. The fleeing kings in Ps 68:12 (MT 68:13) hearkens back to Josh 10:16, along with overtones of Deborah's Judg 5 song of triumph (see esp. the kings in Judg 5:19).

Psalm 68:12–14 (MT 68:13–15) are difficult verses to interpret, with a variety of possibilities, textual difficulties, and scholarly conjectures. In my translation I have rendered 68:12b (MT 68:13b) as it stands in BHS, but ESV and CSB amend the term "pasture" to a form that refers to a woman at home. The reference to plunder again recalls Judg 5 (see Judg 5:19, 28–30). The cryptic image of men lying among the sheepfolds in 68:13 (MT 68:14) seems to allude to Judg 5:16, and the comments about the wings of the dove covered with silver, the pinions with shimmering gold appears to describe the plunder that has been under discussion. VanGemeren suggests that the snow on Zalmon in 68:14 (MT 68:15) is a poetic depiction of "the corpses of the victims and their weaponry ... lying like scattered snowflakes on the mountains."[225]

The combination of this imagery joins God's victory over Egypt to his victory over Canaan and puts the women celebrating after the Red Sea in Exod 15 together with Deborah's song after God's victory over his enemies in the land in Judg 5. This joining of exodus and conquest and the celebrations of the women indicates again that the way God saved in the past is the way he will save in the future: those strong in worldly strength will be unexpectedly destroyed, and God's people, led by the ladies, will sing God's praise.

### 68:15–23 (MT 68:16–24), To the Holy Mountain

Mount Sinai was also called Mount Horeb and "the mountain of God" in Exod 3:1. The mountain of God in Ps 68:15 (MT 68:16), however, is Mount Zion. This reference to Mount Zion in the first phrase of 68:15 (MT 68:16), is then followed by a vocative address to Mount Bashan. Bashan is asked in 68:16 (MT 68:17) why it envies Zion, where Yahweh chose to put his dwelling place, the temple.

David depicts "the chariot of God with twice ten thousand, thousands of repetition" in Ps 68:17 (MT 68:18). Ezekiel describes Yahweh's chariot throne (Ezek 1), as does Daniel, and in Daniel the chariot throne is accompanied by thousands upon thousands and ten thousand times ten thousand standing before the Ancient of Days (Dan 7:9–10).

Psalm 68 opens with the words of Moses when the ark set out on the journey from Sinai to the land of promise (the quotation of Num 10:35–36 in 68:1 [MT 68:2]). God is then identified as "the one of Sinai" in

---

[225] VanGemeren, *Psalms*, 519.

68:8 (MT 68:9), and Sinai's status as the mountain of God is transferred to Zion in 68:15 (MT 68:16). All of this builds to the final statement of 68:17 (MT 68:18), where David asserts, "Sinai is in the holy place." The holy place is God's new dwelling place on Mount Zion in Jerusalem, and the point is that everything significant about Sinai has been transferred to Zion.

At Sinai Yahweh was uniquely present, making it the mountain of God. And God gave the law at Sinai. Now God is uniquely present in Jerusalem, and the law given at Sinai goes forth from Zion. This aspect of what David is getting at in Ps 68 is accurately interpreted by Isaiah, "for from Zion will go the Torah, and the word of Yahweh from Jerusalem" (Isa 2:3).

In Ps 68:18 (MT 68:19) David speaks of the way Israel at Sinai made freewill offerings that were used to build the tabernacle. These freewill offerings were drawn from the plunder of the Egyptians, and the captives David mentions were the liberated Israelites. It is not altogether clear who did the ascending. This could refer to Moses or Yahweh. Moses went up the mountain, and the gifts were given to Yahweh with Moses as the mediator between God and Israel. Alternatively, Yahweh led the people in the pillar, and then he could be the one depicted as ascending the mountain. Either way, the verse seems to refer to the way that God gave Israel the plunder of Egypt, which Israel then devoted to the Lord in the freewill offerings used for the tabernacle. That tabernacle was then given to Israel as the place where they would meet Yahweh.

This pattern of the plunder of the enemies being used for the building of the dwelling place of God is repeated when David stockpiles the wealth of the nations for Solomon to use in the construction of the temple, and the pattern will be fulfilled when Jesus plunders Satan and makes the liberated captives the construction materials for the new dwelling place of God, the church.

This fulfillment is what Paul has in view in Eph 4:8–12. The fact that God gave Israel the plunder of Egypt, which Israel then gave back to God for the building of the tabernacle, which was then given back to Israel, resolves the superficial change Paul makes to Ps 68:18 (MT 68:19) in Eph 4:8. In Ps 68:18 (MT 68:19) the one who ascended receives gifts, whereas in Eph 4:8 Jesus is the one who ascends, and he then gives gifts. On the understanding presented here, Jesus is the fulfillment of all that Moses typified, and he is the incarnation of Yahweh. And whichever of these two, Moses or Yahweh, does the ascending in Ps 68:18 (MT 68:19), though he receives the material for the building of the dwelling of God he then turns around and gives the dwelling of God to the people. The change in verb, then, from *receive* in Ps 68 to *give* in Eph 4, can be understood as an accurate interpretation of what is happening in Ps 68.[226]

Psalm 68:19–20 (MT 68:20–21) sits at the center of the psalm's chiastic structure. Here God is blessed as the one who sustains Israel, carrying his people day by day (68:19 [MT 68:20]), and celebrated as the God of salvation to whom belong "goings out" from death. The God of the Bible is the one who provides a way out when all hope is gone, even when life is gone.

Psalm 68:21–23 (MT 68:22–24) presents the means whereby Yahweh establishes his triumph over the archenemy who laid claim to Yahweh's dominion. In fulfillment of Gen 3:15, Ps 68:21 (MT 68:22) asserts that Yahweh will crush the head of the seed of the serpent. Whereas the first line of 68:21 (MT 68:22) speaks of Yahweh's enemies in the plural, the second line speaks of the one who walks in his guilt in the singular. This captures the dynamic between the singular archenemy and his corporate seed and asserts that Yahweh will defeat the serpent and all who belong to him.

Because those being brought back in 68:22 (MT 68:23) are brought back for an individual Israelite to strike his feet in their blood in 68:23 (MT 68:24), we can draw several conclusions here. First, these appear to be enemies being brought back. Second, there is one Israelite who is going to strike his feet in their blood, and this singular individual would appear to be Yahweh's triumphant warrior. Given the way that David led Israel to victory over Goliath and the Philistines, the descendant of David was likely expected to lead God's people to victory in the future. These verses, then, seem to speak to the way that God's champion will visit God's justice on God's enemies, and when he does so their heads will be smashed as the champion smashes his foot in their blood. Psalm 68:21 and 23 (MT 68:22 and 24) seem to indicate that the seed of the woman will crush the heads of the seed of the serpent and bruise his heel in the stomping as he achieves God's victory.

God establishes his temple in Zion (68:15–18 [MT 68:16–19]). God delivers his people even from death (68:19–20 [MT 68:20–21]). And this comes

---

[226] For discussion of the targum on Ps 68, see Edwards, *Exegesis in the Targum of Psalms*, 171–73, where he concludes, "The Targum cannot serve as an example of an early tradition that is reflected in Ephesians, since it is doing something quite different."

about as the seed of the woman crushes the head of the seed of the serpent (68:21–23 [MT 68:22–24]).

### 68:24–35 (MT 68:25–36), To Which the Nations Stream

The procession celebrating Yahweh's triumph in 68:11–14 (MT 68:12–15) is now paralleled by a procession of worshipers making their way into the holy place in 68:24–27 (MT 68:25–28). The procession of God the king in 68:24 (MT 68:25) is seen by all as he is accompanied by his people: the singers lead the way, with the musicians last, and the young women with tambourines in the middle (the same term, "timbrel/tambourine" appears in Exod 15:20).

David summons the great congregation that has its source in Yahweh, Israel's fountain, to bless Yahweh in Ps 68:26 (MT 68:27). He then observes in 68:27 (MT 68:28) how little Benjamin leads the way, with the princes of Judah, Zebulun, and Naphtali.

In Ps 68:28–31 Yahweh's triumph over the nations includes his defeat of Egypt, the beasts in the reeds (68:30 [MT 68:31]). He scatters the inhabitants of Canaan (68:30 (MT 68:31) and establishes the temple in Jerusalem (68:29 [MT 68:30]). The nobility of the nations brings tribute to him in Zion (68:31 [MT 68:32]).

David first asserts in 68:28 (MT 68:29) that God has commanded Israel's strength, then he calls on God to be strong in what he has done for his people. David next asserts that the kings of the earth will bring him gifts because of the way he has established his dwelling place at the temple in Jerusalem (68:29 [MT 68:30]). The beast in the reeds and the congregation of bulls among the calves of the nations seem to be ciphers for Egypt in 68:30 (MT 68:31). The peoples delighting in wars and trampling bars of silver in 68:30 (MT 68:31) seem to be the inhabitants of the land with their greedy and warlike ways. In 68:31 (MT 68:32) David describes how all-powerful Egypt will be reduced to bringing tribute to Yahweh.

The final section of Ps 68, verses 32–35 (MT 33–36), summons all nations to praise God. David calls the kingdoms of the earth to sing and psalm his Lord in 68:32 (MT 68:33). He then matches the description of Yahweh as the Desert Rider in 68:4 (MT 68:5) with a description of him as the Sky Rider in 68:33 (MT 68:34). He comes on the clouds, and his mighty voice issues from his unparalleled lungs. To this great God David commands all that they must ascribe strength in 68:34 (MT 68:35), for his majesty waves like a banner over Israel and his strength is on display in the clouds. David concludes in 68:35 (MT 68:36) by addressing the God who is fearsome from his holy places, the God of Israel, who gives strength and fullness of might to his people. Having mused on the identity of God, he exclaims: Blessed be God!

BRIDGE

In Ps 68 the contemplation of God's triumph at the exodus, his giving of the law at Sinai, and his conquest of the land leads to a projection into the future of the way that God will again subdue hostile powers, establish his dwelling place, from which the law will go forth, and conquer all his enemies such that they render him tribute and praise.

The authors of the New Testament present the triumph of Christ as the fulfillment of the new exodus pattern, the gospel going forth in the church as the word of the Lord going forth from Jerusalem, and the making of disciples from all nations as their being gathered into God's kingdom, built into a holy temple for the Lord. These things will be consummated when Christ comes as king, when every knee will bow, when the procession to fulfill all processions will take place as the kings come marching in with the wealth of the nations to enrich the ever-living King of kings. And we will praise him forever.

## Psalm 69

OVERVIEW AND STRUCTURE OF PSALM 69

Psalm 69 is a chiasm:

69:1–4 (MT 69:2–5), Mire, Flood, Deep
   69:5–7 (MT 69:6–8), Guilt, the Remnant
      69:8–12 (MT 69:9–13), Rejected
         69:13–15 (MT 69:14–16), Muck, Flood, Deep
         69:16–21 (MT 69:17–22), Answer Me
      69:22–28 (MT 69:23–29), Imprecations
   69:29–33 (MT 69:30–34), Sacrifice of Praise and Thanks, Remnant
69:34–36 (MT 69:35–37), Praise for Salvation

We will exposit the psalm under the following subheads:

   69:1–12 (MT 69:2–13), The Rejected King

69:13–21 (MT 69:14–22), Calls on the Lord
69:22–36 (MT 69:23–37), For Vindication

SCRIPTURE

CSB                                              Author's translation

For the choir director: according to          [1] For the Preeminent One.
"The Lilies." Of David.                        On Lilies.
                                               Of David.

[1] Save me, God,
for the water has risen to my neck.            [2] Save me, O God, for the waters have
[2] I have sunk in deep mud, and there is          come to my soul.
    no footing;                                [3] I sink in mire of the deep, and there
I have come into deep water,                       is no place to stand.
and a flood sweeps over me.                    I have come into the depths of the
[3] I am weary from my crying;                     waters, and the torrent flooded
my throat is parched.                              over me.
My eyes fail, looking for my God.              [4] I am weary in my calling out, my
[4] Those who hate me without cause                throat is hoarse.
are more numerous than the hairs of            My eyes fail waiting for my God.
    my head;                                   [5] More in number than the hairs of
my deceitful enemies, who would                    my head are those who hate me
    destroy me,                                    without cause.
are powerful.                                  Those who would destroy me are
Though I did not steal, I must repay.              mighty, those at enmity with me in
                                                   deception.
[5] God, you know my foolishness,              What I did not steal, then I restore.
and my guilty acts are not hidden
    from you.                                  [6] O God, you know my folly,
[6] Do not let those who put their hope        and the points where I am guilty are
    in you                                         not hidden from you.
be disgraced because of me,                    [7] Do not let those who wait for you
Lord GOD of Armies;                            be put to shame because of me, my
do not let those who seek you                      Lord, Yahweh of hosts.
be humiliated because of me,                   Do not let those who seek you
God of Israel.                                 be humiliated because of me, O God
[7] For I have endured insults because             of Israel
    of you,                                    [8] Because on account of you I have
and shame has covered my face.                     borne reproach.
[8] I have become a stranger to my             Humiliation has covered my face.
    brothers
and a foreigner to my mother's sons           [9] I am estranged from my brothers
[9] because zeal for your house has            and a foreigner to the sons of my
    consumed me,                                   mother,

and the insults of those who insult
  you
have fallen on me.
¹⁰ I mourned and fasted,
but it brought me insults.
¹¹ I wore sackcloth as my clothing,
and I was a joke to them.
¹² Those who sit at the city gate talk
  about me,
and drunkards make up songs about
  me.

¹³ But as for me, LORD,
my prayer to you is for a time of favor.
In your abundant, faithful love, God,
answer me with your sure salvation.
¹⁴ Rescue me from the miry mud; don't
  let me sink.
Let me be rescued from those who
  hate me
and from the deep water.
¹⁵ Don't let the floodwaters sweep over
  me
or the deep swallow me up;
don't let the Pit close its mouth over
  me.
¹⁶ Answer me, LORD,
for your faithful love is good.
In keeping with your abundant
  compassion,
turn to me.
¹⁷ Don't hide your face from your
  servant,
for I am in distress.
Answer me quickly!
¹⁸ Come near to me and redeem me;
ransom me because of my enemies.

¹⁹ You know the insults I endure—
my shame and disgrace.
You are aware of all my adversaries.
²⁰ Insults have broken my heart,
and I am in despair.
I waited for sympathy,
but there was none;

¹⁰ because zeal for your house has
  consumed me,
and the reproaches of those who
  reproach you have fallen on me.
¹¹ When I wept in the fasting of
  my soul, it became grounds to
  reproach me.
¹² When I gave as my garment
  sackcloth,
then I became for them a proverb [a
  ruler's statement].
¹³ Those who sit in the gate complain
  about me,
and the mocking songs of those who
  drink alcohol!

¹⁴ But as for me, my prayer is to you,
  Yahweh, at the time of favor.
O God, in the abundance of your
  lovingkindness answer me in the
  truth of your salvation.
¹⁵ Deliver me from the muck, and do
  not let me sink!
I will be delivered from those who
  hate me and from the depths of the
  waters.
¹⁶ Do not let the torrent of water flood
  over me;
and do not let the deep swallow me;
and do not let the pit close its mouth
  over me.

¹⁷ Answer me, O Yahweh, for your
  lovingkindness is good.
According to the abundance of your
  mercies turn to me.
¹⁸ And do not hide your face from
  your servant;
because of the distress to me, hasten!
  Answer me!
¹⁹ Draw near to my soul; redeem it.
On account of those at enmity with
  me, ransom me.
²⁰ You know my reproach and my
  shame and my humiliation.

for comforters, but found no one.
²¹ Instead, they gave me gall for my
food,
and for my thirst
they gave me vinegar to drink.

²² Let their table set before them be a
snare,
and let it be a trap for their allies.
²³ Let their eyes grow too dim to see,
and let their hips continually quake.
²⁴ Pour out your rage on them,
and let your burning anger overtake
them.
²⁵ Make their fortification desolate;
may no one live in their tents.
²⁶ For they persecute the one you
struck
and talk about the pain of those you
wounded.
²⁷ Charge them with crime on top of
crime;
do not let them share in your
righteousness.
²⁸ Let them be erased from the book
of life
and not be recorded with the
righteous.

²⁹ But as for me—poor and in pain—
let your salvation protect me, God.
³⁰ I will praise God's name with song
and exalt him with thanksgiving.
³¹ That will please the Lᴏʀᴅ more than
an ox,
more than a bull with horns and
hooves.
³² The humble will see it and rejoice.
You who seek God, take heart!
³³ For the Lᴏʀᴅ listens to the needy
and does not despise
his own who are prisoners.

³⁴ Let heaven and earth praise him,
the seas and everything that moves
in them,

All my adversaries are before you.
²¹ Reproach has broken my heart, and
I am sick.
When I waited for pity, there was
none;
and for those who show compassion,
and I found none.
²² And they gave as my food gall,
and in my thirst they caused me to
drink vinegar.

²³ May their table before them be a
snare, and in their times of *shalom*
a trap.
²⁴ May their eyes be dark and
unseeing, and their loins
continually cause to waver.
²⁵ Pour out upon them your
indignation,
and may the burning of your nose
overtake them.
²⁶ May their camp be desolate.
In their tents may there be no
dwellers.
²⁷ For you, the one you strike, they
pursue.
They recount the wound of those
pierced by you.
²⁸ Give iniquity upon their iniquity,
and do not let them come into your
righteousness.
²⁹ May they be wiped out of the book
of life,
and with the righteous let them not
be written.

³⁰ And as for me, afflicted and pained,
may your salvation, O God, set me
on high.
³¹ I will praise the name of God in song,
and I will make him great with
thanksgiving.
³² And that will be better to Yahweh
than an ox or bull with horns and
hoofs.
³³ The afflicted will see and be glad.

<sup>35</sup> for God will save Zion
and build up the cities of Judah.
They will live there and possess it.
<sup>36</sup> The descendants of his servants will
inherit it,
and those who love his name will live
in it.

Those who seek God, may their hearts
live!
<sup>34</sup> For Yahweh hears the needy, and
his prisoners he does not despise.

<sup>35</sup> May the heavens and earth praise
him, the seas and all that creeps in
them.
<sup>36</sup> For God will cause salvation for Zion
and build the cities of Judah,
and they will dwell there and possess
it.
<sup>37</sup> And the seed of his servants will
inherit it,
and those who love his name will
dwell in it.

CONTEXT: VERBAL AND THEMATIC LINKS WITH SURROUNDING PSALMS

David's difficulties continued right down to the end of his life. He suffered, was delivered, then was plunged into new difficulties. The final four psalms of Book 2 have David once again experiencing rejection and affliction in Ps 69, crying out to Yahweh in the language of Ps 40 in Ps 70 (see "Context" on Psalm 70), seeking vindication in Ps 71, then praying that God will keep his promises for his son Solomon in Ps 72.

Psalm 69, The Rejected King
    Psalm 70, Make Haste to Help Me
    Psalm 71, Let Them Be Put to Shame (Not Me)
Psalm 72, Give the King Your Justice and Blessing

EXPOSITION

### 69:1–12 (MT 69:2–13), The Rejected King

The superscription of Ps 69 gives no indication of the circumstances of David's life that prompted this prayer. If it is correct that Books 1 and 2 of the Psalter are tracking with David's life, with Book 3 transitioning to the reign of Solomon and those who came after, then Ps 69 can be seen as responding either to Absalom's revolt (2 Sam 15–19) or Sheba's rebellion (2 Sam 20).

David opens Ps 69 by describing his difficulties metaphorically as a flood (69:1–3 [MT 69:2–4]) before stating the problem in explicit terms:

he is outnumbered by enemies (69:4 [MT 69:5]). David seems to depict something like Noah's flood rushing over him in Ps 69:1–2 (MT 69:2–3): the waters threaten his life; he has no place to stand; in the deeps the torrents wash over him. He then speaks to his exhaustion in 69:3 (MT 69:4), describing how he has grown hoarse crying out to God, saying that his eyes have failed he has been waiting so long.

David clarifies in 69:4 (MT 69:5) that the deluge of water, the baptism he has undergone, is not a literal flood but a tide of surging enemies. David describes the number of those who hate him without cause (cf. same expression in 35:19) as being more than the hairs of his head. This impressionistic figure of speech is David's way of saying that he is "outgunned, outmanned, outnumbered, outplanned."[227] David will acknowledge his guilt in 69:5 (MT 69:6), but here he insists that the hatred of his enemies is groundless. Their opposition to him is evidently not in response to his iniquity. David characterizes his enemies as powerful, deceptive, and unjust. The line about him being required to restore what he did not steal at the end of 69:4 (MT 69:5) captures the implacable caprice of those set on David's destruction. They do not seek justice but his destruction.

In Ps 69:5–7 (MT 69:6–8) David acknowledges his guilt and folly before God and prays it will have no ill affect upon the people of God. David confesses his foolishness and the ways it has made him guilty in 69:5 (MT 69:6), and he shows love for God and neighbor in 69:6–7 (MT 69:7–8). The love for neighbor can be seen in the prayer in 69:6 (MT 69:7) that those who wait for God might not be put to shame because of what he has done. David does not want God's people dishonored because of the way their king, David, failed to be wise and blameless.

The connection between David's guilt in 69:5 (MT 69:6) and him saying that he bore reproach for God's sake in 69:7 (MT 69:8) seems to be as follows: rather than deny his guilt by redefining right and wrong, and rather than refusing to confess his sin and try to keep it swept under the rug, David has openly confessed himself to be worthy of reproach. He did this for God's sake. Fear of God kept him from saying that what he had done was not wrong, and fear of God kept him from refusing to acknowledge his sin. Thus, fear of God put him out in public as a sinner worthy of reproach.

---

[227] Miranda and McCarter, *Hamilton.*

David's sin complicates things because it compromises his position of strength. His enemies are not opposed to him because of his sin, but his sin does weaken him against his enemies. His sin makes it easier for people to be unsympathetic to his plight.

This lack of sympathy and solidarity is the subject of Ps 69:8–12 (MT 69:9–13). In 69:8 (MT 69:9) David states the extreme rejection he feels in two ways. He first says that he is estranged from his brothers, then says that he is a foreigner to the sons of his mother. This twofold statement that not even his family sides with him stresses the ostracism and rejection David feels.

David goes on to assert that the ostracism he faces springs from his commitment to the Lord. He explains in 69:9 (MT 69:10) that he is alienated and rejected because he is eaten up with zeal for the house of God (cf. 132:1–5). This has resulted in a situation where the vituperation and hatred people feel for God finds a visible target in the person of David. The enemies of God vent their spleen on God's king, David.[228]

Psalm 69:10–12 (MT 69:11–13) illustrates the way that inveterate enemies see anything as validation of their hatred. David's tearful fasting prompted his enemies to reproach him (69:10 [MT 69:11]). David's clothing of himself in sackcloth prompted his enemies to speak of him as a proverbial byword (69:11 [MT 69:12]). Meanwhile in 69:12 (MT 69:13) David relates that people high and low had no regard for him: those who sit in the gate are the elders of the land, respected people, and they complained about him, while the drunkards at their cups with their riotous songs mocked him.

David knows that he is a sinner (69:5 [MT 69:6]), but he also knows that those who hate him are not prompted by righteous indignation against his sin: They hate him without cause (69:4 [MT 69:5]). The hatred arises from David's commitment to God and God's house (69:7, 9 [MT 69:8, 10]), and it leaves David feeling alienated and alone (69:8 [MT 69:9]). The animosity makes David feel as though a flood is sweeping over him, drowning him (69:1–2 [MT 69:2–3]), and his concern is that God's people would not be dishonored because of him (69:6 [MT 69:7]).

---

[228] See the "Bridge" section below for discussion of the citation of this text in John 2:17 and Rom 15:3.

## 69:13–21 (MT 69:14–22), Calls on the Lord

David opened Ps 69 with a cry for God to save him (69:1 [MT 69:2]), and now having described his predicament he renews his pleas for deliverance in 69:13 (MT 69:14). He prays to Yahweh "at the time of favor" (cf. Ps 5:12; 30:6 [MT 5:13; 30:7]; Isa 49:8), and he calls on the Lord to "answer" in the abundance of God's lovingkindness.

The urgency of David's prayer here is communicated by a threefold call on God to answer him (69:13, 16, 17 [MT 69:14, 17, 18]). David specifically calls on God to answer him in the "truth/faithfulness" (אמת) of God's salvation. David's references to God's abounding lovingkindness and truth indicate that he appeals to God's own proclamation of his character in Exod 34:6–7. This shows that when God acts to save David, God will be acting in accordance with his own character, keeping his own promises, upholding his own standards.

David next resumes the language of Ps 69:2 (MT 69:3) in 69:14–15 (MT 69:15–16). Here again the "muck" and the "depths of the waters" and the "torrent" that would "flood over" David are all figurative ways of describing the distress caused by his enemies. When God delivers David from "those who hate" him (69:14 [MT 69:15]), he will be rescued from the baptismal flood, and the pit will not close its mouth over him (69:15 [MT 69:16]).

The resumption of the language from the opening statements of the psalm mark the turning point at its chiastic center, and David again appeals for God to answer him in accordance with his character in 69:16–21 (MT 69:17–22). In 69:16 (MT 69:17) David appeals to God to answer because of the goodness of God's lovingkindness and in keeping with his abundant mercy (cf. Exod 34:6–7).

David petitions the Lord not to hide his face (Ps 69:17 [MT 69:18]), implicitly calling on the Lord to be present with him and to behold his situation, which he goes on to detail. He speaks of his distress and his need for God to answer him quickly at the end of 69:17 (MT 69:18), and he pleads with the Lord to draw near to ransom and redeem him because of his enemies in 69:18 (MT 69:19). Appealing to God's compassion for him, David affirms in 69:19 (MT 69:20) that God knows his reproach, shame, and dishonor, and God knows all his adversaries too. Seeking to provoke God's sympathy, David outlines the way that reproach has broken his heart and left him sick, the way he hoped for pity and there was none, for compassion and found none (69:20 [MT 69:21]). The wretched way that his enemies have treated him then culminates in 69:21 (MT 69:22), as David recounts how when he was hungry and thirsty his enemies gave him gall to eat and vinegar to drink.[229]

Throughout this central section of Ps 69 David has appealed for God to answer him in accordance with his character to deliver him from the flood and from death in the face of merciless opposition.

### 69:22–36 (MT 69:23–37), For Vindication

David unleashes a blistering string of imprecatory maledictions in Ps 69:22–28 (MT 69:23–29). These curses fit the wickedness of the enemies of God who direct their fury against the Lord and his king, David. What David prays here is directed against the enemies of God, and he prays for God to be just against them. God's justice against the wicked will restrain evil and promote goodness, in keeping with God's purposes and character. An unstated assumption here is that these enemies of God will not repent. Often in the Bible, however, God's justice is precisely what leads sinners to repentance, and it goes without saying that if those against whom David prays here were to repent they would receive God's mercy rather than his wrath (see Ps 83:16–18 [MT 83:17–19]). Their repentance, it should be noted, would take the form of them genuinely aligning themselves with David, submitting to him as their king.

The point made throughout these imprecatory prayers is that God's enemies have no right to God's blessings. God's enemies should expect God's curses, and David calls on the Lord to render to them what they deserve. If the wicked do not experience justice against their sin, they will see no incentive to repent. This Isaiah declares when he says, "If the wicked man is shown favor, he does not learn righteousness. In a righteous land he acts unjustly and does not see the majesty of the Lord" (Isa 26:10 CSB).

David prays in Ps 69:22 (MT 69:23) that when his enemies sit down to eat in peace they would find themselves trapped and ensnared.[230] This may represent a desire to see the intrigues and evil practices of his enemies result in them poisoning one another's food. Alternatively, if the "table" is a mat spread on the ground, the food could be likened to bait

---

[229] See the "Bridge" section below for the resonance of these statements with the narratives of the crucifixion of Jesus.

[230] The citation of this text in Rom 11:9 is discussed in the "Bridge" below.

placed upon it, with the mat covering an open pit designed to entrap those lured by the bait.[231]

David prays against the physical health of his enemies in 69:23 (MT 69:24), asking that their eyes might be darkened and unseeing, that their loins might always tremble. It is a biblical theme that sin deadens perceptive capacities and ruins health, so David prays here that the wicked would get what they deserve.[232]

In Ps 69:24 (MT 69:25) David moves away from specific expressions of God's wrath to call for the thing itself, petitioning the Lord to pour out his indignation upon his enemies, for God to allow the burning of his nose to overtake the wicked. If God does so, it will have the affects upon their health he has articulated in previous verses as well as the affects upon their community in the ensuing.

The wicked gathered together against Yahweh and his anointed will be dispersed and rendered ineffectual if Yahweh answers David's prayer to make their camp a desolation with no inhabitants in their tents in 69:25 (MT 69:26).[233] David's prayer arises from the fact that health and community are blessings of God that the wicked do not deserve to enjoy. They have rejected the giver of the gifts, so the giver should end their enjoyment of his gifts.

David returns to the reason the wicked should be punished in 69:26 (MT 69:27): The wicked persecute the one God struck down, celebrating the wounding of the one God pierced. Interestingly the word "pierced" (חלל) in 69:26 (MT 69:27) is a term Isaiah will use to describe the piercing of the servant (Isa 53:5). In the context of Ps 69, David is the sufferer, so he is the one whom God has struck and pierced in discipline for his sin. This prayer indicates that David understands his difficulties, the difficulties from which he has been praying to be delivered, to come from God as discipline for the transgressions he confessed in 69:5 (MT 69:6).

David prays in 69:27 (MT 69:28) that the wicked would reap what they have sown: they have sown to the flesh, cultivated appetites for evil, so they deserve to reap iniquity upon iniquity, punishment upon punishment. They do not deserve to be declared righteous, nor do they deserve

---

[231] For sketches of such snares, see Keel, *Symbolism of the Biblical World*, 91.

[232] See Beale, *We Become What We Worship*.

[233] The "Bridge" discussion below deals with the citation of this passage in Acts 1:20.

to enter into God's righteous presence, and David prays that God would vindicate him by treating the wicked with perfect justice.

David's imprecations reach their logical conclusion in Ps 69:28 (MT 69:29), where David calls on the Lord to banish the wicked to the unclean realm of the dead where they belong. Their destiny is in keeping with their actions and behavior. They have no place in the book of life or among the righteous. These people have set themselves up as the enemies of God, and David prays that they would receive the reward of the enemies of God rather than the reward of the friends of God. They are not God's friends. They are rebels. They will get what rebels deserve.

The series of imprecations against his enemies in 69:22–28 (MT 69:23–29) stands across from David's description of himself as rejected and alienated in 69:8–12 (MT 69:9–13). If God will do what David prays for, the wrong will be set right. David is humble and repentant and should experience the congregation of the righteous and the blessing of God. The wicked are proud and rebellious and should not enjoy God's favor. In these imprecatory prayers, it is as though David prays for the music to be put back on key, back in rhythm, back in tune with the melody, making things the way they should be.

In Ps 69:29–33 (MT 69:30–34) David balances his earlier confession of sin and statement of concern for the remnant (69:5–7 [MT 69:6–8]) with promises of praise and thanks, which are better than sacrifice for sin, and a life-giving testimony for the remnant.

In 69:29 (MT 69:30) David confronts God with a choice: he can vindicate the righteous by defeating the wicked or allow injustice to continue. David stresses the fact that he is afflicted, and though at some level his affliction is God's discipline, at the human level the wicked are afflicting him. He calls on God to save him and set him on high—out of the muck and mire, out of the floodwaters.

David asserts in Ps 69:30 (MT 69:31) that if God will do this, he will offer praise and thanks to God. he goes on to say in 69:31 (MT 69:32) that the praise and thanks will please God more than sacrificial animals. This shows David's correct understanding that what God wants is not sacrifices but mercy. God wants hearts that understand how to respond to mercy by giving God glory and gratitude.

Those who are like David, humbled by their afflictions, will see what God has done for David and be glad over it, and these people who seek God will experience life in their hearts (69:32 [MT 69:33]). This indicates that David understands that his own life is a kind of exemplary, life-giving paradigm for the people of God. They will see what God does for David and rejoice over it, and their hearts will be made alive by it. They will understand from what happens to David what David articulates in 69:33 (MT 69:34): Yahweh hears the prayers of the needy and does not despise his people who have been taken captive.

David's final prayers in Ps 69:34–36 (MT 69:35–37) match the opening prayer in 69:1–4 (MT 69:2–5) and also link the prayers of this psalm to broader themes in biblical hope. The realization of God's purposes will entail exactly what David prays for in 69:34 (MT 69:35), all living things, every creeping thing, in heaven and on earth and in the seas, praising God. This will further involve what David describes God doing in 69:35–36 (MT 69:36–37). Zion will be the capital of the world, with all the cities of Judah flourishing, inhabited by their rightful possessors. The terminology in 69:35 (MT 69:36) is reminiscent of the many promises that Israel would dispossess the inhabitants of Canaan, indicating that the fulfillment of the conquest is in view. That idea is reinforced in 69:36 (MT 69:37), where David describes the seed of the woman, the seed (CSB "descendants;" ESV "offspring") of God's servants, inheriting the land attained by the new conquest and inhabiting it as those who love God's name and renown.

BRIDGE

The use of Ps 69 in the New Testament indicates that this psalm presents David's experience as a typological foreshadowing of what his greater son would endure. The promised king from David's line, Jesus, would also be consumed by zeal for God's house (see the quotation of Ps 69:9 [MT 69:10] in John 2:17).[234] He too would be the object of the scorn of the enemies of God, experiencing the reproaches of those who reproach God falling on him (see the quotation of Ps 69:9 [MT 69:10] in Rom 15:3). Just as David's enemies gave him sour wine/vinegar to drink (Ps 69:21 [MT 69:22]), sour wine was given to Christ on the cross (Matt 27:34; Mark 15:36; Luke 23:36; John 19:29).

The wrath of God visited at the Genesis flood (Gen 6–9) seems to have resulted in flood imagery being employed to depict God's wrath even when people and armies, rather than water, threaten destruction (see esp.

---

[234] For the layers of meaning of this quotation in John, see James M. Hamilton, "John," in *John-Acts*, ESVEC (Wheaton, IL: Crossway, 2019), 64–66.

Ps 124:2, 4; Isa 8:5–8). This imagery appears throughout the Psalter (e.g., Pss 18:4 [MT 18:5]; 29; 88:7, 16–17 [MT 88:8, 17–18]) including Ps 69 (see verses 1–2, 14–15 [MT 2–3, 15–16]). The flood and the reuse of flood imagery throughout the Old Testament inform Jesus describing his experience of God's wrath as a "baptism" he has to undergo (Mark 10:38–39). David was, figuratively speaking, baptized in the waters of God's disciplinary judgment, and David's greater son experienced the fulfilment of baptism into the flood of God's wrath when he was crucified (see also the discussion in this commentary of the psalm texts referenced in this paragraph).

The quotation of Ps 69:9 (MT 69:10) in Rom 15:3 just mentioned is yet another place in the New Testament where the words of David in a psalm are placed directly on the lips of Jesus, as though Jesus himself is the speaker. The explanation for this seems to be that as David spoke of himself in the Psalms, he understood himself to be typifying the seed of promise that God pledged to raise up from his line. When Jesus came as that seed of promise, the words of David, who spoke of himself as a type and shadow of the one to come, flow naturally from the lips of the one who fulfills what David typified.

Along the same lines, the death of Judas is interpreted in Acts 1:20 as a fulfillment of the imprecations David prayed against his enemies in Ps 69:25 (MT 69:26), and Paul cites the imprecation David prays in Ps 69:22–23 (MT 69:23–24) against those who have rejected Jesus in Rom 11:9. These quotations make sense because just as David was a type of Jesus, those aligned with David typified those who follow Jesus, while those who opposed David typified those who would oppose Jesus and his church.

## Psalm 70

OVERVIEW AND STRUCTURE OF PSALM 70

Psalm 70 opens and closes with calls for Yahweh to make haste to help and deliver David (70:1, 5 [MT 70:2, 6]), and in the middle are requests for David's enemies to be put to shame (70:2–3 [MT 70:3–4]) and for his friends to be made glad (70:4 [MT 70:5]). Thus the chiastic structure:[235]

70:1 (MT 70:2), Make Haste to Help and Deliver
   70:2–3 (MT 70:3–4), Let My Enemies Be Put to Shame

---

[235] Similarly Alden, "Chiastic Psalms (II)," 196.

70:4 (MT 70:5), Let All Who Seek You Be Glad
70:5 (MT 70:6), Make Haste to Help and Deliver

SCRIPTURE

CSB

Author's translation

For the choir director. Of David. To
bring remembrance.

¹ For the Preeminent One.
Of David.
For causing remembrance.

¹ God, hurry to rescue me.
LORD, hurry to help me!

² God, to deliver me, O Yahweh, to my
help make haste!

² Let those who seek to kill me
be disgraced and confounded;
let those who wish me harm
be turned back and humiliated.
³ Let those who say, "Aha, aha!"
retreat because of their shame.

³ Let them be ashamed and abashed,
those who seek my life.
Let them be turned back and
humiliated, the ones who delight in
my evil.
⁴ Let them return because of their
shame, those who say, "Aha! Aha!"

⁴ Let all who seek you rejoice and be
glad in you;
let those who love your salvation
continually say, "God is great!"
⁵ I am oppressed and needy;
hurry to me, God.
You are my help and my deliverer;
LORD, do not delay.

⁵ Let them exult and be glad in you, all
who seek you.
And let them say continually, "May
God be great," those who love your
salvation.

⁶ And as for me, afflicted and needy, O
God make haste to me.
My help and the one who delivers me
are you.
O Yahweh do not delay.

CONTEXT: VERBAL AND THEMATIC LINKS WITH SURROUNDING PSALMS

As we near the end of Book 2 of the Psalter, we find David in difficulties
similar to those reflected near the end of Book 1.²³⁶ This impression is
strengthened by the fact that Ps 70 repeats Psalm 40:13–17 (MT 40:14–18)
nearly word for word. The fact that the superscription of Ps 70 includes

---

²³⁶ Rightly Zenger: "The composition made up of Psalms 69–71 is thus a deliberate imi-
tation of the final part of the first Davidic Psalter (Psalms 40–41)," in Hossfeld and Zenger,
*Psalms 2*, 188.

the term להזכיר, "For causing remembrance," indicates that the repetition of the verses from Ps 40 in Ps 70 is meant to bring to remembrance the situation recounted in Ps 40. Interestingly, Ps 40:6–8 (MT 40:7–9) seems to deal with the transition from Saul to David, whereas the superscription of Ps 72 and Ps 72:20 conjoin to point to the transition from David to Solomon.[237]

As we move from the end of Book 1 into Book 2 of the Psalter, we seem to be at the turning point from the days of David being persecuted by Saul to his being enthroned as king. Book 2 opens with a series of psalms of the sons of Korah (Pss 42–49), and the sons of Korah ministered at the house of God after David brought the ark into Jerusalem (1 Chr 6:31).

Just as David was persecuted by Saul before being enthroned as king, at the end of his life he was persecuted by Absalom (2 Sam 15–19). And then prior to Solomon being designated king there was trouble from Adonijah (1 Kgs 1). The prayer for Solomon that concludes the prayers of David in Ps 72 seems to correspond to the anointing of Solomon as king and the establishment of his rule in 1 Kgs 1–2.

If Pss 69–72 comprise a final subunit in Book 2, Pss 70 and 71 cry out for help and vindication before the prayer for the future king in Ps 72.

Psalm 69, The Rejected King
 Psalm 70, Make Haste to Help Me
 Psalm 71, Let Them Be Put to Shame (Not Me)
Psalm 72, Give the King Your Justice and Blessing

Psalm 68 seems to celebrate the triumphant procession of Yahweh from Mount Sinai to Mount Zion. Psalm 69 includes several statements quoted in the crucifixion narratives. Psalm 70 is a cry for God to make haste to deliver and help, and Ps 71 has language that sounds like God will raise the dead (see 71:20). This culminates in the prayer for the Davidic king to bring to pass the blessing of Abraham in Ps 72.

EXPOSITION

The words of Ps 40:13–17 (MT 40:14–18) resonated with Ps 35:4, 21, 25, and 26 and stood at the end of Book 1, speaking of David's utter reliance

---

[237] In Heb 10 these statements in Ps 40:6–8 are cited with reference to another transition, that from the old covenant to the new.

on Yahweh as help and deliverer as he petitioned for his enemies to be humiliated and his friends rejoiced. If it is the case that the flow of thought in the Psalms is tracking with the story of David's life in Samuel and the early narrative of Kings, then the enemies in view in Ps 40 were Saul and his henchmen.

In the new setting in Ps 70, the statements about enemies seem to refer to Absalom and Adonijah, and once again David petitions the Lord to shame his foes and rejoice his friends. With Ps 70 superscripted, "To cause remembrance," the psalm invites remembrance of David's earlier praying of this prayer and comparison with the new circumstances.

Commenting on the word order of the clauses in verses 2–4 (MT 7:3–5), Stephen Dempster notes (private communication): "Note all the verbs in first position and the subjects in last position. The psalmist is desperate for God to act."

The repetition of the words of Ps 40 in the body of Ps 70 indicates that David prayed the same kinds of things about the same kinds of enemies on different occasions in his life. The parallels between the persecutors, the persecuted one, and the prayers prayed in response suggest a perception of similar patterns. These patterns provide the basis for David's typological interpretation of his own experiences.

The repetition of such instances of persecution, prompting the repetition of the same prayer, would lay a foundation of expectation that the future king from David's line would also be persecuted unjustly, in response to which he would rely on God and pray as David did.

### Bridge

David, the seed of the woman, faced opposition from Israelites who proved themselves to be seed of the serpent on multiple occasions in his life, resulting in the repetition of Ps 40:13–17 (MT 40:14–18) in Ps 70. These patterns of persecution and prayer build expectation that the future king will similarly pass through suffering on the way to exaltation. Like David, Jesus, the seed of the woman, was opposed by Israelites who showed themselves to be of their father the devil (John 8:44), seed of the serpent. The prayers of David could rightly be prayed by his greater son, as the New Testament presents him doing (Rom 15:3; Heb 2:12; 10:5–7).

## Psalm 71

OVERVIEW AND STRUCTURE OF PSALM 71

Psalm 71 is unsuperscripted and continues in the vein of prayer seen in Ps 70, even repeating words from 70:1 (MT 70:2) in 71:12, with the result that the first-person singular statements throughout have a Davidic feel.[238] The psalmist opens with a prayer that he not be put to shame (71:1), in the middle he prays for his enemies to be put to shame (71:13), and at the end he says they have been put to shame (71:24). In between are matching statements on how the psalmist has trusted God from youth to old age (71:4–9, 17–21). The full chiastic structure seems to fall out as follows:[239]

71:1–3, Let Me Not Be Put to Shame
  71:4–6, Trust from Youth
    71:7–9, Do Not Cast Me Off in Old Age
      71:10–11, They Think Me God-Forsaken
        71:12–13, Let Them Be Put to Shame
      71:14–16, I Will Praise You
    71:17–18, From Youth to Old Age Forsake Me Not
  71:19–21, You Will Give Life from Death
71:22–24, I Will Praise; They Are Put to Shame

SCRIPTURE

| CSB | Author's translation |
|---|---|
| [1] LORD, I seek refuge in you; let me never be disgraced. [2] In your justice, rescue and deliver me; listen closely to me and save me. [3] Be a rock of refuge for me, where I can always go. Give the command to save me, for you are my rock and fortress. | [1] In you, O Yahweh, I take refuge. Let me not be put to shame to the age. [2] In your righteousness deliver and rescue me. Incline to me your ear and save me. [3] Be to me a rock of habitation to go continually. You commanded to cause salvation for me, |

---

[238] The Greek translation adds a superscription to Ps 71 (LXX Ps 70), Τῷ Δαυιδ. υἱῶν Ιωναδαβ καὶ τῶν πρώτων αἰχμαλωτισθέντων, "Of David. Of the sons of Jonadab and the first carried into captivity." Pietersma argues this was a later development and excludes it from his NETS translation of Psalms. See Pietersma, "Superscriptions of the Greek Psalter," 121–22.

[239] Similarly Alden, "Chiastic Psalms (II)," 197.

⁴Deliver me, my God, from the power
  of the wicked,
from the grasp of the unjust and
  oppressive.
⁵For you are my hope, Lord G{ᴏᴅ},
my confidence from my youth.
⁶I have leaned on you from birth;
you took me from my mother's womb.
My praise is always about you.
⁷I am like a miraculous sign to many,
and you are my strong refuge.
⁸My mouth is full of praise
and honor to you all day long.

⁹Don't discard me in my old age.
As my strength fails, do not abandon
  me.
¹⁰For my enemies talk about me,
and those who spy on me plot
  together,
¹¹saying, "God has abandoned him;
chase him and catch him,
for there is no one to rescue him."
¹²God, do not be far from me;
my God, hurry to help me.
¹³May my adversaries be disgraced
  and destroyed;
may those who intend to harm me
be covered with disgrace and
  humiliation.
¹⁴But I will hope continually
and will praise you more and more.
¹⁵My mouth will tell about your
  righteousness
and your salvation all day long,
though I cannot sum them up.
¹⁶I come because of the mighty acts of
  the Lord G{ᴏᴅ};
I will proclaim your righteousness,
  yours alone.

¹⁷God, you have taught me from my
  youth,
and I still proclaim your wondrous
  works.
¹⁸Even while I am old and gray,

for my high ridge and my stronghold
  you are.

⁴ My God, deliver me from the hand of
  the wicked,
from the palm of the perverter and
  the one who makes bitter.
⁵ For you are my hope, my Lord.
  Yahweh is my trust from my youth.
⁶ Upon you have I leaned from the
  belly of my mother.
From the womb of my mother you are
  the one who cut me.
In you is my praise continually.

⁷ As a portent I am to many, and you
  are my refuge of strength.
⁸ My mouth is full of your praise, all
  the day your beauty.
⁹ Do not cast me away in the time of
  old age.
When my strength is finished do not
  forsake me.

¹⁰ For those at enmity spoke against me.
Those who watch for my soul took
  counsel together,
¹¹ saying, "God has forsaken him.
Pursue and seize him for there is
  none who will deliver."

¹² O God, be not far from me. My God,
  to my help make haste.
¹³ Let them be ashamed and humiliated,
  those who accuse my soul.
Let them be wrapped in reproach and
  humiliation, the ones who seek my
  evil.

¹⁴ But as for me, continually I wait,
  and I will add to your praise.
¹⁵ My mouth will recount your
  righteousness.
All the day your salvation, for I do not
  know the numbers.
¹⁶ I will go in the mighty deeds of my
  Lord Yahweh.

God, do not abandon me,
while I proclaim your power
to another generation,
your strength to all who are to come.
¹⁹ Your righteousness reaches the
heights, God,
you who have done great things;
God, who is like you?
²⁰ You caused me to experience
many troubles and misfortunes,
but you will revive me again.
You will bring me up again,
even from the depths of the earth.
²¹ You will increase my honor
and comfort me once again.
²² Therefore, I will praise you with a
harp
for your faithfulness, my God;
I will sing to you with a lyre,
Holy One of Israel.
²³ My lips will shout for joy
when I sing praise to you
because you have redeemed me.
²⁴ Therefore, my tongue will proclaim
your righteousness all day long,
for those who intend to harm me
will be disgraced and confounded.

I will cause your righteousness to be
remembered, yours alone.

¹⁷ O God, you have taught me from my
youth,
and until now I proclaim your
wonders.
¹⁸ And even to old age and hoary head,
O God do not forsake me until I
proclaim your arm to a generation,
to all who will come your might.

¹⁹ And your righteousness, O God,
unto the height!
You who have done mighty acts, O
God, who is like you?
²⁰ You who have shown us many evil
distresses, you will turn:
you will give us life;
and from the depths of the earth you
will turn:
you will bring me up.
²¹ Multiply my greatness, and come
around:
you will comfort me.

²² Then I will praise you with an
instrument of a harp: your truth,
my God!
I will psalm you with a lyre, O holy
one of Israel.
²³ My lips will shout, for I will psalm
you; and my soul, which you
redeemed.
²⁴ Also my tongue, all the day, will
mutter your righteousness,
for they are ashamed and abashed,
those who seek my evil.

CONTEXT: VERBAL AND THEMATIC LINKS WITH SURROUNDING PSALMS

Psalm 71:1–3 largely repeats Ps 31:1–3. This repetition of material from earlier in David's life reinforces the idea that the kind of persecution he experienced at the beginning has returned at the end. Psalm 71, as noted above, also flows seamlessly (no superscription on Ps 71) from

Ps 70 (which itself reprised Ps 40). The phrase "to my help make haste" in 71:12 is an exact match with the same in 70:1 (MT 70:2), and the call for the enemies to be "ashamed and humiliated" in 71:13 shares language with the same petition in 70:2 (MT 70:3). It is also interesting to observe that just as language from Pss 1 and 2 recurred near the end of Book 1 in Ps 41 (אשרי משכיל ["blessed is the one who causes wisdom"] in 41:2, cf. 1:1; 2:10), language from Pss 1 and 2 recurs near the end of Book 2 (הגה ["mutter"] in 71:24, cf. 1:2; 2:1).

In the discussion of Ps 70 I suggested that the reuse of language from Ps 40, which falls at the end of Book 1, in Ps 70, which falls at the end of Book 2, suggests that the difficulties David had with Saul before he was enthroned are being juxtaposed with the difficulties he had with Absalom and Adonijah at the end of his life. Psalm 71 seems to reinforce these ideas. As the narrative of Kings opens, David is old and incapacitated. Adonijah tries to seize the kingdom, but David's friends help him ensure the enthronement of Solomon, Yahweh's choice (2 Sam 12:24–25).

This sequence is matched by the references in Ps 71 to the speaker, presumably David, being old (71:9, 18). In fact, the phrase "when my strength is finished" in 71:9 employs the same verb that will appear in the statement that the prayers of David are ended in 72:20.

In the narrative of Kings, the threat from Adonijah prompts the anointing of Solomon (1 Kgs 1–2). This seems to be matched in Pss 70–72 as the aged David calls on the Lord to make haste to help him (Ps 70), to put his enemies to shame (Ps 71), and to give his justice to the royal son, to Solomon (Ps 72).

### Exposition

As we have seen him do throughout the Psalter, in Ps 71:1–3 David relies utterly upon the Lord. David opens by asserting that he takes refuge in Yahweh, calling on God not to let him be put to shame (71:1). This idea of not being put to shame will recur throughout the psalm, returning as David calls on the Lord to put his enemies to shame in 71:13, then when he notes that they have been put to shame in 71:24.

Because David has been faithful to the Lord, it is righteous for him to be vindicated and his enemies confounded. This David acknowledges in 71:2 as he calls on the Lord to deliver him in righteousness, and he will reference the Lord's righteousness again in 71:15, 16, 19, and 24.

The Lord's command that causes salvation for David in Ps 71:3 is in keeping with the promises God has made to David and his seed. Those promises guarantee that the Lord will defend David and his house. In keeping with God's character (righteousness in 71:2 and promises-command in 71:3) then, David appeals to the Lord to be a strong and safe place for him to find refuge (71:1, 3).

As so often in the Psalms, the opening cry for deliverance, in this case 71:1–3, will be matched by the closing paean of praise in 71:22–24.

If the Psalter is tracking with David's life as narrated in Samuel and Kings, then the wicked of whom David speaks in 71:4 would be Adonijah and his cabal who sought to seize the kingdom in David's waning days. In this scenario, when David prays for God to rescue him from the hand of the wicked, from the palm of the perverter who makes bitter in 71:4, he prays that the putsch would be put down. From the youthful encounters with a bear against his father's sheep or Goliath against God's people, David's hope and trust has been Yahweh (71:5), thus he leans on and praises the Lord (71:6).

The affirmation of lifelong trust in 71:4–6 is matched in the psalm's chiastic structure by the David's confidence that God will raise the dead in 71:19–21.

David's appeal in 71:7–9 is that the Lord would not cast him off in old age (71:9). He first asserts that he has been "a portent" to many. This term "portent" (מוֹפֵת) is often used to describe the "signs and *wonders*" God did in Egypt through Moses (e.g., Exod 4:21; 7:3, 9; 11:9, 10). This term also appears when Isaiah says that he himself and the children the Lord has given him are "signs and *portents*" (Isa 8:18). The term is used to speak of Ezekiel also as a portent (e.g., Ezek 12:6, 11), and Zechariah uses it to describe Joshua the high priest as a portent (Zech 3:8). These instances of the term in prophetic literature are in cases where the people described as portents are in themselves indicators of what God will do in the future. Isaiah himself typifies things that will be fulfilled in Jesus, and one of his sons is named "Shear Jashub," which means, "a remnant shall return." The boy's name declares that the nation is going into exile, but a remnant will return. His other son's name, "Maher Shalal Hash Baz," indicates that the enemies will swiftly plunder Israel when they send the people into exile. Similar things can be noted about the instances of the term in Ezekiel and Zechariah.

When David declares that he himself is a portent, then, he would appear to affirm that his own life is an installment in the pattern of the righteous sufferer, who is persecuted before being exalted to deliver God's people. This pattern was seen prior to David in the lives of Joseph and Moses. David himself is an installment in this pattern, which points forward to the one in whom the pattern will be fulfilled, the king God promised to raise up from David's line.

Though David is a suffering servant who serves as a portent of things to come, he declares in 71:7 that the Lord has been a strong refuge for him. His mouth is full of God's praise, and his experience of the beauty of the Lord is such that he can talk of it all the day (71:8). Now that he has grown old in God's service, he prays the Lord would not cast him off (71:9).

David's prayer that the Lord not cast him off in old age in 71:7–9 is matched in the psalm's chiastic structure by his appeal in 71:17–18 that he not be cast off now that his hair is hoary and his years many.

The prospect of being forsaken or cast away arises not from any indication that the Lord is only faithful to the young but from the slanders of David's enemies, whom David reports making this claim in Ps 71:10–11. The enemies doing this—taking counsel together to speak these lies about David being cast off in 71:10–11—recalls the description of them gathering together against Yahweh and his anointed in 2:1–3.

The enemy lies and schemes about David's being forsaken in 71:10–11 are matched in the psalm's chiastic structure by David's praise for God in his righteousness and mighty deeds of salvation in 71:14–16.

The center of the chiastic structure of Ps 71 is the twofold prayer in 71:12–13, where David prays that God would be near him and make haste to come to his help (71:12; cf. 70:1, 5 [MT 70:2, 6]), then prays that God would put his enemies to shame (71:13).

Because David's prayers are based squarely on God's character and promises, he is confident that they will be answered. This confidence can be seen in David's jubilant asseveration that he will continue to hope in God and praise him all the more (71:14), his mouth telling of God's righteousness and "all-day" salvation, the numbers of which cannot be known (71:15). David asserts that God's mighty deeds are what will bring him to his destination, and he declares his intention to make all remember God's righteousness and God's alone (71:16).

David recounts in 71:17–18 how he has been taught by the Lord from his youth and still proclaims God's fearsome deeds (71:17), then he again asks not to be forsaken in old age that he might proclaim God's might to the rising generation, to all who will come (71:18). In this psalm and the others, David has proclaimed the Lord's character and work to every generation, and he continues to speak.

In 71:19–21 David declares that God's righteousness is on high, demonstrated in the mighty acts he has done, establishing that there is none like him (cf. Exod 15:11). What better way to speak of the ineffable majesty of the unerring, unmatched rectitude of the Righteous One? His beauty is enough to occupy us all the day (Ps 71:8), his acts on our behalf are innumerable (71:15), and his righteousness soars to the heights.

David speaks of the afflictions he has endured in 71:20 and asserts his confidence that God will give him life, bringing him up from the depths of the earth. This giving of life, bringing up from the depths of the earth, seems most likely to speak of a renewal of life after death, that is, bodily resurrection. God promised to make David's name great in 2 Sam 7:9 (cf. Gen 12:2), and in Ps 71:21 David calls on the Lord to keep that promise (taking the verb as an imperative, rather than an indicative). David further speaks of the Lord's presence and comfort, showing that what he wants is the Lord himself, not merely the making great of his own name. David desires God's presence and the realization of God's purposes, which God has promised to bring about.

At the end of Ps 71, David speaks to how he will respond when God brings about the plan he has promised to enact. In 71:22 he declares that God's truth will prompt him to praise God with harp and lyre, for he is the Holy One of Israel. His redeemed soul will express itself through lips that shout for joy in God, psalming him (71:23), and his tongue will do what Ps 1:3 spoke of with the muttering/meditation on the Torah, muttering out God's righteousness (הגה, 71:24), for at long last the wicked have been put to shame as they deserved (71:24).

BRIDGE

In Ps 71:7 David declares himself a portent, a signifier of what is to come. He is a persecuted servant of the Lord who finds refuge in God, satisfies himself with God's beauty, praises God's righteousness, and from youth to old age walks in God's ways. The enemies of God would put him to shame, but they deserve to have their evil intent rebound upon their own heads, which it will do. God will put them to shame, and the pattern seen in David's life will be fulfilled in the king God raised up from his line, Jesus.

God's people can learn from Ps 71 to pray in accordance with God's character and promises, to know that ephemeral rebellion against God will evaporate before his holy presence, and to answer evil with worship. Ps 71 also testifies that God will raise the dead and that God's beauty is such to occupy us all the day, his deliverances are innumerable, and his righteousness is on high. All this calls us to worship, praise, and render thanks in transfixed wonder.

## Psalm 72

OVERVIEW AND STRUCTURE OF PSALM 72

Psalm 72 seems to be structured along the following chiastic lines:

72:1–4, Justice and Righteousness
   72:5–7, Lasting Shalom
      72:8–11, Worldwide Adamic Dominion
      72:12–14, Justice Executed
   72:15–17, Lasting Reign
72:18–20, Blessed Be Yahweh, May His Glory Fill the Earth

We will pursue the exposition of the psalm according to the following subdivisions of the text:

     72:1–7, The King, Justice, and Shalom
     72:8–14, Adamic Dominion and Justice
     72:15–20, The Davidic King and the Blessing of Abraham

SCRIPTURE

| CSB | Author's translation |
|---|---|
| Of Solomon. | [1] Of Solomon. |
| [1] God, give your justice to the king and your righteousness to the king's son. | O God, your justice to the king give, and your righteousness to the son of the king. |
| [2] He will judge your people with righteousness and your afflicted ones with justice. | [2] May he judge your people in righteousness, and your afflicted ones in justice. |
| [3] May the mountains bring well-being to the people | [3] May the mountains bear shalom for the people, and the hills in righteousness. |

and the hills, righteousness.
⁴ May he vindicate the afflicted among
 the people,
help the poor,
and crush the oppressor.

⁵ May they fear you while the sun
 endures
and as long as the moon, throughout
 all generations.
⁶ May the king be like rain that falls on
 the cut grass,
like spring showers that water the
 earth.
⁷ May the righteous flourish in his
 days
and well-being abound
until the moon is no more.

⁸ May he rule from sea to sea
and from the Euphrates
to the ends of the earth.
⁹ May desert tribes kneel before him
and his enemies lick the dust.
¹⁰ May the kings of Tarshish
and the coasts and islands bring
 tribute,
the kings of Sheba and Seba offer gifts.
¹¹ Let all kings bow in homage to him,
all nations serve him.

¹² For he will rescue the poor who cry
 out
and the afflicted who have no helper.
¹³ He will have pity on the poor and
 helpless
and save the lives of the poor.
¹⁴ He will redeem them from
 oppression and violence,
for their lives are precious in his sight.

¹⁵ May he live long!
May gold from Sheba be given to him.
May prayer be offered for him
 continually,

⁴ May he execute justice for the
 afflicted of the people;
may he cause salvation for the sons of
 the needy;
and may he crush the oppressor.

⁵ May they fear you with the sun,
and before the moon, generation of
 generations.
⁶ May he come down like rain on the
 mown grass,
like abundant showers dripping on
 the earth.
⁷ May the righteous sprout up in his
 days,
and abundance of shalom until the
 moon is no more.

⁸ May he have dominion from sea to
 sea,
and from the river to the ends of the
 earth.
⁹ Before him may the desert dwellers
 bow down,
and may those at enmity with him
 lick the dust.
¹⁰ May the kings of Tarshish and the
 islands bring tribute,
the kings of Sheba and Seba draw
 near with gifts.
¹¹ And may all kings bow down to him.
May all the nations serve him.

¹² For he will deliver the needy who
 cries for help,
along with the afflicted who has no
 helper.
¹³ He will have compassion on the
 poor and needy,
and for the souls of the needy he will
 cause salvation.
¹⁴ From oppression and violence he
 will redeem their soul,
and their blood will be precious in his
 eyes.

and may he be blessed all day long.
¹⁶ May there be plenty of grain in the
    land;
may it wave on the tops of the
    mountains.
May its crops be like Lebanon.
May people flourish in the cities
like the grass of the field.
¹⁷ May his name endure forever;
as long as the sun shines,
may his fame increase.
May all nations be blessed by him
and call him blessed.

¹⁸ Blessed be the Lᴏʀᴅ God, the God of
    Israel,
who alone does wonders.
¹⁹ Blessed be his glorious name
    forever;
the whole earth is filled with his glory.
Amen and amen.
²⁰ The prayers of David son of Jesse are
    concluded.

¹⁵ And may he live! And may he give
    to him from gold of Sheba,
and may he pray for him continually,
    all the day may he bless him.
¹⁶ May there be abundance of grain on
    the earth,
on the head of the mountains may it
    wave, like the Lebanon its fruit;
and may they blossom from the city
    like the green things of the earth.
¹⁷ May his name be to the age; before
    the sun may his name produce
    shoots.
And may they be blessed in him, all
    the nations call him blessed.

¹⁸ Blessed be Yahweh God, God of
    Israel, who alone does wonders.
¹⁹ And blessed be the name of his
    glory to the age,
and may his glory fill the whole of the
    earth. Amen, and amen.
²⁰ The prayers of David the son of
    Jesse are completed.

Cᴏɴᴛᴇxᴛ: Vᴇʀʙᴀʟ ᴀɴᴅ Tʜᴇᴍᴀᴛɪᴄ Lɪɴᴋs ᴡɪᴛʜ Sᴜʀʀᴏᴜɴᴅɪɴɢ Psᴀʟᴍs

Standing at the end of Book 2, Ps 72 brings to a close the prayers of David,
son of Jesse (72:20). Whereas the superscriptions of Books 1 and 2 (Pss
1–72) have sometimes included historical reference points that allow us
to sync the psalm with historical narratives in Samuel or Kings, there are
no such historical points of reference in the superscriptions of Books 3
or 4 and only one in Book 5 (Ps 142). This creates the impression that we
have tracked with the life of the historical David through Books 1 and
2, and that when we enter upon Book 3 we transition to the kings from
David's line.

This transition seems to begin with what appears to be a prayer of
David for Solomon in Ps 72. Psalm 72 joins with the preceding psalms to
hint at the final period of David's life, which included Adonijah's attempt
to seize power, prompting David to install Solomon as his successor and
charge him to keep the Torah as narrated in 1 Kgs 1–2. Whereas 1 Kgs
2:1–9 recounts David's charge to Solomon, Ps 72 seems to stand as David's
prayer for Solomon as he passed the throne to him.

Psalm 72 stands at the end of Book 2, and it reaches back to both Pss 1 and 2 (see also "Context" on Ps 71 for how that psalm does the same). The nations will bless the king from David's line in 72:17 with a term (אשר) from the same root used to describe the blessed man in Ps 1:1 (אשרי), and the worldwide dominion described in 72:8–11 is exactly what the Lord said he would give the anointed one in Ps 2:7–9.

EXPOSITION

### 72:1–7, The King, Justice, and Shalom

The superscription of Psalm 72, "Of Solomon," could indicate that Solomon wrote the psalm. On the basis of the content of the psalm and the reference to the prayers of David being completed in 72:20, however, it seems to me that Ps 72 is a prayer of David for Solomon. As Zenger notes, " 'Of David' is missing from Psalm 72, but the superscription 'For Solomon' is an implicit attribution to David inasmuch as David prays Psalm 72 for his son Solomon."[240] The similarity between what David prays for here in Ps 72 and what is narrated about Solomon in Kings may indicate that the author of Kings was influenced by Ps 72.[241]

The terms "justice" (משפט) and "righteousness" (צדק) join with related concepts to dominate the first four verses of Ps 72. The term "justice" seems to derive from the verb "judge" (שפט), indicating that justice is established through righteous judgment. The term "righteousness" refers to God's upright character and the way his standards of right and wrong are upheld and enforced in the world.

David petitions the Lord to give his own justice to the king in 72:1a, and in what seems to be a parallel statement in 72:1b, he asks for God to give his own righteousness to the son of the king. Parallel terms in 72:1 are "justice" and "righteousness" and "the king" and "the son of the king." This creates the impression that the son of the king has now begun to reign as king, and joined to the superscription "Of Solomon," it seems here that David asks the Lord to give Solomon the ability to apply God's righteous character when he enacts justice by executing judgment.

The petitions that follow after the first seem to flow from it logically: If God answers David's prayer and gives Solomon the ability to

---

[240] Hossfeld and Zenger, *Psalms 2*, 2 n. 2.
[241] Cf. Hossfeld and Zenger, *Psalms 2*, 211 n. 23, "For v. 1 cf. 1 Kgs 3:5–9; for v. 2 cf. 1 Kgs 3:9; for vv. 5–7 cf. 1 Kgs 3:14; for vv. 10–11 cf. 1 Kgs 5:15–26 [ET 5:1–12]; 9:10–14; 10:1–13."

bring God's righteous character to bear in judgment, then the blessings of the covenant and the realization of God's purposes in creation will follow. Throughout the rest of Ps 72 David prays that God would bring to pass both what God set out to accomplish when he made the world and the blessings God promised to Israel when he entered into covenant with them.

The terms "justice" and "righteousness" from 72:1 recur in reverse order in 72:2, as David prays that the king would judge (דִּין) God's people in righteousness and give justice to the afflicted. The term "afflicted" connotes those whose circumstances have humbled them, making them poor, perhaps even desperate. Often such people lack resources and connections, which means that there will be neither financial benefit nor social capital gained from helping them. As a result, they are easily overlooked, or worse, oppressed. This prayer, then, seeks God to make the king one who does justice even for those from whom he stands to gain nothing. Equality before the law, without regard for social standing or the capacity to pay bribes, is precisely what establishes true justice.

David prays in 72:3 that the mountains might lift up *shalom* for the people, and that the hills might do the same, in righteousness. This seems to be a request that God would use the mountains and the hills to hold up the things that make for a holistic enjoyment of God's blessings in God's ways in God's place. Shalom cannot be enjoyed if the land is defiled by sin or if the curses promised to covenant breakers prevail. Thus David prays for the geographical features (mountains and hills) of the land itself to carry *shalom* to God's people in righteousness.

David returns to justice for the afflicted and the needy in 72:4. He adds here that justice for them will give them deliverance, praying also that the righteous king would crush the oppressor, establishing the impression that the needy and afflicted are easily taken advantage of and abused. When David prays that the oppressor would be "crushed," he uses one of the verbs (דכא) that refract the imagery of the seed of the serpent having their heads smashed in Gen 3:15.[242]

The prayers that the king will establish justice and righteousness in Ps 72:1–4 lay the groundwork for the prayers for lasting *shalom* in 72:5–7.

This lasting peace will only be established under the blessing of God, and God blesses those who recognize that he will judge justly in keeping

---

[242] See Hamilton, "Skull Crushing Seed of the Woman."

with his righteous character and respond with a respectful regard for God's commands. That is to say, God blesses those who fear him. Thus David prays in 72:5 that the people would fear God always, as long as the sun and moon remain in the skies, from generation to generation.

The imagery of Ps 72:6, where David prays that the king would be like rain on a cultivated field, is reminiscent of David's description of the just ruler in 2 Sam 23:3–4, which also compares a good king to rain that gives growth to the grass of the field. Like abundant showers on the earth, the good king nourishes the life of the people. The simile captures the beautiful symbiosis between a righteous king and a virtuous populace. People who fear God will experience such a king the way the grass of the field welcomes the dew of the morning and the rain in its season. If the people fear God, they will be pious themselves. And pious people rejoice over righteous leaders. The shared values of the king and the people are thus depicted through an image of organic harmony between the foliage of a fertile land and the water that gives it life.

The imagery of 72:6 continues in 72:7, where David prays that the righteous might sprout up like a healthy plant in the days of the king. Bookending this section of verses, David closes 72:7 the way he opened 72:5, with a prayer that the shalom of the king might abound for as long as the moon haunts the night sky.

In essence, David prays that the reign of the king promised to him might last as long as the world lasts. The expectation that any kingdom might stand so long grows out of the promise in 2 Sam 7:13, where God said the he would establish the throne of the seed of David forever.

## 72:8–14, Adamic Dominion and Justice

The fulfillment of the 2 Sam 7:13 promise to David will also accomplish God's purpose announced at the creation of man in Gen 1:28. God blessed the man and woman and commanded them to "exercise dominion" or "rule" (רדה) over God's creation (Gen 1:28). Using the same verb from Gen 1:28, David prays in Ps 72:8 that the king from his line would have dominion over all the dry lands.

The juxtaposition of these prayers shows that the everlasting Davidic kingdom promised in 2 Sam 7:14 is the worldwide Adamic dominion commanded in Gen 1:28. By means of these prayers, David communicates his hope, based on his understanding of Scripture, that God's purposes for humanity will be achieved through the king from his line.

The figures of speech used to describe the extent of the king's reign in Ps 72:8 speak of all the land between the seas, from the heart of civilization at the great river Euphrates to the farthest reaches of the dry lands.[243] David prayed these words as Solomon took power around 971 BC, and over four hundred years later the prophet Zechariah quoted them around 520 BC to point forward to the king from the line of David whom the faithful continued to expect (see Zech 9:10c, cf. Zech 9:9–10). David prays that the king from his line will reign over all the earth, and the implication that all other kings will be subject to him is traced out in Ps 79:9–11.

Not only do the coastlands bow in Ps 72:9, but also the king's enemies lick the dust (cf. Isa 49:23; Mic 7:17). This poetic reformulation of God's Gen 3:14 words to the serpent (that dust would be his food) significantly interprets both the king and his enemies. Because Gen 3:15 goes on to speak of the enmity between the seed of the woman and the seed of the serpent, the reference to the enemies licking the dust means that those at enmity with the king will come under the same curses that fell on their father the devil. The enemies are hereby identified as the seed of the serpent, and the king is correspondingly identified as the seed of the woman.

The enemies licking the dust allusion to Gen 3:14 in Ps 72:9 immediately follows the reference to Adamic dominion in Ps 72:8, inviting reflection on the way that by his sin Adam forfeited dominion and set up a situation in which the devil would be referred to as "the ruler of this world" (John 12:31). The word of judgment to the serpent in Gen 3:15 indicates that the seed of the woman would defeat him, and the promise to Abraham that God would curse those who dishonor him and bless all the world through him and his seed (Gen 12:3; 18:18, etc.) points to the seed of the woman taking back dominion. In Ps 72:8–9 David prays that the king from his line would bring this to pass as the seed of the woman who would defeat the serpent and his seed and exercise the dominion God gave to Adam.

As faraway places such as coastlands bow to the king in 72:9, the kings of Tarshish, Sheba, and Seba come with gifts of tribute in 72:10. In this scene the kings come marching in and the nations stream to Zion, offering

---

[243] Alternatively, Keel points to "the so-called Babylonian Map of the World," which appears to depict the earth "as circular ... a flat disc ... surrounded by a similarly circular band, the bitter flood." Keel suggests that rather than referring to the Euphrates, "from the river" in Ps 72:8 may point to this circular band around the earth, *Symbolism of the Biblical World*, 20–21. Either way, these phrases describe the entirety of the dry land, the whole world.

their wealth and service to the high king. In Ps 72:11 David makes it explicit that he wants the king's reign to be comprehensive as he prays that *all* kings might bow, *all* nations serve. The term used to describe all kings bowing down before the king from David's line (יִשְׁתַּחֲווּ) is the same used when Joseph dreams that his brothers will bow to him (Gen 37:7, 9, 10) and when Jacob blesses Judah with the words, "the sons of your father will bow to you" (Gen 49:8). Joseph typifies David and Jesus in significant ways, and the king from David's line arises in fulfillment of the blessing of Judah.[244] If God answers David's prayer, the king from his line will be Lord of all.

And he will be worthy. This is not a king who neglects his responsibilities, fails to attend to justice, or uses his power to increase his own luxury and comfort. This king, rather, is one who will hear the cries for help that come from lowly mouths in Ps 72:12. When he reigns, those who have no helper, those who lack resources—those from whom the king will gain nothing—they will gain redress for their wrongs because this king will have God's justice and righteousness (72:1). Psalm 72:13 states that the king's concern for the lowly will spring from a heart of compassion. He will understand the plight of the poor and needy, see their anguish, and rise to make recompense. Psalm 72:14 states that he will redeem the souls of the needy from oppression (just as David prayed that the king would crush oppressors in 72:4). And unlike those hard-hearted rulers who cover their own sins even at the cost of the lives of their loyal subjects (cf. 2 Sam 11:14–24), in the eyes of this king even the blood of nobodies will be precious.

### 72:15–20, The Davidic King and the Blessing of Abraham

The hope that this king will reign forever, a hope based on God's 2 Sam 7:13 promise to establish his throne forever, prompts David to call on God to establish his promise, as he prays in 72:15, "And may he live!" The other prayers in 72:15 seem to be ecstatic exclamations that summarize the glory of the king's reign: the gold of Sheba will be brought to him, prayer will be made for him continually, and God will bless him. I take

---

[244] Hamilton, "Was Joseph a Type of the Messiah?" Samuel C. Emadi argues that the presentation of blessing of Judah intentionally recalls Joseph's dreams because Joseph functions as "a 'narrative prefiguration' of Judah's seed," "Covenant, Typology, and the Story of Joseph: A Literary-Canonical Examination of Genesis 37–50" (PhD diss., Southern Baptist Theological Seminary, 2016), 79.

these statements in 72:15 to express what David wants God to do for the king from his line.

As earlier in the psalm when David prayed that the righteousness of the king would bring the blessings of the covenant (72:2–7), so now the blessings of the covenant are epitomized in 72:16. Here David prays for the grain to be so abundant that it will wave on the mountaintops and be comparable to the fruit of Lebanon. The second line of 72:16 again uses agricultural imagery to speak of the flourishing of the people as David prays that from the city the people would blossom like the blooms of the earth.

The first petition of this section in Ps 72:15 was that the king would live, that his reign might be lasting. David returns to that idea in 72:17 as he calls on the Lord also to keep the 2 Sam 7:9 promise to give him a great name, which reiterates the Lord's Gen 12:2 promise to Abraham to make his name great. David prays that the name of the king from his line would stand to the age to come, and that in the light of the sun his name would be like a plant sending out shoots of new growth. Translations take this to be a prayer that the king's fame would spread and last as long as the sun shines.

The second line of Ps 72:17 picks up the promise God made to Abraham in Gen 12:3, "in you shall all the families of the earth be blessed." When that promise is repeated through the book of Genesis, it is clarified that in Abraham *and in his seed* all the families of the earth will be blessed (Gen 18:18; 22:18; 26:4; 28:14).[245] In a profound affirmation that the blessing of Abraham will be brought to pass by the king from the line of David, David prays, "And may they be blessed in him, all the nations call him blessed." The first statement points to the fulfillment of Gen 12:3 in the seed of David who is the seed of Abraham, blesser of the nations. The second statement identifies this future king from David's line with the blessed man of Ps 1, as the statement "all nations call him blessed" uses a verb built from the same root (אשׁר) as the term employed in Ps 1:1 to announce, "blessed is the man" (אשׁרי). The Ps 1 blessed man is the Ps 72 king from David's line, seed of Abraham in whom all nations will be blessed.

Psalm 72 constitutes a soaring prayer, a pinnacle of Old Testament theology communicating Old Testament hope, as the sweet psalmist of Israel calls on the Lord to keep his promises, along the way interpreting

---

[245] See Hensley, *Covenant Relationships*, 185–89.

the relationships between the statements God has made about what he will do and the means he will use to bring about fulfillment. The crystallization of so much promise and hope into the poetry of Ps 72 can only resolve into doxology, as it does in 72:18–19. The doxology fits the context of Ps 72, but it also stands at the conclusion of Book 2 in the same way that the other books in the Psalter are closed with doxologies (41:13 [MT 41:14]; 89:52 [MT 89:53]; 106:48; Pss 146–150).

David opens the doxology in 72:18 by blessing Yahweh, God of Israel, asserting that he alone does wonders. The wonders in view would seem to be those prayed for in Ps 72. We can summarize the wonders as the fulfillment of God's purposes through the reestablishment of Adamic dominion in fulfillment of Gen 3:15 and the promise to Abraham (Gen 12:1–3) through the reign of the future king from David's line (2 Sam 7). On the one hand, David prays this for Solomon, but on the other hand, the Lord promised to build him a "house" (2 Sam 7:11), which seems to suggest a dynasty, a succession of kings. The promise then goes on to speak of *the* seed whose throne would be established forever (2 Sam 7:13), seeming to point to one future king in whom the hopes would be realized.[246]

David then communicates his desire to see God's glorious name blessed forever in 72:19, praying that the whole earth might be filled with God's glory. Given the context of Ps 72, this is precisely what God has said he will do. Adding a twofold Amen to say "may it be so," the psalm concludes in 72:20 with the note that the prayers of David, son of Jesse, are completed.[247] Hensley observes,

> It is striking that David is cited in genealogical terms with the qualifier בֶּן יִשַׁי [son of Jesse]. This identifies him as the "histor-

---

[246] The quotation of Ps 72:8 in Zech 9:10 referenced above supports the idea that the expectations and hopes prayed for in Ps 72 were not limited to Solomon but extended to the future king from David's line.

[247] David Willgren suggests that Ps 72:20 found its way into the text of Ps 72 not from the hand of the psalm's author, nor even from that of the anthologist/editor who put the finishing touches on the whole book of Psalms, but rather from the hand of a scribe who put the notation there to mark the end of the scroll containing Pss 1–72. David Willgren, "Psalm 72:20: A Frozen Colophon?," *JBL* 135 (2016): 49–60. Willgren proposes that the book of Psalms would have been copied on two scrolls, in which case we might expect a similar colophon at the end of Ps 150. Lacking that, or any other analogous instance of a scribal notation becoming part of the text of Psalms (or of other Scripture), it seems better to regard Ps 72:20 not as a scribal colophon but as part of the author-intended, Spirit-inspired, final form of the canonical text.

ical" David with whom YHWH made his covenant promises in 2 Sam 7. Strikingly, we find the same genealogical expression (דוד בן ישי [David son of Jesse]) in 2 Sam 23:1, which introduces David's *final* words there (ואלה דברי דוד האחרנים [and these are the last words of David]). I propose, then, that editors understood 72:20 as marking the last prayer of the original, *historical* David ben-Jesse.[248]


Bridge

In Ps 72 David prays that the dominion Adam forfeited to the snake would be reclaimed by the seed God promised to raise up from his line (Gen 1:28; Ps 72:8). He prays that the seed of the serpent, the enemies of the Davidic king, might eat dust like their father the devil (Gen 3:14; Ps 72:9). He likewise prays, echoing the head wound to the serpent promised in Gen 3:15, that the seed of the woman, king from his line, would crush the oppressor (Ps 72:4). He prays that God would keep the promises made to him in 2 Sam 7 and make the name of the king from his line great (Ps 72:17; 2 Sam 7:9), and that as God promised to establish the throne of his descendent forever, the king from his line would reign forever (Ps 72:5, 7, 15, 17; 2 Sam 7:13). David prays that as God promised to bless all nations through Abraham and his seed, God would bless all people in the king from his line (Ps 72:17; Gen 12:3; 22:18, etc.). David asks that the king from his line would establish justice, and that the world would be filled with God's glory through his reign (Ps 72:1, 19), thus accomplishing all God's purposes.

The significance of the content of Ps 72 only grows when we consider its strategic location in the Psalter. Psalm 1 introduced the blessed man, and Ps 2 identified him as the Lord's anointed, opposed by God's own enemies, but destined to rule the world. Psalm 72 presents David's prayer for the Lord's anointed, and his worldwide reign will result in nothing less than God's glory covering the dry lands as the waters cover the sea.

God answered the prayer of David in Ps 72 by raising up the Lord Jesus, the righteous one, who will fill the world with God's glory.

---

[248] Hensley, *Covenant Relationships*, 53 (emphasis original).

# BIBLIOGRAPHY

Alden, Robert L. "Chiastic Psalms: A Study in the Mechanics of Semitic Poetry in Psalms 1–50." *JETS* 17 (1974): 11–28.

———. "Chiastic Psalms (II): A Study in the Mechanics of Semitic Poetry in Psalms 51–100." *JETS* 19 (1976): 191–200.

———. "Chiastic Psalms (III): A Study in the Mechanics of Semitic Poetry in Psalms 101–150." *JETS* 21 (1978): 199–210.

Alexander, T. Desmond. "Further Observations on the Term 'Seed' in Genesis." *TynBul* 48 (1997): 363–67.

———. "Genealogies, Seed, and the Compositional Unity of Genesis." *TynBul* 44 (1993): 255–70.

———. "The Old Testament View of Life After Death." *Them* 11.2 (1986): 41–46.

———. *The Servant King: The Bible's Portrait of the Messiah.* Leicester: Inter-Varsity Press, 1998.

Allen, Ronald B. *And I Will Praise Him: A Guide to Worship in the Psalms.* Grand Rapids: Kregel, 1999.

Alter, Robert. *The Book of Psalms: A Translation with Commentary.* New York: Norton, 2007.

———. "Introduction." Pages ix–xlviii in *The Five Books of Moses: A Translation with Commentary.* Translated by Robert Alter. New York: Norton, 2004.

Amzallag, Nissim. "Psalm 67 and the Cosmopolite Musical Worship of YHWH." *BBR* 25 (2015): 171–87.

Athanasius. "The Letter of St. Athanasius to Marcellinus on the Interpretation of the Psalms." Pages 97–119 in *On the Incarnation: The Treatise De incarnatione Verbi Dei.* Crestwood, NY: St. Vladimir's Seminary Press, 1998.

Augustine of Hippo. *Expositions on the Book of Psalms.* NPNF 1/8.

Baker, David W. "Meshech." Page 711 in vol. 4 of *Anchor Bible Dictionary.* Edited by David Noel Freedman. 6 vols. New York: Doubleday, 1992.

Balla, Peter. "2 Corinthians." Pages 753–83 in *Commentary on the New Testament Use of the Old Testament.* Edited by D. A Carson and G. K. Beale. Grand Rapids: Baker Academic, 2007.

Barré, Lloyd M. "Recovering the Literary Structure of Psalm XV." *VT* 34 (1984): 207–11.

Barshinger, David P. *Jonathan Edwards and the Psalms: A Redemptive-Historical Vision of Scripture.* New York: Oxford University Press, 2014.

Basson, Alec. *Divine Metaphors in Selected Hebrew Psalms of Lamentation.* FAT 2/15. Tübingen: Mohr Siebeck, 2006.

Bates, Matthew W. *The Birth of the Trinity: Jesus, God, and Spirit in New Testament and Early Christian Interpretations of the Old Testament.* New York: Oxford University Press, 2015.

———. *The Hermeneutics of the Apostolic Proclamation: The Center of Paul's Method of Scriptural Interpretation.* Waco, TX: Baylor University Press, 2019.

Beale, G. K. *The Temple and the Church's Mission: A Biblical Theology of the Dwelling Place of God.* NSBT 17. Downers Grove, IL: InterVarsity Press, 2004.

———. *We Become What We Worship: A Biblical Theology of Idolatry.* Downers Grove, IL: InterVarsity Press, 2008.

Beckwith, Roger T. "The Early History of the Psalter." *TynBul* 46 (1995): 1–27.

———. *The Old Testament Canon of the New Testament Church and Its Background in Early Judaism.* Grand Rapids: Eerdmans, 1985.

Brenton, Lancelot C. *The Septuagint with Apocrypha: Greek and English.* Peabody, MA: Hendrickson, 1986.

Brotzman, Ellis R. *Old Testament Textual Criticism: A Practical Introduction.* Grand Rapids: Baker, 1994.

Brouwer, Wayne. "Understanding Chiasm and Assessing Macro-Chiasm as a Tool of Biblical Interpretation." *CJT* 53 (2018): 99–127.

Brown, William P. "The Psalms: An Overview." Pages 1–23 in *The Oxford Handbook of the Psalms.* Edited by William P. Brown. New York: Oxford University Press, 2014.

Bullock, C. Hassell. "The Shape of the Torah as Reflected in the Psalter, Book 1." Pages 31–50 in *From Creation to New Creation: Essays in Honor of G. K. Beale.* Edited by Daniel M. Gurtner and Benjamin L. Gladd. Peabody, MA: Hendrickson, 2013.

Butterfield, Rosaria. "How Psalm 113 Changed My Life." *9Marks*, December 10, 2019. https://www.9marks.org/article/how-psalm-113-changed-my-life/.

Carr, David M. *Writing on the Tablet of the Heart: Origins of Scripture and Literature.* New York: Oxford University Press, 2005.

Carter, Craig A. *Interpreting Scripture with the Great Tradition: Recovering the Genius of Premodern Exegesis.* Grand Rapids: Baker Academic, 2018.

Charry, Ellen T. *Psalms 1–50: Sighs and Songs of Israel.* BTCB. Grand Rapids: Brazos, 2015.

Chase, Mitchell L. "From Dust You Shall Arise: Resurrection Hope in the Old Testament." *SBJT* 18.4 (2014): 9–29.

Chesterton, G. K. *Orthodoxy.* Colorado Springs: Waterbrook, 2001.

Ciampa, Roy E. "The History of Redemption." Pages 254–308 in *Central Themes in Biblical Theology: Mapping Unity in Diversity.* Edited by Scott J. Hafemann and Paul R. House. Grand Rapids: Baker Academic, 2007.

Cole, Robert L. *Psalms 1-2: Gateway to the Psalter.* HBM 37. Sheffield: Sheffield Phoenix, 2013.

———. *The Shape and Message of Book III (Psalms 73-89).* JSOTSup 307. Sheffield: Sheffield Academic, 2000.

Compton, Jared. *Psalm 110 and the Logic of Hebrews.* LNTS 537. New York: T&T Clark, 2015.

Cook, Edward M., trans. *The Psalms Targum: An English Translation.* 2001. http://www.targum.info/pss/tg_ps_index.htm.

Craigie, Peter C. *Psalms 1-50.* WBC 19. Waco, TX: Word, 1983.

Crutchfield, John C. *Psalms in Their Context: An Interpretation of Psalms 107-118.* PBM. London: Paternoster, 2011.

Damico, Matt. "Congregational Worship Should Be Peculiar." Center For Baptist Renewal. May 8, 2017. http://www.centerforbaptistrenewal.com/blog/2017/5/1/congregational-worship-should-be-peculiar.

Dempster, Stephen G. *Dominion and Dynasty: A Biblical Theology of the Hebrew Bible.* NSBT 15. Downers Grove, IL: InterVarsity Press, 2003.

———. "An 'Extraordinary Fact': Torah and Temple and the Contours of the Hebrew Canon, Part 1." *TynBul* 48 (1997): 23–56.

———. "The Servant of the Lord." Pages 128–78 in *Central Themes in Biblical Theology: Mapping Unity in Diversity.* Edited by Scott J. Hafemann and Paul R. House. Grand Rapids: Baker Academic, 2007.

Dolezal, James E. *All That Is in God: Evangelical Theology and the Challenge of Classical Christian Theism.* Grand Rapids: Reformation Heritage Books, 2017.

Dostoyevsky, Fyodor. *Crime and Punishment.* Translated by Richard Pevear and Larissa Volokhonsky. New York: Knopf, 1993.

Douglas, Mary. *Thinking in Circles: An Essay on Ring Composition.* Terry Lectures. New Haven: Yale University Press, 2010.

Edenburg, Cynthia. "Intertextuality, Literary Competence and the Question of Readership: Some Preliminary Observations." *JSOT* 35 (2010): 131–48.

Edwards, Timothy. *Exegesis in the Targum of Psalms: The Old, the New, and the Rewritten.* GDBS 28. Piscataway, NJ: Gorgias, 2007.

Eller, Vernard. *The Language of Canaan and the Grammar of Feminism.* Grand Rapids: Eerdmans, 1982.

Emadi, Matthew Habib. "The Royal Priest: Psalm 110 in Biblical-Theological Perspective." PhD diss., Southern Baptist Theological Seminary, 2016.

Emadi, Samuel Cyrus. "Covenant, Typology, and the Story of Joseph: A Literary-Canonical Examination of Genesis 37–50." PhD diss., Southern Baptist Theological Seminary, 2016.

Freedman, David Noel. *Psalm 119: The Exaltation of Torah.* BJSUCSD 6. Winona Lake, IN: Eisenbrauns, 1999.

Galbraith, Robert. *The Cuckoo's Nest.* New York: Little, Brown, 2013.

Gallagher, Edmon L., and John D. Meade. *The Biblical Canon Lists from Early Christianity: Texts and Analysis.* Oxford: Oxford University Press, 2018.

Gay, Jason. "Here's Stephen Curry's Best Shot." *Wall Street Journal*, April 15, 2015. http://www.wsj.com/articles/heres-stephen-currys-best-shot-14291 37846.

Gelston, Anthony. "Editorial Arrangement in Book IV of the Psalter." Pages 165–76 in *Genesis, Isaiah and Psalms: A Festschrift to Honour Professor John Emerton for His Eightieth Birthday*. Edited by Katharine J. Dell, Graham Davies, and Yee Von Koh. VTSup 135. Leiden: Brill, 2010.

Gentry, Peter J. "The Septuagint and the Text of the Old Testament." *BBR* 16 (2006): 193–218.

———. "The Text of the Old Testament." *JETS* 52 (2009): 19–45.

Gentry, Peter J., and Stephen J. Wellum. *Kingdom through Covenant: A Biblical-Theological Understanding of the Covenants*. 2nd ed. Wheaton, IL: Crossway, 2018.

Ginsburg, Mirra. "On the Translation." In *Notes from Underground*. By Fyodor Dostoyevsky. New York: Bantam, 1974.

Goldingay, John. *Psalms 1–41*. BCOTWP. Grand Rapids: Baker Academic, 2006.

———. *Psalms 90–150*. BCOTWP. Grand Rapids: Baker Academic, 2008.

Goldsworthy, Graeme. *Prayer and the Knowledge of God: What the Whole Bible Teaches*. Leicester: Inter-Varsity Press, 2003.

Grant, Jamie A. *The King as Exemplar: The Function of Deuteronomy's Kingship Law in the Shaping of the Book of Psalms*. AcBib 17. Atlanta: Society of Biblical Literature, 2004.

Gray, Alison Ruth. *Psalm 18 in Words and Pictures: A Reading through Metaphor*. BibInt 127. Leiden: Brill, 2014.

Gergory of Nazianzus. *On God and Christ: The Five Theological Orations and Two Letters to Cledonius*. Translated by Frederick Williams and Lionel Wickham. Crestwood, NY: St Vladimirs Seminary Press, 2002.

Gregory of Nyssa. *Gregory of Nyssa's Treatise on the Inscriptions of the Psalms*. Translated by Ronald E. Heine. OECS. Oxford: Clarendon, 1995.

Gundersen, David Alexander. "Davidic Hope in Book IV of the Psalter (Psalms 90–106)." PhD diss., Southern Baptist Theological Seminary, 2015.

Gunkel, Hermann. *The Psalms: A Form-Critical Introduction*. Translated by Thomas M. Horner. Facet Books 19. Philadelphia: Fortress, 1967.

Gurnall, William, and John Campbell. *The Christian in Complete Armour*. London: Tegg, 1845.

Hafemann, Scott J. "The Covenant Relationship." Pages 20–65 in *Central Themes in Biblical Theology: Mapping Unity in Diversity*. Edited by Scott J. Hafemann and Paul R. House. Grand Rapids: Baker Academic, 2007.

Hahn, Scott W. *Kinship by Covenant: A Canonical Approach to the Fulfillment of God's Saving Promises*. ABRL. New Haven: Yale University Press, 2009.

Hamilton, James M. "Canonical Biblical Theology." Pages 59–73 in *God's Glory Revealed in Christ: Essays in Honor of Thomas R. Schreiner*. Edited by Denny Burk, James M. Hamilton, and Brian J. Vickers. Nashville: Broadman & Holman, 2019.

———. "God with Men in the Prophets and the Writings: An Examination of the Nature of God's Presence." *SBET* 23 (2005): 166–93.

———. "God with Men in the Torah." *WTJ* 65 (2003): 113–33.

———. *God's Glory in Salvation through Judgment: A Biblical Theology.* Wheaton, IL: Crossway, 2010.

———. *God's Indwelling Presence: The Holy Spirit in the Old and New Testaments.* NAC Studies in Bible and Theology. Nashville: Broadman & Holman, 2006.

———. "John." Pages 17–308 in *John-Acts.* ESVEC 9. Wheaton, IL: Crossway, 2019.

———. "The Lord's Supper in Paul: An Identity-Forming Proclamation of the Gospel." Pages 68–102 in *The Lord's Supper: Remembering and Proclaiming Christ until He Comes.* Edited by Thomas R. Schreiner and Matthew R. Crawford. Nashville: Broadman & Holman, 2010.

———. "Original Sin in Biblical Theology." Pages 189–208 in *Adam, the Fall, and Original Sin: Theological, Biblical, and Scientific Perspectives.* Edited by Hans Madueme and Michael Reeves. Grand Rapids: Baker Academic, 2014.

———. "The Seed of the Woman and the Blessing of Abraham." *TynBul* 58 (2007): 253–73.

———. "The Skull Crushing Seed of the Woman: Inner-Biblical Interpretation of Genesis 3:15." *SBJT* 10.2 (2006): 30–54.

———. *Song of Songs: A Biblical-Theological, Allegorical, Christological Interpretation.* Focus on the Bible. Fearn: Christian Focus, 2015.

———. "Still Sola Scriptura: An Evangelical View of Scripture." Pages 215–40 in *The Sacred Text: Excavating the Texts, Exploring the Interpretations, and Engaging the Theologies of the Christian Scriptures.* Edited by Michael Bird and Michael W. Pahl. Gorgias Précis Portfolios. Piscataway, NJ: Gorgias, 2010.

———. "That the Coming Generation Might Praise the Lord." *Journal of Family Ministry* 1 (2010): 10–17.

———. "Was Joseph a Type of the Messiah? Tracing the Typological Identification between Joseph, David, and Jesus." *SBJT* 12.4 (2008): 52–77.

———. *What Is Biblical Theology? A Guide to the Bible's Story, Symbolism, and Patterns.* Wheaton, IL: Crossway, 2014.

———. "Who Can Be Saved? A Review Article." *TJ* 28 (2007): 89–112.

———. *With the Clouds of Heaven: The Book of Daniel in Biblical Theology.* NSBT 32. Downers Grove, IL: InterVarsity Press, 2014.

———. *Work and Our Labor in the Lord.* Short Studies in Biblical Theology. Wheaton, IL: Crossway, 2017.

Hamilton, Jill. "Psalm 135:5–7." Page 385 in *Women at Southern: A Walk through Psalms.* Edited by Jaye Martin and Alyssa Caudill. Louisville: Southern Baptist Theological Seminary Press, 2010.

Harman, Allan M. "The Exodus and the Sinai Covenant in the Book of Psalms." *RTR* 73 (2014): 3–27.

Hays, Richard B. *Reading Backwards: Figural Christology and the Fourfold Gospel Witness.* Waco, TX: Baylor University Press, 2014.

Hensley, Adam D. *Covenant Relationships and the Editing of the Hebrew Psalter.* LHBOTS 666. New York: T&T Clark, 2018.

Homer. *The Iliad*. Translated by Robert Fagles. New York: Viking, 1990.

Hossfeld, Frank-Lothar, and Erich Zenger. *Psalms 2: A Commentary on Psalms 51–100*. Hermeneia. Minneapolis: Fortress, 2005.

———. *Psalms 3: A Commentary on Psalms 101–150*. Hermeneia. Minneapolis: Fortress, 2011.

House, Paul R. "The Day of the Lord." Pages 179–224 in *Central Themes in Biblical Theology: Mapping Unity in Diversity*. Edited by Scott J. Hafemann and Paul R. House. Grand Rapids: Baker Academic, 2007.

Howard, David M. "Psalms Study Notes." Pages 968–1187 in *NIV Zondervan Study Bible*. Edited by D. A. Carson. Grand Rapids: Zondervan, 2015.

———. *The Structure of Psalms 93–100*. BJSUCSD 5. Winona Lake, IN: Eisenbrauns, 1997.

Huffmon, Herbert B. "The Treaty Background of Hebrew *Yāda'*." BASOR 181 (1966): 31–37.

Hutchinson, James Hely. "The Psalter as a Book." Pages 23–45 in *Stirred by a Noble Theme: The Book of Psalms in the Life of the Church*. Edited by Andrew G. Shead. Nottingham: Apollos, 2013.

Janse, Sam. *You Are My Son: The Reception History of Psalm 2 in Early Judaism and the Early Church*. CBET 51. Leuven: Peeters, 2009.

Jobes, Karen, and Moisés Silva. *Invitation to the Septuagint*. Grand Rapids: Baker Academic, 2000.

Joüon, Paul. *A Grammar of Biblical Hebrew*. Translated and revised by T. Muraoka. 2 vols. SubBi 14. Rome: Pontifical Biblical Institute, 1996.

Joyce, James. *Finnegans Wake*. Penguin, 1999.

Keel, Othmar. *The Symbolism of the Biblical World: Ancient Near Eastern Iconography and the Book of Psalms*. New York: Seabury, 1978.

Keller, Timothy, and Kathy Keller. *The Songs of Jesus: A Year of Daily Devotions in the Psalms*. New York: Viking, 2015.

Kidner, Derek. *Psalms 1–72: An Introduction and Commentary*. TOTC. London: Inter-Varsity Press, 1973.

———. *Psalms 73–150: A Commentary on Books III–V of the Psalms*. TOTC. London: Inter-Varsity Press, 1975.

Kimelman, Reuven. "Psalm 145: Theme, Structure, and Impact." *JBL* 113 (1994): 37–58.

Kselman, John S. "Psalm 77 and the Book of Exodus." *JANESCU* 15 (1983): 51–58.

Kugel, James L. *The Idea of Biblical Poetry: Parallelism and Its History*. Baltimore: Johns Hopkins University Press, 1981.

Kwakkel, Gert. *According to My Righteousness: Upright Behaviour as Grounds for Deliverance in Psalms 7, 17, 18, 26, and 44*. OTS 46. Leiden: Brill, 2002.

Kynes, Will. *My Psalm Has Turned into Weeping: Job's Dialogue with the Psalms*. BZAW 437. Berlin: de Gruyter, 2012.

———. *An Obituary for "Wisdom Literature": The Birth, Death, and Intertextual Reintegration of a Biblical Corpus*. Oxford: Oxford University Press, 2019.

Leithart, Peter J. *Deep Exegesis: The Mystery of Reading Scripture*. Waco, TX: Baylor, 2009.

————. *A Son to Me: An Exposition of 1 & 2 Samuel*. Moscow, ID: Canon, 2003.

"*Les Miserables* Musical Lyrics." https://www.allmusicals.com/l/lesmiserables.htm.

Levenson, Jon D. *Resurrection and the Restoration of Israel: The Ultimate Victory of the God of Life*. New Haven: Yale University Press, 2008.

————. "The Sources of Torah: Psalm 119 and the Modes of Revelation in Second Temple Judaism." Pages 559–74 in *Ancient Israelite Religion: Essays in Honor of Frank Moore Cross*. Edited by Patrick D. Miller, Paul D. Hanson, and S. Dean Mcbride. Philadelphia: Fortress, 1987.

Lewis, C. S. *The Discarded Image: An Introduction to Medieval and Renaissance Literature*. Cambridge: Cambridge University Press, 1964.

————. *Inspirational Writings of C. S. Lewis: Surprised by Joy, Reflections on the Psalms, the Four Loves, the Business of Heaven*. New York: Inspiration Press, 1991.

————. *Mere Christianity*. New York: Macmillan, 1952.

Lohfink, Norbert, and Erich Zenger. *The God of Israel and the Nations: Studies in Isaiah and the Psalms*. Translated by Everett R. Kalin. Collegeville, MN: Liturgical Press, 2000.

McFall, Leslie. "The Evidence for a Logical Arrangement of the Psalter." *WTJ* 62 (2000): 223–56.

Mckelvey, Michael G. *Moses, David and the High Kingship of Yahweh: A Canonical Study of Book IV of the Psalter*. GDBS 55. Piscataway, NJ: Gorgias, 2010.

McRaven, William H. "Adm. McRaven Urges Graduates to Find Courage to Change the World." *UT News*, May 16, 2014. http://news.utexas.edu/2014/05/16/admiral-mcraven-commencement-speech.

Meacham, Jon. *Thomas Jefferson: The Art of Power*. New York: Random House, 2012.

Millar, J. Gary. *Calling on the Name of the Lord: A Biblical Theology of Prayer*. NSBT 38. Downers Grove, IL: InterVarsity Press, 2016.

Miranda, Lin-Manuel, and Jeremy McCarter. *Hamilton: The Revolution*. New York: Grand Central Publishing, 2016.

Mitchell, David C. *The Message of the Psalter: An Eschatological Programme in the Book of Psalms*. JSOTSup 252. Sheffield: Sheffield Academic, 1997.

Morales, L. Michael. *Who Shall Ascend the Mountain of the Lord? A Biblical Theology of the Book of Leviticus*. NSBT 37. Downers Grove, IL: InterVarsity Press, 2015.

Morgan, Robert, ed. *The Nature of New Testament Theology: The Contribution of William Wrede and Adolf Schlatter*. SBT 2/25. Naperville, IL: Allenson, 1973.

Motyer, Stephen. "The Psalm Quotations of Hebrews 1: A Hermeneutic-Free Zone?" *TynBul* 50 (1999): 3–22.

Muilenburg, James. "Introduction." Pages iii–ix in *The Psalms: A Form-Critical Introduction*. By Hermann Gunkel. Translated by Thomas M. Horner. Philadelphia: Fortress, 1967.

O'Callaghan, Roger. "Echoes of Canaanite Literature in the Psalms." *VT* 4 (1954): 164–76.

Packer, J. I. *Knowing God*. Downers Grove, IL: InterVarsity Press, 1993.

Peterson, David G. *Commentary on Romans*. Biblical Theology for Christian Proclamation. Nashville: Broadman & Holman, 2017.

Pietersma, Albert. "Exegesis and Liturgy in the Superscriptions of the Greek Psalter." Pages 99–138 in *X Congress of the International Organization for Septuagint and Cognate Studies.* Edited by Bernard A. Taylor. SCS 51. Atlanta: Society of Biblical Literature, 2001.

Piper, John. *God's Passion for His Glory: Living the Vision of Jonathan Edwards, with the Complete Text of The End for Which God Created the World.* Wheaton, IL: Crossway, 1998.

Plumer, William S. *Psalms: A Critical and Expository Commentary with Doctrinal and Practical Remarks.* Philadelphia: Lippincott, 1867. Repr. Carlisle, PA: Banner of Truth, 2016.

Potter, Harry. "The New Covenant in Jeremiah XXXI 31–34." *VT* 33 (1983): 347–57.

"Psalm 145." Wikipedia, April 3, 2018. https://en.wikipedia.org/w/index.php ?title=Psalm_145&oldid=833919731.

Rahlfs, Alfred. *Psalmi cum Odis.* SVTG 10. Göttingen: Vandenhoeck & Ruprecht, 1979.

Rashi. *Commentary on Psalms.* Translated by Mayer I. Gruber. Philadelphia: Jewish Publication Society, 2008.

Rendtorff, Rolf. "The Psalms of David: David in the Psalms." Pages 53–64 in *The Book of Psalms: Composition and Reception.* Edited by Peter W. Flint and Patrick D. Miller. VTSup 99. Leiden: Brill, 2005.

Rieff, Philip. *Freud: The Mind of the Moralist.* Chicago: University of Chicago Press, 1979.

Robar, Elizabeth. *The Verb and the Paragraph in Biblical Hebrew: A Cognitive-Linguistic Approach.* SSLL 78. Leiden: Brill, 2015.

Robertson, O. Palmer. *The Flow of the Psalms: Discovering Their Structure and Theology.* Phillipsburg, NJ: P&R, 2015.

Ross, Allen P. *A Commentary on the Psalms: 1–41.* Grand Rapids: Kregel, 2012.

———. *A Commentary on the Psalms: 90–150.* Grand Rapids: Kregel, 2016.

Sarna, Nahum M. *On the Book of Psalms: Exploring the Prayers of Ancient Israel.* New York: Schocken Books, 1993.

Schaper, Joachim. *Eschatology in the Greek Psalter.* WUNT 2/76. Tübingen: Mohr Siebeck, 1995.

Schreiner, Thomas R. "The Commands of God." Pages 66–101 in *Central Themes in Biblical Theology: Mapping Unity in Diversity.* Edited by Scott J. Hafemann and Paul R. House. Grand Rapids: Baker Academic, 2007.

———. *Commentary on Hebrews.* Evangelical Biblical Theology Commentary. Bellingham, WA: Lexham Press, 2020.

Seitz, Christopher R. "Psalm 34: Redaction, Inner-Biblical Exegesis and the Longer Psalm Superscriptions—'Mistake' Making and Theological Significance." Pages 279–98 in *The Bible as Christian Scripture: The Work of Brevard S. Childs.* Edited by Christopher R. Seitz and Kent Harold Richards. Atlanta: Society of Biblical Literature, 2013.

Sequeira, Aubrey Maria. "The Hermeneutics of Eschatological Fulfillment in Christ: Biblical-Theological Exegesis in the Epistle to the Hebrews." PhD diss., Southern Baptist Theological Seminary, 2017.

Sharwood, Anthony. "Lionel Messi Is 'Still Cool Even with a Tarantula in His Shorts.' " *Huffington Post*, April 24, 2017. http://www.huffingtonpost. com.au/2017/04/24/lionel-messi-is-still-cool-even-with-a-tarantula-in-his-shorts_a_22052703/.

Sherrin, Ned, ed. *Oxford Dictionary of Humorous Quotations*. 4th ed. New York: Oxford University Press, 2008.

Snearly, Michael K. *The Return of the King: Messianic Expectation in Book V of the Psalter*. LHBOTS 624. New York: T&T Clark, 2016.

Spurgeon, Charles Haddon. *The Treasury of David*. 3 vols. Peabody, MA: Hendrickson, 2008.

Stec, David M. *Targum of Psalms*. ArBib 16. Collegeville, MN: Liturgical Press, 2004.

Stevens, Wallace. "Sunday Morning." Poetry Foundation. https://www.poetry-foundation.org/poetrymagazine/poems/13261/sunday-morning.

Steymans, Hans Ulrich. "Harry Potter's Preservation and Horus' Protective Power: The Semiotic of the Horus-Stelae and the Semantic of Psalm 91:13." Pages 126–46 in *Psalms and Mythology*. Edited by Dirk J. Human. LHBOTS 462. New York: T&T Clark, 2007.

Swale, Matthew E. "Structure, Allusion, Theology, and Contemporary Address in Psalm 106." *BSac* 176 (2019): 400–17.

Talshir, Zipora. "Several Canon-Related Concepts Originating in Chronicles." *ZAW* 113 (2001): 386–403.

Tate, Marvin E. *Psalms 51-100*. WBC 20. Nashville: Nelson, 1991.

Taylor, Charles. *A Secular Age*. Cambridge: Belknap, 2007.

Tiessen, Terrance L. *Who Can Be Saved? Reassessing Salvation in Christ and World Religions*. Downers Grove, IL: InterVarsity Press, 2004.

Tigay, Jeffrey H. *The Evolution of the Gilgamesh Epic*. Philadelphia: University of Pennsylvania Press, 1982.

Tomasino, Anthony. "עוֹלָם." Pages 345–51 in vol. 3 of *New International Dictionary of Old Testament Theology and Exegesis*. Edited by Willem VanGemeren. 5 vols. Grand Rapids: Zondervan, 1997.

Tov, Emanuel. *Textual Criticism of the Hebrew Bible*. 3rd ed. Minneapolis: Fortress, 2011.

Tsumura, David Toshio. *The First Book of Samuel*. NICOT. Grand Rapids: Eerdmans, 2007.

VanGemeren, Willem A. *Psalms*. EBC 5. Grand Rapids: Zondervan, 2008.

Walford, Nancy deClaisse-, Rolf A. Jacobson, and Beth LaNeel Tanner. *The Book of Psalms*. NICOT. Grand Rapids: Eerdmans, 2014.

Waltke, Bruce K., and Michael P. O'Connor. *An Introduction to Biblical Hebrew Syntax*. Winona Lake, IN: Eisenbrauns, 1990.

Wardlaw, Terrance R. *Elohim within the Psalms: Petitioning the Creator to Order Chaos in Oral-Derived Literature*. LHBOTS 602. New York: Bloomsbury, 2015.

Watson, Francis. *Text and Truth: Redefining Biblical Theology*. Edinburgh: T&T Clark, 1997.

Watson, Rebecca S. *Chaos Uncreated: A Reassessment of the Theme of "Chaos" in the Hebrew Bible*. BZAW 341. New York: de Gruyter, 2005.

Watson, Wilfred G. E. *Classical Hebrew Poetry: A Guide to Its Techniques.* JSOTSup 26. New York: T&T Clark, 2001.

Wellum, Stephen J. *God the Son Incarnate: The Doctrine of Christ.* Foundations of Evangelical Theology. Wheaton, IL: Crossway, 2016.

Wenham, Gordon J. *Psalms as Torah: Reading Biblical Song Ethically.* Grand Rapids: Baker Academic, 2012.

———. *The Psalter Reclaimed: Praying and Praising with the Psalms.* Wheaton, IL: Crossway, 2013.

———. "Sanctuary Symbolism in the Garden of Eden Story." Pages 399–404 in *I Studied Inscriptions from before the Flood: Ancient Near Eastern, Literary, and Linguistic Approaches to Genesis 1–11.* Edited by Richard Hess and David Toshio Tsumara. SBTS 4. Winona Lake, IN: Eisenbrauns, 1994.

Wesselschmidt, Quentin F., ed. *Psalms 51–150.* ACCS 8. Downers Grove, IL: InterVarsity Press, 2007.

Willgren, David. "Psalm 72:20: A Frozen Colophon?" *JBL* 135 (2016): 49–60.

Wilson, Gerald Henry. *The Editing of the Hebrew Psalter.* SBLDS 76. Chico, CA: Scholars Press, 1985.

Wilson, Victor M. *Divine Symmetries: The Art of Biblical Rhetoric.* Lanham, MD: University Press of America, 1997.

Wittstruck, Thorne. *The Book of Psalms: An Annotated Bibliography.* 2 vols. Books of the Bible 5. New York: Garland, 1994.

Wright, N. T. *The New Testament and the People of God.* Christian Origins and the Question of God 1. Minneapolis: Fortress, 1992.

Zenger, Erich. "The Composition and Theology of the Fifth Book of Psalms, Psalms 107–45." *JSOT* 80 (1998): 77–102.

# SCRIPTURE INDEX

## OLD TESTAMENT

## OTHER ANCIENT WITNESSES